CONTENTS

P9-AEY-714

20 Deconstructing the State: Dictatorship and the Origins of Neoliberal Markets 510

21 Transcending Neoliberalism: Electoral Engaños and Popular Resistance to the Dictatorship of Markets 535

22 **The Two Americas: United States–Latin American Relations** 574

Maps

PREFACE

THE NINTH EDITION of *A History of Latin America* offers teachers and students of Latin American history a text based on the best recent scholarship, enriched with data and concepts drawn from the sister social sciences of economics, anthropology, and sociology. Because the book is a history of Latin American *civilization*, it devotes considerable space to the way of life adopted at each period of the region's history.

To achieve its goal, this book sets Latin American history within a broad interpretive framework based on the "dependency theory." The dependency theory is the most influential theoretical model for social scientists concerned with understanding Latin America. Not all followers of the theory understand it in precisely the same way, but most probably agree with the definition of *dependency* offered by the Brazilian scholar Theotonio dos Santos: "A situation in which the economy of certain countries is conditioned by the development and expansion of another economy to which the former is subject."

Dependency theory has been criticized intermittently over the last seventy years by scholars who feel it does not adequately describe Latin America's historical struggle for development in the twenty-first-century global context. Those who reject the dependency approach typically favor one of a number of alternative paradigms for explaining Latin America's historical struggle for development. In particular, in the first decades following World War II, modernization theory informed and dominated discussions in the United States and Western Europe. Drawing on their own postwar national experiences, scholars espousing modernization theory assumed that "underdevelopment" and "economic backwardness" were conditions common to all societies at one time in their evolution. The key to unlocking the mystery of development, for these scholars, was to contrast conditions in the developed countries with those in undeveloped areas. This produced a prescription for social, political, cultural, and economic change that sought to bring the developmental benefits of modernity to all. Modernizationists concluded that the undeveloped world suffered from a lack of personal freedom, excessive government regulation, highly politicized states, weak civil societies, a shortage of "entrepreneurial values," and the survival of powerful "antimodern" cultural traditions that stressed cooperative communal, rather than competitive individualistic, values.

For the modernization theorists, then, Latin America's failure to develop was largely a consequence of its own internal problems and its reluctance to open itself to the forces of modernity emanating from Western Europe and the United States. Some scholars have even suggested that this failure was the product of a distinct tradition in Latin America, informed by a historic legacy of militarism, local political bosses (*caudillaje*), indigenous communalism, and insular Iberic Catholic culture. To combat these perceived deficiencies in the developmental experiences of Latin America, the modernizationists prescribed a bitter medicine that largely mirrored neoliberal recommendations to dismantle state bureaucracies, reduce budget deficits, cut spending on social services, deregulate private business, privatize national resources, provide incentives to foreign investors, promote free trade, encourage entrepreneurial education, and reduce the political power of so-called antimodern social sectors.

A rapid glance at the results of more than a decade of application of neoliberal therapy to Latin America's problems suggests that in all essential respects the area's economic and social crisis worsened and its dependency on the core capitalist powers deepened. In this book, we draw on a critical synthesis of these two intellectual traditions and emphasize both internal and external factors that have shaped Latin America's historic struggle for development. We challenge the developmentalist belief that all countries have been equally underdeveloped in their historic past and that the developed countries achieved modernity by promoting personal freedom, free trade, and unfettered foreign direct investment. The text unambiguously shows that European and U.S. modernity relied on a five-century legacy of brutal conquest, enslavement, exploitation, and unequal trade enforced alternately by military and market coercion. Moreover, unlike classical dependency theory, which emphasizes transnational social forces and institutional structures of power that seemingly rendered inconsequential all forms of popular resistance, this text documents the powerful role that internal class, racial, gender, ethnic, and interest group struggles have played in shaping the region's development.

Unlike both classical dependency and modernizationist formulations, this text's revised dependency approach also draws on recent feminist theory that defines women as the "last colony," whose shared experiences, according to feminist scholars Christine Bose and Edna Acosta-Belén, include unwaged and low-wage labor, extreme poverty, and "structural subordination and dependency." However, women, like colonial peoples more generally, have not been passive victims in the developmental process. They have been active in the spheres of both production and reproduction. As producers of material wealth in Latin America, women have played a significant, but largely neglected, historical role, working endless hours without pay in household activities that have been an essential source of private capital accumulation.

Historically, men largely assigned women to the family household, where they were responsible for reproduction—i.e., to rear, nurture, and educate the next generation of workers. Once freed from these constraints to seek employment in the marketplace, however, many working-class women experienced double exploitation: first, as poorly paid wage earners whose collective hard work outside the home produced great value that enriched their employers; second, as traditional unwaged household labor that sustained working-class families as the bedrock of classical capital accumulation. This text both highlights the transition of women's roles in Latin America and documents women's demand for state regulation of market activities to protect their developmental contributions in the vital areas of production and reproduction.

Finally, like classical dependency writers who originally blamed global markets for Latin America's poverty and doubted the region's developmental potential in the absence of socialism, we conclude that market expansion often has created economic growth at the expense of development. Unlike these classical dependency theorists, however, we stress the key role of popular social movements in taming markets, restraining inequities produced by their unregulated activities, and transforming them into agents of development. Contrary to modernizationists who argued that market expansion was key to development, this text shows that markets in and of themselves are not nearly as important as how they were regulated. Historical struggles, in turn, have shaped the specific nature of these regulations. In socialist Cuba, for example, the expansion of market activities since the collapse of the Soviet Union and its global trading partners had a decidedly different developmental impact than it had in neoliberal Argentina or Peru. Similarly, Brazil, Chile, and Venezuela regulated global markets differently, with correspondingly different developmental impacts.

More to the point, after 2002, Latin Americans elected a wave of progressive nationalist governments in Argentina, Bolivia, Brazil, Chile, Ecuador, Nicaragua, Paraguay, Uruguay, and Venezuela. Known as the "Pink Tide," these democratically elected governments, despite their many differences, shared a collective commitment to oppose neoliberalism and expand the state's control of market forces. The resulting combination of state regulation, outright nationalization, growing regional integration, increased Chinese market demand, relatively high international export prices, and significant expansion of state antipoverty programs started slowly to reverse the social losses experienced during the neoliberal decade of the 1990s. Our text documents these conclusions in historic detail, underlining the general collapse of the neoliberal, modernizationist model and simultaneously reinforcing the relevance of our revised dependency perspective.

Organization and Revisions

A History of Latin America is published in two volumes as well as in a complete version. Volume 1 includes Latin American history from ancient times to 1910, and Volume 2 covers Latin American history from independence to the present.

This text has developed organically in response to valuable feedback from students and faculty. Early on we decided not to try to cover the postindependence history of the twenty Latin American republics in detail and have avoided cataloging every single general who ever passed through a presidential palace. Most teachers will agree that such content can discourage students by miring them in a bog of tedious facts. Accordingly, the text limited coverage of the national period in the nineteenth century to Argentina, Brazil, Chile, and Mexico, whose histories best illustrate the major issues and trends of the period. In addition to covering these four countries, the survey of the twentieth century later broadened to include the central Andean area, with a special concentration on Peru and Cuba, the scene of a socialist revolution with continental repercussions.

The second edition added a chapter on Central America, where a revolutionary storm, having toppled the U.S.-unsupported Somoza tyranny in Nicaragua, threatened the rickety structures of oligarchical and military rule in Guatemala and El Salvador. The fourth edition recognized the political and economic importance of the Bolivarian lands of Colombia and Venezuela by including a chapter on the modern history of those countries. The seventh edition more fully integrated the discussion of the Andean and Central American regions, the

Bolivarian republics, and Cuba into the text's original layout. Because teachers rarely have time to cover all the Latin American countries in their survey classes, this organization provides greater flexibility, without sacrificing historical continuity, as instructors select those nations on which students should focus. This ninth edition preserves this historical detail, which supplies a foundation for the case study approach, but revisions aim to satisfy the needs of instructors who are interested in a comparative or thematic course design.

Responding to readers' suggestions, we made significant changes to the eighth edition to facilitate its use in course designs that employ both case study and comparative approaches. Part Two included a more detailed overview that highlights the major themes covered in the chapters on nineteenth-century Latin America. It also expanded the coverage with a new chapter on the roles of slavery and emancipation in shaping the postcolonial search for independent national identities. Veteran readers of this text found material on literary traditions that reflected nineteenth- and twentieth-century cultural developments posted to a robust website that accompanies the text. Part Three likewise offered greater comparative cohesion without sacrificing the unique historical details that distinguish each country's national development.

After a more robust overview introducing major themes in the twentieth-century history of Latin America, the text offers successive chapters on the history of liberalism and populism in the Andean Republics, Argentina, Brazil, Central America, Chile, Cuba, Colombia, Mexico, and Venezuela. The focus of Chapter 12 is the Mexican Revolution, the first social revolution in the twentieth century, which decisively shaped Mexico's quest for a unified national identity and bequeathed various institutions, ideologies, and interests that later influenced populism elsewhere. Chapter 13 examines Getulio Vargas and the populist movement unleashed by Brazil's 1930 Revolution, including its historical antecedents and legacies. Chapter 14 explores the origin and evolution of the distinctive postwar populist experience in Argentina under Juan Domingo Perón and his charismatic wife Evita.

Chapter 15 analyzes the 1959 Cuban Revolution, its causes and effects, to explain how it aimed to transcend the limitations of populism and promote an authentically independent national development. As an alternative both to the failures of populism and the Cuban Revolution, Chapter 16 discusses the development of the Andean region's flirtation with military socialism and the military's role in Peru's 1968 "Revolution from Above." Chapter 17 focuses on the populist experience and its role in shaping Chile's distinctive road to national development in 1970 under the leadership of Salvador Allende, the region's first democratically elected Socialist president. Chapter 18 discusses the roles of armed revolution and prolonged popular war as historically particular struggles to promote national liberation in Central America during the 1980s. Chapter 19 concentrates on the historical sources of Venezuela's Bolivarian Revolution in the 1990s and contrasts this with the protracted guerrilla war in Colombia, concluding that both offered different strategies for securing an elusive unified national development. Neoliberalism, yet another strategy to transcend the limitations of a failed populism, is the focus of Chapters 20 and 21, which examine respectively its historical evolution and common experiences in the 1990s and beyond. Finally, Chapter 22 explores the historical role of the United States, its regional and global objectives, and the impact of its foreign policies on Latin American national development.

The ninth edition continues the reorganization of the text that began with the eighth edition and updates the history of the region since 2008, stressing especially the roles of regional integration and the Chinese market in Latin America's recovery from the 2009 global recession. The histories of all the countries discussed in this edition have been brought up to date, and the rest of the book has been thoroughly revised to reflect current scholarship, particularly the respective roles of race, class, and gender in the region's historical development. This edition especially emphasizes such topics as the impact of neoliberal economic policies and the gathering revolt against them, the effects of the North American Free Trade Agreement, the growing urgency of environmental issues, the heightened visibility of the women's movement, and the significance of popular culture.

Website Resources

Newly available with the ninth edition is Cengage Learning's History CourseMate website with interactive learning, study, and exam preparation tools that support *A History of Latin America*. The History CourseMate website includes an integrated e-book, primary sources, quizzes, flashcards, glossary terms, and Engagement Tracker, a first-of-its-kind tool that monitors student engagement in the course. A collection of related full-color maps and video clips relevant to specific chapters of the book are also included. Learn more at www.cengagebrain.com. An online version of the Instructor's Resource Manual and a test bank are available on the Instructor website.

Acknowledgments

Although my friend and comrade Benjamin Keen has not been involved physically in revisions to this book for more than a decade, his spirit still lives in its ideas and interpretations; it will be his book forever. This edition has benefited from the careful scrutiny of the eighth edition by fellow Latin American History professors: Frank Argote-Freyre, Kean University; Eileen Ford, California State University, Los Angeles; Greg Landau, City College of San Francisco; and Angela Vergara, California State University, Los Angeles. We want to acknowledge a special debt of gratitude to Professor Asunción Lavrín, who graciously shared her photo archive on Latin American feminism. Jim Livingston of Rutgers University and Carl Swidorski of the College of Saint Rose provided special guidance and support. We wish to recall, too, the many students, graduate and undergraduate, who helped us to define our views on Latin American history through the give-and-take of classroom discussion and the reading and discussion of their papers and theses.

Benjamin Keen
Keith Haynes

INTRODUCTION

The Geographic Background of Latin American History

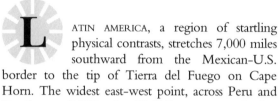

LATIN AMERICA, a region of startling physical contrasts, stretches 7,000 miles southward from the Mexican-U.S. border to the tip of Tierra del Fuego on Cape Horn. The widest east-west point, across Peru and Brazil, spans 3,200 miles. This diverse geography has helped produce the distinctive development of each Latin American nation.

Latin America has two dominant physical characteristics: enormous mountains and vast river systems. The often-snowcapped and sometimes volcanic mountain ranges—the three Sierra Madre ranges in Mexico and the 4,000-mile-long Andes in South America that make a western spine from Venezuela to Tierra del Fuego—form the backbone of the landmass. Nearly impassable for most of their length, these mountain ranges boast many peaks of more than 22,000 feet. The mountains have presented a formidable barrier to trade and communications in Mexico and the nations of the southern continent. The mountain ranges not only separate nations from each other but also divide regions within nations.

The enormous rivers most often lie in lightly populated areas. Three mammoth river systems (the Amazon, the Orinoco, and the Río de la Plata) spread over almost the entire South American continent east of the Andes. The size of the Amazon River basin and the surrounding tropics—the largest such area in the world—has posed another impediment to the development of transportation and human settlement, although some rivers are navigable for long distances. Only with the advent of modern technology—railroads, telegraph, telephones, automobiles, and airplanes—has geographic isolation been partly overcome, a condition that has helped create markets and forge independent states.

Latin America encompasses five climatological regions: high mountains, tropical jungles, deserts, temperate coastal plains, and temperate highlands. The first three are sparsely populated, whereas the latter two tend to be densely inhabited. With the exception of the Maya, all the great ancient civilizations arose in the highlands of the Andes and Mexico.

The varied climate and topography of South America, Mexico, and Central America have produced this highly uneven distribution of population. Three notable examples—the gargantuan Amazonian region of mostly steamy tropical forests and savannah, the vast desert of Patagonia in southern Argentina, and the northern wastelands of Mexico—support few inhabitants. In contrast to these inhospitable regions, a thin strip along Brazil's coast, the plain along the Río de la Plata estuary in Argentina, and the central plateau of Mexico contain most of the people in these countries. Thus, these nations are overpopulated and underpopulated at the same time.

In western South America, the heaviest concentration of people is found on the inland plateaus. None of its major cities—including Santiago, Chile; Bogotá and Medellín, Colombia; Quito, Ecuador; and Lima, Peru—are ports; the Pacific coast is home to few good natural harbors. By contrast, in eastern South America, the major cities—including Buenos Aires, Argentina; São Paulo–Santos, Rio de Janeiro, Bahia, and Recife, Brazil; and Montevideo, Uruguay—are situated on the Atlantic coast. The majority of people in Argentina, Brazil, and Uruguay reside on the coastal plains. Guadalajara, Mexico City, and Monterrey, Mexico's largest cities, are inland. Almost all these cities have a population of more than 1 million, with Mexico City, the largest, having more than 20 million.

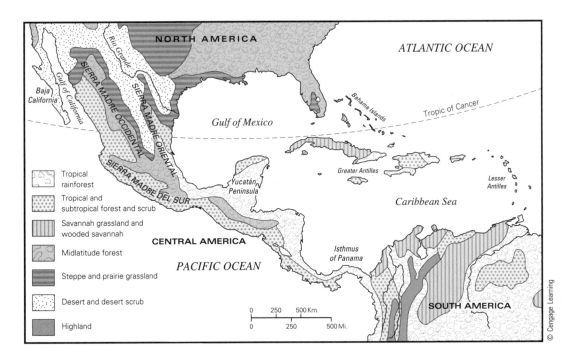

The maps on these two pages form an overall picture of the natural geographic features of Latin America: Middle America (*above*), composed of Mexico, Central America, and the Caribbean region; and South America (*next page*).

The number of waterways and the amount of rainfall vary greatly from region to region. Mexico has no rivers of importance, but Brazil contains the huge Amazon network. Lack of rain and rivers for irrigation in large areas makes farming impossible. Barely 10 percent of Mexico's land is fertile enough to farm; rainfall is so uncertain in some cultivable areas that drought strikes often and for years at a time. Mexico, with too little water, contrasts with Brazil, with too much. Much of Brazil's vast territory, however, is equally uncultivable, as its tropical soils have high acidity and have proved infertile and incapable of sustaining agricultural crops.

On the other hand, Latin America has enormous natural resources for economic development. Mexico and Venezuela rank among the world's largest oil producers. Mexico may have the biggest petroleum reserves of any nation other than Saudi Arabia. Bolivia, Ecuador, Colombia, and Peru also produce oil. Over the centuries, Latin American nations have been leading sources of copper (Chile and Mexico), nitrate (Chile), silver (Mexico and Peru), gold (Brazil), diamonds (Brazil), and tin (Bolivia). Much of the world's coffee grows on the fertile highlands of Central America, Colombia, and Brazil. Much of the world's cattle pasture on the plains of northern Mexico, southern Brazil, and central Argentina. Argentina's immense plains, the Pampas, are among the planet's most fertile areas, yielding not only cattle but sheep, wheat, and soy beans as well. Over the past five centuries, the coastal plains of Brazil have produced enormous amounts of sugar, but they now have transformed the nation into the world's second largest producer of soy beans. In addition, human ingenuity has converted geographic obstacles into assets. Some extensive river systems have the potential for hydroelectric power and provide water for irrigation as well, as has been done in Mexico's arid regions.

The historical record shows that the richness of Latin America's resources has had a significant impact

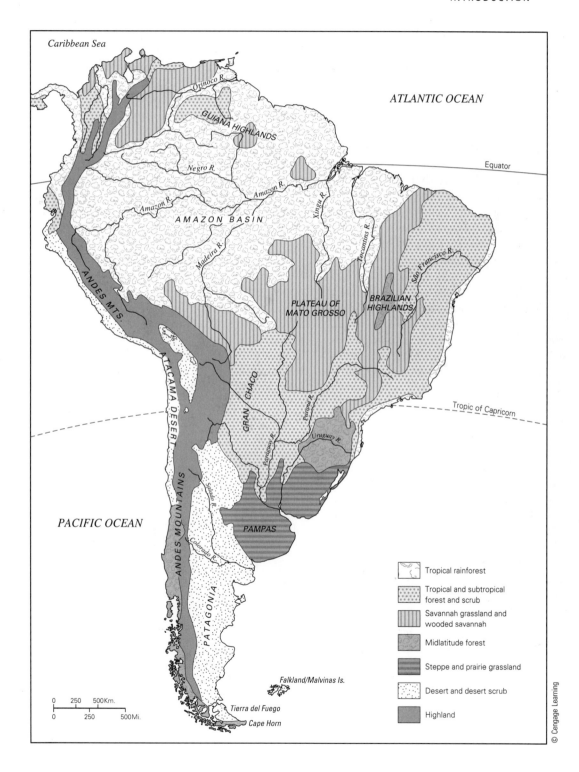

Caribbean Sea

ATLANTIC OCEAN

Orinoco R.

GUIANA HIGHLANDS

Negro R.

Equator

Amazon R.

Amazon R.

Xingu R.

AMAZON BASIN

Tocantins R.

São Francisco R.

Madeira R.

PLATEAU OF MATO GROSSO

BRAZILIAN HIGHLANDS

ANDES MTS.

ATACAMA DESERT

GRAN CHACO

Paraguay R.

Paraná R.

Uruguay R.

Tropic of Capricorn

PACIFIC OCEAN

ANDES MOUNTAINS

Salado R.

Colorado R.

PAMPAS

PATAGONIA

Falkland/Malvinas Is.

Tierra del Fuego

Cape Horn

0   250   500 Km.

0   250   500 Mi.

Tropical rainforest

Tropical and subtropical forest and scrub

Savannah grassland and wooded savannah

Midlatitude forest

Steppe and prairie grassland

Desert and desert scrub

Highland

© Cengage Learning

on the economic and political development of Europe and North America. The gold and silver of its New World empire fueled Spain's wars and diplomacy in Europe for four hundred years. Many scholars trace the origins of the Industrial Revolution in such nations as Great Britain and the Netherlands to resources extracted from Latin America by its colonial masters, Spain and Portugal.

Latin America's resources have affected economic development elsewhere, but how these resources have been developed and by whom and in which ways has profoundly changed the history of the nations in this area. Geography has perhaps narrowed historical alternatives in Latin America, but the decisions of people determined its development. Going back to the colonization by Spain and Portugal, exploitation of its peoples and its natural resources has marked Latin America's history. Imperial Spain's policy to drain its conquered lands of gold, silver, and other resources fixed the pattern for later exploiters. With European dominance came the decision to subjugate the indigenous peoples and often force them to labor under subhuman conditions in mines and on large estates, where many died. In the more recent era, external market demand has caused foreign companies and local producers to grow bananas on the coastal plains of Central America instead of corn or other staples of the local diet. This has made export profitable, usually for North American concerns, but this land use has left many, like the Guatemalans, without sufficient food. Meanwhile, the uncontrolled expansion of capitalism in the area has led to an ecological crisis, reflected in massive deforestation, severe soil exhaustion, and growing agricultural and industrial pollution. These developments have contributed to rapid depletion of renewable resources, lack of clean water and air, and major epidemics of contagious diseases and other health problems.

The work that follows is a history of the development of Latin America's economy, politics, and society viewed primarily from the perspective of ordinary people, who endured exploitation and oppression but steadfastly resisted and continued to struggle for social justice. It is the story of the events and forces that produced the alternatives from which Latin Americans created their world.

PART TWO

1823	Rise of liberal republics in independent Spanish America
1829–1852	Establishment of Juan Manuel de Rosas's conservative rule in Argentina
1830	Creation of conservative rule in Chile under influence of Diego Portales
1835–1837	Revolution of Ragamuffins in Brazil and popular protests against aristocratic rule and slavery
1838	Destruction of liberal United Provinces of Central America and consolidation of conservative rule under Rafael Carrera
1839–1852	Spread of slave revolts throughout Venezuela, prompting legal abolition of slavery in 1854
1844	Spread of slave rebellions across Cuba, some led by enslaved Afro-Cuban women
1846–1848	U.S. invasion of Mexico, Treaty of Guadalupe Hidalgo, and surrender of half of Mexico's territory
1854–1862	War of the Reform, pitting Mexican Liberals led by Benito Juárez against the Conservatives
1860s	Expansion of abolitionist movement and agitation against the emperor in Brazil
1862–1868	French intervention and occupation of Mexico under Emperor Ferdinand Maximilian
1864	War of Triple Alliance and destruction of two decades of Paraguayan development initiated by Dr. José Gáspar de Francia
1868–1878	Ten Years' War, seeking abolition of slavery and political independence for Cuba and Puerto Rico
1870–1900	Expansion of foreign investment and rise of Liberal *caudillos* like Antonio Guzmán Blanco in Venezuela (1870–1899), Porfirio Díaz in Mexico (1876–1910), Rafael Núñez in Colombia (1879–1888), and Julio Roca in Argentina (1880–1904)
1871	Passage of Rio Branco law in Brazil, manumitting newborn slave children but requiring them to remain with their masters until age twenty-one
1880	Abolition of slavery in Cuba and establishment of *patronato*, an eight-year apprenticeship for liberated slaves
1889	Overthrow of Dom Pedro II and establishment of Brazilian Republic

Latin America in the Nineteenth Century

Coffee Plantation, 1935, by Candido Portinari

INDEPENDENCE LEFT MUCH of the colonial social structure intact. This fact was very apparent to liberal leaders of the Postindependence Era. "The war against Spain," declared the Colombian liberal Ramón Mercado in 1853, "was not a revolution.... Independence only scratched the surface of the social problem, without changing its essential nature." After winning their independence, the new Latin American states began a long, uphill struggle to achieve economic and political stability. They faced immense obstacles, for independence did not bring economic and social changes that could spur rapid progress—for example, no redistribution of land and income in favor of the lower classes took place. The large estate, which generally relied on primitive methods and slave or peon labor, continued to dominate economic life. Far from diminishing, the influence of the landed aristocracy actually increased because of the leading military role it had played in the wars of independence and the passing of Spanish authority. We should not, however, minimize the extent and importance of the changes that did take place. Independence may not have produced a major social upheaval, but it did produce a minor one. It opened wide fissures within the elite, dividing aristocratic supporters of the old social order from others who wanted a more democratic, bourgeois order. Their struggle is an integral aspect of the first half-century after the end of Spanish and Portuguese rule. Independence also enabled such formerly submerged groups as artisans and gauchos to enter the political arena, although in subordinate roles, and even allowed a few to climb into the ranks of the elite. The opening of Latin American ports to foreign goods also established a relatively free market in ideas, at least in the capitals and other cities. With almost no time lag, such new European doctrines as utopian socialism, romanticism, and positivism entered Latin America to propose solutions to the continent's problems. These new doctrinal winds, blowing through what had lately been dusty colonial corridors, contributed to the area's intellectual renovation and promoted further social change.

Verbally, at least, the new republican constitutions established the equality of all before the law, destroying the legal foundations of colonial caste society. Because little change in property relations took place, however, the racial, ethnic, and social class lines of division remained essentially the same. Wealth, power, and prestige continued to be concentrated in the hands of a ruling class that reproduced colonial racial structures and identified itself with whiteness; in some countries, such as Venezuela, however, it included individuals of darker skin who had managed to climb the social ladder through their prowess in war or politics.

Of all the groups composing the old society of castes, the status of indígenas changed least of all. Mexican historian Carlos María Bustamante was one of the few creole leaders who recognized that independence had not freed them from their yoke. "They still drag the same chains," he wrote, "although they are flattered with the name of freemen." Even native tribute and forced labor, abolished during or after the wars of independence, soon reappeared in many countries under other names. Still worse, indigenous communal landholding, social organization, and culture, which Spanish law and policy had to some extent protected in colonial times, came under increasing attack. Liberals especially believed that these communal traditions constituted as much of an obstacle to progress as the Spanish system of castes and special privileges did.

Until about 1870, however, large, compact indigenous populations continued to live under the traditional communal landholding system in Mexico, Central America, and the Andean region. Then, the rapid growth of the export economy, the coming of the railroads, and the resulting rise in land values and demand for labor caused "white" and mestizo landowners and landowner-dominated governments to launch a massive assault on native lands. The expropriation of these lands was accompanied by a growth of peonage and tenantry. Employers used a variety of devices, ranging from debt servitude to outright coercion, to attach laborers to their estates. In some areas, an indigenous serfdom arose that closely resembled the classic European model. In the Andean region, for example, Aymara tenants, in addition to working their masters' land, had to render personal service in their households, sometimes at the hacienda, sometimes in the city. Their masters also had the right to give or sell them to friends during the term of domestic service. This and other forms of serfdom survived well into the twentieth century.

The master class, aided by the clergy and local magistrates, sought to reinforce the economic subjugation of indigenous peoples with psychological domination. There evolved a pattern of relations and role-playing that assigned to the *patrones* the role of benevolent figures who assured their peons or tenants of a livelihood and protected them in all emergencies in return for their absolute obedience. In countries with large indigenous populations, the relations between masters and peons often included an elaborate ritual that required natives to request permission to speak to *patrones*, to appear before them with head uncovered and bowed, and to seek their approval for all major personal decisions, including marriage.

Nonetheless, not all indigenous peoples accepted these relationships and attitudes of submission and servility, which were more characteristic of resident peons. In the Andean area, Mexico, and elsewhere during the second half of the nineteenth century, the surviving native landowning communities fought stubbornly to prevent the absorption of their lands by advancing haciendas and to halt the process by which they became landless laborers. They fought with all the means at their disposal, including armed revolts as a last resort. Landowners and government officials called the revolts that occurred in Mexico in the 1860s and 1870s "communist" and sought to crush them with superior military force.

The greater freedom of movement that came with independence, the progressive disappearance of autonomous indigenous communities, and the growth of the hacienda, in which natives mingled with mestizos, strengthened a trend toward acculturation that had begun in the late colonial period. This acculturation reflected a growth of bilingualism: Indigenous peoples increasingly used

Spanish in dealing with criollos, reserving their native languages for use among themselves. To the limited extent that public schools entered their regions, they contributed to the adoption of Spanish as a second language or sometimes led to total abandonment of their native tongues. Mexican historian Eduardo Ruiz recalled that as a child he spoke only Tarascan but had forgotten it during his twelve years of study at the colegio: "I did not want to remember, I must confess, because I was ashamed of being thought to be an Indian." Some acculturation also occurred in dress, with frequent abandonment of regional fashions in favor of a quasi-European style, sometimes enforced by legislation and fines. Over much of Mexico, for example, the white trousers and shirt of coarse cotton cloth and the broad-brimmed hat became almost a native uniform.

Yet pressures toward indigenous acculturation or assimilation failed to achieve integration into criollo society that well-meaning Liberals had hoped to secure through education and employment in the modern world of industry and trade. At the end of the nineteenth century, the processes of acculturation had not significantly reduced the size of the indigenous sector in the five countries with the largest native populations: Mexico, Guatemala, Ecuador, Peru, and Bolivia. The various reasons for this included the economic stagnation and political troubles of the early postindependence decades, which tended to reinforce the isolation and cultural separateness of their communities. When the Latin American economies revived because of the expansion of the export sector, indigenous peoples suffered most because this revival served mainly to accentuate their poverty and backwardness. Their economic marginality; their almost total exclusion from the political process; the intense exploitation to which white and mestizo landowners, priests, and officials subjected them; and the barriers of distrust and hatred that separated them from the white world prevented any thorough-going acculturation, much less integration.

Indigenous communities made such concessions to the pressures for assimilation as were necessary but preserved their traditional housing, diet, social organization, and religion, which combined indigenous and Christian features. In some regions, the pre-Conquest cults and rituals, including occasional human sacrifice, survived. The existence in a number of countries of large native populations, intensely exploited and branded as inferior by the ruling social Darwinist ideology, constituted a major obstacle to the formation of a national consciousness in those lands. With good reason, pioneer Mexican anthropologist Manuel Gamio wrote in 1916 that Mexico, rather than a unified nation in the European sense, was really a collection of numerous small nations, differing in speech, economy, social organization, and psychology.

The wars for independence, by throwing "careers open to talent," enabled a few natives and a larger number of mestizos of humble origins to rise high on the military, political, and social scales. The liberal caudillos, Vicente Guerrero and Juan Alvarez in Mexico, and such talented leaders as Juan José Flores of Ecuador, Andrés Santa Cruz of Bolivia, and Ramón Castilla of Peru illustrate the ascent of mixed-race people.

The rise of these mestizo or mulatto leaders inspired fears in some members of the creole elite, beginning with Bolívar, who gloomily predicted a race war that would also be a struggle between haves and have-nots. Bolívar revealed his obsessive race prejudice in his description of the valiant and generous Mexican patriot Vicente Guerrero as the "vile abortion of a savage Indian and a fierce African." These fears proved groundless; although some mixed-race leaders, like Guerrero and Alvarez, remained to one degree or another loyal to the humble masses from which they had sprung, the majority soon declared their allegiance to the creole aristocracy and firmly defended its interests.

Conversely, creole politicians of the Postcolonial Era had to take account of the new political weight of the mixed-race middle and lower classes, especially the artisan groups. Despite promises to satisfy the aspirations of the masses, white elites exploited them politically and failed to fulfill their pledges. This happened in Bogotá, where Colombian liberals courted the artisans in their struggle against Conservatives, and in Buenos Aires, where Juan Manuel Rosas demagogically identified himself with provincial mixed-race gauchos and urban artisans against the aristocratic liberal *unitarios*, who favored a centralized national government that monopolized customs revenues collected in the port city.

After mid-century, the growing influence of European racist ideologies, especially Spencerian biological determinism, led to a heightened sensitivity to color. From Mexico to Chile, members of the so-called white elite and even the middle class claimed to be superior to natives and mestizos. Dark skin increasingly became an obstacle to social advancement. Typical of the rampant pseudoscientific racism by the turn of the century was the remark of the Argentine Carlos Bunge, son of a German immigrant, that mestizos and mulattos were "impure, atavistically anti-Christian; they are like the two heads of a fabulous hydra that surrounds, constricts, and strangles with its giant spiral a beautiful, pale virgin, Spanish America."

As a rule, neither Liberals nor Conservatives were free from the pervasive racism of the time. Carried away by his enthusiasm for what he called "civilization," the Argentine liberal Domingo Sarmiento identified it with the European bourgeois order and white supremacy. "It may appear unjust to exterminate savages, destroy nascent civilizations, and conquer peoples who occupy land that is rightly theirs, but thanks to this injustice," he proclaimed, "America, instead of being abandoned to savages who are incapable of progress, is today occupied by the Caucasian race, the most perfect, intelligent, beautiful, and progressive of all the races that inhabit the earth." A handful of Latin American intellectuals dissented from such a view. One was the Chilean Francisco Bilbao, who condemned "the great hypocrisy of covering up every crime and outrage with the word *civilization*" and pointedly referred to Sarmiento's war against native peoples and gauchos. Another was the Cuban José Martí, who denounced "the pretext that 'civilization,' the name commonly given to the present state of Europe, has the natural right to seize the land of 'barbarians,' the name that those who hunger for other people's land give to everyone who is not European or of European descent."

Even before the wars of independence, black slavery had declined in various parts of Latin America. This occurred in part because of economic developments that made slavery unprofitable and favored manumission or commutation of slavery to tenantry. An even more significant reason, perhaps, was the frequent flight of slaves to remote jungles and mountains, where they formed self-governing communities. For example, in 1800, officials estimated that Venezuela held some eighty-seven thousand slaves, but some twenty-four thousand had escaped to freedom in the inaccessible hinterland. Of course, arguably the most powerful force shaping the movement to abolish slavery was enslaved Africans and their descendants who, following the lead of Toussaint L'Ouverture and his comrades in Haiti, took up arms to secure their collective freedom from Latin American slavery.

The wars of independence gave a major stimulus to emancipation. Patriot commanders like Bolívar and San Martín and royalist officers frequently offered slaves freedom in return for military service, and black slaves sometimes formed a majority of the fighting forces on both sides. About a third of San Martín's army in the campaign of the Andes was black. Moreover, the confusion and disorder produced by the fighting often led to a collapse of plantation discipline, easing the flight of slaves and making their recovery difficult if not impossible.

After independence, slavery further declined, partly because of its patent incompatibility with the libertarian ideals proclaimed by the new states, but the hostile attitude of Great Britain, which had abolished the slave trade in all its possessions in 1807, also brought pressure for similar action by all countries still trading in slaves. British pressure on Brazil further contributed to the crisis of Brazilian slavery and its ultimate demise.

Emancipation came most easily and quickly in countries where slaves were a negligible element in the labor force; thus, Chile, Mexico, and the Federation of Central America (1823–1839) abolished slavery between 1823 and 1829. In other countries, the slave owners fought a tenacious rear-guard action. For example, Venezuela adopted a gradual manumission law in 1821 but did not finally abolish slavery until 1854. Ramón Castilla abolished slavery in Peru in 1855. After a long and violent struggle to subdue rebellious slaves, the Spanish Cortes finally decreed the end of slavery in Puerto Rico in 1873 and in Cuba in 1880, but the Cuban institution continued in a disguised form (the ***patronato***, a period of apprenticeship) until 1886, when it finally ended.

The record of Latin American slavery in the nineteenth century does not support the thesis of some historians that cultural and religious factors made Hispanic slavery inherently milder than the North American variety. In its two main centers of Cuba and Brazil, under conditions of mounting demand for Brazilian coffee and Cuban sugar and a critical labor shortage, ample evidence exists of systematic brutality with the use of the lash to make the enslaved work longer and harder. The enslaved responded with a resistance that varied from slowdowns to flight to open rebellion—a resistance that contributed to the final demise of the institution.

Patriarchal family organization, highly ceremonial conduct, and leisurely lifestyle continued to characterize the landed aristocracy and Latin American elites after independence. The kinship network extended beyond the large patriarchal family because of ***compadrazgo*** (the Spanish cultural institution that established a relationship of patronage and protection on the part of an upper-class godparent toward a lower-status godchild and his or her parents). The lower-class family members in turn formed part of the godparent's following and devoted themselves to the godparent's interests.

As in colonial times, great landowners generally resided most of the time in the cities, leaving their estates in the charge of administrators (who often scrutinized account books and were equally concerned with considerations of profit and loss). From the same upper class came a small minority of would-be entrepreneurs who challenged the traditional agrarian bias of their society. In the words of historian Richard Graham, they were "caught up by the idea of capitalism, by the belief in industrialization, and by a faith in work and practicality." Typical of this group was the Brazilian Viscount Mauá, who created a banking and industrial empire between 1850 and 1875 against the opposition of traditionalists. Mauá's empire collapsed, however, partly because the objective conditions for capitalist development in Brazil had not fully matured and partly because of official apathy and even disfavor. The day of the entrepreneur had not yet come; the economic history of Latin America in the nineteenth century is strewn with the wrecks of abortive industrial projects. These fiascos also represented defeats for the capitalist mentality and values.

After mid-century, with the gradual rise of a neocolonial order based on the integration of the Latin American economy into the international capitalist system, the ruling class, although retaining certain precapitalist traits, became more receptive to bourgeois values and ideals. An Argentine writer of the 1880s noted that "the latifundist no longer has that semibarbarous, semifeudal air; he has become a scientific administrator, who alternates between his home on the estate, his Buenos Aires mansion, and his house in Paris." In fact, few *estancieros* or hacendados became "scientific administrators." They preferred to leave the task of managing their estates to others, but the writer accurately identified this gradual Europeanization of elites under way throughout the continent.

The process began right after independence but greatly accelerated after mid-century. Within a decade after independence, marked changes in manners and consumption patterns had occurred. "Fashions alter," wrote Fanny Calderón de la Barca, Scottish-born wife of the Spanish minister to Mexico, who described Mexican upper-class society in the age of Santa Anna in a series of sprightly letters. According to Calderón de la Barca, "The graceful mantilla gradually gives place to the ungraceful bonnet. The old painted coach, moving slowly like a caravan, with Guido's Aurora painted on its gaudy panels, is dismissed for the London-built carriage."

The old yielded much more slowly and grudgingly to the new in drowsy colonial cities like Quito, capital of Ecuador, but yield it did, at least in externals. The U.S. minister to Ecuador in the 1860s, Friedrich Hassaurek, who was harshly critical of Quitonian society and manners, noted that, "in spite of the difficulty of transportation, there are about one hundred and twenty pianos in Quito, very indifferently tuned." Another U.S. visitor to Quito in this period, Professor James Orton, observed that "the upper class follow *la mode de Paris*, gentlemen adding the classic cloak of Old Spain." He added sourly that "this modern toga fits an Ecuadorian admirably, preventing the arms from doing anything, and covers a multitude of sins, especially pride and poverty."

Under the republic, as in colonial times, dress was an important index of social status. Orton reported that "no gentleman will be seen walking in the streets of Quito under a poncho. Hence citizens are divided into men with ponchos and gentlemen with cloaks." Dress even served to distinguish followers of different political factions or parties. In Buenos Aires under Rosas, the artisans who formed part of the dictator's mass base were called *gente de chaqueta* (wearers of jackets), as opposed to the aristocratic Unitarian Liberals, who wore dress coats. In the gaucho army of Justo José de Urquiza, Rosas's conqueror, the only Argentine officer dressed as a European was Sarmiento, a strange sight in his frock coat and *kepi* (a French military cap) among the gauchos with their lances and ponchos. For Sarmiento, writes John Lynch, "it was a matter of principle, a protest against barbarism, against Rosas and the caudillos.... 'As long as we do not change the dress of the Argentine soldier,' said Sarmiento, 'we are bound to have caudillos.'"

By the close of the century, European styles of dress had triumphed in such great cities as Mexico City and Buenos Aires and among all except native peoples. Attitudes toward clothes continued to reflect aristocratic values, especially scorn for manual labor. In Buenos Aires, for example, at the turn of the century, a worker's blouse would bar the entrance of its wearer to a bank or the halls of Congress. As a result, according to James Scobie, "everyone sought to hide the link with manual labor," and even workingmen preferred to wear the traditional coat and tie.

After 1880, European immigrants swarmed into Argentina, Uruguay, and Brazil and, in lesser numbers, into such countries as Chile and Mexico. Combined with growing urbanization and continued expansion of the export sector, this helped accelerate the rate of social change. These developments helped

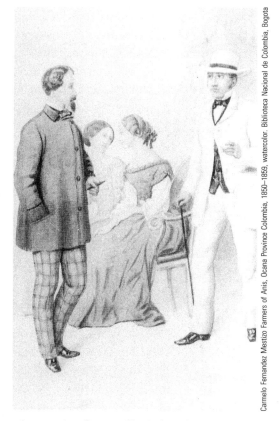

These fine sketches of Colombian mestizo farmers and upper-class figures effectively make the point that, in nineteenth-century Latin America, clothes still made the man.

create a small, modern industrial working class and swelled the ranks of blue-collar and middle-class white-collar workers.

However, aside from that minority of the working class that adopted social-ist, anarchist, or syndicalist doctrines, the immigrants posed no threat to the ex-isting social structure or the prevailing aristocratic ideology; instead, many surrendered to that ideology. The foreigners who entered the upper class as a rule already belonged to the educated or managerial class. Movement from the middle class of immigrant origin to the upper class was extremely difficult and rare, and for the lower-class immigrant it was almost impossible. A few immi-grants made their fortunes by commerce or speculation. Their children or grand-children took care to camouflage the origins of their wealth and to make it respectable by investing it in land. These nouveaux riches regarded natives and workers with the same contempt as their aristocratic associates.

Independence did not better the status of women. Indeed, their civil status probably worsened because of new bourgeois-style law codes that strengthened husbands' control over their wives' property. More than ever, men relegated women to the four walls of their houses and household duties. Church and parents taught women to be submissive and sweetly clinging, and to have no wills of their own. Typical of the patriarchal attitudes that prevailed with regard to relations be-tween the sexes was the advice that Colombian Mariano Ospina Rodríguez gave in an 1864 letter to his daughter María on the eve of her marriage to José Mariano Roma y Batres. "Your happiness," he wrote, "depends ... on the sincere and con-stant practice of these modest virtues: humility, patience, resignation, abnegation, and ... the proper conduct of the domestic relations that depend on those same Christian virtues." Mariano Ospina went on to caution his daughter,

> One of your first cares must be to study your husband's inclinations,
> habits, and tastes, so that you never contradict them. Never seek to
> impose your will or make him give up his habits or tastes, no matter
> how insignificant they may seem; on the contrary, act in such a manner
> that he may continue them without disturbance.... Frequently you will
> find that you have different tastes and habits; never hesitate for a mo-
> ment to sacrifice your own tastes and habits in favor of his.

The double standard of sexual conduct prevailed; women were taught to deny their sexuality and believe that procreation was the sole purpose of sexual intercourse. However, women's actual conduct did not necessarily conform to the law and ideology. Silvia Arróm has shown, for example, that these restric-tions did not deter women in early nineteenth-century Mexico from engaging in extramarital affairs.

Few Latin American women of the elite class, however, strayed so far beyond the bounds of propriety as did Flora Tristán (1803–1844), pioneer feminist and socialist. Daughter of an aristocratic Peruvian landowner and a French mother, she spent most of her life in France, but Peruvian feminists and socialists regard her as one of their own. A woman of striking beauty, she separated early from her husband and became active in French feminist and socialist circles. In 1835, she published a novel, *Méphis*, which proposed the transformation of society on socialist and feminist principles, and in 1840, she published *Promenades in London*, a description of the monstrous contrasts between wealth and poverty in the English metropolis. In her last book, *The Workers' Union* (1844), she called on "the working men and women of the world" to unite, anticipating by four years Marx's appeal in *The Communist Manifesto*. Tristán clearly identified the gendered layers of exploitation. "The most oppressed male can oppress another human being who is his own wife," she wrote. "Woman is the proletariat of the proletariat." She also presaged theoretical formulations of twentieth-century feminists, arguing that "the liberation of women is the necessary condition for the liberation of men."

The democratic, liberal movements of the first half-century after independence stimulated some developments in favor of women. In Argentina, Sarmiento wrote that "the level of civilization of a people can be judged by the social position of its women"; his educational program envisaged a major role for women as primary-school teachers. In Mexico, the triumph of the Reforma led to promulgation of a new school law that called for the establishment of secondary schools for girls and normal schools for the training of women primary-school teachers. In both countries after 1870, small feminist movements, largely composed of schoolteachers, arose and formed societies, edited journals, and worked for the cultural, economic, and social improvement of women.

Even in a backward slave society like Brazil, a women's rights press was created, pioneered by Joana Paula Manso de Noronha, who stated in the introductory editorial to *O Jornal das Senhoras* (1852) her intention to work for "social betterment and the moral emancipation of women." In the last decades of the century, with the development of industry, women in increasing numbers entered factories and sweatshops, where they often were paid half of what male workers earned, becoming a source of superprofits for capitalist employers. By 1887, according to the census of Buenos Aires, 39 percent of the paid workforce of that city was composed of women.

The church, which in some countries had suffered discredit because of the royalist posture of many clergy during the wars of independence, experienced a further decline in influence because of increasing contacts with the outside world and a new and relatively tolerant climate of opinion. In country after country, Liberals pressed with varying success for restrictions on the church's monopoly over education, marriage, burials, and the like. Because the church invariably aligned itself with the conservative opposition, liberal victories brought reprisals in the form of heavy attacks on its accumulated wealth and privileges.

The colonial principle of monolithic religious unity dissolved because of the need to allow freedom of worship to the prestigious and powerful British merchants. In fact, the reactionary Rosas, who disliked foreigners and brought the Jesuits back to Argentina, himself donated the land on which the Anglicans built their first church in Buenos Aires. Despite the efforts of some fanatical clergy to incite the populace against foreign heretics, a system of peaceful coexistence between Catholics and dissenters gradually evolved, based on reciprocal goodwill and tact.

The Inquisition, whose excesses had made it odious even to the faithful, disappeared during the wars of independence. In many countries, however, the civil authorities assumed its right to censor or ban subversive or heretical writings. Occasionally, governments exercised this right. In the 1820s, clerical and conservative opposition forced the liberal vice president of Gran Colombia, Francisco de Paula Santander, to authorize the dropping of a textbook by the materialist Jeremy Bentham from law school courses. In Buenos Aires, Rosas publicly burned subversive books and other materials. According to Tulio Halperin-Donghi, however, a reading of the press advertisements of Buenos Aires booksellers suggests that this repression was singularly ineffective. In Santiago in the 1840s, the public hangman burned Francisco Bilbao's fiery polemic against Spain and Catholicism. According to Sarmiento, however, the violent, strident tone of Bilbao's book, not its content, caused this reaction; Bilbao, he added, had been justly punished for his clumsiness.

After mid-century, with the enthronement of positivism, which glorified science and rejected theology as an approach to truth, efforts to suppress heretical or anticlerical writings diminished or ended completely in many countries. In general, during the last half of the nineteenth century, there existed in Latin America a relatively free market in ideas—free, that is, as long as these ideas were couched in theoretical terms or referred primarily to other parts of the world and did not threaten an incumbent regime. Governments often were quick to suppress and confiscate newspapers and pamphlets whose contents they considered dangerous to their security, but they remained indifferent to the circulation of books containing the most audacious social theories. By way of example, the Díaz dictatorship in Mexico struck at opposition journalists and newspapers but permitted the free sale and distribution of the writings of Marx and anarchist theoretician Peter Kropotkin.

Because of the ascendancy of positivism, the church suffered a further decline in influence and power. Conservative victories over liberalism sometimes produced a strong proclerical reaction, typified by Gabriel García Moreno, who ruled Ecuador from 1860 to 1875 and carried his fanaticism to the point of dedicating the republic to the Sacred Heart of Jesus. Rafael Núñez, dictator of Colombia from 1880 to 1894, drafted a concordat with the Vatican that restored to the church most of the rights it had enjoyed in colonial times. Nonetheless, such victories failed to arrest the general decline of the church's social and intellectual influence among the literate classes. Anticlericalism became an integral part of the ideology of most Latin American intellectuals and a large proportion of other upper-class and middle-class males, including many who were faithful churchgoers and observed the outward forms and rituals of the church. However, church influence continued to be strong among women of all classes, indigenous peoples, and the submerged groups generally.

After independence, economic life initially stagnated, for the anticipated large-scale influx of foreign capital did not materialize and the European demand for Latin American staples remained far below expectations. Free trade brought increased commercial activity to the coasts, but it also caused the near destruction of some local craft industries that could not compete with cheap, factory-made European imports. The sluggish pace of economic activity and the relative absence of interregional trade and true national markets encouraged local self-sufficiency, isolation, political instability, and even chaos.

Because of these factors, the period from about 1820 to about 1870 was for many Latin American countries an age of violence, alternating dictatorship and revolution in a collective postcolonial struggle to construct distinctive national identities. Its symbol was the caudillo (strongman), whose power always depended on force, no matter what kind of constitution the country had. Usually the caudillo ruled with the aid of a coalition of lesser caudillos, each supreme in his region. Whatever their methods, the caudillos generally displayed some regard for republican ideology and institutions. Political parties, bearing such labels as "Conservative" and "Liberal," "Unitarian" and "Federalist," were active in most of the new states. Conservatism drew most of its support from the great landowners and their urban allies. Liberalism typically attracted provincial landowners, professional men, and other groups that had enjoyed little power in the past and were dissatisfied with the existing order. As a rule, Conservatives sought to retain many of the social arrangements of the Colonial Era and favored a highly centralized government. Liberals, often inspired by the example of the United States, usually advocated a federal form of government, guarantees of individual rights, lay control of education, and an end to special privileges for the clergy and military. Neither party displayed much interest in the problems of the native peasantry and other lower-class groups.

Beginning around 1870, the accelerating tempo of the Industrial Revolution in Europe stimulated more rapid change in the Latin American economy and politics. European capital flowed into the area and created the facilities needed to expand and modernize production and trade. The pace and degree of economic progress of the various countries were uneven and depended largely on their geographic position and natural resources.

Extreme one-sidedness was a feature of the new economic order. One or two products became the basis of each country's prosperity, making these commodities highly vulnerable to fluctuations in world demand and price. Meanwhile, other sectors of the economy remained stagnant or even declined through diversion of labor and land to other industries.

The late-nineteenth-century expansion had two other characteristics: In the main, it took place within the framework of the hacienda system of land tenure and labor, and it accompanied a steady growth of foreign control over the natural and human-made resources of the region. Thus, by 1900 a new structure of dependency, or colonialism, had arisen, called neocolonialism, with Great Britain and later the United States replacing Spain and Portugal as the dominant powers in the area.

The new economic order demanded peace and continuity in government, and after 1870 political conditions in Latin America grew more stable. Old party lines dissolved as Conservatives adopted the positivist dogma of science and progress, whereas Liberals abandoned their concern with constitutional methods and civil liberties in favor of an interest in material prosperity. A new type of liberal caudillo—Porfirio Díaz in Mexico, Rafael Núñez in Colombia, Antonio Guzmán Blanco in Venezuela—symbolized the politics of acquisition. The cycle of dictatorship and revolution continued in many lands, but the revolutions became less frequent and less devastating.

These major trends in the political and economic history of Latin America in the period extending from about 1820 to 1900 accompanied other changes in the Latin American way of life and culture. In Part Two, we present short histories of Argentina, Brazil, Chile, Cuba, Gran Colombia, Mexico, Peru, and the United Provinces of Central America in the nineteenth century. These histories all contain themes and problems common to Latin America in that period, but each displays variations that reflect its distinctive struggle to define the newly emerging postcolonial nation.

Decolonization and the Search for National Identities, 1821–1870

9

FOCUS QUESTIONS

- How did the wars of independence affect the landed aristocracy, the military, and foreign dependence?
- What were the economic and social roots of *caudillismo?*
- What were the principal differences between Liberals and Conservatives in early nineteenth-century Latin America?
- How did the liberal ideas of the Mexican Reforma change?
- How was Paraguay's early nineteenth-century development different from Argentina's?
- How did foreign interventions and class, racial, and ethnic conflicts shape the development of early nineteenth-century national identities in the United Provinces of Central America?

INDEPENDENCE DID NOT bring Latin America the ordered freedom and prosperity for which the liberators had hoped. In most of these newly emerging states, decades of civil strife followed the passing of Spanish and Portuguese colonial rule. Bolívar reflected the disillusionment of many patriot leaders when he wrote in 1829, "There is no good faith in America, nor among the nations of America. Treaties are scraps of paper; constitutions, printed matter; elections, battles; freedom, anarchy; and life, a torment." The contrast between Latin American stagnation and disorder and the meteoric advance of the former English colonies—the United States—intensified the pessimism and self-doubt of some Latin American leaders and intellectuals.

The Fruits of Independence

Frustration of the great hopes with which the struggle for liberation began was inevitable, for indepen-

dence did not produce the economic and social changes that could shatter the colonial mold. Aside from the passing of the Spanish and Portuguese trade monopolies, the colonial economic and social structures remained intact. The hacienda, fazenda, or estancia, employing archaic techniques and a labor force of peons or slaves, continued to dominate agriculture; no significant class of small farmers arose to challenge the economic and political might of the great landowners. Indeed, the independence wars strengthened the power of the landed aristocracy by removing the agencies of Spanish rule—viceroys, audiencias, intendants—and by weakening among the landowners the ingrained habits of obedience to a central authority. In contrast, all other colonial elites—the merchant class, weakened by the expulsion or emigration of many loyalist merchants; the mine owners, ruined by wartime destruction or confiscation of their properties; and the church hierarchy, often in

1814–1840	Paraguayan dictator Dr. Francia establishes state-owned farms called *estancias de la patria* and promotes balanced agricultural and industrial development
1815–1817	José Artigas declares independence of Banda Oriental (Uruguay) and calls for redistribution of royalist lands to landless people
1818–1823	Bernardo O'Higgins establishes liberal rule in Chile
1821–1823	Rise and fall of Agustín Iturbide's conservative empire in Mexico
1821–1827	Rise and fall of Bernardino Rivadavia's liberal state in the United Provinces of La Plata (Argentina)
1823–1842	Emergence of the United Provinces of Central America under the liberal leadership of Francisco Morazán
1830–1837	Era of conservative rule under Diego Portales in Chile
1831–1852	Juan Manuel de Rosas establishes conservative rule in the United Provinces of La Plata
1834–1854	Antonio de Santa Anna inaugurates conservative rule in Mexico
1839–1847	Caste War of Yucatán combines resistance to conservative rule with demands for indigenous autonomy and defense of ancestral lands
1842–1865	Rafael Carrera defeats Morazán, dissolves United Provinces of Central America, and brings conservative rule to Guatemala
1846–1848	North American Invasion (Mexican War) ends with Treaty of Guadalupe Hidalgo that surrenders one-half of Mexican territories to United States
1854–1862	Juan Álvarez announces Plan de Ayutla, inaugurating War of the Reform, a decade of civil war and liberal rule
1862–1868	French intervention and restoration of Mexican empire under the rule of Maximilian and Carlota; establishment of Argentine Republic under leadership of liberal Bartolomé Mitre
1865–1870	War of the Triple Alliance destroys Paraguayan development
1868–1876	Expulsion of French occupation and creation of Mexico's Restored Republic under liberals Benito Juárez and Sebastián Lerdo de Tejada

disgrace for having sided with Spain—emerged from the conflict with diminished weight.

To their other sources of influence, members of the landed aristocracy added the prestige of a military elite crowned with the laurels of victory, for many revolutionary officers had arisen from its ranks. The militarization of the new states because of years of destructive warfare and postwar instability ensured a large political role for this officer group. Standing armies that often consumed more than half of the national budgets arose. Not content with the role of guardians of order and national security, military officers became the arbiter of political disputes, usually deciding in favor of the conservative landowning interests and their allies among the urban elites.

ECONOMIC STAGNATION

Independence leaders had expected that a vast expansion of foreign trade would follow the passing of Spanish commercial monopoly and aid economic recovery. In fact, some countries, favored by their natural resources or geographic position, soon recovered from the revolutionary crisis and scored modest to large economic advances; these included Brazil (coffee and sugar), Argentina (hides), and Chile (metals and hides). Others, such as Mexico, Bolivia, and Peru, whose mining economies had suffered shattering blows, failed to recover colonial levels of production.

Several factors accounted for the economic stagnation that plagued many of the new states in the first half of the nineteenth century. Independence did not usher in a redistribution of land and income that might have stimulated a growth of internal markets and productive forces. The anticipated large-scale influx of foreign capital also did not materialize—partly because political disorder discouraged foreign investment and partly because Europe and the United States, then financing their own industrial revolutions, had little capital to export. Exports of Latin American staples remained below expectations, for Europe still viewed Latin America primarily as an outlet for manufactured goods, especially English textiles. The resulting flood of cheap, factory-made European products damaged local craft industries and drained the new states of their stocks of gold and silver, creating a chronic balance-of-trade problem. The British conquest of the Latin American markets further weakened the local merchant class, which was unable to compete with its English rivals. By mid-century, the wealthiest and most prestigious merchant houses, from Mexico City to Buenos Aires and Valparaíso, bore English names. Iberian merchants, however, continued to dominate the urban and provincial retail trade in many areas.

Taken together, these developments retarded the development of native capitalism and capitalist relations and reinforced the dominant role of the hacienda in the economic and political life of the new states. Aggravated by the lack of roads and by natural obstacles to communication (such as jungles and mountains), the deepening stagnation in their respective interiors intensified tendencies toward regionalism. This also enhanced local rule by *caudillos* (powerful political bosses) great and small, who usually were large landowners.[1] The sluggish tempo of economic activity encouraged these caudillos to employ their private followings of peons and retainers as pawns in the game of politics and revolution on a national scale. Indeed, in some countries, politics and revolution became a form of economic activity that compensated for the lack of other opportunities. Having gained control of the all-important customhouse (which collected duties on imports and exports) and other official sources of revenue, the victors often rewarded themselves and their followers with government jobs, contracts, grants of public land, and other favors. This reliance by members of the elite on political and military activity as a career and on the customhouse as a source of government revenue had two negative results. One was the rise of bloated military and bureaucratic establishments that diverted resources from economic development, and the other was

a stress on foreign trade that intensified the trend toward dependency.

POLITICS: THE CONSERVATIVE AND LIBERAL PROGRAMS

The political systems of the new states made large formal concessions to the liberal ideology of the nineteenth century. With the exception of Brazil, all the new states adopted the republican form of government (Mexico had two brief intervals of imperial rule) and paid their respects to the formulas of parliamentary and representative government. Their constitutions provided for presidents, congresses, and courts; often they contained elaborate safeguards of individual rights.

These façades of modernity, however, poorly concealed the dictatorial or oligarchical reality behind them. Typically, the chief executive was a caudillo whose power rested on force, no matter what the constitutional form; usually, he ruled with the support of a coalition of lesser caudillos, each more or less supreme in his own domain. The supposed independence of the judicial and legislative branches was a fiction. As a rule, elections were exercises in futility. Because the party in power generally counted the votes, the opposition had no alternative but revolt.

Literacy and property qualifications disfranchised most natives and mixed-race peoples, and if they had the right to vote, the *patrón* (master) often herded them to the polls to vote for him or for his candidates. The lack of the secret ballot (voting was usually open, with colored ballots) made coercion of voters easy. Whether Liberal or Conservative, all sections of the ruling class agreed on keeping the peasantry, gauchos, and other "lower orders" on the margins of political life, on preventing their emergence as groups with collective philosophies and goals. The very privileges that the new creole constitutions and law codes granted indigenous

---

1. The term *caudillo* commonly applies to politico-military leaders who held power on the national and regional level in Latin America before more or less stable parliamentary government became the norm in the area beginning about 1870. Military ability and charisma were qualities often associated with caudillos, who, although assuming many guises, did not all possess the same traits.

peoples—equality before the law, the "right" to divide and dispose of their communal lands—weakened their solidarity and their ability to resist the creole world's competitive individualism. But especially gifted, ambitious, and fortunate members of these marginal groups were sometimes co-opted into the creole elite and provided some of its most distinguished leaders; two examples are the Zapotec Benito Juárez in Mexico and the mestizo president Andrés Santa Cruz in Bolivia.

At first glance, the political history of Latin America in the first half-century after independence, with its dreary alternation of dictatorship and revolt, seems pointless and trivial. Nonetheless, the political struggles of this period were more than disputes over spoils between sections of a small upper class. Genuine social and ideological cleavages helped produce those struggles and the bitterness with which they were fought. Such labels as "Conservative" and "Liberal," "Unitarian" and "Federalist," assigned by the various parties to themselves or each other, were more than masks in a pageant, although opportunism contributed to the ease with which some leaders assumed and discarded these labels.

Conservatism generally reflected the interests of the traditional holders of power and privilege, men who had a stake in maintaining the existing order. Hence, the great landowners, the upper clergy, the higher ranks of the military and the civil bureaucracy, and monopolistic merchant groups tended to be Conservatives. Liberalism, in contrast, appealed to those groups who in colonial times had little or no access to the main structures of economic and political power and were naturally eager to alter the existing order. Thus, liberalism drew much support from provincial landowners, lawyers and other professionals (the groups most receptive to new ideas), shopkeepers, and artisans; it also appealed to ambitious, aspiring indígenas and mixed-race people. Nonetheless, regional conflicts and clan or family loyalties often cut across the lines of social and occupational cleavage, complicating the political picture.

Liberals wanted to break up the hierarchical social structure inherited from the colonial period. They had a vision of their countries remade into dynamic middle-class states on the model of the United States or England. Inspired by the success of the United States, they usually favored a federal form of government, guarantees of individual rights, lay control of education, and an end to a special legal status for the clergy and military. In their modernizing zeal, Liberals sometimes called for the abolition of entails (which restricted the right to inherit property to a particular descendant or descendants of the owner), dissolution of convents, confiscation of church wealth, and abolition of slavery. The **federalism** of the Liberals had a special appeal for secondary regions of the new states, which were eager to develop their resources and free themselves from domination by capitals and wealthy primary regions.

Conservatives typically upheld a strong centralized government, the religious and education monopoly of the Roman Catholic Church, and the special privileges of the clergy and military. They distrusted such radical novelties as freedom of speech and the press and religious toleration. Conservatives, in short, sought to salvage as much of the colonial social order as was compatible with the new republican system. Indeed, some conservative leaders ultimately despaired of that system and dreamed of implanting monarchy in their countries.

Neither Conservatives nor Liberals displayed much interest in the problems of the indigenous, black, and mixed-race masses that formed the majority of the population in most Latin American countries. Liberals, impatient with the supposed backwardness of indigenous peoples, regarded their communalism as an impediment to the development of a capitalist spirit of enterprise and initiated legislation providing for the division of communal lands—a policy that favored land grabbing at the expense of indigenous villages. Despite their theoretical preference for small landholdings and a rural middle class, Liberals recoiled from any program of radical land reform. Conservatives correctly regarded the great estate as the very foundation of their power. As traditionalists, however, the Conservatives sometimes claimed to continue the Spanish paternalist policy toward indigenous communities and often enjoyed their support.

This summary of the conservative and liberal programs for Latin America in the first half-century after independence inevitably overlooks variations from the theoretical liberal and conservative norms, variations that reflected the specific conditions and problems of the different states. A brief examination of the history of Mexico, Argentina, Chile, and the United Provinces of Central America reveals not only certain common themes but also a rich diversity of political experience.

Mexico

The struggle for Mexican independence, ironically begun by the radical priests Hidalgo and Morelos, ended with Agustín de Iturbide, who headed a coalition of creole and peninsular Conservatives. These men were terrified at the prospect of an imperial government that sought in 1820 to reestablish the liberal Spanish constitution of 1812. Independence, achieved under such conservative auspices, meant that Mexico's economic and social patterns underwent little change. To be sure, the popular insurgency begun by Hidalgo had at least a short-term impact on the social, economic, and political patterns of Mexican development. John Tutino, for example, has shown that in the Bajío the insurgency destroyed commercial hacienda production, which generated profit by storing maize until prices peaked with scarcity. It also forced a shift to tenant ranchero production, which maximized maize production, bringing "real and enduring benefits to both rural producers and urban consumers of maize across the Bajío during the first half-century of national life." Similarly, Florencia Mallon and Peter Guardino stress the revolutionary participation of popular urban and rural groups in Mexican nineteenth-century political struggles, revealing their long-term impact on Mexican state formation and peasant consciousness.

Nonetheless, the great hacienda continued to dominate the countryside in many areas. Although indigenous villages managed to retain substantial community lands until after mid-century and even improved their economic and political position somewhat with the passing of Spanish centralized authority, the trend toward usurpation of indigenous lands grew stronger because of the lapse of

Spanish protective legislation. Peons and tenants on the haciendas often suffered from debt servitude, miserable wages, oppressive rents, and excessive religious fees. At the constitutional convention of 1856–1857, the liberal Ponciano Arriaga declared:

> With some honorable exceptions, the rich landowners of Mexico ... resemble the feudal lords of the Middle Ages. On his seigneurial lands, with more or less formalities, the landowner makes and executes laws, administers justice and exercises civil power, imposes taxes and fines, has his own jails and irons, metes out punishments and tortures, monopolizes commerce, and forbids the conduct without his permission of any business but that of the estate.

An anonymous contemporary writer similarly reflected the disillusion of the lower classes with the fruits of independence: "Independence is only a name. Previously they ruled us from Spain, now from here. It is always the same priest on a different mule. But as for work, food, and clothing, there is no difference."

THE MEXICAN ECONOMY

The ravages of war had left mineshafts flooded, haciendas deserted, and the economy stagnant. The end of the Spanish commercial monopoly, however, brought a large increase in the volume of foreign trade; the number of ships entering Mexican ports jumped from 148 in 1823 to 639 in 1826. However, exports did not keep pace with imports, leaving a trade deficit that had to be covered by exporting precious metals. The drain of gold and silver aggravated the problems of the new government, which had inherited a bankrupt treasury and had to support a swollen bureaucracy and an officer class ready to revolt against any government that suggested a cut in their numbers or pay. The exodus of Spanish merchants and their capital added to the economic problems of the new state. Complicating those problems was the disorder that was a legacy of the war; according to Fanny Calderón de la Barca, bands of robbers made travel on the roads so unsafe that "whether coming or going from Puebla or Veracruz, the Mexico City traveler expected to be robbed."

Foreign loans appeared to be the only way out of the crisis. In 1824–1825, English bankers loaned Mexico 32 million pesos, guaranteed by Mexican customs revenues. Of this amount, the Mexicans received only a little more than 11 million pesos, as the bankers went bankrupt before they paid all the money due to Mexico from the loan. By 1843, unpaid interest and principal had raised the nation's foreign debt to more than 54 million pesos. This growing foreign debt created crushing interest burdens, threatened Mexico's independence, and endangered its territorial integrity, for behind foreign capitalists stood governments ready to intervene militarily in case of default.

Foreign investments, however, mainly from Britain, made possible a partial recovery of the decisive mining sector. Old mines, abandoned and flooded during the wars, reopened, but the available capital proved inadequate, the technical problems of reconstruction were greater than anticipated, and production remained relatively low.

An ambitious effort to revive and modernize Mexican industry also got under way, spurred on by the founding in 1830 of the *Banco de Avío*, which provided government assistance to industry. Manufacturing, paced by textiles, made some limited progress in the three decades after independence. Leading industrial centers included Mexico City, Puebla, Guadalajara, Durango, and Veracruz. But shortages of capital, lack of a consistent policy of protection for domestic industry, and a socioeconomic structure that sharply limited the internal market hampered the growth of Mexican factory capitalism. By 1843, the Banco de Avío had to close its doors for lack of funds. The Mexican economy, therefore, continued to rely heavily on mining and agriculture. Mexico's principal exports were precious metals, especially silver, and such agricultural products as tobacco, coffee, vanilla, cochineal, and henequen (a plant fiber used in rope and twine). Imports consisted primarily of manufactured goods that Mexican industry could not supply.

POLITICS: LIBERALS VERSUS CONSERVATIVES

A Liberal–Conservative cleavage dominated Mexican political life in the half-century after independence. That conflict was latent from the moment that the "liberator" Iturbide, the former scourge of insurgents, rode into Mexico City on September 27, 1821, flanked on either side by two insurgent generals, Vicente Guerrero and Guadalupe Victoria, firm republicans and Liberals. The fall of Iturbide in 1823 cleared the way for the establishment of a republic. But it soon became apparent that the republicans were divided into Liberals and Conservatives, Federalists and Centralists.

The constitution of 1824 represented a compromise between liberal and conservative interests. It appeased regional economic interests, which were fearful of a too-powerful central government, by creating nineteen states that possessed taxing power; their legislatures, each casting one vote, chose the president and vice president for four-year terms. The national legislature was bicameral, with an upper house (Senate) and a lower house (Chamber of Deputies). By ensuring the creation of local civil bureaucracies, the federalist structure also satisfied the demand of the provincial middle classes for greater access to political activity and office. However, the constitution also had a conservative tinge: Although the church lost its monopoly on education, it declared Catholicism the official religion and specifically confirmed the fueros of the church and the army.

A hero of the war of independence, the liberal general Guadalupe Victoria won the first presidential election under the new constitution. Anxious to preserve unity, Victoria brought the conservative Lucas Alamán into his cabinet, but this era of good feeling was short-lived; by 1825, Liberals forced Alamán out of the government. The Liberal–Conservative cleavage now assumed the form of a rivalry that reflected the Anglo-American competition for economic and political influence in Mexico. Founded by the American minister Joel Roberts Poinsett, the York Rite Masonic lodge favored Liberals and Federalists, who regarded the United States as a model for their own reform

Latin America, 1830

program. Its rival, the Scottish Rite lodge, sponsored by the British chargé d'affaires Henry Ward, appealed to the Conservative Party, which represented the old landed and mining aristocracy, the clerical and military hierarchy, monopolistic merchants, and some manufacturers. Its intellectual spokesman and organizer was Lucas Alamán, statesman, champion of industry, and author of a brilliant history of Mexico from the Conservative point of view.

The Liberal Party represented a creole and mestizo middle class—provincial landowners, professional men, artisans, the lower ranks of the clergy and military—determined to end special privileges and the concentration of political and economic power in the upper class. A priest-economist, José María Luís Mora, presented the liberal position with great force and lucidity. However, the Liberal Party was divided: The *moderados* (the moderate wing) wanted to proceed slowly and sometimes joined the Conservatives, whereas the *puros* (literally, the pure people) advocated sweeping antifeudal, anticlerical reforms.

During the first decade after independence, none of these factions consolidated its control over the nation, but the year 1833 was a high-water mark of liberal achievement. Aided by Mora, his minister of education, the puro President Valentín Gómez Farías pushed through Congress a series of radical reforms. These included abolition of the special privileges and immunities of the army and church (meaning that officers and priests would now be subject to the jurisdiction of civil courts), abolition of tithes, secularization of the clerical University of Mexico, creation of a department of public instruction, reduction of the army, and creation of a civilian militia. These measures accompanied a program of internal improvements designed to increase the prosperity of the interior by linking it to the capital and the coasts. In their use of the central government to promote education and national economic development, the Liberals showed that they were not doctrinaire adherents of **laissez-faire**.

This liberal program inevitably provoked clerical and conservative resistance. Army officers began to organize revolts; priests proclaimed from their pulpits that the great cholera epidemic of 1833 was a sign of divine displeasure with the works of the impious Liberals. Meanwhile, Gen. Antonio López de Santa Anna, a classic caudillo who earlier had supported liberal movements, now placed himself at the head of the conservative rebellion, occupied the capital, and sent Gómez Farías and Mora into exile. Assuming the presidency, he summoned a hand-picked, reactionary congress that repealed the reform laws of 1833 and suspended the constitution of 1824. The new conservative constitution of 1836 reduced the states to departments completely dominated by the central government, ensured upper-class control of politics through high property and income qualifications for holding office, and restored the fueros of the church and army.

Santa Anna and the Conservatives ruled Mexico for the greater part of two decades, 1834 to 1854. Politically and economically, the conservative rule subordinated the interests of the regions and the country as a whole to a wealthy, densely populated central core linking Mexico City, Puebla, and Veracruz. The Tariff Act of 1837 reflected its centralist trend. It restored the alcabala, or sales tax system, inland customhouses, and the government tobacco monopoly, ensuring the continuous flow of revenues to Mexico City.

Thereafter, conservative neglect and abuse of outlying or border areas like northern Mexico and Yucatán contributed to the loss of Texas in 1836 and almost led to the loss of Yucatán. Santa Anna's destruction of provincial autonomy enabled American colonists in Texas, led by Sam Houston, to pose as patriotic Federalists in a revolt against Santa Anna's tyranny. In Yucatán, the Caste or Social War of 1839 combined elements of a regional war against conservative centralism and an indigenous war against feudal landlords. For almost a decade, Yucatán remained outside Mexico.

After the United States annexed Texas in 1845, the North American Invasion or Mexican War (1846–1848) marked another conservative disaster. Its immediate cause was a dispute between Mexico and the United States over the boundary of Texas, but the decisive factor was the Polk administration's determination to acquire California and New Mexico. The war ended in catastrophic Mexican defeat, largely because Conservatives, dreading the mobilization of peasant armies in a prolonged guerrilla war against the U.S. invasion, concluded a hasty surrender. "The Mexican government," says Mexican historian Leticia Reina, "preferred coming to terms with the United States rather than endanger the interests of the ruling class." By the treaty of Guadalupe Hidalgo (1848), Mexico gave up half the country, ceding Texas, California, and New Mexico to the United States; in return, Mexico received $15 million and the cancellation of certain claims against it.

Naturally, puro leaders, including Benito Juárez, Melchor Ocampo, and Ponciano Arriaga, urged continued resistance. "Give the people arms," said Ocampo, "and they will defend themselves." In some regions of the country, peasant revolts broke out that combined demands for division of large haciendas among the peasantry and other reforms with calls for a continued resistance to the invaders. Congressional opposition mobilized against ratification of the treaty and urged continuing the war. In his "Observations on the Treaty of Guadalupe Hidalgo," the liberal Manuel Rejón predicted that the treaty would mean the inevitable economic conquest of Mexico by the United States. He foresaw that the new boundary, bringing American commerce closer to the Mexican heartland, would lead to the Americanization of Mexico; he argued that "we will never be able to compete in our own markets with the American imports.... The treaty is our sentence of death." Finally, in view of the intense American racism, he questioned whether the new U.S. government in the ceded territories would protect Mexican citizens in their civil and property rights as the treaty promised.

Rejón's fears concerning the treatment of Mexican citizens in the newly annexed territories were soon justified. The gold rush in California caused a wave of attacks by Anglo-American miners against native Californians. In his reminiscences, Antonio Coronel, from Los Angeles, described "stabbings, extortions, and lynchings as commonplace American reactions to native Californios, whom they regarded as interlopers." Even worse was the fate of indigenous Californians, whom the constitution of 1824 considered full Mexican

citizens. Denied the protection specified in the treaty of Guadalupe Hidalgo, they "became the victims of murder, slavery, land theft, and starvation." In two decades, the indigenous population of the state declined by more than one hundred thousand. "Genocide," writes Richard Griswold del Castillo, "is not too strong a word to use in describing what happened to the California Indians during that period." In New Mexico, which became a territory rather than a state, Hispanic inhabitants did not gain citizenship status until New Mexico achieved statehood in 1912, and it continued to deny its native peoples the vote until 1953.

A major grievance of many Mexican Americans was (and remains) violation of their land rights, the protection of which the treaty of Guadalupe Hidalgo promised. Claiming that the great majority of Mexican land grants in the ceded territory were "imperfect," American courts ruled that the U.S. government had inherited the right to complete the process of land confirmation. In California and New Mexico, this process, creating for Mexican American landowners an immense expense of litigation and legal fees, aggravated by usurious interest rates and falling cattle prices, resulted in the loss of their land by most rancheros. Even the few who survived the confirmation process came under great pressure from squatters, mostly wealthy and influential Anglo-Americans, to surrender their land. In New Mexico, writes historian Richard Griswold del Castillo, a fraternity of predatory lawyers and politicians, the so-called Santa Fe Ring, "used the long legal battles over land grants to acquire empires extending over millions of acres." Here, the struggle of Mexican Americans to regain the lost lands of their ancestors, on the basis of the claim that the United States violated the articles of the treaty of Guadalupe Hidalgo that guaranteed the citizenship and property rights of Mexicans, continues into the twenty-first century.

LA REFORMA, CIVIL WAR, AND THE FRENCH INTERVENTION

The disasters suffered by Mexico under conservative rule had created widespread revulsion against conservative policies and stimulated a revival of puro liberalism. In 1846, during the war, liberal administrations came to power in the states of Oaxaca and Michoacán. In Michoacán the new governor was Melchor Ocampo, a scholar and scientist whom Rousseau and French utopian socialist thought profoundly influenced. In Oaxaca, Benito Juárez, a Zapotec lawyer, became governor and earned a reputation for honesty, efficiency, and democratic simplicity.

Ocampo and Juárez were two leaders of a renovated liberalism that ushered in the movement called *La Reforma*. Like the older liberalism of the 1830s, the Reforma sought to destroy feudal vestiges and implant capitalism in Mexico. Its ideology, however, was more spirited than the aristocratic, intellectual liberalism of Mora. Puros like Ponciano Arriaga and Ignacio Ramírez transcended liberal ideology with their attacks on the latifundio, the defense of labor and women's rights, and other advanced ideas. Meanwhile, Santa Anna returned to power in 1853 and, accompanied by a terrorist campaign against all dissenters, proclaimed himself "His Most Supreme Highness." This spurred a gathering of opposition forces, including many disgruntled moderados and Conservatives. In early 1854, the old liberal caudillo, Juan Alvarez, and the moderado general Ignacio Comonfort issued a call for revolt: the Plan of Ayutla, which demanded the end of the dictatorship and the election of a convention to draft a new constitution. Within a year, Santa Anna, seeing the handwriting on the wall, went into exile for the last time, and a puro-dominated provisional government took office. Alvarez became provisional president and named Benito Juárez as minister of justice and Miguel Lerdo de Tejada as treasury minister.

One of Juárez's first official acts was to issue a decree, the *Ley Juárez*, proclaiming the state's right to limit clerical and military fueros to matters of internal discipline. The *Ley Lerdo* (Lerdo Law) of 1856, drafted by Lerdo de Tejada, also struck a heavy blow at the material base of the church's power: its landed wealth. The law barred the church from holding land not used for religious purposes and compelled the sale of all such property

to tenants. It also auctioned unrented real estate to the highest bidder, with payment of a large sales tax to the government.

The law aimed to create a rural middle class, but because it made no provision for division of the church estates, the bulk of the land passed into the hands of great landowners, merchants, and capitalists, both Mexican and foreign. Worse, the law barred indigenous villages from owning land and ordered the sale of such land in the same manner as church property, excepting only land and buildings designed exclusively for the public use of the inhabitants and for *ejidos* (communal pastures). As a result, land-grabbers descended on the native villages, "denounced" their land to the local courts, and proceeded to buy it at auction for paltry sums. The law provided that the native owners should have the first opportunity to buy property, but few could pay the minimum purchase price. When they responded with protests and revolts, Lerdo explained in a circular that the intent of his law was to ensure that community lands should be divided among the natives, not sold to others. But he insisted that "the continued existence of the Indian communities ought not to be tolerated …, and this is exactly one of the goals of the law."

Lerdo was also adamant that those who rented indigenous lands had the right to buy them if they chose to do so. Consequently, during the summer and fall of 1856, many *pueblos* (towns) lost crop and pasturelands from which they had derived revenues vitally needed to defray the cost of their religious ceremonies and other communal expenses. Indigenous resistance and the Liberals' need to attract popular support in their struggle with the conservative counterrevolution and French interventionists in the decade 1857–1867 slowed enforcement of the Lerdo Law as it applied to native villages. However, the long-range tendency of liberal agrarian policy compelled division of communal lands, facilitating their acquisition by hacendados and even small and mid-size farmers. This strengthened the latifundio and increased the size of the rural middle class.

Meanwhile, a constitutional convention dominated by moderate Liberals drafted the constitution of 1857, which proclaimed freedom of speech, press, and assembly; limited fueros; forbade ecclesiastical and civil corporations to own land; and proclaimed the sanctity of private property. It restored the federalist structure of 1824, but it replaced the bicameral national legislature with a single house and eliminated the office of vice president. A few voices denounced the land monopoly, peonage, and immense inequalities of wealth. "We proclaim ideas and forget realities," complained the radical delegate Ponciano Arriaga. "How can a hungry, naked, miserable people practice popular government? How can we condemn slavery in words, while the lot of most of our fellow citizens is more grievous than that of the black slaves of Cuba or the United States?" Despite his caustic attack on the land monopoly, Arriaga offered a relatively moderate solution: The state should seize and auction off large uncultivated estates. The conservative opposition promptly branded Arriaga's project "communist"; the moderate majority in the convention passed over it in silence.

Because the new constitution incorporated the Lerdo Law and the Juárez Law, the church now openly entered the political struggle by excommunicating all public officials who took the required oath of loyalty. Counterrevolution had been gathering its forces for months, and the Three Years' War soon erupted in 1857. As the struggle progressed, both sides found themselves in serious financial difficulties. The Conservatives, however, had the advantage of generous support from the church. In July 1859, Juárez struck back at the clergy with reform laws that nationalized without compensation all ecclesiastical property except church buildings; the laws also suppressed all monasteries, established freedom of religion, and separated church and state.

By the middle of 1860, although conservative bands in the provinces continued to make devastating raids, the tide of war had turned in favor of the Liberals. The war was effectively over, but diehard reactionaries now looked for help abroad. The conservative governments of England, France, and Spain had no love for the Mexican Liberals and Juárez. Moreover, both sides had ample pretexts for intervention, for they both had seized or destroyed foreign property without compensation, and foreign bondholders were clamoring for payments from an empty Mexican treasury. The three European powers demanded compensation for damages to their nationals and payment of just debts. Noting the dubious nature of some of the claims, Juárez vainly pleaded poverty, but the three powers nonetheless invaded and occupied Veracruz in 1862. France wanted more than payment of debts, however. A group of Mexican conservative exiles had convinced Napoleon III that the Mexican people would welcome a French army of liberation and the establishment of a monarchy. Napoleon had visions of a French-protected Mexican empire that would yield him great political and economic advantages. It remained only to find a suitable unemployed prince like Archduke Ferdinand Maximilian of Hapsburg, brother of Austrian emperor Franz Josef.

To prepare the ground for the arrival of the new ruler of Mexico, the French army advanced from Veracruz into the interior toward Puebla, where, instead of a festive welcome as liberators, the invaders met determined resistance from a poorly armed Mexican garrison and suffered heavy losses. Mexicans still celebrate the date—Cinco de Mayo de 1862—as a national holiday to commemorate the struggle against imperialism. Nonetheless, the French soon secured control of some major cities, but republican guerrilla detachments controlled most of the national territory.

Meanwhile, a delegation of conservative exiles called on Maximilian to offer him a Mexican crown, which he and his wife Carlota gratefully accepted in 1864. The conservative conspirators had counted on Maximilian to help them recover their lost wealth and privileges, but the emperor, mindful of realities, would not consent to their demands; the purchase of church lands by native and foreign landlords and capitalists had created new interests that Maximilian refused to antagonize. Confident of conservative support, Maximilian even wooed moderate Liberals.

But the hopes of both conservatives and misguided Liberals were built on quicksand. The victories of Maximilian's generals could not destroy the fluid and elusive liberal resistance, firmly grounded in popular hatred for the invaders and aided by Mexico's rugged terrain. In 1865, with its triumph over the Confederacy, the Union government demanded that the French evacuate Mexico, a region regarded by Secretary of State William Seward as a U.S. zone of economic and political influence. Facing serious domestic and diplomatic problems at home, Napoleon decided to cut his losses and liquidate the Mexican adventure. Abandoned by his Mexican and French allies, Maximilian and his leading generals, Miguel Miramón and Tomás Mejía, were captured, found guilty of treason, and executed by a *Juarista* firing squad.

Postwar Transformation of *La Reforma*

Juárez, symbol of Mexican resistance to a foreign usurper, assumed the presidency in August 1867. His government inherited a devastated country. Agriculture and industry were in ruins; as late as 1873, the value of Mexican exports was below the level of 1810. To reduce the state's financial burdens and end the danger of military control, Juárez dismissed two-thirds of the army, an act that produced discontent

Mexico's José Clemente Orozco celebrated Mexican national resistance to French colonialism and the heroic leadership of Benito Juárez in this painting entitled *The Triumph of Juarez*. It depicts ordinary Mexican citizens rising to assist outgunned and overmatched Mexican regular army soldiers in a great victory over the French Legion at the Battle of Puebla on May 5, 1862.

and uprisings that his generals managed to suppress. He also devoted the state's limited resources to the development of a public school system, especially on the elementary level; by 1874, eight thousand schools with some three hundred fifty thousand pupils were in operation.

Juárez's agrarian policy continued the liberal program that aimed to implant capitalism in the countryside, at the expense of indigenous communities, not the haciendas. Indeed, the period of the Restored Republic (1868–1876) saw the federal government's intensified effort to implement the Lerdo Law by compelling dissolution and partition of indigenous communal lands, opening the way for a new wave of fraud and seizures by neighboring hacendados and other land-grabbers. The result was a series of nationwide peasant revolts, the most serious occurring in the state of Hidalgo (1869–1870). Denouncing the rebels as communists, the hacendados, aided by state and federal authorities, restored order by the traditional violent methods. A few Liberals like Ignacio Ramírez raised their voices in protest, but they were ignored. Ramírez condemned the usurpation and fraud practiced by the hacendados with the complicity of corrupt judges and officials and called for suspension of the law.

Reelected president in 1871, Juárez put down a revolt by a hero of the wars of the Reforma, Gen. Porfirio Díaz, who charged Juárez with attempting to become a dictator. Juárez died the next year of a heart attack and Sebastían Lerdo de Tejada, chief justice of the Supreme Court, succeeded him as acting president. He governed until 1876 when Díaz, aided by a group of Texas capitalists with strong links to New York banks, successfully overthrew him.

Díaz seized power in the name of the ideals of the Reforma, but thereafter, he embraced a new, profoundly antirevolutionary ideology of positivism, which ranked order and progress above freedom. This ideological change reflected the material transformation of the Mexican **bourgeoisie** from a revolutionary class into a ruling class that was more predatory and acquisitive than the old creole aristocracy. The remnants of that aristocracy speedily adapted to the ways of the new ruling class and merged with it. The interests of the old and the new rich required political stability, a docile labor force, internal improvements, and a political and economic climate that was favorable to foreign investments. This was the mission of Porfirio Díaz's government—what Porfirista intellectual Francisco Cosmes called an "honorable tyranny."

Argentina

In 1816, delegates to the congress of Tucumán proclaimed the independence of the United Provinces of the Río de la Plata. "Disunited," however, would have better described the political condition of the La Plata area, for the creole seizure of power in Buenos Aires in 1810 brought in its wake a dissolution of the vast viceroyalty of the Río de la Plata.

THE LIBERATION OF PARAGUAY, URUGUAY, AND UPPER PERU

Paraguay was the first to repel the Buenos Aires junta's efforts to liberate it, and, under the dictatorial rule of the creole lawyer José Gaspar Rodríguez de Francia, it declared its own independence. Thereafter, Francia effectively sealed it off from its neighbors to avoid submission and payment of tribute to Buenos Aires, which controlled Paraguay's river outlets to the sea. Francia did permit a limited licensed trade with the outside world by way of Brazil, chiefly to satisfy military needs.

Francia's state-controlled economy brought certain benefits: The planned diversification of agriculture, which reduced the production of such export crops as yerba maté, tobacco, and sugar, ensured a plentiful supply of foodstuffs and the well-being of the indigenous and mestizo masses. An interesting feature of Francia's system was the establishment of *estancias de la patria* (state farms or ranches) that successfully specialized in the raising of livestock and ended Paraguay's dependence on livestock imports from the Argentine province of Entre Ríos. Those who suffered most under Francia's dictatorship were Spaniards, many of whom he expelled or penalized in various ways, and creole aristocrats, who were kept under perpetual surveillance and subjected to severe repression.

The gaucho chieftain José Artigas also resisted the efforts of the Buenos Aires junta to dominate the area and led Uruguay, then known as the Banda Oriental, toward independence. In 1815, the junta abandoned these efforts, evacuated Montevideo, and turned it over to Artigas. No ordinary caudillo, Artigas defended Uruguayan nationality and sought to achieve social reform. In 1815, he issued a plan for distributing royalist lands to the landless, with preference shown to blacks, indigenous peoples, zambos, and poor whites. He did not, however, have the opportunity to implement this radical program. In 1817, a powerful Brazilian army invaded Uruguay and soon had a secure grip on the Banda Oriental. Occupied by foreign armies until 1828, Uruguay became independent only after Great Britain, unwilling to see it fall under the control of either Brazil or Argentina, intervened to negotiate its liberation.

Upper Peru, the mountainous northern corner of the old viceroyalty of La Plata, also escaped the grasp of Buenos Aires after 1810. Three expeditions into the high country won initial victories and then retreated under pressure from Spanish counteroffensives. Logistical problems, the apathy of the native population, and the hostility of the creole aristocracy, which remained loyal to Spain until it became clear that the royalist cause was doomed, contributed to the patriot defeats. Not until 1825 did Gen. Antonio José de Sucre, Bolívar's lieutenant, finally liberate Peru. Renamed Bolivia in honor of the liberator, it began its independent life the next year under a complicated, totally impractical constitution drafted by Bolívar.

THE STRUGGLE FOR PROGRESS AND NATIONAL UNITY

Even among the provinces that had joined at Tucumán to form the United Provinces of La Plata, discord grew and threatened the dissolution of the new state. The efforts of the wealthy port and province of Buenos Aires to impose its hegemony over the interior met with tenacious resistance. The end of the Spanish trade monopoly brought large gains to Buenos Aires and lesser gains to the littoral provinces of Santa Fe, Entre Ríos, and Corrientes; their

exports of meat and hides increased, and the value of their lands rose. However, the wine and textile industries of the interior, which the colonial monopoly had protected, suffered from the competition of cheaper and superior European wares imported through the port of Buenos Aires.

The interests of the interior provinces required a measure of autonomy, or even independence, to protect their primitive industries, but Buenos Aires preferred a single free-trade zone under a government dominated by the port city. This was one cause of the conflict between Argentine *federales* (Federalists) and **unitarios** (Unitarians). By 1820, the federalist solution had triumphed: The United Provinces had in effect dissolved into a number of independent republics, with the interior provinces ruled by caudillos, each representing the local ruling class and having a gaucho army behind him.

A new start toward unity came in 1821 when Bernardino Rivadavia, an ardent liberal who acknowledged the strong influence of English philosopher Jeremy Bentham, launched an ambitious program of education, social, and economic reform. He promoted primary education, founded the University of Buenos Aires, abolished the ecclesiastical fuero and the tithe, and suppressed some monasteries. Rivadavia envisioned a balanced development of industry and agriculture, with a large role assigned to British investment and colonization. The obstacles to industrialization proved too great, however, and little came of efforts in this direction. The greatest progress occurred in cattle raising, which expanded rapidly southward into territory formerly claimed by native peoples. To control the large floating population of gauchos, Rivadavia enacted vagrancy laws requiring them to have passports for travel and to have written permission from the *estanciero* to leave his ranch.

In 1822, hoping to raise revenue and increase production, Rivadavia introduced the system of **emphyteusis**, a program that distributed public lands to leaseholders at fixed rentals. Some writers have seen in this system an effort at agrarian reform, but the size of grants was not limited, and the measure actually contributed to the growth of latifundios. The lure of large profits in livestock raising

General Rosas.

Although he cultivated the populist image of a *gaucho*, Juan Manuel Rosas was a wealthy *estanciero* and military *caudillo*, whose policies inevitably defended the interests of Argentina's landed aristocracy.

Mary Evans Picture Library/Alamy

induced many native and foreign merchants, politicians, and members of the military to join the rush for land. The net result was the creation not of a small-farmer class but of a new and more powerful estanciero class that was the enemy of Rivadavia's progressive ideals.

Rivadavia's planning went beyond the province of Buenos Aires; he had a vision of a unified Argentina under a strong central government that would promote the rounded economic development of the whole national territory. In 1825, a constituent congress met in Buenos Aires at Rivadavia's call to draft a constitution for the United Provinces of the Río de la Plata. Rivadavia, who was elected president of the new state, made a dramatic proposal to federalize the city and port of Buenos Aires. The former capital of the province would henceforth belong to the whole nation, with the revenues of its customhouse used to advance the general welfare.

Rivadavia's proposal reflected his nationalism and the need to mobilize national resources for a war with Brazil (1825–1828) over Uruguay. Congress approved Rivadavia's project, but the federalist caudillos of the interior, fearing that the rise of a strong national government would mean the end of their power, refused to ratify the constitution and even withdrew their delegates from the congress. In Buenos Aires, a similar stand was taken by the powerful estancieros, who had no intention of surrendering the privileges of their province and regarded Rivadavia's program of social and economic reform as a costly folly. Defeated on the issue of the constitution, Rivadavia resigned the presidency in 1827 and went into exile. The liberal program for achieving national unity had failed.

After an interval of factional struggles, the federalism espoused by the landed oligarchy of Buenos Aires triumphed in the person of Juan Manuel Rosas, who became governor of the province in 1829. In 1831, he forged a federal pact under which Buenos Aires assumed representation for the other provinces in foreign affairs but left them free to run their own affairs in all other respects. Federalism, as defined by Rosas, meant that Buenos Aires retained the revenues of its customhouse for its exclusive use and controlled trade on the Río de la Plata system for the benefit of its merchants. A network of personal alliances between Rosas and provincial caudillos, backed by the use of force against recalcitrant leaders, ensured for him a large measure of control over the interior.

Rosas's long reign saw a reversal of Rivadavia's policies. For Rosas and the ruling class of estancieros, virtually the only economic concern was the export of hides and salted meat and the import of foreign goods. The dictator also showed some favor to wheat farming and artisan industry, which he protected by the Tariff Act of 1835, but the competition for land, pressure from the cattle industry, and the primitive character of artisan manufacturing combined to prevent both from taking much advantage of the act. Rosas himself was a great estanciero and owner of a *saladero* (salting plant) for the curing of meat and hides. He vigorously pressed the conquest of indigenous territory, bringing much new land under the control of the province of Buenos Aires; his government then sold it at low prices to estancieros, quickly abandoning Rivadavia's policy of state ownership of land.

Although he professed to favor the gauchos, Rosas enforced the vagrancy laws against them even more rigorously, seeking to convert so-called idlers into ranch hands or soldiers for his army. Contrary to some historians who argue that Rosas represented the rural masses against the urban aristocracy, Rosas clearly acknowledged his fear of the masses and his tactical support of gauchos and urban blacks to control them. "As you know," he wrote in a letter, "the dispossessed are always inclined to rise against the rich and the powerful. So … I thought it very important to gain a decisive influence over this class in order to control and direct it." Rosas's "populism," his cultivation of gaucho manners and dress, did nothing to improve the condition of the poor majority. Under Rosas, discipline on the estancias relied on punishments inherited from the colonial past that included torture, the lash, the stocks, and staking delinquent peons out "like hides in the sun." His government, observes John Lynch, was a seigneurial regime based on an informal alliance of estancieros and militia commanders, often the same people.

By degrees, Rosas cowed or destroyed the press and all other potential dissidents. To enforce the dictator's will, a secret organization known as the *Mazorca* (ear of corn—a reference to the close unity of its members) arose. In collaboration with the police, this terrorist organization assaulted and sometimes murdered Rosas's opponents. The masthead of the official journal and all official papers carried the slogan "Death to the savage, filthy unitarians!" Even horses had to display the red ribbon that was the federalist symbol. Those opponents who did not knuckle under to escape death fled by the thousands to Montevideo, Chile, Brazil, or other places of refuge.

Under Rosas, the merchants of the city and the estancieros of the province of Buenos Aires enjoyed a measure of prosperity, but it bore no proportion to the possibilities of economic growth. Technical backwardness marked all aspects of livestock raising and agriculture, and port facilities were totally inadequate.

Meanwhile, the littoral provinces, which had experienced some advance of livestock raising and agriculture, became increasingly aware that Rosas's brand of federalism was harmful to their interests and that free navigation of the river system of La Plata was necessary to ensure their prosperity. In 1852, the anti-Rosas forces formed a coalition that united liberal émigrés with the caudillo Justo José de Urquiza of Entre Ríos, who together defeated Rosas's army and sent him fleeing to an English exile.

Victory over Rosas did not end the dispute between Buenos Aires and the other provinces or between federalism and unitarianism. Only the slower process of economic change would forge the desired unity. A rift soon arose between the liberal exiles, who assumed leadership in Buenos Aires, and the caudillo Urquiza of Entre Ríos, who still sported the red ribbon of federalism. A sincere convert to the gospel of modernity and progress, he had proposed a loose union of the provinces, with all of them sharing the revenues of the Buenos Aires customhouse. However, the leaders of Buenos Aires feared the loss of their economic and political predominance to Urquiza, whom they wrongly considered a caudillo of the Rosas type.

After Urquiza had attempted unsuccessfully to make Buenos Aires accept unification by armed force, the two sides agreed to a peaceful separation. As a result, delegates from Buenos Aires were absent from the constitutional convention that met at Santa Fe in Entre Ríos in 1852.

The constitution of 1853 reflected the influence of the ideas of the journalist Juan Bautista Alberdi on the delegates. His forcefully written pamphlet, *Bases and Points of Departure for the Political Organization of the Argentine Republic*, offered the United States as a model for Argentina. The new constitution strongly resembled that of the United States in certain respects. The former United Provinces became a federal republic, presided over by a president with significant power who served a six-year term without the possibility of immediate reelection. It vested legislative functions in a bicameral legislature, a senate and a house of representatives. It proclaimed Catholicism the official religion of the nation, but assured freedom of worship for non-Catholics. The states could elect governors and legislatures and frame their own constitutions, but the federal government had the right of intervention—including armed intervention—to ensure respect for the provisions of the constitution. General Urquiza became the first elected president of the Argentine Republic.

The liberal leaders of Buenos Aires, joined by the conservative estancieros who had been Rosas's firmest supporters, refused to accept the constitution of 1853, for they feared the creation of any state they did not control. As a result, two Argentinas arose: the Argentine Confederation, headed by Urquiza, and the province of Buenos Aires. For five years, the two states maintained their separate existences. In Paraná, capital of the confederation, Urquiza struggled to repress gaucho revolts, stimulate economic development, and foster education and immigration. Modest advances occurred, but the tempo of growth lagged far behind that of the wealthy city and province of Buenos Aires, which prospered on the base of a steadily increasing trade with Europe in hides, tallow, salted beef, and wool.

Hoping to increase the confederation's scanty revenues, Urquiza began a tariff war with Buenos Aires, levying surcharges on any goods that landed at the Paraná River port of Rosario if duties had been paid on them at Buenos Aires. Buenos Aires responded with sanctions against ships sailing to Rosario and threatened to close commerce on the Paraná altogether. In 1859, war between the two Argentine states broke out, and the forces of Bartolomé Mitre, governor of Buenos Aires, emerged victorious.

The military and economic superiority of Buenos Aires, the need of the other provinces to use its port, and awareness on all sides of the urgent need to achieve national unity dictated a compromise. At an 1862 congress representing all the provinces, it finally was agreed that the city should be the provisional capital of both the Argentine Republic and the province and that the Buenos Aires custom-

house should be nationalized, with the proviso that for a period of five years the revenues of the province would not fall below the 1859 level. Bartolomé Mitre—distinguished historian, poet, soldier, and statesman—was elected the first president of a united Argentina.

Mitre promoted economic progress and consolidated national unity. He nationalized the customhouse, as he had promised, and made plans for the federalization of the capital. The construction of railways and telegraph lines that forged closer links between Buenos Aires and the interior had begun, and European immigrants arrived in growing numbers. His government made some progress in the establishment of a public school system, but great problems remained, the most difficult of which was the long, exhausting Paraguayan War (1865–1870).

THE PARAGUAYAN WAR

On the death of the dictator Francia in 1840, power in Paraguay passed to a triumvirate, in which Carlos Antonio López soon emerged as the dominant figure. In essence, López continued Francia's dictatorial system but gave it a thin disguise of constitutional, representative government. Because he had inherited a stable, prosperous state, López could afford to rule in a less repressive fashion than his predecessor did. More flexible than Francia, too, with a better understanding of the outside world, López made a successful effort to end Paraguay's diplomatic and commercial isolation. After the fall of Rosas, a stubborn enemy of Paraguayan independence, López obtained Argentine recognition of his country's independence and opened the Paraná to Paraguayan trade. López also established diplomatic relations with a series of countries, including England, France, and the United States.

The end of the policy of isolation accompanied a major expansion of the Paraguayan economy. Although agriculture (especially the production of such export crops as tobacco and yerba maté) continued to be the principal economic activity, López assigned great importance to the development of industry. One of his proudest achievements in this field was the construction of an iron foundry, the most modern enterprise of its type in Latin America. Transportation improved with the building of roads and canals, the creation of a fleet of merchant ships, and the construction of a short railroad line.

Continuing Francia's policy, López enlarged the role of the state sector in the national economy. In 1848, he transferred to state ownership forest-lands that produced yerba maté and other commercial wood products and much arable land. The lucrative export trade in yerba maté and some other products became a government monopoly, and the number of state-owned ranches rose to sixty-four. López promoted education as well as economic growth; by the time of his death, Paraguay had 435 elementary schools, with some twenty-five thousand pupils, and a larger proportion of literate inhabitants than any other Latin American country.

At the same time, López took advantage of his position to concentrate ownership of land and various commercial enterprises in his own hands and those of his children, relatives, and associates; thus, a bourgeoisie arose that profited by its close connection with the state. Few large private estates, however, existed; small or mid-size farms cultivated by owners or tenants, sometimes with the help of a few hired laborers, dominated the private agricultural sector. In contrast with the situation in other Latin American countries, peonage and debt servitude were rare, and the regime gradually abolished slavery with an 1842 manumission law. The relative absence of peonage and other feudal survivals contributed to a rapid growth of Paraguayan capitalism and the well-being of its predominantly indigenous and mestizo population. When López died in 1862, Paraguay was one of the most progressive and prosperous states in South America.

His son, Francisco Solano, succeeded him as dictator. The younger López inherited a tradition of border disputes with Brazil that erupted into open war when Brazil sent an army into Uruguay in 1864 to ensure the victory of a pro-Brazilian faction in that country's civil strife. López could not be indifferent to this action, which threatened the delicate balance of power in the basin of La Plata. López also feared that Brazilian control of

Uruguay would end unrestricted Paraguayan access to the port of Montevideo, which would make Paraguayan trade dependent entirely on the goodwill of Buenos Aires.

When the Brazilian government disregarded his protests, López declared war, and Brazil quickly concluded a Triple Alliance with Argentina and Uruguay; a separate secret treaty between Brazil and Argentina provided for the partition of more than half of Paraguay's territory between them. Paraguay thus faced a coalition that included the two largest states in South America, with an immense superiority in manpower and other resources.

Yet the war dragged on for five years, for at its outset Paraguay possessed an army of some seventy thousand well-armed and disciplined soldiers that outnumbered the combined forces of its foes. By 1870, however, the Triple Alliance had depleted Paraguay's economic strength and defeated its military forces. Perhaps as much as 20 percent of Paraguay's prewar population of some three hundred thousand perished because of military action, famine, disease, and a devastating Brazilian occupation. The peace treaty assigned much Paraguayan territory to the victors and burdened Paraguay with extremely heavy reparations. Brazil, the occupying power, installed a puppet regime that radically reconstructed the Paraguayan economy and state.

The essence of the new policy was to liquidate the progressive changes made under the Francia and López regimes. The new regime sold most state-owned lands to land speculators and foreign businesses at bargain prices, with no restriction on the size of holdings. It expelled tenants who could not present the necessary documents, even though they and their forebears had cultivated the land for decades. By the early 1890s, the state-owned lands were almost gone. Foreign penetration of the economy through loans, concessions, and land purchases soon deprived Paraguay of its economic as well as its political independence.

PROGRESS AND DEVELOPMENT UNDER SARMIENTO

The Paraguayan War also changed Argentina, which obtained its share of Paraguayan reparations

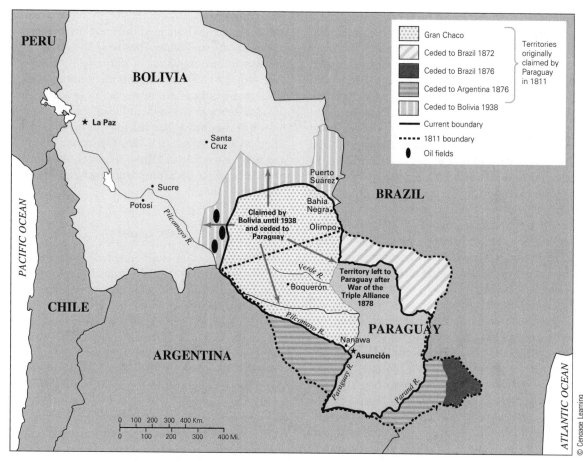

War and National Development in Paraguay and Bolivia, 1864–1938

and territorial concessions (Formosa, Chaco, and Misiones). Politically, it ushered in a transfer of power to Domingo Faustino Sarmiento (1868–1874), a gifted essayist, sociologist, and diplomat, who worked for Argentine unity and economic and social progress.

Even more important, however, a flood of technological change began to sweep over Argentina. Railways penetrated the interior, extending the stock-raising and farming area. The gradual introduction of barbed-wire fencing and alfalfa ranges made possible a dramatic improvement in the quality of livestock. In 1876, the arrival of an experimental shipload of chilled carcasses from France prepared the way for the triumph of frozen over

salted meat. This led to a vast expansion of European demand for Argentine beef and greater need for labor to exploit the rapidly expanding pasturelands and farmlands. As a result, Sarmiento's administration promoted immigration, and some three hundred thousand immigrants poured into the country. Sarmiento, believing it necessary to educate the citizens of a democratic republic, expanded the public school system and introduced to Argentina teacher-training institutions of the kind his friend Horace Mann had founded in the United States. But Sarmiento's policies had a dark side as well. Regarding native peoples and gauchos as obstacles to the advance of "civilization," he waged a war of extermination against indigenous communities and used vagrancy laws, press gangs, and other repressive measures to control the gauchos.

When Sarmiento left office, Argentina presented the appearance of a rapidly developing, prosperous state, but clouds soon invaded the generally bright Argentine sky. The growth of exports and the rise in land values did not benefit the majority of European immigrants or the forlorn gauchos, aliens in a land over which they once had freely roamed. Immigrants rarely acquired homesteads, and those who wished to farm usually found the price of land out of reach; as a result, many preferred to remain in Buenos Aires or other cities of the littoral, where they began to form an urban middle class largely devoted to trade. Meanwhile, foreign economic influence grew because of increasing dependence on foreign capital—chiefly British—to finance the construction of railways, telegraph lines, gasworks, and other needed facilities. Colonial patterns of land tenure and trade soon reemerged with the growing concentration of landownership, the tightening British control of markets and national economic infrastructure, and increasing dependence on a foreign metropolis, with London replacing Seville as the commercial center. Nevertheless, Mitre, Sarmiento, and other builders of the new Argentina celebrated their successes in nation-building. They believed wrongly that this climate of prosperity was permanent, and they did not suspect the extent of the problems in the making, nor did they anticipate the nature of the problems future generations of Argentines would face.

Chile

The victories of José de San Martín's Army of the Andes over royalist forces at Chacabuco and Maipú in 1817 and 1818 gave Chile its definitive independence. From 1818 until 1823, Bernardo O'Higgins, a hero of the struggle for Chilean liberation and a true son of the Enlightenment, ruled the country with the title of supreme director. O'Higgins energetically pushed a program of reform designed to weaken the landed aristocracy and the church and promote rapid development of the Chilean econ-

omy along capitalist lines. His abolition of titles of nobility and entails angered the great landowners of the fertile Central Valley between the Andes and the Pacific; his expulsion of the royalist bishop of Santiago and his restrictions on the number of religious processions and the veneration of images infuriated the church. Dissident Liberals who resented his sometimes heavy-handed rule joined the opposition to O'Higgins. In 1823, O'Higgins resigned and went into exile in Lima. There followed seven turbulent years, with presidents and constitutions rising and falling.

PORTALES AND ECONOMIC GROWTH

In Chile, as in other Latin American countries, the political and armed struggle gradually assumed the form of a conflict between Conservatives, who usually were Centralists, and Liberals, who generally were Federalists. The Conservative–Centralists were the party of the great landowners of the Central Valley and the wealthy merchants of Santiago; the Liberal–Federalists spoke for the landowners, merchants, and artisans of the northern and southern provinces, who were resentful of political and economic domination by the wealthy central area. By 1830, the Conservatives emerged victorious under the leadership of Joaquín Prieto and his cabinet minister Diego Portales.

Until 1837, Portales, who never held an elective office, indelibly stamped his ideas on Chilean politics and society. A business executive of aristocratic origins and owner of a successful import house, he faithfully served the interests of an oligarchy of great landlords and merchants that dominated the Chilean scene for decades. Although Portales expressed atheist views in private, he supported the authority of the church as an instrument for keeping the lower classes in order. He understood the importance of trade, industry, and mining and promoted their interests by removing remaining obstacles to internal trade. He introduced income and property taxes to increase the state's revenues and trimmed government spending by dismissing unnecessary employees. High tariffs on agricultural imports protected Chilean agriculture.

His government improved port facilities, strengthened the Chilean merchant marine, and, in 1835, supported construction of a steamship line to connect Chilean ports. Under the fostering care of the conservative regime and in response to a growing European demand for Chilean silver, copper, and hides, the national economy made steady progress in the 1830s.

Measures designed to stimulate economic growth complemented others that fortified the social and political power of the oligarchy. Portales restored the privileges the church had lost under liberal rule and normalized the troubled relations between Chile and the papacy.

In 1833, a conservative-dominated assembly adopted a constitution that further consolidated the power of the oligarchy. It made elections indirect, with the suffrage limited to men of twenty-five years or over who could satisfy literacy and property qualifications. It required still higher property qualifications for the lower and upper houses. The constitution restored entails, ensuring the perpetuation of the latifundio, declared Catholicism the state religion, and gave the church control over marriage. The president enjoyed an absolute veto over congressional legislation, appointed all high officials, and could proclaim a state of siege. The process of amending the constitution was so difficult as to be virtually impossible. Because the president controlled the electoral machinery, the outcome of elections was a foregone conclusion.

ECONOMIC EXPANSION UNDER BULNES

In 1841, Gen. Manuel Bulnes succeeded Prieto to the presidency and won reelection to a second five-year term in 1846. Victorious at home and abroad, the conservative leadership decided it could relax the strict discipline of the Portales period. Chile's economic life began a renewed advance. Commerce, mining, and agriculture prospered as never before. The Crimean War and the gold rushes to California and Australia of the 1850s created large, new markets for Chilean wheat, stimulating a considerable expansion of the cultivated area. In 1840, a North American, William Wheelright, established

a steamship line to operate on the Chilean coast, using coal from newly developed hard coal mines. Wheelright also founded a company that in 1852 completed Chile's first railroad line, providing an outlet to the sea for the production of the mining district of Copiapó. The major Santiago-Valparaíso line, begun in 1852, was not completed until 1863. Foreign capital—especially British—began to penetrate the Chilean economy; Britain dominated foreign trade and had a large interest in mining and railroads, but Chilean capitalists constituted an important, vigorous group and displayed much initiative in the formation of joint stock companies and banks.

The great landowners were the principal beneficiaries of this economic upsurge; their lands appreciated in value without any effort on their part. Some great landowners invested their money in railroads, mining, and trade. However, the essential conservatism of the landed aristocracy and the urge to preserve a semifeudal control over its peons discouraged the transformation of the great landowners into capitalist farmers. A pattern of small landholdings arose in southern Chile, to which German as well as Chilean colonists came in increasing numbers in the 1840s and 1850s. The rich Central Valley, still dominated by the latifundio, reflected inefficient techniques and reliance on the labor of *inquilinos* (tenants who also had to work the master's fields). Thus, alongside an emerging capitalist sector composed of mining, trade, banking, intensive agriculture, and some industry, a semifeudal sector flourished; it drew on the latifundio, peonage, and an aristocracy that hindered the development of Chilean capitalism.

Although Chile appeared more progressive than most other Latin American states, militants like José Victorino Lastarria—historian, sociologist, and a deputy of the Liberal Party—were dissatisfied with the new Conservatives' modest concessions to modernity. They wanted to accelerate the rate of change and demanded both a radical revision of the constitution of 1833 and an end to oligarchical rule.

To the left of Lastarria stood the firebrand Francisco Bilbao, author of a scorching attack on the church and Hispanic heritage, "The Nature of

This David Siqueiros mural, *Death to the Invader*, depicts the fused bodies of Chile's indigenous warriors Lautaro, Galvarino, and Caupolicán, joined with Francisco Bilbao, the mid-nineteenth-century crusader for freedom and social justice. In the background, Bernardo O'Higgins and José Manuel Balmaceda join in the fight against foreign invasion.

Chilean Society" (1844). Later, he spent several years in France, where utopian socialist and radical republican thought profoundly influenced him. He returned to Chile in 1850 to found, with Santiago Arcos, the Society of Equality, uniting radical intellectuals and artisans, which advocated these advanced ideas. The society carried on an intensive antigovernmental campaign and within a few months had a membership of four thousand.

MONTT'S MODERATE REFORMS

The Society of Equality emerged on the eve of the 1850 election, for which President Bulnes had des-ignated Manuel Montt his heir. Despite Montt's progressive educational policies and patronage of the arts and letters, Liberals identified him with the repressive system of Portales and the constitution of 1833. Liberals like Lastarria and radical democrats like Bilbao proclaimed the impending election a fraud and demanded constitutional reforms. The government responded by proclaiming a state of siege and suppressing the Society of Equality. Regarding these acts as a prelude to an attempt to liquidate the opposition, groups of Liberals in Santiago and La Serena rose in revolts that the government quickly crushed. Lastarria was exiled, and Bilbao and Arcos fled to Argentina. Montt became president and immediately crushed another liberal revolt but thereafter took steps to resolve future crises by granting amnesty to the insurgents and abolishing both entails and tithes.

The abolition of entails, which aimed to encourage the breakup of landed estates among the children of the great landowners, affected a dwindling number of great aristocratic clans. Its effects were less drastic than the anguished cries of the affected parties suggested, for other latifundists almost invariably acquired the divided estates, and the condition of the inquilinos who worked the land remained the same. The elimination of the tithe and Montt's refusal to allow the return of the Jesuits greatly angered the reactionary clergy. Responding to their attacks, Montt promulgated a new civil code in 1857 that placed education under state control, gave the state jurisdiction over the clergy, and granted non-Catholics the right of civil marriage.

The abolition of entails and tithes represented a compromise between Liberals and Conservatives, between the new bourgeoisie and the great landowners. In the process, the bourgeoisie gained little, and the landowners lost almost nothing; the chief loser was the church. Although Montt's reforms alienated the most reactionary elements of the Conservative Party, they gained him the support of moderate Liberals, who joined with moderate Conservatives to form a new coalition, the National Party. Its motto was the typically positivist slogan "Freedom in Order."

In the last years of his second term, President Montt faced severe economic and political problems. The 1857 depression caused a sharp fall in the price of copper and reduced Australian and Californian demand for Chilean wheat. The economic decline fed the fires of political discontent, and another large-scale revolt erupted in January 1859. The rebels included radical intellectuals, northern mining capitalists and their workers, artisans, and small farmers, all groups with grievances against the dominant Central Valley alliance of great merchants and landowners. Their demands included a democratic republic, state support for mining and industry, the splitting up of the great estates, and

abolition of the semifeudal *inquilinaje* system of peonage as incompatible with democratic principles. Before it ended, the revolt had taken five thousand lives. Thereafter, Montt imprisoned some of the revolt's bourgeois leaders, deported others, and still others fled into exile, but a large number of miners, artisans, and peasants were executed. Maurice Zeitlin regards it as a crucial turning point in Chilean history: "Defeat of the revolutionary bourgeoisie amounted to virtual suppression of an alternative and independent path of capitalist development for Chile—a realm of objective historical possibilities unfulfilled because of the failure of the bourgeois revolution."

By 1861, the depression had lifted and another boom began, creating new fortunes and bringing large shifts of regional influence. A growing stream of settlers, including many Germans, flowed into southern Chile, founding cities and transforming woodlands into farms.

Nonetheless, Chile's true center of economic gravity became the desert north, rich in copper, nitrates, and guano; the last two, in particular, were objects of Europe's insatiable demand for fertilizers. The major nitrate deposits, however, lay in the Bolivian province of Antofagasta and the Peruvian province of Tarapacá. Chilean capital, supplemented by English and German capital, began to pour into these regions and soon dominated the Peruvian and Bolivian nitrate industries. In the north, an aggressive mining capitalist class demanded a place in the sun for itself and its region. A rich mine owner, Pedro León Gallo, abandoned the Liberals to form a new middle-class party called Radical, which fought more militantly than the Liberals for limited constitutional changes, religious toleration, and an end to repressive policies.

LIBERAL CONTROL

The transition of Chile's political life to liberal control, begun under Montt, culminated in 1871 with the election of the first liberal president, Federico Errázuriz Zañartú. Between 1873 and 1875, a coalition of Liberals and radicals pushed through the congress a series of constitutional reforms: reduction of senatorial terms from nine to six years; direct election of senators; and freedom of speech, press, and assembly. These victories for enlightenment also represented a victory of new capitalist groups over the old merchant-landowner oligarchy that traced its beginnings back to colonial times. By 1880, of the fifty-nine Chilean personal fortunes of more than 1 million pesos, only twenty-four were of colonial origin, and only twenty had made their fortunes in agriculture; the rest belonged to coal, nitrate, copper, and silver interests or to merchants whose wealth had been formed only in the nineteenth century. Arnold Bauer has observed that the more interesting point is "not that only twenty made their fortune in agriculture, but that the remaining thirty-nine—designated as miners, bankers, and capitalists—subsequently invested their earnings in rural estates. This would be comparable to Andrew Carnegie sinking his steel income into Scarlett O'Hara's plantation." Bauer's comment points to the "powerful social model" that the Chilean agrarian oligarchy continued to exert. For the rest, the victories of the new bourgeoisie brought no relief to the Chilean masses, the migrant laborers and tenant farmers on the haciendas, and the young working class in Chile's mines and factories.

During the first half-century after independence in Chile, collective fear of subaltern social sectors caused liberal and conservative elites to overcome their considerable differences and create a national political identity that stressed oligarchic unity and collaboration with foreign capitalists. Meanwhile, the great majority of Chilean peasants, propertyless wage workers, and indigenous communities, all of whom were largely excluded from this definition of citizenship, mobilized around issues of democracy, equality, and anticolonialism to promote their rival vision of a more inclusive nation-state. Ironically, José Manuel Balmaceda, himself born to a wealthy aristocratic family, soon became a national voice for this growing reform movement.

United Provinces of Central America

On the eve of independence, the five republics—Guatemala, El Salvador, Honduras, Nicaragua, and Costa Rica[2]—were provinces of the captaincy general of Guatemala, with its capital at Guatemala City. Under the captain general and his audiencia, a small group of wealthy creole merchants, organized in a powerful consulado, had dominated the economic, social, and political life of the colony. Spain's hold over its American colonies had weakened after 1800, however, because of its involvement in European wars, the resulting disruption of trade, and growing political turmoil at home. Central America drifted toward independence. When Mexico proclaimed its independence in 1821, Central America followed suit. City after city declared its independence, not only from Spain but from Guatemala and rival cities and towns, as well. The captaincy general dissolved into a multitude of autonomous *cabildo* (municipal) governments. The transition to independence grew more complicated because of Agustín de Iturbide's efforts to incorporate Central America into his Mexican empire, efforts supported by Central American Conservatives and opposed by many Liberals. In 1822, a majority of cabildos supported union with Mexico, but Iturbide's overthrow the next year permanently ended the Mexican connection.

INDEPENDENCE AND THE FAILURE OF UNION, 1810–1865

Despite provincial rivalries and resentment against Guatemalan domination, a tradition of Central American unity remained, which liberals sought to strengthen. In 1823, a constituent assembly met and created the federal republic of Central America out of the five former provinces: Guatemala, Honduras, Nicaragua, Costa Rica, and El Salvador. The constitution provided for a federal government with free and independent state governments and

---

2. Although, for descriptive convenience, Belize and Panama usually are included in Central America, the former was a British colony and the latter a province of Colombia. Therefore, neither had historical links to the region.

had a strong liberal tinge: It abolished slavery and the special privileges of the clergy and established the principles of laissez-faire, free trade, and free contract of labor. The next year, a Salvadoran liberal, Manuel José Arce, won the election as the first president of the republic. Meanwhile, the states were forming their own governments. On the state as on the federal level, Conservatives and Liberals struggled for power: Conservatism—the ideology of the old monopolistic merchant clique, many great landowners, and the church—had its base in Guatemala; liberalism was the dominant doctrine among many large and small landowners of the other states and the small middle class of artisans, professionals, and intellectuals. Behind the façade of elections and universal male suffrage, great landowning and mercantile families held power throughout the area, and they often mobilized their private armies of retainers and tenants in a struggle for control of regions and states.

The superficial unity of Central America soon dissolved as it became clear that the states were neither willing nor able to finance both their own governments and the federal government in Guatemala City. Efforts by Arce's federal government to assert its prerogatives by the establishment of a strong army and the collection of taxes led him to abandon liberalism, which ignited a destructive civil war between 1826 and 1829. The struggle ended with the defeat of the national government and its conservative leadership by liberal forces headed by Francisco Morazán and the reorganization of the union on a basis of liberal hegemony.

Morazán, elected president of the federal republic and commander of its armed forces, both based in San Salvador, defended it against conservative plots and attacks. At the same time, a former Conservative turned Liberal, Mariano Gálvez, the governor of Guatemala, launched a program for the economic and social reconstruction of his state. The program included establishment of civil marriage and divorce, secular schools on all levels, anticlerical measures that allowed nuns to leave their orders, and fewer church holidays. It also granted large land concessions to British companies that were to colonize the land with foreign immigrants

and develop basic economic infrastructure. It even provided an agrarian reform that allowed squatters to buy land for half its value and permitted natives to settle on vacant land. Gálvez also sought to reform Guatemala's judicial system by providing for trial by jury and *habeas corpus* and by vesting power to appoint all judges in the governor of the state. This last feature alienated powerful landed interests who often served as *jefes políticos* (local officials who combined judicial and administrative functions and claimed a share of tax collections as compensation).

The loss of the support of local landed interests combined with the ravages of a cholera epidemic that spread over Central America in 1837 to bring down the Gálvez regime and its ambitious reform program. Stirred up by local clergy who proclaimed the epidemic to be divine retribution for the heresies of civil marriage and divorce, the native and mixed-race masses rose in revolt against Gálvez's radical innovations in law and taxation, attacks on their landholdings by creole landowners, and sanitary measures instituted to prevent the spread of disease. Led by the mestizo Rafael Carrera, the principal revolt in February 1838 mobilized an army of indígenas and castas who cried, "Long live religion, and death to all foreigners!"

Carrera took Guatemala City, defeated Morazán in 1842, and ended the federal republic. He then established a conservative regime in Guatemala, which he controlled until his death in 1865. In 1854, dispensing with the formality of elections, he had Congress name him president for life. Thereafter, he implemented a reactionary program that revived the authority of the church, returned church and indigenous communal properties to their original owners, brought back native forced labor, and even changed the title of local officials from jefe político to the old colonial title of corregidor. What had begun as a lower-class protest against modernization and the spoliation of communal lands, however, soon changed into a conservative government controlled by a merchant oligarchy that provided the taxes Carrera needed to pay his army and foreign loans. Conservative ministers drawn from the elite surrounded the dictator. Alongside the traditional labor arrangements, free labor and a money economy existed, along with landless natives and mestizos working, sometimes under debt peonage, on the plantations.

Similar trends prevailed throughout Central America in the age of Carrera, although labor was freer in most of the area than it was in Guatemala. By the 1850s, an increasing world demand for coffee stimulated expansion of the crop, which had been grown on a large scale in Costa Rica since the 1830s, and spurred attacks on indigenous communal lands. Coffee in Costa Rica and El Salvador, along with indigo, made for relative political stability in those countries. In the more backward republics of Nicaragua and Honduras, where cattle barons warred with each other, little centralized authority existed.

The discovery of gold in California gave a new importance to Central America as a transoceanic transit route and sharpened the rivalry of the United States and Great Britain in the area. The threat to the sovereignty and territorial integrity of the Central American republics grew acute because of the folly of Nicaraguan Liberals, who in 1855 invited William Walker, an adventurer from the United States, to help them overthrow a conservative regime. Having brought the Liberals to power, Walker, supported by a band of some three hundred compatriots, staged a coup, proclaimed himself president, legalized slavery, and made English the official language. By mid-1856, in a rare display of unity, Nicaraguan Liberals and Conservatives, joined by all the other Central American republics, had combined in the National War against the Yankee intruders, but the Central American army that opposed Walker was essentially a conservative army. Defeated in 1857, Walker returned to the United States. He nevertheless made two more attempts to conquer Central America, the last ending with his death before a Honduran firing squad in 1860.

The National War revived the moribund movement for Central American unity. The liberal Salvadoran president Gerardo Barrios was a leading advocate of federation. His efforts to realize Morazán's dream provoked Carrera, who was determined to maintain conservative domination over Central America and to send troops into El Salvador and its ally Honduras. The war ended with Barrios's defeat and exile; every Central American republic now had conservative regimes. In 1865, Barrios attempted to make a comeback, but his enemies captured and executed him. Carrera died in the same year. With his death, the violence-filled formative period of Central American history ended.

Clearly, the wars of independence failed to effect major changes in colonial economic and social structures in Mexico, Argentina, Chile, and Central America. In the difficult process of decolonization, these young republics faced extraordinary obstacles, including regionalism, economic stagnation, and political instability, that challenged the capacity of each to create a distinctive national identity. The republican political systems adopted by these new states functioned in practice very differently from the political theory that informed them. A Conservative–Liberal cleavage, with its roots in the conflicting interests and ideals of various elite groups, dominated political, economic, and cultural life. Although these same elite conflicts also characterized the experience of decolonization and the postcolonial reconstruction of national identities in Brazil, Cuba, Peru, and Gran Colombia, popular opposition to slavery and the demand for freedom decisively shaped the process in those countries.

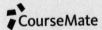 Go to the CourseMate website at **www.cengagebrain.com** for primary sources, additional study tools, and review materials—including audio and video clips—for this chapter.

10

Race, Nation, and the Meaning of Freedom, 1821–1888

FOCUS QUESTIONS

- How did movements to abolish slavery variously affect the development of national identities in Brazil, Peru, Cuba, and Gran Colombia?
- What were the causes of the crisis of Brazilian slavery after mid-century?
- Why did the creole elite in Peru oppose the movement of national liberation led by San Martín and Bolívar?
- How did conflicts over race and slavery within the rebel community affect the nineteenth-century evolution of Cuban nationalism?
- How did the struggle over emancipation affect the rivalry between Liberals and Conservatives in Venezuela and Colombia?

WITH THE ACHIEVEMENT OF INDEPENDENCE, the new nations then under construction immediately faced questions that their successful struggle for home rule had not answered. Who would rule at home, how, and through what institutions of the state? Who was a citizen, and what did it mean to be free? How would the state limit individual freedom and regulate relations among diverse social classes, racial and ethnic groups, and foreign interests? In the process of resolving these questions and building the postcolonial institutions that expressed the national interest, the colonial legacy of slavery and **race** played an influential role. Enslaved Africans and their descendants in the Americas actively participated in this postcolonial struggle to fashion unified nation-states out of societies that historically were divided by region, class, race, ethnicity, and gender. A popular desire for freedom from the slaveholder easily translated into calls for freedom from **patriarchy**, foreign control, and aristocratic class rule. This struggle, along with elite conflicts between Liberals and Conservatives, shaped the meaning of citizenship and the contours of new nationalities emerging in Brazil, Cuba, Peru, and Gran

Colombia. Although their motives often varied greatly, black slaves, free people of color, peasants, urban workers, merchants, radical intellectuals, and others joined together to demand the abolition of slavery, but they faced the equally determined resistance of slaveholders. In this conflict, race informed the negotiations that structured institutional relations between citizen and state, defining these new nations in the nineteenth century and beyond.

Initially, historians like Frank Tannenbaum argued that, contrary to the experience of emancipation in the United States, creole independence leaders like Simón Bolívar enthusiastically supported abolitionism, which consequently "was achieved in every case without violence, without bloodshed, and without civil war." Since then, historians have examined postcolonial elite decision making and concluded that political and military expediency, rather than moral enthusiasm, largely drove abolitionism in Latin America. According to this view, republican elites mostly embraced the idea of abolitionism to recruit black soldiers, counter royalist recruitment strategies, or curry favor with foreigners like Haiti's Alexandre Petion,

1812	Aponte slave rebellion in Cuba
1821	Congress of Cúcuta in Gran Colombia preserves slavery but decrees "free wombs" and encourages voluntary manumission
1823–1889	Independent empire of Brazil preserves the essential institutions of its colonial past
1823–1826	In Peru, Bolívar restores slavery, which San Martín had abolished
1829	José Antonio Páez dissolves Gran Colombia and preserves slavery in independent republic of Venezuela
1835–1845	Local Brazilian uprisings like the *cabanagem* and Sabinada revolts, Balaiada Rebellion, and Revolution of the Ragamuffins demand independence, republican government, racial equality, and abolition of slavery
1844	Cuban creole elite and Spanish colonial officials suppress Escalera slave conspiracy
1851	Brazil ends slave trade; slave revolt in Peru's Chicama Valley mobilizes abolitionist movement; José Hilario López abolishes slavery in Colombia
1854	Ramón Castilla abolishes slavery and indigenous tribute in Peru; Venezuela abolishes slavery
1858–1863	Federal War in Venezuela mobilizes poor majority against wealthy propertied elite
1868–1878	Ten Years' War, initially led by Cuban creoles like Carlos Manuel de Céspedes, mobilizes Afro-Cubans like Antonio Maceo to demand freedom from Spain, slavery, and social injustice
1871	Brazil passes Rio Branco law, freeing newborn slave children and encouraging voluntary manumission
1878	Pact of Zanjón ends Ten Years' War without winning Cuban independence or ending slavery and racial discrimination
1886	Cuba formally abolishes slavery
1888	Brazil abolishes slavery

who provided food and munitions in exchange for Bolívar's 1816 pledge to liberate all slaves. Although this offered a more critical and nuanced interpretation than Tannenbaum, it still focused on elite ideas and actions, thereby effectively silencing the voices of enslaved Africans and their descendants.

More recently, however, a new generation of historians, increasingly interested in recovering this lost voice, have asked new questions and examined new archival collections. Although they agree that elites mostly lacked the moral conviction that slavery was wrong (or failed independently to act on it), they stress the active role of enslaved and free people of color in opposing slavery and forcing reluctant elites to abolish it. Their study of Afro-Latino culture, religion, and family life reveals that the enslaved and free people of color pursued both legal and extralegal strategies in their relentless search for freedom. Court records, for example, show that slaves, grounding their arguments in appeals to republican laws, routinely petitioned the government for their liberty. Still more frequently, however, slaves employed the strategy of what W. E. B. Du Bois famously called "the general strike": they defied legal constraints, refused to work, escaped to join **maroon** communities called *palenques* or quilombos, engaged in social banditry, and, less frequently, openly rebelled against the institution of slavery. Taken together, this history of popular resistance decisively shaped both the institutions of government and citizen participation in the newly developing nations.

In general, a new consensus on the origins and implications of emancipation has emerged. First, it is clear that independence did not immediately produce the abolition of slavery. Second, creole independence leaders vigorously debated the morality of slavery and ultimately sought compromise that effectively prolonged its existence for decades. This most commonly involved passage of "Free Womb" laws that freed the children of enslaved women, required slave owners to support them (and control their labor) until adulthood, and thereafter paid the slaveholders compensation for their liberation. Third, slave owners accepted abolition only after the enslaved and free people of color rebelled, often violently, and threatened the long-term security of private property rights in the new republics. Elite fears of social revolution from below fueled reform programs that gradually abolished slavery, but they simultaneously established income and literacy requirements that limited free people's political participation. Finally, decades of civil strife and political mobilization of cross-class, multiracial coalitions ultimately prepared the way for emancipation, but the experience effectively silenced the struggle for racial justice, as citizen activists abandoned the divisive idea of race in favor of the unifying language of nation. As a result, emancipation generally compensated slave owners for their losses, and the newly emerging nations preferred not to speak about the enduring racial inequalities that remained for future generations of black and mixed-race peoples.

Naturally, the specific historical experiences of these nations varied, depending on local traditions, availability of land, proximity to transatlantic markets, reliance on slave labor, the size of the population of free people of color, and the influence of foreign nations. A careful study of this complex history therefore requires an examination of particular events in Peru, Gran Colombia, Cuba, and Brazil, where slave populations were largest and the iniquitous institution endured the longest.

Brazil

Brazil took its first major step toward independence in 1808, when the Portuguese crown and court, fleeing before a French invasion of Portugal, arrived in Rio de Janeiro to make it the new capital of the Portuguese empire. Formal national independence came in 1822 when Dom Pedro, who ruled Brazil as regent for his father, João VI, rejected a demand that he return to Portugal and issued the famous Cry of Ipiranga: "Independence or Death!"

DOM PEDRO, EMPEROR

Dom Pedro acted with the advice and support of the Brazilian aristocracy, which was determined to preserve the autonomy Brazil had enjoyed since 1808. It was equally determined to make a transition to independence without the violence that marked the Spanish American movement of liberation elsewhere. The Brazilian aristocracy had its wish; Brazil made a transition to independence with comparatively little disruption and bloodshed. But this meant that independent Brazil retained its colonial social structure: monarchy, slavery, large landed estates, monoculture, an inefficient agricultural system, a highly stratified society, and a free population that was 90 percent illiterate.

Dom Pedro had promised to give his subjects a constitution, but the constituent assembly he summoned in 1823 drafted a document that placed excessive limits on his power. In response, he dissolved the assembly and assigned a handpicked commission the task of making a new constitution, which he promulgated by imperial proclamation. This constitution, under which Brazil was governed until the fall of the monarchy in 1889, concentrated great power in the hands of the monarch. In addition to a Council of State, it provided for a two-chamber parliament: a lifetime Senate, the members of which the emperor chose, and a Chamber of Deputies who were elected only by voters who met certain property and income requirements that effectively disenfranchised the great majority. The emperor had the right to appoint and dismiss ministers and summon or dissolve parliament at will. He also appointed the provincial governors or presidents.

Resentment over Dom Pedro's high-handed dissolution of the constituent assembly and the highly centralist character of the constitution of 1824 was particularly strong in Pernambuco, a center of republican and federalist ferment. Here in 1824, a group of rebels, led by the merchant Manoel de Carvalho, proclaimed the creation of a Confederation of the Equator that would unite the six northern provinces under a republican government. A few leaders voiced antislavery sentiments, but they did nothing to abolish slavery, partly because they feared that this would mobilize the enslaved and free people of color to produce a revolutionary outcome modeled on the Haitian experience. This fear deprived the movement of the potential support of a large slave population, and, within a year, imperial troops had smashed the revolt.

Dom Pedro had won a victory, but resentment of his autocratic tendencies continued to smolder, and his popularity steadily waned. Once again, the issue of slavery loomed large. The emperor's foreign policies contributed to this growing discontent. In 1826, in return for recognition of Brazilian independence and a trade agreement, Dom Pedro signed a treaty with Great Britain that obligated Brazil to end the slave traffic by 1830. Despite this ban and the British Navy's efforts to seize the slave ships, the trade continued with the full knowledge and approval of the Brazilian government. Nonetheless, British policing practices caused the price of slaves to rise sharply. The prospering coffee growers of Rio de Janeiro, São Paulo, and Minas Gerais could afford to pay high prices for slaves, but the cotton and sugar growers of the depressed north could not compete with them for workers and blamed Dom Pedro for their difficulties.

News of the July Revolution of 1830 in France, a revolution that toppled an unpopular, autocratic king, produced rejoicing and violent demonstrations in Brazilian cities. *Exaltados* (radical Liberals) placed themselves at the head of the revolt and called for the abolition of the monarchy and the establishment of a federal republic. In the countryside, enslaved and free people of color seized the opportunity to demand the abolition of slavery, which had long functioned as the bedrock of a fragile elite provincial unity. In the face of the growing crisis, Dom Pedro abdicated in favor of his five-year-old son Pedro, and, two weeks later, he sailed for Portugal, never to return. These developments, eliminating the dominant influence of Portuguese merchants and Portuguese-born courtiers under Emperor Pedro I, completed the transition to full Brazilian independence.

REGENCY, REVOLT, AND A BOY EMPEROR

The revolution had been the work of radical Liberals, who viewed Dom Pedro's downfall as the first step toward the establishment of a federal republic, but the moderates enjoyed its fruits. In effect, the radicals had played the game of the monarchist Liberals, who had guided the movement of secession from Portugal and later lost influence at court because of Dom Pedro's embrace of conservative *fazendeiros*. Dom Pedro's departure was a victory for these moderates, who hastened to restore their ascendancy over the central government and prevent the revolution from getting out of hand.

As a first step, parliament appointed a three-man regency composed of moderate Liberals to govern for the child emperor until he reached the age of eighteen. Another measure created a national guard, recruited from the propertied classes, to repress urban mobs and slave revolts. Simultaneously, the new government began work on a project of constitutional reform designed to appease the strong federalist sentiment. After a three-year debate, parliament approved the Additional Act of 1834, which gave the provinces elective legislative assemblies with broad powers, including control over local budgets and taxes. This provision ensured that the great landowners had a large measure of control over their regions and abolished the Council of State, long identified with Dom Pedro's reactionary rule. The regency did not abandon centralism, however, for the national government continued to appoint provincial governors with a partial veto over the acts of the provincial assemblies.

Almost immediately, the regency government struggled against a rash of revolts, mostly in the northern provinces, where the economy suffered from a loss of markets for their staple crops, sugar and cotton. None occurred in the central southern zone (the provinces of Rio de Janeiro, São Paulo, and Minas Gerais), whose coffee economy prospered and whose planter aristocracy had secure control of the central government. These revolts had a variety of local causes. Some were elemental, popular revolts, such as the so-called *cabanagem* (from the word *cabana*, meaning "cabin") of Pará, which originated in the grievances of small tradesmen, farmers, and lower-class elements against the rich Portuguese merchants who monopolized local trade. Others, like the republican and separatist

Sabinada revolt in Bahia (1837–1838), reflected the frustrations of the planter aristocracy of this once-prosperous area over its loss of economic and political power, but it also mobilized the large majority of black and mixed-race people who had long advocated slavery's abolition. A slaveholders' petition complained about "insubordination" on plantations where "slaves walk around with arms and there is to be feared some sad incident, besides the bad example they give to the neighboring fazendas, especially when, because of the events of Bahia, the slaves in general are losing their deference which is so necessary." Another measure of the regency's fear of these abolitionist rebellions was its 1834 decree of the death penalty for insurgent slaves.

Most serious of all was the revolt that broke out in 1835 in the province of Rio Grande do Sul. Although it was dubbed the *Revolução Farroupilha* (Revolution of the Ragamuffins) in contemptuous reference to its supposed lower-class origins, cattle barons who more or less controlled the gauchos—the rank-and-file of the rebel armies—actually led the movement. An intense regionalism, resentment over taxes and unpopular governors imposed by the central government, and the strength of republican sentiment all induced the revolt that established the independent republic of Rio Grande in 1836. The presence of considerable numbers of Italian exiles such as Giuseppe Garibaldi—ardent republicans who opposed slavery—gave a special radical tinge to the revolt. For almost a decade, two states—one a republic and one an empire—existed on Brazilian territory.

The inability of imperial troops to quell the Rio Grande revolt further weakened the regency government, and, in 1838, the Balaiada rebellion raged across the northern provinces of Maranhão, Piauí, and Ceará. Initiated in Maranhão, the province with the greatest share of slaves (some 55 percent of the population), this revolt began as a lower-class protest against conscription and blossomed into an insurgency that appealed to black slaves, indigenous people, free people of color, and well-established maroon communities. One maroon leader, Cosme Bento das Chagas, recruited a slave army of two thousand and forced local plantation owners to free their slaves. According to historian Matthias Röhrig Assunção, another mixed-race leader, Raimundo Gomes, proclaimed "equal rights for all people of colour, *cabras* [dark mulattos], and **caboclos** [poor, usually landless, people of mixed indigenous and European descent]."

Doubtlessly, the revolt's increasingly radical, egalitarian program reflected the broad cross-class, multiracial nature of its rebel army, which government officials confirmed. For example, military commander Luis Alves de Lima described Gomes as a rebel leader who "claimed that he did not want to ally himself to the insurrected negroes, but now, without resources and always persecuted, tries to attract them." This growing subaltern alliance clearly threatened the monarchy, the plantation oligarchs, and the private property rights that secured them. To preserve their power and privilege, these elites used the issue of race to divide the rebels, promising amnesty to all free rebels in exchange for their agreement to "hunt down" runaway slaves. According to Lima, "in order to avoid further insurrections," his amnesty proposal aimed "to excite the hate between slaves and free rebels."

While the army tried to restore order on the battlefield, moderate Liberals, who favored concessions to federalism, sought political accommodation with a Conservative Party that preferred to strengthen the central government. On such essential issues as the monarchy, slavery, and the maintenance of the status quo in general, these Liberals and Conservatives saw eye to eye. They also agreed on the need to suppress the Rio Grande rebellion and other regional revolts in the north. The Rio Grande experiment in republican government and its offer of freedom to all slaves who joined the republic's armed forces posed an especially serious threat to monarchy and slavery. To strengthen the central government in its war against these subversive and separatist movements, Liberals and Conservatives decided to call the young Pedro to rule before his legal majority. In 1840 the two legislative chambers orchestrated a parliamentary coup d'état and proclaimed the fourteen-year-old Dom Pedro emperor. He empowered a conservative government that dismantled the federalist reforms in the

Slavery in Brazil by Jean-Baptiste Debret depicts the cruelty that characterized Brazilian slavery and produced the Balaiada Rebellion, named for the Afro-Brazilian basket weaver Manuel Francisco dos Anjos Ferreira, who led thousands of Afro-Brazilians in a movement to abolish slavery and establish an independent republic.

Additional Act of 1834, sharply curtailed the powers of provincial assemblies, and stripped locally elected judges of their judicial and police powers.

Thereafter, the government undertook to settle scores with the rebels of Rio Grande. Because of internal squabbles and the cessation of aid from friendly Uruguay after Argentina invaded it in February 1843, the situation of the republic became extremely difficult. Facing the prospect of military defeat, the republican leaders accepted an offer from Rio de Janeiro to negotiate a peace, and they signed a peace treaty in February 1845. It extended amnesty to all rebels but annulled all laws of the republican regime. The cattle barons won certain concessions, including the right to nominate

their candidate for provincial governor and retain their military titles.

The last large-scale revolt in the series that shook Brazil in the 1830s and 1840s was the uprising of 1848 in Pernambuco. Centered in the city of Recife, its causes included hostility toward the Portuguese merchants who monopolized local trade, the appointment of an unpopular governor by the conservative government, and hatred for the greatest landowners of the region, the powerful Cavalcanti family. The rebel program called for the removal from Recife of all Portuguese merchants, expansion of provincial autonomy, work for the unemployed, and division of the Cavalcanti lands. Even this radical program, however, contained no reference to the abolition of slavery. The movement collapsed after imperial troops captured Recife in 1849. Many captured leaders were condemned to prison for life, but all were amnestied in 1852.

Underlying these rebellions and armed conflicts of the 1830s and 1840s was economic stagnation caused by the weakness of foreign markets for Brazil's traditional exports. Coffee, already important in the 1830s but flourishing after 1850, expanded into the center-south, which strengthened the hand of the central government with increased revenues and laid the foundation for a new era of cooperation between regional elites and the national government. The new coffee prosperity, confirming the apparent viability and rationality of the neocolonial emphasis on export agriculture, also discouraged any thought of taking the more durable but difficult path of Brazilian autonomous development.

THE GAME OF POLITICS AND THE CRISIS OF SLAVERY

By 1850, Brazil seemed at peace. The emperor presided over a pseudo-parliamentary regime, exercising his power in the interests of a tiny ruling class. He paid his respects to parliamentary forms by alternately appointing conservative and liberal prime ministers at will; if the new ministry did not command a majority in parliament, he obtained one by holding rigged elections. Because the ruling class united on essential issues, the only issue at stake in party struggles was patronage, the spoils of office. An admirer of Dom Pedro, Joaquim Nabuco, described the operation of the system in his book *O abolicionismo*:

> The representative system, then, is a graft of parliamentary forms on a patriarchal government, and senators and deputies only take their roles seriously in this parody of democracy because of the personal advantage they derive therefrom. Suppress the subsidies, force them to stop using their positions for personal and family ends, and no one who had anything else to do would waste his time in such shadow boxing.

The surface stability of Brazilian political life in the decades after 1850 rested on the prosperity of the coffee-growing zone of Rio de Janeiro, São Paulo, and Minas Gerais, itself the product of growing demand and good prices for Brazilian coffee. But the sugar-growing northeast and its plantation society continued to decline because of exhausted soil, archaic techniques, and competition from foreign sugars.

The crisis of the northeast grew more acute because of English pressure on Brazil to enforce the Anglo-Brazilian treaty banning the importation of slaves into Brazil after November 7, 1831. Before 1850, slavetraders virtually ignored this treaty and enslaved more than fifty thousand people a year in Brazil during the 1840s. In 1849 and 1850, however, the British government pressured Brazil to pass the Queiroz anti-slave-trade law and instructed its warships to enter Brazilian territorial waters if necessary to destroy Brazilian slave ships. By the middle 1850s, the importation of slaves had virtually ended.

Abolition of the slave trade had major consequences. Because poor food, harsh working conditions, and other negative factors produced high mortality among the enslaved, natural reproduction could not maintain the slave population, which ensured the slave system's eventual demise. The end of the slave trade created a serious labor shortage, with large numbers of slaves moving from the north to the south because of the coffee planters' greater capacity to compete for slave labor. This movement aggravated the imbalance between the declining north and the prosperous south-central zone. By the 1860s, a growing number of Brazilians had become convinced that slavery brought serious discredit to Brazil and insisted on its abolition. The abolition of slavery in the United States after the Civil War, which left Brazil and the Spanish colonies of Cuba and Puerto Rico the only slaveholding areas in the Western Hemisphere, sharpened sensitivity to the problem. The Paraguayan War also promoted the cause of emancipation. In an effort to fill the gaps caused by heavy losses at the front, the emperor issued a decree granting freedom to government-owned slaves who agreed to join the army, and some private slave owners followed the official example.

Criticism of slavery increasingly morphed into criticism of the emperor, whom abolitionists censured for his cautious posture on slavery. Although the monarchy believed it might survive the abolition of slavery, it greatly feared the growing independent organizations of "blacks, mulattos, caboclos, etc." that accompanied abolitionism. In the words of a royal councilor, Pimenta Bueno,

> Political experience teaches us that the best rule is not to talk about this. If one allows the principle to exist, then it will develop, and there will be consequences. Distinctions or divisions based on caste are always bad; homogeneity, if not real at least supposed, is the desired goal of nationalities.

This idea epitomized Brazil's nineteenth-century struggles and ultimately led historians like Sidney Chalhoub to conclude that they bequeathed a legacy of political exclusion for peoples of African descent.

Alongside the antislavery movement, a nascent republican movement arose. In 1869, the Reform Club, a group of militant Liberals, issued a manifesto demanding restrictions on the powers of the emperor and the grant of freedom to the newborn children of enslaved mothers. The crisis of slavery was fast becoming a crisis of the Brazilian empire.

THE ANTISLAVERY MOVEMENT

From the close of the Paraguayan War (1870), the slavery question surged forward, becoming the dominant issue in Brazilian political life. Dom Pedro, personally opposed to slavery, was caught in a crossfire between slave owners who were determined to postpone the inevitable as long as possible and a growing number of liberal leaders, intellectuals, urban middle-class groups, and free people of color—not to mention the enslaved themselves—all of whom demanded emancipation. In 1870, Spain freed all newborn and aged slaves in Cuba and Puerto Rico, leaving Brazil the only nation in the Americas to retain slavery in its original colonial form. Fearing the perpetual social instability promised by the slaves' defiant resistance to slavery, a conservative ministry soon yielded to pressure

and pushed the Rio Branco Law through parliament in 1871. This measure freed all newborn children of enslaved women but obligated their masters to care for them until they reached the age of eight. At that time, owners could either release the children to the government in return for an indemnity or retain them as laborers until they reached the age of twenty-one. The law also freed all slaves belonging to the state or crown and created a fund to compensate slaveholders for the manumission of their slaves.

The Rio Branco Law was a tactical retreat designed to put off a final solution of the slavery problem. As late as 1884, when Brazil still had more than 1 million slaves, Brazil's Free Womb legislation had freed only 113.

Abolitionist leaders denounced the law as a sham and illusion, and advanced ever more vigorously the demand for total and immediate emancipation. From 1880 on, the antislavery movement developed great momentum. Concentrated in the cities, it drew strength from the process of economic, social, and intellectual modernization under way. To the new urban groups, slavery was an anachronism, glaringly incompatible with modernity.

Among the slave owners, divisions of opinion appeared. In the north, where slavery had become economically inefficient, a growing number of planters shifted to wage labor, drawing on the *sertanejos* (inhabitants of the interior), poor whites and mixed-race people, who lived on the fringes of the plantation economy. Another factor in the decline of the enslaved population in the northeast was the great drought of 1877–1879, which caused many of the region's wealthier folk to sell their slaves or abandon the area, taking their slaves with them. Where native and mixed-race workers vastly outnumbered a few black slaves, provinces like Amazonas and Ceará abolished slavery within their borders in 1884. By contrast, the coffee planters of Rio de Janeiro, São Paulo, and Minas Gerais, joined by northern planters who trafficked in slaves, selling them to the coffee zone, offered the most tenacious resistance to the advance of abolition.

The abolitionist movement produced leaders of remarkable intellectual and moral stature. One

Slaves drying coffee on a plantation in Terreiros, in the state of Rio de Janeiro, about 1882.

was Joaquim Nabuco, the son of a distinguished liberal diplomat of the empire, whose eloquent dissection and indictment of slavery, *O abolicionismo*, had a profound impact on its readers. Another was a mulatto journalist, José de Patrocinio, a master propagandist noted for his fiery, biting style. Another mulatto, André Rebouças, an engineer and teacher whose intellectual gifts won him the respect and friendship of the emperor, was a leading organizer of the movement. For Nabuco and his comrades-in-arms, the antislavery struggle was the major front in a larger struggle for the transformation of Brazilian society. Abolition, they hoped, would pave the way for the attainment of other such goals as land reform, public education, and political democracy.

Yielding to mounting pressure, parliament adopted another measure on September 28, 1885, which liberated all slaves when they reached the age

of sixty but required them to continue to serve their masters for three years and forbade them to leave their place of residence for five years. These conditions, added to the fact that few slaves lived beyond the age of sixty-five, implied little change in the status of the vast majority of slaves. The imperial government also promised to purchase the freedom of the remaining slaves in fourteen years—a promise that few took seriously in light of their experience with the Rio Branco Law. Convinced that the new law was just another tactical maneuver, the abolitionists spurned all compromise solutions and demanded immediate, unconditional emancipation. By the mid-1880s, the antislavery movement had assumed massive proportions and a more militant character. Large numbers of slaves voted for freedom with their feet; they received assistance from abolitionists who organized an underground railroad that helped them escape from São Paulo to

Ceará, where slavery had ended. Efforts to secure the return of fugitive slaves encountered growing resistance. Army officers, organized in a *Club Militar*, protested against the use of the army for the pursuit of fugitive slaves.

In February 1887, São Paulo liberated all slaves in the city with funds raised by popular subscription. Many slave owners, seeing the handwriting on the wall, liberated their slaves on the condition that they remain at work for a certain period. By the end of 1887, even the diehard coffee planters of São Paulo were ready to adjust to new conditions by offering to pay wages to their slaves and improve their working and living conditions; they also increased efforts to induce European immigrants to come to São Paulo. These efforts were highly successful; the flow of immigrants into São Paulo rose from sixty-six hundred in 1885 to more than thirty-two thousand in 1887 and to ninety thousand in 1888. As a result, coffee production reached record levels. With its labor problem solved, São Paulo was ready to abandon its resistance to abolition and even joined the abolitionist crusade.

On May 13, 1888, Brazil finally abolished slavery, but contrary to a traditional interpretation, this decision was not the climax of a gradual process of slavery's decline and slave owners' peaceful acceptance of the inevitable. The total slave population dropped sharply only after 1885, as a result of abolitionist agitation, mass flights of slaves, armed clashes, and other upheavals that appeared to threaten anarchy. In effect, abolition had come not through reform but by revolution.

The aftermath of abolition refuted the dire predictions of its foes. Freed from the burdens of slavery and aided by the continuance of very high coffee prices all over the world (until about 1896), Brazil made more economic progress in a few years than it had during the nearly seven decades of imperial rule. Fazendeiros replaced freedmen with immigrants on the coffee plantations; in the cities, black artisans lost their jobs to immigrants. For the former slaves, however, little had changed. The abolitionist demand for the grant of land to the freedmen was forgotten. Relationships between former masters and slaves in many places remained largely unchanged; racist traditions and the economic and political power of the fazendeiros gave them almost absolute control over their former slaves. Denied land and education, freedmen faced a future in which the "whip of hunger" now compelled them to labor at the hardest, most poorly paid jobs. Moreover, political reforms that established high income and literacy requirements for citizen participation effectively disenfranchised the freedmen, but they also dramatically reduced voting among free people of color and poor whites. In a society in which, according to the 1872 census, only 16 percent of the people were literate, this legislation disfranchised 99 percent of eligible voters and set the stage for a century of covert, race-based discrimination.

Peru

The liberation of Peru from Spanish rule had come from without, for the creole aristocracy, whose wealth was derived from the forced labor of indigenous peoples and enslaved Africans in mines, workshops, and haciendas, rightly feared that revolution might set fire to this combustible social material. The liberators, General José de San Martín and Simón Bolívar, had attempted to reform the social and economic institutions of the newly created Peruvian state. Before he left to meet Bolívar in Guayaquil, San Martín had decreed a ban on slave importation, the automatic emancipation of all children born of slaves in Peru, the abolition of native tribute, and the end of all other forms of indigenous forced labor; he also proclaimed that all inhabitants of Peru, whether native or creole, were Peruvians.

Because these reforms did not conform to the interests of elite creoles, however, they never implemented them after San Martín left Lima to meet Bolívar in Guayaquil. When Bolívar assumed power in Peru in 1823, he enacted reforms that reflected the same liberal ideology. Wishing to create a class of independent small-holders, he decreed the dissolution of indigenous communities and ordered the division of communal lands into individual parcels; each family was to hold its plot as private property, with the surplus to become part of the public domain. While attacking communal property, Bolívar left alone feudal property, the great haciendas serviced by yanaconas or **colonos** (native sharecroppers or serfs), who were required to pay their landlords a rent that amounted to as much as 50 to 90 percent of the value of their crops.

The well-intentioned Bolivarian land reform played into the hands of hacendados, public officials, and merchants, who used it to build up vast estates at the expense of indigenous communal lands; the process began slowly but gathered momentum as the century advanced. Bolívar's efforts to abolish native tribute had no greater success. After he left Peru in 1826, Peru's creole government reinstituted the tribute for **serranos** (inhabitants of the sierra) under the name of the **contribución de indígenas** (a head tax levied on indigenous peoples), and, for good measure, it also reintroduced the *contribución de castas* for the mestizo population of the coast.

The new government's heavy dependence on such tribute as a source of revenue reflected the stagnant condition of the Peruvian economy. The revolution completed the ruin of the mining industry and coastal plantation agriculture, both of which had been declining since the close of the eighteenth century, and the scanty volume of exports could not pay for the much greater volume of imports of manufactured goods from Britain. As a result, the new state, already burdened with large wartime debts to English capitalists, developed a massive trade deficit with Great Britain, its largest trading partner. Wool exports increased after 1836, and, in 1840, a new economic era opened on the coast with the exploitation of guano; in its first stage, however, the guano cycle failed to provide the capital accumulation needed to revive coastal agriculture.

PERUVIAN POLITICS AND ECONOMY

Peru's backward, stagnant economy, the profound cleavage between the sierra and the coast, and the absence of a governing class (such as arose in Chile)

that could give reliable and intelligent leadership to the state produced chronic political turbulence and civil wars. This provided abundant opportunities for slaves to initiate their self-liberation. First, urban slavery increasingly emerged as an alternative to the declining productivity of coastal agriculture and highland mining. Rural slaveholders could secure profits by renting their slaves in Lima and other cities, where they performed a broad range of skilled jobs and earned money to pay their owners or purchase their freedom. Second, urban slavery afforded black slaves greater mobility and weakened the slaveholder's direct control. Urban slaves took advantage of this position to challenge their owners in court, claiming that their masters had abused them physically in violation of republican laws. One even claimed the right of manumission because his owner was English and Protestant, an argument designed to appeal to the prejudices of Catholic criollo magistrates in Lima. Third, urban slaves also participated in various conspiracies like the 1835 plot, led by Juan de Dios Algorta, who sought to "overthrow the government and assassinate the whites in Lima." Lastly, although relatively rare by comparison to Caribbean slave revolts, black slaves played leading roles in armed rebellions like the Chicama Revolt of 1851. In the context of what anthropologist James Scott calls "everyday forms of resistance" to slavery, this violent armed rebellion doomed the "peculiar institution" in Peru. Elite property owners could no longer tolerate the social instability that slavery seemed to produce, especially when its economic advantages had long since disappeared.

Under these conditions, military caudillos, sometimes men of plebeian origin who had risen in the ranks during the wars of independence, came to play a decisive role in the political life of the new state. Some were more than selfish careerists or instruments of aristocratic creole cliques. The ablest and most enlightened of the military caudillos was the mestizo general Ramón Castilla, who served as president of Peru from 1845 to 1851 and again from 1855 to 1862. Castilla presided over an advance of the Peruvian economy that relied on the rapid growth of guano exports. British capitalists dominated this export trade and obtained the right to sell guano to specified regions of the world in return for loans to the Peruvian government (secured by guano shipments). Exorbitant interest and commission rates swelled their profits. Castilla contemplated direct government exploitation of some guano deposits, establishment of state controls over price and production, and reinvestment of guano revenues in state development projects, but he never acted on any of these ideas. The guano boom, however, stimulated some growth of native Peruvian commerce and banking and created the nucleus of a national capitalist class. Guano prosperity also financed the beginnings of a modern infrastructure; thus, in 1851 the first railway line began to operate between Lima and its port of Callao.

The rise of guano revenues enabled Castilla to carry out a series of social reforms that also contributed to the process of nation-building. In 1854, he abolished slavery and indigenous tribute, relieving natives of a heavy fiscal burden and freeing enslaved Africans, who numbered some twenty thousand. Abolition was advantageous to the planter aristocracy, who received compensation of up to 40 percent of their slaves' value. With these indemnities, planters could buy seeds, plants, and Chinese coolies brought to Peru on a contract basis that made them virtual slaves. Meanwhile, the freed blacks often became sharecroppers who lived on the margins of the hacienda and supplied a convenient unpaid labor force and a source of rent. Stimulated by these developments, cotton, sugar cane, and grain production expanded on the coast. Highland economic life also quickened, though on a smaller scale, with the rise of extensive livestock breeding for the export of wool and leather through Arequipa and Lima.

The general upward movement of the Peruvian economy after 1850 benefited greatly from such favorable factors as the temporary dislocation of the cotton industry of the southern United States and large inflows of foreign capital. As a result, exports of cotton and sugar increased sharply. The coastal latifundia continued to expand at the expense of indigenous communities, sharecroppers, and tenants, all of whom were expelled from their lands. This process accompanied the modernization of coastal agriculture through the introduction of cotton gins, boilers, refinery equipment for sugar, and steam-driven tractors.

Although profits from the agricultural sector enabled the commercial and landed aristocracy of Lima to live in luxury, the Peruvian state sank even deeper into debt. The unrestrained exploitation of guano deposits, Peru's collateral for its foreign borrowings, depleted this nonrenewable resource at an ever-accelerating rate, and the bulk of the proceeds from these loans went to pay interest on old and new debts. In 1868, during the administration of the military caudillo José Balta, his minister of the treasury, Nicolás de Piérola, devised a plan to extricate Peru from its difficulties and provide funds for development. The project eliminated the numerous consignees to whom the state had sold guano rights and awarded a monopoly of guano sales in Europe to the French firm of Dreyfus and Company. In return, the Dreyfus firm agreed to service its foreign debt and to make Peru a loan that would tide over its immediate difficulties. The contract initiated a new flow of loans that helped create a boundless euphoria, an invincible optimism, about the country's future.

U.S. adventurer and entrepreneur Henry Meiggs, who had made a reputation as a railway builder in Chile, easily convinced Balta and Piérola that they should support the construction of a railway system to tap the mineral wealth of the sierra. As a result, much of the money obtained under the Dreyfus contract, and a large part of the proceeds of the dwindling guano reserves, poured into railway projects that could not show a profit in the foreseeable future.

PARDO AND THE CIVILIANIST PARTY

The good fortune of Dreyfus and Company displeased the native commercial and banking bourgeoisie that had arisen in Lima. A group of these men—headed by the millionaire business executive Manuel Pardo and including former guano consignees whom the Dreyfus contracts had eliminated—challenged the legality of the contract before the

Supreme Court. They argued that assignment of guano sales to their corporation of native consignees would be more beneficial to Peru's economic development. This native bourgeoisie suffered defeat, but in 1871 they organized the *Civilista*, or Civilianist Party (in reference to their opposition to military caudillos), which ran Pardo as its candidate for president. An amalgam of "an old aristocracy and a newly emerging capitalist class," the Civilianist Party opposed clerical and military influence in politics and advocated a large directing role for the state in economic development. Pardo won handily over two rivals and took office in 1872.

Pardo presided over a continuing agricultural boom, with exports reaching a peak in 1876. Foreign capital poured into the country. In those years, an Irish immigrant, W. R. Grace, began to establish an industrial empire that included textile mills, a shipping line, vast sugar estates, and Peru's first large-scale sugar-refining plants. Whereas private industry prospered, the government sank ever deeper into a quagmire of debts and deficits. The guano cycle was nearing its end, with revenues steadily declining because of falling prices, depletion of guano beds, and competition from an important new source of fertilizer: nitrates exploited by Anglo-Chilean capitalists in the southern Peruvian province of Tarapacá. In 1875, wishing to control the nitrate industry and make it a dependable source of government income, Pardo expropriated the foreign companies in Tarapacá and established a state monopoly over the production and sale of nitrates. This measure angered the Anglo-Chilean entrepreneurs, whose holdings Pardo had nationalized and indemnified with bonds of dubious value. Meanwhile, because of unsatisfactory market conditions in Europe, the nationalization measure failed to yield the anticipated economic benefits.

In 1876, Peru felt the full force of a worldwide economic storm. Within a few months, it had forced all the banks of Lima to close; by the following year, the government had to suspend payments on its foreign debt and issue worthless paper money. A military disaster, the War of the Pacific, followed the economic collapse. Despite heroic resistance, Peru suffered a crushing defeat at the hands of a Chilean state that enjoyed a more advanced economic organization, political stability, and the support of British capitalists. The war completed the work of economic ruin begun by the depression. The Chileans occupied and ravaged the economically advanced coastal area: They levied taxes on the hacendados; dismantled equipment from the haciendas and sent it to Chile; and sent troops into the sierra to exact payment from hacendados, towns, and villages. Their extortions infuriated the native peasantry. Led by Gen. Andrés Cáceres, they began to wage an effective guerrilla war of attrition against the Chilean occupiers. The 1883 Treaty of Ancón finally ended the war.

Cuba

Because of its distinctive colonial past, Cuba's nineteenth-century development differed markedly from that of most other Latin American countries. For three centuries after Christopher Columbus landed in 1492, the island served primarily as a strategic stopover for the Spanish treasure fleet. Largely isolated from expanding transatlantic markets and without precious metals or a large indigenous population to exploit, Cuba remained a neglected, sparsely populated outpost of the empire. The island's inhabitants engaged, for the most part, in small-scale farming for domestic consumption. Unlike the sugar-producing islands of the Caribbean, at the end of the seventeenth century, Cuba had few slaves (its population of African descendants numbered 40,000, only one-tenth that of Haiti), many of whom worked in nonagricultural occupations, often as skilled artisans.

ECONOMIC AND SOCIAL CHANGE: THE BITTER HARVEST OF KING SUGAR

The second half of the eighteenth century, however, had brought profound economic and social change as Cuba transformed into a classic case of **monoculture** (an area dependent on the production and export of a single crop for its economic livelihood). Spurred on by the short-lived British occupation of Havana in 1762 and further stimulated by the growing U.S. market produced by independence in 1783, the island experienced a commercial awakening. Most important, Cuba developed into a major sugar producer and slave importer in the aftermath of the Haitian Revolution of the 1790s, which ruined that island as a sugar producer (until then, it had been the world's leader). During the next half-century, sugar production in Cuba skyrocketed, and nearly six hundred thousand enslaved Africans arrived on its shores. From 1774 to 1861, the island's population leaped from 171,620 to 1,396,530, some 30 percent of whom were of African descent.

Initially, the transfer to sugar did not stimulate the creation of the latifundio because much of the land converted to sugar was the underused acreage of large cattle haciendas. Moreover, many farmers did not change over to sugar, preferring instead to produce coffee and tobacco, which then enjoyed high prices resulting from the abolition of the royal monopoly on these commodities. Furthermore, the sugar mills themselves stimulated demand for livestock (to turn the mills) and food crops for the slaves. During the first decades of the nineteenth century, the number of farm proprietors increased markedly, and the leaders of Cuban society came from their ranks for the next century.

By 1800, the economic boom that had followed the destruction of Haitian sugar production ended because other Caribbean islands expanded and initiated production in response to the same stimuli, thereby creating an enormous glut on the market. Just as the industry recovered from this setback, diplomatic maneuvering during the Napoleonic wars closed U.S. ports. Shortly thereafter, two new challenges to the Cuban economy arose: the introduction of beet sugar in Europe and the British campaign to end the slave trade. England forced Spain to end the trade in 1821. Further impediments resulted from the restrictions imposed by Spanish hegemony: high tariffs, scarce and expensive credit, and the disruptions brought on by the Spanish American wars of independence.

By 1820, the first of a series of technological innovations began to transform the character of the sugar industry in Cuba. Mill owners had to expand operations and invest heavily in steam-operated machinery to compete with beet sugar. The larger the mill, the more sugar it could process, the more fuel it consumed, and the more labor it needed. Smaller and less efficient mills were at a severe competitive disadvantage. Modern machinery allowed the mills to expand in size, but they could do so only gradually because of limited transportation facilities. Because railroads were enormously expensive, and in any case capital was insufficient on the island and in Spain for large projects of this type, they did not become important until much later. The mills also carried a huge overhead because they largely lay idle during the off-season, but mill owners still had to feed and shelter their slaves and livestock even when they did not generate new revenues. The problem of fuel for the mills also slowed their expansion. The forests close to the mills quickly disappeared, and transport of wood to the mills proved prohibitively costly.

In response to the need for *centrales* (bigger mills), large plantations also developed in Cuba. Sugar production traditionally had been set up in one of two ways: Resident or temporary labor cultivated the land, or farmers, known as colonos, worked parcels of land for a salary or a share of the crop. They planted and harvested the cane and brought it to the mill, which processed it in exchange for a share of the sugar. Now, to satisfy market demand, successful planters expanded the land under cultivation and deployed massive numbers of enslaved Africans to work more than sixteen hours per day, clearing land, planting and cutting cane, and transporting it to the mills. Not surprisingly, given this high level of exploitation, most slaves died within eight years. This trend toward concentration in the ownership of land and increased capitalization of sugar plantations was a direct result of market-induced changes in the sugar industry.

As a result, sugar production expanded in the first half of the century through an increase in the size of plantations, the number of mills, and enslaved Africans. In 1827, one thousand mills were in operation; two decades later, more than fourteen hundred; and by 1860, two thousand. During the first few decades of the nineteenth century, a reinvigorated African slave trade increased the enslaved population from 18,000 in 1788 to 125,000 in 1810; Spanish slave traders sold 161,000 Africans into slavery between 1811 and 1820, and thereafter some two hundred thousand newly enslaved Africans worked the Cuban sugar plantations.

The expansion of trade and the introduction of large-scale sugar production created a fantastic economic boom and delayed the development of a creole rebellion against Spanish rule that swept the rest of Spanish America. Cuba stayed loyal to Spain during the Spanish American wars of independence, for its creole leaders feared slave rebellions and saw no reason to tamper with their newfound prosperity. Meanwhile, discontent grew among enslaved and free blacks because of the rise of an increasingly harsh plantation system. In addition to everyday acts of resistance, such as work slowdowns, feigned illness, equipment sabotage, and abortion, enslaved African men and women periodically punctuated their daily protests against enslavement with major slave revolts like the Aponte Rebellion in 1812 and La Escalera in 1844. Very much influenced by the Haitian Revolution and other slave insurrections throughout the Caribbean world, these rebellions united enslaved Africans, Cuban-born black slaves, free blacks, and free people of color to seek the destruction of slavery and plantation agriculture.

By the last half of the nineteenth century, however, wealthy creoles became increasingly

© Bettmann/CORBIS

An Afro-Cuban woman called Black Carlota led a fearsome slave rebellion in 1843 that terrified Spanish officials and creole plantation owners, who relied on enslaved African labor to work the sugar plantations, as depicted in this 1830 image.

resentful of corrupt Spanish officialdom, which was determined to enforce continued obedience from Spain's last and richest colony in the New World. The colony grew increasingly dissatisfied with repressive Spanish rule and less dependent economically on the mother country. As Cuba turned increasingly toward the United States as a market for its products and a source of needed imports, schemes for the annexation of Cuba to the United States emerged both on the island and in some North American circles. In Cuba, conservative creole planters saw annexation as an insurance policy against the abolition of slavery; in the United States, some proslavery groups regarded annexation as a means of gaining a vast new area for the expansion of plantation slavery. Some even dreamed that carving Cuba into three or five states would give the South increased power in the U.S. national government, but the Civil War ended these projects.

During the 1860s, a developing national and class consciousness intensified and spread creole discontent. The creole elite rejected various reform proposals offered by an ineffectual Spanish government that internal dissension and economic difficulties had weakened. It became increasingly clear to the creoles that Spanish economic and political policies severely restricted Cuban development—a feeling sharpened by a serious economic downturn.

Meanwhile, Cuba's sugar economy had developed a sectional specialization. To the east, a sparse population, predominantly composed of free whites with a relatively small share of black slaves, worked on cattle ranches that produced meat for consumption on the slave-based sugar plantations that dominated western Cuba. Creole landowners in the east, less dependent on slave labor, feared slave rebellions less than they feared Spanish domination. As a result, on October 10, 1868, in the small town of Yara in Oriente Province, Carlos Manuel de Céspedes, a creole landowner, voluntarily freed those he had enslaved and launched Cuba's first movement for independence from Spanish colonialism. During the Ten Years' War that followed, race increasingly divided the rebel movement, as free black and mixed-race leaders like Antonio Maceo predominated. Their demands were simple and straightforward: They wanted independence, the abolition of slavery, and the establishment of a postcolonial racial equality.

Even as the Spanish sought to divide the rebels by manipulating creole planters' racial fears, the movement's increasingly black military leadership celebrated the idea of nation over race. In 1869, the rebel movement drafted a constitution that declared "all inhabitants of the Republic entirely free" and granted citizenship to all "soldiers of the Liberation Army," a majority of whom were Afro-Cuban. But some creole rebel leaders, fearing the radicalism of the Afro-Cuban demand for freedom from Spain and slave masters alike, sought to amend the Constitution to require Cuban citizens to lend their "services according to their aptitudes," a clear attempt to discriminate against Afro-Cubans. They also drafted the *Reglamento de Libertos* that "assigned" freedmen to "pro-Cuban owners" or "other masters." Naturally, this alienated Afro-Cuban rebels, who refused to compromise on the issues of abolition, independence, and racial equality. For them, *cubanidad* (Cuban national identity) transcended race; to be Cuban meant equality and freedom from oppression, whether from Spain, the creole slave master, or self-described white men.

The Ten Years' War

The Ten Years' War, a long, bitter, devastating guerrilla struggle, ended ignominiously in 1878 when Cuban creole leaders accepted a peace that granted them some autonomy but withheld independence. The Pact of Zanjón ended hostilities, but some rebel leaders, like the black revolutionary Antonio Maceo, the "Bronze Titan," rejected the settlement because it recognized the freedom only of slaves who had fought in the rebel army; it did not achieve the main goals of the revolution: complete independence and the abolition of slavery. Consequently, Afro-Cubans refused to surrender arms, more slaves escaped to maroon communities, and those who remained enslaved refused to work or obey plantation masters. New Spanish colonial laws sought to suppress this post-Zanjón rebelliousness by restricting movements of the enslaved, punishing the enslaved for communication with outsiders, prohibiting the enslaved from possession of machetes, and regulating sales of the enslaved.

Notwithstanding these efforts, however, Afro-Cuban resistance ultimately resulted in a new conflict, the 1879 *Guerra Chiquita* (Little War), which distinguished itself by the absence of creole participation and the prominence both of black military and political leadership that demanded abolition and equal rights. Desperate to stabilize the island, preserve Spanish colonial authority, and prevent a second black republic in the Caribbean, the Spanish government sought the loyalty of free Afro-Cubans by abolishing slavery in 1880, with provision for an eight-year **patronato** (period of apprenticeship) for the liberated slaves. Ironically, the abolition of slavery removed the last major factor that made creole planters loyal to Spain. Thereafter, the prospect of independence, offering free, unlimited trade with the United States, became increasingly attractive.

The Ten Years' War and the Guerra Chiquita had a far-reaching impact on the development of Cuban society. First, the conflicts decimated the creole landowning class, hindering the formation of a traditional Latin American landed elite on the island. Second, they convinced future Cuban independence leaders—black and white—that success required the abolition of race and the substitution of national identity. To that end, Cuban nationalists like José Martí and the Afro-Cuban journalist Juan Gualberto Gómez produced war memoirs that deracialized black insurgents in the Ten Years' War and instead celebrated them as "national heroes." According to historian Ada Ferrer, these counter-hegemonic discourses contradicted Spanish propaganda about a future "black republic" and depicted images of faithful blacks who were "grateful" for "white generosity."

Naturally, this image of passive black insurgents starkly contradicted the reality of black political activism between 1886 and 1895. Afro-Cubans, drawing on their political experiences during the previous decade, organized the *Directorio Central*

de las Sociedades de las Clases de Color, a group whose principal objective was to promote racial equality on the island. They aimed to create free public schools, abolish segregated civil registers and "titles of courtesy," and secure equal access to public roads, transportation, and public accommodations.

Third, the shakeout of mills during the war, the financial crisis of 1885–1890, and the expansion of the island's railroad network combined to stimulate the spread of latifundios. As they grew, the mills required more sugar cane, which came from a wider geographic area than they previously had. At the same time, the introduction of cheap rails spurred railroad construction in Cuba (and all around the world). In their quest for more cane, owners of centrales began to lay their own track, and a competition among centrales for cane, a condition previously unknown because of transportation limitations, resulted.

The owners of centrales confronted the necessity of guaranteeing enough cane at the lowest possible prices for the *zafra* (harvest). They could do this either by reducing the independence of the colonos or by acquiring their own cane land. The first method transformed the once-free farmers into satellites of the giant mills. The second led to the proliferation of latifundia. Small and midsize growers fell by the wayside, replaced by tenants or day laborers. The colonos managed to hold their own until independence, after which time the massive influx of foreign capital into the sugar mills overwhelmed them. With their dwindling financial resources, they were doomed.

Entrepreneurs from the United States filled the vacuum created by the ruin of the creole aristocracy and the bankruptcy of Spanish interests by the war. Thousands of North Americans accompanied their investment dollars to the island to run the sugar mills and merchant houses. The McKinley Tariff Act of 1890, which abolished import duties on raw sugar and molasses, greatly increased American trade with and economic influence in Cuba; by 1896, U.S. interests had invested $50 million in Cuba and controlled the sugar industry. The United States purchased 87 percent of Cuba's exports. The growth of U.S. investment in Cuba also brought about an increasing concentration of sugar production, a trend signaled by the entry of the "Sugar Trust" (the American Sugar Refining Company of Henry Q. Havemeyer) into the island in 1888.

Although the Ten Years' War had transformed Cuba into a haven for North Americans, it had done nothing to eliminate racial segregation and discrimination, even after emancipation. Elite Spanish and creole white supremacists dominated late-nineteenth-century Cuba and routinely blamed Afro-Cubans for all manner of Cuban social ills, denied them access to education and adequate health care, engaged in employment discrimination, and created obstacles to full citizenship. Interracial marriage, prohibited by law until 1881, remained socially stigmatized thereafter.

This racial apartheid created two Cubas—one steeped in Spanish cultural traditions and ritual practices like Catholicism and Freemasonry, and the other centered in African *santería* (a syncretic popular religion) and *ñáñigos* (secret mutual aid societies). According to historian Aline Helg, Afro-Cubans, frustrated by limits imposed on their ability to rise in Spanish society, increasingly relied on their African heritage to protect themselves and to organize social protest movements that demanded their "rightful share."

Gran Colombia

The early history of Venezuela and Colombia is indistinguishable from the life's work of the liberator Simón Bolívar. Venezuela was his homeland, and Colombia (then called New Granada) and Venezuela were the theaters of his first decisive victories in the war for Latin American independence. Bolívar sought to unite Venezuela and New Granada into a single large and powerful state and looked toward the creation of a vast federation of all the Spanish American republics, extending from Mexico to Cape Horn. In 1819, the Congress of Angostura (in Venezuela) approved the formation of the state of Colombia (later called Gran Colombia, or Greater Colombia) that would combine Venezuela, New

Granada, and Ecuador (then still in Spanish hands). In 1821, at Cúcuta on the Venezuelan-Colombian border, the revolutionary congress formalized the union and outlined a liberal reform program. It included the gradual abolition of slavery, the abolition of native tribute, the division of indigenous communal lands into private parcels (a "reform" that opened the door to land-grabbing), the suppression of smaller male convents and the seizure of their property for the support of public secondary education, and a general expansion of education. It also adopted a centralized constitution that guaranteed citizenship rights to all people, irrespective of gender or race.

Drafted according to Bolívar's wishes, the constitution created a nation-state that reflected his indictment of Spain's colonial domination. For him, Spain had functioned as a tyrannical father who enslaved his children for his own profit and thereby refused to allow them to develop into mature adults. As a result, he argued that the new republic, controlled by its enlightened "Founding Fathers," was obligated to prepare its rebellious children for the responsibilities of self-government before they could secure full and equal citizenship rights. Committed to the contradictory ideas of liberty, equality, property, and security, Bolívar's generation of wealthy propertied creoles aimed to create a patriarchal nation that would protect property and order against the chaotic protests of women, poor whites, and peoples of African descent, all of whom yearned for freedom and equality.

Arguably, the most pressing issue that faced the young republic was slavery. Naturally, enslaved Africans and their descendants variously had accommodated and resisted slavery since its introduction in the early colonial period. This included slave revolts; escape to *cumbes* (remote, autonomous village communities) or palenques; and other everyday acts of resistance. During the independence wars, Bolívar and his comrades had encouraged slave emancipation by recruiting them to service in the liberation army. Free blacks and pardos (mixed-race people) flocked to military service. However, in the aftermath of independence, women, slaves, free blacks, and pardos all seized on republican laws

Mural by Ian Pierce/Courtesy of Encontrarte

Slave rebellions marked Gran Colombia's transition from colony to republic and shaped the nature of nineteenth-century debates over citizenship in Colombia and Venezuela. One rebellion, led by José Leonardo Chirino, a free zambo, occurred in 1795 and was immortalized by the Chilean artist Ian Pierce, whose mural at the Colegio Andrés Bello in Caracas commemorates the event.

and the rhetoric of national liberation to petition the government for their emancipation. In response to this general clamor for equal citizenship rights, creole leaders aimed to fashion laws and political institutions that would protect private property and patriarchy.

The movement to abolish slavery offers a powerful example of this negotiation among creole elites and between them and subalterns. In 1820, pursuant to military exigencies and congressional proclamations that "no man can be the property of another," Bolívar had ordered Francisco de Paula Santander, a leading general under his command, to recruit an army of some five thousand slaves in the provinces of Antioquía and Chocó by promising emancipation. This naturally excited great enthusiasm

among the enslaved population, but it alienated mine owners and other proprietors who depended on slave labor. To reconcile these conflicting interests, Santander limited his recruitment to three thousand and directed all remaining slaves to return to their masters.

A similar compromise at the Congress of Cúcuta effectively prolonged the institution of slavery. It passed a law that called for the gradual abolition of slavery through a complicated process of manumission. Thereafter, all children born of enslaved mothers would be free, but they were required to work for their mother's master until age eighteen. The law also created a series of local **juntas de manumisión** (committees composed of local notables), who were responsible for collecting tax monies necessary to pay slaveholders compensation for their loss. The juntas, notoriously inefficient and largely representing the interests of slave owners, failed to liberate many slaves.

Nonetheless, slaves continued to pressure Bolívar and his creole nation by organizing revolts that swept across the republic between 1824 and 1827. Fearing the nation's imminent collapse, Bolívar issued an 1828 decree that effectively centralized control over the juntas and assessed financial penalties against local junta members who failed to act. This contributed to a growing chorus of criticism from elites and local military caudillos like José Antonio Páez, the pardo leader, who denounced Bolívar's "dictatorial" actions and called for the dissolution of Gran Colombia in 1829. In addition to the conflict over slavery, Gran Colombia's survival was doomed by its geographic, economic, and social realities. Immense distances separated its component parts, and a mountainous terrain made communication difficult; it took about a month for a letter to reach Bogotá from Caracas. These conditions also hindered the development of economic ties among Venezuela, New Granada, and Ecuador; Caracas and other Venezuelan coastal cities communicated more easily with Europe than overland via the Andes with Bogotá. Finally, the Venezuelan elite of cacao planters, merchants, and military leaders or caudillos had little sympathy for Bolívar's idea of fusing several independent Spanish American republics into one and even less for his vision of a confederation that would unite all the Spanish American states.

PÁEZ, THE CONSERVATIVE–LIBERAL SPLIT, AND THE FEDERAL WAR IN VENEZUELA, 1830–1863

On May 6, 1830, a congress assembled in Valencia to provide the independent state of Venezuela with a constitution, the third in the country's short history. The document limited suffrage to males who were twenty-one, were literate, and had a high income. These requirements excluded most of the population, numbering under 900,000, from participation in political life. Of these, some 60 percent were descended from Africans. Another 15 percent

were natives, and a quarter identified as white. A tiny minority of these, about ten thousand, composed the ruling class of wealthy merchants, great landowners, high officeholders, and military officers, who usually also owned large landed estates. The members of this class, often linked through family networks, dominated politics.

Military hero, longtime champion of Venezuelan independence, and former ranch hand José Antonio Páez was elected president, a post he combined with that of supreme army commander. His rise illustrated the renewal of the old colonial ruling class through the admission of a new elite of military caudillos, frequently of humble origins. The Venezuelan society and economy over which Páez presided essentially resembled the colonial social and economic order. The latifundio continued as the basic unit of economic activity; concentration of landownership increased after independence because of the rapid acquisition of royalist estates and public lands by a small group of military caudillos. A decree of October 15, 1830, compelling the sale of so-called uncultivated indigenous lands, gave the latifundists more opportunities to expand their landholdings. Labor relations in the countryside continued to rely heavily on slavery, peonage, and various forms of tenancy, including sharecropping and obligatory personal service.

Slavery in Venezuela, as in other parts of Latin America, had long been in decline. Enslaved Africans' defiant opposition to enslavement, either through passive forms of resistance, rebellions, or escape to *cumbes* (runaway slave settlements), had made slavery socially destabilizing and less economically efficient. Nonetheless, slave owners continued to insist on the protection of their property rights, which, under the terms of the 1821 law, would have required manumission of the first generation of free-born blacks in 1839. So the Venezuelan Constituent Congress of 1830 adopted a manumission law that extended their masters' control until the age of twenty-one. Thereafter, another decree established a mandatory "apprenticeship" program that prolonged the age of manumission from twenty-one to twenty-five and secured the patrón's control over his labor force. Continuing a tendency that began in the late colonial period, however, many slave owners found it more profitable to free their slaves voluntarily, because they generally remained on their former masters' land as tenants or peons bound by debts and other obligations. By 1841, fourteen thousand had been freed in this manner—one hundred fifty of them only because they had reached the age of manumission—but some forty thousand slaves remained in 1844.

The long revolutionary war had caused immense material damage and loss of life—the population declined by 262,000—and destroyed the fragile economic links between the country's different regions. By the 1830s, however, Venezuela experienced an economic boom, rooted in the switch from cacao to coffee as its principal export and the country's integration into the capitalist world market, which henceforth absorbed about 80 percent of Venezuela's exports of coffee, cacao, indigo, tobacco, and hides.

The high coffee prices that accompanied the 1830s boom made planters hungry for credit to expand production by obtaining new land. Foreign merchant capitalists, the Venezuelan export-import merchants who were their agents, and native moneylenders were happy to oblige, using coffee crops and the planters' estates as security, but colonial legislation that regulated interest rates and punished usury posed an obstacle. The Venezuelan congress removed this impediment by passing a credit law in 1834 that abolished all traditional Spanish controls on contracts; the state then enforced legally executed contracts, no matter how exorbitant the interest rates. By the late 1830s, with the world price of coffee in decline, the Venezuelan economy was in serious trouble. Creditors refused to refinance their debtors, plunging Venezuela into a severe depression.

The economic crisis caused a rift in the elite, with the emergence of factions that turned into political parties in the 1840s. One called itself Conservative, but opponents dubbed its members *godos* (Goths) to identify them with the unpopular Spanish colonial rule. Páez was its acknowledged leader, and it represented the views and interests of the export-import merchants and their foreign partners, the moneylenders, the high civil and military bureaucracy, and

some great landowners. The Liberal Party was led by Antonio Leocadio Guzmán and was a loose coalition of debt-ridden planters, the urban middle class, artisans, intellectuals seeking reform, and disaffected caudillos who resented Páez's long reign.

Guzmán's rhetorical press attacks on conservative economic policies contributed to the growing social tension. A series of popular uprisings and slave revolts between 1839 and 1852, which Páez described as open warfare against private property, terrified the Conservatives, who raised the specter of a general social race war waged by pardos and slaves. Although Conservatives blamed Guzmán's inflammatory propaganda, in fact the Liberals feared social revolution as much as their opponents and had no links to these popular revolts. Nonetheless, the government, determined to crush them at their supposed source, brought Guzmán to trial, found him guilty of instigating the revolutionary movements, and sentenced him to death.

By 1854, popular unrest, slave revolts, and passive resistance to slavery had dramatically raised its cost, which, combined with the downturn in global coffee prices, threatened planters' profits. Conservatives thereafter sought to assist their allies by supporting congressional passage of several laws designed to give relief to distressed planters. One of these laws abolished slavery in Venezuela, guaranteeing compensation to slave owners, some of whom already were voluntarily freeing their slaves to avoid paying their support.

In effect, abolition aimed to end an economically costly and socially destabilizing popular movement, but emancipation brought little change in the lives of most freedmen. In the absence of a modern factory system to provide alternative employment or any program for distributing land to them, most were doomed to remain on their former owners' estates as tenants burdened with heavy obligations. Others earned scanty wages paid in *vales* (tokens) redeemable only for goods purchased in the **tienda de raya** (estate store) at inflated monopoly prices.

Hard times continued in the late 1850s. Depressed coffee prices and elite fears of a social explosion persuaded Conservatives and Liberals to join forces momentarily, but the coalition soon fell apart. A group of extreme Conservatives seized power, installed a repressive government, and imprisoned or deported many Liberals, who responded with an uprising that began the Federal War (1858–1863).

The term *federal* as used here had different meanings for the liberal elite and its rank-and-file followers, most of whom were pardos or blacks who rallied to the federalist battle cry "Death to the whites." However, whereas Conservatives denounced the liberal elite for fomenting a "race war," the "colored population" saw it as a war of the poor majority against the wealthy, propertied elite. After their victory, liberal leaders gave the country a new constitution (1864) with many reforms, including universal male suffrage and increased autonomy for the twenty states. Nevertheless, without substantive social reform, these rights were virtually meaningless. Federalism under these conditions simply meant the continued supremacy of the local caudillo, who often was a great landowner.

However, for peasants and artisans who rose in spontaneous revolt against the conservative regime and rallied to the liberal leadership's slogan of federalism, the term had a different meaning. A manifesto by Ezequiel Zamora, a veteran guerrilla fighter, brilliantly captured their vague hopes for revolutionary change. Zamora supported the occupation of large estates by their former peons and tenants, creation of federal states, and election of local governments by the citizenry. Zamora's death by an assassin's bullet in 1860 cut short the life of a leader who represented a genuinely democratic, social revolutionary tendency in the Federal War.

Fearing the growing power of peasant revolutionists, Conservatives and Liberals agreed to a negotiated peace. The 1863 Treaty of Coche ended the war, which had cost some fifty thousand lives, inflicted immense damage on the economy, and destroyed many haciendas. The cattle herds of the llanos virtually had disappeared because of wartime depredations and neglect. Like the War of Independence, the Federal War produced limited social changes. The old conservative oligarchy disintegrated, and victorious liberal military officers, some of plebeian background, occupied their

estates. For the revolutionary rank-and-file, however, the war's end forced them to surrender the parcels of land and return as peons to the great estates that they once had occupied.

SANTANDER AND THE BIRTH OF A TWO-PARTY SYSTEM IN COLOMBIA, 1830–1850

Following the secession of Venezuela and Ecuador from Gran Colombia in 1830, the remaining territory went its separate way under the name of the Republic of New Granada (present-day Colombia plus Panama). Led by Bolívar's old ally Francisco de Paula Santander, New Granada adopted a constitution that provided for a president elected for four years, a bicameral Congress, and provincial legislatures. The constitution granted suffrage to all free males who were married or age twenty-one and were not domestic servants or day laborers. In practice, a small aristocratic ruling class dominated political life.

The geographic, economic, and social conditions of the new state posed even greater obstacles to the creation of a true national society. Dominated by the towering Andean cordillera, whose ranges, valleys, and plateaus were home to a million people, the country's difficult geography offered formidable barriers to communication and transport.

New Granadan industry displayed many precapitalist features. Working in their homes, women chiefly produced most industrial activity, including weaving and spinning, pottery making, and shoe manufacture. In Bogotá, many state-sponsored efforts to establish factories producing soap, glassware, textiles, and iron ended in failure. By the 1840s, sizable artisan groups had arisen in larger towns like Bogotá, Medellín, and Cali, but despite moderate tariff protections for local industries, they had difficulty competing with imported foreign goods. The backwardness of economic life was most apparent in transportation; in parts of the country, porters and pack mules typically dominated the local transport industry well into the twentieth century. Even after steamboat navigation became regular on the Magdalena River, it took between four and six weeks to make the voyage from Atlantic ports to Bogotá. The limited development of productive forces and the sluggish tempo of economic activity produced modest wealth even for the elite. In the first half of the nineteenth century, the income of Bogotá's upper class came to about $5,000 per capita, and the number of individuals whose capital exceeded $100,000 was exceedingly small.

The lack of a dynamic export base to stimulate the economy and provide resources for a strong nation-state was a major factor in Colombia's economic and political difficulties in its first half-century. Efforts to replace declining gold production with tobacco, cotton, and other export products generated a series of short booms that quickly collapsed because of shrinking markets, falling prices, and growing foreign competition. The absence of an export base and a nationally dominant elite helps explain the "economic archipelago" or regional isolation and self-sufficiency that developed. A corollary of this economic autarchy was political autarchy, an almost permanent instability punctuated by frequent civil wars or threats of war and even secession by hacendado-generals, who could mobilize private armies of peons to settle scores with rival caudillos or the weak central government.

The large hacienda or plantation, mainly dedicated to growing wheat, barley, potatoes, and raising cattle, dominated agriculture, the backbone of the economy. Their labor force usually consisted of mestizo peons or tenants who paid rent in labor or in kind for the privilege of cultivating their own small parcels of land; debts restricted their freedom of movement, and sometimes they owed personal service to their patrón.

Alongside these haciendas and on marginal lands and mountain slopes lived other peasants whose precarious independence came from subsistence farming and supplying food to nearby towns. The northwest region of Antioquia, with its rugged terrain and low population, had few haciendas and numerous small and midsize landholdings; a more independent peasantry had also arisen in neighboring Santander. The Spanish had enslaved thousands of Africans and their descendants to labor on plantations and in gold-mining districts in the western states and on the Caribbean coast. However, the

institution, greatly weakened by independence wars, slave resistance, and Free Womb legislation, was in decline. Nonetheless, slave owners zealously defended their property rights and sought to limit both the pace of abolition and the rights of *libertos* (freedmen) born to slave mothers after 1821. To ensure their mothers' masters a plentiful supply of cheap labor, an 1842 law limited freedmen's mobility, enforced prison penalties for violation of vagrancy laws, and sanctioned *concertaje* (a mandatory "apprenticeship" program) that placed freedmen in a "trade craft, profession, or useful occupation" until age twenty-five.

Naturally, slaves and libertos resisted these efforts to control their labor by rebelling violently or running away. Moreover, they also joined together with merchants, artisans, peasants, and freedmen to create a cross-class, multiracial coalition dedicated to immediate emancipation. Some black freedmen even scandalized Liberals and Conservatives by their insistence upon what anthropologist Michael Taussig calls a "radical Catholic utopia, anarchist and egalitarian." Organized into Democratic Societies, this mass movement relentlessly pressured the liberal government of José Hilario López to abolish slavery, which he finally did in 1851, but not before quieting a slaveholders' rebellion by guaranteeing them full compensation. The measure, freeing about twenty-five thousand individuals, had its most severe impact on gold-mining areas, which generally relied heavily on slave labor.

The Liberals, however, always had equated emancipation with *mestizaje* (a homogenized mixed-race culture) that required the sacrifice of distinct African and indigenous ethnic identities and the invention of an idealized unified Hispanic national culture, perhaps best reflected in the Colombian motto of "one God, one race, one tongue." This secured the power and property of liberal elites, but it presumed the surrender of indigenous and African communal lands and their autonomous political traditions. Thereafter, the Liberals intensified the attack on *resguardos* (native communal lands), and land "liberated" by forced division often passed into the hands of neighboring hacendados by legal or illegal means. Natives made landless by such means often became peons forced to serve the hacendados.

To fashion a unified mestizo national identity, Liberals sought to distinguish themselves clearly from their conservative rivals. Until the late 1840s, the difference between the ideologies and programs of the two groups was far from absolute. Actually, both represented upper-class interests but accepted the formal democracy of representative, republican government; both had faith in social and technological progress, believed in the freedoms of speech and of the press as well as other civil liberties, and in economic policy accepted laissez-faire and liberal economics. Neither party cared about the agrarian problem or other problems of the rural and urban masses. The only genuine issue separating them was the relation between church and state and the church's role in education. The emergent Liberal Party was distinctly anticlerical, regarding the church as hostile to progress; however, they favored freedom of worship and separation of church and state. The nascent Conservative Party endorsed religious toleration but favored cooperation between church and state, believing that religion promoted morality and social peace.

In the struggle over emancipation, however, the ideological gap between Liberals and Conservatives widened, and three new political factions emerged: urban artisans, Gólgotas, and *Draconianos*, military from the lower officer ranks, who later aligned themselves with the artisans. Shaped by the rapid expansion of tobacco cultivation, the beginnings of the coffee cycle, and a resulting growth of foreign and domestic trade, the Gólgotas were the sons of a merchant class whose population increased to 2 million by 1850. Well-educated and influenced by antislavery agitation, French romanticism, utopian socialism, and the Revolution of 1848 in France, they developed a peculiar sentimental brand of liberalism that drew heavily on a romantic interpretation of Christianity in which Christ, described as the "Martyr of Golgotha," appeared as a forerunner of nineteenth-century secular reformism. This ideology's practical essence was its demand for the abolition of slavery, the ecclesiastical and military fuero, compulsory tithing, and all restraints on free enterprise.

Urban artisans, whose numbers also had increased in the preceding decade, faced growing competition from foreign imported manufactures, which caused serious unemployment. Attributing their distress to lower tariffs that benefited conservative slave owners and their plantations, these artisans readily identified with the language of freedom and equality that shaped the political struggle against slavery. In 1847, they created a network of Democratic Societies, beginning with the Democratic Society of Bogotá, which had almost four thousand members. These mutual-aid societies carried on education and philanthropic activities, but they also served as important political vehicles for the liberal leadership, enabling the new merchant elite, with large support from regional landed oligarchies, to seek the triumph of laissez-faire and modernity.

Clearly, struggles against slavery provided the historical context within which Brazil, Cuba, Peru, Colombia, and Venezuela defined their respective national identities, but the closely related issues of race and property played equally powerful roles. Ultimately, Liberals seized on the language of freedom and equality, always explicit in the abolitionist movements throughout the region, to insist on the emancipation of slaves. They also created a national discourse that demanded freedom from foreign domination and state regulation, conditions necessary to protect their class privileges and property. This language of nation sought to silence more radical demands for racial equality and mass democratic participation.

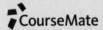

Go to the CourseMate website at **www.cengagebrain.com** for primary sources, additional study tools, and review materials—including audio and video clips—for this chapter.

11

The Triumph of Neocolonialism and the Liberal State, 1870–1900

FOCUS QUESTIONS

- What was neocolonialism, and what were its characteristic economic and political features? What role did the liberal state play in promoting national economic growth between 1870 and 1900?

- What were the policies of Mexico's Porfirio Díaz regarding indigenous communities, land, labor, trade, and foreign investment?

- What were the policies of Argentina's Julio Roca regarding indigenous communities, land, labor, and foreign investment?

- What were the major elements of Justo Rufino Barrios's liberal reform program in Guatemala?

- How did Antonio Guzmán Blanco's program in Venezuela compare with Rafael Núñez's plan in Colombia, and how did each affect national economic development?

- How did these liberal programs contrast with the developmental policies of José Manuel Balmaceda in Chile?

- How did liberal development programs affect subaltern social classes, especially peasants and workers?

B EGINNING ABOUT 1870, the quickening tempo of the Industrial Revolution in Europe stimulated a more rapid pace of change in the Latin American economy and politics. Responding to mounting demand for raw materials and foodstuffs, Latin American producers increased their output of those commodities. Increasing political stability, itself the result of the consolidation of the liberal state, facilitated the region's growing trade with Europe and the United States.

Encouraged by the increased stability and liberal economic policies, European capital flowed into Latin America, creating railroads, docks, processing plants, and other facilities needed to expand production and trade. Latin America became integrated into an international economic system in which it exchanged raw materials and foodstuffs for the factory-made goods of Europe and North America. Gradual adoption of free-trade policies by many Latin American countries, which marked the abandonment of efforts to create a native factory capitalism, hastened the area's integration into this international division of labor.

The New Colonialism

This "neocolonial" economic system fastened a new dependency on Latin America, with Great Britain and later the United States replacing Spain and Portugal in the dominant role. Despite its built-in flaws

1873–1885	Justo Rufino Barrios inaugurates liberal dictatorship in Guatemala
1876–1885	Rafael Zaldívar established liberal dictatorship in El Salvador
1879–1883	Chile wins the War of the Pacific and seizes mineral-rich lands from Peru and Bolivia, which becomes land-locked
1881	Revolt of the Comuneros in Nicaragua protests privatization of indigenous communal lands; Zaldívar abolishes communal land tenure in El Salvador
1883	*Ley de deslindes* privatizes public lands in Mexico; Chile expropriates Araucanian ancestral lands
1886–1891	President Balmaceda promotes national industrial and agricultural development in Chile despite opposition from latifundistas and foreign investors
1889	Benjamin Constant leads overthrow of Dom Pedro II in Brazil to create the First Republic
1891	Chilean oligarchy and foreign capitalists overthrow Balmaceda
1893–1910	José Santos Zelaya creates liberal dictatorhip in Nicaragua
1894	*Ley de terrenos baldíos* privatizes Mexican public lands
1896	Canudos Rebellion resists Brazil's oligarchic republic and abolishes private property
1899–1908	Cipriano Castro seizes dictatorial power in Venezuela
1906	Major labor strike at Cananea Copper Company in Mexico; Brazilian Labor Confederation protests oligarchic republic
1909	Rio Blanco strikes in Mexico close down textile production; Luis Emilio Recabarren organizes Chilean Workers' Federation
1912	Argentine oligarchy passes Sáenz Peña Law

and local breakdowns, the neocolonial order displayed a certain stability until 1914. By disrupting the markets for Latin America's exports and making it difficult to import the manufactured goods that Latin America required, World War I marked the beginning of a general crisis of neocolonialism and the liberal state.

Although the period from 1870 to 1914 saw rapid overall growth of the Latin American economy, the pace and degree of progress were uneven, with some countries (like Bolivia and Paraguay) joining the advance much later than others. A marked feature of the neocolonial order was its one-sidedness (monoculture). One or a few primary products became the basis of prosperity for each country, making it highly vulnerable to fluctuations in the world demand and price of these products. Argentina and Uruguay depended on wheat and meat; Brazil on coffee, sugar, and briefly rubber; Chile on copper and nitrates; Honduras on bananas; Cuba on sugar.

In each country, the modern export sector became an enclave that was largely isolated from the rest of the economy and that actually accentuated the backwardness of other sectors by draining off their labor and capital. The export-oriented nature of the modern sector shaped the pattern of national railway systems, which as a rule aimed to satisfy the transportation needs of export industries, rather than integrate each country's regional markets into a unified national network. In addition, the modern export sector often rested on extremely precarious foundations. Rapid, feverish growth, punctuated by slumps that sometimes ended in a total collapse, formed part of the neocolonial pattern; such meteoric rise and fall is the story of Peruvian guano, Chilean nitrates, and Brazilian rubber.

The triumph of neocolonialism in Latin America in the late nineteenth century was not inevitable or predetermined by Europe's economic "head start" or the area's past history of dependency. The leap from a feudal or semifeudal economy and society to an autonomous capitalist system, although difficult, is not impossible, as the case of Japan makes clear. Following independence, the new states had to choose between the alternatives of autonomy or dependency, or in the words of historian Florencia Mallon, "between focusing on internal production and capital formation, on the one hand, and relying increasingly on export production, foreign markets, and ultimately foreign capital, on the other." However, the formation of the dynamic entrepreneurial class and the large internal market required by autonomous capitalism could not be achieved without such sweeping reforms as the breakup of great estates, the abolition of peonage and other coercive labor systems, and the adoption of a consistent policy of supporting native industry. Such reforms required a powerful, activist nation-state committed to the regulation of market forces and the redistribution of material resources. Most sections of the elite, however, found them too costly and threatening. Instead, they embraced the liberal developmental creed that stressed the need to privatize public resources, reduce government expenditures, dismantle state bureaucracies, provide incentives to foreign investors, and encourage export trade. Most Latin American elites, therefore, chose the easier road of continued dependency, with first Great Britain and later the United States replacing Spain as the metropolis.

Latin America in the nineteenth century, however, produced some serious efforts to break with this pattern of dependence. We already described two such efforts. A remarkable and temporarily successful project for autonomous development was launched in Paraguay under the rule of Dr. Francia and the Lópezes, father and son. Their state-directed program of agrarian reform and industrial diversification transformed Paraguay from a backward country into a relatively prosperous and advanced state, but the disastrous Paraguayan War interrupted this progress and returned Paraguay to a state of backwardness and dependency. In Chile, in the 1850s, an alliance of mining capitalists, small farmers, and artisans attempted to overthrow the landed and mercantile oligarchy and implement a radical program of political and social reform; their "frustrated bourgeois revolution" was drowned in blood. In this chapter, we examine a second Chilean effort to achieve autonomous development under the slogan "Chile for the Chileans"; it too ended in defeat and in the death of the president who led it.

Expansion of the Hacienda System

The neocolonial order evolved within the framework of the traditional system of land tenure and labor relations. Indeed, it led to an expansion of the hacienda system on a scale far greater than the colonial period had known. As the growing European demand for Latin American products and the growth of national markets raised the value of land, the great landowners in country after country launched assaults on the surviving indigenous community lands. In part at least, this drive reflected an effort to eliminate indigenous competition in the emerging market economy. In Mexico, the Reforma laid the legal basis for this attack in the 1850s and 1860s; it reached its climax in the era of Porfirio Díaz. In the Andean region, similar legislation turned all communal property into individual holdings, leading to a cycle of indigenous revolt and bloody government repressions. However, not all native peoples opposed the nineteenth-century drive to dissolve the ancient communal landholding system. In both Mexico and the Andean regions, where market relations had induced significant socioeconomic differentiation within villages, indigenous leaders often willingly accepted privatization of communal lands, viewing it as a road to personal enrichment.

Seizure of church lands by liberal governments also contributed to the growth of the latifundio. Mexico again offered a model, with its Lerdo Law and the Juárez anticlerical decrees. Following the Mexican example, Colombian liberal governments confiscated church lands in the 1860s, the liberal dictator Antonio Guzmán Blanco seized many church estates in Venezuela in the 1870s, and Ecuadoran Liberals expropriated church lands in 1895.

Expansion of the public domain through railway construction and wars also contributed to the growth of great landed estates. Liberal states typically expropriated lands from the church or from indigenous communities and usually sold them to buyers in vast tracts at nominal prices. Concentration of land, reducing the cultivable area available to native and mestizo small landowners, accompanied a parallel growth of the *minifundio* (an uneconomical small plot worked with primitive techniques).

The seizure of indigenous community lands, to use immediately or to hold for a speculative rise in value, provided great landowners with another advantage by giving them control of the local labor force at a time of increasing demand for labor. Expropriated natives rarely became true wage earners paid wholly in cash, for such workers were too expensive and independent in spirit. A more widespread labor system was debt peonage, in which workers were paid wholly or in part with vouchers redeemable at the *tienda de raya* (company store), whose inflated prices and often devious bookkeeping created a debt that was passed on from one generation to the next. The courts enforced the obligation of peons to remain on the estate until they had liquidated their debts. The landowners' private armies, local police, or military authorities typically punished peons who protested low wages or the more intensive style of work demanded by the new order.

In some countries, the period saw a revival of the colonial repartimiento system of draft labor for indigenous peoples. In Guatemala, this system required able-bodied natives to work for a specified number of days on haciendas. The liberal president Justo Rufino Barrios issued instructions to local magistrates to see to it "that any Indian who seeks to evade his duty is punished to the full extent of the law, that the farmers are fully protected, and that each Indian is forced to do a full day's work while in service."

As we have seen, slavery survived in some places well beyond mid-century—for example, in Peru until 1855, in Cuba until 1886, and in Brazil until 1888. Closely akin to slavery was the system of bondage, under which contract labor companies imported some ninety thousand Chinese coolies into Peru between 1849 and 1875 to work on the guano islands and in railway construction. The term *slavery* equally applies to the system under which Mexican authorities sent political deportees and captured native rebels to labor in unspeakable conditions on the coffee, tobacco, and henequen plantations of southern Mexico.

More modern systems of agricultural labor and farm tenantry arose only in such regions as southern Brazil and Argentina, whose critical labor shortage required the offer of greater incentives to the millions of European immigrants who poured into those countries between 1870 and 1910.

Labor conditions were little better in the mining industry and in the factories that arose in some countries after 1890. Typical conditions were a workday of twelve to fourteen hours, miserable wages frequently paid in vouchers redeemable only at the company store, and arbitrary, abusive treatment by employers and supervisors. Latin American law codes usually prohibited strikes and other organized efforts to improve working conditions, and police and the armed forces commonly intervened to break strikes, sometimes with heavy loss of life.

FOREIGN CONTROL OF RESOURCES

The rise of the neocolonial order accompanied a steady growth of foreign corporate control over the natural and human-made resources of the continent. The process went through stages. In 1870, foreign investment was still largely concentrated in trade, shipping, railways, public utilities, and government loans; at that date, British capital enjoyed an undisputed hegemony in the Latin American investment field. By 1914, foreign corporate ownership had expanded to include most of the mining industry and had deeply penetrated real estate, ranching, plantation agriculture, and manufacturing; by that date, Great Britain's rivals had effectively challenged its domination in Latin America. Of these rivals, the most spectacular advance was made by the United States, whose Latin American investments had risen from a negligible amount in 1870 to more than $1.6 billion by the end of 1914 (still well below the nearly $5 billion investment of Great Britain).

Foreign economic penetration went hand in hand with a growth of political influence and even armed intervention. The youthful U.S. imperialism proved to be the most aggressive of all. In the years after 1898, a combination of "dollar diplomacy" and armed intervention transformed the Caribbean into an "American lake" and reduced

Cuba, the Dominican Republic, and several Central American states to the status of dependencies and protectorates of the United States.

THE POLITICS OF ACQUISITION

The new economy demanded new politics. Conservatives and Liberals, fascinated by the atmosphere of prosperity created by the export boom, the rise in land values, the flood of foreign loans, and the growth of government revenues, put aside their ideological differences and joined in the pursuit of wealth. The positivist slogan "Order and Progress" now became the watchword of Latin America's ruling classes. The social Darwinist idea of the struggle for survival of the fittest and Herbert Spencer's doctrine of "inferior races," frequently used to support racist claims of the inherent inferiority of the native, black, mestizo, and mulatto masses, also entered the upper-class ideological arsenal.

The growing domination of national economies by the export sectors and the development of a consensus between the old landed aristocracy and more capitalist-oriented groups caused political issues like the Federalist–Centralist conflict and the Liberal–Conservative cleavage to lose much of their meaning; in some countries, the old party lines dissolved or became extremely tenuous. A new type of liberal caudillo—Porfirio Díaz in Mexico, Rafael Núñez in Colombia, Justo Rufino Barrios in Guatemala, and Antonio Guzmán Blanco in Venezuela—symbolized the politics of acquisition.

As the century ended, dissatisfied urban middle-class, immigrant, and entrepreneurial groups in some countries combined to form parties, called Radical or Democratic, that challenged the traditional domination of politics by the creole landed aristocracy. They demanded political, social, and education reforms that would give more weight to the new middle sectors. But these middle sectors—manufacturers, shopkeepers, professionals, and the like—were in large part a creation of the neocolonial order and depended on it for their livelihood; therefore, as a rule they did not question its viability. The small nationalist, socialist, **anarchist**, and **syndicalist** groups that arose in various Latin American countries

in the 1890s challenged capitalism, neocolonialism, and the liberal state, but the full significance of these movements lay in the future.

These trends lend a certain unity to the history of Mexico, Argentina, Chile, Brazil, Central America, Venezuela, and Colombia in the period from 1870 to 1914. Each, however, presents significant variations on the common theme—variations that reflect distinctive historical backgrounds and conditions.

Mexican Politics and Economy

DICTATORSHIP UNDER DÍAZ

Gen. Porfirio Díaz seized power in 1876 with the support of disgruntled regional caudillos and military personnel, Liberals angered by the old regime's patronage politics, and indigenous or mestizo small landholders who believed that Díaz would protect them. He also owed his success to the open support of American capitalists, army commanders, and great Texas landowners who, regarding his predecessor as "anti-American," supplied Díaz with arms and cash. Thereafter, Díaz erected the *Porfiriato*, one of the longest personal dictatorships in Latin American history.

However, the construction of the dictatorship was a gradual process. During his first presidential term, Congress and the judiciary enjoyed a certain independence, and the press, including a vocal radical labor press, was free. The outlines of Díaz's economic and social policies, however, soon became clear. Confronted with an empty treasury, facing pressures from above and below, Díaz decided in favor of the great landowners, moneylenders, and foreign capitalists, whose assistance could ensure his political survival. In return, he assured these groups that he would protect their property and other interests. Díaz, who had once proclaimed that in the age-old struggle between the people and the haciendas, he was firmly on the side of the people, now sent troops to suppress peasant resistance to land seizures. Moreover, although he had denounced generous concessions to British capitalists before taking power, Díaz granted even more lavish subsidies for railway construction to North American companies a few years later. Economic growth had become for Díaz the great object, the key solution to his own problems and those of the nation.

Economic growth required political stability; accordingly, Díaz promoted a policy of conciliation, described by the formula *pan o palo* (bread or the club). This consisted of offering an olive branch and a share of spoils to all influential opponents, no matter what their political past or persuasion. A dog with a bone in its mouth, Díaz cynically observed, neither kills nor steals. In effect, Díaz invited all sections of the upper class and some members of the middle class, including prominent intellectuals and journalists, to join the great Mexican barbecue, from which he barred only the poor and humble. Opponents who refused Díaz's bribes—political offices, monopolies, and the like—suffered swift reprisal. His regime beat up, murdered, or arrested and imprisoned dissidents in the damp underground dungeons of San Juan de Ulúa or the grim Belén penitentiary, a sort of Mexican Bastille. An important instrument of this policy was a force of *rurales* (mounted police), originally composed of former bandits and vagrants who gradually were replaced by artisan and peasant recruits dislocated by the large social changes that took place during the Porfiriato. Aside from chasing unrepentant bandits, the major function of the rurales was to suppress peasant unrest and break strikes.

By such means, Díaz virtually eliminated all effective opposition. The 1857 constitution and the liberties it guaranteed existed only on paper. Elections to Congress, in theory the highest organ of government, were a farce; Díaz simply circulated a list of his candidates to local officials, who certified their election. The dictator contemptuously called Congress his *caballada* (stable of horses). Díaz appointed the state governors, usually from the ranks of local great landlords or his generals. In return for their loyalty, he gave them a free hand to enrich themselves and terrorize the local population. Under them were *jefes políticos* (district heads), petty tyrants appointed by the governors with the approval of Díaz; below the jefes were municipal presidents who ran the local administrative units. One feature of the Díaz Era was a mushrooming of the

coercive apparatus; government administrative costs during this period soared by 900 percent.

The army naturally enjoyed special favor. Higher officers received good salaries and enjoyed many opportunities for further enrichment at the expense of the regions in which they resided, but the Díaz army was pathetically inadequate for purposes of national defense. The regime appointed generals and other high officers for their loyalty to the dictator, not for their ability. Discipline, morale, and training were extremely poor. It recruited a considerable part of the rank-and-file from the dregs of society; the remainder included young native conscripts. These soldiers, often used for brutal repression of strikes and agrarian unrest, themselves endured harsh treatment and miserable pay: ranks below sergeant earned $0.50 a month.

The church became another pillar of the dictatorship and agreed to support Díaz in return for his disregard of anticlerical Reforma laws. Monasteries, nunneries, and church schools reappeared, and wealth again accumulated in the hands of the church. Faithful to its bargain, the church hierarchy ignored the complaints of the lower classes and taught complete submission to authorities.

The Díaz policy of conciliation targeted prominent intellectuals as well as more wealthy and powerful figures. A group of such intellectuals, professional men, and business leaders made up a closely knit clique of Díaz's advisers. Known as **Científicos**, they got their name from their insistence on "scientific" administration of the state and were especially influential after 1892. About fifteen men made up the controlling nucleus of the group. Their leader was Díaz's all-powerful father-in-law, Manuel Romero Rubio, and after his death in 1895, the position passed to the new minister of finance, José Yves Limantour.

For the Científicos, the economic movement was everything. Most Científicos accepted the thesis of the inherent inferiority of the native and mestizo population and the consequent necessity for relying on the native white elite and on foreigners and their capital to lead Mexico out of its backwardness. In the words of the journalist Francisco G. Cosmes, "The Indian has only the passive force of inferior

Beginning in the 1920s, with considerable support from the state, there arose in Mexico a school of socially conscious artists who sought to enlighten the masses about their bitter past and the promise of the revolutionary present. One of the greatest of these artists was David Alfaro Siqueiros, whose painting depicts with satire the former President Porfirio Díaz, who tramples on the constitution of 1857 as he diverts his wealthy followers with dancing girls.

races, is incapable of actively pursuing the goal of civilization."

CONCENTRATION OF LANDOWNERSHIP

At the opening of the twentieth century, Mexico was still predominantly an agrarian country; 77 percent of its population of 15 million still lived on the land. The laws of the Reforma already had promoted the concentration of landownership, and under Díaz, this trend greatly accelerated. The rapid advance of railway construction increased the possibilities of production for export and therefore stimulated both a rise in land values and the growth of land-grabbing in the Díaz period.

A major piece of land legislation was the 1883 *Ley de Deslindes* that provided for the survey of

public lands. The law authorized real estate companies to survey such lands, retain one-third of the surveyed area as compensation, and sell the remainder for low fixed prices in vast tracts, usually to Díaz's favorites and their foreign associates. The 1883 law opened the way for vast territorial acquisitions. One individual alone obtained nearly 12 million acres in Baja California and other northern states. Nonetheless, the acquisition of such lands did not satisfy the land companies. In 1894, the *Ley de Terrenos Baldíos* declared that a parcel of land without legal title was vacant land, opening the door to expropriation of untitled land cultivated by indigenous villages and other small landholders from times immemorial. If the victims offered armed resistance, Díaz sent troops against them and sold the vanquished rebels like slaves to labor on henequen plantations in Yucatán or sugar plantations in Cuba. This was the fate of the Yaquis of the northwest, defeated after a long, valiant struggle.

Another instrument of land seizure was an 1890 law designed to give effect to older Reforma laws requiring the distribution of indigenous village lands among the villagers. The law created enormous confusion. In many cases, land speculators and hacendados cajoled illiterate villagers into selling their titles for paltry sums. Hacendados also used other means, such as cutting off a village's water supply or simply brute force, to achieve their predatory ends. By 1910, the process of land expropriation was largely complete. More than 90 percent of the indigenous villages of the central plateau, the most densely populated region of the country, had lost their communal lands. Only the most tenacious resistance enabled villages that still held their lands to survive the assault of the great landowners. Landless peons and their families made up 9.5 million of a rural population of 12 million.

As a rule, the new owners did not use the land seized from indigenous villages or small landholders more efficiently. Hacendados let much of the usurped land lie idle, waiting for a speculative rise in value or an American buyer. By keeping land out of production, they helped keep the price of maize and other staples artificially high. The technical level of hacienda agriculture generally was extremely low, with little use of irrigation, machinery, and commercial fertilizer, although some new landowning groups—northern cattle raisers and cotton growers, the coffee and rubber growers of Chiapas, and the henequen producers of Yucatán—employed more modern equipment and techniques.

The production of foodstuffs stagnated, barely keeping pace with population growth, and per capita production of such basic staples as maize and beans actually declined toward the end of the century. This decline culminated in three years of bad harvests, 1907 to 1910, principally because of drought. As a result, the importation of maize and other foodstuffs from the United States steadily increased in the last years of the Díaz regime. Despite the growth of pastoral industry, per capita consumption barely kept pace, for a considerable proportion of the livestock was destined for the export market.

The only food products for which the increase exceeded the growth of population were alcoholic beverages. The growth of bars in Mexico City from fifty-one in 1864 to fourteen hundred in 1900 reflected this increased consumption of alcohol. At the end of the century, the Mexican death rate from alcoholism—a common response to intolerable conditions of life and labor—was approximately six times that of France. Meanwhile, inflation, rampant during the last part of the Díaz regime, greatly raised the cost of the staples on which the mass of the population depended. Without a corresponding increase in wages, the situation of agricultural and industrial laborers deteriorated sharply.

THE ECONOMIC ADVANCE

Whereas food production for the domestic market declined, production of food and industrial raw materials for the foreign market experienced vigorous growth. By 1910, Mexico had become the largest producer of henequen, a source of fiber in great demand in the world market. Mexican export production increasingly catered to the needs of the United States, which was the principal market for sugar, bananas, rubber, and tobacco produced on foreign-owned plantations. U.S. companies dominated the mining industry, whose output of copper, gold, lead, and zinc rose sharply after 1890. The oil industry, controlled by U.S. and British interests, developed spectacularly, and by 1911 Mexico was third among the world's oil producers. French and Spanish capitalists virtually monopolized the textile and other consumer goods industries, which had a relatively rapid growth after 1890.

Foreign control of key sectors of the economy and the fawning attitude of the Díaz regime toward foreigners gave rise to a popular saying: "Mexico, mother of foreigners and stepmother of Mexicans." The ruling clique of Científicos justified this favoritism by citing the need for a rapid development of Mexico's natural resources and the creation of a strong country capable of defending its political independence and territorial integrity. Thanks to an influx of foreign capital, the volume of foreign trade greatly increased, a modern banking system arose, and the country acquired a relatively dense network of railways linking the interior to overseas markets. But these successes were achieved at a heavy price: a brutal dictatorship, the pauperization of the mass of the population, the stagnation of food agriculture, the strengthening of the inefficient latifundio, and the survival of many feudal or semi-feudal vestiges in Mexican economic and social life.

LABOR, AGRARIAN, AND MIDDLE-CLASS UNREST

The survival of feudal vestiges was especially glaring in the area of labor relations. Labor conditions varied from region to region. In 1910, forced labor and outright slavery, as well as older forms of debt peonage, were characteristic of the southern states of Yucatán, Tabasco, Chiapas, and parts of Oaxaca and Veracruz. The rubber, coffee, tobacco, henequen, and sugar plantations of this region depended heavily on the forced labor of political deportees, captured indigenous rebels, and contract workers kidnapped or lured to work in the tropics by a variety of devices.

In central Mexico, where a massive expropriation of village lands had created a large, landless native proletariat, tenantry, sharecropping, and the use of migratory labor had increased and living standards had declined. The large labor surplus of this area diminished the need for hacendados to tie their workers to their estates with debt peonage. In the north, the proximity of the United States, with its higher wage scales, and the competition of hacendados with mine owners for labor made wages and sharecropping arrangements somewhat more favorable and weakened debt peonage. In all parts of the country, however, agricultural workers endured hardships and abuses of every kind.

Labor conditions in mines and factories were little better than in the countryside. Workers in textile mills labored twelve to fifteen hours daily for a wage ranging from $0.11 for unskilled women and children to $0.75 for highly skilled workers. Employers found ways to reduce even these meager wages. They discounted wages for alleged carelessness in the use of tools or machines or for defective goods; they usually paid workers wholly or

in part with vouchers good only in company stores, the prices of which were higher than in other stores. Federal and state laws banned trade unions and strikes. Troops shot down scores of workers, both men and women, and broke the great textile strike in the Orizaba (Veracruz) area in 1909 and the strike at the U.S.-owned Consolidated Copper Company mine at Cananea (Sonora) in 1906. Despite such repressions, the trade union movement continued to grow in the last years of the Díaz Era, and socialist, anarchist, and syndicalist ideas began to influence the still-small urban working class.

The growing wave of strikes and agrarian unrest in the last, decadent phase of the Díaz Era indicated an increasingly rebellious mood among even broader sections of the Mexican people. Alienation spread among teachers, lawyers, journalists, and other professionals, whose opportunities for advancement were sharply limited by the monolithic control of economic, political, and social life by the Científicos, their foreign allies, and regional oligarchies. In the United States in 1905, a group of middle-class intellectuals, headed by Ricardo Flores Magón, called for the overthrow of Díaz and advanced a radical program of economic and social reforms.

Even members of the ruling class soon joined the chorus of criticism. These upper-class dissidents included national capitalists, like the wealthy hacendado and business executive Francisco Madero, who resented the competitive advantages enjoyed by foreign companies in Mexico. They also feared that the static, reactionary Díaz policies could provoke the masses to overthrow the capitalist system itself. Fearing revolution, these upper-class critics urged Díaz to end his personal rule, shake up the regime, and institute modest reforms needed to placate popular protest and preserve the existing economic and social order. When their appeals failed, some of these bourgeois reformers reluctantly prepared to take the road of revolution.

The simultaneous advent of an economic recession and a food crisis sharpened this growing discontent. The depression of 1906–1907, which spread from the United States to Mexico, caused a wave of bankruptcies, layoffs, and wage cuts. At the same time, the crop failures of 1907–1910 provoked a

Striking workers at the Rio Blanco textile works in Mexico in 1909; the business was controlled by French capital. Troops broke up the strike, and much blood was shed.

dramatic rise in the price of staples like maize and beans. By 1910, Mexico's internal conflicts had reached an explosive stage. The workers' strikes, the agrarian unrest, the agitation of middle-class reformers, and the disaffection of some great landowners and capitalists all reflected the disintegration of the dictatorship's social base. Despite its superficial stability and posh splendor, the house of Díaz was rotten from top to bottom. Only a slight push was necessary to send it toppling to the ground.

Argentine Politics and Economy

Although the principal source of conflict in Argentina remained rivalry between provincial caudillos and Buenos Aires, Julio Roca and other oligarchs sought to unify the nation by forging stronger economic links between the port city and interior provinces. In Argentina, like Porfirian Mexico, the

consolidation of a liberal state was the key to neocolonial economic growth.

CONSOLIDATION OF THE STATE

Julio Roca institutionalized this new unification by carrying out a long-standing pledge to federalize the city of Buenos Aires, which now became the capital of the nation, while La Plata became the new capital of the Buenos Aires province. The interior seemed to have triumphed over Buenos Aires, but that apparent victory was an illusion; the provincial lawyers and politicians who carried the day in 1880 had absorbed the commercial and cultural values of the great city and wished not to diminish but rather to share in its power. Far from losing influence, Buenos Aires steadily gained in wealth and power until it achieved an overwhelming ascendancy over the rest of the country.

The federalization of Buenos Aires completed the consolidation of the Argentine state, the new leaders of which closely identified with and often emerged from the ruling class of great landowners and wealthy merchants. The "generation of 1880," or the Oligarchy, as it was called, shared a faith in economic development and the value of the North American and European models, but it also reflected a deep cynicism, intense egotism, and a profound distrust for the popular classes. These autocratic Liberals prized order and progress above freedom. They regarded the gauchos, indigenous peoples, and the mass of illiterate European immigrants flooding Argentina as unfit to exercise civic functions. Asked to define universal suffrage, a leading oligarch, Eduardo Wilde, replied, "It is the triumph of universal ignorance."

The new rulers identified the national interest with the interest of the great landowners, wealthy merchants, and foreign capitalists. Regarding the apparatus of state as their personal property or as the property of their class, they used their official connections to enrich themselves. Although they maintained the forms of parliamentary government, they were determined not to let power slip from their hands and organized the *unicato* (one-party rule) to monopolize political control in their newly formed National Autonomist Party. Extreme concentration of power in the executive branch and systematic use of fraud, violence, and bribery were basic features of the system.

ECONOMIC BOOM AND INFLATION

Roca presided over the beginnings of a great boom that appeared to justify the oligarchy's optimism. Earlier, Roca had led a military expedition—the so-called Conquest of the Desert—southward against native peoples of the pampa in 1879–1880. This conquest added vast new areas to the province of Buenos Aires and to the national public domain. The campaign, devastating to the region's indigenous communities, had created an opportunity to implement a democratic land policy directed toward the creation of an Argentine small-farmer class. Instead, the Roca administration sold off the

area in huge tracts for nominal prices to army officers, politicians, and foreign capitalists.

Coming at a time of steadily mounting European demand for Argentine meat and wheat, the Conquest of the Desert triggered an orgy of land speculation that drove land prices ever higher and caused a prodigious expansion of cattle raising and agriculture. This expansion took place under the sign of the latifundio. Few of the millions of Italian and Spanish immigrants who entered Argentina in this period realized the common dream of becoming independent small landowners. Although some immigrants established agricultural colonies in the provinces of Santa Fe and Entre Ríos in the 1870s and 1880s, by the mid-1890s, with wheat prices now declining, small-scale farming shifted to extensive tenant farming. The traditional unwillingness of the estancieros to sell land forced the majority of would-be independent farmers to become ranch hands or tenant farmers, whose hold on the land was precarious. Because leases usually were limited to a few years, these immigrants broke the virgin soil, replaced the tough pampa grass with the alfalfa pasturage needed to fatten cattle, and produced the first wheat harvests but then had to move on, leaving the landowner in possession of all improvements.

As a result, the great majority of new arrivals settled in Buenos Aires, where the rise of meat-salting and meat-packing plants, railroads, public utilities, and many small factories created a growing demand for labor. True, the immigrant workers received very low wages, worked long hours, and crowded with their families into one-room apartments in wretched slums. In the city barrio, however, they lived among their own people, free from the loneliness of the pampa and the arbitrary rule of great landowners, and had some opportunity of rising in the economic and social scale. As a result, the population of Buenos Aires shot up from 500,000 in 1889 to 1,244,000 in 1909. The great city, which held the greater portion of the nation's wealth, population, and culture, grew at the expense of the interior—particularly the northwest—which was impoverished, stagnant, and thinly peopled. Argentina, to use a familiar metaphor, became a giant head set on a dwarf body.

Foreign capital and management played a decisive role in the expansion of the Argentine economy in this period. The creole elite obtained vast profits from the rise in the price of their land and the increasing volume of exports but showed little interest in plowing those gains into industry or the construction of the infrastructure required by the export economy, preferring a lavish and leisurely lifestyle to entrepreneurial activity. Just as they left to English and Irish managers the task of tending their estates, so too they left to English capital the financing of meatpacking plants, railroads, public utilities, and docks and other facilities. As a result, most of these resources remained in British hands. Typical of the oligarchy's policy of surrender to foreign interests was the decision of Congress in 1889 to sell the state-owned Ferrocarril Oeste, the most profitable and best-run railroad in Argentina, to a British company. Service on a growing foreign debt claimed an increasingly larger portion of the government's receipts.

Meanwhile, imports of iron, coal, machinery, and consumer goods grew much faster than exports. Combined with the unfavorable price ratio of raw materials to finished goods, the result was an unfavorable balance of trade and a steady drain of gold. New loans with burdensome terms brought temporary relief but aggravated the long-range problem. The disappearance of gold and the government's determination to keep the boom going at all costs led to the issue of great quantities of unbacked paper currency and a massive inflation.

The great landowners did not mind, for their exports earned French francs and English pounds, which they could convert into cheap Argentine pesos for the payment of local costs; besides, inflation caused the price of their lands to rise. The sacrificial victims of the inflation were the urban middle class and the workers, whose income declined in real value.

THE FORMATION OF THE RADICAL PARTY

In 1889–1890, just as the boom was turning into a depression, the accumulated resentment of the urban middle class and some alienated sectors of the elite over the catastrophic inflation, one-party rule, and official corruption produced a protest movement that took the name *Unión Cívica* (Civic Union). Although the new organization had a middle-class base, its leadership united such disparate elements as disgruntled urban politicians like Leandro Além, its first president; new landowners and descendants of old aristocratic families denied access to patronage; and Catholics outraged by the government's anticlerical legislation. Aside from the demand for effective suffrage, the only thing uniting these heterogeneous elements was a common determination to overthrow the government.

The birth of the new party in 1890 coincided with a financial storm: The stock market collapsed, bankruptcies multiplied, and in April the cabinet resigned. Encouraged by this last development, and counting on support from the army, the leaders of the Unión Cívica planned a revolt that ended in defeat for the rebels.

The oligarchy now showed its ability to maneuver and divide its enemies. It appeased disgruntled elements of the elite by revising the system of state patronage and sought to improve economic conditions by a policy of retrenchment that reduced inflation, stabilized the peso, and revived Argentine credit abroad. Thanks to these measures and a gradual recovery from the depression, popular discontent began to subside.

These reforms isolated Leandro Além and other dissidents, who now formed a new party committed to a "radical" democracy—the *Unión Cívica Radical*. The party knew that rigged voting made electoral victory impossible, so they prepared for another revolt—a move that effectively was squelched by the government's decision to deport Além and other Radical leaders.

On his return from exile, Além organized a third revolt in July 1893. The rebels briefly seized Santa Fe and some other towns, but after two and a half months of fighting, the revolt collapsed for lack of significant popular support. Depressed by his failures and the intrigues of his nephew, Hipólito Yrigoyen, to seize control of the Radical Party, Além committed suicide in 1896. Until 1910, the Radical Party, now led by Yrigoyen, proved unable to achieve political reform by peaceful or revolutionary means, as the reunited oligarchy consolidated its power.

In Yrigoyen, however, the Radicals possessed a charismatic personality and a masterful organizer who refused to admit defeat. Yrigoyen, a one-time police superintendent in Buenos Aires, was formerly a minor politician who used his official party connections to acquire considerable wealth, which he invested in land and cattle. As a Radical caudillo, Yrigoyen was the architect of a program whose vagueness was dictated by the party's need to appeal to diverse elements and by its wholehearted acceptance of the economic status quo. "Abstention," refusal to participate in rigged elections, and "revolutionary intransigence," the determination to resort to revolution until free elections were achieved, were the party's basic slogans.

The Radical Party represented a dependent bourgeoisie that did not champion industrialization, economic diversification, or nationalization of foreign-owned industries. Far from attacking the neocolonial order, the Radical Party proposed to strengthen it by promoting cooperation between the landed aristocracy and the urban sectors, which challenged the creole elite's monopoly of political power. The Radical Party went into eclipse after the debacles of 1890 and 1893 but gradually revived after 1900, in part because of Yrigoyen's charismatic personality and organizing talent. The most important factor, however, was the steady growth of an urban and rural middle class largely composed of immigrant children. The domination of the export sector, which limited the growth of industry and opportunities for entrepreneurial activity, increasingly focused middle-class ambitions on government employment and the professions, two fields dominated by the creole elite. Signs of growing unrest and frustration in the middle class included a series of student strikes in the universities, caused by efforts of creole governing boards to restrict enrollment of students of immigrant descent.

ELECTORAL REFORM AND THE GROWTH OF THE LABOR MOVEMENT

Meanwhile, a section of the oligarchy had begun to advocate electoral reform. These aristocratic reformers argued that the existing situation created a permanent state of tension and instability; they feared that even-tually the Radical efforts at revolution would succeed. Therefore, they believed that the concessions demanded by the Radicals would open up the political system and gain for the ruling party—now generally called Conservative—the popular support and legitimacy it needed to remain in power. Moreover, the Conservative reformers, aware of a new threat from the labor movement and especially its vanguard—the socialists, anarchists, and syndicalists—hoped to make an alliance with the bourgeoisie against the revolutionary working class. They therefore supported a series of measures known collectively as the Sáenz Peña Law (1912). The new law established universal and secret male suffrage for citizens when they reached the age of eighteen. This law, which historian David Rock calls "an act of calculated retreat by the ruling class," opened the way for a dependent bourgeoisie to share power and the spoils of office with the landed aristocracy.

The principal political vehicle for working-class aspirations was the Socialist Party, founded in 1894 as a split-off from the Unión Cívica Radical by the Buenos Aires physician and intellectual Juan B. Justo, who led the party until his death in 1928. Despite its professed Marxism, the party's socialism was of the parliamentary reformist kind, appealing chiefly to highly skilled, native-born workers and the lower-middle class. The majority of workers, foreign-born noncitizens who still dreamed of returning someday to their homelands, remained aloof from electoral politics but readily joined trade unions that valiantly resisted deteriorating wages and working conditions; the government crushed a series of great strikes with brutal repression and deported the so-called foreign agitators. Despite these defeats, the labor movement continued to grow and struggle, winning such initial victories as the ten-hour workday and the establishment of Sunday as a compulsory day of rest.

Chilean Politics and Economy

NITRATES AND WAR

In 1876, the Liberal president Aníbal Pinto inherited a severe economic crisis (1874–1879). Wheat and copper prices dropped, exports declined, and unemployment grew. The principal offset to these unfavorable developments was the continued growth of nitrate exports from the Atacama Desert because of a doubling of nitrate production between 1865 and 1875. Nevertheless, nitrates, the foundation of Chilean material progress, also became the cause of a major war with dramatic consequences for Chile and its two foes, Bolivia and Peru.

The nitrate deposits exploited by the Anglo-Chilean companies lay in territories belonging to Bolivia (the province of Antofagasta) and Peru (the province of Tarapacá). In 1866, a treaty between Chile and Bolivia defined their boundary in the Atacama Desert as the twenty-fourth parallel, gave Chilean and Bolivian interests equal rights to exploit the territory between the twenty-third and twenty-fifth parallels, and guaranteed each government half of the tax revenues obtained from the export of minerals from the whole area. Anglo-Chilean capital soon poured into the region, developing a highly efficient mining-industrial complex. A second treaty of 1874 left Chile's northern border with Bolivia at the twenty-fourth parallel. Chile relinquished its rights to a share of the taxes from exports north of that boundary but received in return a twenty-five-year guarantee against increase of taxes on Chilean enterprises operating in the Bolivian province of Antofagasta.

Chile had no boundary dispute with Peru, but aggressive Chilean mining interests, aided by British capital, soon extended their operations from Antofagasta into the Peruvian province of Tarapacá. By 1875, Chilean enterprises in Peruvian nitrate fields employed more than ten thousand workers, engineers, and supervisory personnel. At this point, the Peruvian government, on the brink of bankruptcy because of an expensive program of public works, huge European loans, and the depletion of the guano deposits on which it had counted to service those loans, decided to expropriate the foreign companies in Tarapacá and establish a state monopoly over the production and sale of nitrates. Meanwhile, Peru and Bolivia had negotiated a secret treaty in 1874 providing for a military alliance in the event either power went to war with Chile.

Ejected from Tarapacá, the Anglo-Chilean capitalists intensified their exploitation of the nitrate deposits in Antofagasta. In 1878, Bolivia, counting on its military alliance with Peru, challenged Chile by imposing higher taxes on nitrate exports from Antofagasta, in violation of the treaty of 1874. When the Chilean companies operating in Antofagasta refused to pay the new taxes, the Bolivian government threatened them with confiscation. The agreement of 1874 provided for arbitration of disputes, but the Bolivians twice rejected Chilean offers to submit the dispute to arbitration.

In February 1879, despite Chilean warnings that expropriation of Chilean enterprises would void the treaty of 1874, the Bolivian government ordered the confiscation carried out. On February 14, the day set for the seizure and sale of the Chilean properties, Chilean troops occupied the port of Antofagasta, encountering no resistance, and proceeded to extend Chilean control over the whole province. Totally unprepared for war, Peru made a vain effort to mediate between Chile and Bolivia. Chile, however, having learned of the secret Peruvian-Bolivian alliance, charged Peru with intolerable duplicity and declared war on both Peru and Bolivia on April 5, 1879.

In this war, called the War of the Pacific, Chile faced enemies whose combined population was more than twice its own; one of these powers, Peru, also possessed a respectable naval force. Chile enjoyed major advantages, however. By contrast with its neighbors, it possessed a stable central government, a people with a strong sense of national identity, and a disciplined, well-trained army and navy. Chile also enjoyed the advantage of being closer to the theater of operations, because Bolivian troops had to come over the Andes and the Peruvian army had to cross the Atacama Desert.

All three powers had serious economic problems, but Chile's situation was not as catastrophic as that of its foes. Equally important, Chile had the support of powerful English capitalist interests, who knew that the future of the massive English investment in Chile depended in large part on the outcome of the war. The prospect of Chilean acquisition of the valuable nitrate areas of Antofagasta and

Tarapacá naturally pleased the British capitalists. British capital also invested in Bolivia and Peru; however, whereas the Chilean government had maintained service on its debt, Bolivia and Peru had suspended payment on their English loans. In addition, the Peruvian nationalization of the nitrate industry in Tarapacá had seriously injured British interests.

With British assistance, Chile won the war in 1883 and imposed its terms. By the Treaty of Ancón (October 20, 1883), Peru ceded the province of Tarapacá to Chile in perpetuity. The provinces of Tacna and Arica would be Chilean for ten years, after which a plebiscite would decide their ultimate fate. The plebiscite never occurred, however, and Chile continued to administer the two territories until 1929, when Peru recovered Tacna, and Arica went to Chile. An armistice signed in April 1884 by Bolivia and Chile assigned the former Bolivian province of Antofagasta to Chile, but for many years, no Bolivian government would sign a formal treaty acknowledging that loss. Finally, in 1904, Bolivia signed a treaty in which Chile agreed to pay an indemnity and to build a railroad that, by 1913, connected the Bolivian capital of La Paz to the port of Arica.

AFTERMATH OF THE WAR OF THE PACIFIC

Chile took advantage of the continued mobilization of its armed forces during the negotiations with Peru to settle scores with the Araucanians, whose struggle in defense of their land against encroaching whites had continued since colonial times. After two years of resistance against unequal odds, the Araucanians were forced to admit defeat and sign a treaty (1883) that resettled them on reservations but retained their tribal government and laws. The Araucanian campaign of 1880–1882, which extended the Chilean southern frontier into a region of mountain and forest, sparked a brisk movement of land speculation and colonization in that area.

The War of the Pacific shattered Peru economically and psychologically, and it left Bolivia more isolated than before from the outside world. However, Chile emerged the strongest nation on the west coast, in control of vast deposits of nitrates

and copper, the mainstays of its economy. Nonetheless, the greater part of these riches soon passed into foreign hands. In 1881, the Chilean government made an important decision: It returned the nitrate properties of Tarapacá to private ownership—that is, to the holders of the certificates issued by the Peruvian government as compensation for the nationalized properties.

During the war, uncertainty as to how Chile would dispose of those properties had caused the Peruvian certificates to depreciate until they fell to a fraction of their face value. Speculators, mostly British, had bought up large quantities of these depreciated certificates. In 1878, British capital controlled some 13 percent of the nitrate industry of Tarapacá, and, by 1890, its share had risen to at least 70 percent. British penetration of the nitrate areas proceeded not only through formation of companies for direct exploitation of nitrate deposits but also through the establishment of banks, which financed entrepreneurial activity in the nitrate area, and through the creation of railways and other companies more or less closely linked to the central nitrate industry. An English railway company with a monopoly of transport in Tarapacá, the Nitrate Railways Company, controlled by John Thomas North, paid dividends of up to 20 and 25 percent, compared with earnings of from 7 to 14 percent for other railway companies in South America.

The Chilean national bourgeoisie, which had pioneered the establishment of the mining-industrial-railway complex in the Atacama, offered little resistance to the foreign takeover. Lack of strong support from the liberal state, the relative financial weakness of the Chilean bourgeoisie, and the profitable relations between Chilean oligarchs and British interests facilitated the rapid transfer of Chilean nitrate and railway properties into British hands. This transformed Chilean mine owners into a dependent bourgeoisie content to share the profits of British companies.

Elsewhere in Chile, the war had energized the national economy and mobilized local manufacturers and workers, who pressed for electoral reform; in 1884, a literacy test replaced the property qualification for voting. Because the great majority

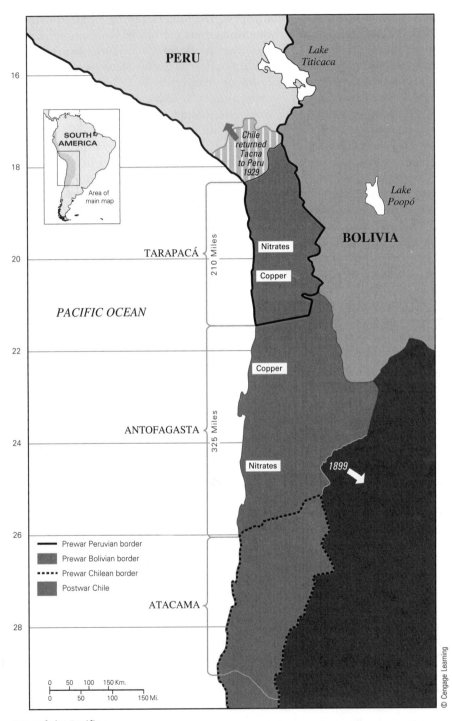

War of the Pacific

of Chilean males were illiterate *rotos* (seasonal farm workers) and inquilinos, this change did not materially add to the number of voters; as late as 1915, out of a population of about 3.5 million, only one hundred fifty thousand persons voted. However, it did secure the 1886 presidential victory of José Manuel Balmaceda, who took office with a well-defined program of state-directed economic modernization. By the 1880s, stimulated by the War of the Pacific, factory capitalism had taken root in Chile. In addition to consumer goods industries—flourmills, breweries, leather factories, furniture factories, and the like—foundries and metalworking enterprises served the mining industry, railways, and agriculture. Balmaceda proposed to consolidate and expand this native industrial capitalism.

BALMACEDA'S NATIONALISTIC POLICIES

Balmaceda came to office when government revenues were at an all-time high: They had risen from about 15 million pesos a year before the War of the Pacific to about 45 million pesos in 1887. The chief source of this government income was the export duty on nitrates. Knowing that the proceeds from this source would taper off as the nitrate deposits diminished, Balmaceda wisely planned to employ those funds for the development of an economic infrastructure that would remain when the nitrate was gone. Hence, public works figured prominently in his program. In 1887, he created a new ministry of industry and public works, which spent large sums to extend and improve the telegraphic and railway systems and to construct bridges, roads, and docks. Balmaceda also generously endowed public education, needed to provide skilled workers for Chilean industry. During his presidency, the total enrollment in Chilean schools rose in four years from some seventy-nine thousand in 1886 to more than one hundred fifty thousand in 1890. He also favored raising the wages of workers but was inconsistent in his labor policy; yielding to strong pressure from foreign and domestic employers, he sent troops to crush a number of strikes.

Central to Balmaceda's program was his determination to "Chileanize" the nitrate industry. In his inaugural address to Congress, he declared that his government would consider what measures it should take "to nationalize industries which are, at present, chiefly of benefit to foreigners," a clear reference to the nitrate industry. Later, Balmaceda's strategy shifted; he encouraged the entrance of Chilean private capital into nitrate production and exportation to prevent the formation of a foreign-dominated nitrate cartel whose interest in restricting output clashed with the government's interest in maintaining a high level of production to collect more export taxes. In November 1888, he scolded the Chilean elite for their lack of entrepreneurial spirit:

> Why does the credit and the capital which are brought into play in all kinds of speculations in our great cities hold back and leave the foreigner to establish banks at Iquique and abandon to strangers the exploiting of the nitrate works of Tarapacá? ... The foreigner exploits these riches and takes the profit of native wealth to give to other lands and unknown people the treasures of our soil, our own property and the riches we require.

Balmaceda waged a determined struggle to end the monopoly of the British-owned Nitrate Railways Company, whose prohibitive freight charges reduced production and export of nitrates. His nationalistic policies inevitably provoked the hostility of English nitrate "kings" like North, who had close links with the Chilean elite and employed prominent liberal politicians as their legal advisers.

Balmaceda had many domestic as well as foreign foes. The clerics opposed his plans to curb church powers. The landed aristocracy resented his public works program because it drew labor from agriculture and drove up rural wages. His proposal to establish a national bank with a monopoly of note issue angered the banks, which had profited from an uncontrolled emission of notes that fed inflation and benefited mortgaged landlords and exporters. The entire oligarchy, Liberals as well as Conservatives, opposed his use of the central government as an instrument of progressive economic and social change.

Meanwhile, the government's economic problems multiplied, adding to Balmaceda's political difficulties by narrowing his popular base. By 1890, foreign demand for copper and nitrates had weakened. Prices in an overstocked world market fell, and English nitrate interests responded to the crisis by forming a cartel to reduce production. Reduced production and export of nitrates and copper sharply diminished the flow of export duties into the treasury and caused growing unemployment and wage cuts even as inflation cut into the value of wages. The result was a series of great strikes in Valparaíso and the nitrate zone in 1890. Despite his sympathy with the workers' demands and unwillingness to use force against them, Balmaceda, under pressure from domestic and foreign employers, sent troops to crush the strikes. These repressive measures ensured much working-class apathy and even hostility toward the president in the eventual confrontation with his foes.

Indeed, Balmaceda had few firm allies at his side when that crisis came. The industrial capitalist group whose growth he had promoted ardently was still weak. The mining interests, increasingly integrated with or dominated by English capital, joined the bankers, the clericals, and the landed aristocracy in opposition to his nationalist program of economic development and independence. The opposition mobilized its forces in parliament, where Balmaceda lacked a reliable congressional majority, forcing him to abolish the system of parliamentary government and return to the traditional system of presidential rule established by the constitution of 1833. His rash act, made without any serious effort to mobilize popular forces, played into the hands of his enemies, who already were preparing for civil war.

On January 7, 1891, congressional leaders proclaimed a revolt against the president in the name of legality and the constitution. The navy, then as now led by officers of aristocratic descent, promptly supported the rebels, who seized the ports and customhouses in the north and established their capital at Iquique, the chief port of Tarapacá.

English-owned enterprises also actively aided the rebels. Indeed, by the admission of the British minister at Santiago, "our naval officers and the British community of Valparaíso and all along the coast rendered material assistance to the opposition and committed many breaches of neutrality." Many nitrate workers, alienated by Balmaceda's repression of their strike, remained neutral, or even joined the rebel army, organized by a German army officer, General Emil Korner. Politically isolated and militarily defeated, Balmaceda sought refuge in the Argentine embassy, and on September 19, 1891, the day on which his legal term of office ended, Balmaceda put a bullet through his head.

The death of Chile's first anti-imperialist president restored the reign of the oligarchy, a coalition of landowners, bankers, merchants, and mining interests closely linked to English capital. A new era began, the era of the so-called Parliamentary Republic. Taught by experience, the oligarchy now preferred to rule through a congress divided into various factions rather than through a strong executive. Such decentralization of government favored the interests of the rural aristocracy and its allies. A new law of 1892, vesting local governments with the right to supervise elections both for local and national offices, reinforced the power of the landowners, priests, and political bosses who had fought Balmaceda's progressive policies.

THE PARLIAMENTARY REPUBLIC, FOREIGN ECONOMIC DOMINATION, AND THE GROWTH OF THE WORKING CLASS

The era of the Parliamentary Republic accompanied a growing subordination of the Chilean economy to foreign capital, confirmed by a steady increase in the foreign debt and foreign ownership of the nation's resources. English investments in Chile amounted to 24 million pounds in 1890 and rose to 64 million pounds in 1913. Of this total, 34.6 million pounds formed part of the Chilean public debt. In the same period, North American and German capital began to challenge the British hegemony in Chile. England continued to be Chile's principal trade partner, but U.S. and German trade with Chile grew at a faster rate. German instructors also acquired a strong influence in the Chilean army, and the flow of German immigrants into southern Chile continued, resulting in the formation of compact colonies dominated by a Pan-German ideology. The revival of the Chilean economy from the depression of the early 1890s brought an increase of nitrate, copper, and agricultural exports, and further enriched the ruling classes, but it left inquilinos, miners, and factory workers as desperately poor as before. Meanwhile, the working class grew from one hundred twenty thousand to two hundred fifty thousand between 1890 and 1900, and the doctrines of trade unionism, socialism, and anarchism achieved growing popularity in its ranks.

Luis Emilio Recabarren (1876–1924), the father of Chilean socialism and communism, played a decisive role in the social and political awakening of the Chilean proletariat. In 1906, Recabarren won an election to Congress from a mining area, but state officials did not allow him to take his seat because he refused to take his oath of office on the Bible. In 1909, he organized the Workers Federation of Chile, the first national trade union movement. Three years later, he founded the Socialist Party, a revolutionary Marxist movement, and became its first secretary.

The growing self-consciousness and militancy of the Chilean working class found expression in a mounting wave of strikes. Between 1911 and 1920, almost three hundred strikes, involving more than three hundred thousand workers, took place, many of which the state crushed with traditional brutal methods that left thousands of workers dead.

Brazilian Politics and Economy

THE FALL OF THE MONARCHY

Abolition of slavery in 1888 sabotaged slavery's sister institution, the monarchy, which had long rested on the support of the planter class, especially the northern planters, who saw in it a guarantee of slavery's survival. Before 1888, the Republican Party had its principal base among the coffee interests, who resented the favor shown by the imperial government to the sugar planters and wished to achieve political power that corresponded to their economic clout. Now, angered by abolition and embittered by the failure of the crown to indemnify

them for their lost slaves, those planters who had opposed abolition joined the Republican movement. The monarchy that had served the interest of regional elites for the previous sixty-seven years had lost its reason for existence.

Republicanism and a closely allied ideology, positivism, also made many converts in the officer class, who were disgruntled by the imperial government's neglect and mistreatment. Many of the younger officers belonged to the new urban middle class or were of aristocratic descent but disagreed with the ways of their fathers. Positivism, it has been said, became "the gospel of the military academy," where a popular young professor of mathematics, Benjamin Constant Botelho de Magalhães, a devoted disciple of Auguste Comte, the doctrine's founder, taught. The positivist doctrine, with its stress on science, its ideal of a dictatorial republic, and its distrust of the masses, fit the needs of urban middle-class groups, progressive officers, and businessmen-fazendeiros, who wanted modernization but without drastic changes in land tenure and class relations. On November 15, 1889, a military revolt led by Benjamin Constant and Marshal Floriano Peixoto overthrew the government, proclaimed a republic with Marshal Deodoro da Fonseca as provisional chief of state, and sent Pedro II into exile in France.

Like the revolution that gave Brazil its independence, the republican revolution came from above; the coup d'état encountered little resistance but also inspired little popular enthusiasm. Representatives of the business, landed, and military elites monopolized political, economic, and social power.

The new rulers promptly promulgated a series of reforms, including a decree that ended corporal punishment in the army, a literacy test that replaced property qualifications for voting (because property and literacy usually went together, this measure did not significantly enlarge the electorate), and successive decrees that established a secular state and civil marriage.

THE NEW REPUBLIC

Two years after the revolt, a constituent assembly met in Rio de Janeiro to draft a constitution for the new republic. It provided for a federal, presidential

Fundação Maria Luisa e Oscar Americano, São Paulo

Allegory of the Departure of Dom Pedro II for Europe After the Declaration of the Republic. This romantic painting suggests the respect and affection many Brazilians, including supporters of the republic, felt for the ousted emperor.

form of government with the customary three branches: legislative, executive, and judicial. The principal debate was between the partisans of greater autonomy for the states and those who feared the divisive results of an extreme federalism. The coffee interests, which dominated the wealthy south-central region, sought to strengthen their position at the expense of the central power. The urban business groups, represented in the convention chiefly by lawyers, favored a strong central government that could promote industry, aid the creation of a national market, and offer protection from British competition.

The result was a compromise tilted in favor of federalism. The twenty provinces in effect became self-governing states with popularly elected governors,

the exclusive right to tax exports (a profitable privilege for wealthy states like São Paulo and Minas Gerais), and the right to maintain militias. The national government received control over the tariffs and the income from import duties, whereas the president obtained significant powers: He could designate his cabinet ministers and other high officers, declare a state of siege, and, in the event of a threat to their political institutions, intervene in the states with the federal armed forces. The constitution proclaimed the sanctity of private property and guaranteed freedom of the press, speech, and assembly.

If these freedoms had some relevance in the cities and hinterlands touched by the movement of modernization, they lacked meaning over the greater part of the national territory. The fazendeiros, former slave owners, virtually monopolized the nation's chief wealth: its land. The land monopoly gave them absolute control over the rural population. Feudal and semifeudal forms of land tenure, accompanied by the obligation of personal and military service on the part of tenants, survived in the backlands, especially in the northeast. Powerful *coronéis* (urban or rural bosses) maintained armies of *jagunços* (full-time private soldiers) and waged war against each other.

In this medieval atmosphere of constant insecurity and social disintegration, there arose messianic movements that reflected the aspirations of the oppressed *sertanejos* (inhabitants of the sertão) for peace and justice. One of the most important of such movements arose in the interior of Bahia, where the principal activity was cattle raising. Here, Antônio Conselheiro (Anthony the Counselor) established a settlement at the abandoned cattle ranch of Canudos. Rejecting private property, Antônio required all who joined his sacred company to give up their goods, but he promised a future of prosperity in his messianic kingdom. All would share in the division of hostile landowners' property and the treasure of the "lost Sebastian," the Portuguese king who had disappeared in Africa in 1478, but soon would return as a redeemer.

Despite its religious coloration, the existence of such a focus of social and political unrest was intolerable to the fazendeiros and the state authorities. When the sertanejos easily defeated state forces sent against them in 1896, the governor called on the federal government for aid. Four brutal military campaigns finally broke the epic resistance of the men, women, and children of Canudos, nearly all of whom perished in the national army's final assault. A Brazilian literary masterpiece, *Os sertões* (*Rebellion in the Backlands*) by Euclides da Cunha (1856–1909), immortalized the heroism of the defenders and the crimes of the victors. It also revealed to the urban elite another and unfamiliar side of Brazilian reality.

THE ECONOMIC REVOLUTION

An enormous historical gulf separated the bleak sertão—where the tragedy of Canudos played out—

from the cities, the scene of a mushrooming growth of banks, stock exchanges, and corporations. In Rio de Janeiro, writes Pedro Calmon, there was "a multitude of millionaires of recent vintage—commercial agents, bustling lawyers, promoters of all kinds, politicians of the new generation, the men of the day." Even the physical appearance of some of Brazil's great urban centers changed. The federal capital of Rio de Janeiro experienced the most marked changes, when Prefect Pereira Passos mercilessly demolished narrow, old streets to permit the construction of broad, modern avenues. At the same time, the distinguished scientist Oswaldo Cruz waged a victorious struggle to conquer mosquito-borne disease by filling in swamps and installing adequate water and sewage systems. Thus, Rio became a beautiful and healthful city between 1902 and 1906.

The economic policies of the new republican regime reflected pressures from different quarters: the planter class, urban capitalists, and the military. Many planters, left in a difficult position by the abolition of slavery, demanded subsidies and credits to enable them to convert to the new wage system. The emerging industrial bourgeoisie, convinced that Brazil must develop an industrial base to emerge from backwardness, asked for protective tariffs, the construction of an economic infrastructure, and policies favorable to capital formation. Within the provisional government, these aspirations had a fervent supporter in the minister of finance, Ruy Barbosa, who believed that the factory was the crucible in which an "intelligent and independent democracy" would be forged in Brazil. Finally, the army, whose decisive role in the establishment of the republic had given it great prestige and influence, called for increased appropriations for the armed services. These various demands far exceeded the revenue available to the federal and state governments.

The federal government initially tried to satisfy these competing demands by resorting to the printing press and allowing private banks to issue notes backed by little more than faith in the future of Brazil. In two years, the volume of paper money in circulation doubled, and the foreign-exchange value of the *milréis* (the Brazilian monetary unit) plummeted disastrously. Because objective economic conditions (the small internal market and the lack of an adequate technological base, among other factors) limited the real potential for Brazilian growth, much of the new capital served highly speculative purposes, including the creation of fictitious companies.

The resulting economic collapse brought ruin to many investors, unemployment and lower wages to workers, and a military coup that replaced President da Fonseca with his vice president, Marshal Floriano Peixoto. The urban middle-class sector thereafter briefly gained greater influence, and inflation continued unchecked. The rise in the cost of many imported items to almost prohibitive levels stimulated the growth of Brazilian manufactures: The number of such enterprises almost doubled between 1890 and 1895.

However, the suppression of a new revolt with strong aristocratic and monarchical overtones increased Peixoto's reliance on the financial and military support of the state of São Paulo, whose coffee oligarchy resolved to use its clout to end the ascendancy of the urban middle classes. The oligarchy distrusted their policies of rapid industrialization and blamed them for the financial instability that had plagued the first years of the republic. In 1893, the old planter oligarchies, whose divisions temporarily had enabled the middle classes to gain the upper hand in coalition with the military, reunited to form the Federal Republican Party, with a liberal program of support for federalism, fiscal responsibility, and limited government. Because they controlled the electoral machinery, they easily captured the presidency and again institutionalized the domination of the coffee interests, relegating urban capitalist groups to a secondary role in political life.

A succession of Liberal governments thereafter gave primacy to export agriculture and fully endorsed the international economic division of labor that rendered Brazil dependent on foreign manufactured imports. "It is time," proclaimed President Manuel Ferraz de Campos Sales (1898–1902), "that we take the correct road; to that end we must strive to export all that we can produce better than other

countries, and import all that other countries can produce better than we." This formula confirmed the continuity of neocolonialism from the empire through the early republic. Determined to halt inflation, the Liberals drastically reduced expenditures on public works, increased taxes, made every effort to redeem the paper money to improve Brazil's international credit, and secured new loans to cover shortfalls in government revenues.

Coffee was king. Whereas Brazil produced 56 percent of the world's coffee output from 1880 to 1889, it accounted for 76 percent from 1900 to 1904. Its closest competitor, rubber, supplied only 28 percent of Brazil's exports in 1901. Sugar, once the ruler of the Brazilian economy, now accounted for barely 5 percent of the nation's exports. Minas Gerais and especially São Paulo became the primary coffee regions, and Rio de Janeiro declined in importance. Enjoying immense advantages—the famous rich, porous *terra roxa* (red soil), an abundance of immigrant labor, and closeness to the major port of Santos—the *Paulistas* harvested 60 percent of the national coffee production.

The coffee boom from the late 1880s through the mid-1890s soon led to overproduction, falling prices, and the accumulation of unsold stocks after 1896. Because coffee trees came into production only four years after planting, the effects of expansion into the western frontier of São Paulo continued to be felt even after prices fell; between 1896 and 1900 the number of producing trees in São Paulo alone went from 150 million to 570 million. Large international coffee-trading firms controlled the world market, and they added to planters' difficulties by paying depressed prices during the height of each season and selling off their reserves in periods of relative shortage when prices edged up.

Responding to the planters' clamor for help, the São Paulo government took the first step for the defense of coffee in 1902, forbidding new coffee plantings for five years. Other steps soon proved necessary. Faced with a bumper crop in 1906, São Paulo launched a coffee price-support scheme to protect the state's economic lifeblood. With financing from British, French, German, and U.S. banks and the eventual collaboration of the federal government, São Paulo purchased several million bags of coffee and held them off the market in an effort to maintain profitable price levels. Purchases continued into 1907; from that date until World War I, the state gradually sold off the stocks with little market disruption. The operation's principal gainers were the foreign merchants and bankers, who, because they controlled the Coffee Commission formed to liquidate the purchased stocks, gradually disposed of them with a large margin of profit. The problem, temporarily exorcised, shortly returned in an even more acute form.

The valorization scheme, which favored the coffee-raising states at the expense of the rest, reflected the coffee planters' political domination. President Campos Sales institutionalized this ascendancy with the so-called *política dos governadores* (politics of the governors). Its essence was a formula that gave the two richest and most populous states (São Paulo and Minas Gerais) a virtual monopoly of federal politics and the choice of presidents. Thus, the first three civilian presidents from 1894 to 1906 came from São Paulo; the next two, from 1906 to 1910, came from Minas Gerais and Rio de Janeiro, respectively.

In return, the oligarchies of the other states enjoyed almost total freedom of action within their jurisdictions, with the central government usually intervening only when it suited the local oligarchy's interest. Informal discussions among the state governors determined the choice of president, whose election was a foregone conclusion because less than 2 percent of the population was eligible to vote. No official candidate for president lost an election before 1930. Similar reciprocal arrangements existed on the state level between the governors and the coronéis, who rounded up the local vote to elect the governors and thereby earned a free hand in their respective domains.

Despite the official bias in favor of agriculture, industry continued to grow. By 1908, Brazil could boast of more than three thousand industrial enterprises. Foreign firms dominated the fields of banking, public works, utilities, transportation, and the export and import trade. On the other hand, native Brazilians and permanent immigrants almost exclusively engaged in manufacturing. This national industry concentrated in the four states of São Paulo, Minas Gervais, Rio de Janeiro, and Rio Grande do Sul. Heavy industry did not exist; more than half of the enterprises were textile mills and food-processing plants. Many of these "enterprises" were small workshops that employed only a few artisans or operated with archaic technology, and Brazilians in the market economy continued to import most quality products. Semifeudal conditions prevailing in the countryside, the extreme poverty of the masses (which sharply limited the internal market), the lack of a skilled and literate labor force, and the hostility of most fazendeiros and foreign interests to industry all limited the quantitative and qualitative development of industry.

Together with industry, a working class arose destined to play a significant role in the life of the country. The Brazilian proletariat formed partly from sharecroppers and minifundio peasants fleeing to the cities to escape dismal poverty and the tyranny of coronéis, but above all, it relied on the flood of European immigrants, who arrived at a rate of one hundred thousand to one hundred fifty thousand each year. Working and living conditions of the working class were often intolerable. Child labor was common, for children could legally seek employment from the age of twelve. The workday ranged from nine hours for some skilled workers to more than sixteen hours for various categories of unskilled workers. Wages were pitifully low and often paid in vouchers redeemable at the company store. Legislation was totally absent to protect workers against the hazards of unemployment, old age, or industrial accidents.

Among the European immigrants, many militants with socialist, syndicalist, or social-democratic backgrounds helped organize the Brazilian labor movement and gave it a radical political orientation. National and religious divisions among workers, widespread illiteracy, and quarrels between socialists and **anarcho-syndicalists** hampered the rise of a trade union movement and a labor party.

Nonetheless, trade unions grew rapidly after 1900, and the first national labor congress, representing the majority of the country's trade unions, met in 1906 to struggle for the eight-hour

workday. One result of the congress was the formation of the first national trade union organization,
the Brazilian Labor Confederation, which organized a number of strikes that authorities and employers tried to suppress by arresting labor leaders,
deporting immigrants, and sending dissidents to
forced labor on a railroad under construction in
distant Mato Grosso. The phrase "The social question is a question for the police" was often used to
sum up the labor policy of Brazil's liberal state.

Central American Politics and Economy

In the last third of the nineteenth century, the three
Central American countries selected for special
study—Guatemala, Nicaragua, and El Salvador—
underwent major economic changes in response
to growing world demand for two products the
area produced in great quantity: coffee and bananas.
The changes included a liberal reform that sought to
promote economic growth but left intact existing
class and property relations. This liberal program
also led to a new dependency on the export of
one or two products, foreign control of key natural
resources, and acceptance of U.S. political hegemony. Throughout Central America, these changes
accompanied concentration of landownership, intensified exploitation of labor, and contributed to a
growing gulf between the rich and the poor.

Guatemala, 1865–1898

Six years of continuous liberal political and military
challenge to Guatemala's conservative rule followed
Rafael Carrera's death in 1865. The Liberals responded to changes in the world economy, in particular to the mounting foreign demand for coffee
and the adjustments this required in Guatemala's
economic and social structures. In 1871, they seized
power, and two years later the energetic Justo Rufino Barrios became president. Barrios and his successors were determined to consolidate state power,
subjugate relatively autonomous indigenous communities, and create a unified national market for
land, labor, and commodities.

Their liberal reform program included major
economic, social, and ideological changes. The
ideological reform introduced doctrines of white
supremacy then current in Europe and the United
States to justify racist immigration policies designed
to "whiten" the population. It also rejected clerical
and metaphysical doctrine in favor of a firm faith in
science and material progress. This called for the
secularization and expansion of education. The
shortage of public funds, however, greatly limited
public education; as late as 1921, the Guatemalan
illiteracy rate was more than 86 percent. Seeking to
reduce the power and authority of the church, the
Liberal governments nationalized its lands, ended its
special privileges, and established freedom of religion and civil marriage.

The economic transformation encompassed
three major areas: land tenure, labor, and infrastructure. A change in land tenure was necessary for the
creation of the new economic order. Thousands of
small and midsize producers had grown the old staples
of Guatemalan agriculture, indigo and cochineal; coffee, however, required significant accumulations of
capital and large expanses of land concentrated in relatively few hands. Barrios began an agrarian reform
designed to make such land available to the coffee
growers. He confiscated Church and monastery lands,
indigenous communal lands, and uncultivated state
holdings, which he divided and either sold cheaply
or granted freely to private interests. Legislation requiring titles to private property provided the legal
basis for this expropriation. The principal native beneficiaries of this process were small and midsize coffee
growers who could purchase or otherwise obtain land
from the government. However, foreign immigrants,
warmly welcomed by the Liberal regimes, also
benefited from the new legislation. By 1914,
foreign-owned (chiefly German) lands produced almost half of Guatemala's coffee. By 1926, concentration of land ownership had reached a point at which
only 7.3 percent of the population owned land.

The land reform helped achieve another objective of the liberal program: the supply of a mass of
cheap labor to the new group of native and foreign
coffee growers. Many highland natives who had lost
their land migrated to the emerging coffee-growing

areas near the coast. The most common labor system was debt peonage—legal under Guatemalan law—in which hereditary debts bound indigenous workers to the *fincas* (plantations). Export agriculture also depended on the recruitment of native peoples who came down from the mountains to work as seasonal laborers on haciendas and plantations to supplement their meager income from their own tiny landholdings. Barrios also revived the colonial system of **mandamientos** (a system of coerced indigenous labor), which required indigenous people to accept offers of work from planters. Local officials maintained registers for this purpose and also used them to conscript natives for military service or public works. Those who could not pay the two-peso head tax—the great majority—had to work two weeks per year on road construction.

Constituting 70 percent of the nation's 1 million people in the late nineteenth century, indigenous peoples naturally resisted this liberal onslaught, occasionally through overt acts of localized rebellion. However, in the face of a ruthless military state prepared to obliterate them, they more commonly survived by deploying "weapons of the weak," modes of resistance designed to limit the risk of annihilation. In rural Guatemala, these indigenous communities relied on **guachibales** (independent religious brotherhoods rooted in colonial Catholic traditions) to maintain their cultural identities, defend their autonomy, and preserve communal customs, ancestral languages, and religious rituals against the homogenizing power of liberalism's unfettered market forces.

NICARAGUA, 1870–1909

A struggle between Liberals and Conservatives also dominated the history of Nicaragua for two decades after the collapse of the Central American federation in 1838. The Liberals' responsibility for inviting William Walker to assist them, followed by Walker's attempt to establish his personal empire in Central America, so discredited them that the Conservatives ruled Nicaragua with little opposition for more than three decades thereafter (1857–1893).

Although coffee was grown commercially as early as 1848, the principal economic activities in Nicaragua until about 1870 were cattle ranching and subsistence agriculture. Indigenous communities still owned much land, a class of independent small farmers lived on public land, and peonage was rare. On the Atlantic coast, however, the autonomous Kingdom of Mosquitia, controlled by the British since 1678, was home to traditional Miskitos, Sumus, and Afro-creoles, who labored at low wages on thriving British- and U.S.-owned banana plantations, timberlands, gold mines, and commercial port facilities. But the sudden growth of the world market for coffee induced the Nicaraguan elite to demand additional land suitable for coffee growing and an expanded supply of cheap labor.

Beginning in 1877, a series of laws required indigenous villages to sell their communal lands and effectively drove the indigenous and mestizo peasants off their land, gradually transforming them into a class of dependent peons or sharecroppers. The passage of vagrancy laws and laws permitting the conscription of native peoples for agricultural and public labor also ensured the supply of cheap labor needed by the coffee growers. These laws provoked a major indigenous revolt, the War of the Comuneros (1881), which ended in defeat for indigenous communities and thereafter unleashed a ferocious repression that took five thousand lives.

The new class of coffee planters was impatient with the traditional ways of the conservative cattle ranchers who had held power in Nicaragua since 1857. In 1893, the planters staged a revolt that brought the Liberal José Santos Zelaya to the presidency. A modernizer, Zelaya ruled for the next seventeen years as dictator-president. He undertook to provide the infrastructure needed by the new economic order through the construction of roads, railroads, port facilities, and telegraphic communications. He reorganized the military, separated church and state, and promoted public education. Like other Latin American Liberal leaders of his time, he believed that foreign investment was necessary for rapid economic progress and granted large concessions to foreign capitalists, especially U.S. firms. By 1909, North Americans controlled much of the production of coffee, gold, lumber, and bananas—the principal sources of Nicaragua's wealth.

EL SALVADOR, 1876–1911

By the mid-nineteenth century, El Salvador already had passed through two economic cycles. The first was dominated by cacao, the prosperity of which collapsed in the seventeenth century; the second by indigo, which entered a sharp decline in the latter half of the nineteenth century, first as a result of competition from other producing areas and then as a result of the development of synthetic dyes. The search for a new export crop led to the enthronement of coffee. Coffee cultivation began at about the time of independence, but it did not expand rapidly until the 1860s. As elsewhere in Central America, expropriation and usurpation of native lands—carried out in the name of private property and material progress—accompanied the rise of coffee because indigenous communities owned most of the land best suited to coffee cultivation.

Unlike indigo, which was planted and harvested every year, coffee trees did not produce for three years. Producers, therefore, had to have capital or credit, and the people with capital or access to credit were the hacendados who had prospered from the growing of indigo. To help these hacendados in their search for land and labor, a government decree of 1856 declared that, if a pueblo did not plant two-thirds of its communal lands in coffee, ownership would pass into the hands of the state. Later, the Liberal president and military strongman, Rafael Zaldívar, directly attacked native landholdings with passage of an 1881 law that ordered the division of all communal lands among the co-owners. This division of land opened the way for the expanding coffee growers to acquire their land by legal or illegal means. Thirteen months later, Zaldívar decreed the abolition of all communal land tenure. The new legislation harmed these communities and **ladino** (mestizo) small farmers. These farmers often relied on municipal **tierras comunes** (the free pasture and woodlot where they could graze their stock) for an important part of their subsistence. In 1879, 60 percent of the people depended on communal properties, which composed 40 percent of arable lands.

The result of this new legislation was a rapid concentration of landownership in the hands of a landed oligarchy often referred to as "the fourteen families." The number, although not an exact figure, expressed symbolically the reality of the tiny elite that dominated the Salvadoran economy and state. Throughout most of the nineteenth century, the great landowners used their own private armies to deal with the problem of recalcitrant peasants. Government decrees of 1884 and 1889 made these private armed forces the basis of the public Rural Police, later renamed the National Police. In 1912 the *Guardia Nacional* (National Guard), modeled after the Spanish National Guard, was established. Like the National Police, the National Guard patrolled the countryside and offered police protection to haciendas.

For the rural poor, the social consequences of the coffee boom were disastrous. A few of the dispossessed peasants were permitted to remain on the *fincas* (new estates) as *colonos*—peons who received a place to live and a *milpa* (garden plot) where they could raise subsistence crops in exchange for their labor. Unlike the old indigo or sugar latifundia, however, which required a large permanent labor force, the need for labor on the coffee plantations was seasonal, so for the most part planters relied on hired hands. This circumstance determined the pattern of life of most Salvadoran campesinos. They might farm a small plot as squatters or as colonos on a plantation, but their tiny plots usually did not provide sufficient subsistence for their families. They therefore tended to follow the harvests, working on coffee fincas during the harvest season, moving on to cut sugar cane or harvest cotton during August and September, and finally returning to their milpas, hopeful that the maize had ripened. This unstable migratory pattern created many social problems.

Venezuelan Politics and Economy

Turmoil in the aftermath of the Federal War ended in 1870 when Antonio Guzmán Blanco, the ablest of Venezuela's nineteenth-century rulers, seized power. Like his father, Guzmán Blanco was a master of demagogic rhetoric. He was a self-proclaimed Liberal and foe of the oligarchy, an anticlerical and devout believer in the positivist creed of science and progress, whose ambition was to create a "practical republic" of "civilized people." To secure this vision, he forged pacts with the Conservative merchant class of Caracas, regional caudillos, and foreign economic interests who profited from his ambitious program to construct roads, railroads, and telegraph systems. In the end, Guzmán Blanco's dream of a developed capitalist Venezuela proved to be a mirage; after two decades of his rule, Venezuela remained rural, monocultural, and dependent, a country in which caudillos again ran rampant as they struggled for power.

Guzmán or "the illustrious American," as his sycophantic Congress and press called him, presided over a system of government that Venezuelan historians often describe as "a national alliance of caudillos." The supreme caudillo replaced the constitution of 1864 with a succession of new constitutions that reinforced the centralization of power. Although Guzmán's dictatorship was mild by comparison with some others in Venezuelan history, he did not hesitate to use repressive measures against his foes.

By his pact with the caudillos, Guzmán secured a relatively stable peace (though several large-scale revolts erupted against him between 1870 and 1888, and local uprisings were common throughout the period). Soon after coming to power, he established a *compañía de crédito* with a powerful group of Caracas merchants. This group gave him the resources needed to initiate a program of public works designed to improve transportation and communication. Between 1870 and 1874, he began fifty-one road-building projects, but local funding did not suffice. Although Guzmán solicited the cooperation of foreign capital, other countries were reluctant to invest in a country where recurrent episodes of civil war had marked its recent history. In 1879, he secured his first foreign contract with a group of British investors for the construction of a railroad to connect Caracas with its major port, La Guaira. By the time he left office, Venezuela had eleven railroad lines completed or under construction, all designed to serve the export-import trade by connecting Caracas and the major agricultural and mining areas with the ports. Given Venezuela's unfavorable terms of trade—the long-term

tendency for the prices of its exports to decline and those of its manufactured imports to rise—the net result was to reinforce Venezuela's economic dependency, promote decapitalization, and leave the country a legacy of large unpaid foreign debt that in time posed a threat of foreign intervention and loss of sovereignty.

Guzmán Blanco's anticlerical policies led to a further weakening of the church. Liberals already had abolished tithing as "an excessive tax burden" on the citizenry, but Guzmán Blanco ended the priestly fuero, established civil marriage and registration of births and deaths, and closed convents and seminaries. His government forbade the church to inherit real estate and seized many church estates. Guzmán Blanco also tried to prohibit black and Asian immigration, even as he enticed Europeans with generous subsidies. Ultimately, this failed, and Venezuela remained a society in which a small, self-proclaimed white wealthy minority ruled a black majority.

For the rest, Guzmán Blanco's development programs caused little change in the country's economic and social structures. In 1894, the population, numbering some 2.5 million, was overwhelmingly rural; only three cities had a population of more than ten thousand. Most of the laboring population worked in agriculture; what little modern industry existed was limited to light industry, such as food processing and textiles. Artisan shops, employing some fifty thousand workers, were economically much more important.

After a chaotic decade following the demise of Guzmán Blanco, Cipriano Castro, an energetic young caudillo from the Andean state of Táchira, seized power with his *compadre* (buddy) Juan Vicente Gómez, a prosperous cattle raiser and coffee grower. Castro's rise reflected the growing economic importance of the Andean coffee-growing region. Although he tried to continue Guzmán Blanco's policy of centralization by establishing a strong national army to replace the old-time personal and state militias, declining coffee prices reduced state revenues and handicapped his program of military reform. This led to a series of caudillo revolts repressed at heavy cost and a major conflict with foreign powers whose blockade of Venezuelan ports deprived the government of a vital source of income: custom duties.

Castro presided over a country in ruin because of devastating civil wars and a prolonged depression. The German and British governments demanded immediate settlement of their nationals' claims for unpaid debts and damages suffered in civil wars, but the government could not pay. In December 1902, despite Castro's offer to negotiate, the two powers sent an Anglo-German squadron of twelve warships into Venezuelan waters with orders to seize or destroy Venezuela's tiny fleet and blockade its ports. The powerful guns of the Anglo-German squadron soon silenced the answering fire of Venezuelan coastal batteries, and the aggressors occupied several Venezuelan ports. The unequal nature of the struggle, the catastrophic economic impact of the Anglo-German blockade, and the continuing internal revolts in some areas of the country made a settlement necessary. Accordingly, Castro asked the U.S. ambassador to mediate in negotiating a settlement. The terms required Venezuela to allocate 30 percent of its customs duties to the payment of claims, provided for an end to the blockade, and reestablished diplomatic relations between the parties, but the settlement denied Venezuela compensation for its losses.

Castro's last years in power were troubled by new clashes with foreign states—France, Holland, the United States—usually caused by his insistence that foreign nationals were subject to Venezuelan courts and laws. As Castro's health declined, Juan Vicente Gómez, with support of foreign powers, notably the United States, ended the Castro regime and launched a new Liberal dictatorship.

Colombian Politics and Economy

Dominating the presidency and Congress in 1853, the Liberals in Colombia authored a new constitution that provided for universal male suffrage, a provision that troubled some Liberals, who feared that illiterate proclerical peasants might vote Conservative. Actually, because in most areas peasants continued to vote the wishes of the local *gamonales* (bosses), the new electoral law did not significantly change anything.

In economics, the Liberals sought a decisive break with the colonial tradition of restriction and monopoly. They abolished the state tobacco monopoly and ceded to the provinces revenues from tithes (hitherto collected by the state but used for support of the church), the quinto tax on gold and other precious metals, and other traditional sources of national state revenue. They also empowered the provinces to abolish these taxes. To compensate for the resulting loss of national revenues, Congress adopted a tax on individuals.

Having achieved these objectives with artisan support, the Liberal elite now ignored their allies' demands for tariff protection. This triggered a new political crisis in 1854 when a coup, supported by artisans who formed workers' battalions to defend the revolution, briefly installed Gen. José María Melo. However, Liberal and Conservative generals, putting aside their differences, raised private armies and defeated Melo in a short campaign. They subsequently imprisoned his artisan allies and deported three hundred to Panama. The economic, political, and military rout of the artisans was complete.

In 1860, Liberals carried their religious and political reforms to their extreme and logical conclusions. They abolished compulsory tithes and ecclesiastical fueros, suppressed all religious orders, closed all convents and monasteries, and seized church wealth. However, the resulting transfer of massive amounts of church land into private hands produced little or no change in the land tenure system; clerical latifundia simply became lay latifundia, contributing to a further concentration of landownership. The principal buyers were Liberal merchants, landowners, and politicians, but Conservatives also participated in the plunder of church land.

In 1863, Liberal political reform reached its climax when a new constitution carried the principle of federalism to great lengths. The nine sovereign states became, in effect, independent nations, each with its own armed forces and possessing all the legislative powers not explicitly granted to the weak central government. The Liberals remained in power until 1885 in a political climate that approximated institutionalized anarchy, as the central government was powerless to intervene against the local revolutions that toppled and set up state governments.

The economic movement and its quest for the export base that could firmly integrate Colombia into the capitalist world economy continued. By the 1870s, tobacco exports were down sharply, but exports of coffee, quinine, and other products made up for this decline. Coffee emerged as the country's major export product, but its development lagged behind that of Brazil, which relied increasingly on European immigrant free labor. In Colombia, coffee production in its principal centers of Santander and Cundinamarca relied on traditional haciendas worked by peons and tenants who lived and labored under oppressive conditions. A more satisfactory situation existed in Antioquia and Caldas, characterized by a mix of haciendas with more enlightened forms of sharecropping and smallholdings, operations marked by high productivity. In these states, the twentieth-century takeoff of the Colombian coffee industry occurred.

The development of coffee as the major export, the growing ties between foreign and domestic merchants and coffee planters, and the stimulus that expropriation of church lands gave to trade and speculation created economic interests that required a new political model. Its principal characteristic was a strong state that could impose order, construct a railroad network, and create the financial infrastructure needed to expand the coffee industry. The Liberal reform had removed many obstacles to capitalist development, but its federalist excesses had created others. By the early 1880s, Conservatives and many moderate Liberals agreed that political and social stability required the consolidation of a centralized nation-state, a project initiated by Rafael Núñez in 1879.

RAFAEL NÚÑEZ, THE "REGENERATION," AND THE WAR OF A THOUSAND DAYS, 1880–1903

Núñez began political life as a radical Liberal and spent thirteen years in the consular service in Europe. He returned home in 1875 and won the presidential election in 1879, governing with a coalition of Liberal and Conservative Parties. Re-elected in 1884, he swiftly crushed a radical Liberal revolt and announced that the 1863 constitution had "ceased to exist." In 1886, he presented the country with a new constitution that replaced the sovereign states with departments headed by governors appointed by the president, extended the presidential term to six years, established literacy and property qualifications for voting for representatives, and provided for indirect election of senators. Under that constitution, personally or through surrogates, Núñez ruled Colombia until his death in 1894.

The foundations of Núñez's authoritarian republic were a strong standing army and a national police force. Earlier regimes had virtually dismantled the regular army; private armies, formed by the great landowners with their tenants and peons, had fought the revolts and civil wars of the federal period. The existence of these regional private armies and militias was incompatible with Núñez's unitary project. The 1886 constitution created a permanent army and reserved to the central government the right to possess arms and ammunition. The national police, organized in 1891, kept a watchful eye on political suspects and disrupted most plots against the government.

Núñez was responsible for two major economic innovations. Claiming that free trade or low tariffs were the cause of economic decadence and poverty, which had caused civil war, he proposed to use tariff protection to stimulate the growth of certain industries. He believed this would create a new middle class that would form a buffer between the governing social class and the unlettered multitude. His implementation of this program was timid and inconsistent. The new policy succeeded, however, in providing a modest level of protection for domestic industry.

Núñez's other innovation was the creation in 1881 of a national bank designed to relieve the financial distress of a government always on the verge of bankruptcy. The bank had the exclusive right to issue money; managed prudently until 1890, this monopoly enabled the state to provide for its needs. Thereafter, its uncontrolled emissions of paper money caused a galloping inflation. An expensive civil war in 1899 provoked the emission of paper money on such a scale that the printers could not keep up with demand, and millions of pesos of depreciated currency flooded the country.

The "Regeneration," as the Núñez Era is known, represented an effort to achieve national unification from above; it was comparable to Bismarck's project for German national unification, a compound of feudal and capitalist elements. Under Núñez, the conditions for the rise of a modern, capitalist state began. An important step in this direction was his creation of a permanent army and the state's monopolistic exercise of force. His removal of internal barriers to trade and his policy of tariff protection, however modest, contributed to the formation of an internal market; his national bank, despite its later scandalous mismanagement, represented an initial effort to create a national system of credit; and he gave impulse to the construction of internal improvements, especially railroads. Finally, he sought to give private enterprise access to frontier lands by formally denying the existence of ethnic Afro-Colombian and indigenous communities, voiding their proprietary claims. These policies, combined with the coffee boom, created national markets in land, labor, and commodities and contributed to a growth of capitalism in Colombia.

When he died, corruption, flagrant rigging of elections, division over freedom of the press and electoral reform, and an economic slump caused by a sharp decline of coffee prices produced a political crisis, followed by a resort to arms. Confident of victory over a thoroughly unpopular government, the Liberals launched a revolt in 1899 that ushered in the disastrous War of a Thousand Days. It raged for three years, caused an estimated loss of one hundred thousand lives, and created immense material damage. It ended in a government victory.

During the last third of the nineteenth century, liberal economic policies shaped the development of the various nations of Latin America. This typically included encouragement of exports, foreign investment, and privatization of public resources like land and subsoil rights. But it also relied on the consolidation of forceful, often brutal, dictatorships that used their monopoly of state power to create a unified national market, control labor, subordinate local caudillos, and conquer indigenous lands. The liberal dictatorships consolidated political authority and promoted economic growth, but they failed to sustain an authentic national development that benefited a broad cross-section of the population. Thus, they bequeathed a legacy of social instability and political discontent that frequently combined to produce violent movements for social reform.

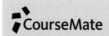

Go to the CourseMate website at **www.cengagebrain.com** for primary sources, additional study tools, and review materials—including audio and video clips—for this chapter.

PART THREE

1898	Spanish-American-Cuban-Filipino War
1910–1920	Mexican Revolution and emergence of populism
1930	Brazilian Revolution, populism, and rise of Getulio Vargas in Brazil
1947–1955	Election of Juan Perón and emergence of Argentine populism
1952–1964	Bolivian Revolution and populism
1959	Cuban Revolution and socialism
1964–1983	Military coup against democratically elected populist government of João Goulart and establishment of dictatorship in Brazil
1968	Peruvian Revolution and military corporatism
1970–1973	Democratic election of Salvador Allende and Chilean path to socialism
1973–1990	Military coup led by Augusto Pinochet and establishment of neoliberal dictatorship in Chile
1975–1983	Military coup led by Jorge Rafael Videla and establishment of neoliberal dictatorship in Argentina
1979–1990	Armed revolutions opposing military rule throughout Central America and triumph of Sandinista Revolution against Somoza dictatorship in Nicaragua
1990–2000	Electoral *engaños* and triumph of neoliberals like Peru's Alberto Fujimori, Argentina's Carlos Menem, Brazil's Fernando Cardoso, and Chile's Patricio Aylwin
1998–2011	Triumph and consolidation of "Bolivarian Democracy" under Venezuela's Hugo Chávez Frías, a defiant opponent of neoliberalism
2002–2011	"Pink Tide" and popular democratic election of opponents to neoliberalism like Brazil's Lula da Silva, Uruguay's Tabaré Vázquez, Argentina's Néstor Kirchner, Bolivia's Evo Morales, Ecuador's Rafael Correa, Chile's Michelle Bachelet, and Nicaragua's Daniel Ortega

Latin America Since 1900

Los explotatores, 1926–1927, by Diego Rivera.

U NDERSTANDING THE COMPLEXITY of Latin America's evolution in the twentieth century requires particular attention to the social, political, economic, and cultural histories of each nation and its integration into the international economic order. Throughout this text, we consistently have emphasized both internal and external factors that have shaped and constrained Latin American development. These have included domestic class conflicts; gender, racial, and ethnic struggles; strategic rivalries among the United States and certain European powers; and the shifting demands of international markets.

Internally, the struggle of Latin America's peoples to eliminate neocolonialism and *latifundismo*, the chief obstacles to the achievement of a more just economic and social order, gives meaning and direction to the turbulent flow of modern Latin American history. Viewed as a whole, that history, with all its contradictory aspects, its gains and setbacks, appears to form a sequence of stages, each representing a higher level of effort to achieve complete economic and political emancipation. Such an overview inevitably ignores the great differences between the Latin American countries, but it clarifies the general unity of problems and the common direction of movement of all the Latin American states.

The single most significant external factor in Latin America's twentieth-century development was the emergence of the United States as first a hemispheric and then a global hegemonic power. Its recurrent military, economic, and diplomatic interventions in the region established the international context within which local events unfolded. Changes in the global economy also affected Latin America greatly, giving rise to three distinct periods.

1900–1930

From 1900 to 1930, a fierce competition among industrially developed capitalist countries for overseas markets led to recurrent imperialist interventions, chiefly by the United States. U.S. and European political leaders and corporate executives continued their competition for privileged access to Latin American markets for strategic raw materials, cheap labor, and direct investment. This typically required alliances with traditional latifundistas and the oligarchical or dictatorial governments that protected their interests. It also reinforced late-nineteenth-century trends toward urbanization, the decline of independent peasantries and relatively autonomous indigenous communities, and the parallel growth of new national bourgeoisies and a wage-earning working class in which women would play an increasingly decisive role. Throughout the region, market forces steadily eroded traditional barriers between public and private life and doubly exploited women—as menial, poorly paid wage earners and as unpaid labor in the patriarchal household. Simultaneously, these same market forces assaulted the rural, relatively isolated, provincial hinterland and drove a steady stream of migrant workers first to urban slums in search of industrial employment and then to new lands as immigrants.

Not surprisingly, these new social actors sought out political alliances and often joined social protest movements that challenged the power of traditional oligarchs like Porfirio Díaz in Mexico, Cipriano Castro and Juan Vicente Gómez in Venezuela, and Gerardo Machado in Cuba. By the end of this period, these opposition groups formed the core constituency of an emerging regional **"populism"** that had taken advantage of political space created by intra-elite conflicts and international rivalries to demand the creation of a more modern nation-state. It sought to regulate private sector relations in a way that promoted greater economic independence, social justice, and political stability.

The Mexican Revolution of 1910 and the start of World War I offer two points of departure for this period. The revolution swiftly developed into the first major effort in Latin American history to uproot the system of great estates and peonage and curb foreign control of the area's natural resources. The famous constitution of 1917 spelled out this social content of the revolution. In the leadership struggle between agrarian and bourgeois revolutionaries, the latter emerged victorious and adopted a program that subordinated the interests of peasants and workers to the goals of rapid capitalist development. Nonetheless, the determined struggles of Mexico's lower classes made lasting contributions to the construction of a new, modern state that incorporated popular demands for reform and political participation. Moreover, despite discrepancies between its professed social ideals and its practical political-economic achievements, the revolution also unleashed creative energies in art, literature, and the social sciences that gave Mexico a leading role in the cultural life of Latin America.

World War I seriously disrupted the markets for Latin America's goods and placed difficulties in the way of importing needed manufactured products. As a result, some local capital and labor shifted from agriculture to manufacturing in an effort to supply these goods. Although the postwar period saw some revival of the export economy, declines in the price levels of Latin America's exports encouraged a further growth of manufacturing. Nonetheless, at the end of this period, industrialization was still almost completely limited to light consumer goods industries.

The United States, which emerged from World War I as the world's principal industrial and financial power, soon replaced Great Britain as the major source of foreign investments in Latin America. Continuing the "big stick" and "dollar diplomacy" policies of their predecessors, Democratic and Republican administrations used armed intervention and economic pressure to expand U.S. control over the Caribbean area. By the end of the period, deep Latin American resentment of these strong-arm tactics had forced Republican policy makers to consider a change in dealing with Latin America.

1930–1970

In rapid succession, the devastation of the Great Depression and World War II brought substantial changes to the nations of Latin America, the world economic order, and the international balance of power. With the emergence of the United States as a global hegemonic power and the absorption of Japanese and European capitalists in the herculean postwar task of national reconstruction, international competition for access to and control over foreign markets in Latin America diminished, at least temporarily. This left traditional latifundista oligarchies vulnerable to the political challenges of popular movements from below and often required military dictatorships to preserve their interests. As an alternative to these dictatorships, newly emerging national industrial bourgeoisies joined with, or even helped mobilize, alienated peasants, militant workers, indigenous peoples, racial minorities, and women's groups to create a new national corporative state committed to an ambiguous notion of collective social justice, the specific elements of which each constituent faction defined differently.

Ultimately, in virtually every Latin American country, these struggles produced a populist state dominated by a new national bourgeoisie. This new state, in turn, typically subsumed a plethora of local class, ethnic, racial, and clientelist identities to fashion a single new national identity, the foundation of which was national private sector industrial and agricultural development that would benefit, however unequally, all domestic social sectors. To secure this objective, populists like Getulio Vargas in Brazil and Juan Perón in Argentina typically advocated a limited agrarian reform, greater social welfare expenditures, nationalistic and state-centered economic policies like import substitution and export-led industrialization, and an expansion of citizenship rights among workers, women, and racial minorities.

Naturally, from country to country, the scope and intensity of these populist reforms varied proportionately with the level of internal popular political mobilization and its success in shaping the ideology and practice of the new bourgeoisies that occupied the corridors of power. Nonetheless, without substantial foreign competition, these new rulers could afford to raise wages, pay higher taxes, and submit to otherwise expensive state regulations by passing these higher costs on to consumers through a protected price system. Despite the obvious tensions and contradictions that divided the social constituents of Latin American populism, these developmental strategies often produced dynamic economies that expanded the local working class, simultaneously fortifying the power of a sometimes fiercely nationalistic bourgeoisie, and consolidating populist political alliances—even as they reinforced the region's capitalist social structures and long-term dependency on external markets.

The Great Depression dramatically exposed the vulnerability of a neocolonial, monocultural economy: The area's foreign markets collapsed, and the price of its raw materials and foodstuffs fell much more sharply than manufactured imports. Latin America's unfavorable balance of trade made necessary exchange controls and other trade restrictions that encouraged the growth of industries to produce goods formerly supplied through importation. World War II, which caused a virtual suspension of imports of manufactured goods, gave further stimulus to the movement for Latin American industrialization.

The nationalist temper of the times also found expression in the formation of state enterprises in such fields as oil exploitation and in efforts to nationalize some foreign-owned utilities and natural resources. The most dramatic example of this trend was the seizure of foreign oil properties in Mexico by President Lázaro Cárdenas in 1938. The new nationalist regimes also made concessions to labor in the form of social legislation but maintained tight control over working-class organizations.

By 1945, the movement for Latin American industrialization could point to some successes. Consumer-goods industries had arisen in all the Latin American republics, and some countries had laid the foundations of heavy industry. However, shortages of capital, lack of advanced technology, and the extremely low purchasing power of the masses hampered industrial development. Latin American economists often related these deficiencies to such background conditions as latifundismo and its corollary of wretchedly *minifundismo* (small farms), widespread disease and illiteracy, and absorption of a large part of the area's economic surplus by foreign investors in the form of dividends, interest, and the like. Meanwhile, aside from the massive assault of Lázaro Cárdenas on the Mexican latifundio, little or nothing occurred in the way of agrarian reform.

In the same period, the United States, reacting to the diplomatic and economic losses caused by the old-style imperialism and a wave of "anti-Yanqui" feeling throughout the continent, adopted the Good Neighbor Policy, which proclaimed the principle of nonintervention by one American state in the affairs of another. But the policy represented more of a change in form than in content. Washington's friendly, cooperative relations with such tyrannies as those of Anastasio Somoza in Nicaragua, Rafael Trujillo in the Dominican Republic, and Fulgencio Batista in Cuba ensured a continuance of North American hegemony in the Caribbean. For the rest, the immense economic power of the United States in Latin America, exercised through investments and its role as the area's main trading partner, usually sufficed to obtain approval of its policies in most parts of the continent.

In the new Postwar Era, the Latin American drive to industrialize continued, but after 1950, with the gradual restoration of competition among the industrially developed capitalist countries, the pace of Latin America's advance slowed and the industrialization process underwent a certain deformation. Perceiving the changes taking place in the Latin American society and economy because of industrialization and the growth of urban markets, foreign firms began to shift the bulk of their new investments from agricultural and mining activities to manufacturing. This shift allowed them to leap over tariff walls and penetrate the Latin American market. The immensely superior resources of foreign firms and their advanced technology gave them a great advantage over national companies. The result was that many small and midsize national companies failed or sold out to subsidiaries of foreign firms.

A favorite device of foreign economic penetration was the mixed company, dominated by foreign capital, with native capitalists reduced to the role of junior partners or directors. The huge sums exported annually by foreign companies in profits, dividends, and other types of income led to a process of "decapitalization" that slowed down the rate of Latin American capital accumulation and industrial growth.

The failure to reform archaic agrarian structures and improve income distribution also held back industrialization. Indeed, the experience of those countries that had the largest growth of capitalism, such as Argentina and Brazil, suggested that the new industrial and financial oligarchies were as fearful of social change, as prone to come to terms with foreign economic interests, as the old landed aristocracy had been. During the 1950s and 1960s, ruling elites in various Central and South American countries increasingly abandoned the populistic, more or less democratic, state-centered, nationalistic strategies of industrialization that earlier had achieved considerable success in modernizing the region.

A similar shift occurred in Mexico, where the successors of President Lázaro Cárdenas pursued policies favorable to big business and large landowners but neglected the peasantry. As a result, a new corporate hacienda arose and soon dominated Mexican agriculture. By the end of the 1960s, the once fashionable hope that a dynamic nationalistic entrepreneurial class could lead Latin America out of dependence and underdevelopment had largely faded.

Meanwhile, the discontent of the masses, sharpened by the "revolution of rising expectations," continued to erupt in revolts. In 1944, a revolution in Guatemala had established a standard of democracy and social justice against which later popular movements there and throughout Latin America measured themselves. A spontaneous rising of Bolivian peasants and miners in 1952 similarly demanded political and economic democracy. Likewise, a 1963 democratic upheaval in Brazil forced a moderate president, João Goulart, to radicalize his policies with a call for nationalization of oil and wholesale land reform. Popular mobilizations in Peru also led to a reformist military coup in 1968. In the same year, the Latin American Bishops' Conference, announcing its intent to exercise "a preferential option for the poor," introduced the idea of Liberation Theology. In Mexico, a general protest against authoritarian politics led to the massacre of university students and workers in Tlatelolco Square. Urban uprisings, led by Montoneros and Tupamaros, spread throughout the industrial cities of Argentina and Uruguay. Finally, in 1970, a popular coalition of Chilean industrial workers, peasants, women, and students freely elected the first avowedly Marxist president in the hemisphere. Nonetheless, the single most important popular mobilization in the region was the armed struggle begun by Fidel Castro and his comrades against the Cuban dictator Fulgencio Batista in July 1953. Their long guerrilla war ended with the victorious entry of the Rebel Army into Havana on January 1, 1959.

The victory of the Cuban Revolution, soon transformed into a socialist revolution, marked a turning point in Latin American history. The swift, thoroughgoing Cuban agrarian reform and nationalization of foreign enterprises and the revolution's successes in raising living standards offered Latin America a radical alternative to development along capitalist lines.

In response to Cuba's threat to the old order in Latin America, Washington embraced a variety of tactics. In 1961, President John F. Kennedy proclaimed the establishment of the Alliance for Progress, designed to show that, with U.S. help, Latin America could achieve social revolution peacefully within the framework of capitalism. Within a few years, however, the failure of the corruption-ridden program to achieve structural change was apparent.

Simultaneously, the U.S. government sought to undermine and destroy the Castro regime, first by economic blockade and political isolation and then by a Central Intelligence Agency (CIA)-sponsored effort by Cuban exiles to invade Cuba (1961), an effort that met with a swift and humiliating defeat. The Soviet Union stepped up its flow of arms to Cuba, which led to the Cuban missile crisis (1962). For ten days, a jittery world lived under the threat of nuclear war between the United States and the Soviet Union. The crisis ended with a U.S. pledge not to invade Cuba in return for the withdrawal of Soviet missiles from the island.

Forced to retreat in Cuba, the United States, supported by the old and new Latin American elites who feared radical social change, redoubled its efforts to prevent a spread of the Cuban "contagion" to other parts of the hemisphere. In 1964, a coalition of reactionary Brazilian military, great landowners, and large capitalists overthrew the mildly progressive government of President João Goulart, whose heresies included a modest program of agrarian and electoral reform. A heavy-handed military dictatorship succeeded it, offered large incentives to foreign investors, and proclaimed its unswerving loyalty to the United States, which responded with generous financial assistance.

Nevertheless, the movement for structural social change and economic independence proved irrepressible. Nationalist military officers sometimes played a leading role in these upheavals, disproving the common assumption that the Latin American officer class was one reactionary group. Thus, the military takeover in Peru in 1968 quickly produced the nationalization of key foreign-owned industries and land reform that transferred many large estates to peasants and workers, who organized into cooperatives. The Peruvian Revolution—a revolution from above, without significant participation by the masses—soon faltered, however, primarily because of its failure to break with the traditional strategy of development that depended on foreign loans and export expansion.

The struggle against neocolonialism scored a temporary major victory with the triumph of the Marxist presidential candidate Salvador Allende and his Popular Unity coalition in Chile in 1970. In three years, it carried out the nationalization of copper mines and banks, organized a massive agrarian reform, and made significant advances in housing, health, and education. The Allende government also made serious errors, however. The most serious was its failure to take preventive action against a reactionary military coup. In September 1973, military plotters overthrew the Allende government. Published evidence thereafter confirmed U.S. complicity in a destabilization of his government that prepared the way for the coup.

1970–2003

By the 1970s, the global marketplace once again had shifted dramatically. The system of international capitalism would no longer tolerate the relatively modest nationalist constraints imposed on foreign corporations in Latin America by populist governments, much less those of democratically elected Socialists like Allende. Japanese and European capitalists, with the assistance of the United States and, ironically, a host of local statist protections, had fully reconstructed their war-ravaged economies and once again looked to overseas markets to acquire strategically valuable raw materials, sell surplus products, invest surplus capital, and exploit cheap labor. Meanwhile, the United States had experienced a serious economic decline and international competitive crisis, largely the product of its expensive investment in a military establishment designed to police the postwar New World order.

Peaceful resolution of these resurgent international capitalist rivalries seemed to require that the core capitalist countries have freer access to the world's resources. Thereafter, through their control of national governments and private organizations like the Trilateral Commission, transnational corporate capitalist elites sought to promote a neoliberal strategy of economic development that emphasized free trade, an open door for foreign investment, state deregulation of business, and privatization. It also favored free convertibility of local currencies, tax and spending cuts beneficial to investors and disastrous to workers, balanced federal budgets, currency devaluation, and liquidation of public sector debt. These new reforms attacked the material foundation of the old populist political alliances that had supported the region's state-led industrialization during the previous forty years.

Latin America's established industrial, commercial, agricultural, and financial elites, all of whom had profited handsomely from the nationalistic policies promoted by populists, now were squeezed between resurgent, aggressive foreign interests and growing domestic popular mobilizations that continued to demand expansion of social programs that redistributed power and wealth. Always suspicious of the goals and methods of these popular social movements, these elites also were increasingly attracted to the relatively low-cost loans and lucrative business partnerships that transnational corporations and core capitalist governments promised.

Populist redistributive policies, whose success always had depended on a dynamic economic expansion, increasingly came to rely on foreign loans. However, under President Ronald Reagan, the Federal Reserve Board raised the prime rate from 9 percent in 1979 to 21.5 percent in January 1981—"the highest interest rate since the birth of Jesus Christ," according to West German chancellor Helmut Schmidt. Trapped by these high floating interest rates, in just three years (1981–1983), Latin America had to pay out $94.8 billion in interest payments, twice the outlay on interest for the whole of the 1970s. Despite the negative impact of the skyrocketing external debt on redistributive policies and state-sponsored economic growth, Latin American elites quickly became enthusiastic champions of foreign-inspired neoliberal strategies. These strategies appeared first in Brazil in 1964, when Gen. Humberto de Alencar Castelo Branco overthrew the democratically elected government of João Goulart, but they reached their fullest expression in the policies of Gen. Augusto Pinochet, who ousted Allende in 1973. His new, openly terrorist military junta, in league with the most reactionary elements of Chile's ruling class and its foreign allies, reversed the progressive policies of the Allende regime and transformed Chile into a concentration camp, torturing and killing thousands of opponents. Its economic policies reduced the living standards of the masses to near-starvation levels.

The destruction of Chilean democracy was part of a general counteroffensive by Latin American elites and their foreign allies to halt and roll back the movement for structural economic and social change. By mid-1976 a block of brutal military dictatorships—Argentina, Bolivia, Brazil, Chile, Paraguay, and Uruguay—had taken shape. These regimes, however, whose policies included the systematic use of torture and assassination against political opponents and the abandonment of the effort to achieve economic independence, offered no solutions for the deep-seated problems of their countries. Their most shining success, the "Brazilian miracle" of steady economic growth since 1964, depended on the reduction of wages to the subsistence level, an annual inflation rate of about 20 percent, and massive foreign investments that hastened the foreign conquest of Brazilian industry. By the mid-1970s, the "Brazilian miracle" had dissipated, and, in 1980, Brazil was in a deep recession, with factories closing, unemployment rising, and a balance-of-payments problem growing steadily worse.

Other military regimes, such as Argentina and Chile, faced similarly grave economic problems during this lost decade. However, the crisis did not afflict dictatorships alone; whatever their political systems, it confronted all the countries that pursued a strategy of dependent development on the basis of foreign loans and investments.

At the heart of the continuing debt problem lay the unequal exchange between Latin America and advanced capitalist countries, such as the United States. A major factor in Latin America's chronic balance-of-payments deficit was the traditional imbalance between the low prices of Latin American export commodities and the high prices of the manufactured goods and oil that most of the countries in the area imported. Falling commodity prices, which were the product of growing global competition, greatly aggravated the problem. These unfavorable terms of trade helped to explain Latin America's mountainous debt.

Certain changes in the Latin American industrialization programs contributed to the growing gap between its exports and imports. Since about 1955, countries like Brazil and Mexico increasingly stressed production of consumer durables and capital goods that required the importation of expensive machinery, equipment, and technical licenses from countries like the United States. The result was a growing surplus of imports over exports. The transnational companies' takeover of much of the Latin American manufacturing sector contributed to the same result. In the 1970s, for every dollar invested in Latin America, transnationals repatriated approximately $2.20 to their home countries. To cover the deficits in their balance of payments, Latin American countries had to borrow from Western bankers at interest rates that reached double-digit figures by 1980.

By 1982, with their national treasuries almost empty of foreign exchange, a number of major Latin American countries faced the prospect of immediate default. This posed immense dangers to the international banking system, because defaults by Brazil and Mexico alone could have wiped out 95 percent of the capital of the nine largest U.S. banks. Western governments and bankers provided emergency aid packages to avert defaults in return for agreements by recipient governments to carry out "austerity" programs that further reduced the living standards of their workers and peasants. Nevertheless, the intervention merely postponed the problem, without resolving it. Latin America had no prospects to repay even a portion of its huge debt without large write-offs and long delays in payment. Meanwhile, the flow of new commercial bank loans sharply declined.

In the later 1980s, many Latin American governments deployed strident populist rhetoric about resisting the tyranny of the International Monetary Fund (IMF), a multilateral institution created after World War II to manage the postwar global economy, and the World Bank, which monitored debtor countries' compliance with what the IMF called "structural adjustment programs." These inevitably required debtor countries to privatize state companies, end subsidies, and open their economies to foreign investment as a condition for new loans. However, this populist rhetoric did little more than demand rescheduling of debt payments and lower interest rates. Efforts by Latin American governments to reduce their debt burdens under the Brady Plan proposed by the United States included debt-bond swaps, in which foreign debt was exchanged at a discount for new government bonds, and debt-equity swaps, in which foreign debt was exchanged for equity—that is, shares in local companies. None of this made a serious dent in the region's foreign debt, which grew between 1990 and 2000 from $439 billion to $774 billion, an increase of 76 percent.

Meanwhile, even as major Western banks reduced their Latin American exposure, the United States, under successive presidents Reagan, Bush, and Clinton, used debt as a weapon of coercion and played a leading role in imposing the neoliberal or structural adjustment system. The logical next step was the incorporation of Latin America into a U.S.-dominated Western Hemisphere common market that would aid the United States in its competition with Japan and the European Community. A major move toward that goal was approval of the North American Free Trade Agreement with Mexico (1993). By eliminating remaining tariffs and restrictions on investment, the pact ensured that Mexico would become a cheap-labor preserve for U.S industry, with a loss of better-paying jobs in the United States. The opening of Mexico to U.S. low-cost agricultural products, especially corn, had a devastating effect on less-efficient and less-productive Mexican small farmers. Other Latin American countries, beginning with Chile, signed similar pacts, but the more ambitious proposal for a Free Trade Area of the Americas (FTAA) faced growing resistance throughout the region.

After decades of experience with neoliberal policies that promised to produce economic growth, reduce poverty, and promote development in Latin

America, the people of the region became increasingly disillusioned. According to polling by Latinobarómetro, by the end of the 1990s, almost half the population described the economic situation as either bad or very bad; 60 percent said that their parents lived better, more than 20 percent described unemployment as the most important problem in their country, and 40 percent described their economic situation as unstable. Even more important, almost 80 percent complained that income distribution was either unfair or very unfair. Even José Manuel Salazar-Xirinachs, a neoliberal trade adviser to the Organization of American States, reluctantly acknowledged that "liberalization was not the miracle or the magic formula that many expected."

The chapters that follow document in detail the staggering economic and social costs of the neoliberal or structural adjustment program for Latin America. Here we offer a few social indicators of Latin American underdevelopment. Between 1980 and 1990, the number of poor people in the region increased by 66 million from 40 to 48 percent of the population, and a decade later, despite a slight decline in that rate, a record 211 million people remained mired in poverty. Moreover, of these, some 89 million lived in extreme poverty, meaning they could not afford to purchase a basic family food basket that cost $1.00 per day. The share of Latin Americans living in extreme poverty increased from 18.6 to 19.4 percent from 1980 to 2002. Even these depressing statistics, however, grossly understated the problem because they measured poverty according to the capacity to purchase subsistence food without considering additional costs associated with housing, health care, education, transportation, clothing, and cooking fuel.

To emerge from underdevelopment, Latin American countries will have to learn from the historical successes and failures of reforms undertaken from the 1930s through the 1970s, when the region, largely left alone to pursue developmental strategies consistent with its internal needs, experienced stable growth and a significant reduction of poverty. For example, Araceli Damián and Julio Boltvinik, in their careful case study of poverty in Mexico, show that by three different measures of poverty, rates fell consistently between 1968 and 1981 and rose steadily thereafter before leveling off in 1996. Sustained growth and social development doubtlessly will require the reinvigoration of positive government and its collaboration with nongovernmental organizations to formulate more autonomous, inward-directed strategies of development on the basis of more rational exploitation of human and natural resources. Such strategies require profound changes in the relations between Latin America and the industrial countries and in Latin America's economic and social structures, particularly in land tenure and use, ownership of industry, and income distribution. They also require powerful, well-organized social movements to spearhead a democratic revitalization of Latin American political life that will allow popular interests and to influence the direction of state economic and social policy.

In the early 1980s, in fact, it appeared that a democratic revival had begun as the reactionary tide of the 1970s receded, and in country after country—Argentina, Bolivia, Brazil, and Uruguay—discredited military regimes gave way to popularly elected governments. By 1990, the last military or personal dictatorships, in Chile and Paraguay, had fallen. In part because of the long repression of progressive political parties and trade union movements, the emerging democratic movements of the 1980s and 1990s as a rule tended to be politically moderate. Often, they cultivated accommodation with the former military rulers, granting pardons or amnesties for their crimes, and thus perpetuated a climate of impunity for human rights abuses. Sometimes, too, the new democratic regimes displayed a broad authoritarian streak, resorting to free use of rule by decree to bypass Congress and other arbitrary measures. Peruvian President Alberto Fujimori's 1992 *autogolpe* (self-coup), the Haitian military's 1991 overthrow of populist President Jean-Bertrand Aristide, the collapse of the Argentine economy and its elected government in 2000, and the 2002 aborted coup against populist Venezuelan President Hugo Chávez all revealed the fragility of this democratic revival.

None of these new democracies initially made a clean break with the failed economic policies of the past. They typically acquiesced in payment of the immense foreign debt and accepted the harsh neoliberal remedies prescribed by the IMF and the World Bank. In particular, the acceptance by Latin America's old and new democracies of privatization and tariff-reduction policies represented a virtual abandonment of a half-century of struggle to achieve independent capitalist development. Throughout this neoliberal period, in countries like Argentina, Bolivia, Brazil, Mexico, and Peru, these policies resulted in higher unemployment and lower living standards, relieved in Bolivia and Peru by a thriving informal or underground economy based on the production of coca and cocaine. The reliance by Bolivia, Colombia, and Peru on the demand for cocaine in the United States and Europe represents a grotesque new kind of Latin American dependency on the industrial countries.

2003–2011

Nevertheless, as the new millennium opened, neoliberalism, which demolished Latin America's statist institutions and the old populist, corporative consensus that underwrote them, failed to fashion a cohesive new social order. In this age of neoliberalism, the fruits of an unregulated marketplace proved incompatible with basic human needs; the signs of discontent proliferated as the insistent political-economic demands of foreign bankers and Latin America's new billionaires conflicted with popular democratic political aspirations. In the Mexican state of Chiapas, the dramatic 1994 revolt led by the self-styled Zapatista Army of National Liberation emerged as what Mexican economist Julio Moguel calls an "armed critique" of Mexico's neoliberal policy.

Electoral opposition to neoliberalism also continued to grow. Brazil's Lula (Luis Inaçio da Silva) of the Socialist Workers' Party won the 2002 presidential elections with the support of women, blacks, and diverse social movements like the Landless People's Movement (MST). In Bolivia and Ecuador, indigenous people, trade union activists, women's organizations, and student groups mobilized to resist neoliberal austerity programs and to elect progressive nationalist presidents like Bolivia's Evo Morales and Ecuador's Rafael Correa.

Environmentalists, indigenous groups, and trade union organizations in Venezuela similarly organized to support the election of President Hugo Chávez, running on a populist platform opposed to neoliberalism. He inaugurated new policies that reinforced state control of the Venezuelan oil industry, whose rising revenues funded a range of antipoverty programs at home and abroad.

In Argentina, neoliberalism produced high rates of unemployment and provoked massive street demonstrations that forced the nation to close its banks and default on its foreign debt payments. Spreading poverty, popular political protest, and food riots quickly swept successive neoliberal presidents from power and ultimately elected a new populist president, Néstor Kirchner, who, like most Argentines, angrily blamed the wealthy bankers and industrialists for the neoliberal debacle. "We're somewhat less popular than serial killers," one banker candidly confessed to *The Economist*.

By 2002 the neoliberal model, for more than a decade the dominant policy prescription for Latin American development, ceased to offer credible solutions to the region's many social, economic, and political problems. Its patent failure to promote genuine development, raise living standards, and reduce the gigantic Latin American foreign debt gave new life to broad regional and national social and political movements. These typically united labor unions, indigenous rights groups, activist women, peasant cooperatives, and community organizations intent on securing social justice and democratic models of development. Even once-stalwart neoliberals like Joseph Stiglitz, the World Bank's chief economist from 1997 to 2000, appeared to have lost faith in the developmental potential of the "free movement of capital."

As the new millennium opened, Latin America appeared perched on the precipice of a new era in its historic struggle for development and social justice.

Within a few short years, popular movements throughout the region had won significant victories, organizing in homes, workplaces, and polling places. By 2009 they had brought to power progressive nationalist governments in Argentina, Bolivia, Brazil, Chile, Costa Rica, El Salvador, Honduras, Guatemala, Nicaragua, Paraguay, Uruguay, and Venezuela. In Mexico, electoral victory proved elusive, but only by a razor-thin margin of 0.56 percent of the vote.

Although these elected governments had considerable ideological and practical political differences—not to mention sometimes-conflicting national interests—they all seemed to agree that their first responsibility was to promote social justice. The primary instrument for their program of national development was the state, either in its capacity as a regulator of private sector market activities or as a direct producer of national wealth. They generally advocated national ownership of the economy's "commanding heights"—the key strategic nonrenewable natural resources on which national development depended. State-funded poverty-eradication programs formed a core component of their national agendas, and they sought to increase public sector spending on education and health services for the poor.

Moreover, they happily embraced regional economic cooperation through established organizations like the Andean Community and Mercosur, the South American common market, or bilateral partnership agreements like Misión Barrio Adentro, a Venezuelan program to provide Cuba with oil in exchange for Cuban doctors to staff medical clinics in poor Venezuelan neighborhoods. In 2010, for example, trade among the Mercosur countries grew 41 percent, which accelerated recovery from the economic crisis that swallowed the region in 2009; intra-Andean trade likewise increased 36 percent. These progressive nationalist governments also sought to reduce their dependence on foreign bankers, especially the IMF, first by renegotiating debt obligations and then, if possible, liquidating them. Thus, between 2002 and 2008, external debt as a share of gross domestic product (GDP) fell by 61 percent among the seven countries that formed the original Pink Tide.

These progressive nationalist governments also intervened forcefully in the domestic economy to engineer a quick recovery. Throughout the region, they invested heavily in basic social and economic infrastructure that expanded employment, increased domestic purchasing power, and stimulated economic growth. In Brazil, for example, one private economist remarked that increased "family consumption" convinced entrepreneurs that "demand growth is sustainable," which caused them to "resume investment plans that will contribute to growth."

Finally, they took maximum advantage of arguably the single greatest transformation in the global political economy since World War II—the emergence of the People's Republic of China as an international economic powerhouse. Its seemingly insatiable industrial demand for the region's agricultural and mineral raw materials, its export of low-cost capital equipment, and its surplus of dollar-denominated investment funds all augured well for Latin American development. This growth, however, required that the region's progressive nationalist governments would continue to resist the lure of a renewed export dependency and sustain a strategy of development that combined nationalist government regulation and a vigorous private sector.

Crouching Tiger, Hidden Dragon

Without doubt, Latin American trade with China cushioned the blow of the global economic collapse in late 2008, which disproportionately affected its traditional markets in the United States and Europe. In 2000, regional trade with China was a paltry $10 billion, but it exceeded $140 billion a decade later. China's voracious demand for copper, zinc, oil, iron ore, and soybeans sparked higher prices and fueled expanded export production, especially in Argentina, Brazil, Chile, and Peru. A World Bank study confirmed that Chinese demand was responsible for 14 percent of export growth in the Southern Cone alone. According to economist Kevin Gallagher, between 2000 and 2007, "Chinese demand accounted for 20 percent of world export growth in metals, 11 percent for copper, 55 percent for iron, and 58 percent for soy." In 2009, China replaced the United States as Brazil's largest trade partner. Moreover, progressive nationalist governments in Brazil and Chile effectively used new revenues generated from their commodity exports to China to establish "stabilization funds," upon which they drew to finance economic stimulus programs in 2009. Brazil channeled its export revenues into its National Bank for Social and Economic Development, which financed domestic industrial expansion and modernization.

Beyond trade, China also increased its loans and investments in the region, lowering interest rates and diversifying the region's historic dependency on U.S. and European markets. Since 2005, Chinese firms invested $25 billion in Latin America, mostly in raw materials production, transportation, and refinery industries. China also became a donor member of the Inter-American Development Bank, to which it gave $350 million in 2009. Even more significantly, however, it made direct loans to developing countries, totaling more than $110 billion since 2008. Unlike IMF or World Bank credits, however, the Chinese loans did not attach stringent free-market, private sector conditions. The Chinese willingly financed state companies, like Brazil's Petrobras, which received $10 billion to finance deep-sea exploration and extraction in exchange for an agreement to ship oil to China for the next ten years. Ecuador likewise borrowed some $3 billion to modernize its oil production facilities and build a hydroelectric dam to generate low-cost electricity. Venezuela also borrowed $20 billion to invest in high-tech oil exploration and production in exchange for contractual agreements to supply oil.

Notwithstanding these positive contributions to Latin America's economic development, however, major problems loomed on the horizon. First, much of China's economic interest in the region reinforced traditional ties of dependency on primary production for export instead of a diversified agro-industrial economy. Second, Chinese low-wage, low-cost manufacturing exports threatened to displace 92 percent of Latin American products or 39 percent of all regional exports from world markets. This especially concerned Mexico, whose broad range of manufactured exports most directly competed with Chinese products, but seventy-seven thousand manufacturing jobs also disappeared in Brazil because of Chinese competition in 2010. Third, Chinese imports grew more rapidly than Latin American exports to China, which converted substantial trade surpluses in the 1990s into a deficit in excess of $32 billion by 2010.

Notwithstanding the China market's new dynamic, the ultimate success of these new progressive nationalist governments to resist the lure of a new dependency and achieve a healthy mix of state and private sector market activities remained uncertain, but one conclusion was inescapable. Over the past century, the historic struggle of Latin American peoples for an elusive national development that combined economic growth and social justice had produced certain unmistakable changes in the region's social structure, political consciousness, and cultural institutions. The following chapters detail these specific national experiences, but a general summary of the major themes is useful.

The New Social Class Structure

Naturally, Latin America's contemporary class structure was very much a product of its historical evolution. Although the capitalist mode of production, based on contractual wage labor, was dominant since about 1880, the area still had not made a clean break with its precapitalist past. Slavery, debt peonage, and other forms of forced labor still survived in various parts of the continent. Such servile or feudal forms of labor typically characterized primary industries like agriculture, cattle raising, and logging. Located in politically and socially less developed regions, great landowners or powerful companies usually dominated the state, and corruption was widespread.

By the middle decades of the twentieth century, industrialization, urbanization, and the commercialization of agriculture had significantly altered the Latin

American social structure and the relative weight of the various classes. These changes included the transformation of the old landed elite into a new latifundista capitalist class, the emergence of a big industrial and financial bourgeoisie with close ties to foreign capital, growth of urban middle sectors, and the rise of a small but militant industrial working class.

In the early twenty-first century, such quasi-feudal conditions still existed in Brazil's Amazon frontier, where landed elites threatened defenders of the rain forest, indigenous peoples, and small farmers with death and murdered with impunity. Thousands of peasants, lured from other parts of the country by promises of good jobs, free housing, and plenty of good food, often found themselves reduced to slavery, felling trees, and tending cattle deep in the jungle. One eyewitness complained that "particularly troublesome workers, especially those who kept asking for their wages, were sometimes simply killed." According to a *New York Times* report, even government officials conceded that "contemporary forms of slavery" flourished in the rainforest for various reasons ranging "from ranchers in cahoots with corrupt local authorities to ineffective land-reform policies and high unemployment." Slavelike conditions of labor existed in other regions of Brazil—for example, in the sugar cane factories of Bahia.

Child labor, in violation of the law, flourished among the 1 million Mexican migrants—*jornaleros* (day laborers)—and their families, who abandoned their homes for part of the year to move north with the harvests. They did not leave their homes, observed a sympathetic *New York Times* reporter, because they were looking for better wages: "they are looking for any wages." They had no jobs at home, and their only means of subsistence was cultivation of beans and corn on their little milpas. The $1,500 that he and his family hoped to take home at the end of the harvest, one migrant said, was just about all the money they would see for the year. "If the whole family," including his three children ages eight, ten, and eleven, "does not work," he explained, "we all starve." In a time of growing unemployment and general instability of labor, illegal forced labor and child labor obviously exerted considerable downward pressure on wages, living standards, and efforts to organize unions. Although neoliberal policies largely neglected the growing problem of child labor, estimated in 1999 at 17.5 million working children between the ages of five and fourteen, progressive nationalists like Lula in Brazil have joined with international organizations like the United Nations (U.N.)-sponsored International Labor Organization to reduce child labor dramatically. In the past four years, the share of child workers in Latin America fell by two-thirds from 17 to 5 percent.

The neoliberal economic policies adopted by most Latin American governments during the 1990s, favoring multinationals and their local allies, also caused a sharp decline in the number and influence of small and midsize national man-ufacturers. The privatization or dismantling of many state enterprises, reduction of social services, and a general downsizing of the state as part of structural ad-justment programs demanded by the IMF also caused growing impoverishment and unemployment among the middle and working classes. A survey of these and other developments suggests the complexity of modern Latin American class alignments and the possible direction of future social and political change.

THE GREAT LANDOWNERS

Although they had to yield first place economically and politically to the new bour-geoisie, with which they maintained close links, the great landowners, Latin Amer-ica's oldest ruling class, retained immense power, thanks to their control over the land and water resources of the area. Over the last century, the latifundio experi-enced a major expansion, especially of new agribusiness, which produced industrial and export crops with the aid of improved technology and wage labor. During the 1990s, the dominant policies of free trade and open doors to foreign investment further spurred the trend toward concentration of landownership and penetration of Latin American agriculture by foreign capital. For example, the Mexican govern-ment's approval in 1991 of an agrarian law that ended land redistribution and legal-ized the sale or rental of communally owned ejido land illustrated the shift toward policies favoring the rise of a new latifundio.

The traditional hacendado was a vanishing breed. His successor was often a cosmopolitan, university-trained type who combined agribusiness with industrial and financial interests. However, the arbitrary and predatory spirit of the old hacendados survived in the new latifundistas. The great landowners continued to be the most reactionary class in Latin American society.

THE NEW BOURGEOISIE

A native commercial bourgeoisie arose in Latin America after independence and consolidated its position with the rise of the neocolonial order after midcentury. In the second half of the nineteenth century, an industrialist class, which in-cluded many immigrants, appeared in response to the demand of a growing ur-ban population for consumer goods. World War I further stimulated the movement for export-led, import-substitution industrialization. Nevertheless, the day of the industrial entrepreneur did not arrive until the great economic crisis of 1930 disrupted the trading patterns of the area. Aided by favorable inter-national and domestic conditions and massive state intervention, the native in-dustrial bourgeoisie quickly gained strength; in many countries, it displaced the landed elite as the dominant social and economic force. As a rule, however, the new bourgeoisie avoided frontal collision with the latifundistas, preferring to form bonds of kinship and interest with the landed elite.

Meanwhile, foreign capital, attracted by the potential of the growing Latin American market, began to pour into the area, particularly after 1945. Possessing immensely superior capital and technological resources, foreign firms absorbed many small and midsize national companies and soon dominated key sectors of the economy of the host countries. Aware, however, that the survival of a national bourgeoisie was essential to their own security, foreign capitalists endeavored to form close ties with the largest, most powerful national firms through the formation of mixed companies and other devices. This dependence on foreign corporations explains why the Latin American new bourgeoisie often lacked enduring nationalist sentiment.

In its youth, some sections of the Latin American national bourgeoisie supported the efforts of such nationalist, populist chieftains as Cárdenas, Perón, and Vargas to restrict foreign economic influence and accepted, although with misgivings, their concessions to labor. But soon the new bourgeoisie adopted the hostility of its foreign allies to restrictions on foreign capital and independent trade unionism. With rare exceptions, these capitalists supported repressive military regimes in such countries as Argentina, Brazil, Chile, and Uruguay, until, convinced that the policies of those regimes threatened the stability of capitalism itself, they became converts to democracy.

Neoliberal policies during the 1990s gave an immense stimulus to the alliance of foreign multinationals and local capitalists, an alliance in which foreign capital played the dominant role. The process was under way in many countries but particularly in Argentina, Brazil, Chile, Mexico, and Venezuela. Privatization became a major instrument for denationalizing the Latin American economy through auctions and debt-equity swaps that virtually donated valuable state companies to foreign firms. Small groups of local capitalists linked to foreign capital and with crony connections to the ruling parties also benefited by the privatization process. In Mexico, for example, after the 1992 privatization of the banking system, "a mere 224 investors held effective control of the Mexican banks.... This oligarchy controls the fundamental instruments of economic—and indirectly—political power in Mexico today." Typical of these aggressive new entrepreneurs was Carlos Slim Helú, ranked third in the *Forbes* 2006 list of the world's richest men. With a fortune estimated to be more than $30 billion, Slim Helú, in partnership with two associates and two foreign firms, bought the Mexican telephone giant Telmex during the administration of his friend and business associate Carlos Salinas. Paying little cash and using credit advanced by a number of banks, he paid a mere $1.7 billion for a company worth close to $12 billion. After the sale, the price of the company stock skyrocketed. Slim Helú also owned the Denny's and Sanborn's restaurant chains and Mexico's most profitable investment firm in 1996, Carso-Imbursa, in addition to having a monopoly on cigarette manufacturing. His cousin Alfredo Harper Helú was one of a group of billionaires who controlled Banamex, one of Mexico's three largest banks.

Narcorevenues produced another crop of Latin American new wealth. Although U.N. agencies estimated the illegal drug industry's annual revenue at $460 billion, roughly the equivalent of 8 percent of total international trade, for obvious reasons, the extent of its wealth was uncertain. Nonetheless, its wealth was vast and its activity—as revealed in a 1998 U.S. money-laundering sting that led to the arrests of about two dozen Mexican bankers—often intersected with the legitimate operations of Latin American entrepreneurs. According to journalist Daniel Lazare, the drug traffic, the neoliberal policies pushed by the IMF, the World Bank, and other agencies, and the U.S. drug war "all intersected in an explosive way." By imposing austerity and privatization measures and by dismantling the Latin American state, he argues, neoliberalism created massive unemployment that generated "thousands of recruits for the drug trade—coca growers, day laborers, smugglers, enforcers." Neoliberalism's emphasis on financial deregulation and trade liberalization also made international borders more porous, created insuperable obstacles to effective interdiction, and facilitated the laundering of drug profits to invest them in legitimate activities.

THE URBAN MIDDLE SECTORS

The urban middle sectors occupied an intermediate position between the new bourgeoisie and the landed elite on the one hand and the peasantry and the industrial working class on the other. The boundaries of this intermediate group with other classes were vague and overlapping. At one end, for example, the group included highly paid business managers whose lifestyles and attitudes identified them with the new bourgeoisie; at the other, it included store clerks and lower-echelon government servants whose incomes often were lower than those of skilled workers.

The longest established urban middle sector consisted of self-employed artisans, shopkeepers, and owners of innumerable small enterprises. White-collar employees formed another large urban intermediate sector. Urbanization, the growth of commercial capitalism, and the vast expansion of the state in the middle decades of the century contributed to the growth of both public and private bureaucracies. Until recently, public employees made up about one-fifth of the economically active population of the area.

University students composed a sizable urban middle sector. Between 1960 and 1970, their number rose from 0.25 million to more than 1 million. The great majority came from middle-class backgrounds, and many combined work and study.

Student discontent with inadequate curricula and teaching methods and the injustices of the social and political order made the university a focal point of dissidence and protest. Ultimately, however, the students were merely transients, in Latin America as elsewhere, and their radical or reformist zeal often subsided after they entered a professional career.

Because of their great size, the ideology of the urban middle sectors and their actual and potential role in social change were issues of crucial importance. Following World War II, many foreign experts on Latin America, especially in the United States, pinned great hopes on the emerging middle sectors (to which they assigned the new industrialist class) as agents of progressive social and economic change. The history of the following decades did not confirm these expectations. The urban middle sectors mushroomed, but with the exception of many students and intellectual workers—teachers, writers, and scientists—they were not a force for progressive social change.

The urban middle sectors were not hopeless reactionaries, however. By their very intermediate nature, they were capable of strong political oscillations, especially in response to the movement of the economy. The "savage capitalism" implanted in many Latin American countries in recent decades by both military and civilian governments played havoc with middle-class living standards and expectations. In the process, it also transformed these traditionally complacent urban middle sectors.

A good example of such a transformation was *El Barzón*, a Mexican middle-class debtors' union that took its name from the leather strap that held the oxen to the plow on the great haciendas of prerevolutionary times. With a membership exceeding half a million Mexicans in thirty-one states and the Federal District, El Barzón became the largest, most militant resistance movement formed in the wake of the peso's crash in 1994. This sent interest rates up more than 100 percent and threatened thousands of farmers, small businesses, and assorted members of the middle class with financial ruin. With a combination of direct action that included the public burning of credit cards and the blocking of entrances to bank branches to shut down their operations, El Barzón stopped foreclosures and imposed a moratorium on the banks. El Barzón also formed links with domestic and foreign trade unions, the Catholic Church, debtors' unions in other Latin American countries, and the Zapatista rebellion in Chiapas. Its national director, Juan José Quirino, became a senator of the progressive nationalist Partido

Revolucionario Democrático (PRD). "It's not just personal debt that we are talking about now—the foreign debt is the mechanism by which the IMF keeps us chained up," says Quirino. "Latin American debtor nations missed the opportunity to unite after 1982. This time we must be ready to fight for a continental moratorium."

THE PEASANTRY

The term *peasantry* refers here to all small landowners, tenants, and landless rural laborers. As documented in the following chapters, the expansion of the new type of latifundio created an unparalleled crisis for the Latin American peasantry. The increased use of tractors and other kinds of mechanized farm equipment already had displaced millions of farmworkers, and the process was accelerating. The removal of trade barriers, opening national markets to competition with more efficient foreign grain producers, threatened the existence of small farmers. Meanwhile, the neoliberal trend reversed land reforms and produced a growing exodus of impoverished peasants to the overcrowded cities or, in the case of Mexican and Central American campesinos, a dangerous and sometimes unsuccessful journey across the border into an increasingly inhospitable United States. Behind these desperate migrations were sharply declining standards of living. Poverty, conservatively estimated by the World Bank at 25 percent in 1981 before the introduction of neoliberal reforms, rose sharply to 69 percent in 2000.

THE INDUSTRIAL WORKING CLASS

The rapid growth of capitalism in Latin America since about 1930 accompanied a parallel growth of the industrial working class. Although miners and factory workers formed the best-organized and most class-conscious detachments of the army of labor, they were a minority of the labor force. Artisans, self-employed or working in shops employing fewer than five persons, constituted the largest group. The predominance of the artisan shop, whose labor relations were marked by paternalism and individual bargaining, hindered the development of workers' class-consciousness and solidarity.

Despite its small size, the industrial working class played a key role in major movements for social and political democracy in Latin America. Armed Bolivian tin miners helped achieve the victory of the 1952 revolution and its program of land reform and nationalization of mines. Cuban workers gave decisive support to the guerrilla struggle against the Batista dictatorship, and their general strike in 1959 helped topple it. The working class of Buenos Aires intervened at a critical moment in 1945 to save Juan Perón from a reactionary coup, and its pressure broadened his reform program. In Chile, the working class led the Popular Unity coalition that brought Salvador Allende to the presidency, ushering in a three-year effort (1970–1973) to achieve socialism by peaceful democratic means.

These advances—particularly the Cuban and Chilean revolutions—provoked a counterrevolutionary reaction that until recently was still ascendant. Many countries under personal or military dictatorships banned all working-class parties, abolished trade unions or placed them under strict government control, and murdered many labor leaders or forced them into exile.

The gradual restoration of formal democracy in the region, accompanied by the imposition of the neoliberal economic model, did not bring full recognition of labor's right to organize and other basic rights. In Chile, for example, the new civilian government retained many features of the Pinochet labor code. In Mexico, workers could not freely join unions of their choice, and most union members were forced to join unions affiliated with the ruling *Partido Revolucionario Institucional* (PRI). Export-processing areas, like Mexico's maquila sector or the Central American and Caribbean free-trade zones, routinely ignored union rights. In Argentina, according to Argentine scholar Daniel Cieza, the election of Carlos Menem in 1989 initiated "a vicious labor counterreform" that gutted the traditional Labor Contracting Law, with the result that nearly 90 percent of new hires were temporary rather than permanent. Changes in workplace accident legislation also caused health and safety conditions to deteriorate dramatically. The stated objective of the law was to create more jobs, but the result was just the opposite, with Argentine unemployment and underemployment estimated at 40 percent of the economically active population.

Nevertheless, Latin American workers continued the struggle for equality and social justice. In Mexico, a new federation with 1.5 million members, the National Workers' Union, led by Francisco Hernández Suárez of the telephone workers' union, challenged the Mexican Confederation of Labor (CTM), which held wages to levels decreed by the government and collaborated with the security forces to repress independent unionists. In Mexico's maquila sector and the Central American garment sweatshop zone, some breakthroughs in trade union organization and improvement of working conditions occurred because of cooperation between independent local unions and their counterparts in the United States. The struggle for workers' rights often targeted neoliberalism, whose downsizing of the state and other structural adjustment policies led to the virtual disappearance of some national industries, a rapid expansion of the informal economy, and the massive unemployment and atomization of labor.

THE SERVICE OR INFORMAL SECTOR

According to the International Labor Organization, from 1980 to 1992, informal-sector employment rose from 40.2 percent to 54.4 percent of total employment and grew 3.9 percent per year thereafter. This made the informal sector the largest source of employment in Latin America, including "a great number of poorly paid domestic servants and a mass of individuals who eke out a precarious living as lottery ticket vendors, car watchers and washers, shoe shiners, and street peddlers." But the meaning of "informal sector" was extremely elastic and the list of occupations that fit the category almost endless. Its main defining elements were self-employment and the irregular and precarious nature of the work. "'Informal sector,'" observes sociologist Tessa Cubitt, "implies a dualist interpretation of the urban economy, since it proposes a dichotomy between a formal modern capitalist sector in which big businesses and multinationals flourish and the mass of the poor who are unable to benefit from participation in this sector."

In fact, many of the activities of the informal sector benefited the modern capitalist sector, and the links between them were exploitative. The garbage pickers of Cali, Colombia, collected wastepaper, which they sold to warehouses, which in turn sold it to the giant paper company Cartón de Colombia, whose main shareholder was the Mobil Oil Company. "Why," asks Cubitt,

> does Cartón de Colombia not directly employ the garbage pickers?
> Clearly, it is cheaper for them to operate like this because they do not
> have regular wage bills to pay. The income the garbage pickers receive
> for each item is extremely low and reduced even further by the com-
> petition between them, which is encouraged by the system that is very
> much a buyer's market.

In effect, the low income of the garbage pickers subsidized the multinational Cartón de Colombia. Similar exploitative relations existed between manufacturers and workers who subcontracted to do work in their own homes and earn money for each completed piece. In all such cases, the companies saved on wages and the costs of social security benefits; this system had the additional benefit of keeping workers weak and divided, unable to present a common front to employers.

The New Political Consciousness

Economic change produced a transformation in family life, race relations, education, and the whole superstructure of society, but the old attitudes and mentalities struggled hard to survive. As a result, Latin America presented dramatic contrasts between customs and mores that were as new as the Space Age and others that recalled the age of Cortés and Pizarro. Increasingly, women, blacks, and indigenous peoples organized themselves politically and demanded their fair share of society's resources.

GENDER

The status of women was a case in point. In some ways, their status had improved; the struggle to obtain the vote, for example, began around World War I and ended successfully when Paraguay granted women suffrage in 1961. More and more Latin American women held appointive and electoral offices, and in increasing numbers they entered factories, offices, and the professions. By 1970, in some countries, notably Brazil and Argentina, the percentage of women classified as professionals was higher than the percentage for men, a significant fact because the proportion of economically active women was much lower than that of men. In Brazil, out of every one hundred women working in nonagricultural services in 1970, eighteen engaged in professional and technical operations, whereas for men, the figure was only six out of every one hundred. The ratios were reversed, however, for positions of higher responsibility, reflecting the persistence of discriminatory attitudes.

The movement for women's rights could claim much less progress in such areas as family patterns, divorce laws, and sexual codes. The traditions of the patriarchal family, of closely supervised courtship and marriage, continued strongly to influence the upper and middle classes. The ideology of machismo, the cult of male superiority with its corollary of a sexual double standard, continued to reign almost everywhere in the continent. "The Mexican family," writes sociologist Rogelio Díaz-Guerrero, "is founded upon two fundamental propositions: (a) the unquestioned and absolute supremacy of the father and (b) the necessary and absolute self-sacrifice of the mother." The flood of economic, political, and social change of almost three decades weakened the force of this statement, but, with some qualifications, it still held for most Latin American republics.

Socialist Cuba, however, made great advances in abolishing sexual discrimination in law and practice. In 1975, it introduced the Family Code, which gave the force of law to the division of household labor. It required working men and women to share housework and child care equally, and a spouse could take her recalcitrant partner to court. Nevertheless, Vilma Espín, head of the Cuban women's movement, admitted that the law was one thing and the way people lived was another:

> Tradition is very strong. But we have advanced. Before, the machismo was terrible. Before, the men on the streets would brag about how their wives took care of them and did all the work at home. They were very

proud of that. At least now we have reached the point where they don't dare say that. That's an advance. And now with young people you can see the difference.

Nicaragua was another country where a liberating revolution transformed the lives and roles of many women. Women, both rural and urban, took part in the struggle against the Somoza tyranny and made an immense contribution to its final triumph in July 1979. Women prepared for the final offensive by stockpiling food, gathering medical supplies, and organizing communications networks to send messages to Sandinista fighters and their families. By the time of the final victory, from one-quarter to one-third of the Sandinista People's Army was female—some as young as thirteen. Three women were guerrilla commanders; two served on the general staff of the People's Army. Following the triumph of the revolution, women assumed responsible positions at all levels of the Sandinista government. A similar process of women's liberation took place as part of the revolutionary struggle in neighboring El Salvador.

In the Southern Cone, women took the lead in the struggle against the military dictatorships that arose in Chile (1973), Uruguay (1973), and Argentina (1976). They embraced this role because of the repressive policies of the dictatorships, the banning of trade unions and political parties, and the murder or disappearance of thousands of male activists. Women paid a price for their sacrifices. Thirteen members of the Argentine human rights movement, including the president of the Mothers of the Plaza de Mayo, who demanded an accounting for their disappeared children, vanished into the death camps.

Despite their services, women in Cuba, Nicaragua, and the countries of the Southern Cone had not achieved full recognition of their equality. Gioconda Belli, a former Nicaraguan guerrilla leader, complained, "We'd led troops into battle, we'd done all sorts of things, and then as soon as the Sandinistas took office we were displaced from the important posts. We'd had to content ourselves with intermediate-level positions for the most part." Her complaint resonated with a Uruguayan trade unionist who had taken part in the struggle against the military dictatorship. "When the men came out of prison or returned from exile," she lamented, "they took up all the spaces, sat down in the same chairs, and expected the women to go back home." And Rosa, one of the Chilean working-class women who played key roles in the resistance to the military dictatorship, wryly remembered, "When the democratic government took over, the men around here said, 'It's okay, Rosa, you can leave it to us now.' We thought, 'Have they forgotten everything we did during the dictatorship?'" Consciously or unconsciously, the old prejudices persisted in the thought patterns of men—even radicals and revolutionaries—from one end of the area to the other.

Women responded to the continuing challenge of machismo by forming a multitude of groups that, whether or not they called themselves feminist, had as their essential goal the end of the old, unequal relations between the sexes. One *encuentro* (meeting) in Nicaragua in March 1992 brought together some five hundred Central American women "who talked about the power Central American women have in their 'public' and 'private' lives, the kind of power they would like to have, and how to go about getting that power." Women were divided by class, however, and Latin American working-class women often criticized traditional feminist organizations as middle class and indifferent to their own practical needs. "We have things in common with middle-class women, but we also have other problems that middle-class women don't have, like the housing shortage, debt problems, unemployment," said one Chilean woman activist, "and we're not going to advance as women if the two things aren't closely linked."

Economic forces, in particular the disastrous impact of neoliberal economic policies on household incomes and living standards, were silently transforming gender and familial relations in many parts of the area. It was becoming increasingly difficult for one wage to support a family. From sheer necessity, women were entering industry in record numbers. According to the Inter-American Development Bank and the Economic Commission on Latin America, the proportion of women in the labor force rose 50 percent, from almost 18 percent in 1950 to just under 27 percent in 1990. By 2003, women composed 46 percent of the region's labor force.

The results were particularly evident in an area like the Caribbean basin, where declining traditional exports such as sugar, coffee, and bananas—industries that employed a predominantly male labor force—gave way to export manufacturing, which typically used poorly paid women workers. Similar economic trends, challenging male dominance in the household, were under way in other countries of the region.

As Latin America entered the twenty-first century, however, a growing gulf appeared between women's legal and social equality. A major legal achievement was the passage of national legislation to prevent and punish violence against women, modeled on the U.N. Convention on the Elimination of All Forms of Discrimination Against Women. Still another was the creation of state bureaucracies to advance women's interests, which sometimes linked to larger agencies responsible for the areas of culture, education, or the family. Finally, in country after country during the 1990s, laws established quotas for women in each party's list of candidates. During Fujimori's ten-year rule in Peru, for example, Congress required political parties to field women candidates in at least 30 percent of local and congressional races, enacted laws against domestic violence, and authorized both a Ministry of Women and a Public Defender for Women. Indeed, during Fujimori's last, brief, and chaotic administration, a governing council composed entirely of women ran Congress.

As Maruja Barrig points out, however, the cause of women's legal equality often advanced without improving their deteriorating social and economic conditions.

> In the 1990s, for example, 70 percent of the Bolivian population was considered poor, climbing to 90 percent in rural areas. In Peru, close to 50 percent of the population is classified as poor. The literacy rate among the female indigenous population, as a group, is the lowest in Latin America. The 1991 national census in Bolivia found that 50 percent of rural women could not read. In Peru, according to the 1993 National Census, the figure was 43 percent.

Moreover, health statistics, Barrig notes, "are no less alarming…. In Bolivia, there are 300 maternal deaths for every 100,000 births, but in Potosí, the number of maternal deaths per 100,000 could reach 600." Noting that Bolivia, Haiti, and Peru had the highest rates of maternal death in Latin America, the U.N. Population Fund described this as "one of the most dramatic representations of social injustice and the inequality among women."

Meanwhile, Salvadoran lawmakers, responding to pressure from prolife groups, eliminated the four legal options for abortion from the country's 1997 legal code, and Nicaragua followed suit in 2006, despite opinion polls that showed public support for a woman's right to choose abortion under some conditions. In Chile, conservative forces defeated a divorce law and retained in the civil code the statutory definition of the husband as the "head" of the family. In response to these defeats and "internal cracks in the institutional structures created for women," Barrig notes that "in the search for the possible, a subtle pragmatism appears to have become lodged in the strategies of feminists playing by the rules proposed by others." Nonetheless, the strategy appeared to pay off in 2004, when Chile finally passed a law recognizing legal divorce. Two years later, Chileans elected the first independent woman president in the Americas, Michelle Bachelet, herself a single mother of three children by two different fathers.

RACE PREJUDICE

Notions of the inferiority of blacks and indigenous peoples were officially disapproved throughout Latin America, but race prejudice remained strong, especially among upper- and middle-class people who identified themselves as white. In Brazil, often touted as a model of racial democracy, sociologist Florestan

Fernandes found that these people clung to "the *prejudice of having no prejudice*, limiting themselves to treating blacks with tolerance, maintaining the old ceremonial politeness in interracial relationships, and excluding from this tolerance any true egalitarian feeling or content." In 2002, Brazilian newspapers carried advertisements from private companies that called for a "good appearance," a code phrase meaning that blacks should not apply. In a 2000 census, only 6 percent of the population of 170 million identified themselves as black, a low figure that proponents of reform attributed to discrimination and a poor racial self-image. A DNA study by Brazilian scientists suggested that as many as 80 percent of Brazilians had African ancestry. Only 2.2 percent of Brazil's 1.6 million college students were black, however, and blacks were almost invisible on television except in menial or exotic roles. Under pressure from the Brazilian Black Movement, the Brazilian Congress debated a 2003 law that reserved 20 percent of university admissions for blacks and applied the same figure to civil service jobs. The plan also required black or mixed-race actors to compose 25 percent of the cast of any theatrical or television production. Thereafter, the progressive nationalist government of Lula da Silva created a new state ministry responsible for eradicating racial inequality and advancing the interests of black Brazilians and *pardos* (mixed-race Brazilians), who together compose roughly half the population.

Unlike the situation in the United States, where people identified as either white or black, a kind of "sliding scale" of prejudice and discrimination existed in Brazil, Colombia, and Venezuela, and other Latin American countries with large black populations. Here, the shade of skin color—varying degrees of whiteness—typically favored pardos over blacks. As a rule, the higher occupations such as medicine, law, upper-level government posts, and the officer and diplomatic corps excluded both categories, but pardos could aspire to become schoolteachers, journalists, bank tellers, low-level municipal officials, and the like. Dark-skinned people predominated in the lowest-paid jobs. The virulent opposition attacks on populist President Hugo Chávez of Venezuela, who boasted of his black and indigenous ancestry, had a clear racist component.

Even in black Haiti, a vast economic and social gulf separated an urban mulatto elite from the rural black masses of poor people and the "black ghetto" of downtown Port-au-Prince. In the neighboring Dominican Republic, the late president Joaquín Balaguer had preached an overt racism, claiming that the "biological imperialism" of Haitian immigrants threatened his "white and Christian" country. In fact, the Dominican Republic was the only true mulatto country in the world. A pervasive Dominican racism, based on a rejection of African ancestry and on supposed links with a superior indigenous Spanish racial heritage, led to many assaults against the large Haitian immigrant community, the most lethal of which was Rafael Trujillo's 1937 massacre of some twenty thousand unarmed Haitians. Meanwhile, only revolutionary Cuba had largely eliminated racism in both theory and practice; here, blacks held high positions in government, the armed forces, and the professions. But the roots of racism in a country with Cuba's history were deep and strong, and Castro himself recognized that racial, gender, and class prejudices persisted.

The indigenous peoples of Latin America remained the principal victims of racist exploitation and violence. In Brazil, according to one recent estimate, the number of indigenous people had dropped from 1 million to 180,000 since the beginning of the twentieth century. This process of cultural destruction in the interests of economic progress continued unabated. Since 1975, gold miners had murdered some one thousand Yanomamis, of the nine thousand living in Brazil, and twelve thousand in Venezuela. Similar wanton killings occurred in the jungle lowlands of Colombia, and land-grabbing hacendados or their *pistoleros* (gunmen) murdered natives with impunity in Mexico, Guatemala, and other countries with sizable indigenous populations. In Guatemala, military regimes practiced systematic genocide against the Maya and attempted to eradicate their culture.

In some countries, the native peasantry endured a many-sided economic, social, and cultural exploitation. "The Indian problem," writes Mexican sociologist Pablo González Casanova, "is essentially one of internal colonialism. The Indian communities are Mexico's internal colonies.... Here we find prejudice, discrimination, colonial forms of exploitation, dictatorial forms, and the separation of a different population, with a different race and culture." Some Mexican social scientists claimed that Mexicans had long been blind to their own racism and discrimination. One cited a paragraph written in 1985 by a leading historian, Enrique Krauze: "Mexico constructed a tradition of natural liberty and equality that was rooted in the culture of the people and freed us very early from slavery, servitude, and racism."

These revisionist scholars assigned much of the blame for this blindness to an indigenous policy that dated from the time of independence and that gave native peoples (and people of African descent) the option of abandoning their cultures or becoming wax figures in a historical museum. The framers of this integrationist policy included such illustrious names in scholarship or politics as Manuel Gamio, Gonzalo Aguirre Beltrán, Alfonso Caso, and the revered Lázaro Cárdenas. Adding a touch of humor, the ethnologist Luz María Martínez Montiel declared that the anthropologists themselves had made the important Instituto Nacional Indigenista "the last encomienda in Mexico." For Martínez, integration of the indigenous peoples consisted not in despoiling them of their identities and cultures but in ensuring their equal rights in the process of production, education, and expression. And it is they, she stressed, who must decide.

In the spring of 2001, the Zapatista Army of National Liberation, led by Subcomandante Marcos, staged an impressive march from Chiapas to Mexico City to demand indigenous autonomy and control of their resources. On the way north, thousands of supporters greeted the Zapatista caravan and received petitions and memorials like the Declaration of the Indigenous Peoples of Morelos:

> What do we want and demand? To be treated with respect as indigenous peoples. That we should not be jailed for defending our land. That there should be true justice. An end to industrial and commercial megaprojects in communal and ejido land. An end to the destruction of our forests, waters, and natural resources. An end to the neoliberal modernization that is causing the disappearance of the indigenous peoples. That we be taken into account when decisions are made. We want to be part of development, not a simple rung on which others step up for their development.

Nonetheless, in the capital, disillusionment awaited the rebels. Congress left the implementation of a list of native rights to the state legislatures, effectively leaving matters as they were. The Zapatista reply was swift and decisive: "If this reform deserves any name, it should be 'the Constitutional Recognition of the Rights and Culture of the Latifundists and Racists.'" Returning to Chiapas, the rebels and their communities faced the same problems of military encirclement and harassment by paramilitary bands in the service of great landowners and reactionary politicians. In a struggle that had now lasted more than a decade, the Zapatistas avoided a suicidal armed project to seize power. However, they also refused to limit their demands to conditions in Chiapas, focusing instead on principles of indigenous self-determination and national democratic reform. By adroit use of the most modern means of communication and a series of national and international meetings, they made their struggle known. In the process, they won sympathy throughout the world, achieving a frontline place in the battle against globalization and neoliberalism. Subcomandante Marcos, the telegenic Zapatista leader, soon became almost as well known in Latin America as Che Guevara.

The indigenous peoples of America were on the march, forming broad coalitions with unions, middle-class groups, and international organizations, and they were winning. In 2001, grassroots movements from around the world came to Cochabamba, the third-largest city in Bolivia. "Cochabamba," writes Sophia Style, "became a key symbol of the struggle against global capitalism, when thousands of local people took to the streets against the privatization of their water supply by the U.S. transnational Bechtel—and won." The victory had its costs. After a mobilization of thirty thousand people had shut down the city center for five days, President Hugo Banzer (former dictator of Bolivia) sent in troops, including a sharpshooter trained at the School of the Americas, who gunned down a seventeen-year-old protester.

One milestone in the struggle of the indigenous peoples of America against old and new forms of exploitation was the decision of the United Nations to declare 1993 the International Year of the Indigenous Peoples of the World. Another was the award of the Nobel Peace Prize to the Guatemalan indigenous leader Rigoberta Menchú (October 1992) in recognition of her work on behalf of the native peoples of America. Shortly thereafter, indigenous-rights organizations in Ecuador and Bolivia successfully mobilized their members to challenge neoliberal agendas and drove from power unpopular presidents in Ecuador and Bolivia. The climax of the broad popular movement for indigenous rights, however, was doubtlessly the 2005 victory of Evo Morales, an Aymara indígena, who became the hemisphere's first modern, democratically elected indigenous president.

Cultural Institutions

Over the course of the twentieth century, Latin America's major cultural institutions—the Catholic Church and the armed forces—underwent considerable change, although neither entirely broke with its colonial and postcolonial past. Buffeted by the alternating winds of a populist nationalism and a neoliberal universalism, these two venerable institutional representatives of oligarchic order experienced divisions that reflected accurately the ideological crisis of modern Latin America.

THE CATHOLIC CHURCH

The new reformist and revolutionary currents that emerged within the Catholic Church since about 1960 had different sources. One was a more liberal climate of opinion within the church brought about by the Second Vatican Council, convened in 1962 under Pope John XXIII. Another was concern on the part of some elements of the hierarchy that the church's traditional collusion with the elites risked a loss of the masses to Marxism. Still another was a crisis of conscience on the part of some clergy, especially working clergy whose experiences convinced them that the area's desperate dilemmas required drastic solutions.

The new ferment within the Latin American church found dramatic expression in the life and death of the famous Colombian priest and sociologist Camilo Torres Restrepo. Born into an aristocratic Colombian family, a brilliant scholar and teacher, Torres became convinced that it was futile to seek reform by peaceful means, and he joined the communist-led guerrilla National Liberation Army. He died in a clash with counterinsurgency forces in February 1966.

The second conference of Latin American bishops, held at Medellín, Colombia, in 1968, hotly debated the proper stand for the church to take in the face of Latin America's structural crisis. The presence of Pope Paul VI at its opening session underlined the meeting's importance. Reflecting the progressive shift of some clergy, the bishops at Medellín affirmed the church's commitment to the task of liberating the people of Latin America from neocolonialism and "institutionalized violence." This violence, declared the bishops, was inherent in the continent's economic, social, and political structures, dependent on what Pope Paul called "the international imperialism of money."

Even before Medellín, a group of Latin American bishops had taken a position in favor of socialism. Their leader was Helder Câmara, archbishop of Recife (Brazil). He and seven other Brazilian bishops had signed a pastoral letter issued by seventeen bishops of the developing world that called on the church to avoid identification of religion "with the oppression of the poor and the workers, with feudalism, capitalism, imperialism." Himself rejecting violence as an instrument of revolutionary change, Câmara expressed sympathy and understanding for those who felt that violence was the only effective tactic.

These developments accompanied the emergence and growing acceptance by many clergy of the so-called theology of liberation, the product of the study and reflection of leading church scholars in various Latin American countries. This doctrine taught that the church, returning to its roots, must again become a church of the poor. It must cease to be an ally of the rich and powerful and commit itself to the struggle for social justice. Its primary responsibility was to raise the consciousness of the masses, to make them aware of the exploitative social system under which they suffered, and to unite them to change an oppressive economic and political order. Liberation theology rejected Marxism's atheist worldview, but it drew heavily on a Marxist analysis of the causes of poverty and oppression in the developing world. On the subject of revolution, although deploring all violence, liberation theologians taught that revolution, or counterviolence, was justified as a last resort against the greater violence of tyrants, an orthodox Catholic teaching that went back to St. Thomas Aquinas. In this spirit, Archbishop Oscar Arnulfo Romero of San Salvador, in one of his last sermons before his murder by a right-wing assassin in 1980, declared, "When all peaceful means have been exhausted, the Church considers insurrection moral and justified."

To implement the teachings of liberation theology, progressive clergy set about developing a new type of Christian organization, the *comunidad de base* (Christian grassroots organization). Composed of poor people in the countryside and the barrios of cities, assisted and advised by priests and students, these communities combined religious study and reflection with efforts to define and solve the practical social problems of their localities. The great landowners and the authorities, frequently branding their activity "subversive," subjected both laity and priests to severe repression. This led to a growing politicization and radicalization of many communities and their involvement in revolutionary movements.

Conflict between this progressive faction and the traditional church hierarchy soon emerged at the third conference of Latin American bishops, convened at Puebla, Mexico, in 1979. Unlike Medellín, where the Progressives had the upper hand, traditionalists controlled the agenda and clearly intended to put down the troublesome liberation theology. They prepared a working paper that urged resignation on the part of the poor in the hope of a better hereafter and placed their trust for the solution of Latin America's great social problems in the failed reformist models of the 1960s. This document raised a storm of criticism among progressive bishops and other clergy.

The unknown element in the equation at Puebla was the position of Pope John Paul II, who inaugurated the conference. Despite the ambiguity of the pope's statements, in general, they tended to reinforce the position of Progressives and Moderates at the Puebla conference. Its final document continued the line of Medellín, especially in its expression of overwhelming concern for the poor: "We identify as the most devastating and humiliating scourge, the situation of inhuman poverty in which millions of Latin Americans live, with starvation wages, unemployment and underemployment, malnutrition, infant mortality, lack of adequate housing, health problems, and labor unrest."

Later, the pope's opposition to liberation theology and the so-called popular church appeared to harden. In Brazil—where many bishops accepted the basic tenets of liberation theology, actively engaged in the struggle for land reform, and enjoyed the support of many thousands of grassroots communities—he denounced their activities as subversive or heretical. The pope sanctioned a popular theologian, Leonardo Boff, and weakened the majority of progressive Brazilian clerics by naming traditional bishops.

The Vatican also joined the Mexican government in efforts to force Bishop Samuel Ruiz of San Cristóbal de las Casas, in Chiapas, to resign. They accused Ruiz, a champion of the poor Maya campesinos of his diocese, of having a

Marxist interpretation of the Gospel and "incorrect theological reflection." The effort collapsed when the Salinas administration asked Ruiz to mediate between the government and the indigenous rebels after the outbreak of the Zapatista revolt in 1994.

Nonetheless, in the course of a historic January 1999 visit to Cuba, the pontiff seemed to signal some change of course. Although he called on the Cuban government to grant greater religious, civil, and political liberties, he praised the social achievements of the Cuban Revolution. Moreover, in what appeared to be a thinly veiled reference to the United States, he urged Cubans to reject the neoliberal capitalist policies of Western nations because such policies led to the creation of a small, wealthy upper class and a large, impoverished underclass. Most striking of all, he repeatedly criticized the U.S. embargo against Cuba as unjust.

With the death of John Paul, however, the ascent of Pope Benedict augured poorly for liberation theology, which he had condemned in the 1980s as "a fundamental threat to the faith of the church." Social activists also anticipated opposition from the church hierarchy. In a 2007 address to the faithful in Brazil, the new pope declared unambiguously that Spain's sixteenth-century "proclamation of Jesus and of His Gospel did not at any point involve an alienation of the pre-Columbus cultures," which had been "silently longing" for Christ "without realizing it." Catholicism was not "the imposition of a foreign culture," the pope insisted. Indigenous people willingly had received the Holy Spirit "who came to make their cultures fruitful, purifying them." Progressive nationalists like Venezuela's Hugo Chávez demanded a papal apology, and politically mobilized indigenous rights activists denounced "the representatives of the Catholic Church of that era [who], with honorable exceptions, were complicit accessories and beneficiaries of one of the more horrible genocides that humanity has seen."

The recent rapid growth in membership and influence of Protestant evangelical or fundamentalist sects posed a major challenge to the religious supremacy of the Catholic Church in Latin America. Between 1981 and 1987, the membership of these sects had doubled to 50 million, increasing to 67 million in 2010. The dramatic economic and social changes that were taking place throughout the continent had much to do with the phenomenal growth of these new churches. Their revivalist preaching and "pie-in-the-sky" message brought color, excitement, and hope to the lives of the uprooted rural immigrants of the shantytowns that ringed every Latin American city. The churches' support networks often provided these "marginalized" people with material assistance as well.

Despite the current pope's hostility toward progressive Catholic social thought, liberation theology still strongly influenced the theory and practice of

Latin American Catholic clergy. For example, a joint statement issued by four bishops of dioceses on the Colombian-Ecuadorian border denounced Plan Colombia, the FTAA, and President George W. Bush's Andean Initiative as part of an unjust system that aggravated the area's poverty and violence. Poverty, they declared, was the primary evil and the principal cause of violence in the area. "What is happening now in Colombia," declared Bishop Arturo Correa of Ipiales, Colombia, "will happen in Ecuador, Peru, Venezuela, Brazil, and all of poor America."

Interestingly, the bishops' statement directly opposed the official Colombian and Ecuadorian governments' support of Plan Colombia, which included permission for the U.S. government to install a military base at the port of Manta to carry out surveillance of drug cultivation and trafficking in Bolivia, Colombia, Peru, and the Caribbean. However, the bishops went farther and rejected "the imposition of an unjust economic system that fails to respect human dignity and attacks the most elemental human rights." They viewed Plan Colombia, the FTAA, and the Andean Initiative as part of the neoliberal economic model, reflecting the ambition of wealthy countries for a redistribution of areas of influence. Ecuadorian Bishop Gonzalo López of Sucumbios saw a connection between the militarization of the drug war and these free-trade initiatives: "One is a military attempt to control the region, while the others will be used to ensure open markets and access to our countries' resources." The bishops stressed that they favored the eradication of illicit crops but demanded "procedures that respect the ecosystem, biodiversity, and especially human life" and called for a different economic plan "based on sustainability and economic solidarity."

THE MILITARY

Within the Latin American armed forces, as within the church, a differentiation occurred. The phenomenon of the reformist or even social revolutionary military officer had a long pedigree. In Brazil, the *tenente* (junior officer) revolts of the 1920s paved the way for the triumph of Getúlio Vargas's reformist revolution of 1930. Juan Perón and other members of the Group of United Officers exemplified a similar tendency within the Argentine officer corps in the 1930s. In Guatemala, in 1944, a group of progressive officers led by Col. Jacobo Arbenz overthrew the Ubico dictatorship and installed a government that enacted a sweeping land reform and other democratic changes. Although the military regimes in Peru (1968), Panama (1968), and Ecuador (1972) differed considerably in the scope and depth of their reforms, they demonstrated the existence of a reformist or even revolutionary officer class.

The massive influx of North American capital into Latin America after 1945, accompanied by the growing political influence of the United States in the area, altered the balance of forces between Conservatives and Progressives within the Latin American military. Many high-ranking officers became fervent converts to the North American system of free enterprise and accepted the inevitability of a mortal struggle between "atheistical communism" and the "free world." By the Treaty of Rio de Janeiro (1947), the Latin American republics committed to join the United States in the defense of the Western Hemisphere. In the context of the cold war, this commitment entailed collaboration with the United States in a global anticommunist strategy, to the extent of justifying military intervention in any country threatened or conquered by "communist penetration." Under the cover of this doctrine, in 1965, Brazilian troops joined U.S. forces in intervening in the Dominican Republic to crush the progressive revolutionary nationalist government of Col. Francisco Caamaño. The integration of Latin American armies into the strategic plans of the Pentagon converted many of these armies into appendages of the North American military machine.

The Pentagon's technical and ideological tutelage over the Latin American military reflected this integration; in particular, it aimed to destroy Latin American revolutionary movements. After the victory of the Cuban Revolution in 1959, this program of training and indoctrination greatly expanded. Thousands of Latin American officers took courses in counterinsurgency warfare at Fort Bragg, Fort Knox, Fort Monmouth, and other installations in the United States and in the Panama Canal Zone. The School of the Americas (SOA), run by the U.S. Army for the training of Latin American officers, continued to play an especially important role. Founded in 1946 in Panama, it moved to Fort Benning, Georgia, in 1984, when the Panama Canal Zone Treaty forced its relocation from Panama. Since its inception, the SOA provided more than fifty-six thousand Latin American soldiers training in the art of waging a "dirty little war."

Dubbed by *Newsweek* as "a school for dictators," SOA's graduates included terrorists like Chile's Gen. Augusto Pinochet, Panama's Manuel Noriega, and El Salvador's Roberto D'Aubuisson, supposed assassin of Archbishop Oscar Romero. According to the U.N. Truth Commission in El Salvador, SOA graduates directed many of the massacres and atrocities committed by the military in that country. Nineteen of the twenty-seven officers implicated in the Jesuit priest killings in 1989 were SOA alumni, as were eight of the twelve officers charged with responsibility for the El Mozote massacre. A folder labeled "Confidential," discovered in Paraguay's so-called Horror Archives, contained a torture manual used at the SOA. The manual taught interrogators how to keep electric shock victims alive and responsive by methods that included dousing their heads and bodies with salt water. In 1997, the number of Mexican military personnel trained at the SOA more than doubled, rising to 305. U.S. Rep. Joseph Kennedy, a harsh critic of the school, claimed that SOA graduates planned the massacre of forty-five indígenas at Acteal, Chiapas. More recently, the U.S. military sought to sanitize the SOA by bestowing on it a new name: the Western Hemisphere Institute of Security Cooperation.

The formation of close ties between high-ranking officers and large foreign and domestic firms contributed to the making of a reactionary military mentality. In Argentina in the 1960s, 143 retired officers of the highest ranks held 177 of the leading posts in the country's largest industrial and financial enterprises, most of which were foreign controlled. Latin America thus developed its own military-industrial complex. Through all these means, the United States acquired an enormous influence over the Latin American military.

The CIA's close links with Latin American military and their counterrevolutionary projects were well known. The CIA's 1954 role in the destruction of the government of Jacobo Arbenz Guzmán, Guatemala's democratically elected reformist president, offers a classic example. Not until May 1997 did the CIA make public the classified records bearing on that intervention. Perhaps the "most chilling document" in the collection, writes Kate Doyle, is an unsigned "Study of Assassination," in which the agency laid out "in excruciating detail" its proposals to murder leading members of the Arbenz government and military. The CIA also compiled hit lists in preparation for the coup. The success of the operation convinced President Eisenhower that such clandestine operations were "a safe, inexpensive substitute for [the use of] armed force." CIA counterinsurgency aid to Guatemala continued until 1995, when evidence surfaced that an "agency asset," Guatemalan Army Col. Julio Roberto Alpiréz, had been involved in the murders of U.S. citizen Michael DeVine and Efraín Bámaca Velásquez, a guerrilla leader married to the Harvard-educated lawyer Jennifer Harbury. The U.S. government still provided counter-drug aid to Guatemala, even though most of the major syndicates uncovered by the Drug Enforcement Agency (DEA) had direct links to Guatemalan military officers.

Revolutionary Cuba was next in line after Guatemala; in 1960, President Eisenhower signed a directive authorizing the CIA to "get rid of Castro." The Bay of Pigs disaster of April 1961 was "a direct descendant" of the Guatemalan operation, devised on the assumption that Castro would suffer the same "loss of nerve" that Arbenz had in 1954. When that failed, the agency launched a terrorist campaign of sabotage against Cuba and unsuccessfully attempted to assassinate Castro. In 1998, the *New York Times* published two sensational reports based on interviews with the anti-Castro Cuban exile Luis Posada Carriles, as well as declassified CIA files. In the interviews, Posada claimed credit for a series of terrorist activities, including a wave of bombings of Cuban hotels and restaurants in 1997 that killed one tourist and alarmed the Cuban government. "The CIA," he said, "taught us everything—everything. They taught us explosives, how to kill, bomb, trained us in sabotage." The CIA, for its part, commended Posada in one document as "of good character, very reliable, security-conscious," and in another said his "performance in all assigned tasks has been excellent." Posada also claimed that he had received considerable financial support for his terrorist activities from the late Jorge Mas Canosa, the millionaire founder of the anti-Castro Cuban American National Foundation, a close political ally of successive U.S. presidents, including President Clinton; evidence in the intelligence files supported his claim.

In Chile, after the election of socialist Salvador Allende as president in 1970, the CIA desperately tried to prevent his inauguration. According to a recently declassified report on the CIA's Chilean Task Force Activities, the agency "focused on provoking a military coup," the principal obstacle to which was the "apolitical, constitutional-oriented inertia of the Chilean military." To overcome this obstacle, President Nixon ordered CIA chief Richard Helms to "make the economy scream" and pursued a two-track policy combining economic destabilization with shipments of arms and money to right-wing army officers. This eventually led to the overthrow and death of Allende and the establishment of a repressive military dictatorship that ruled for two decades and still casts its long shadow over a supposedly "democratic" Chile.

In 2001, the sons of former Chilean Commander-in-Chief René Schneider, killed in 1970 in a failed attempt to kidnap him, filed suit in a U.S. federal court seeking more than $3 million in damages. The suit named Henry Kissinger, President Nixon's national security adviser at the time; Richard Helms, former CIA director; and the U.S. government, who together were responsible for "summary execution," assault, and civil rights violations. Citing recently declassified CIA documents, the suit charged that U.S. authorities conspired to remove Schneider because he stood in the way of their planned military coup to prevent Salvador Allende from taking office as Chile's elected president. Judges in Chile and Argentina unsuccessfully sought to secure Kissinger's testimony regarding his knowledge of Operation Condor, a vast operation organized between 1970 and 1980 by the dictatorships of Latin America's Southern Cone to aid each other in the elimination of their political opponents, without regard for national borders.

In 1981, the CIA turned Honduras into a base for a secret war against Sandinist Nicaragua and, with the cooperation of the Honduran military, created a new army intelligence unit called Battalion 316 to counter subversion.

Declassified documents revealed that the CIA trained the unit in surveillance, interrogation, and torture. The battalion learned well, torturing hundreds of Honduran citizens and "disappearing" many others.

The militarization of U.S. foreign policy clearly had a decisive impact on the military in Latin America. Over the course of the late twentieth century, it increasingly abandoned its nationalist character and embraced its new role as a neoliberal guardian of private property and foreign investment. It remained unclear whether, in the face of a growing popular democratic movement against neoliberalism, the Latin American military would remain in its barracks or reprise its earlier role.

12

Forging a New Nation: The Mexican Revolution and the Populist Challenge

FOCUS QUESTIONS

- What were the major factions in the Mexican Revolution? What were their programs, and how did their rivalry shape Mexico's new nationalist state?

- What were the policies of the Reconstruction Era (1920–1933), and how did they affect development?

- What was Cárdenas's reform program (1934–1940), and how did it affect workers and peasants?

- What role did women play in the Revolution, and how did it affect their struggle for equality?

- What were the major trends in Mexico after 1940, and how did they affect development?

THE MEXICAN REVOLUTION was the first popular, social revolution in twentieth-century Latin America. Although historians still debate its precise meaning, most agree that it transformed a mechanical peace imposed by the iron fist of Porfirio Díaz's liberal dictatorship into a cohesive social order formed on the basis of genuine popular support. Díaz had created a unified nation-state with clearly defined borders and uniform laws that regulated land, labor, and commodities, but considerable popular resistance remained. As long as domestic peace depended on the fear of armed force, a lasting social stability rooted in national **hegemony** (that is, a widespread popular identification with, and voluntary deference to, the authority of a powerful national state) was impossible. However, such hegemony required a new nationalist ideology and a nation-state that would protect all sectors of society rather than merely secure the interests of a tiny, wealthy, privi-

leged, and light-skinned elite. As always, however, this new nationalism was a product of conflict and negotiation among groups and social classes with distinctly different interests. This was the primary achievement of the Mexican Revolution, and it soon became a model for other Latin American nations that were undergoing similar changes in the late nineteenth and early twentieth centuries.

On the eve of the 1910 presidential election, signs of unrest multiplied in Mexico. Peasant risings and workers' strikes became more frequent, and the Mexican Liberal Party (PLM), founded and led by the exiled revolutionary journalist Ricardo Flores Magón, intensified its conspiratorial activities. Drawn by the PLM's programmatic commitment to "equality between the sexes" and repelled by miserably low wages, abusive working conditions, and legal discrimination, women like Juana Gutiérrez de Mendoza and Dolores Jiménez became influential activists, organizers, and propagandists

1910	Wealthy landowner Francisco Madero overthrows dictatorship of Porfirio Díaz
1911	Zapata, a peasant leader from Morelos, demands immediate re-distribution of lands to landless peasants
1912	Madero wins presidential election but fails to control peasant revolutionaries, alienating oligarchs
1913	Victoriano Huerta overthrows Madero and executes him
1914	Peasant revolutionaries, Villa and Zapata, join forces at Convention of Aguascalientes; U.S. troops invade Veracruz to protect oil fields
1915	U.S. unofficially recognizes Carranza's government
1916	Villa attacks U.S. military base in Columbus, New Mexico, to provoke U.S. invasion of Mexico and discredit Carranza
1917	Populist Constitution limits foreign investment rights and protects Mexican workers
1921–1928	Obregón and Calles institutionalize the achievements of their populist revolution by creating a National Bank and establishing the National Revolutionary Party
1934–1940	Cárdenas announces populist reforms, including land redistribution, protection of workers' rights, and nationalization of both oil and railroad industries
1940–1952	Wartime prosperity and state-centered import-substitution industrialization policies promote national industrial expansion
1968	Tlatelolco Square Massacre ignites *guerra sucia* (dirty war) against popular resistance
1971	Avándaro Music Festival disintegrates into youthful lower-class violence against inequality and authoritarian State

in this growing opposition to Porfirio Díaz's dictatorial regime. Divisions soon appeared within the oligarchy. Bernardo Reyes, a foe of the Científicos and the powerful governor of Nuevo León, whose rule combined iron-fisted repression with reformist rhetoric, announced his candidacy for the post of vice president. Reyes saw this office as a stepping-stone to the presidency when Díaz, who was eighty years old in 1910, died or retired.

In an unusual atmosphere of political ferment and debate, there appeared a tract for the times: *The Great National Problems* (1909) by the lawyer Andrés Molina Enríquez. Financed by Reyes, the book combined the customary eulogies of Díaz with incisive criticism of his political system and especially of his agrarian policy. Its denunciation of the latifundio and appeal for land reform anticipated the radical slogans of the coming revolution.

Díaz had contributed to this ferment by announcing in 1908 that Mexico was now ready for democracy and that he would welcome the emergence of an opposition party. Francisco Madero, a Coahuila hacendado whose extensive family interests included cattle ranches, wheat farms, vineyards, textile factories, and mines, took Díaz at his word. A member of the elite, Madero was no revolutionary, but he feared that continuance of the existing political order would inevitably breed social revolution. Madero made clear, however, that by "democracy," he meant control by an elite. "The ignorant public," he wrote, "should take no direct part in determining who should be the candidate for public office."

Madero criticized Díaz's social policies—his genocidal wars against indigenous communities and violent repression of strikes—as counterproductive; in place of those brutal tactics, he proposed a policy of modest concessions to peasants and workers to reduce mounting tensions and check the growth of radical ideas. Madero regarded democracy as an instrument of social control that would promote the acceptance of capitalism through the grant of limited political and social reforms, with a large stress on education.

In December 1909, Madero began to tour the country, making speeches in which he explained his reform program. In April 1910, an opposition antireelectionist party formed and announced Madero as its candidate for president. Díaz at first refused to take Madero seriously but soon, alarmed by his growing popularity, ordered his arrest. In early June, he charged Madero with preparing an armed insurrection; arrests of many of his supporters followed. Shortly after the June 21 election, the government announced that Díaz and his hand-picked vice-presidential candidate, Ramón Corral, had won the election by an almost unanimous vote.

Thereafter, Díaz no longer considered Madero dangerous and released him on bail. Convinced that peaceful means could not remove the dictator, Madero also feared the demands of radical women, peasants, and workers; in September 1910, for example, Dolores Jiménez, a working-class leader of the feminist Daughters of Cuauhtémoc, advocated women's empowerment in their "economic, physical, intellectual, and moral struggles." Caught between the Scylla of reaction and the Charybdis of lower-class revolution, Madero opted for armed struggle.

On October 7, he fled across the border to Texas and from there announced the Plan of San Luis Potosí. Declaring the recent elections null and void, Madero assumed the title of provisional president of Mexico but promised to hold free elections as soon as conditions permitted. The plan made a vague reference to the return of usurped peasant lands, but most of its articles dealt with political reforms. That U.S. authorities allowed Madero to organize the revolution on U.S. soil with little interference suggests the U.S. government's displeasure with Díaz. Fearing that North American domination of investments in Mexico threatened Mexican economic and political independence, the dictator recently had favored British over North American capitalists in granting concessions and had given other indications of an anti-U.S. attitude. The Taft administration evidently hoped that Madero would display a more positive attitude toward U.S. interests.

The Great Revolution, 1910–1920

The Great Revolution got off to a shaky start when Francisco Madero, having crossed back into Mexico,

found only twenty-five supporters waiting for him and hurriedly returned to Texas. Nonetheless, it soon gathered momentum as two major movements of peasant revolt responded to his call. In the huge northern border state of Chihuahua, where peons and small farmers suffered under the iron rule of the Terrazas-Creel clan, masters of a vast landed empire, the rising began under the leadership of Pascual Orozco, a mule driver, and Pancho Villa, a bandit with a reputation for taking from the rich to give to the poor. By the end of 1910, guerrilla armies had seized control of most of the state from federal troops.

Another seat of rebellion was the mountainous southern state of Morelos, where indigenous communities had long waged a losing struggle against encroaching sugar haciendas. Here the mestizo insurgent leader Emiliano Zapata, attracted by the promise of land reform in the Plan of San Luis Potosí, proclaimed his loyalty to Madero.

Meanwhile, in March 1911, former PLM leaders Camilo Arriaga and Dolores Jiménez, now *maderistas* (Madero's supporters), organized Mexico City's Complot de Tacubaya, an urban revolt against Díaz that advocated a revolutionary social agenda that included protection of indigenous rights, agrarian reform, an eight-hour workday, equal pay for equal work, and equal access to education. In the political context of a countryside in arms, the Tacubaya uprising, although prematurely betrayed and suppressed, nonetheless successfully undermined Díaz's confidence in his ability to rule and led directly to a decision to seek compromise with Madero a month later.

In May 1911, moreover, the Zapatistas won two decisive victories. Rather than face an invasion of the poorly defended capital by Zapata's dreaded agrarian rebels, Díaz and his advisers decided to reach an agreement with Madero. Disregarding urgent warnings by the left wing of the revolutionary movement against compromises with the Díaz regime, Madero signed the Treaty of Ciudad Juárez on May 21, which provided for the removal of Díaz but left intact all existing institutions. It was completely silent on the subject of social change. On May 25, the aged dictator resigned the presidency, and a few days later, he left for Europe. Francisco León de la Barra, the

Mexican ambassador to the United States, assumed the interim presidency.

On June 7, 1911, Madero entered Mexico City in triumph, but the rejoicing of the crowds who thronged into the streets to greet the "apostle of democracy" was premature. The provisional president was loyal to the old regime and had no sympathy with the revolution. The *Porfirista* aristocracy and its allies had not given up hope of regaining power; they regarded the compromise that made León de la Barra provisional president a tactical retreat, a means of gaining time to allow the revolutionary wave to subside so they could prepare a counterblow. Under the interim president, the huge Díaz bureaucracy remained largely intact. The reactionary officer corps remained in command of the federal army and burned for revenge over the revolutionary peasant armies that had defeated it.

Social conditions throughout the country remained largely unchanged. The provisional government sought to disband the revolutionary troops and restore the status quo. León de la Barra sent federal forces into Morelos to initiate hostilities against the Zapatistas, who had confiscated large estates and distributed land to the villages. Madero's ineffective efforts to halt the fighting and mediate between Zapata and León de la Barra only deepened the reactionaries' hatred for the visionary meddler who had unleashed anarchy in Mexico. However, the revolutionary wave was still running strong, and reaction had to bide its time. In October 1911, overwhelming majorities elected Madero and his running mate, José María Pino Suárez, president and vice president. Despite numerous public protests and petitions, led by leaders like Juana Gutiérrez de Mendoza and her *Amigas del Pueblo* (AP), feminists failed to secure voting rights, but their political agitation in support of the "apostle of democracy" was undiminished.

MADERO'S PRESIDENCY: INADEQUACY AND REVOLT

It soon became evident that the "apostle" had no fundamental solutions for Mexico's grave social and economic problems. Even on the political plane,

Madero's beliefs were not progressive. His conception of democracy was a formal democracy that would give the masses the illusion of power and participation in political life but would vest all decision making in the hands of an elite.

In regard to economic and social democracy, his vision was even more limited. Madero allowed workers to organize trade unions and to strike and permitted workers to form a national center, the *Casa del Obrero Mundial*, in Mexico City. However, his answer to the agrarian problem was a totally inadequate program to purchase land from large landowners and recover national land for distribution among landless peasants. In fact, Madero, who believed that large landholdings were essential to modernize Mexican agriculture, totally opposed land reform at the expense of the haciendas. Madero's retreat on the land issue led to a break with his most faithful ally, Emiliano Zapata. Zapata urged Madero to carry out the agrarian provisions of the Plan of San Luis Potosí. Madero refused, arguing that the treaties that set up the interim government of León de la Barra obliged him to accept the legality of the legal and administrative decisions of the Díaz regime. Madero also demanded the total surrender and disarmament of Zapata's peasant troops.

Convinced that Madero did not intend to carry out his pledges to restore land to the villages, Zapata announced his own program on November 28, 1911. The Plan of Ayala called for the immediate return of "the lands, woods, and waters usurped by the hacendados, Científicos, or caciques through tyranny and venal justice." The Zapatista movement soon spread to other states in central and southern Mexico. Historian John Womack paints a vivid portrait of these peasant armies and their commanders, one of which was a woman warrior known as "La China." Clad "in rags, some in plundered finery, wearing silk stockings and dresses, sandals, straw hats, and gun belts," these armed women so terrorized federales and hacendados in the region that even veteran Zapatista commanders "treated La China with respect." Madero sent a series of generals against Zapata and his allies but failed to crush the revolt.

Library of Congress

The *soldaderas* (women who joined their lovers or husbands and often fought at their side) made their own contribution to the victory of the Mexican Revolution.

Madero's failure to carry out a genuine agrarian reform lost him the trust and support of the revolutionary peasantry without mollifying the reactionaries, who resented his modest concessions to labor and his efforts to transform Mexico into a bourgeois democracy with freedom of speech and press and the rule of law. They also feared that under pressure from the peasantry and under the influence of urban middle-class reformers like Luis Cabrera, a strong advocate of land reform, Madero might move farther to the left.

The aristocracy, its possessions and influence almost intact, dreamed of restoring the lost paradise of Don Porfirio, when peasants, workers, and natives knew their place. Almost from the day that Madero took office in November 1911, therefore, counterrevolutionary revolts sprouted in various parts of Mexico. Most serious was a revolt in the north led by Pascual Orozco, who was encouraged and bribed by conservative elements in Chihuahua, especially the Terrazas-Creel clan. Federal troops under Gen. Victoriano Huerta crushed the Orozco revolt in a series of battles, but Huerta's victory, joined with the alienation of Zapata and other of Madero's old revolutionary allies, increased Madero's dependence on an officer corps whose loyalty to his cause was highly dubious.

Abortive revolts followed one after another throughout the rest of 1912. The danger to Madero increased as it became clear that he had lost the support of the United States. Although Madero had made it apparent that he favored foreign investments and guaranteed their security, he refused to show special favors to U.S. capitalists and warned foreign investors that the crony system that had operated under Díaz was dead. This independent spirit, plus Madero's legalization of trade unions and strikes and his inability to cope with the peasant revolution and establish stability, alienated the United States, whose foreign policy, originally favorable to Madero, turned against him.

U.S. Ambassador Henry Lane Wilson became increasingly hostile to Madero. In February 1912, a hundred thousand U.S. troops were stationed along the border, and throughout the year, Wilson made vehement threats of intervention if the Madero government failed to protect U.S. lives and property.

Meanwhile, preparations for a coup d'état were under way in the capital. The blow fell on February 9, 1913, when the military garrison at Tacubaya "pronounced" against Madero and marched on the National Palace. Meanwhile, the U.S. ambassador, in complete sympathy with the counterrevolutionary revolt, sent Madero a sharp protest against the conduct of military operations in Mexico City because they threatened U.S. life and property. At his urging, the British, German, and Spanish representatives sent similar demands. As the crisis moved toward a climax, Wilson became feverishly active. On February 14, he demanded that the Mexican government begin negotiations with the other warring parties; otherwise, U.S. Marines would occupy Mexican ports. The same day, Wilson invited other foreign diplomats to a conference at which they agreed to force Madero to resign and sent him a message to that effect, but Madero firmly rejected the demand. He would rather die, he said, than allow foreign intervention.

HUERTA'S DICTATORSHIP

Ambassador Wilson, clearly coordinating his activities with the conspirators, encouraged Huerta to arrest the president and other members of his government. Wilson also mediated a dispute over who should head the new regime, and a meeting at the U.S. embassy produced an agreement that Huerta should head a provisional government. To give some semblance of legality to his usurpation, Huerta obtained the "voluntary" resignations of Madero and Pino Suárez in return for the promise

that they would then be free to leave Mexico. An intimidated Congress accepted the resignations and recognized Huerta as provisional president, almost without dissent. The question of what to do with Madero remained. Asked by Huerta for his advice, the U.S. ambassador replied that he should do "what was best for the country." Despite urgent requests by other members of the diplomatic corps and Madero's wife that he intercede to save Madero's life, Wilson refused. On the evening of February 22, Huerta's forces murdered Madero and Pino Suárez during their transfer from the National Palace to the penitentiary.

Huerta's seizure of power, which the landed aristocracy, big Capitalists, and the church greeted with rejoicing, restored the Díaz system of personal dictatorship. Hoping to broaden its social base and conceal its reactionary character as long as possible, Huerta for a time continued Madero's labor policies, but as the terrorist nature of the regime became more apparent and labor increasingly allied itself with the anti-Huerta movement, he proceeded to arrest its leaders and eventually closed down the Casa del Obrero Mundial.

THE OPPOSITION: ZAPATA, VILLA, CARRANZA, AND OBREGÓN

Huerta had counted on a quick victory over the peasant revolutionaries of the south and favorable reception of his coup d'état by conservative economic and political interests in the north. The revolutionary wave, still running strong, rose even higher in reaction to Madero's brutal murder and the imposition of Huerta's terrorist regime. Zapata intensified his struggle against local great landowners, Huerta's allies, and federal troops. In the northern border states of Sonora, Chihuahua, and Coahuila, meanwhile, an anti-Huerta coalition of disparate social groups—liberal hacendados, middle classes, miners, industrial workers, *vaqueros* (cowboys), and peasants—began to take form. By forcing Huerta to commit a considerable part of his troops to the campaign in the south, Zapata ensured the success of the revolutionary movement that sprang up anew in the north.

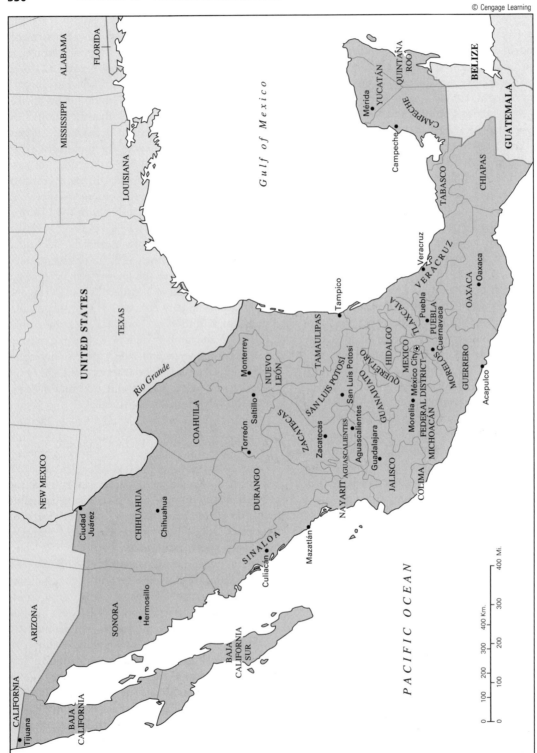

© Cengage Learning

Modern Mexico

Pancho Villa assumed leadership of the Constitutionalists, as Huerta's northern opponents called themselves. Enjoying an immense popularity among the state's vaqueros, he soon controlled almost all Chihuahua and imposed a revolutionary new order on the state. He employed his soldiers as a civil militia and administrative staff to restore normal life. Villa ordered a reduction of meat prices and distributed money, clothing, and other goods to the poor. Education was a passion with the almost illiterate Villa. According to the U.S. correspondent John Reed, who accompanied him, Villa established some fifty new schools in Chihuahua City.

Clearly, Villa's social policies were radical by comparison to other Constitutionalist leaders in the neighboring states of Sonora and Coahuila. In December 1913, he expropriated without compensation the properties of the pro-Huerta oligarchy in Chihuahua. His agrarian program, however, differed in significant ways from that of Zapata. Whereas Zapata confiscated estates and promptly distributed them among the peasants, Villa's decree provided that they should remain under state control until the victory of the revolution. He used the revenues from these estates to finance the revolutionary struggle and support the widows and orphans of revolutionary soldiers. After the revolutionary victory, the funds would finance pensions for these widows and orphans, compensation for veterans, restoration of village lands that the hacendados had usurped, and payment of taxes left unpaid by the hacendados.

Meanwhile, Villa gave his lieutenants control of some confiscated haciendas, and the state administered the rest. He sold cattle in the United States to secure arms and ammunition for his army, and he distributed meat on a large scale to the urban unemployed, to public institutions like orphanages and children's homes, and for sale in the markets. The agrarian programs of Villa and Zapata differed because the economy of the north relied on cattle raising, not on subsistence agriculture, and required large economic units to be administered by the state or on a cooperative basis. In addition, the percentage of peasants in the population was much smaller in the north and the problem of land hunger much less acute.

In the neighboring state of Coahuila, meanwhile, the elderly Venustiano Carranza, a great landowner who abandoned Díaz in 1911 to join Madero, now led a revolt against Huerta. On March 26, 1913, he announced his Plan of Guadalupe, which called for the overthrow of the dictator and the restoration of constitutional government but did not mention social reforms. Carranza assumed the title of first chief of the Constitutionalist Army.

Meanwhile, within Mexico City, Huerta also faced clandestine opposition, led by prominent intellectuals like José Vasconcelos and Martín Luís Guzmán. Just as troublesome, however, was the public resistance of the feminist Loyalty Club, headed by María Árias Bernal, which protested the regime's brutality and organized a public demonstration at the site of Madero's tomb.

INTERVENTION BY THE UNITED STATES

By the beginning of 1914, the Constitutionalist revolt had assumed significant proportions, and Huerta's fall appeared inevitable. Meanwhile, in March 1913, Woodrow Wilson had succeeded Taft as president of the United States. Alone among the great powers, Wilson's government refused to recognize the Huerta regime, although it continued to embargo revolutionary arms purchases while permitting U.S. arms sales to Huerta to consolidate his rule. Wilson justified his nonrecognition policy with moralistic rhetoric, refusing to recognize a government that had come to power illegally. More important, he believed that Huerta could not provide the stable political climate that U.S. interests required in Mexico. Noting Huerta's strong support among European governments, Wilson also suspected that Huerta had cut a deal to grant British and German investors privileged access to Mexican markets at the expense of U.S. business. In the first six months of his regime, Huerta clearly favored British interests, thereby solidifying his support in London and further alienating Washington.

Wilson's concern with a suitable political climate for U.S. investments emerged in a note sent to British officials in November 1913. He assured them that his U.S. government "intends not merely to force Huerta from power, but also to exert every influence it can exert to secure Mexico a better government under which all contracts and business concessions will be safer than they have been."

Shortly thereafter, growing tensions between England and Germany, ultimately leading to World War I, dramatically affected the Huerta regime's security and international backing. Both nations now openly courted the United States and began to distance themselves from Huerta. By yielding to a British request for uniform rates on all goods shipped through the nearly completed Panama Canal, Wilson obtained an end of British support for Huerta in early 1914. As a result, Huerta's financial position became increasingly difficult. Seeking to avert a catastrophe, he suspended payment on the interest on the national debt for six months, but that extraordinary measure only increased Huerta's difficulties. Foreign creditors began to demand the seizure of Mexican customhouses, and some even clamored for immediate intervention. By February 1914, Wilson decided to use force. After receiving assurances from Carranza's agent in Washington that the Constitutionalists would respect foreign property rights, including "just and equitable concessions," Wilson lifted the existing embargo on arms shipments to the Carranza forces.

Wilson found a pretext for intervention when local officials arrested U.S. sailors from the cruiser *Dolphin*, who had landed in a restricted area of Tampico. Huerta ordered their immediate release with an apology, but the ship's commander, under orders from Washington, demanded a formal disavowal of the action, severe punishment for the responsible Mexican officer, and a twenty-one-gun salute to the U.S. flag. For Huerta to grant these demands might have meant political suicide, and he refused.

President Wilson now sent a fleet into the Gulf of Mexico, and on April 21, 1914, learning that a German merchant ship loaded with munitions was headed for Veracruz, he ordered the seizure of the city. When Mexican batteries at the fortress of San Juan de Ulua attempted to prevent a landing, U.S. ships silenced them. Huerta's forces evacuated Veracruz the same day, but the local population and

cadets of the naval academy continued a courageous resistance until April 27, when U.S. troops occupied Veracruz, setting off a wave of anti-Yankee sentiment in Mexico and a number of Latin American countries. Meanwhile Carranza, whom Wilson had hoped to control, bitterly denounced the U.S. action and demanded the immediate evacuation of Veracruz.

Shortly thereafter, the Huerta regime's collapse seemed imminent. Recognizing that his situation had become hopeless, Huerta took flight for Europe on July 15. Huerta's fall deprived the United States of any pretext for continuing its armed intervention, but Wilson delayed the evacuation of Veracruz as long as possible in the hope of securing commitments from Carranza that effectively would have prevented any basic changes in Mexico's social and economic structure. Despite hints that "fatal consequences" might follow, Carranza resolutely rejected these demands and continued to insist on the end of the military intervention. U.S. troops finally evacuated Veracruz on November 23, 1914.

FIGHTING AMONG THE VICTORS

As the day of complete victory drew near, differences emerged within the Constitutionalist camp, especially between Carranza and Villa. More important than such personal factors as Carranza's jealousy of Villa as a potential rival was Carranza's failure to define his position on such fundamental issues as the agrarian question, the role of the church, and the new political order. Villa, however, sought a revolutionary agreement that clearly defined "the present conflict as a struggle of the poor against the abuses of the powerful." He also wanted the Constitutionalist leaders to agree "to implant a democratic regime ... to secure the well being of the workers, to emancipate the peasants economically, making an equitable distribution of lands or whatever else is needed to solve the agrarian problem."

Under pressure from his generals, who recognized the potential dangers of an open break with Villa, Carranza permitted his representatives to sign the agreement containing this radical idea, which he personally found unacceptable. Villa, however, continued to distrust Carranza, whose actions, notably his unilateral occupation of the capital, confirmed this distrust. Relations also deteriorated between Carranza and Zapata, who had waged war against Huerta independently and refused to recognize Carranza's leadership; a Zapatista manifesto announced the Plan of Ayala and proclaimed the removal of all the old regime's officials.

In October 1914, a convention of revolutionary leaders and their delegates met at Aguascalientes to settle the conflict between Carranza and Villa. The *Villistas* insisted on inviting Zapata to attend, and presently a delegation from "the Liberating Army of the South" arrived. The convention endorsed the Plan of Ayala, assumed supreme authority, called for the resignation of Carranza as first chief, and appointed Gen. Eulalio Gutiérrez provisional president of the nation. Gutiérrez was a compromise candidate pushed by delegates equally opposed to Carranza and Villa. Because Aguascalientes swarmed with Villa's troops, Gutiérrez had no choice but to name Villa commander in chief of the Conventionist Army.

However, Carranza refused to accept the decisions of the Aguascalientes convention, claiming it had no authority to depose him. When he failed to meet the deadline for his resignation—November 10—the armies of Zapata and Villa advanced on the capital and occupied it. Carranza retreated with his depleted forces to Veracruz, which the Americans had evacuated shortly before. According to historian John Hart, although the United States remained suspicious of Carranza's nationalism, its decision to withdraw from Veracruz in favor of the Constitutionalists reflected U.S. fears of the revolutionary convention's radical threat to U.S. economic interests, especially investments in Mexican oil production. Veracruz became a safehouse for *Carrancista* forces led by Álvaro Obregón, a popular young ranchero commander who had remained loyal to Carranza and rebuilt his army with the aid of arms and munitions stockpiled during the U.S. occupation.

Although the peasant revolutionaries controlled the capital and much of the country, they could not consolidate their successes. Unskilled in

politics, they entrusted state power to the unreliable provisional president, Gutiérrez, a former general in Carranza's army, who sabotaged the Conventionist's war effort and opened secret negotiations with Obregón. Meanwhile, Conservatives at the convention strongly opposed land reform, expropriation of foreign properties, and other radical social changes. Villa's sympathies on land reform were with the radicals, but he avoided taking sides in the dispute, probably because he believed that unity was necessary to gain both a rapid military victory and recognition by the United States, which he also regarded as essential to his final triumph. For these reasons, the convention proved unable to forge a clear national program of socioeconomic reforms that could unite the interests of the peasantry, industrial workers, and the middle class. His later attempts to broaden his program to attract labor, the middle class, and even national Capitalists were too little and too late.

The Constitutionalists did not make the same mistake. At the insistence of Obregón and intellectuals like Luís Cabrera, who were aware of the need for broadening the social base of the Constitutionalist movement, Carranza adopted a program of social reforms that aimed to win the support of peasants and workers. In December 1914, during the darkest days of the Constitutionalist cause, Carranza issued his "Adiciones" to the Plan of Guadalupe, promising agrarian reform and better conditions for industrial workers. Other decrees followed: On January 6, 1915, he restored lands usurped from the villages and expropriated additional needed land from haciendas. (Simultaneously, Carranza secretly promised the hacendados that he would return the haciendas that had been confiscated by revolutionary authorities—promises that he ultimately would keep.) Carranza's agrarian decrees gained him a certain base among the peasantry. Carranza courted labor support by the promise of a minimum-wage law applying to all branches of industry and by affirming the right of workers to form trade unions and to strike. He also appealed for women's support, and thousands flocked to his ranks from diverse social classes. According to historian Shirlene Soto, working-class radicals like Artemisa Sáenz Royo, a

In early December 1914, Pancho Villa (*on throne*) met with Emiliano Zapata (*center right, with sombrero*) in Mexico City, where both attended the installation of a new president. Earlier, Villa and Zapata had reached an agreement on a course of action for the revolution, but the arrangement soon fell apart.

labor organizer who later served in the "red battalions," joined with middle-class feminists such as Hermila Galindo de Topete, Carranza's private secretary, to demand "women's complete equality, including sexual equality."

After Obregón's troops reoccupied Mexico City in January 1915, an alliance formed between the Carranza government and the Casa del Obrero Mundial, which reorganized after Huerta's fall. Members of the Casa agreed to join "the struggle against reaction," meaning above all the revolutionary peasantry. Six "red battalions" of workers formed and made an important contribution to the offensive launched by Obregón against Villa and Zapata in January 1915. Inadequate under-

standing on the part of the peasant and working-class leaders of their common interests and the skillful opportunism of the middle-class politicians in Carranza's camp contributed to this disastrous division between labor and the peasantry.

With growing support from a diverse, cross-class political constituency, and emboldened by financial and arms transfusions from the United States, the Constitutionalists benefited from a dramatic shift in the balance of forces in Mexico. Carranza's troops forced Villa to evacuate Mexico City on January 19, and a few months later, Obregón decisively defeated Villa's forces in the battle of Celaya. Shortly thereafter, Carranza loyalists inflicted heavy losses on the Zapatistas.

In October 1915, after unsuccessful efforts to play off the revolutionary chiefs against each other or to achieve a coalition under U.S. leadership, President Wilson acknowledged Carranza's ascendancy and extended de facto recognition of his regime; equally important, he placed an arms embargo on Carranza's opponents. However, the United States had not abandoned its efforts to influence the course of the Mexican Revolution. A memorandum to Carranza dictated the conditions he must meet before he could obtain *de jure* recognition. These conditions amounted to protection of foreign economic rights, religious freedom, and democratic elections. These demands were as unacceptable to Carranza in October 1915 as they had been a year before.

In early 1916, relations between the United States and Mexico deteriorated sharply. In part, this resulted from initial efforts by Mexican federal and state authorities to regulate the operations of foreign oil companies. A crisis arose in March when Villa, angered by the arms embargo and wrongly convinced that Carranza had bought U.S. recognition by agreeing to a plan to convert Mexico into a U.S. protectorate, raided Columbus, New Mexico, in an apparent effort to force Carranza to show his hand. The Wilson administration responded by ordering Gen. John Pershing to pursue Villa into Mexico. The United States counted on the enmity between Villa and Carranza to secure the latter's neutrality. However, Carranza denounced the invasion, demanded the immediate withdrawal of U.S. forces, and prepared for war. In a note to other Latin American nations, the Mexican government affirmed its commitment to repel the "foreign invasion," defended Mexican sovereignty, and condemned the U.S. intervention because it aimed to restore privileged treatment of foreign capital.

The United States had anticipated an easy victory, but Pershing's hot pursuit of the elusive Villa proved a fiasco, and Wilson accepted Carranza's offer to negotiate a settlement. Wilson was unsuccessful in his efforts to link the evacuation of U.S. forces with acceptance of the U.S. formula for Mexican domestic policy. In January 1917,

influenced by the troubled international scene and his conviction that a war with Mexico would involve at least half a million men, Wilson decided to liquidate the Mexican venture. Mexican nationalism had won a major victory over yet another effort by the United States to impose its hegemony.

THE CONSTITUTION OF 1917

In the fall of 1916, Carranza called for the election of deputies to a convention to frame a new constitution and prepare the way for his election as president. The convention opened in Querétaro on December 1, 1916. Because it effectively excluded women and those who had not sworn loyalty to his 1913 Plan of Guadalupe, the constitution likely would reflect Carranza's ideas. Consequently, the initial draft did not contemplate a radical agrarian reform; for labor, it merely proclaimed workers' rights to form organizations for "lawful purposes," to hold "peaceful" assemblies, and to work.

However, these abstract proposals were unsatisfactory to a majority of the deputies, who formed the radical wing of the convention. The principal representative of this left wing was Francisco J. Múgica, a young general who helped make the first land distribution of the revolution. The radicals obtained majority approval to create a commission to revise Carranza's project. Múgica himself was largely responsible for Article 3, which struck a heavy blow at church control of education by specifically forbidding "religious corporations" and "ministers of any cult" to establish or conduct schools.

Hermila Galindo and other women revolutionaries were quite interested in Articles 34 and 35, which dealt with citizenship and voting rights. Addressing the convention, Galindo appealed to the delegates' "sense of justice as popular representatives" and argued that women should have an equal right to vote and hold office precisely because working women paid taxes, obeyed the same laws as men, and participated fully in the revolutionary struggle for social justice. But others, especially the more radical delegates like Luís Monzón and Inés Malváez, early supporters of the PLM and principled proponents of gender equality, opposed women's suffrage for practical political reasons. They feared that the vast majority of women, sheltered from the harsh realities of the working world (less than 20 percent worked for wages in 1917) and seduced by a conservative Catholic Church, would use the franchise to restrain the revolution's radical anticapitalist, anticlerical tendencies. Fear triumphed over principle, and the constitutional convention denied women citizenship and political rights.

Nonetheless, wage-earning women did win important protections in Article 123, which dealt with the rights of labor. Carranza had asked only to empower the federal government to enact labor legislation, but the convention went much further. It provided for the eight-hour day; secured childbirth benefits for women, including paid prenatal and postnatal maternity leaves; and required companies that had more than fifty women employees to provide on-site childcare. It abolished the *tienda de raya*, (company store) and debt servitude and guaranteed the right of workers to organize, bargain collectively, and strike, making it the most advanced labor code in the contemporary world.

Article 27, which dealt with property rights, had an equally advanced character. It proclaimed the nation the original owner of all lands, waters, and the subsoil; the state could expropriate them, but only with compensation to the owners. National ownership of water and the subsoil was inalienable, but individuals and companies could obtain concessions for their exploitation. Foreigners granted this privilege must agree to obey Mexican laws and not invoke the protection of their governments. Of prime importance were the same article's agrarian provisions. It annulled all measures passed since 1856 that alienated ejidos (communal lands); if the pueblos needed more land, they could acquire it by expropriation from neighboring haciendas.

These and other provisions of the constitution of 1917 made it the most progressive law code of its time. It laid legal foundations to attack the latifundio, weaken the power of the church, and regulate the operations of foreign capital in Mexico, but the constitution was not anticapitalist. It protected private property, sought to control, rather than eliminate, foreign enterprises, and created favorable conditions for the development of national capitalism.

CARRANZA'S PRESIDENCY

As president, Carranza soon made it clear that he did not intend to implement the reform articles of the constitution. He distributed only a trifling amount of land to the villages. Carranza returned many confiscated haciendas to their former owners, and others he turned over to his favorite generals. Official corruption existed on a massive scale. The working class suffered severe repression. Carranza shut down the Casa del Obrero Mundial and ignored the constitution's promise of free education. Only in Carranza's foreign policy, marked by a genuine revolutionary nationalism, did the spirit of the constitution live. Carranza staunchly resisted U.S. pressure to guarantee that Article 27 of the constitution would not damage foreign interests. He kept Mexico neutral in World War I and insisted on an independent Mexican diplomatic position in the hemisphere, postures that the United States regarded as unfriendly.

Carranza also appealed to upper- and middle-class women with decrees that legalized civil divorce, established alimony rights, and authorized women to own and manage property. On April 9, 1917, he signed the Law of Family Relations, which guaranteed women equal rights to exercise guardianship and child custody, file lawsuits, and sign contracts. However, cultural taboos against divorce and other legal inequities institutionalized what historian Shirlene Soto calls a "sexual double standard" in Mexico.

Meanwhile, Carranza continued to battle the tenacious Zapatista movement in the south and Villa in the north. Against the Zapatistas, Carranza's favorite general, Pablo González, launched campaign after campaign. Zapata's forces diminished, and the territory under his control shrank to the vanishing point, but he remained unconquerable, supported by the affection and loyalty of the peasantry. His fall came through treachery. Proclaiming his loyalty to Zapata, a Carrancista officer arranged to meet with the Tiger of the South, and assassinated him on April 10, 1919. But his people continued their struggle for *tierra y libertad* (land and liberty).

After an unsuccessful effort to extend his power in 1920, Carranza fell victim to a revolt led by his former ally, Álvaro Obregón, who assumed the presidency and restored peace to Mexico, but the work of national reconstruction was yet to begin. It would not be an easy task. The great wind that swept through Mexico had left a devastated land, with hundreds of thousands dead or missing; the Mexican population had actually declined by 1 million since 1910. The constitution of 1917 offered a blueprint for a new and better social order, but major obstacles to change remained.

Reconstructing the State: Rule of the Millionaire Socialists

OBREGÓN AND REFORM

With Obregón, a group of northern generals and politicians came to power to begin the work of economic and social reconstruction that Madero, Huerta, and Carranza were unable or unwilling to achieve. Obregón and his successor, Calles, were of middle-class or even lower-class origins—Obregón had been a mechanic and farmer, Calles a schoolteacher. Both were products of a border region where U.S. cultural influence was strong and where capitalism and capitalist relations were more highly developed than in any other part of Mexico. Obregón and Calles thus possessed a pragmatic business mentality as far removed from the revolutionary agrarian ideology of Zapata as it was from the aristocratic reformism of Carranza. These men deliberately set out to lay the economic, political, and ideological foundations of a Mexican national capitalism.

Aware that the revolution had radicalized the masses, aware of the appeal of socialism and anti-imperialism to the workers on whose support they counted, Obregón and Calles employed a revolutionary rhetoric designed to mobilize popular support and conceal the insignificance of the social changes that took place. In practice, Obregón's program was revolutionary only by contrast with the reactionary trend that characterized the last years of Carranza's rule. Far from promoting socialism, Obregón sought accommodation with all elements of Mexican society except the most reactionary clergy and landlords. He allowed exiles of the most varied political tendency to return to Mexico, and radical intellectuals rubbed shoulders with former Científicos in his government. A ruling class of wealthy generals, capitalists, and landlords held power. Labor and the peasantry were the government's obedient clienteles.

Regarding agrarian reform as a useful safety valve for peasant discontent, Obregón distributed some land to the pueblos, but the process faced intense opposition from hacendados and the church, which condemned it for its neglect of the "just rights of the landlords." Litigation by landlords, their use of armed force to resist occupation of expropriated land, and the opposition of the clergy slowed down the pace of land reform.

Even after a village received land, its prospect for success was poor, for the government failed to provide the peasants with seeds, implements, and adequate credit facilities or modern agricultural training. Any credit assistance they received usually came from government rural banks, which exercised close control over land use, intensifying the client status of the peasantry, or from rural loan sharks. The Obregón land reform was neither swift nor thoroughgoing; by the end of his presidency, he had distributed only some 3 million acres among 624 villages, whereas 320 million acres remained in private hands.

Obregón also encouraged labor to organize, for he regarded trade unions as useful for stabilizing labor-capitalist relations and as an important bulwark of his regime. The principal trade union organization was the *Confederación Regional Obrera Mexicana* (CROM), formed in 1918. Despite the rhetoric of its leaders about "class struggle" and freedom from the "tyranny of capitalism," CROM was about as radical as the American Federation of Labor, with which it maintained close ties. Its perpetual boss was Luis Morones, known for his flashy dress, diamonds, and limousines. As the only labor organization sponsored and protected by the government, CROM had virtually official status. Despite this official protection, Morones's method of personal negotiation with employers yielded scanty benefits to labor; wages barely kept pace with the rising cost of living.

Perhaps the most solid achievements of the Obregón regime were in the areas of education and culture. The creation of a native Mexican capitalism demanded the development of a national consciousness, which meant the integration of indigenous peoples—still made up of so many small nations—into the national market and the new society. From this point of view, they were a key problem of Mexican reconstruction. Because incorporating them into the modern world required a thorough understanding of their past and present conditions of life, the revolutionary regimes encouraged *indigenismo* (a counterhegemonic developmental ideology) on the basis of scientific study of indigenous peoples.

An integral part of indigenismo was a reassessment of indigenous cultural heritage. To insist on the greatness of the old native arts was one way of asserting the value of one's own, of revolting against the tyranny of the pallid, lifeless French and Spanish academicism over Mexican art during the last decades of the Díaz Era. From Europe returned two future giants of the Mexican artistic renaissance, Diego Rivera and David Alfaro Siqueiros, to join another gifted artist, José Clemente Orozco, in creating a militant new art that drew much of its inspiration from the indigenous peoples and their ancient art. Believing that "a heroic art could fortify the will to reconstruction," Obregón's brilliant young secretary of education, José Vasconcelos, offered the walls of public buildings for the painting of murals that glorified the natives, past and present.

The "Indianist" cult had great political significance. The revolution's enemies, unregenerate Porfiristas, clericals, and reactionaries of all stripes, looked back to Spain as the sole source of enduring values in Mexican life. They regarded Cortés as the creator of Mexican nationality, but partisans of the revolution tended to idealize Aztec Mexico (sometimes beyond recognition) and elevated the last Aztec warrior-king, Cuauhtémoc, to the status of a demigod.

Convinced that the school was the most important instrument for unifying the nation—that "to educate was to redeem"—Vasconcelos, with ample financial support from Obregón, launched an imaginative program of cultural missions designed to bring literacy and health to indigenous villages. Professor Elena Torres, a founding member of the Mexican National Council of Women and a fiery socialist feminist, supervised the training of more than four thousand rural teachers, most of whom were women commissioned to bring the gospel of sanitation and literacy to remote pueblos. Torres acquired practical experience in this field during her collaboration with Yucatán state governor Felipe Carrillo Puerto, whose progressive reform agenda included "socialist education," state-supported birth control, women's suffrage, and civil equality.

Vasconcelos also founded teacher-training colleges, agricultural schools, and other specialized schools. An achievement in which he took special pride was the publication of hundreds of classic works in cheap editions for free distribution in the schools. Although these state education programs aimed to promote capitalist land and labor relations by building a patriarchal solidarity with peasants who otherwise were hostile to this goal, the result was much more ambiguous. According to historian Mary Kay Vaughan, the rural literacy crusades "injected new notions of women's work and personhood" into traditional rural images of women, thereby empowering **campesinas** (poor, politically powerless rural women) and their local communities in ways unanticipated by national leaders. These villagers soon took advantage of the growing institutional rivalry between church and state to expand their autonomy.

The new, secular, nationalist school provoked clerical anger, for it threatened to supplant the priest with the teacher as the guiding force of the rural community. The church fought back with all the means at its disposal. Some priests denounced secular education from their pulpits and threatened parents with excommunication if they sent their children to state schools. This campaign induced fanatical villagers to attack teachers, some of whom they killed. Still, Obregón made no effort to implement Article 3 of the constitution, which banned religious primary schools, for he believed that in the absence of enough resources on the part of the state, it was better that Mexican children receive instruction from priests than remain illiterate.

The Catholic issue joined with other issues to aggravate Obregón's relations with the United States. For three years, the U.S. government withheld diplomatic recognition from Obregón in an effort to force him to recognize that Article 27 of the constitution should not apply to mineral concessions obtained by foreigners before 1917. Like Carranza, Obregón respected the principle of nonretroactivity but refused to formalize it in a treaty as a condition of U.S. diplomatic recognition, which he considered humiliating and politically destabilizing.

Obregón's practical policies, however, confirmed his interest in securing the rights of private property essential to foreign investment and capitalist growth. He signed agreements that renewed Mexico's foreign debt service payments, returned the National Railways to private ownership, and resolved various indemnity claims; he also secured Supreme Court rulings that declared unconstitutional any attempt to apply Article 27 retroactively. Faced with Obregón's uncompromising demand for unconditional U.S. recognition and a growing counterrevolutionary insurgency that threatened once again to destabilize Mexico, thereby undermining these agreements, the United States formally recognized the Mexican government in August 1923. When the expected revolt broke out in December, the United States allowed Obregón to procure large quantities of war materiel. Together with the help of the organized labor and peasant movements, this aid enabled Obregón to crush the uprising that reactionary landowners, clergy, and military supported. On November 30, 1924, Obregón's handpicked successor, Plutarco Elías Calles, assumed the presidency of Mexico.

CALLES'S REGIME

In and out of office, as legal president or de facto dictator, Calles dominated the next decade of Mexican politics. Building on the foundations Obregón had laid, he continued his work with much the same methods. His radical phraseology tended to conceal the pragmatic essence of his policy, which was to promote the rapid growth of Mexican national capitalism, whose infrastructure he helped to establish. To strengthen the fiscal and monetary system, he created the Bank of Mexico, the only bank permitted to issue money; a national road commission; and a national electricity code to aid the electric power industry. These measures stimulated the growth of construction and consumer goods industries, in which members of Calles's official family—or the "revolutionary family," as the ruling elite came to be called—were heavily involved. His government generously extended protective tariffs, subsidies, and other forms of aid to industry, both foreign and domestic. In 1925, an assembly plant of the Ford Motor Company began operations in Mexico after Calles and the company negotiated an agreement providing for numerous concessions.

Calles showed more enthusiasm for land reform than Obregón, and the tempo of land distribution increased sharply during his presidency. Like Obregón, Calles regarded land reform as a safety valve for peasant unrest. During the four years of his term, Calles distributed about twice as much land as Obregón had, but less than one-fourth of that amount consisted of arable land because he did not require the hacendados to surrender productive land. Calles also failed to make a serious effort to provide the peasantry with irrigation, fertilizer, implements, or seed. He established an agricultural development bank that was supposed to lend money to the ejidos, promote modern farming techniques, and act as agents for the sale of their produce. Nonetheless, it lent four-fifths of the bank's resources to hacendados who had much superior credit ratings, and many of the bank's agents took advantage of their position to enrich themselves at the expense of the peasants.

Under these conditions, the land reform soon appeared to be a failure. By 1930, grain production had fallen below the levels of 1910, and Calles, concluding that peasant proprietorship was economically undesirable, announced the abandonment of land distribution. Meanwhile, on his own large estates, Calles introduced machinery and other modern agricultural techniques and advised other large landowners to do the same.

Like Obregón, Calles regarded labor unions as desirable because they helped stabilize labor-capitalist relations and avert radical social change. However, by the end of the *Callista* decade, Mexican labor, disillusioned with a corrupt leadership that kept wages at or below the subsistence level, had begun to break away from CROM and form independent unions.

Although Calles had announced his rhetorical support for women's rights, he did little to advance them, prompting women to organize themselves to secure their political, social, and economic liberation. Socialist Elvia Carrillo Puerto, sister of the Yucatecan caudillo, and communist María "Cuca" García organized women government employees; Elena Torres joined García to establish the Mexican Feminist Council, and the Mexican Feminist League appeared a few years later. At successive national and international conferences, however, these women inevitably clashed over issues of class. For example, when a middle-class delegate argued for prohibitions on begging, García objected, "How can one prevent begging when there is no work, when salaries are so meager, and you have the poor in complete helplessness?" Carrillo Puerto concluded the ensuing debate, scorning "the people of class" as "parasites that suck the lifeblood from the country."

Calles continued the Carranza and Obregón policies of asserting Mexico's right to regulate the conditions under which foreign capital could exploit its natural resources, but he was far from hostile to foreign capital. Indeed, he gave assurances that "the government will do everything in its power to safeguard the interests of foreign capitalists who invest money in Mexico."

Nevertheless, a serious dispute with the United States arose in 1925 when the Mexican Congress passed laws to implement Article 27. The most important of these measures required owners of oil leases to exchange their titles for fifty-year concessions dating from the time of acquisition, to be followed, if necessary, by a thirty-year renewal, with the possibility of yet another extension if needed. No Mexican oil well had ever lasted more than eighty years. Far from injuring the foreign oil companies, the law eliminated the vagueness of their status under Article 27, gave them firm titles emanating from the government, and served to quiet more radical demands for outright nationalization. A number of U.S. oil companies denounced the law as confiscatory, however, and threatened to continue drilling operations without confirmatory concessions.

The U.S. State Department vigorously protested the restrictive legislation, and the U.S. ambassador, James R. Sheffield, pursued a hardline, uncompromising policy. By late 1926, the United States appeared to be moving toward war with Mexico. Fortunately, the interventionist policy came under severe attack from progressive Republican senators, the press, church groups, and the academic world. President Calvin Coolidge and Secretary of State Kellogg, realizing that war with Mexico had little national support, sought a way out of the impasse and relied on U.S. international bankers, who had a firmer grasp of Mexican policies and intentions. The appointment of Dwight Morrow, a partner in the financial firm of J. P. Morgan, as ambassador to Mexico in September 1927 marked a turning point in the crisis. Morrow managed to persuade Calles that portions of the oil law had the potential to injure foreign property rights, with the result that the Mexican Supreme Court found unconstitutional that portion of the law setting a time limit on concessions. As rewritten, however, the law still provided for confirmatory concessions and reaffirmed national ownership of the subsoil.

In addition, a serious domestic dispute arose because of the government's alienation of peasant communities disadvantaged by its market reforms and the growing opposition of the church to the whole modernizing thrust of the revolution. Under Calles, this opposition assumed the proportions of a civil war. In January 1926, the church hierarchy signed a letter declaring that the constitution of 1917 "wounds the most sacred rights of the Catholic Church" and disavowed the document. Calles responded by enforcing the anticlerical clauses of the constitution, which had lain dormant. The Calles Law ordered the registration of priests with the civil authorities and the closing of religious primary schools. The church struck back by suspending church services throughout Mexico, a powerful weapon in a country so overwhelmingly Catholic.

Neither this strike nor the boycott organized by the church, which urged the faithful to buy no goods or services except absolute necessities, brought the government to its knees. By the end of 1926, militant Catholics, in frequent alliance with local hacendados, had taken up arms. Guerrilla groups were formed, with the mountainous backcountry of Jalisco the main focus of their activity. Government schools and young teachers sent into remote areas were frequent objects of clerical fury that led to the torture and murder of many teachers. The total number of Catholic guerrillas, known as *Cristeros* from their slogan *Viva Cristo Rey* (Long Live Christ the King), was small, but federal commanders helped keep the insurrection alive by the brutality of their repressions. By the summer of 1927, however, the revolt had largely burned out.

In 1929, after a fanatical Catholic assassinated president-elect Obregón, Calles named a succession of interim presidents to complete his term, crushed a rebellion led by regional military caudillos, and organized the National Revolutionary Party (PNR) to pacify the country and institutionalize the political rule of the "revolutionary family." Under different names and with leaderships of differing composition, this party dominated Mexican politics for six decades. The official party's candidates for president did not lose an election until 2000.

However, the PNR was not immune to conflict. In fact, the Great Depression immediately challenged it by exposing the bankruptcy of capitalist economics and increasing the misery of Mexican peasants and workers. Their growing unrest created fears of a new revolutionary explosion. Rumblings of protest echoed even within the

ruling party. A new generation of young, middle-class reformers demanded vigorous implementation of the constitution of 1917. Some were intellectuals influenced by Marxism and the success of the Soviet example, especially its experience with economic planning, but their basic message was the need to resume the struggle against the latifundio, peonage, and economic and cultural backwardness.

This message resonated loudly at successive meetings of the National Congress of Women Workers and Peasants in the early 1930s. Here, "Cuca" García, for example, accused the Callistas of murdering campesinos and denounced their neglect of poor peasant women: "The agrarian legislation," she thundered, "condemns them always to live in their father's, husband's, or brother's poverty," denying them the "economic independence [that] is the foundation of women's political independence." García was promptly arrested but was later released when thousands of women rallied to her defense at the jail. Despite rancorous debate, these meetings typically demanded progressive state action to expand indigenous rights, protect women workers, raise the minimum wage, accelerate land reform, and promote women's suffrage.

By 1933, the influence of the progressive wing within the PNR had grown. Its acknowledged leader was Gen. Lázaro Cárdenas, governor of Michoacán, who had established an enviable record for honesty, compassion, and concern for commoners. He had spent almost 50 percent of his budget on education, doubling the number of schools in the state. Despite his progressive ideas, he enjoyed the support of the "revolutionary family's" inner circle in 1933. Although there was no doubt that he would be elected, Cárdenas campaigned vigorously, visiting the most remote areas of the country, patiently explaining to workers and peasants his Six-Year Plan to strengthen the ejidos, build modern schools, and develop workers' cooperatives.

Cárdenas and the Populist Interlude

Under Cárdenas, the Mexican Revolution resumed its advance. Land distribution to the villages on a massive scale accompanied a many-sided effort to raise agricultural productivity and improve the quality of rural life. He encouraged labor to replace the old, corrupt leadership with militant leaders and to struggle for improved conditions. A spirit of service began to pervade at least a part of the governmental bureaucracy. Cárdenas set an example to subordinates by displaying the democratic simplicity of his manners, cutting his own salary in half, and making himself available to the delegations of peasants and workers who thronged the waiting rooms of the National Palace.

LAND REFORM

Having consolidated his political control, Cárdenas proceeded to implement his reform program. He privileged agrarian reform and distributed land to the peasantry in a variety of ways, according to the climatic and soil conditions of the different regions. The principal form was the ejido, the communal landholding system under which land could not be mortgaged or alienated (except under special conditions), with each *ejidatario* (member of the community who owned lands in common) entitled to use a parcel of community land. The ejido was the focal point of the agrarian reform, but Cárdenas also distributed land in the form of the *rancho* (the individual smallholding widely prevalent in the northern Mexican states). Finally, in regions where natural conditions favored large-scale cultivation of such commercial crops as sugar, cotton, coffee, rice, and henequen, he organized large cooperative farms (collective ejidos) on a profit-sharing basis. The government generously endowed these enterprises with seeds, machinery, and credit from the *Banco de Crédito Ejidal*.

The Cárdenas government distributed some 45 million acres of land to almost twelve thousand villages. Its distribution program struck a heavy blow at the traditional, semifeudal hacienda and peonage, satisfied the land hunger of the Mexican peasantry for the time being, and promoted a general modernization of Mexican life and society. By 1940, thanks to the land reform and supplemented by the provision of villages with schools, medical care, roads, and other facilities, the standard of

living of the peasantry had risen, if only modestly. These progressive changes in turn contributed to the growth of the internal market and therefore of Mexican industry. The land reform also justified itself in terms of productivity; average agricultural production during the three-year period from 1939 to 1941 was higher than it had been at any time since the beginning of the revolution.

Notwithstanding these benefits and Cárdenas's excellent intentions, the land reform suffered from certain structural defects. To begin with, it primarily aimed to satisfy land hunger by granting or returning land to the villages, and it overlooked the need to establish agricultural units that would be viable from an economic point of view. In many cases, the *ejidal* parcel, especially in areas of dense population, was so small as to form a minifundio. Much of the distributed land was of poor quality (the agrarian law always allowed the landowner to retain a portion of his estate, and naturally landowners kept the best portions for themselves), and aid in the form of seeds, technical assistance, and credit was frequently inadequate.

In addition, peasants received their land from the government, which controlled their activities through the operations of the *Departamento Agrario*, the Banco de Crédito Ejidal, and officially organized peasant leagues; thus, they were increasingly dependent on public authorities. Under Cárdenas, officials of these agencies worked to develop peasant collective initiative and democracy, but they also sought to enmesh the peasantry and its organizations in a bureaucratic network that manipulated them to satisfy the state's own interests. After 1940, Mexican governments increasingly favored large private property and neglected the ejido. In concert with the structural defects of the land reform, this produced a gradual decline of the ejido system and a parallel growth of large landed property, leading to the emergence of a new latifundio.

LABOR REFORM

Cárdenas also revitalized the labor movement. Aware of the sympathetic attitude of the new regime, workers struck in unprecedented numbers for higher wages and better working conditions; in 1935, there were 642 strikes, more than twice the number in the preceding six years. In 1936, the young radical intellectual Vicente Lombardo Toledano organized a new labor federation, the *Confederación de Trabajadores Mexicanos* (CTM), to replace the dying and discredited CROM. Labor supported Cárdenas and he returned the favor.

Labor, the peasantry, and the army became the three main pillars of the official party, reorganized in 1938 and renamed the Party of the Mexican Revolution (PRM). The power of the generals declined because of a policy that raised wages and improved the morale of the rank-and-file and distributed weapons to peasant militia.

Like the land reform, the labor reform had structural flaws that created serious problems for the future. In return for concessions from a paternal government, labor, like the peasantry, incorporated itself into the official apparatus and offered automatic, obligatory support to a government that fundamentally represented the interests of the national bourgeoisie. In the domestic and international situation of the 1930s, the interests of that bourgeoisie and Mexican labor largely coincided. In the changed conditions after 1940, however, labor's loss of independence and the meshing of its organizations with the official apparatus led to a revival of corruption and reactionary control of the trade unions.

ECONOMIC REFORM

Although Cárdenas was sympathetic to labor's demands for better conditions, he was not averse to private enterprise, despite efforts by his foes to link him to socialism and communism. In fact, industrial capitalism made significant strides under Cárdenas, who supported labor's efforts to raise wages if the financial condition of an enterprise warranted it, but he also favored Mexican industry with government loans and protective tariffs that ensured the creation of a captive market for high-priced consumer goods. In 1934, his government established the *Nacional Financiera*, a government bank and investment corporation that used funds supplied by the federal government and domestic investors to

make industrial loans, finance public welfare projects, and issue its own securities. The coming of World War II, which sharply reduced the availability of imports, greatly stimulated the movement toward industrialization and import substitution.

Mexico's struggle for economic sovereignty reached a high point under Cárdenas. In 1937, a dispute between North American and British oil companies and the unions erupted into a strike, followed by legal battles between the contending parties. When the oil companies refused to accept a much-scaled-down arbitration-tribunal wage finding in favor of the workers, Cárdenas intervened. On March 18, 1938—a date celebrated by Mexicans as marking their declaration of economic independence—the president announced in a radio speech that the properties of the oil companies had been expropriated in the public interest. With support from virtually all strata of the population, Cárdenas was able to ride out the storm caused by economic sanctions against Mexico on the part of the United States, England, and the oil companies. The oil nationalization was a major victory for Mexican nationalism. It provided cheap, plentiful fuel for Mexican industry, and the needs of the nationalized oil industries further stimulated industrialization. But the oil nationalization did not set a precedent; some 90 percent of Mexico's mining industry remained in foreign hands.

WOMEN'S RIGHTS

Pressured by a well-organized, increasingly cohesive women's movement, Cárdenas supported constitutional reform "to grant equal rights" and pledged to create a women's section of the PNR to guarantee that "working women have the right to participate in electoral struggles." Meanwhile, women consolidated their organizational efforts in the United Front for Women's Rights, under the leadership of veteran feminist "Cuca" García and other socialist and communist women. The Front, incorporating some eight hundred women's groups with more than fifty thousand members, demanded women's right to vote and hold office, civil equality, protective legislation for women workers, social integration of indigenous women, and women's centers for cultural education and vocational training.

In 1937, even though the law forbade women to hold elective office and the PNR refused to slate her, the Front supported García's successful primary race for a seat in the Chamber of Deputies. It also secured congressional and state legislative approval of a constitutional amendment permitting women's suffrage beginning in 1939, but thereafter the PNR-dominated Congress, split by fractious party infighting and fearful of a resurgent Catholic conservatism that might have benefited politically from women's enfranchisement, neglected to pass the necessary enabling legislation. Women's suffrage would have to wait until 1953, when a more conservative ruling party had reached a *modus vivendi* with the Catholic Church.

CÁRDENAS'S GROWING MODERATION AND THE ELECTION OF 1940

Education, especially the rural school system, made considerable progress under Cárdenas. Of Tarascan origin, Cárdenas displayed much concern for indigenous welfare. He created a *Departamento de Asuntos Indígenas* to protect their interests and encouraged the study of their past and present culture by founding the *Instituto Nacional de Antropología de México*.

However, in the last years of his presidency, in apparent deference to clerical and conservative opposition, Cárdenas abandoned many reforms and soft-pedaled the so-called socialist character of Mexican education. He also slowed down the pace of land distribution and displayed a conciliatory attitude toward the entrepreneurial class, assuring its members that he regarded them as part of the *fuerzas vivas* (vital forces) of the country and that they need not fear for the safety of their investments.

The Big Bourgeoisie in Power, 1940–1976: Erosion of Reform

The Cárdenas Era was the high-water mark of the struggle to achieve the social goals of the revolution.

During those years, the material and cultural condition of the masses had improved, if only modestly; peasants and workers managed to secure a somewhat larger share of the total national income. Under his successors, the social conquests of the Cárdenas years slowly eroded. After 1940, the new rulers of Mexico favored a development strategy that sharply restricted trade union activity, slowed the tempo of agrarian reform, and reduced the relative share of total income of the bottom two-thirds of the Mexican population.

Ironically, Gen. Manuel Ávila Camacho, a Cárdenas loyalist and devout Catholic, presided over the first phase (1940–1946) of this policy reversal. Regarding unlimited private profit as the driving force of economic progress, he proposed to create a favorable climate for private enterprise. In practice, this meant the freezing of wages, the repression of strikes, and the use of a new weapon against dissidents, a vaguely worded law dealing with the "crime of social dissolution."

Meanwhile, World War II stimulated both the export of Mexican raw materials and import-substitution industrialization. Mexico made significant advances in food processing, textiles, and other consumer goods industries, and the capital goods industry, centered in the north, expanded considerably. Steel production increased, with Monterrey Steel and other companies producing structural and rolled steel for buildings, hotels, highways, and steel hardware. The Nacional Financiera played a leading role in this process of growth through loans to industry for plant construction and expansion. In view of this spontaneous economic growth, the concept of planning dissolved, the second Six-Year Plan remained on paper, and the government made no effort to produce a balanced development of the Mexican regions (instead, most of the development took place in the Federal District and the surrounding area). Meanwhile, land distribution declined sharply.

In 1946, the official party changed its name to the PRI (*Partido Revolucionario Institucional*), and the lawyer Miguel Alemán (1946–1952) succeeded Ávila Camacho as president. Alemán made every effort to continue the policies of his predecessor;

he encouraged private investment through tariff protection, import licensing, subsidies, and government loans. This favorable economic climate attracted domestic and foreign investors looking for outlets for their surplus capital after World War II. A characteristic of the new foreign capital investment was that it flowed primarily into manufacturing rather than the traditional extractive industries.

Alemán and his successor, Adolfo Ruiz Cortines (1952–1958), neglected land distribution and efforts to increase the productivity of the ejidos in favor of large, private landholdings. To provide an incentive to capitalist entrepreneurs, Alemán had Article 27 of the constitution amended. This "reform" consisted in the grant of certificates of "inaffectibility" to landowners, which exempted them from further expropriation for holdings up to 100 hectares of irrigated land or 200 hectares of land with seasonal rainfall. For the production of certain specified crops, the size of inaffectible holdings grew even larger.

A massive program of irrigation contributed to the explosion of capitalist agriculture that began in this period. The irrigation projects were concentrated in northern and northwestern Mexico, where prominent Mexican politicians, their friends, and relatives owned much of the land directly or indirectly. Alemán presided over a great boom in public works construction, accompanied by an orgy of plunder of the public treasury by entrepreneurs and officials; his was probably the most corrupt administration in modern Mexican history.

A new hacienda, technically efficient and often arrayed in modern corporate guise, soon arose and accounted for the bulk of Mexico's commercial agricultural production. It shared its profits with processing plants that usually were subsidiaries of foreign firms. By 1961, fifty years after the revolution began, less than 1 percent of all farms possessed 50 percent of all agricultural land. Meanwhile, increasing numbers of small landholders, starved for credit and lacking machinery, had to abandon their parcels of land and become peons on the new haciendas or migrate to the cities in search of work in the new factories.

Industry continued to grow but foreign capital increasingly penetrated and controlled it. A favorite device for foreign penetration of Mexican industry was the mixed, or joint, company, which had a number of advantages. First, it satisfied the requirement of Mexican law that Mexican nationals hold 51 percent of most companies operating in Mexico. Second, it camouflaged actual domination of such enterprises by the foreign partners through control of patents, licensing agreements, and other sources of technological and financial dependence. Finally, it formed strong ties between foreign capitalists and the native industrial and financial bourgeoisie.

Popular Culture and Resistance

The economic and social policies of Presidents Adolfo López Mateos (1958–1964) and Gustavo Díaz Ordaz (1964–1970) did not differ significantly from those of their predecessors. Under Díaz Ordaz, discontent among workers mounted as their real income shrank because of chronic inflation, a virtual freeze on wages, and *charrismo* (the official control of trade union organizations). Demetrio Vallejo of the independent railway workers epitomized this growing instability and led a series of strikes that quickly spread to other workers. The teachers' strike was especially disturbing to the PRI's authoritarian state and its proponents, such as the newspaper *Excelsior*, which promptly lamented the lack of respect for "authority" that this inculcated among students who consequently were not taught about "the inviolable and absolute respect for private property."

The 1957 death of Pedro Infante also gave voice to this growing social alienation. Arguably Mexico's premier entertainer, Infante, born to poverty, became famous for his good looks, quick wit, anarchic lifestyle, enormously popular films, and *ranchera* songs that proclaimed, "It's better to die while dreaming than to live in reality." According to cultural historian Anne Rubenstein, his funeral and the riots that it occasioned among his mostly working-class fans represented this same social turmoil and growing popular resistance to Mexico's authoritarian state. Angered at his sudden death in an airplane crash, Infante's working-class fans empathized with their hero, whom they saw as a victim of the same forces of modernization that daily assaulted their lives. As a result, they lashed out at Mexico City's police, the most visible and proximate representatives of an authoritarian state that had relentlessly promoted modernization in the postwar world.

Popular resistance to modernization also characterized the experience of Mexican workers at the General Motors plant in Mexico City, which further illustrated the impact of global market changes in the 1960s. For many years, General Motors had been the symbol par excellence of postwar modernity, the populist state's import-substitution industrialization strategy, and paternalistic transnational corporate managerial relations with workers. The company, according to historian Steven Bachelor, traditionally had prided itself on creating a family environment with which Mexican workers would readily identify. This included relatively high wages, paid vacations, educational scholarships for workers' children, and company-sponsored baseball, soccer, and bowling leagues. These collaborative relationships began to deteriorate, however, as international markets for automobile production became increasingly competitive and domestic demand grew in response to the 1962 Integration Decree, which required domestic production of all cars sold in Mexico. Thereafter, GM's corporate management forcibly retired older workers, hired younger replacements at half the wages, restricted employees' bathroom breaks, and dramatically increased the speed of assembly line operations to maximize productivity and profits. One worker, unable to endure the relentless pressure of the accelerated assembly line, broke down in tears. Others naturally resisted these pressures through open acts of defiance: One, whose boss refused to authorize a bathroom break, simply urinated on the spot; others, like Clemente Zaldívar, sabotaged the assembly line. By 1965, these tensions exploded into a month-long strike against General Motors that won some considerable wage benefits but failed to achieve the workers' goal of greater control over production decisions.

Student unrest also grew. Historian Eric Zolov argues that this was, at least in part, the consequence of the invasion of British and U.S. rock-and-roll music in the late 1950s and 1960s. Initially embraced by López Mateos's government as a symbol of Mexico's newly achieved modernity, Mexico's cultural industries celebrated rock-and-roll, along with other musical imports like *cha-cha-chá* and *mambo* from Cuba and **cumbia** (a musical genre drawing on traditional West African dance) from Colombia. Epitomized by the lyrics, facial expressions, and body movements of Elvis Presley, however, upper- and middle-class Mexican youth seemed more interested in rock's sneering contempt for traditional values, associated in Mexico with **buenas costumbres** (good behavior). Because this threatened the stability of the nation's patriarchal, authoritarian power, the official press quickly denounced it as *"rebeldismo sin causa"* (rebellion without a cause), and an effort to discredit foreign rock shortly ensued. For example, rumors soon circulated that Presley had said he would "rather kiss three black girls than a Mexican," and an advertising campaign entitled "Die Elvis Presley" soon began.

Nonetheless, this did not dampen the enthusiasm of Mexican middle-class youth for rock-and-roll music. On the contrary, it became more popular than ever. Mexican bands like Los Loud Jets, Los Rebeldes del Rock, and Los Teen Tops became national icons, at least in part because of nationalistic laws that placed high tariffs on foreign imports and required radio stations to feature Mexican artists. Ironically, the popularity of these Mexican bands was a reflection of their skill at producing *refritos* (accurate English-language covers) of British and U.S. rock songs by bands like the Doors, the Beatles, the Rolling Stones, Jimi Hendrix, and Janis Joplin, whose music increasingly celebrated freedom, rebellion, and disrespect of tradition. By the end of the 1960s, the rock music that flourished in Mexico City's **cafés cantantes** (coffeehouses) unleashed *La Onda* (the Wave), which became Mexico's counterculture, championing alike the cultural contributions of Che Guevara, Allen Ginsberg, and Mick Jagger. Denouncing these coffeehouses as "centers of perversion" that were influenced by decadent foreigners, the authorities organized a campaign to close them down in 1965 and instructed border officials to deny visas to "dirty, long-haired North American youth."

The student protest movement of 1968 unfolded against this cultural background. Many of those who rallied in support of student demands for an end to state repression initially were attracted to the movement by its association with the rock-and-roll subculture that had developed over the previous decade. Zolov interviewed one student who confessed that in his early teens he had known little about the movement except that it was composed of students from the national university who "listened to rock." Others recalled that the student movement recruited supporters for its opposition to an authoritarian patriarchal social order by invoking state and parental repression of rock music: "Isn't it true they don't let you listen to rock?"

This student movement denounced police brutality against student protesters and violations of the constitutional autonomy of the national university. The student protest broadened into a nationwide movement demanding democratization of Mexican economic and political life. In response, the government ordered a savage armed assault on a peaceful assembly of students and others in the Plaza of Three Cultures in Mexico City (October 2, 1968), leaving a toll of dead and wounded running into the hundreds.

This massacre of students at Tlatelolco Square ignited a fierce repression of popular resistance that forced political opposition underground and channeled it into cultural forms. The student movement fractured into two groups: political radicals and *jipitecas* (youth who joined foreign "hippies" in their common search for psychedelic mushrooms and an escape from the modern world into the "pristine poverty" of indigenous Mexico). During the next decade, Mexico's angry, young, urban working class laid its claim to the rebellious rock-and-roll culture that middle- and upper-class youth increasingly abandoned after 1968. Nurtured in the *hoyos fonquis* (funky holes), bands like Los Dug-Dugs, with their "dirty and disheveled look" and "insolent gestures that offend," used these urban "raves" to reflect

and represent their youthful working-class protest, which found its ultimate outlet at the Avándaro music festival in 1971. Here, Mexican rock bands attracted an audience of more than two hundred thousand that included *fresas* (wealthy, privileged elites), middle-class *onderos*, and a large number of *nacos* (lower-class youth from the "proletarian neighborhoods of the Federal District"). Critics on the left and right alike denounced the cultural anarchy unleashed at Avándaro, but the participants more closely identified with one of the featured bands, Three Souls in My Mind, who insisted that "Rock isn't about peace and love; rock is about revolution." Although the rock subculture was self-consciously—and even aggressively—antipolitical, it gave voice to anti-authoritarian popular protest and provided a potentially powerful instrument of political organization that seemingly transcended class barriers. "Avándaro," according to Zolov, "had revealed the political dangers of rock." Not surprisingly, the PRI thereafter tried to close it down.

The economic strategy of the Díaz Ordaz administration aimed to provide the greatest possible incentives to private investment, foreign and domestic. The foreign debt grew alarmingly, with the volume of foreign loans reaching a figure four times that of the Ruiz Cortines Era. This heavy influx of loans increased the dependent character of the Mexican economy.

The official presidential candidate, Luís Echeverría, took office in 1970 amid deepening political, social, and economic storm clouds. Echeverría signaled a tactical shift when he released a large number of students and intellectuals imprisoned after the 1968 student disturbances, promised to struggle against colonialism and corruption, and condemned the unjust distribution of land and income in Mexico. However, recent publication of archival materials, memoirs, and other testimony removed any doubt about Echeverría's leading role in the Tlatelolco massacre and the *guerra sucia* (dirty war) thereafter waged by PRI regimes against leftist opposition.

Conservative Mexican capitalists, closely linked with foreign capital, struck back by withholding investment funds from the market, setting off a serious recession. Under intense pressure from the

Avándaro Music Festival. Published in 1971 by Piedra Rodante. Photo courtesy of Alberto Cruz Molina

Rock-and-roll music offered alienated Mexican youth a forum for their collective protest against cultural conformity, social inequality, and political repression. Organized in the aftermath of the Mexican government's slaughter of rebellious students at Tlatelolco Square, the 1971 Avándaro Music Festival provided more than 200,000 young people an opportunity to express their enthusiasm for a music that defied Mexico's established traditions.

right, Echeverría retreated. During his last three years in office, he reverted to traditional policies and methods, poorly concealed by a populist rhetoric. He publicly denounced colonialism and multinational corporations, but his government did its utmost to attract foreign investments, especially from the United States. These investments also brought growing foreign penetration and domination of strategic sectors of Mexican industry. By the mid-1970s, 70 percent of earnings from the capital goods industry went to foreign capital, leaving 20 percent for public firms and 10 percent for national private companies.

As the investments increased, so too did Mexico's indebtedness and the drain of its capital in the form of dividends, interest, and other returns on foreign investment. By June 1976, Mexico's foreign debt had reached $25 billion. Mexico and Brazil shared the distinction of having the highest foreign debts among developing countries. By September of that year, the growing trade deficit had forced the government to order a 60 percent devaluation of the peso, causing a sharp rise in inflation and greater hardship for the masses. The problems of landlessness or inadequate land and rural unemployment and underemployment remained as stubborn as ever. Some 6 million peasants were landless.

Prospects for the solution of Mexico's urgent problems through the electoral process appeared dim because the PRI, dominated by the industrial and financial oligarchy, had an unshakable grip on power. That power rested on a system of institutionalized coercion and fraud, but it also depended on co-optation of dissidents into the state apparatus, which provided greater access to medical services, schools, low-cost housing, and other benefits to state employees, professionals, and organized workers. The state also orchestrated the paternalistic distribution of goods and services to the urban poor and generated a populist rhetoric that identified the ruling party with the great ideals of the Revolution. These policies slightly reduced mass poverty and income inequalities in Mexican society, but they reinforced a precarious popular base and legitimacy for the PRI's monopoly of political power. By the 1970s, however, rampant inflation and a stagnant economy threatened both.

This was the legacy of Mexico's new nationalism, born of the 1910 revolution. It had produced a new activist state dominated by a nationalistic bourgeoisie, but an armed, racially and ethnically diverse, politically mobilized peasantry still insisted on the satisfaction of its needs. This produced what social scientists have called a **social corporatism**, which guided Mexican national development throughout the twentieth century. This corporatism generated stable growth and a measure of development, but only as long as international export prices were high or relatively low-cost foreign loans were abundant. As we shall read in Chapters 13 and 14, similar global conditions accompanied by vastly different domestic racial, class, ethnic, and gender struggles led to more distinctively populist or **state corporatist** institutions in Argentina and Brazil. In the absence of favorable external conditions, however, all three nations faced uncertain futures.

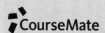 Go to the CourseMate website at **www.cengagebrain.com** for primary sources, additional study tools, and review materials—including audio and video clips—for this chapter.

13

Brazil: Populism and the Struggle for Democracy in a Multiracial Society

FOCUS QUESTIONS

- What were the economic, social, and political conditions that led to Brazil's 1930 revolution?
- How did immigration and women's growing participation in the urban labor movement affect Brazil's national development?
- What was Vargas's populist program, how did it evolve, and how did it affect various sectors of Brazilian society?
- How did changing race relations affect Brazilian populism?

Although the Mexican Revolution pioneered a new nationalism and activist regulatory state in Latin America, the Brazilian populist experiment inaugurated by Getulio Vargas in 1930 more fully developed them. Under his leadership, the national state became a dominant force in Brazilian society, regulating the often-contradictory interests of foreign investors, large plantation owners, local industry, workers, peasants, women, Afro-Brazilians, and indigenous communities.

On the eve of World War I, as revolution raged in Mexico, Brazil's economic, political, and social structures also showed growing strain and instability. Between 1910 and 1914, the Amazonian rubber boom began to fade because of competition from the new and more efficient plantations of the Far East. The approaching end of the rubber cycle revealed the vulnerability of Brazil's monocultural economy to external factors beyond its control and heightened its dependence on coffee. The coffee industry was plagued by recurrent crises of overproduction that required periodic resort to **valorization**—that is, government intervention to maintain coffee

prices by withholding stocks from the market or restricting plantings.

Violence was endemic over large areas of the country. In the backcountry, feudal coronéis with private armies recruited from dependents and *jagunços* (hired gunmen) maintained a patriarchal but frequently tyrannical rule over the peasantry. Over large areas of the country, peasants lived in feudal bondage, obligated to give one or more days per week of free labor as homage to the landowners. Lacking written contracts, they could be evicted at any moment and could find work elsewhere only on the same conditions. The interior was also the scene of mystical or messianic movements that sometimes assumed the character of peasant revolts. Banditry, especially widespread in the northeast, was another response to the tyranny of rural coronéis and the impotence of officials. A few *cangaceiros* (outlaws) took the part of the peasantry against their oppressors; most, however, served as mercenaries in the coronéis's private wars.

Violence was not confined to the countryside. Even in the growing cities, proud of their European culture and appearance, popular anger at the arbitrary

1912–1916	Contestado Rebellion seeks to defend *caboclo* lands against large landowners
1922	Modern Art Week, *Tenentes* Rebellion, and Berta Lutz's Brazilian Federation for the Advancement of Women reflect popular discontent with the Old Republic
1930	Revolution led by Getulio Vargas inaugurates populist reforms
1934	New populist constitution guarantees the rights of labor, women, and state intervention in the economy
1937	Vargas creates Estado Novo, populist dictatorship that combines social welfare and state control of industry
1940–1945	Five Year Plan produces national industrial development
1942–1946	Vargas creates state-owned iron ore, steel, automotive, and energy companies
1945	Military coup crushes São Paulo Textile workers strike and Brazilian Communist Party
1951	Vargas wins presidential election, running as progressive populist opposed to military and foreign business interests
1954	Military forces Vargas's resignation, but his suicide unleashes popular opposition
1956–1961	Kubitschek wins presidency and supports state intervention to produce rapid economic growth
1960	Kubitschek builds new capital, Brasilia, stimulating economic growth
1960	Quadros wins presidential election but soon resigns in favor of vice-president João Goulart
1961–1964	Goulart's progressive populist agenda includes land reform, limits on foreign investment, and workers' rights
1964	With U.S. support, Brazilian military ousts Goulart

rule of local oligarchies, or divisions within those oligarchies, sometimes flared up into civil war. Intervention by the federal government in these armed struggles on the side of its local allies greatly enlarged the scale of violence and ultimately produced a populist revolution under the charismatic leadership of Getulio Vargas.

Decline and Fall of the Old Republic, 1914–1930

ECONOMIC IMPACT OF WORLD WAR I

The outbreak of World War I in August 1914 initially had a negative impact on Brazil. Exports of coffee, a nonessential product, declined, and in 1917 the government came to the rescue of the planters with a new valorization (price maintenance) program. However, by 1915, the growing demand of the Allies for sugar, beans, and other staples had sparked a revival that turned into a boom.

The war accelerated some changes under way in Brazilian economic life. It weakened British capitalism and therefore strengthened the North American challenge to British financial and commercial preeminence in Brazil. The virtual cessation of imports of manufactured goods also gave a strong stimulus to Brazilian industrialization. Profits derived from coffee, an industry protected by the state, provided a large part of the resources needed for industrialization. Favored by its wealth, large immigrant population, and rich natural resources, the state of São Paulo led the movement, replacing Rio de Janeiro as the foremost industrial region. Brazil doubled its industrial production during the war, and the number of enterprises (which stood at about three thousand in 1908) grew by 5,940 between 1915 and 1918. But these increases were concentrated in light industry, especially food processing and textiles, and most of the new enterprises were small shops.

The advance of industry and urbanization enlarged and strengthened both the industrial bourgeoisie and the working class, which became racially, sexually, and ethnically more diverse. After emancipation, Brazil's late-nineteenth-century white supremacist policies, drawing on foreign ideologies and elite fears of Afro-Brazilian power, had discriminated against blacks. They encouraged European immigration to "whiten" the country's labor force and undermine the black majority's ability to negotiate favorable wages and working conditions. Thus, immigrant women, especially from Italy, played a central role in the early development of Brazil's industrial working class and dominated employment in the rapidly expanding textile industry. Of the nine thousand workers hired in thirty-one representative textile mills in São Paulo in 1912, almost seven thousand were women.

In response to wartime inflation that eroded the value of workers' wages, the trade union movement grew, and strikes became more frequent. In 1917, a general strike—the first in Brazilian history—gripped the city and state of São Paulo. Women weavers, whose paid and unpaid work responsibilities in the factory and in the home made them especially aware of the negative impact of wartime inflation on workers' wages, organized and initiated the strike. They therefore demanded a 20 percent wage increase, "more respect" from male supervisors, improvement of working conditions, and a promise that "in everything there should be reason and justice." These women's grievances rapidly spread to other factories, mobilized thousands of strikers who won significant concessions from the city's industrialists, and energized the national labor movement. Although the strike wave of 1917 to 1920 forced many employers to grant higher wages, the living conditions of most workers did not permanently improve. The labor movement, composed largely of foreign-born workers, remained small and weak, without ties with the peasantry, who formed the overwhelming majority of the Brazilian people.

The economic expansion associated with the war also had a dramatic impact on the development of Brazilian culture. Displaced from their homelands and lured by new economic opportunities in Brazil, new immigrants from Japan and the Ottoman empire joined with migrants of African descent from the nation's hinterland, especially the drought-ridden Northeast, in search of high-paying jobs that never seemed to materialize. Together they gathered in the urban centers of Rio de Janeiro and São Paulo in the *favelas* (sprawling slums also known as *morros*) and gave birth to the *samba* (a song and dance that drew heavily on Angolan and Congolese cultural traditions). The samba was closely associated with the ritualistic celebration of *carnival* (a popular street festival that preceded the Lenten season of self-sacrifice and created a safe public space for the lower classes to challenge established social hierarchies and to mock the customs, attitudes, dress, and beliefs of their social rivals). In its early days, the wanton sexuality and the wild, irrepressible, and defiant behavior associated with carnival scandalized the Brazilian aristocracy, which greatly feared the unruliness of its exploited workforce.

Samba lyrics similarly raised serious social and political issues, often using clever word play, double entendre, and the juxtaposition of contrasting images to scorn the arrogant power of the upper classes. In 1917, for example, one of Brazil's greatest samba artists, Ernesto dos Santos, better known as Dongo, recorded the first samba, "*Pelo telefone*" ("On the Telephone"), which simultaneously celebrated the new technology and lamented its use by police officials to harass a poor man. During the postwar period, the radio broadened the popular appeal of the samba, repeatedly broadcasting the songs produced by competing *escolas da samba* (samba schools), the neighborhood clubs that organized community participation in carnival. Suddenly, the precise meaning of what it meant to be Brazilian had ceased to be as clear as the traditional light-skinned, Eurocentric plantation elites had imagined it. Change was in the air.

POSTWAR INDUSTRY AND LABOR

Industrialization and urbanization further weakened the foundations of the neocolonial order, which stressed the primacy of agriculture and dependence on foreign markets and loans, but it emerged from the war essentially intact, although its stabilization proved temporary and precarious. A chronically adverse balance of trade and a declining rate of exchange against foreign currencies gave Brazilian industry a competitive advantage in goods of popular consumption. It continued to grow, but it had little support from a central government dominated by the coffee interests. Bitter debates between the friends and foes of tariff protection for industry marked the political life of the 1920s.

As that decade opened, Brazil remained an overwhelmingly rural country. A few export products—coffee, sugar, cotton—dominated Brazilian agriculture, which otherwise neglected food production so that the country had to import four-fifths of its grain. The concentration of landownership was extreme: 461 great landowners held more than 27 million hectares of land, whereas 464,000 small and midsize farms occupied only 15.7 million hectares. Archaic techniques prevailed in agriculture: The hoe was still the principal farming instrument and the wasteful slash-and-burn method the favored way of clearing the land. Even relatively progressive coffee planters gave little attention to care of the soil, selection of varieties, and other improvements. As a result, the productivity of plantations rapidly declined, even in regions of superior soil.

In the cities, most workers toiled and lived under conditions that recalled those of the early Industrial Revolution in Europe. In 1920, the average industrial worker in São Paulo earned about four milréis ($0.60) a day; for this wage he or she worked ten to twelve hours, six days a week. Women earned only 60 percent of men's wages and suffered from abusive patriarchal power in the workplace. Historian Joel Wolfe documents the case of one such woman, Ambrosina Pioli, whose supervisor beat her savagely when she complained about his threats to fire her to make room for his lover.

Malnutrition, parasitic diseases, and lack of medical facilities limited Brazilians' average life span in 1920 to twenty-eight years. In the same year, more than 64 percent of the population over the age of fifteen was illiterate. Because literacy was a requirement for voting, the general lack of schools kept the people ignorant and politically powerless.

As expanding market forces dissolved traditional rural patron-client social relations, the impoverished peasantry often sought refuge in a culture of resistance that focused on daily survival strategies. Although periodically engaged in overt acts of sedition like the Contestado Rebellion of 1912–1916, peasants typically did not organize to transform Brazilian society.

CULTURAL CRISIS AND POLITICAL UNREST

The task of transforming society fell to the rapidly growing urban bourgeois groups, and especially to the middle class, which began to voice ever more strongly its discontent with the rule of corrupt rural oligarchies. In the early 1920s, a many-faceted movement for the renovation of Brazilian society and culture arose. Intellectuals, artists, junior military officers, professional men, and a small minority of radical workers participated in this movement, but they had no common program and did not comprehend the convergence of their aims.

Three seemingly unrelated events of 1922 illustrate the diverse forms that the ferment of the times assumed.

First, in February, São Paulo intellectuals organized a Modern Art Week to commemorate the centenary of Brazilian independence. Influenced by rebellious European artists, these young poets, painters, and composers rejected the staid traditions of naturalism that had dominated the late-nineteenth-century Brazilian art world, declared their independence from old forms and content, and insisted on the need to develop indigenous Brazilian culture. Among the young intellectuals who gathered there were Heitor Villa-Lobos, who became the nation's premier samba artist, and Oswaldo de Andrade. He later shocked Brazilian audiences by proclaiming the need to become "cultural cannibals"—that is, to consume foreign artistic ideas, mix them with Brazil's digestive enzymes, and thereby produce an authentically Brazilian national cultural identity that was neither xenophobic nor nativist.

Second, in March 1922, after the appearance of Marxist groups in a number of cities, a congress in

Rio de Janeiro founded the Brazilian Communist Party and began a struggle against the anarcho-syndicalist doctrines that still dominated much of the small labor movement.

Third, in July, *tenentes* (junior officers) at the Copacabana garrison in Rio de Janeiro rose to prevent the seating of Artur da Silva Bernardes, who had won the presidential election according to the agreement between the two dominant states of São Paulo and Minas Gerais. The rebel program denounced the rule of the coffee oligarchy, political corruption, and electoral fraud. Government forces easily crushed the revolt, but it left a legend when a handful of insurgents refused to surrender and fought to the death against overwhelming odds.

The officers' revolt signaled the beginning of a struggle by the Brazilian bourgeoisie to seize power from the rural oligarchy. Given the closed political system, it inevitably assumed the character of an armed struggle, spearheaded by a nationalist young officer group, mostly of middle-class origins, who called for democratic elections, equal justice, and similar political reforms.

President Bernardes (1922–1926) took office amid growing economic and political turmoil. Because of a massive increase in coffee plantings between 1918 and 1924, the industry again suffered from overproduction and falling prices. In 1924, another military revolt, organized by junior officers, broke out in São Paulo. The city's large working class was sympathetic to the revolt, but its conservative leaders rejected the workers' request for arms.

Meanwhile, the revolt had spread to other states. Another group of rebels in Rio Grande do Sul, led by Captain Luís Carlos Prestes, moved north to join the insurgents from São Paulo, and their combined forces, known in history as the Prestes column, began a prodigious 14,000-mile march through the interior. The tenentes hoped to enlist the peasantry in their struggle against Bernardes, but they knew little of the peasants' problems and offered no program of agrarian reform. The peasants, for their part, had no interest in fighting the "tyrant" Bernardes in distant Rio de Janeiro.

The long march had much educational value for the officers who took part in it. For the first time in their lives, many of these young men came face to face with the reality of rural Brazil and began to reflect on its problems. As a result, the tenente reform program acquired an economic and social content. It began to speak of the need for economic development and social legislation, including agrarian reform as well as minimum wages and maximum working hours.

Naturally, these conflicts provided additional political space for lower-class mobilization in the 1920s. Black Brazilians in Salvador da Bahia and elsewhere joined Marcus Garvey's black power movement, prompting the government to solicit the covert assistance of the Federal Bureau of Investigation (FBI) in the United States to monitor and disrupt their activities. Meanwhile, others flocked to the practice of **candomblé** (a popular religion that evoked consciousness of the African past and created a spiritual community of resistance to white supremacist policies).

Brazilian women likewise mobilized in the militant tradition of nineteenth-century feminist Motta Diniz, who had declared that "in all the world, barbarous or civilized, woman is a slave." In 1922, women's rights activist Berta Lutz organized the Brazilian Federation for the Advancement of Women (FBPF). Largely composed of middle-class professionals, it nonetheless advocated state intervention against market forces and called on the Bernardes government to protect "female labor, which has been subject to inhuman exploitation, reducing women to an inferior position in the competition for industrial and agricultural salaries."

Although Bernardes survived this political opposition, he continued to be plagued by economic problems, with the coffee problem paramount. Bernardes applied the now orthodox remedy of valorization, but he gave it a decentralized form. The central government turned over the supervision of the scheme to the individual coffee-producing states. The state of São Paulo established an agency, the Coffee Institute, that undertook to control the export trade in coffee by regulating market offerings to maintain a balance between supply and demand. It withdrew unlimited stocks of coffee, stored

NOTIMEX/PHOTO/JUENVIGNOLES/FRE/ACE/Newscom

One of the original organizers of Brazil's famous "Modern Art Week" in 1922 and a pioneer of Brazilian modernism was Emiliano di Cavalcanti. His *Samba* (1925) broke with artistic traditions that stressed the nation's European origins and instead celebrated Brazil's African and indigenous cultural roots.

them in warehouses, and released them according to the needs of the export trade. The plan required financing the producers of coffee withheld from the market. The program appeared to work, for prices rose and remained stable until 1929, but the burdens of valorization steadily grew because high prices stimulated production, required new withdrawals, and called for new loans to finance the unsold output. To make matters worse, the high coffee prices attracted Brazil's competitors—

especially Colombia—and they expanded their own output.

ECONOMIC CRISIS

In 1926, Bernardes turned over the presidency to the Paulista Washington Luís de Sousa Pereira (1926–1930). His administration made a series of new loans to support the valorization program. This especially alienated the nation's industrial bourgeoisie, whose interests and power had continued to expand. The coffee oligarchs and their foreign bankers siphoned off financial and labor resources needed by industry. High, state-sponsored coffee prices created greater demand for labor, which led to high turnover rates and increased costs in urban industry. By 1930, foreign loans had produced an external debt of $1,181 million, and Brazil had to pay $200 million annually—one-third of the national budget—to service the debt. Squeezed between the conflicting demands of coffee planters and militant workers, these industrialists relied on local repression and privately funded social welfare programs to co-opt and control their labor force, even as they increasingly pressured the state to regulate economic activity in their interests.

By 1930, U.S. investment in Brazil had reached $400 million, considerably larger than the British total, and the United States had supplanted England as Brazil's chief trading partner. But Brazil's heavy dependence on foreign markets and loans made it extremely vulnerable to the crisis that shook the capitalist world after the New York stock market collapsed in October 1929. Coffee prices fell from $0.225 to $0.08 a pound between 1929 and 1931, and immense stocks of coffee piled up in the warehouses. By the end of 1930, Brazil's gold reserves had disappeared, and the exchange rate plummeted to a new low. As foreign credit dried up, it became impossible to continue to finance the valorization program, which collapsed, leaving behind a mountain of debt.

The presidential campaign and election of 1930 took place against a background of economic crisis, the principal burdens of which—unemployment, wage cuts, and inflation—fell chiefly on the working classes. Nevertheless, the crisis sharpened all class and regional antagonisms, especially the conflict between the coffee oligarchy and the urban bourgeois groups, who regarded the Great Depression as proof of the bankruptcy of the old order. A rift even appeared within the coffee oligarchy, and the traditional alliance of São Paulo and Minas Gerais fell apart. This emboldened a new coalition, the Liberal Alliance, which linked urban groups, great landowners (like the ranchers of Rio Grande do Sul,

who resented São Paulo's dominant position), and disaffected politicians from Minas Gerais and other states. It named Getúlio Vargas, a wealthy rancher and politician from Rio Grande do Sul, as its candidate.

The working class was not a participant in the Liberal Alliance, but many workers sympathized with its program and openly pressured Vargas to improve working conditions, establish a minimum wage and mandatory vacations, organize consumer cooperatives, and regulate labor relations. Women's groups, in search of freedom from the tyranny of market forces, also lobbied the antioligarchical movement. Berta Lutz and the FBPF announced their Thirteen Principles, which advocated women's suffrage, civil equality, equal pay for equal work, paid maternity leave for working women, affirmative action in government employment, a minimum wage, the eight-hour day, paid vacations, and medical, disability, and retirement insurance. All these provisions eventually became part of the 1934 constitution.

The Vargas campaign, although careful not to offend its latifundist supporters, stressed the need to promote industrialization, advocated high tariffs to protect Brazilian industry using local raw materials, and called on Brazilians to "perfect our manufactures to the point where it will become unpatriotic to feed or clothe ourselves with imported goods." Reflecting the influence of the tenentes, Vargas advanced a program of social welfare legislation and political, judicial, and educational reform. He even made a cautious pledge of "action with a view to the progressive extinction of the latifundio, without violence, and support for the organization of small landed property through the transfer of small parcels of land to agricultural laborers."

When the coffee oligarchs sought to deny Vargas the presidency, he overthrew the Washington Luís government. The successful revolt meant that the Old Republic, born in 1889 and dominated since 1894 by the coffee oligarchy, was dead. A new era had begun that may with fair accuracy be called the era of the bourgeois revolution. The political career of its chieftain, Getúlio Vargas, faithfully mirrored its advances, retreats, and ultimate defeat.

Vargas and the Bourgeois Revolution, 1930–1954

The liberal revolution of 1930 represented a victory for the urban bourgeois groups who favored industrialization of Brazil's economic, political, and social structures. But the bourgeoisie had gained that victory with the aid of allies whose interests had to be taken into account. Getúlio Vargas presided over a heterogeneous coalition that included fazendeiros—who had joined the revolution from jealousy of the overweening Paulista power but feared radical social change—and intellectuals and tenentes who called for agrarian reform, the formation of cooperatives, and the nationalization of mines. Women's groups and others disadvantaged by oligarchical rule and market forces pressured Vargas to endorse their campaign for liberation. The Brazilian Black Front (FNB), established in 1931, organized massive protests against racial discrimination, advocated laws to require racial integration of all public places, educated Afro-Brazilians about Pan-Africanist political movements, and sought black representation in the national Congress. The working class, vital to the development of Brazilian capitalism, remained a potential threat to its very existence. Finally, Vargas had to take account of foreign capital interests, temporarily weakened but capable of applying great pressure on the Brazilian economy when the capitalist world emerged from the depths of the Great Depression. Vargas's strategy of attempting to balance and reconcile these conflicting interests helps to explain the contradictions and abrupt shifts of course that marked his career.

VARGAS'S ECONOMIC AND POLITICAL MEASURES

The most pressing problem facing the new government was finding a way out of the economic crisis. Vargas did not abandon the coffee industry, the base of his political enemies, to its fate; he attempted to revive it by such classic valorization measures as the restriction of plantings, the purchase of surplus stocks, and the more drastic expedient of burning excess coffee. Nonetheless, the level of coffee exports and prices remained low throughout the

1930s. The government had more success with efforts to diversify agriculture. Production of cotton, in particular, grew with the aid of capital and labor released by the depressed coffee industry, and cotton exports rose steadily until 1940, when the outbreak of war interrupted their advance. Such diversification of agriculture, however, could not compensate for the steep decline in Brazil's import capacity. The key to recovery was import-substitution industrialization.

The Great Depression did not create Brazilian industrialization, but it created the conditions for a new advance. Beginning as a spontaneous response to the loss of import capacity that resulted from the catastrophic decline of exports and a falling rate of exchange, industrialization received a fresh impetus from Vargas, who encouraged industry through exchange controls, import quotas, tax incentives, lower duties on imported machinery and raw materials, and long-term loans at low interest rates. Thanks to the combination of favorable background conditions and the Vargas policy of state intervention, Brazilian industrialization, based entirely on production for the home market, made notable strides in a few years: Industrial production doubled between 1931 and 1936. As early as 1933, when the United States was still deep in the Great Depression, Brazil's national income had begun to increase, which indicated that for the moment, at least, the economy no longer depended on external factors but on internal ones.

Meanwhile, Vargas sought to centralize political power by making strategic concessions to his coalition allies. He appeased the political elite of São Paulo with ministerial appointments. He also tried to conciliate São Paulo's workers, who, again sparked by the women weavers in the textile industry, openly rebelled against industrialists in May 1932, demanding an eight-hour day, 20 percent wage increases, night-work bonuses, equal pay for equal work, prohibition of forced overtime, and recognition of their local bargaining units called "factory commissions." Tens of thousands joined the general strike, and Vargas was forced to intervene, co-opting the workers' movement by agreeing to most of their demands but requiring that

Thomas D. McAvoy/Time & Life Pictures/Getty Images

Employed in one of the many state-owned companies created by the populist president Getulio Vargas, skilled workers walked past a statue of Vargas that commemorated the first decade of nationalizing action in the Amazonian region of Madeira-Mamoré.

future disagreements over working conditions be negotiated peacefully by tripartite conciliation commissions composed of workers, employers, and government appointees.

In February 1932, Vargas had promulgated an electoral code that established the secret ballot, lowered the voting age from twenty-one to eighteen, and extended the vote to working women, but the code still denied illiterates the vote. Although these electoral reforms left 95 percent of Brazilians ineligible to vote, they expanded suffrage sufficiently to allow women to get elected in eighteen of twenty state legislatures. Moreover, reflecting women's new political muscle, the state government of Rio de Janeiro appointed women

to the cabinet portfolios of Labor and Education. The constituent assembly elected under this code also drafted a new constitution, which was promulgated on July 16, 1934. This document retained the federal system but considerably strengthened the powers of the executive. The assembly, constituting itself the first Chamber of Deputies, elected Vargas president for a term extending to January 1938.

The section of the constitution on "economic and social order" stressed the government's responsibility for economic development. Article 119 declared that "the law will regulate the progressive nationalization of mines, mineral deposits, and waterfalls or other sources of energy, as well as of the industries considered as basic or essential to the economic and military defense of the country."

The section on the rights and duties of labor revealed Vargas's patriarchal relationship with the working class, which he courted through concessions but denied independence of action. The constitution of 1934 established a labor tribunal system, gave the government power to fix minimum wages, and guaranteed the right to strike. Subsequent decrees set the working day at eight hours in commerce and industry, fixed minimum wages throughout the country, and created an elaborate social security system that provided for pensions, paid vacations, safety and health standards, and employment security.

In exchange for these gains, the working class lost its freedom of action. The trade unions, formerly subject to harsh repression, but militant and jealous of their autonomy, became official agencies controlled by the Ministry of Labor. The workers had no voice in the drafting of labor legislation. Police and security agencies brutally repressed strikes not approved by the government.

The labor and social legislation, moreover, was unevenly enforced, and employers frequently evaded the law. The legislation did not apply to the great majority of agricultural workers, who made up 85 percent of the labor force. Determined to maintain his alliance with the fazendeiros in his coalition, Vargas left intact the system of patrimonial servitude that governed labor relations in the countryside, just as he preserved the latifundio and abandoned campaign promises of agrarian reform.

Vargas's shift in favor of the fazendeiros grew more pronounced in 1934 and alienated tenentes, intellectuals, radical workers, and the Communist Party, founded in 1922 by Luís Carlos Prestes. As honorary president of the *Aliança Nacional Libertadora* (National Liberation Alliance, or ANL), a popular front movement that attracted middle-class as well as working-class support, Prestes advocated the liquidation of the latifundio, nationalization of large foreign companies, and cancellation of imperialist debts.

Meanwhile, Vargas harassed the leftist opposition as "subversive." In 1935, after Prestes attacked Vargas's failure to implement the tenente ideals and called for the creation of a truly "revolutionary and anti-imperialist government," Vargas responded by banning the ANL and ordering the arrest of many leftist leaders.

VARGAS AS DICTATOR

The repression of the left paved the way for the establishment of Vargas's personal dictatorship. On November 10, he canceled the 1938 presidential elections, dissolved Congress as an "inadequate and costly apparatus," and assumed dictatorial power under a new constitution patterned on European fascist models. On December 2, he abolished all political parties.

The new regime, baptized the *Estado Novo* (New State), copied the constitutional forms of the fascist regimes and their repressive tactics. It established strict press censorship and filled prisons with workers, teachers, military officers, and others suspected of subversion. The apparatus of repression included a special police force for hunting down and torturing dissidents. The Estado Novo also dealt women workers a decided setback in their struggle for freedom and equality by actively soliciting their return to the private patriarchal province of home and family. The tax code penalized single women and childless families, while other laws provided special protections to mothers and children and actively discouraged women from

working outside the home or joining trade unions. Yet little organized resistance to the regime emerged. Neutralized by a paternalist social legislation and doped by populist rhetoric, labor, its most likely opponent, remained passive or even supported Vargas.

In international affairs, Vargas sought economic rapprochement with Germany and Italy to open up new markets for Brazil and to strengthen his hand in bargaining with the United States. Despite its authoritarian, repressive aspects, the Estado Novo continued the struggle against neocolonialism to achieve economic independence.

Indeed, under the new regime, the state intervened more actively than before to encourage the growth of industry and provide it with the necessary economic infrastructure. Rejecting laissez-faire, the Estado Novo pursued a policy of planning and direct investment for the creation of important industrial complexes in the basic sectors of mining, oil, steel, electric power, and chemicals. In 1940, the government announced a Five-Year Plan whose goals included the expansion of heavy industry, the creation of new sources of hydroelectric power, and the expansion of the railway network. In 1942, the government established the *Companhia Vale do Rio Doce* to exploit the rich iron ore deposits of Itabira; in 1944, it created a company for the production of materials needed by the chemical industry; and, in 1946, the National Motor Company began the production of trucks. In the same year, Vargas saw the realization of one of his cherished dreams: The National Steel Company began production at the Volta Redonda plant between Rio de Janeiro and São Paulo. Aware of the need of modern industry for abundant sources of power, Vargas created the National Petroleum Company in 1938 to press the search for oil.

By 1941, Brazil had 44,100 plants employing 944,000 workers; the comparable figure for 1920 was 13,336 plants with about 300,000 workers. Aside from some export of textiles, the manufacturing industries served the domestic market almost exclusively. State and mixed public-private companies dominated the heavy and infrastructural industries, and private Brazilian capital predominated in manufacturing, but the 1930s also saw a significant growth of direct foreign investment as foreign corporations sought to enlarge their share of the internal market and overcome tariff barriers and exchange problems by establishing branch plants in Brazil. By 1940, foreign capital represented 44 percent of the total investment in Brazilian stock companies. Vargas made no effort to check the influx of foreign capital, perhaps because he believed that the growth of Brazilian state and private capitalism would keep the foreign sector in a subordinate status.

The Estado Novo banned strikes and lockouts but retained and even expanded the body of protective social and labor legislation. In 1942, it consolidated the labor laws into a labor code, regarded as one of the most advanced in the world, but its uneven enforcement brought no benefits to the great mass of agricultural workers. Moreover, spiraling inflation created a growing gap between wages and prices; prices rose 86 percent between 1940 and 1944, whereas between 1929 and 1939, they had risen only 31 percent. In effect, inflation, by transferring income from workers' wages to capitalists' profits, provided much of the financing for the rapid economic growth of the 1940s.

World War II accelerated that growth through the new stimulus it gave to industrialization. Brazil exported vast quantities of foodstuffs and raw materials, but the industrial countries, whose economies focused on war production, could not pay for their purchases with machinery or consumer goods. As a result, Brazil built up large foreign exchange reserves, $707 million in 1945. Most of the economic advance of the war years was due to expansion and intensive exploitation of existing plants or the technical contributions of Brazilian engineers and scientists.

Vargas adroitly exploited great power rivalries to secure financial and technical assistance from the United States for the construction of the huge state-owned integrated iron and steel plant at Volta Redonda. U.S. companies and government agencies were notably cool to requests for aid to establish heavy industry in Latin America, but Vargas's hints that he might have to turn for help to Germany removed all obstacles. Volta Redonda was a great victory for the Vargas policies of economic nationalism and state intervention in economic life. In return for its assistance, Vargas allowed the United States to lease air bases in northern Brazil even before it entered the war against the Axis.

The paradox of Brazil's participation in an antifascist war under an authoritarian regime was not lost on Brazilians; the demands for an end to the Estado Novo grew stronger as the defeat of the Axis drew near. Although the dictatorship and war had limited the political agenda of women's rights groups, their organizational strength continued to grow under the auspices of the Women's Division of the League for National Defense, whose members staffed neighborhood committees to monitor food prices and demand social justice. This led to the creation of the Woman's Committee for Amnesty, which by war's end had built a broad coalition to restore civil liberties and secure political liberalization. During the war, the struggle for Afro-Brazilian rights also took refuge in cultural organizations like the Black Experimental Theater (TEN), which rooted "antiracist civil and human rights demands" in the cultivation of African consciousness among blacks.

Likewise, a simmering worker discontent, blunted by repression and wartime co-optation of union leadership, could express itself only in popular protest sambas, clandestine factory commissions, spreading absenteeism, and personal appeals to Vargas for justice. Nevertheless, in February 1945, this dissatisfaction boiled over in a riot involving hundreds of protestors. In the summer, women textile workers in São Paulo again led a strike movement that mobilized thousands, destabilized Brazilian industrial society, and threatened Vargas's regime. Ever sensitive to changes in the political climate and the balance of forces, Vargas announced an amnesty for political prisoners, promulgated a law allowing political parties to function openly, and set December 2 as the date for presidential and congressional elections.

A MILITARY COUP

Vargas announced that he would not run for president, but he set the stage for a well-organized campaign by his supporters, called *queremistas* (from the Portuguese verb *querer*, "to want"), who wanted Vargas to declare himself a candidate in the forthcoming election. Soon after issuing the decrees restoring political freedom, Vargas, proclaiming himself the "father of the poor," authorized the expropriation of any organization whose practices were harmful to the national interest.

The authorization decree, which aimed to keep down the cost of living, inspired alarm in conservative foreign and domestic circles. Senior military officers regarded Vargas's leftward move with growing uneasiness. The wartime alliance with the United States had accentuated their inherent conservatism and made them ready to accept the gospel of free enterprise and U.S. leadership in the cold war against the Soviet Union and world communism.

On October 29, 1945, generals Goes Monteiro and Eurico Dutra staged a coup, forced Vargas to resign, promptly repealed Vargas's authorization decree, and suppressed the Communist Party. They refused to expand the vote to illiterates and organized elections that guaranteed the victory of President Eurico Dutra (1946–1951), under whom neocolonial interests regained much of the influence they had lost under Vargas. In his foreign and domestic policies, Dutra displayed a blind loyalty to the anticommunist creed propounded by Washington.

In the 1945 elections, the Communist Party (PCB) had polled more than half a million votes, and two years later the Brazilian Women's Federation, the country's leading feminist organization, joined the Communist-sponsored Women's International Democratic Federation. Alarmed by the growing influence of the Communist Party, Dutra outlawed it, and Congress followed by expelling the party's elected representatives. Dutra exploited the resulting witch-hunt to smash the independent, labor movement and declared the Workers' Federation illegal; meanwhile, the government intervened in a large number of unions to eliminate "extremist elements." The imposition of a wage freeze and the failure to raise the officially decreed minimum wage caused the real income of workers to drop sharply.

Regarding economic development, Dutra pursued a laissez-faire policy that meant the virtual abandonment of the Vargas strategy of a state-directed movement toward economic independence. Dutra removed all import and exchange controls and allowed the large foreign exchange reserves accumulated during the war—reserves that Vargas had proposed to use to reequip Brazilian industry—to be dissipated on imported consumer goods, luxury goods in large part.

Attracted by the new economic climate, foreign capital flowed into Brazil. Meanwhile, seeking to curb inflation according to the prescription of U.S. advisers, the government pursued a restrictive credit policy harmful to Brazilian entrepreneurs and industrial growth.

Despite these setbacks, popular movements continued to organize and agitate for progressive reform. Afro-Brazilians, for example, created the National Black Convention and the Black Women's National Congress to expose the hypocrisy of the government's claim that Brazil was a "racial democracy." After years of public pressure—culminating in 1950 with a well-publicized incident in which a São Paulo hotel refused to accommodate the famous African American choreographer Katherine Dunham but reserved a room for her white secretary—the Dutra regime finally adopted a relatively timid, but nonetheless significant, anti-discrimination law: the Afonso Arinos Act.

VARGAS'S RETURN TO POWER

In 1950, having assured himself of the neutrality of the armed forces, Vargas drew on this popular dissatisfaction and ran for president with the support of a broad coalition of workers, industrialists, and members of the urban middle class. His campaign stressed the need to accelerate industrialization and expand social welfare legislation. Riding a wave of discontent with the economic and social policies of the Dutra regime, Vargas easily defeated his two opponents.

Vargas inherited a difficult economic situation. After a brief boom in coffee exports and prices in 1949–1951, the balance of trade again turned unfavorable and the inflation rate increased. In the absence of other major sources of financing for his developmental program, Vargas had to rely largely on a massive increase in the money supply, with all its inevitable social consequences. Meanwhile, his national program of state-directed industrialization encountered increasing hostility from neocolonial interests at home and abroad. In the United States, the Eisenhower administration decided that the Vargas government had not created the proper climate for private investment and terminated the Joint United States–Brazilian Economic Commission. Within Brazil, Vargas's program faced sabotage at the hands of the rural fazendeiros that continued to dominate the majority of state governments and Congress. This hardening of attitudes greatly reduced Vargas's options and his capacity for maneuvering among different social groups.

Nonetheless, Vargas pursued his populist program. He created a mixed public-private petroleum corporation, called *Petrobrás*, which gave the state a monopoly on the drilling of oil and new refineries. Petrobrás illustrated Vargas's belief that the state must own the commanding heights of the economy and represented an attempt to reduce the balance-of-payments deficit by substituting domestic sources of oil for imported oil. Vargas sought to appease domestic and foreign opponents by leaving the distribution of oil in private hands and allowing existing refineries to remain privately owned. Vargas also proposed to create *Electrobras*, a similar agency to produce electric power.

Vargas's labor policy became another political battleground. Under Vargas, labor regained much of the freedom of action it had lost during the Dutra years. In December 1951, under pressure from militant workers, the government decreed a new minimum wage that compensated for the most recent price rises. In 1953, three hundred thousand workers went on strike for higher wages and other benefits. In June of that year, Vargas appointed a young protégé, João Goulart, minister of labor. Goulart, a populist in the Vargas tradition, was sympathetic with labor's demands. In January 1954, Goulart recommended a doubling of the minimum wage.

The battle lines between Vargas and his foes grew ever more sharply. In speeches to Congress, Vargas criticized foreign investors for aggravating Brazil's balance-of-payments problem by their massive remittances of profits and claimed that invoicing frauds had cost Brazil at least $250 million over an eighteen-month period. Meanwhile, conservative attacks on him grew even more bitter. On August 24, the military ordered him to resign or be deposed. Isolated and betrayed, the seventy-two-year-old Vargas found the way out of his dilemma by suicide, but he left a message that was also his political testament. It ended with the words:

> I fought against the looting of Brazil. I fought against the looting of the people. I have fought bare-breasted. Hatred, infamy, and calumny did not beat down my spirit. I gave you my life. Now I offer my death. Nothing remains. Serenely I take the first step on the road to eternity and I leave life to enter history.

As in life, so also in death, Vargas remained a controversial figure, but a woman textile worker, Odette Pasquini, offered perhaps the most astute epitaph for Vargas and his populist programs. "Vargas," she opined, "oh, he was the 'father of the poor,' as they used to say on the radio, but of course he was truly the mother of the rich!"

Reform and Reaction, 1954–1964

The death of Vargas foreshadowed the demise of the nationalist, populist model of independent capitalist development over which he had presided for the better part of a quarter-century. That model, based on a strategy of maneuver and compromise, of reconciling the clashing interests of the national bourgeoisie, fazendeiros, foreign capitalists, and the working class, of avoiding such structural changes as agrarian reform, had about exhausted its possibilities.

Two options remained. One was for Vargas's political heirs to mobilize the working class and the peasantry for the realization of a program of structural changes, including agrarian reform, that could impart a new dynamic to Brazilian national capitalism. The alternative was for Vargas's political enemies to impose a streamlined neocolonial model on the basis of the denationalization and modernization of Brazilian industry, on its transformation into an extension of the industrial park of the great capitalist powers, accompanied by a shift in emphasis from the export of raw materials to the export of manufactured goods. Because such a course entailed immense sacrifices for the Brazilian people, it also required the imposition of a dictatorship of the most repressive kind. The balance of forces in 1954 already favored the second option. For a decade, however, Brazil would sway uncertainly between the two alternatives.

THE KUBITSCHEK ERA

The presidential election of 1955 took place under the watchful gaze of the military. Juscelino Kubitschek, governor of Minas Gerais, with João Goulart as his running mate, stressed the defense of democracy and the acceleration of economic growth. Kubitschek was not an economic nationalist in the Vargas mold, but the nationalist and reformist groups, knowing the limits of military tolerance, gave him their support. As the campaign progressed, a clamor for a coup grew on the right to prevent the victory of Kubitschek and Goulart. They won the election in October, however, with the popular Goulart polling more votes than the president-elect.

Kubitschek took office in January 1956 with a promise of "fifty years of progress in five," but he aimed to achieve this progress with the aid of massive foreign investments, to which Kubitschek offered most generous incentives. Foreign capital flowed into Brazil; the total inflow between 1955 and 1961 amounted to $2.3 billion. The bulk came from the United States, whose investments in Brazil reached $1.5 billion in 1960.

This influx of capital, which benefited from advantages denied to Brazilian enterprises, promoted a rapid foreign conquest of Brazilian national industry. In the process, the native entrepreneurs frequently became directors or partners of the foreign-controlled firms. The takeover concentrated on the most modern and fastest-growing industries: chemical, metallurgy, electrical, communications, and automotive. In 1960, foreign investment accounted for 70 percent of the capital invested in the thirty-four largest companies and more than 30 percent in the six hundred and fifty corporations with capital of $1 million or more.

The Kubitschek Era was a heady time of unprecedented economic growth that averaged 7 percent per year between 1957 and 1961. By 1960, he had transformed Brazil from an agrarian country into an agrarian-industrial nation with a base of heavy industry, for it could boast that it produced half of its heavy-industry needs. Construction of a series of great dams provided much of the power needed by Brazil's growing industry. Kubitschek's decision to build a new capital, Brasilia, in the frontier state of Goias reflected his exuberant optimism about Brazil's future. Completed in three years, he inaugurated the new capital on April 21, 1960. A network of what he called "highways of national unity" linked Brasilia with the rest of the country but failed to solve the many difficulties—housing and resettlement problems, cultural isolation, and the like—that faced its inhabitants.

A high cost accompanied these triumphs of development. A major source of financing was foreign loans, which swelled Brazil's already large foreign debt from $1.6 billion in 1954 to $2.7 billion in 1961. Service of the foreign debt took an ever-increasing share of the national budget, rising from $180 million to $515 million (more than half the value of Brazil's exports) in the same period. This source of financing had its limits; by 1959, the International Monetary Fund (IMF) threatened to withhold loans if Brazil did not adopt a stabilization program and live within its means. Kubitschek responded by breaking off negotiations with the IMF and increasing the money supply. The result was an unprecedented inflation rate and a catastrophic decline in the value of the cruzeiro. This in turn greatly diminished the value of Brazil's exports. Inflation, like foreign loans, appeared to have reached its limits as a source to finance Brazilian development.

This economic growth, the resulting expansion of Brazil's middle class, and the ideology of modernity that accompanied both also affected Brazilian culture. *Bossa nova* (literally, the new beat), which emerged from fashionable cabarets in middle- and upper-class communities, sought to rescue Brazilian national music from the wild, seemingly uncontrollable, undulating rhythms of the samba, traditionally associated with mixed-race popular classes. Instead, it redefined Brazil's cultural identity in a way that emphasized modernity, personal freedom, and the pursuit of individual pleasure. Like the country's modernization during the 1950s, bossa nova relied heavily on imports from the United States—in this case, syncopated jazz rhythms that artists like Antonio Carlos (Tom) Jobim, João Gilberto, and Nara Leão fused with a samba drumbeat. Lyrically, bossa nova music like the internationally renowned "Girl from Ipanema," written by Brazilian beat poet extraordinaire Vinicius de Moraes, celebrated the bohemian lifestyles of young, middle-class men who were more interested in the beach, beautiful girls, and drinking whiskey than the daily struggles of Brazil's popular classes, which samba songs traditionally memorialized.

The Quadros Regime

The election of 1960 took place amid growing social unrest and intense debate over domestic and foreign policy. Women actively participated in this national dialogue, demanding civil equality and organizing a massive protest demonstration to commemorate the tenth anniversary of the Brazilian Women's Federation, which Kubitschek had outlawed in 1956. Workers also agitated for an end to inflation, corruption, and foreign control of the economy. Brazilian popular culture reflected and reinforced this social turmoil. According to cultural historian Eduardo Carrasco Pirard, bossa nova songs, which had eschewed controversial subjects like exploitation, inequality, and oppression, now increasingly discussed "social themes which presented a rather idealized and paternalistic vision of the black favela-dweller and the worker from the fringe areas of the big cities." Songs like "The

Farmworker's Funeral," by Chico Buarque de Holanda, sarcastically lamented the misfortunes of a peasant who finally won in death that which in vain he had sought in life: a plot of latifundio land "large enough for a grave, not too big, not too deep!"

The campaign oratory and programs of all the principal candidates reflected the ascendancy that the nationalist, populist ideology had gained over public opinion. Even Conservatives supported the presidential candidacy of the flamboyant Jânio da Silva Quadros, former governor of São Paulo, whose populist campaign denounced "foreign exploiters" and promised to "sweep out of the government the corrupt elements, the thieves and exploiters of the people."

Without breaking with the traditional dependence on the capitalist countries for markets and loans, Quadros sought to reduce that dependence by developing new trade and diplomatic relations with the socialist countries and the developing world. Accordingly, he initiated negotiations for the resumption of diplomatic relations with the Soviet Union, sent a trade mission to the People's Republic of China, and denounced the Central Intelligence Agency–backed Bay of Pigs invasion of Cuba in April 1961. Although he stressed the need for foreign investments and guaranteed their security, Quadros opposed foreign investment in Brazilian oil and proposed to modify the "laws and regulations which place the Brazilian company in an inferior position." He also restricted the remittance of profits abroad.

Quadros's policies quickly aroused the hostility of military and civilian Conservatives. An increasingly recalcitrant Congress, dominated by fazendeiros, compounded his problems. Determined to break the legislative deadlock by some dramatic act, Quadros submitted his resignation on August 25, 1961, after only seven months of rule. His resignation message claimed that hostile foreign forces had obstructed his program of Brazil for the Brazilians. Convinced that the military would not permit the prolabor vice president Goulart to succeed him, Quadros evidently believed that public clamor for his return would bring him back to office with the powers he needed to govern, but he had miscalculated.

Led by war minister Odílio Denys, military officers took control of the government and declared that, for reasons of "national security," Goulart, whom they distrusted as a dangerous radical, should not return from his trade mission to China. Naturally, this ignited a national popular uprising that caused a split within the military. In Goulart's home state of Rio Grande do Sul, the commander of the Third Army announced his support for Goulart, and the governor of the state rallied the population to defend the constitution and ensure Goulart's elevation to the presidency. The threat of civil war loomed, but the military ministers, facing divisions within the armed forces and feeling the pressure of public opinion, agreed to a compromise. Goulart took office, but a constitutional amendment restrained the power of democracy and required the president to share power with a parliamentary council drawn from the anti-Goulart legislature.

GOULART'S PRESIDENCY

Taking office in September 1961, Goulart steered a cautious course designed to allay conservative suspicions at home and abroad. In April 1962, he paid a visit to Washington, D.C. Addressing a joint session of Congress, he promised reasonable treatment of foreign-owned utilities in Brazil. The United States provided $131 million in aid for Brazil's depressed northeast, but the IMF, whose approval was a condition for the cooperation of private bankers, remained skeptical of Goulart's intentions.

The first year and a half of Goulart's rule under the parliamentary system saw few major legislative achievements. One was passage of a Brazilian civil code that, under pressure from women's rights groups, prohibited gender discrimination in employment, gave married women legal control over their earnings, and guaranteed shared ownership of commonly acquired property. Another law established Electrobras, the national agency proposed by Vargas for the control of the production and distribution of electric power. Still another required

foreign capital to register with the Brazilian government and barred profit remittances abroad in excess of 10 percent of invested capital, certainly not a radical measure. Yet it produced a sharp drop in foreign investments, from $91 million in 1961 to $18 million in 1962. Lacking other sources for financing development, Goulart had to resort to the Kubitschek formula of a massive increase in the money supply. The new inflationary spiral brought the collapse of the cruzeiro, a wave of strikes, food riots, and a growing radicalization of labor, but the economic slowdown, apparent since 1961, continued. Import substitution as a stimulus to industrialization appeared to have reached its limits, and the small domestic market, the inequities of Brazilian income distribution, and the drain of capital through debt repayment and profit remittances blocked further advance.

With the advice of the brilliant young economist Celso Furtado, who had directed an ambitious effort to develop Brazil's backward, poverty-ridden northeast, Goulart drafted a program of structural reforms that aimed to expand Brazil's democracy and impart a new dynamism to its faltering economy. Reform of the archaic land tenure system would expand the domestic market and increase agricultural production. Tax reform would reduce the inequities of income distribution and provide funds needed for public education and other social welfare purposes. The grant of votes to illiterates aimed drastically to reduce the power of the rural oligarchy in the national and state legislatures.

To implement these changes, however, the legislative deadlock in Congress had to be broken, so in mid-1962, Goulart launched a campaign for a plebiscite to let the people choose between presidential and parliamentary government. Under great public pressure, Congress agreed to the plebiscite, and on January 1, 1963, more than 12 million voters decided by a three-to-one majority to restore to Goulart his full presidential powers under the constitution of 1946.

Goulart's victory only deepened a growing polarization of opinion in the country, however, with the bourgeoisie and the middle class joining the landed oligarchy in opposition to Goulart's domestic program. Goulart's moderate reform proposals in reality favored the industrial bourgeoisie and should have enjoyed its support. But the dynamic industrialist class that had arisen and thrived under Getúlio Vargas was now much weaker. The progressive foreign conquest of Brazilian industry had greatly reduced that class's influence as more and more national entrepreneurs gave up an unequal struggle and solved their personal problems by becoming directors or associates of foreign-owned firms. This dependent bourgeoisie shared its foreign and rural allies' fears of social change. Even the more militant nationalists within the ranks of the progressive industrial bourgeoisie—industrialists long affiliated with organizations like the Industrial Social Service (SESI) and the National Service for Industrial Training (SENAI), which had collaborated with *getulista* populism—feared a growing radicalism of Brazil's peasant and urban industrial working class. As historian Barbara Weinstein argues, by the late 1950s and early 1960s, workers had become a more significant political force: They had expanded their autonomy from state controls, they increasingly relied on strikes and uncompromising demands for wage hikes to secure their interests, and they tended to elect leftist union leaders less inclined to collaborate with industrialists or the state.

The industrialists' apprehension increased because of the spread of radicalism to the countryside. Under the leadership of the lawyer Francisco Julião, peasants in the bleak northeast, afflicted by drought, famine, and oppressive land tenure and labor systems, joined Peasant Leagues and invaded fazendas. Their activities and Goulart's proposals to enfranchise illiterates and enact agrarian reform all endangered the latifundio.

By the end of 1963, the forces on the right—the fazendeiros, the big bourgeoisie, the military, and their foreign allies—had begun to mobilize against the threat from the left. Industrialists had long cultivated support among army officers, inviting generals like Humberto Castelo Branco, the future dictator, to speak at their Forum Roberto Simonsen, a regular meeting sponsored by the São Paulo Federation of Industrialists. But, in early

1962, they began plotting in earnest and by March of 1964, according to Weinstein, the industrialists "had collected more than 1.5 billion cruzeiros equal to more than a million dollars, to aid the armed forces in the seizure of power."

Meanwhile, under strong pressure from impatient radicals, Goulart moved to the left. Appearing at a mass rally in Rio de Janeiro in March 1964, he signed two decrees. One nationalized all private oil refineries. The other made liable to expropriation all large and underutilized estates close to federal highways or railways and lands of more than seventy acres near federal dams, irrigation works, or drainage projects. At the same meeting, Goulart announced that he would shortly issue a decree on rent control. He asked Congress to pass reforms that included tax reform, the vote for illiterates and enlisted men, an amendment to the constitution providing for land expropriation without immediate compensation, and legalization of the Communist Party.

By the middle of March, the military-civilian conspiracy for Goulart's overthrow was well advanced. The governors of some important states met to plan the installation of a "legalist government" in São Paulo to compete with Goulart's regime for official recognition. An emissary returned from the United States with assurances from the State Department that it would immediately recognize the new government. Then, if it became necessary, the legalist government would solicit aid from the United States, and the dispatch of U.S. troops would not constitute intervention but rather a response to a legitimate government's request for aid to suppress communism and subversion.

On March 31, army units in Minas Gerais and São Paulo began to march on Rio de Janeiro. The U.S. ambassador to Brazil, Lincoln Gordon, was well informed of the conspiracy; five days before the coup he cabled Secretary of State Dean Rusk, naming Gen. Humberto de Alencar Castelo Branco as the probable head of the new military junta. Published documents also show that the United States prepared to give military aid, if needed, to the rebels, but Operation Uncle Sam (its code name) proved unnecessary; the Goulart regime fell almost without a struggle on April 1, and the president fled into exile in Uruguay.

As the new military regime consolidated its power, the generals sought to install an alternative to the nationalist economic model that successfully had promoted Brazil's initial industrialization. Their neocolonial vision, based on thorough integration of a dependent Brazilian economy into the international capitalist economy, pursued rapid growth of Brazilian industry and agriculture without regard to its social consequences. Because of the regime's combination of brutally repressive policies with primary economic and political dependence on the United States, the Brazilian scholar Hélio Jaguaribe

aptly calls it "colonial fascism." Ironically, the Brazilian experiment quickly became a model favored by Argentine generals in their 1976 effort to topple Latin America's other major populist regime, which originally was inaugurated in 1947 by the distinguished career military officer, Juan Domingo Perón, and his charismatic wife, Evita.

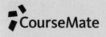

Go to the CourseMate website at **www.cengagebrain.com** for primary sources, additional study tools, and review materials—including audio and video clips—for this chapter.

14

Argentina: Populism, the Military, and the Struggle for Democracy

FOCUS QUESTIONS

- How did Argentina's agricultural export economy affect its political and social development?

- How did the tango's history represent Argentina's ideological identification with European culture in contrast to notions of "racial democracy" in Brazil and indigenismo in Mexico?

- How did the military, urban trade unions, and global economy affect the evolution of Argentine populism?

- Who were Juan and Evita Perón, what was their program, and how did it affect Argentine national development?

- How did market expansion affect women and their role in the nation's political economic life?

A S IN BRAZIL, POPULISM became the defining characteristic of twentieth-century Argentina, but unlike its neighbor, the Argentine military played a much more influential role in shaping its evolution. Peronism, a form of populism identified with Col. Juan Domingo Perón, dominated the political, economic, and cultural landscape of Argentina for two decades. In contrast to the mythologies of Brazil's "racial democracy" and Mexico's "*indigenismo*," however, Argentina's leaders aimed to repress its multiracial, multiethnic past and sought to invent an Argentine national identity that self-consciously celebrated working-class culture and its European origins. Nonetheless, Argentina's experience with export agriculture shared much in common with the other Latin American nations.

By the first decade of the twentieth century, after thirty years of explosive economic growth and sustained political stability, Argentina seemed ready to take a place among the industrial nations. Argentines proudly claimed to be the world's greatest exporter of grain and a leading exporter of meat; they boasted of a railroad network unsurpassed outside Western Europe and the United States; and their capital, Buenos Aires, ranked among the world's most beautiful and cultured cities. Argentines were seemingly prosperous, relatively well educated, and increasingly urban. The burgeoning population (nearly 8 million in 1910) and transportation system promised to create an internal market that would stimulate the rise of native manufacturing and elevate Argentina to the position of one of the world's modern industrial countries.

The full flowering of democracy, too, seemed close at hand. The landed oligarchy, known as estancieros, historically had monopolized Argentine politics by relying on military force and restricting the vote to propertied males, most of whom traditionally resided on rural estates. By the early

1900	Alicia Moreau de Justo founds the Socialist Feminist Center to advocate for women's rights
1916	Radical Party's Yrigoyen wins presidency, calling for minimum wage and workers' rights
1917–1919	Strikes by Maritime Workers' Federation lead to *Semana Trágica*, violent repression by Yrigoyen and Argentine Patriotic League
1924	Women's Rights Association and Socialist Feminist Center win an eight-hour workday for women, forty-eight hour workweek, and prohibitions on night work
1930	Uriburu leads military coup to overthrow Yrigoyen and begins Infamous Decade, characterized by state repression, wage cuts, and state-centered economic activity
1943	Group of United Officers (GOU) seizes power and Perón becomes Minister of Labor
1946	Perón wins presidency promising higher wages, women's rights, and social security
1951	Perón easily wins reelection, campaigning on populist themes
1952	Perón's wife, Eva dies of cancer, and his popular support declines
1955	September coup kills thousands and restores Constitution of 1853
1958	Frondizi wins presidency calling for "Peronism without Perón"
1966	Onganía coup leads to military dictatorship that slashes workers' wages and favors foreign capital
1972	Perón returns to presidency from twenty-year exile and arranges Social Pact with labor to freeze wages and prices
1974	Perón dies, and political violence grows under his successor, Spanish-born wife, Isabel
1976	Military coup led by Gen. Videla

twentieth century, however, Argentina had become a much more urban society, and a propertied middle class consisting of shopkeepers, artisans, manufacturers, and government bureaucrats emerged. New political organizations like the Radical Party soon developed and began to compete effectively for this new constituency. Moreover, with the gradual professionalization of the army, the social composition of the officer corps also changed. Middle-class men, mostly the sons of immigrants, replaced the old officer groups, and the oligarchy gradually lost its predominance. These developments and a series of unsuccessful Radical coups apparently convinced the estancieros that the time had come for electoral reform. Consequently, in the hope of attracting a significant share of newly enfranchised voters, they embraced the Saenz Peña Law, which provided for universal male suffrage and a secret ballot.

The appearance of prosperity and emerging democracy, however, proved illusory. Stagnation, interspersed with periods of depression and runaway inflation, marked the Argentine economy during succeeding decades. Military coups, disorder, and brutal repression afflicted the nation's politics. At the base of these problems lay Argentina's structural dependence on foreign markets and capital, a dependence that placed the country's economy at the mercy of foreign events and decisions made abroad. Although the populist policies implemented by Juan Perón and his successors aimed to promote a genuine national development, their failure to break the country's structural dependence perpetuated a deformed social and political system.

The Export Economy

Argentina's dynamic economic growth during the last quarter of the nineteenth century and the early twentieth century was due to three factors. First, a large market developed in Europe for its primary exports: wool, mutton, beef, and wheat. Second, the inflow of millions of immigrants provided cheap labor for the expanding agricultural sector. Third, the influx of large quantities of foreign investment capital facilitated railroad construction, put more land under cultivation, and established food (mainly meat) processing plants. The nation's prosperity depended on its ability to export huge amounts of agricultural commodities, to import the manufactured goods it required, and to attract a steady stream of large-scale foreign investment.

Consequently, Argentina was critically vulnerable to fluctuations in international market and finance conditions. Any reduction in overseas trade reverberated disastrously throughout the economy. Because Argentines usually imported more than they exported—a tendency made worse by the fact that the market price for raw materials remained steady or declined while the prices of manufactured goods rose—the country suffered from chronic trade deficits that habitually depleted the national economy of circulating coin and restricted local market development. To attract new sources of wealth, successive Argentine governments had opened Argentina to foreign capital.

Foreign investment reached enormous proportions in the first decades of the twentieth century. During the years 1900 to 1929, foreigners came to control between 30 and 40 percent of the nation's fixed investments. Argentina absorbed nearly 10 percent of all foreign investment carried out by capital-exporting nations, one-third of all the foreign investment in Latin America, and more than 40 percent of the total foreign investment of Great Britain, the world's leading capitalist power. Investment was concentrated in railroads and government bonds, the proceeds from which subsidized the construction of railroads and public works.

Although foreign investment unquestionably helped fuel economic growth, it simultaneously created immense economic difficulties. Huge interest payments on foreign debts and the profit remittances of foreign-owned companies, often representing between 30 and 50 percent of the value of Argentina's exports, produced serious balance-of-payments problems. Because government bodies owed much of the foreign debt, a substantial portion of government revenue went to service payments. Rigid interest rates and repayment schedules meant that the burden remained the same, even when state revenues declined because of adverse economic conditions. Moreover, governments dependent on foreign bondholders could not easily divert revenues earmarked for debt service to other areas.

Every sector of the Argentine economy depended on exports. Agriculture and livestock raising employed 35 percent of the workforce. The nation's greatest agricultural area, the pampas, exported 70 percent of its production. Argentine industry centered on food processing, mainly meat packing. As late as 1935, foodstuff processing accounted for 47 percent of all industrial production, and textiles for another 20 percent. The transportation industry—railroads and coastal shipping—handled mostly export commodities.

Rich and poor alike relied on the export economy for their livelihood. The ruling elite included large landowners, who produced almost entirely for the export trade. Their income and their political power rested squarely on the export economy. In addition to large numbers of farm laborers, many urban and industrial workers depended on exports for their jobs. The major trade and industrial unions in Argentina arose in those industries—coastal shipping, railroads, dock work, and packinghouses—whose workers owed their well-being to overseas trade. Because the government relied on revenues derived from import taxes, significant numbers of white-collar workers and professionals employed by the government also depended on the export economy.

Foreign control and influence permeated the economy. Foreign businesses either owned or were affiliated with most of the large merchant houses that carried on the all-important export-import trade. British or U.S. companies owned and operated the major shipping lines (both intercoastal and interoceanic), the railroads, and the *frigoríficos* (meat-packing plants).

The export economy brought indisputable benefits to Argentina, but those benefits were unequally distributed. Sharp differences in economic development, for exampled, existed among regions. Whereas the pampas and Buenos Aires boomed, most of the interior provinces stagnated. Mendoza and Tucumán with their wine and sugar made some headway, but all the other central and northwestern provinces—Jujuy, La Rioja, Santiago del Estero, and Salta—experienced social and economic decline.

The inequalities of property and income between the various classes were equally glaring. The rich were very rich and growing richer; the poor grew poorer. In the countryside, the estancieros, masters of thousands of acres of rich land, built palaces, while the majority of foreign-born immigrant sharecroppers eked out a miserable living. In Buenos Aires, wealthy landowners, merchants, and lawyers gathered at the sumptuous Jockey Club, while laborers struggled to make ends meet as inflation eroded their already insufficient paychecks.

The expansion of market forces also dissolved traditional barriers between private and public spheres, forcing women into low-paid, menial positions in urban factories and sweatshops without releasing them from their unpaid responsibilities in the home. According to a late-nineteenth-century Buenos Aires census, women composed 39 percent of the paid workforce, and a 1904 report by Dr. Juan Bialet Masse confirmed that, in an industrial environment generally characterized by intolerable working conditions and low wages, Argentine women "suffered the most intense discrimination and exploitation." Apparently, male employers preferred women workers because they were cheaper, more reliable, more efficient, and more docile than men. A 1913 report for the National Labor Department revealed that, on average, children employed in industry received half the wages of women, whose income, in turn, was half that of men.

Argentina's greatest treasure was its land, but only a few Argentines owned sizable portions of it. In 1914, farm units larger than 2,500 acres accounted for only 8.2 percent of the total number of farms but held 80 percent of the nation's farm area. Tenants worked more than 40 percent of farms, most on terms that were less than favorable. In 1937, a mere 1 percent of the active rural population controlled more than 70 percent of Argentina's farmland, much of which they left idle. Yet the land was fertile and suitable for intensive agriculture. Thousands of immigrants came to Argentina in search of land

only to discover that the estanciero oligarchy had long since monopolized virtually all of it.

Income distribution followed the same pattern. Less than 5 percent of the active population garnered 70 percent of the gross income derived from agriculture. Not only did workers and rural laborers receive little benefit from the export system, but the operation of the system's finances and taxation eroded what little return they did receive for their labor. Faced with chronic deficits in the balance of payments and unwilling or unable to tax the land or income of the landed elite, the government had no alternative but to resort to the printing press to finance its costs. The result was inflation. Exporters also demanded a fluctuating currency-exchange rate, which had an adverse effect on wage earners. Finally, the tax structure burdened the mass of consumers with high sales taxes that discouraged internal market expansion.

Argentine Society

Argentine society divided roughly into three classes—upper, middle, and lower. The upper class acquired its wealth and prestige through its virtual monopoly of landownership. These large landholders used the late-nineteenth-century export boom to solidify and enhance their power. Cattle fatteners, who supplied beef for both the domestic and foreign markets, constituted the most powerful faction within this elite. This inner circle included approximately four hundred families who were allied closely through social clubs and business associations. Geographically, most of the wealth was located in the cattle and cereal regions of the pampas near Buenos Aires. From 1880 to 1912, this landed oligarchy also controlled national politics. It used its control over the government to promote meat and grain exports, guarantee easy credit for members, and provide more favorable taxation and currency policies. The other great institutions of Argentine society, the military and the church, also reflected the views of the elite.

Late-nineteenth-century economic growth stimulated urbanization, which transformed the nation's class structure. An urban middle class arose. This middle class, heavily concentrated in the bureaucracy and professions, depended on the export economy and attached itself to the Radical Party.

The lower class divided into two groups: urban marginals and workers. Urban marginals were a racially and ethnically diverse group, composed largely of immigrant foreigners, including Eastern European Jews, against whom regular employers routinely discriminated. Not surprisingly, according to historian Donna Guy, women constituted a large share of this underclass, a considerable number of whom became involved in prostitution, which the Argentine government had legalized in 1875. For elites, legalized prostitution—which required prostitutes to undergo regular medical examinations and restricted their activities to particular urban zones—aimed to stabilize the patriarchal family by providing a safe, secure outlet for the release of men's sexual frustrations. It also enabled elites to collect revenues from, and establish control over, a population considered dangerous. For the prostitutes and pimps, these licensed bordellos became a means of survival and, ironically, gave birth to a cultural form —the tango—that eventually defined Argentina's national identity.

The tango, first as dance and later as song, had emerged in the early nineteenth century among the nation's lower classes, especially its black population, which composed 25 percent of Buenos Aires. According to historian John Charles Chasteen, enslaved Africans originally performed the dance to celebrate their individual black kings and distinguish their African national identities. Later, it evolved into *candombe*, a dance style typical of the Argentine black community, and by the middle of the nineteenth century, Argentine elites adopted it to mock Afro-Argentine culture. By the early twentieth century, however, the tango or *milonga* had become, according to the *Dictionary of Argentine Expressions*, "a dance found only among people of the lower orders." It appeared routinely in the brothels, nightclubs, and *academios* (dance halls) of Buenos Aires, where poor women mixed with men of all social classes. Its songs typically addressed themes about life in the *conventillos* (tenements), criminals, slum

dwellers, and the relentless intrusion of poverty on the dreams of young girls.

By contrast, most members of the working class labored in small factories, where Argentina's industrial expansion was concentrated until 1914. (The primary exception to the predominance of small industries was the frigorífico.) A considerable number of workers were employed by the shipping industry, railroads, and urban tramways in the Port of Buenos Aires, where organizations like *La Fraternidad*, the railroad workers' union, and the Maritime Workers' Federation were especially strong. Numerous strikes occurred after the turn of the century and throughout the first Radical regime (1916–1922). However, disputes about political activity and internecine rivalries among Socialists, anarchists, and syndicalists weakened the labor movement.

The Radical Era, 1916–1930

THE RISE OF THE RADICAL PARTY

Naturally, increasing social inequality produced growing unrest among the urban middle class, university students, women, workers, ethnic minorities, and small groups of junior military officers. The Radicals drew on this discontent in their efforts to overthrow the oligarchy by force in 1905. Despite their failure, the Radicals attracted growing popular support in the decade that followed.

Radical Party strength rested on twin pillars: its local urban organization, which acted to meet the needs of the middle class, and its leader, Hipólito Yrigoyen, who played a dual role as the titular head of the Radical Party. First, he was the great mediator who managed to reconcile the conflicting interests of the middle class and large landowners who made up his political coalition. Second, although inarticulate and a recluse, Yrigoyen managed to project an austere democratic image that made him the party's charismatic leader. This clever dealmaker and manipulator symbolized for the middle class the Radical dedication to democracy. Despite a checkered past that included shady business deals, he furnished the party with much of its moral appeal.

Modern South America

The Radical propaganda effectively presented an image of a national party, transcending the narrow regional and class interests that previously had governed Argentine politics. The Radical program was purposely vague. It straddled the line between its two major constituencies: the middle class and the landed elite. The Radicals therefore never challenged the basic premises of the export economy and its dependence on foreign capital. The party advocated neither land reform nor industrialization.

During the Radical Era, Argentine women, who historically had been treated like children or, worse, as *patria potestad* (the legal property of men), continued to organize and agitate for equality both within and outside the formal structure of political parties. Cecelia Grierson, Argentina's first female doctor, formed the National Women's Council to lobby for women's greater access to education and professional employment. These women's groups, like others in Latin America, typically sought to protect and conserve the primary power of women within the family. Although some viewed this as an implicitly "conservative" role, in the context of a traditional society battered by unfettered market forces, the communal maternal values of family life quickly translated into civic actions, which Francesca Miller calls "social motherhood."

This meant that, irrespective of class, ethnic, racial, or regional identity, women activists came to expect the state to intervene to monitor, regulate, protect, and harmonize the interests of all members of the Argentine national family, especially when outsiders threatened them. "The aristocratic women and the proletarian women are equally victims," thundered Carolina Muzzilli, a prominent feminist. "It is time that the Argentine woman recognizes that she is not inferior to men and, even if she has a different mission, her civil and natural rights must be restored."

In practice, however, class interests often distinguished the activities of various women's organizations. For example, feminist leaders like Alicia Moreau de Justo, founder of the Socialist Feminist Center in 1900, pressured her husband, Juan Bautista Justo, the nation's premier Socialist, and his male colleagues to sponsor Law 5291, which attempted to regulate working conditions for women and children, providing them special legal protections against the ravages of unfettered market forces.

By 1910, these and other women's organizations had coalesced to sponsor Argentina's first International Feminist Congress, which attracted women's groups throughout Latin America to its agenda for civil equality, better working conditions for women, equal pay for equal work, school reform, and revision of divorce laws to allow divorced mothers custody of themselves, their children, and their property. Not content merely with equality of opportunity, delegates from the Socialist Women's Center argued that this would only reinforce the existing inequality of social condition between men and women; they consequently called on male leaders in government, business, and education to institute affirmative action in support of women's issues. They demanded special treatment that would consider women's historical responsibilities in both public and private realms; for example, they wanted a special commercial school for women and legal provisions that would give wage-earning women thirty-four days of paid leave before and after giving birth.

European ethnic immigrant groups also protested against the elite's discriminatory laws designed to "ghettoize," stigmatize, and limit the civil rights of the non-native-born, who also—not coincidentally—happened to be either prosperous small farmers, urban petty proprietors, or organized proletarians. Ironically, the late-nineteenth-century white supremacist oligarchy had encouraged their arrival in Argentina to "whiten" the nation's population and provide relatively cheap labor on the great estates and in export-oriented urban industry. However, continuous harassment greeted those immigrants who either resisted acculturation, demanded worker rights, or successfully competed against the creole estancieros. Swiss and German immigrant farmers, for example, organized a revolt in the province of Santa Fe to denounce the oligarchy's discriminatory policies. Similarly, Jewish schools, especially in the province of Entre Ríos, had been the target of racist violence in 1910, which prompted Jewish organizations to protest.

Carolina Muzzilli and Alicia Moreau were militant Argentine feminists who agitated for civil and political equality, social justice, and international solidarity in the early twentieth century.

Finally, a coalition of immigrant groups including Italians, Germans, and Russian Jews, many of whom were sympathetic to socialist, anarchist, and trade unionist ideas, challenged the Social Defense Law of 1910, which authorized the expulsion of foreign "agitators" and defined some immigrant groups as "undesirable elements."

THE FIRST RADICAL GOVERNMENT: YRIGOYEN, 1916–1922

With a finely tuned grassroots political organization, a well-known presidential candidate, and a vague program promoting "class harmony," the Radicals won the 1916 presidential elections, but their tenuous bond with the landowner elite limited their success. The elite controlled the military and the major agricultural lobbying groups and had close contacts with powerful foreign business interests. Yrigoyen continually walked an unsteady tightrope between the middle class, which wanted a piece of the governmental pie, and the oligarchy, which was still wary of the party that had rebelled three times in three decades and that had won an election campaigning against the selfish interests of that oligarchy. He could not push too hard too fast, or the oligarchy would surely overthrow him.

The Radical government's program combined a conservative fiscal policy and moderate social reforms designed to secure political stability, in return for which the oligarchy was to allow the middle class wider access to the government bureaucracy and the professions. This strategy had inherent contradictions. First, expansion of access to government employment meant that government expenditures necessarily had to increase, but this violated the tenet of fiscal conservatism, unless the economy continued to expand at a rapid rate. Second, Yrigoyen had to maintain the fragile alliance of landowners and members of the middle class within his own party. In sum, the key to the Radicals' staying in power was Yrigoyen's ability to distribute the fruits of Argentine economic growth to the middle class without antagonizing the oligarchy.

Discontent was growing on the part of the middle class, too, because the decline in government revenues from imports meant fewer government jobs for its members. Yrigoyen's balancing act became even more difficult with the emergence of labor agitation for improved wages and working conditions. Wartime demand for Argentine exports had brought on inflation, and as a result, the purchasing power of wages seriously declined. Yrigoyen had to move cautiously in attempting to alleviate labor's plight, for the oligarchy looked on such moves as interference in its economic domain. The problem grew more complicated because much of the labor agitation targeted foreign-owned companies with close ties to the elite. Facing bitter opposition from the ruling elite, Yrigoyen abandoned his modest efforts to incorporate labor into his coalition.

Consequently, from 1916 to 1919, political expediency and, in the last analysis, the degree of pressure exerted by the landed elite clearly determined Yrigoyen's policy toward workers' struggles. Major strikes occurred against foreign-owned companies engaged in export-related enterprises. Because Argentine governments often sent in the police and armed forces to break strikes, the attitude of the Yrigoyen regime was decisive. The Maritime Workers' Federation struck twice, in 1916 and 1917, for higher wages. The first strike coincided with harvest shipments. In both instances, the union gained access to Yrigoyen, the government kept out of the dispute, and the union won; but in late 1917, the government abandoned the unions when a general strike jeopardized export interests. With the strike threatening the entire harvest, the British government and the elite brought joint pressure on Yrigoyen to intervene and use troops to break the strike. The frigorífico strike of 1917–1918 met the same fate when the government sent in marines to subdue the strikers.

The climactic episode, known in Argentine history as the *Semana Trágica* (Tragic Week), came in January 1919. Its name refers to the heavy loss of life that followed when Yrigoyen, apparently fearing the army's intervention to topple his government, abandoned his original conciliatory position and sent police and armed forces to break a general strike that had grown out of a strike in a metal factory. This violence accompanied a wave of brutal pogroms against Russian Jewish immigrants by members of the elite and the middle class, organized in an Argentine Patriotic League. Instead of denouncing the anticommunist witch-hunt, the Radical government added its voice to the hysterical cry that the strike was a revolutionary conspiracy and even encouraged party members to join the vigilante bands. Thereafter, Yrigoyen strengthened his popular electoral base and catered to his middle-class constituency by increasing patronage.

The Radicals also faced growing opposition among women, who, according to the 1914 national census, composed 22 percent of the total workforce. These women activists continued to press the government for greater access to the professions and government jobs, equal pay, the right to vote and hold office, and a variety of regulations designed to protect women from the brutality of unfettered market forces. In 1919, Elvira Rawson de Dellepiane, a veteran feminist leader, organized the Women's Rights Association (ADF) to rally women, regardless of political affiliation, around this progressive platform. Within a relatively short time, the ADF claimed some eleven thousand members and worked closely with other feminist organizations like the Women's Union and Labor Group to pressure the Yrigoyen administration. The last three years of Yrigoyen's term were a struggle merely to survive.

The Argentine university reform of 1918, which had continental reverberations, reflected Yrigoyen's desire to cater to his middle-class constituency. The series of events leading to this famous reform began with a student strike at the University of Córdoba; the students demanded, among other changes, simplification of the entrance requirements and secularization of the curriculum.

When the strike deteriorated into violence, Yrigoyen intervened and acceded to the student demands. But he went further, establishing a series of new universities that increased middle-class access to the professions and the government jobs for which so many middle-class aspirants hungered. This especially benefited Argentine women. The Radicals also sought to strengthen their electoral position by expanding the patronage system and removing provincial governors on the pretext that they had violated the federal constitution.

By 1921, the boom unleashed by World War I had ended, and depression followed. The union movement disintegrated. Layoffs eroded union membership, and internal bickering rendered the unions ineffective. The Radicals actually experienced some success in recruiting workers during the depression because their local committees provided charitable services.

THE SECOND RADICAL GOVERNMENT: ALVEAR, 1922–1928

Despite adverse economic conditions, Marcelo de Alvear, Yrigoyen's hand-picked successor, became president. Immediately, however, the party began to come apart. Although couched in personal terms —Alvear against Yrigoyen—the division more accurately reflected the growing split between the middle-class and elite sectors of the party.

Alvear cut the payroll to trim expenses and hiked tariff rates to increase revenue. The tariff increase also aimed to reduce imports and alleviate the balance-of-payments problem to satisfy the middle class. A balanced budget, however, appealed to estancieros but directly contradicted middle-class demands for even more government employment opportunities. In 1924, the Radicals split into two factions, with the Anti-Personalist wing under Alvear's leadership.

Meanwhile, although largely excluded from these debates, subordinate social sectors nonetheless sought to organize popular movements to take advantage of the political discord within the Radical Party and between propertied elites and the middle class. Although workers, women's rights organizations, and ethnic minorities were often internally divided, the devastating impact of external market forces on their daily lives mobilized a common agenda that occasionally managed to intrude on the national political discourse. In 1924, for example, a coalition of trade unions and women's groups, including the Socialist Feminist Center and the Women's Rights Association, successfully secured the passage of Law 11.317, which established an eight-hour workday for women, limited a woman's workweek to forty-eight hours, and prohibited night work.

The law also required large, typically foreign-owned, companies to obey special rules for pregnant workers, including a stipulation that factories with at least fifty women employees should provide facilities for nursing mothers. Two years later, women's groups pressured Argentina's patriarchal political parties to pass another law, this time empowering adult married women to sign contractual agreements and pursue personal, educational, and career goals without their husbands' permission. Naturally, none of this legislation protected women employed in agriculture or domestic service, nor did it address the gender wage gap. But these victories, no matter how seemingly modest, laid the foundation for future state intervention on behalf of women and other historically oppressed people disadvantaged by an unregulated market.

The decade also pioneered the expansion of radio, a new technology that assisted the Radicals in their efforts to fashion a unified national culture. Although Argentine traditions had precluded "decent" women from participation in Argentina's rich cultural nightlife, the radio brought the tango from the dance halls and brothels into middle-class homes, where women thrilled to its raunchy disrespect for an established social order that confined them to their kitchens and bedrooms. Moreover, the French had widely acclaimed the tango in Paris, which lent it still greater credibility as a national cultural expression acceptable to Francophile elites and the middle-class folk who simultaneously envied and mimicked their lifestyle. From this moment onward, the tango became the new symbol of Argentine modernity and national identity.

Yrigoyen's Second Term, 1928–1930

Yrigoyen made a smashing comeback in 1928, winning his second presidential term with an overwhelming 57 percent of the vote, but the Great Depression hit Argentina in October 1929. The Radicals, whose strength had been increasing, suffered a mortal blow. Exports dropped 40 percent, foreign investment stopped, and unemployment was widespread. Government efforts to spark a recovery served only to induce inflation. The decline in imports severely undermined the government's fiscal position, because it relied on import duties for most of its revenue.

The government incurred a huge deficit, which it tried to cover by borrowing. As a result, it found itself in the position of competing for increasingly scarce credit resources with the landed elite, which desperately needed money to ride out the decline in the export market. Yrigoyen's policy threatened the interests of the landed elite, and he became expendable. Furthermore, his meddling with the military had seriously undercut his standing with that powerful institution. Finally, the Great Depression destroyed his personal popularity among the middle class, his main base.

Yrigoyen became the scapegoat. His enemies pictured him as senile and corrupt, incapable of ruling the nation in a time of crisis. The Great Depression ruined the party apparatus, which lacked the resources necessary to dispense patronage. The political situation continued to disintegrate, and violence increased. A military coup overthrew Yrigoyen on September 6, 1930.

The Infamous Decade, 1930–1943: Military Intervention and the State

The coup marked the end of Argentina's short experiment with democracy and the entry of the military into the nation's politics; it ushered in a period of harsh repression and corruption, known as the Infamous Decade. Lt. Gen. José F. Uriburu, who had led the group of conspirators that overthrew Yrigoyen, became the head of a coalition of widely diverse elements, including traditional Conservatives, right-wing Nationalist-Fascists, and such center and left parties as the Progressive Democrats, Independent Socialists, and Socialists. These strange bedfellows had agreed on the elimination of Yrigoyen, but little else. Consequently, the loosely built alliance soon fell apart.

Following the coup, Uriburu conducted a campaign of brutal repression against opponents of his provisional government. He especially targeted prostitutes, whose defiance of established law had spread venereal disease and undermined the patriarchal family. Their scandalous behavior threatened public authority and led the military to abolish prostitution in 1934. Fearful that the abrupt abolition of the sex industry would create a new wave of unemployed in the midst of a global depression, however, the military government passed the Law of Social Prophylaxis, which offered former prostitutes state-sponsored medical care and employment opportunities in the public and private sector. The military also strictly controlled radio, decreeing the Dry Law, which censored electronic broadcasts that featured tango music, soap operas, and other lewd activities that corrupted public morality.

With its political and social opposition dispersed and defenseless, the military sought to reorganize Argentina's civilian political institutions and created a new coalition, the *Concordancia*, which united landed aristocrats, dissident Radicals, the Catholic Church, and the military. With the help of fraud, the intimidation tactics of goon squads and gangsters, and the general apathy of an embittered and cynical electorate, the Concordancia won control of the national government.

The Great Depression, the first modern crisis of the international capitalist system, powerfully proclaimed the fragility of the nation's economically dependent, externally oriented national development policies and ushered in a new era of internal sociopolitical struggle that dramatically transformed Argentine society. The global economic collapse bankrupted Argentina's largest companies and inundated the nation with a tidal wave of unemployment, which, not surprisingly, disproportionately afflicted women, who lost jobs at a much higher rate than men.

The Great Depression also precipitated a pronounced demographic shift in the social origins of the national labor force. Before 1930, urban industrial and rural agricultural employers alike had relied on more than 6 million European immigrants, half of whom had arrived after 1880; in the ensuing decades, expansion of Argentine industry and agriculture would have to depend on internal migration from rural to urban areas.

Naturally, women constituted an increasingly important segment of this population; during the Great Depression and World War II, twice as many women as men migrated to Buenos Aires and other cities. This reflected both the destructive impact of market forces on rural life and the patriarchal nature of Argentine families. Unable to make a living in rural areas, men who lost their jobs or small agricultural plots often abandoned their families as well. Under these circumstances, single female heads of households could not sustain their families' subsistence in the low-paying jobs traditionally available to women in agriculture, where wages were one-fourth those of urban industry. Not surprisingly, women's nationwide employment increased 27.4 percent from 1935 to 1939. In the textile, tobacco, and clothing industries, women composed a majority of the labor force by the end of the decade.

Although the military's intrusion into Argentine politics during the 1930s effectively reduced opportunities for democratic popular participation, trade union leaders still organized and agitated in defense of male workers' rights and for state regulation of the market. Here, women's groups, reflecting their increased visibility in the public sector, joined them to demand an activist national government that recognized their political rights and protected their socioeconomic interests. That is why the Argentine Association for Women's Suffrage, founded by Carmela Horne de Burmeister in 1932 and claiming a membership of eighty thousand, campaigned vigorously for women's right to vote, state-subsidized subsistence, maternity leave and health-care benefits, and child care for working mothers. Argentina's Concordancia faced one inescapable conclusion: It could not impose an

enduring social stability militarily; this required an expanding economic pie, which the unfettered international market forces of a dependent capitalism no longer guaranteed.

Abandoning the liberal, free-trade, laissez-faire economic doctrines on which the prewar export economy relied, the Concordancia's economic policy established state intervention as a decisive factor in the economy. Its basic aim was to protect the nation from the cyclical effects of the world capitalist economy. To accomplish this, they sought to protect their main foreign market, Great Britain; limit production of farm commodities; and restrict imports through indirect methods, such as the establishment of a currency-exchange system that discriminated against non-British imports. They also sought to establish new import-substitution industries primarily through foreign investment.

In this period, discovering they could not export manufactured goods to Argentina on a competitive basis because of high tariffs and the discriminatory exchange system, U.S. manufacturers established plants in Argentina. As a result, foreign capital played an increasingly important role in the economy during the 1930s, accounting for 50 percent of the total capital invested in Argentine industry. Foreign companies virtually monopolized the meat-packing, electric power, cement, automobile, rubber, petroleum, pharmaceutical, and several other industries.

The British market for beef and grain was critical for the Argentine export economy. During the late 1920s and early 1930s, the British government was under constant pressure to reduce Argentine imports to protect producers within the empire. The result of Argentine efforts to secure the British market was the controversial Roca-Runciman Treaty of 1933. By this treaty, Britain guaranteed Argentina a fixed, although somewhat reduced, share of the chilled beef market. It also promised to eliminate tariffs on cereals. Argentina, in return, lowered or eliminated tariffs on British manufactures. It also agreed to spend its earnings from the British market on British imports into Argentina.

The economy improved after 1934, and, by 1936, the crisis had passed. Cereal prices rose gradually on the world market until 1937, when they again dropped. Meat prices rose until 1936 and then remained steady. Industrial investment reached pre-Depression levels. Although real wages declined, unemployment fell sharply because of public works and industrial investment. In general, Argentines were relatively well off during the 1930s. Consumption of consumer goods and food rose considerably.

The process of industrialization accompanied a growth of native industrialists and a parallel increase in the size of the working class and its organizations, which heightened political tensions within Argentine society. For its part, the Argentine industrial bourgeoisie was profoundly dissatisfied with the economic policies of the landed oligarchy and, although still relatively small and unorganized, the working class was rapidly gaining in self-consciousness and developing new political aspirations that challenged both industrialists and the estancieros. In 1930, the General Confederation of Labor arose from the merger of two large unions, and by 1943 trade union membership totaled between three hundred and three hundred fifty thousand. With the Concordancia government apparently helpless in the face of a brewing social revolution, the Group of United Officers (GOU), a secret military officers' lodge, organized a coup d'état and overthrew the Concordancia regime in 1943. Thereafter, they established a ruling military junta headed successively by generals Arturo Rawson, Pedro P. Ramírez, and Edelmiro Farrell.

The Perón Era, 1943–1955

PERÓN'S RISE TO POWER

The 1943 military coup had deep and tangled roots. The fraud and corruption that tainted both oligarchic and Radical politics in the Infamous Decade no doubt offended military sensibilities. During the 1930s, the officer corps of the Argentine armed forces, predominantly middle class in its social origins, had developed an ardent nationalism that saw the solution for Argentina's problems in industrialization

and all-around technical modernization. The interest of the military in industrialization also reflected its desire to create a powerful war machine capable of creating a Greater Argentina that could exercise hegemony in a new South American bloc. Industrialization required Argentines to end the nation's neocolonial status, to free it from dependence on foreign markets. Many officers developed a pro-German attitude, partly influenced by the German military instruction that they had received. Some also admired the supposed successes of the Nazi New Order but sympathized with Germany even more because they believed that its great power rivals, England and the United States, had conspired to keep Argentina a rural economic colony. Their pro-German attitude did not translate into a desire to enter the war on Germany's side; instead, they sought to keep Argentina neutral in the great conflict.

World War II had a lasting impact on the ideology and practical political-economic needs of Argentina's military leaders. First, absorbed with waging global war, the United States, Great Britain, France, Germany, and Japan could not intervene effectively in Argentina's internal affairs. Second, with the war's disruption of international commercial trade and the conversion of the great powers' industrial production to military needs, an externally dependent Argentina lacked the essential inputs—capital equipment, technology, replacement parts, and private sector investment—necessary to sustain economic expansion and social stability. In the absence of any organized and effective foreign opposition, and pressed by domestic popular movements for a social justice based on economic growth, these military leaders had no alternative except to expand the state-centered, import-substitution industrialization policies inaugurated during the 1930s.

Consequently, the military proposed a massive government investment in industrialization and technical modernization, even though it feared the social changes and forces that such transformations might unleash. In particular, it feared the revolutionary potential of the working class. In effect, the military proposed to build Argentine industrial capitalism with a thoroughly cowed, docile working class.

As a result, one of the first acts of the military regime was to launch an offensive against organized labor. The government took over the unions, suppressed newspapers, and jailed opposition leaders. It also sought to silence women's public voice and force them to return to their gendered lives as mothers, wives, and daughters—to be the familial anchor of a revitalized Catholic morality within their private households. Here, gender discrimination aimed to undermine class solidarity by blaming male workers' economic difficulties on women's highly visible presence in the workplace. This policy of direct confrontation and collision with labor and women had disastrous results and threatened to wreck the industrialization program. An astute young colonel, Juan Domingo Perón, saved the military from itself and took over the Department of Labor in October 1943. He promptly raised it to the status of the Ministry of Labor and Welfare and opened a new bureau, the Women's Division of Labor and Assistance. As he noted in his inaugural speech, Perón wanted officially to recognize that "more than 900,000 Argentine women are part of the paid work force."

Born in 1895, the son of immigrant and creole parents of somewhat marginal economic status (his father was a farmer), Perón entered the military college at sixteen and slowly rose in rank to captain in 1930. During the next decade, he spent several years in Europe, where the German and Italian dictatorships much impressed him. In 1941, Perón joined the Group of United Officers; although only a junior colonel, he quickly rose to its leadership ranks.

His genius lay in his recognition of the potential of women, ethnic minorities, and the working class and the need to broaden the social base of the nationalist movement. He became the patron of the urban proletariat and, under considerable pressure from a well-organized and vocal women's rights movement, immediately courted its support by endorsing women's suffrage. Within a year, he submitted such legislation to the Congress, which approved it in 1947. Perón secured the enactment of protective legislation designed to increase women's access to education and improve their wages

and working conditions. Not surprisingly, from 1941 to 1950, the number of women admitted to universities more than doubled.

As Minister of Labor in 1944, Perón established a minimum wage for piecework produced in the home, largely by women; naturally, this raised the issue of a broader minimum wage, and workers in the food industry, mostly women, received this protection the following year. By 1949, women constituted 45 percent of the industrial workers in Buenos Aires. In this year, again pressed by women's groups and apparently recognizing the potential divisiveness of a gendered wage gap between men and women workers, Perón supported legislation to require equal pay for equal work in Argentina's flourishing textile industry. As a result, by 1959 the wage differential between men and women ranged between 7 and 15 percent, which historian Nancy Caro Hollander characterizes as "one of the lowest in the non-Socialist world."

Perón also cultivated a political constituency among Argentina's male work force. He encouraged workers to organize and favored them in bargaining negotiations, in which his department participated. As a result, workers' wages not only rose in absolute terms, but their share of the national income also grew. This, of course, increased mass purchasing power and thereby promoted the process of industrialization. Perón also created a state system of pensions and health benefits, with the result that employers' contributions for pensions, insurance, and other benefits rose steadily until Perón's fall in 1955. In return for these real gains, however, the unions lost their independence and became part of a state-controlled apparatus in Perón's hands.

Naturally, Perón's progressive social policies created considerable opposition both within certain factions of the military and among the landed oligarchy. In October 1945, these groups staged a coup that led to Perón's imprisonment. But the organizers of the coup were divided and unclear about their objectives, and Perón's followers mobilized rapidly. Loyal labor leaders organized the Buenos Aires working class for massive street demonstrations to protest Perón's jailing. The workers virtually took over the city, encountering no opposition from the armed forces. The bewildered conspirators released Perón from prison. Thereupon, he resigned from his various government posts, retired from the army, and began his campaign for the presidency in the 1946 elections.

In preparation for those elections, Perón, taking due account of the defeat of fascism in Europe, cast himself in the role of a democrat. He created a Labor Party to mobilize the working class, the principal component in a class alliance whose other major elements were the national industrial bourgeoisie and the army. Perón's chief opponent was a heterogeneous coalition of landed elites, middle-class Radicals, Socialists, and Communists. Greatly assisted by U.S. foreign policy blunders, Perón won easily.

Once in office, Perón confronted what his movement identified as a new cultural threat. *Fútbol* (soccer) had displaced the tango as Argentina's national obsession after the Great Depression and the advent of movie theaters had bankrupted many small cabarets frequented by middle- and working-class men. Whereas the tango had celebrated unbridled heterosexual passion, soccer had emerged as an all-male sport in its appeal to participants and spectators alike. According to historian Donna Guy, the Peronistas increasingly feared what appeared to be an increase in homosexual relationships and their open representation in national artistic and cultural expression. They therefore determined to use state power to revive the tango and legal prostitution in the hope that this would stimulate more interest in heterosexuality. According to historian Donald Castro, Perón understood the tango's popular appeal and fostered its reemergence for his own political ends. During his administration, the state-owned movie company produced *La historia del tango* and three films that celebrated the life of Argentina's most famous tango artist, Carlos Gardel.

Postwar Economics

After the war, the United States bestrode the emerging new world order like a colossus, but its extraordinary economic output found ample demand in war-torn Europe, Asia, and Africa, where domestic policies focused on internal socioeconomic reconstruction. Consequently, Argentine industrialists and landed oligarchies alike faced relatively little postwar competition as they sought to develop internal markets and expand agricultural raw materials exports. International prices remained high, profits were secure, and domestic tariff protection meant that local companies could afford to pay higher wages and benefits to workers without jeopardizing their control over production.

This postwar boom enabled Perón to keep his coalition together. The export sector produced large surpluses in the balance of payments, making available funds for industrialization, mainly in labor-intensive manufactures. Perón also nationalized railroads and public utilities and created powerful state-owned companies that dominated local shipping, steel, and banking industries. Between 1945 and 1948, industrial workers' real wages rose 20 percent. Personal consumption also rose. Because there was only a slight decline in the share of the national income that went to profits, the redistribution of income to the working class did not come at the expense of any other segment of the alliance. Industrialists kept profits up and benefited from increased domestic consumption, which provided a growing market for their products. The only sector of the economy that suffered was agriculture.

Perón managed to win over a considerable sector of the dependent middle class through his use of government patronage, just as Yrigoyen had done before. He kept the military happy by his commitment to industrialization, which was an important aspect of the military's desire for national self-sufficiency, and by providing it with generous salaries and the latest equipment for modern warfare.

One of Perón's greatest allies was his beautiful and stylish wife, Eva Duarte de Perón, whom the Argentines affectionately called "Evita" (little Eva). Evita relished her role as Juan's liaison to the working class. "The people can be sure," she triumphantly announced to admiring throngs at Perón's presidential inaugural, "that between them and their government, there could never be a separation, because in this case, in order to divorce himself from his people, the President would have to first divorce his wife!" Shortly after the enfranchisement of women in 1947, Evita joined with other feminists to create the Peronist Feminist Party, an organization to mobilize women in support of the Peronist political platform. She also formed the Eva Perón Foundation, a charitable institution that distributed large sums of money to neighborhood groups; financed various women's centers to link impoverished women to vital social, medical, and legal services; and built a large patronage army for Peronism.

Although her role as a feminist in Argentina's history is controversial, one thing is indisputable: Eva Perón's activism showed women and her working-class supporters, the adoring *descamisados* (shirtless ones), that they should not rely on the beneficence of any politician to defend their rights. "Just as only workers could wage their own struggle for liberation," she insisted, "so too could only women be the salvation of women." In the 1951 presidential election, this was a lesson that was not lost on women or the working class. Ninety percent of registered women, eligible to vote for the first time, went to the polls, and some 65 percent cast their votes for Perón, but they also elected seven women senators and twenty-four women deputies, the largest female delegation of government representatives in the Americas. Evita's vision of a government and people linked by her marriage to Perón seemed prophetic, but a year later, death, not divorce, intervened; Evita's tragic demise in 1952 at the age of thirty-two dramatically weakened the populist caudillo's attachment to Argentine workers and women.

Perhaps more significant, the global economy had begun to shift, as did Perón's policies. Except for a short-lived recovery during the Korean War, Argentina entered a period of severe recession, which included several drought-induced bad harvests. The late 1940s brought the first signs that Argentina would face serious long-term economic difficulties. Its export commodities began to confront increased competition from the United States and from revitalized Western European agriculture. Later, the advent of the Common Market worsened Argentina's position. Balance-of-payments

deficits replaced the large surpluses that had financed the nation's import-substitution industrialization. Industrial production fell, as did per capita income. Real wages dropped 20 percent from the 1949 level in 1952–1953. It was in this decline that Perón's political failure was rooted.

PERÓN'S DOWNFALL

After his reelection in 1952 and in response to the economic crisis of the early 1950s, Perón formulated a new plan (the Second Five-Year Plan, 1953–1957) that largely reversed his previous strategy. He tried to expand agricultural production by paying higher prices to farmers for their produce and by buying capital equipment for this sector (tractors and reapers). He sought to increase the agricultural production available for export by means of a wage freeze that he hoped would restrict domestic consumption. Although real wages declined slightly, workers did not suffer proportionately more than other groups. But the industrial bourgeoisie was unhappy because labor productivity fell more sharply than wages that the regime's prolabor policies supported. The industrialists, supported by a considerable portion of the army, wanted economic deregulation to lower wages. The industrial sector's major problem was lack of capital, however, because the agricultural sector no longer generated a large surplus.

To solve the capital shortage, Perón abandoned his previously ultranationalistic stand and actively solicited foreign investment. In 1953, the government reached an agreement with a North American company, the Standard Oil Company of California, for exploration, drilling, refining, and distribution rights in Argentina. Perón hoped thereby to reduce the adverse effect of oil purchases abroad on the balance of payments. Foreign capital, however, used the most modern technology and machines, which required fewer workers and tended to create unemployment in the affected industrial sectors.

To maintain government expenditures and a bloated bureaucracy in the face of declining revenues, Perón printed more money. The amount in circulation increased from 6 to 45 billion pesos

Juan and Evita Perón, 1952.

during his two terms. By 1954, he had had some success in stabilizing the economy; he achieved a balance-of-payments surplus, and capital accumulation showed an upward curve, but his new economic strategy had alienated key elements of his coalition of workers, industrialists, and the armed forces. Perón then sought to divert attention from economic issues—with disastrous results.

Perón adopted two new strategies. First, he attempted to enhance his moral and ideological appeal. Second, he began to employ greater coercion to suppress a growing opposition. The vehicle for his ideological and moral appeal was *justicialismo* (Perón's ideal of justice for all), a third route to development that was neither communist nor capitalist.

Perón's strategy included attacking the church. Starting in 1951 the regime grew more repressive. The government suppressed and took over Argentina's most famous newspaper, *La Prensa* (1951). Furthermore, Perón used his National Liberating Alliance, a private army of thugs, and the thirty-five-thousand-man federal police force to intimidate the political opposition. Torture, imprisonment, censorship, purges, and exile became the order of the day. After 1954, even the General Confederation of Labor became a coercive force, whose prime function seemed to be to suppress opposition within the labor movement.

Perón's reluctance to go along with the industrialists' desire to push down wages and increase productivity alienated that group; the industrial bourgeoisie then joined forces with the agrarian interests that always had bitterly opposed Perón. This desertion ended Perón's once highly successful coalition. Inevitably, Perón's hold on the working class loosened as the wage freeze and inflation reduced the value of their wages.

Despite economic adversity, Perón's presidency could have survived if the military had not abandoned him. For the better part of a decade, he had masterfully balanced, divided, and bribed the military. Most of the senior officers owed him both their rank and their prosperity. The army was heavily involved in industrial production, and this provided an excellent means to become rich. In addition, to win its allegiance, Perón had showered the military with expensive military hardware and excellent wages. However, his relations with the armed forces began to disintegrate when he altered his economic policy to lessen emphasis on industrialization and self-sufficiency. On this score, his concession to Standard Oil in 1953 was the last straw for the nationalist military.

Thus, in struggling to extricate the nation from an economic quagmire, Perón undermined the multiclass coalition that had brought him to power and sustained him there. When the final successful revolt took place in 1955, enough of the working class was alienated to ensure the military's success. Perón briefly threatened to arm the descamisados but instead fled into exile.

Although considerable scholarly debate about Perón and his populist policies continues, he solved none of the country's major economic problems and the principal roadblocks remained. Transportation was still inadequate and obsolete, and a scarcity of electric power hindered industrial modernization. Argentina did not produce enough fuel to meet domestic needs, and this created an enormous drain on the balance of payments. The nation's industry remained limited for the most part to import-substitution light industry. Despite his anti-imperialist rhetoric, Perón did not nationalize key foreign-owned industries like meat packing and sugar refining. Most serious of all, Perón did nothing to break the hold of the latifundio on the land.

As a result, inefficient land use marked agriculture and impeded long-range development.

Collapse of Populism: In the Shadow of Perón, 1955–1973

ECONOMIC STAGNATION

The gradual restoration of global economic competition among the leading capitalist countries led to chronic, sometimes violent, economic fluctuations during this period. The source of these difficulties was a balance-of-payments deficit that the decline in agricultural prices caused. The nation could not earn enough from its exports to pay for the large expenditures necessary to fuel domestic industry. Acute depressions invariably followed periods of rapid economic growth and wiped out all previous gains. Runaway inflation accompanied these cyclical conditions.

The governments of this period, whether military or civilian, tended to promote the inflow of foreign investment as a development strategy. Arturo Frondizi (1958–1962), for example, won the election on a political platform of "Peronismo without Perón"—that is, nationalism and state regulation of market forces. Nonetheless, he quickly bowed to pressure from the U.S. State Department and the International Monetary Fund (IMF). These agencies promised low-interest loans to ease the economic pain produced by mounting trade deficits, but in return, they insisted that Frondizi break his political promises to the Argentine people and slash social welfare spending, deregulate private sector business, and expand investment opportunities for foreign capital.

Nonetheless, this development strategy had severe drawbacks. Foreign companies tended to monopolize credit opportunities, certain key industries became concentrated in foreign hands, and profits earned by foreign subsidiaries and remitted to the home company added to the balance-of-payments deficits. Moreover, since the IMF's principal concern was inflation, its stabilization programs invariably increased the cost of credit, deepened economic recessions, and contributed to growing business failures. Finally, foreign investment was usually technologically intensive and therefore created unemployment. Consequently, during the post-Perón Era of development spurred by foreign capital, Argentina experienced chronic problems with large numbers of underemployed and unemployed urban workers.

This economic insecurity was politically untenable for working men and women who recurrently joined with students, small businesspersons, and other disadvantaged groups in publicly protesting these intolerable policies that disproportionately benefited wealthy foreigners and Argentine elites. The resulting political disorder inevitably led to a cycle of political violence and periodic military coups d'état against Frondizi in 1962 and his civilian successor, Arturo Illia, in 1966.

THE MILITARY IN POLITICS

In the past, military interventions had been brief, largely designed to destroy popular political opposition, intimidate the lower classes, and reconstruct civil society so that civilian governments favorable to the ruling elites could win elections. However, Gen. Juan Carlos Onganía, who replaced Illia, aimed to govern longer. Consequently, he suspended the constitution; dismissed all civilian government entities, including the Congress, the Supreme Court, and provincial governors; abolished all political parties; and purged the universities of moderates and leftists, reserving a special hatred for Jewish intellectuals.

As minister of the economy, Onganía sought foreign investment by removing all restrictions on profit remittances; he also stimulated the process of industrial denationalization by devaluing the peso by 40 percent. This meant that many local companies could no longer afford expensive capital imports and royalty payments to owners of foreign technology. These local companies disappeared, leaving their share of the market to foreign firms. In this way, Coca-Cola and Pepsi gained control of 75 percent of the soft-drink market. Between 1963 and 1971, foreign interests bought out fifty-three Argentine companies that represented almost every

industrial sector, particularly the automotive, chemical, petrochemical, metallurgical, and tobacco industries. Meanwhile, the regime froze wages, although prices continued their steady rise.

Growing outrage on the part of workers and students over the government's economic program, especially its policy of industrial denationalization and the wage freeze, erupted into violence in the interior in the spring of 1969. Major riots took place in Rosario, Corrientes, and Córdoba, the most industrialized city of Argentina. There, workers and students rose in the famous Cordobazo revolt, occupying major sectors of the city until troops ousted them. At the same time, urban guerrilla activity by groups like the Montoneros, who represented the left wing of the Peronist movement, surged. Their tactics included raids on police stations, assassinations, and robberies.

Onganía's failure to cope with the mounting wave of guerrilla activity precipitated the 1970 military coup, which installed Gen. Roberto M. Levingston as president. An expert in military intelligence and counterinsurgency, Levingston decreed the death penalty for terrorist acts and kidnappings, but his repressive decrees failed to establish a permanent social peace that could restore investors' confidence and reverse Argentina's 1970–1971 economic decline.

THE RETURN OF PERÓN

Displeased with a resurgence of labor unrest, the military ousted Levingston in March 1971. His replacement, Gen. Alejandro Lanusse, carried out a dual policy that combined brutal repression of leftist guerrillas with a general liberalization of the political climate. In effect admitting the military's failure to renovate Argentine politics, Lanusse undertook negotiations that led to the restoration of political activity and the return of the Peronists to full electoral participation for the first time since 1955.

The military briefly held out hope that the moderate political parties would unite to stand against the Peronists, but the latter's superior organization and their leader's unchallenged popularity ensured their victory. At the heart of the Peronist program were formal agreements with labor (*Pacto Social*) and industry (*Acto Compromiso del Campo*) that pledged compliance with a wage and price freeze. This cooperation lasted for about a year, while the Argentine economy, buoyed by high world-market prices for beef and grain, boomed. These populist agreements disintegrated in mid-1974 with the onset of renewed inflation brought on by a huge increase in international oil prices.

Even before these economic arrangements ended, the Perónist movement had begun to disintegrate, divided between radical and moderate factions. By the time Perón died in July 1974, the level of violence had increased. In 1975, thugs representing both factions reportedly killed eleven hundred people. In the face of this escalating violence and economic chaos, the military stepped in again and installed Gen. Jorge Rafael Videla as president.

Once again, as in Brazil, populism's failure to embrace revolutionary structural change left its reform agenda at the mercy of uncontrollable international markets. Unable to afford to finance its state-centered development project with low-cost foreign loans or high export prices, the Peronists fought with each other and with their long-time political rivals. The seemingly endless cycles of violence thereafter created an opportunity for the military to intervene, only this time to create an enduring dictatorship that abandoned populism in favor of a new neoliberal faith. Cuba would not make the same mistakes as Mexico, Brazil, and Argentina.

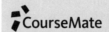

Go to the CourseMate website at **www.cengagebrain.com** for primary sources, additional study tools, and review materials—including audio and video clips—for this chapter.

15

Cuba: The Revolutionary Socialist Alternative to Populism

FOCUS QUESTIONS

• How did U.S. intervention in Cuba affect the development of Cuban national identity?

• How did the struggle of Afro-Cubans and women for equality affect Cuban national development?

• What were the causes of the 1933 Cuban Revolution, and how did it lay the political foundation for Cuban populism?

• What were the primary structural changes produced by the 1959 Revolution, and how did they affect Cuba's national development?

• How did the Cuban Revolution resolve the dilemmas confronted by populist regimes in Mexico, Brazil, and Argentina, respectively, in the 1960s?

IKE THE OTHER Latin American nations we have examined, Cuba suffered historically from dependency and the cyclical nature of world market demand for its products. Moreover, Cuba endured the additional burdens of almost total economic domination and repeated prolonged military occupation by the United States. But in 1959, Cuba—an island ninety miles from Key West and ruled by one of the region's most firmly entrenched dictatorships—became the scene of the most successful social revolution in Latin America during the twentieth century. Under the banner of Marxism and with the military, economic, and political support of the Soviet Union, until recently, the revolutionary government made great progress toward the elimination of such problems as illiteracy, mass unemployment, and unequal distribution of income and wealth. However, the collapse of the Soviet Union and Cuba's other trading partners in the socialist bloc, combined with an intensified effort by the United States to bring about its downfall, produced the most serious crisis in socialist Cuba's history, a crisis it is still struggling to overcome.

Independence and the Spanish-Cuban-American War

JOSÉ MARTÍ AND THE REVOLUTIONARY MOVEMENT

By the early 1890s, a global economic crisis, compounded by high U.S. tariffs on Cuban sugar imports, reduced external demand for sugar, destroyed sugar planters' profits, swelled unemployment, and inflamed long-simmering class, racial, and gender animosities. Afro-Cubans, workers, women, colonos, creole elites, and U.S. investors in Cuba increasingly identified Spanish imperial authority as the principal source of this injustice and therefore revived the movement for independence.

1895	José Martí leads a second war of independence
1898	United States declares war on Spain, taking Cuba and Puerto Rico
1902	Tomás Estrada Palma becomes president, but Platt Amendment limits Cuban sovereignty
1906–1909	United States orders Second Intervention to end Gómez rebellion
1912	United States participates in racist massacre of Afro-Cubans
1917–1923	Gen. Enoch Crowder leads Third U.S. intervention
1924	Gerado Machado wins presidential election and becomes dictator
1933	Ramón Grau San Martín and Sgt. Fulgencio Batista overthrow Machado dictatorship
1940–1944	Batista wins presidential election in coalition with Cuban Communists
1944–1952	Auténticos govern an unstable Cuba awash in corruption
1952	Batista overthrows Auténticos and imposes a brutal dictatorship
1953	Fidel Castro leads failed attack on Batista army at Moncada Barracks
1956	26th of July Movement directs guerrilla war led by Castro brothers, Che Guevara, and Camilo Cienfuegos
1959	Revolution defeats Batista, redistributes land, and offers free education and health care
1960	Vilma Espín organizes Cuban Women's Federation to lead campaign against illiteracy
1961	United States plans failed invasion by Cuban exiles at the Bay of Pigs
1962	Soviet nuclear missiles deploy to protect Cuba from further U.S. aggression
1970	"Ten-Million-Ton Harvest" of sugar fails miserably

The spiritual, intellectual, and organizational leader of the revolutionary movement was José Martí (1853–1895). As a lad of sixteen, Martí had spent six years in prison for supporting the 1868 independence revolt. Exiled in 1871, he moved to New York, where he earned his living as a brilliant journalist and worked tirelessly to unite Cuban émigré revolutionary groups. In 1892, he founded *El Partido Revolucionario Cubano* (the Cuban Revolutionary Party), which proposed to obtain, "with the united effort of all men of good will, the absolute independence of the island of Cuba, and to foment and aid that of Puerto Rico." He then recruited such military veterans of 1868 as Máximo Gómez and Antonio Maceo in preparation for an invasion of the island. In April 1895, Martí landed on a Cuban beach with a group of insurgents; a little more than a month later, he died in a skirmish with a Spanish patrol.

Despite the loss of its charismatic leader, the revolution spread, and the National Liberation Army achieved major successes with the aid of time-proven guerrilla tactics. Afro-Cubans played particularly prominent roles in the armed struggle. In every rebellious province except Camaguey, Afro-Cubans constituted a majority of the soldiers, known as *mambises*, and they fought in integrated battalions, often under the command of black officers like Maceo, his brother José, and Agustín Cebrerco. This prompted some Afro-Cubans to conclude that in the army, where "nobody cares about the color of a man," the *Cuba Libre* movement was "putting the principles of democracy into practice." This wartime experience reaffirmed Afro-Cubans' long-standing commitment to equality and social justice.

Women also shaped the independence struggle in decisive ways. Some, like university graduate Adela Azcuy, distinguished themselves in battle, whereas peasant women, despite Spanish attempts to enclose them in concentration camps, continued to provide food and intelligence information to the liberation army. This "women's war" shaped the consciousness of the revolutionary generation and led to a political demand for women's suffrage, public employment, and educational opportunity.

At the beginning of 1896, a new Spanish commander, Gen. Valeriano Weyler, instituted counterinsurgency measures that colonial powers later employed against twentieth-century rebels in Algeria, the Philippines, and Vietnam. He set up population concentration centers and free-fire zones,

José Martí (*left*), a brilliant writer and thinker, became a towering figure in Latin American history when he joined with Antonio Maceo (*right*), the Bronze Titan, to lead the revolutionary movement for Cuban independence.

which resulted in enormous hardships and losses to the peasantry. His successes were transient and counterproductive, serving mostly to intensify popular hatred for Spanish rule, and whole provinces remained under the absolute control of the liberating army. The failure of Weyler's military policies and growing pressure from the United States led Spain to promise autonomy to Cuba in late 1897.

INVOLVEMENT BY THE UNITED STATES

As the rebellion spread over Cuba, it became an increasingly volatile issue in the United States. Inevitably, the fighting destroyed or damaged property, and this brought complaints from powerful U.S. business leaders and financiers with interests in Cuba. These leaders, who were white supremacists, also feared the possibility that Cuba's "race war," as Spanish propagandists depicted it, might transform the island into another Haiti and simultaneously inflame the African American community. Nonetheless, the Cuban struggle for independence struck a sympathetic chord with some Americans, particularly among the working class. William Randolph Hearst and Joseph Pulitzer, then engaged in a newspaper circulation war in New York City, helped keep popular interest high by running lurid stories of Spanish brutality.

Meanwhile, enthusiastic expansionists like Theodore Roosevelt in the McKinley administration believed that the Cuban situation raged out of control, that the autonomy proposal sponsored by the United States had failed, and that, if the United States did not intervene, an unmanageable Cuban revolutionary government might take over from the collapsing Spanish

Modern Caribbean Nations

regime. In the midst of this ferment, the *USS Maine* blew up in Havana Harbor on February 15, 1898, with heavy loss of life. This incident helped spur McKinley to a more belligerent stance; he demanded that Spain terminate the concentration camp policy, offer an armistice to the rebels, and accept the United States as a final arbiter between the parties. He did not mention Cuban independence. When Spain delayed its response to U.S. demands, McKinley sent a message to Congress asking it to authorize U.S. military intervention in Cuba. Congress, after considerable debate, adopted a joint resolution to that effect.

However, Cubans did not rejoice: Almost every major revolutionary figure—Martí, Maceo, Gómez—opposed U.S. entry into the war, fearing it would result in direct or indirect U.S. political and economic control of Cuba. "The Cuban war," Martí wrote in 1895, "has broken out in America in time to prevent … the annexation of Cuba to the United States." All they sought from the United States was recognition of Cuban belligerency and the right to purchase arms in the United States. McKinley, of course, had worked feverishly to defeat the Turpie-Foraker bill, recognizing Cuban belligerency, and had unsuccessfully opposed the 1898 Teller Amendment that prohibited U.S. annexation of Cuba.

The ensuing war was short and nasty. U.S. commanders ignored their Cuban counterparts, excluding Cuban generals from decision making and relegating Cuban soldiers to sentry and cleanup duties. Although incompetence was the key feature of both Spanish and U.S. war efforts, the U.S. Army—wretchedly led, scandalously provisioned, and ravaged by tropical disease—swiftly defeated a demoralized, dispirited Spanish army and snatched the fruits of victory from the Cuban mambises, who had fought gallantly in a struggle of three years' duration. The exclusion of Cuban leaders from both war councils and peace negotiations foreshadowed the course of U.S.-Cuban relations for the next sixty years.

The First U.S. Occupation, 1899–1902

The U.S. Army occupied Cuba from January 1899 to May 1902. The occupation had three basic goals. First, the United States sought to make Cuba into a self-governing colony, an arrangement designed to secure liberal economic policies and political stability without the administrative burdens of an outright colonial occupation. To this end, the U.S. military sought to pacify the island without serious conflict with the Cuban army, which was still intact and in control of much of rural Cuba. The revolutionary army, however, did not resist the U.S. takeover, as did Emilio Aguinaldo and his insurgent forces in the Philippines at the same time. Cuban passivity in part reflected the fact that the years of struggle had taken their toll; the leading Cuban generals, such as Calixto García and Máximo Gómez, were tired old men, and many of the younger men who could have led a resistance movement had died in battle.

In addition, U.S. authorities bought off the army by offering to purchase its arms, an offer that hungry, unemployed soldiers found difficult to refuse. They also offered key rebel leaders well-paid positions and ably manipulated the volatile issue of race to divide and conquer Cuba Libre. At the same time, the occupation government established a Rural Guard, largely devoid of Afro-Cubans, most of whom could not meet eligibility requirements, which included literacy, a recommendation from propertied elites, and sufficient wealth to purchase a uniform, equipment, and horse. The Guard's primary purpose was to eradi-

cate banditry and protect foreign property—in the words of Gen. Leonard Wood, to put down the "agitators who began to grow restive at the presence of the Americans."

After political stability, necessary to attract U.S. capital, the second major goal was to repair the destruction wrought by the war and provide the services needed to sustain the U.S. occupation and promote economic recovery. Gen. Leonard Wood, appointed governor general in 1899, launched a program of public works and sanitation that led to a major achievement of the occupation—the conquest of yellow fever. Taking its lead from a Cuban doctor, Carlos Finlay, whose theory correctly attributed the transmission of the dread disease to the mosquito, the American Sanitary Commission succeeded in eliminating it. Another major accomplishment of the Wood administration was the creation of a Cuban national education system, vastly superior to what had existed under Spain but designed to inculcate U.S. principles; even the textbooks were translations of U.S. textbooks. The Cuban treasury paid for all these programs as well as the expenses of the U.S. troops.

Ruling with arbitrary methods and largely ignoring the former revolutionaries, especially the Afro-Cubans, in favor of Spaniards and creole planters who had opposed independence, Wood imposed a new electoral law that empowered the "better class" by restricting the franchise to literate adult males with property worth $250. Elihu Root, McKinley's secretary of war, especially celebrated the law's impact on Afro-Cubans: "Limited suffrage," he wrote, effectively excluded "so great a proportion of the elements which have brought ruin to Haiti and San Domingo." Elections for a constitutional convention, not surprisingly, produced an assembly that, under intense U.S. pressure, adopted a document that included the so-called Platt Amendment. This amendment limited the ability of independent Cuba to conduct foreign policy and to borrow money abroad. It authorized the United States to maintain a naval base at Guantánamo Bay, and, most important, gave the United States the right to intervene in Cuba for the "preservation of Cuban independence" and for the "maintenance of a government adequate for the protection of life, property, and individual liberty."

The third goal of the occupation was to absorb Cuba into the United States' economic sphere of influence. Because the Platt Amendment assured U.S. business executives of protection and a generally favorable investment climate on the island, capital poured into sugar and railroad construction. A reciprocal trade agreement signed by the two nations in 1903 was the final step in bringing Cuba under U.S. hegemony. This treaty cut by 20 percent the tariff on Cuban sugar exported to the United States; in return, Cuba reduced the duties on imported U.S. goods.

The end of Spanish rule and the U.S. occupation also transformed Cuban society by removing the final obstacle to the development of the latifundio in Cuba. Two processes worked hand in hand in the following decades: the concentration of land and mills and the **proletarianization** (a violent social process that expelled peasants from the land) of the sugar workers. The two wars of independence had devastated small mills: The total number fell from two thousand in 1860 to one thousand in 1877 to only two hundred in 1899. The rapid and huge influx of foreign—mostly U.S.—investment into sugar enabled the larger mills to buy up surrounding cane land and reduce the colono to circumstances close to slavery. Ramiro Guerra y Sánchez has estimated that the great mills owned perhaps 20 percent of the island's area in 1927.

The expansion of the latifundio impoverished the island's rural masses and kept the colonos at subsistence levels, deeply indebted to the mill, and in constant fear of eviction. The wages of rural workers remained low because the mills imported cheap labor from other Caribbean islands. As a result, a considerable reserve pool of labor was available; even those lucky enough to find jobs worked only four months of the year during the harvest period. Displaced farmers had two choices: They could remain and work for small wages on a seasonal basis for the sugar mills (*centrales*), or they could emigrate to the cities, where jobs also were scarce. Small independent growers were at a severe disadvantage, for the mills squeezed the price paid

for their cane to a minimum. In addition, the mills controlled the transportation network.

The ruin of the small mills and farmers and the low wages paid rural labor, which reduced the purchasing power of the masses, sharply limited the domestic market for manufactured goods and commercial services. Thus, Cuban industrialization lagged. Sugar companies monopolized the railroads and operated them solely for their own benefit, often without regard to the public interest. Although Cuba's railroad network exceeded that of most Latin American nations, it was inadequate to develop an internal market.

U.S. companies, which had poured money into Cuban sugar during the first occupation, had invested $200 million by 1913, predominantly in sugar. This accounted for nearly one-fifth the total U.S. investment in all of Latin America.

Dependent Development and Popular Struggle, 1902–1953

INTERVENTION, CORRUPTION, AND POPULAR RESISTANCE, 1902–1924

Cuba's political life, afflicted by its status as a U.S. "protectorate" and suffering from interventions, had a weak and stunted growth. Its first president, Tomás Estrada Palma, the aging former head of the government-in-exile during the Ten Years' War, had not even lived in Cuba for twenty-five years and consequently relied heavily on U.S. support to secure his election in 1901. Without a loyal Cuban constituency even among the "better class," Estrada set an enduring pattern in twentieth-century Cuban politics by implementing U.S.-sponsored policies and currying favor among local elites through patronage, graft, fraud, corruption, and intimidation.

Although these tactics served Estrada well in his 1905 reelection bid, they also alienated propertied elites excluded from the public dole; meanwhile, lower-class Cubans—*guajiros* (racially mixed peasants), workers, and Afro-Cubans—seethed at the government's neglect of the national liberation struggle's original goals: independence, equality, and social justice. The combination of elite and popular discontent, always a volatile mix, produced a series of revolts (in 1906, 1912, 1917, and 1921) that caused weak Cuban governments to invite U.S. military intervention.

In 1906, President William Howard Taft responded by sending in the Marines, and shortly afterward appointed Charles Magoon, a judge from Minnesota, to preside over a U.S. provisional government. Magoon's solution for the problem of factional violence was to divide patronage more equitably among contending Cuban groups. During the second occupation, elite resistance to U.S. domination virtually disappeared, in large part because of this new system of institutionalized corruption, which united all sections of the elite in the eager pursuit of U.S. favor and protection.

Magoon's provisional government also reformed the Cuban Army and reinvigorated the decade-old racist immigration policy of "whitening," which prohibited "races of color" but encouraged Spanish immigrants with travel subsidies and promises of public employment. According to the 1907 census, this significantly reduced the proportion of Afro-Cubans to less than 30 percent of the total population. Magoon also attacked **brujería** (witchcraft)**, ñáñiguismo** (religious brotherhoods), and santería, the cultural centers of Afro-Cuban resistance; purged political partisans from the Rural Guard; reorganized the Cuban Army as a political counterweight to it; and developed both as institutions designed to protect private property and elite rule in Cuba.

Nonetheless, the lower classes remained restive. Workers, irrespective of race and gender, continued to organize trade unions and press their agenda for social justice. Meanwhile, Afro-Cuban mambises like José Isabel Herrera complained that U.S. investors, Spanish immigrants, and loyalist elites "took over the businesses, factories, and public jobs that we had just brought to independence." The case of Quintín Banderas was instructive: An Afro-Cuban who fought for thirty years against Spanish colonialism and rose to the rank of general, he died penniless and propertyless, unable even to secure a janitorial job with the government of independent Cuba.

In 1908, under the leadership of Evaristo Estenoz, a veteran of Cuba Libre, Afro-Cubans organized the Independent Party of Color (PIC) to defend the interests of black Cubans, promote integration and racial democracy, and protest against monopolization of the material rewards of independence by white elites and foreigners. The PIC denounced white supremacy and demanded an end to racial discrimination, expansion of public employment and education programs, establishment of the eight-hour day, agrarian reform, and "Cuba for the Cubans." Despite official efforts to disrupt its activities, the PIC continued to expand until 1912, when, fearing imminent threats to capitalist labor and property relations, U.S. Marines joined the Cuban Army in what historian Aline Helg calls a "racist massacre" that left thousands of blacks dead and thereafter forced Afro-Cubans to pursue social justice through class and anti-imperialist struggles.

WORLD WAR I AND THE DANCE OF THE MILLIONS

Cuba's greatest sugar boom and bust occurred because of World War I. The fighting in Europe, which disrupted sugar production on the continent, from the first caused large price increases: Prices nearly doubled in the first two months alone. Eventually, the Allies became totally dependent on Cuban sugar production because they were fighting their major former supplier, Austria-Hungary. This demand spurred further expansion of Cuban sugar production, with planters moving into previously uncultivated land. The last great surge of mill construction also occurred. As production spread into virgin land, centrales were built, and new towns sprang up.

The Allies attempted to keep commodity prices from skyrocketing by establishing purchasing committees to handle the acquisition of raw materials and food. Nonetheless, Cuban production rose in 1916 to 3 million tons at an average price of $0.04 a pound. Expansion created a severe labor shortage on the island, and Cubans imported laborers from Jamaica and other Caribbean islands to fill the void. The colonos staged a comeback, and a few actually prospered.

Biblioteca Nacional José Martí

This 1912 cartoon, entitled "Today's Trendy Sport," depicts a U.S. Marine and a white Cuban soldier playing soccer with the heads of Evaristo Estenoz and Pedro Ivonnet, leaders of the Afro-Cuban insurrection in Oriente Province. The caption reads, "Is this how 'football' will be played in Oriente?"

The war accelerated the trend toward the concentration of the industry in U.S. hands. By 1919, U.S. companies owned approximately half the island's mills and produced more than half the total sugar. The boom also led to the integration of sugar mills and plantations with distributors and companies that were large sugar users. Giants such as Coca-Cola, Hershey (chocolate), and Hires (root beer) bought up producers to guarantee their supplies. Producers, in turn, purchased distributors and refiners.

The postwar years of 1918 to 1920 brought unprecedented prosperity to Cuba as sugar prices soared and Eastern European sugar-producing areas were slow to recover from the war. After the Allied purchasing committees deregulated prices in 1920, they began an incredible upward spiral called the "Dance of the Millions." In February 1920, the price of sugar stood at $0.09125 per pound. By mid-May the price had climbed to $0.225. But soon prices collapsed as a result of a worldwide depression and Europe's agricultural recovery; by December, Cubans were getting $0.0375 per pound—the prewar price level.

The precipitous rise and equally sudden collapse of sugar prices caused chaos in the Cuban economy. Mills had contracts to buy large quantities of sugar at high prices, prices that were now far higher than the world market. Producers and processors had taken out loans to expand—loans based on anticipated high prices. Banks began to call in these loans. In April 1921, the island's largest bank, the *Banco Nacional*, closed, and others throughout the country followed suit. Simultaneously, the United States raised its tariff on sugar by $0.01, thereby inflicting another blow on the already devastated industry. In 1921, the First National City Bank of New York—long heavily involved with U.S. sugar interests in Cuba—took more than nearly sixty bankrupt mills. The harvest reached 4 million tons in 1922, but prices stayed low. The following year, prices rose to $0.05 a pound because of the crisis over the French invasion of the Rhineland. Prices did not reach that level again for three decades.

In late 1920, with the collapse of sugar prices and growing political unrest in Cuba, the U.S. military again intervened, and Gen. Enoch Crowder, in effect, ruled Cuba from his headquarters on board the battleship *Minnesota* until 1923, when he became U.S. ambassador. This experience revived Cuban nationalism. Crowder's blatant meddling in Cuban politics and the postwar collapse of Cuban sugar revealed the disastrous consequences of foreign domination and monoculture. Searching for solutions to these problems, Cuban university students, one-quarter of whom were women, entered the political arena in the postwar period. Believing that to change society they must change the university, they directed their first attacks against inept and corrupt professors and administrators; in 1922, students at the University of Havana demonstrated for reforms along the lines of the 1918 university reform in Argentina. Students would henceforth play an important role in Cuban politics.

Women also played increasingly influential roles in Cuba. Economic growth, especially in household services, textiles, and the tobacco and sugar-refining industries, created greater employment for women outside the home. Nonetheless, as they moved "from the house to the streets," in the words of historian Lynn Stoner, women brought to their public activities a communal consciousness forged in family life. Even the Women's Club, organized in 1917 and composed primarily of upper- and middle-class women, insisted that the state, the *pater familias* of Cuban society, should regulate domestic social relations consistent with the common welfare. It therefore supported women's suffrage, equal pay for equal work, greater access to education, and civil equality.

However, for Cuban elites and U.S. policymakers, the growing political activism of students and women was not their greatest concern. In the 1920s, a much larger cultural struggle emerged over Cuban national identity that could have had grave implications for the future security of property rights and U.S. hegemony. Historically, Spanish and criollo elites alike had sought to identify the island's culture with Spain and racist doctrines of white supremacy. The various U.S. military occupations, reflecting their own racial and class prejudices, thereafter reinforced these efforts and joined criollo elites in fashioning an image of Cuba as a white Spanish woman menaced by its black population. A "national music" identified with Spain and the *danzón*, a rigidly structured dance favored by Cuba's upper class, reinforced this image of whiteness. Nevertheless, popular sectors in Cuba, especially in Oriente Province, long a stronghold of Afro-Cuban culture, had contested this elite vision of Cuba's national identity and preferred the multicultural sound of **son** (a musical style that joined traditional Spanish melodies with African rhythms to reimagine a racially diverse Cuban national culture).

Initially denounced by criollo elites like composer Luis Casas Romero as a "true disgrace" and suppressed by the Cuban government, postwar working-class Cubans defiantly resisted the elite's cultural hegemony and thrilled to the pulsating beat of son and the *rumba*, the dance it inspired. Together, son and the rumba, which pantomimed sexual intercourse, gave voice to a popular culture that sought to liberate Afro-Cubans and the lower classes from social controls imposed by the dominant class. During the 1920s, the development of radio and recording industries soon created a new audience for this music and dance that, according to historian Louis Pérez, previously had existed only in "working-class bars, waterfront cafés, and dance halls." Boaz Long, the U.S. Minister to Cuba, perhaps best expressed elite fears of this spreading cultural rebellion in a 1920 letter that scorned Cubans' growing affection for the "syncopated music of Africa" and specifically deplored the social dangers of the rumba, which would "often become indecent" and "have the effect of developing a mob spirit." More to the point, however, Long was especially concerned that "in the case of the negro, they may arouse a sense of racial solidarity."

MACHADO, 1925–1933

Taking advantage of growing nationalistic sentiment and appealing for women's support with promises of enfranchisement, Gerardo Machado y Morales won the 1924 presidential election. Despite his nationalistic declarations, however, Machado had close links to U.S. economic interests, for until his election he had been vice president of a U.S.-owned utility in Havana. Even before he took office, Machado visited the United States to assure President Calvin Coolidge of his government's good intentions. Likewise, Machado neglected his promise of suffrage for women, although he authorized breaks for working mothers to nurse their children and established some female hiring quotas.

Machado began his term auspiciously. He embarked on an ambitious program of public works and attempted to institute a system of controls for sugar production designed to protect small and midsize producers against severe price declines. Thanks to these and similar efforts, Machado enjoyed unparalleled popularity and faced virtually no opposition for two years.

Already, however, disturbing signs of tyranny and economic instability were evident. The number of political assassinations increased alarmingly. Police shot strikers to break a wave of strikes during 1925, and a Machado gunman murdered the nation's most prominent Communist leader, Julio Antonio Mella,

in his Mexican exile. Machado's secret police routinely eliminated his opponents by throwing them to the sharks in Havana Harbor.

Meanwhile, the sugar industry entered a long period of stagnation and decline. It became clear that the Cuban economy was painfully vulnerable not only to world-market fluctuations but also to U.S. political conditions. During this decade, Cuba lost much of its U.S. market because it encountered the powerful interests of sugar-beet farmers in the western United States. To make matters worse, sugar consumption stayed constant as international competition increased supply. Consequently, the 1926 Cuban harvest reached nearly 5 million tons, but it brought an average of only $0.022 per pound. Unable to sustain profits, many companies closed mills and threw people out of work all over the island.

This growing economic instability encouraged mounting opposition from a broad coalition that included university students, women, Communists, labor unions, Afro-Cuban *negristas* (intellectuals associated with the Negritude literary movement) like Nicolás Guillén, and many old-line politicians. To secure his power in the face of such resistance, Machado responded with increasingly harsh repression that included tightened censorship and stepped-up terror tactics by his secret police, the *Porra*.

By 1933, the U.S. government had become seriously concerned about the spreading violence, which appeared to threaten U.S. economic interests. In April, incoming President Franklin Roosevelt dispatched Sumner Welles in an unsuccessful attempt to negotiate agreement between Machado and the "responsible" opposition, which effectively excluded popular organizations like the Student Directory and the National Confederation of Cuban Workers (CNOC). Then in the summer, a bus drivers' strike in Havana mushroomed into a general strike that nearly paralyzed the city. After the police massacred several demonstrators in August, Machado's position seriously deteriorated, for he had lost the support of Welles and the army, both of whom lacked confidence in his ability to contain the revolutionary storm. On August 12, Machado resigned and fled into exile.

THE REVOLUTION OF 1933

For the next three weeks, a provisional government headed by Carlos Manuel de Céspedes struggled unsuccessfully to end the escalating violence. However, in August, two hundred thousand sugar workers, led by Afro-Cuban Communist León Álvarez, joined student protests and seized a sugar mill in Camaguey province, sparking similar actions throughout Cuba; within a month, workers organized into rural **soviets** that controlled fully 30 percent of Cuban sugar production. With the old regime rapidly unraveling, a group of army sergeants, led by Fulgencio Batista, overthrew the government. The Student Directory immediately allied itself with the sergeants, and together they formed a revolutionary junta.

The new junta had no organized political backing, and its two main components, the noncommissioned officers and the Student Directory, had sharply divergent aims. The sergeants were concerned only with defending their newly won dominant position against any challenge, whereas the students sought genuine reforms but were unsure just how to achieve them. Within a week, the junta turned over the reins of government to Dr. Ramón Grau San Martín, a well-known physician and long-time opponent of Machado. Grau; Antonio Guiteras Holmes, a leader of the Student Directory; and Batista were dominant figures in the new alignment.

The first move of the new government was to abrogate the onerous Platt Amendment. A flurry of decrees produced more social legislation than in all the previous history of independent Cuba: an eight-hour day for labor, a labor department, an end to the importation of cheap labor from other islands in the Caribbean, and greater access for children from lower-income groups to the university. Additional measures redistributed land to peasants, eliminated usury, and gave women the vote. Thus empowered, seven newly elected women congressional representatives helped expand the revolution's social achievements by legislating protections for working mothers, including a twelve-week maternity leave, mandatory employer-provided child care for infants, and prohibitions against firing women for getting married.

Ultimately, however, the revolutionary coalition soon disintegrated, leaving the Grau government caught in the classic bind of the reformer. Some like the Student Directory and Communists were dissatisfied because the reforms were not sufficiently radical. Meanwhile, moderates like the ABC, a group of middle-class intellectuals, opposed Grau because his program had become "too radical," and the Machadistas opposed all reform. Grau also alienated U.S. financial and agricultural interests when he suspended repayment of several loans owed to the Chase National Bank of New York and seized two mills of the Cuban-American Sugar Company. The U.S. government adamantly refused to recognize the Grau government.

The behavior of Sumner Welles throughout the Grau interregnum was extraordinarily similar to the conduct of U.S. Ambassador Henry Lane Wilson in Mexico during the Madero administration. Welles persistently falsified reports and misrepresented the Cuban government to Secretary of State Cordell Hull and President Roosevelt. As Wilson had befriended Huerta and helped him to power, so too Welles had allied himself with Batista. Eventually, Roosevelt recalled Welles in November 1933, but he had seriously undermined the Grau government. As the economic and political situation worsened, Welles's successor, Jefferson Caffery, maneuvered with Batista to form a new government that was acceptable to the United States. In January 1934, Grau, unable to rule effectively in the face of U.S. opposition, went into exile and Carlos Mendieta replaced him, but Batista ruled from the shadows.

POPULIST INTERLUDE, 1938–1952

Fulgencio Batista y Zaldívar, the sergeant-stenographer mulatto son of a sugar worker, dominated Cuban politics for the next decade, ruling the island through puppet presidents from 1934 to 1940 and as elected president from 1940 to 1944. Although Batista alienated many of the "respectable" elements of the middle and upper classes, he was extremely popular among the masses. During these early years, he endorsed a mild populist reform program with some effort at land redistribution, distanced himself from the United States, and openly courted the support of labor unions and Communists. Moreover, in late 1939, Batista permitted the election of a constituent assembly to draft the 1940 constitution, which contained progressive provisions that protected labor, guaranteed women equal rights, and limited private property rights when they conflicted with public interests.

Batista financed these populist reforms in part with higher sugar prices negotiated by the world's sugar-producing nations, which met in London to divide global markets, limit production, and stabilize costs. They formed an International Sugar Council, which allotted Cuba 29 percent of the U.S. market, half its share in 1929. The bulk of the profits generated by Cuba's sugar economy continued to flow out of the country, however, because foreign companies accounted for 80 percent of Cuban production (U.S. companies controlled 56 percent), whereas Cubans owned barely 20 percent.

World War II brought on another economic boom. In 1944, production reached its highest level since the Great Depression. In 1946, as part of its efforts to aid European recovery, the United States agreed to purchase the entire sugar harvest for $0.037 a pound. During the Korean War, the price of sugar soared to $0.5 a pound. Inevitably, however, Cuba's competitors, especially the Philippines, expanded production. The market soon became glutted with sugar, and prices fell. Wartime prosperity not only had deepened Cuba's trade dependence on sugar and U.S. markets (sugar exports accounted for 80 percent of all Cuban export earnings, 69 percent of which came from U.S. sales), but it also swelled company profits and government tax receipts, creating a fund to support intra-elite corruption and populist social programs without unduly burdening business, foreign or domestic. These modest reform programs typically aimed to stabilize capitalist labor and property relations.

Grau, elected president in 1944, continued this tradition. A symbol of Cuban regeneration and de-

mocracy, he offered hope to Cuban workers, peasants, women, and fledgling industrialists. He especially acknowledged his political debt to Cuban women voters and declared that "my government is a government of women." Unfortunately, Grau did little to make good on his promises and instead presided over an unparalleled reign of corruption. True, the Grau government initiated some reforms, the most significant of which was encouragement of trade-union organizing. By the end of his presidential term, 30 to 50 percent of the workforce had joined unions in the key industries of sugar, tobacco, textiles, transportation, and light manufacturing. These workers used their collective bargaining power and the favorable market conditions to demand higher wages and better working conditions, but Grau made no attack on such key problems as agrarian reform and monoculture.

In 1947, a charismatic populist leader, Eddie Chibás, launched a new campaign against government oppression and corruption. A former ardent supporter of the Auténticos, Chibás had become disillusioned with its corruption and formed the *Ortodoxo* Party, which featured a mild program of social reform and clean politics. Extremely popular, he posed a serious threat to the Auténticos, whose 1948 presidential candidate, Carlos Prío Socorrás, former leader of the Student Directory, nonetheless won easily because he controlled the election machinery. Prío became another in a long line of Cuban country-club presidents who spent much of his time serving his guests daiquiris at his opulent farm in the suburbs of Havana. The corruption, gangsterism, and spoils system characteristic of his predecessor's regime showed no letup. As under Grau, the prosperity brought on by high sugar prices concealed Prío's mismanagement.

However, a dramatic postwar contraction of overseas sugar markets and collapse of international sugar prices, intensified by U.S. laws that reduced the Cuban sugar quota to protect domestic sugar producers, spread economic depression throughout Cuba. This produced growing unrest among the lower class and increasing opposition among foreign and Cuban businesses that could no longer afford to finance the Auténticos' insatiable corruption or expensive populist reforms. Foreign investors especially insisted that the Auténticos rein in militant workers; an executive at the Cuban subsidiary of Bethlehem Steel, for example, noted with obvious displeasure that "the problem during the Grau and Prío Governments was labor strikes."

Even worse, the unorthodox populist Eddie Chibás, a leading candidate for the presidency in 1952, anticipated that either a military coup or fraud would prevent his election. Seeking to ignite a popular uprising against corruption and foreign influence, he killed himself during a nationwide radio broadcast, plunging the nation into political pandemonium. Six months later, Fulgencio Batista, with tacit U.S. support, overthrew the Prío government, outlawed the Cuban Communist Party, violently suppressed labor strikes, abolished recalcitrant unions, and eliminated earlier populist restrictions on business freedom.

THE RETURN OF BATISTA AS DICTATOR, 1952–1959

Batista's new minister of labor, Dr. Carlos Saladrigas, seeking to reassure Cuban business elites and U.S. investors, immediately announced that the coup's goal was to "bring about a radical change in labor-employer relations and remove obstacles for investment of national and foreign capital." A week later, the U.S. government officially recognized the Batista regime, and corporate leaders praised his policies: "When Batista took over, there were no more strikes," a Bethlehem Steel executive told historian Morris Morley. "I found economic conditions under Batista more stable." A Merrill-Lynch executive likewise praised Batista for permitting "business, the competitive system, the free enterprise system to operate."

Although the policies protected by Batista's political terrorism found much favor among business elites, they remained highly unpopular with most Cubans. Moreover, like his contemporaries, Carlos Ibáñez in Chile, Getúlio Vargas in Brazil, and Juan Perón in Argentina, Batista soon discovered that ruling a second time would prove more difficult than the first. A new generation of revolutionaries

rose to replace the discredited leaders of 1933. Unlike Grau or Prío, they would not be bought off or collaborate with the dictator. Several groups opposed Batista, including the Federation of University Students (FEU) and the Auténticos, who plotted from their havens in Florida. The 26th of July Movement, led by Fidel Castro, unsuccessfully tried to overthrow the government in 1953 by assaulting the Moncada army barracks. Despite the activities of the students and Castro's guerrilla group, the dictator seemed to be firmly entrenched, but his greatest vulnerability remained the structural weakness of the economy, produced by reliance on a single crop: sugar.

Meanwhile, Cuba's sugar industry had stagnated, and the resulting malaise had spread throughout the economy. Agriculture had not become diversified because the land was concentrated in a very few hands—twenty-two companies held one-fifth of the island's farmland. Much of the land remained idle in case sugar prices should ever boom. Industry was almost nonexistent, for a series of reciprocal trade agreements with the United States—which guaranteed Cuba's sugar market—made it impossible to compete with U.S. imports. These same treaties also stunted agriculture by permitting a flow of agricultural products from the United States, the low prices of which barred potential Cuban competition. Because of its stagnant economy and the peculiar nature of the sugar industry, Cuba suffered from structural unemployment and underemployment. Most sugar workers were needed only during the harvest; even if well paid during this four-month period, they went jobless and often hungry during the other eight months of the year. These structural deficiencies and the economic injustices created by them helped lay the foundation for the Cuban Revolution.

The Revolution

The Cuban Revolution was deeply rooted in the history of the island, for the movement headed by Fidel Castro continued the revolutionary traditions of 1868, 1898, and 1933. By no coincidence, both before and after gaining power, Castro often cited the ideals of José Martí and the principles of the 1940 constitution. Yet profound disillusionment accompanied those traditions, for Cuba's past revolutions had invariably failed; either its leaders had succumbed to the temptations of great wealth or the United States had intervened to thwart their programs. In large part, the complex development of the Cuban Revolution reflected a combination of loyalty to those revolutionary traditions and a fear of falling into their errors.

Fidel Castro Ruz, the son of a wealthy Spanish farmer in northwest Cuba, was born in 1927. He attended the famous Jesuit school of Belén in Havana and acquired a reputation as a fine athlete. In 1945, he went off to the University of Havana, where he soon became involved in the frequently violent politics that then plagued the university. In 1947, he participated in an ill-fated invasion of the Dominican Republic, sponsored by student political groups that sought to overthrow dictator Rafael Trujillo. Later, he became a follower of Eddie Chibás, to whose Ortodoxo Party he belonged from 1947 to 1952.

On July 26, 1953, Castro, in hopes of sparking a rebellion against the Batista dictatorship, led a small band of lower-middle-class and working-class rebels in an attack of the Moncada army barracks near Santiago de Cuba. The rebel's program called for a return to the constitution of 1940, land reform, education reform, and an end to the vast waste caused by government corruption and large weapons expenditures. Although the assault failed, with heavy casualties, and Batista captured Castro, the drastic acts of repression the government carried out in its wake and Castro's eloquent defense speech at his trial ("History Will Absolve Me") made him a national hero.

Castro spent the next nineteen months in prison on the Isle of Pines. During this period, the 26th of July Movement formed, led largely by women compatriots like Haydée Santamaría, a founding member of the 1952 anti-Batista resistance, and Melba Hernández, the intrepid lawyer who had defended Castro at trial. They forged political alliances with other anti-Batista groups like the Association of United Cuban Women, led by Gloria Cuadras, and the Women's Martí Civic Front, organized by Carmen Castro Porta, whose antidictatorial activities were rooted in struggles against the Machado regime in the 1920s.

Together, these anti-Batista groups built a network of urban and rural women who served the revolution as lawyers, interpreters, medical aides, grassroots organizers, educators, spies, messengers, and armed combatants. In addition to Celia Sánchez, perhaps Cuba's best-known woman guerrilla, the revolution also spawned a female combat unit known as the Mariana Grajales Brigade, in honor of the "heroic mother" of the Afro-Cuban independence fighter, Antonio Maceo.

By 1955, these women had produced and distributed some ten thousand copies of Castro's "History Will Absolve Me," which enhanced his reputation. Batista's general amnesty freed him in 1955, and, shortly thereafter, he went to Mexico to organize a new attack on the dictatorship. While in Mexico, Castro's group received support from ex-president Prío and Venezuelan exile Rómulo Betancourt (later president of Venezuela). Late in 1955, Castro met Ernesto (Che) Guevara, who was to become the revolution's second-in-command and its greatest martyr.

Castro was determined to return to the island to renew the struggle. In 1956, he and his band departed from Mexico aboard a small yacht, the *Granma*, with eighty-two persons aboard. Originally, the rebels had planned to coordinate the landing in Oriente Province with an uprising in Santiago, but, plagued by betrayal and logistical problems, a small group of survivors barely escaped to the Sierra Maestra. From these mountains, the rebels carried out guerrilla raids and repelled attacks by vastly superior forces.

In February 1957, with Vilma Espín, wealthy daughter of a Bacardí rum company executive, acting as interpreter, Castro granted an interview in his mountain hideout to Herbert Matthews, a well-known reporter for the *New York Times*. The resulting articles enhanced Castro's credibility in the United States and assured the Cuban people that he was still alive, despite government claims to

Haydeé Santamaría and Celia Sánchez, along with Vilma Espín, were among the prominent women in the revolutionary leadership and played critical roles especially in the urban underground that directed revolutionary strategy through 1957. Here they are pictured counting cash that they raised in support of the guerrilla war in the Sierra Maestra.

the contrary. The articles overstated the numerical strength and success of the movement and thereby helped win adherents to the rebel cause all over the island. The guerrillas continued to conduct raids throughout the spring of 1957, picking up recruits and gaining increased sympathy and support from the peasants of Oriente, who rendered invaluable assistance in the form of supplies and intelligence information about government forces.

Although Castro and the guerrillas in the sierra received most of the publicity, the urban underground led by Santamaría, Espín, Sánchez, Frank País, and Armando Hart was largely responsible for tactical planning. By mid-1957, violence, especially in Havana, had become endemic as various groups, many unaffiliated with the 26th of July Movement, attacked the regime and met with bru-

tal retaliation. Even women revolutionaries, insulated from earlier repression by the regime's sexism, experienced wholesale arrests, torture, and imprisonment. But they maintained a sense of humor; when their lawyer, Margo Aniceto Rodríguez, was also imprisoned for denouncing Batista's terrorism, other jailed rebels joked that "Margo is such a good lawyer that, if she cannot free us, she at least comes to stay with us in prison."

Terrorism and strikes completely disrupted life in Santiago and Oriente Province, and civil war increasingly gripped Cuba. In the fall, junior naval officers at Cienfuegos staged an abortive uprising. Batista used bombers and other military equipment to crush the revolt; this military response alienated some of his U.S. support, as the terms of Cuba's military assistance agreement with the United States expressly forbade using this equipment for domestic purposes.

After the new year, the trend of events turned decisively against Batista. The United States suspended arms shipments to the Cuban government in March 1958. The middle class abandoned the dictator. In May, Batista launched a major effort to dislodge the guerrilla army from its base in the Sierra Maestra, and the resulting defeat doomed his regime. Rebel forces inflicted heavy losses on the government troops. Withered by corruption and led by incompetent cronies of Batista, the army was no match for the guerrillas and their clandestine urban allies.

As Batista's plight grew desperate, frantic negotiations involving the U.S. embassy began with a view toward staving off a revolutionary victory by the creation, through a coup or fraudulent elections, of a new government, which the U.S. government would recognize and assist militarily. Batista actually held presidential elections, printing up filled-in ballots in advance, and readied a president to take office in February, but the strong drive of rebel forces frustrated these maneuvers. By the end of December 1958, the *barbudos* (bearded revolutionaries) were on the outskirts of Havana. On January 1, 1959, abandoned by his U.S. allies, Batista and his closest aides fled to Miami.

Thus, a rebel band, numbering fewer than three hundred until mid-1958 and scarcely three thousand when the old regime fell, won a great victory because they were persistent and disciplined and gained the sympathy of all the people—peasants, workers, and the middle class. They also faced an army wracked by favoritism and incompetence. Batista's army, when put to the test, proved able to terrorize unarmed citizens but disintegrated when confronted with a formidable insurgency.

The Revolution in Power, 1959–2003

During its first four years (1959–1962), the revolution consolidated its domestic political position, began the socialization of the economy, and established a new pattern of foreign relations. In 1959, the rev-

olutionary leaders made a series of decisions that determined the course of the revolution for the next decade. First, they concluded that parliamentary democracy was inappropriate for Cuba at that time. The Fundamental Law of the Republic, decreed in February 1959, concentrated legislative power in the executive. As prime minister and, later, as first secretary of the Communist Party, Castro held the decisive posts in the government and the ruling party of the Cuban state. Within eighteen months, the revolutionary regime had suppressed the right of free press and the centuries-old autonomy of the University of Havana. The revolutionaries conducted public trials of former *Batistianos* and executed a large number of Batista's henchmen.

Second, the revolutionaries moved to consolidate their political support and accomplish their economic goals: land reform, income redistribution, agricultural diversification, and economic independence from the United States. The radicalism of their economic program and the concentration of political power in the hands of the close-knit 26th of July Movement alienated middle-class supporters like Maj. Huber Matos and President Manuel Urrutía, who resigned in July 1959. In October, Matos, one of the revolution's foremost military leaders and a violent anticommunist, was charged with treason and imprisoned. At the same time, the revolutionaries allied with the Popular Socialist (Communist) Party, seeking its help in administering the country.

In January 1960, the regime purged moderate elements from the leadership of Cuban labor unions and cultivated the Soviet Union as an ally to diversify the nation's economic dependence and protect the revolution from U.S. intervention. Soviet deputy premier Anastas Mikoyan agreed that the Soviets would purchase 425,000 tons of Cuban sugar in 1960 and 1 million tons the next year. In May, Cuba resumed diplomatic relations with the Soviet Union.

UNITED STATES–CUBAN RELATIONS

Meanwhile, Cuban relations with the United States, already suffering from the unfavorable publicity brought by the trials and the expropriation of large estates, reached a crisis in May 1960. The Cuban government requested that the major petroleum refineries, owned by Texaco, Standard Oil, and Royal Dutch Shell, process Soviet crude oil, which the Cubans had obtained at a lower price than the three companies charged for their oil. At the urging of the U.S. State Department, the companies refused, forcing Cuba to expropriate the refineries. The United States retaliated by abolishing the Cuban sugar quota, and Cuba in turn expropriated numerous U.S.-owned properties.[1] In October, all U.S. exports to Cuba were banned—an embargo that has not yet been lifted. This action set off a new wave of expropriations of U.S. property, including that of Sears, Roebuck; Coca-Cola; and the enormous U.S. government–owned nickel deposits at Moa Bay.

As relations between the two nations deteriorated, the Central Intelligence Agency (CIA) funneled money to various exile groups for arms and set up a training camp in Guatemala to prepare an invasion force. On January 3, 1961, the outgoing Eisenhower administration severed diplomatic relations with Cuba, and three months later, President John F. Kennedy authorized the exile invasion at the Bay of Pigs on April 15. The revolutionary army swiftly crushed the attack, which U.S. officials had poorly planned and executed. On the basis of the false assumption that the Cuban people would revolt in support of the exile invasion, the Bay of Pigs fiasco immeasurably increased Castro's prestige and gave new impetus for radical reconstruction of the Cuban economy and society.

What had begun as a program of social and political reform within a framework of constitutional democracy and capitalism evolved into a Marxist revolution. One month after the Bay of Pigs, Castro proclaimed allegiance to socialism, and the Soviet Union, pledging to defend Cuba in the event of another U.S. attack, stepped up its flow of arms to the island.

These arms included missile emplacements and aircraft capable of delivering atomic weapons throughout most of North and South America. Although Cuba and the Soviet Union argued that the missiles had a defensive, deterrent character, the United States claimed that they were offensive weapons, ordered a naval quarantine of Cuba, and demanded the dismantling of the missile sites. For a time it appeared as if Kennedy was losing control of his military, which was pressing to use force against Cuba. After several days, during which the world came close to nuclear war, the two superpowers reached a compromise by which the Soviet Union agreed to remove its missiles from Cuba in return for a pledge from the United States not to invade Cuba and to remove its own missiles from Turkey. However, the United States continued to subvert and harass the Cuban Revolution with the aid of counterrevolutionary Cuban exiles; this included CIA-sponsored raids against refineries and ports, infiltration of enemy agents, and even some bizarre attempts to assassinate Castro.

REVOLUTIONARY ECONOMICS

The Cuban Revolution benefited from advantages few other socialist revolutions have enjoyed. The guerrilla war (in contrast to that of China or Vietnam) was relatively short and caused little destruction of human life or property. Moreover, Cuba had well-developed communications and transportation systems, including an extensive railroad network and excellent primary roads. The character of Cuba's rural population promised to make the process of socialist land reform easier than it had been in Russia, for example. Because the sugar industry had proletarianized much of the agricultural workforce, farm workers did not demand their own land but sought improved working conditions and wages. Cuba also had considerable unused land and industrial capacity that the government quickly employed to raise living standards and increase productivity. Finally, by 1959, a number of developed socialist states existed that could offer Cuba substantial assistance, thus momentarily offsetting

---

1. The government had previously taken over only the operation of these properties.

the severe negative effects of the U.S. embargo on exports.

Nonetheless, the revolution faced serious problems. To begin with, the revolutionaries, inexperienced in economic affairs, made mistakes. The socialist reorientation of the economy inevitably caused disruptions, and the U.S. embargo caused crippling shortages of parts and other difficulties, which the development of new patterns of trade with countries in the socialist camp (and with some capitalist countries) only gradually overcame. Moreover, many of Cuba's ablest technicians joined the first wave of refugees that fled to the United States. Finally, revolutionary leaders initially spurned material incentives that more traditional Marxists endorsed as the best spur to production, in favor of moral incentives, which would give rise to the "new socialist man." Application of this theory caused considerable economic damage before a more pragmatic mix of material and moral incentives replaced it in 1969.

The first goal of the revolutionary government was to redistribute income to the rural and urban working class. During the first three years, it met with considerable success, raising wages 40 percent and overall purchasing power 20 percent. It virtually eliminated unemployment. These benefits accrued predominantly to areas outside Havana, for the revolutionaries aimed to reverse the trend toward **hyperurbanization** (the process whereby national populations become concentrated in one city), which was characteristic of Latin America.

The first Law of Agrarian Reform in May 1959 facilitated redistribution of land. It restricted the size of estates, authorized the government to expropriate private holdings in excess of stated limits, and indemnified the owners on the basis of the tax-assessed value of the property. The revolutionaries immediately seized estates of Batistiano government officials, confiscated the great cattle estates when their owners resisted, and distributed the expropriated land in small plots or established cooperatives, which the Institute of Agrarian Reform (INRA) administered. Much of the land redistribution occurred in Oriente Province, where peasants had provided early and crucial support for the 26th of July Movement. Eighty-five percent of all Cuban farms fell under the jurisdiction of the reform law because landownership was so highly concentrated under the old regime.

During the first year of its rule, the Cuban government experimented with various types of agrarian holdings. Eventually, all became *granjas del pueblo* (state farms). Administered by INRA, they usually employed the same workers who had toiled on them before the revolution, but workers earned better wages and enjoyed improved working conditions.

The redistribution of income to workers and peasants resulted in some long-range problems. With more money to spend, Cubans demanded more food, especially meat, the consumption of which rose 100 percent. This rising demand led to the overkilling of cattle, which seriously damaged the ability of the government to supply meat in later years. The government lowered rents and utility rates and supplied many services free of charge, which increased disposable income even more. Inevitably, shortages arose because Cuba no longer imported consumer goods and foodstuffs. Rather than limit consumption inequitably by raising prices, the government began rationing in March 1962. The revolutionaries also poured large sums into rural housing, roads, and other improvements, but poor planning wasted scarce resources.

Two other important programs had mixed success during the first three years: agricultural diversification and industrialization. The revolutionary government sought to become more self-sufficient by transferring cane land and idle fields to the production of cotton, vegetable oils, rice, soybeans, and peanuts, which would save badly needed foreign exchange on these previously imported commodities. Industrial reforms began slowly; the government at first took over the management of just one major foreign company: the extremely unpopular telephone company. However, U.S. efforts to sabotage the revolution ultimately led to sweeping expropriations of U.S.-owned refineries, factories, utilities, and sugar mills. Next, the government took over the banking system and most urban housing. Finally, the revolutionary regime expropriated native-owned businesses. It postponed more ambitious industrial development plans that proved too costly and difficult to implement.

The revolutionaries encountered serious problems in agriculture after 1961 because of their inability to organize, plan, and administer the economy. Although they set up the Central Planning Agency (Junta Central de Planificación [JUCEPLAN]) in February 1961, more often than not Castro ignored or circumvented it with "special" plans. For a long time, the government also ignored the private agricultural sector, a critical oversight because more than half the farmland remained in private hands. In early 1961, to overcome this neglect, the government established the National Association of Small Farmers (ANAP), which tried to coordinate the production of small farms with national goals. It also furnished credit, set up stores, and organized various associations.

THE RETURN TO SUGAR, 1963–1970: THE TEN-MILLION-TON HARVEST

Experience had shown that Cuba lacked the resources and the administrative or technical expertise to industrialize rapidly. Consequently, Cuban leaders decided in 1963 to reemphasize agriculture and return to intensive sugar production while they developed a more gradual diversification program. Increased agricultural production aimed to generate large earnings that eventually could underwrite future industrialization.

Unfortunately, agriculture, especially sugar, had suffered enormously from well-intentioned but shortsighted policies. The sugar harvests of 1960 and 1961 were extraordinarily successful because they benefited from favorable weather and because the island's cane was at the age of peak yield. They also harvested the entire crop, for the first time in a decade; however, the sugar harvest of 1962 was the worst since 1955, and subsequent harvests continued to be disappointing. The essential problem was that the revolutionaries, in their fervor to diversify, had ripped up some of the best cane land. They had not replanted cane in two years, and as a result, most Cuban cane was well past its peak yield. Moreover, the inexperienced revolutionaries badly administered equipment and manpower. Transportation and dis-

tribution were in chaos, and they left damaged sugar mills unrepaired for years. As a result, from 1962 to 1969, agricultural production fell 7 percent.

The government made considerable efforts to correct the situation. The regime decreed the second Law of Agrarian Reform in October 1963; under this law, it expropriated thousands of midsize farms. State farms became the dominant form of agriculture, controlling 70 percent of the land and taking responsibility for all the major export crops. The government also forced the remaining small farmers to sell their crops at low cost. Cuba put a remarkable portion of its gross national product (GNP) into investment, but largely wasted it because of inefficient administration and poor planning. The state abandoned many unfinished projects and often failed to maintain those that it did complete.

Thereafter, Cuba launched a new campaign of socialization that centralized the administration of the economy. The most visible symbol of this policy change was the ill-fated, ten-million-ton sugar harvest of 1970. Designed to model the effectiveness of a socialist developmental strategy that stressed "moral" over "material" incentives for workers, it also aimed to produce the largest sugar harvest in Cuba's history and to use the anticipated foreign exchange bonanza to invest in the nation's independent industrial development. Confronted with the reality of a severely damaged and underdeveloped agricultural infrastructure capable of producing at best 6 million tons of sugar, however, the effort was doomed to fail. Ironically, even revolutionary successes contributed to its failure: The revolution had created considerable employment opportunities outside the sugar industry, but this left it with one-fifth the former number of professional cane cutters in 1959 and required a mobilization of nonagricultural labor that seriously depleted resources and destabilized the national economy.

FAILURE, REASSESSMENT, AND INSTITUTIONALIZED REVOLUTION, 1970–1990

The ballyhooed "ten-million-ton harvest" of 1970 failed to reach its acclaimed goal and in the process did extensive damage to the Cuban economy as a whole. To get the 8.5 million tons they did eventually harvest, the revolutionaries virtually ruined the sugar industry, and subsequent harvests generally were poor. They siphoned off resources and labor from other sectors, causing disruption and turmoil.

Even more significantly, however, these disastrous economic policies—and the centralized authoritarian state whose administration they seemed to require—began to separate the revolutionary leadership from its base of popular support. No matter how much U.S.-sponsored counterrevolutionary terrorism may have justified it in these years, the regime's blatant disregard for civil liberties and its authoritarian manner remained a permanent stain on an otherwise laudable revolutionary record. Many Cubans, especially young people excited by the revolution's democratic promise, refused to accept these practical constraints on their liberty. Slowly, a new popular antiauthoritarian cultural movement emerged around the *canción de protesta* (protest song). This movement attracted youth who believed in the revolution's goal of social justice but increasingly opposed the hierarchical nature of state decision making, especially its personalist association with Fidel Castro. Ironically, it drew inspiration from African and Asian anticolonial struggles, the celebration of indigenous folk cultures in Chile and Argentina, and especially Brazilian popular resistance to military dictatorship—all of which the Cuban revolutionary regime also promoted.

Protest songs marked a distinctive development in Cuban music and culture. In the early 1960s, folk artists like Carlos Puebla and Los Compadres (The Godfathers) had combined son and traditional Cuban country music (*música guajira*) with lyrics that sang the praises of the revolution and its guerrilla heroes. Los Compadres's popular song "Se acabarán los bohíos" ("The Shacks Will Disappear"), for example, celebrated the revolution's promise of "a living wage, an apartment for every family, hard work," and the eradication of *bohíos* (traditional thatched-roof shacks), except those that "remain as museum pieces." The protest singers of the late 1960s, however, identified with the revolution's idealistic and humanitarian goals but criticized its failures, especially its authoritarianism and restraint of artistic freedom.

Silvio Rodríguez, one of the movement's principal voices, captured this sense of revolutionary patriotism and youthful alienation when he denounced state bureaucrats as "bosses who said one thing and did another, squares, those who didn't trust the young, guys with all the perks, enemies of culture, the establishment cowards who were ruining the revolution that I carried inside of me." For Rodríguez and thousands of other young Cubans, the revolutionary leadership was hypocritical to encourage Latin American, Asian, and African peoples to rebel against tradition but simultaneously to restrain youthful Cuban rebels, who expressed their dissatisfaction by wearing long hair, hippie clothing, and tattoos.

Some within the revolutionary state agreed. Haydée Santamaría, a veteran of the Sierra Maestra and the 1953 attack on Moncada, refused to surrender to bureaucratic pressures and sought to protect these young protest artists. As the head of the Casa de las Américas, a revolutionary state institution that coordinated cultural exchanges with the rest of Latin America, she organized a series of international music festivals that gave voice to protest songs and, for a time, secured their access to state radio and television programming. However, in general, failed sugar harvests and jailed protest singers signaled bleak years for the revolutionary economy, cultural expression, and political freedoms.

The great failure of the 1970 sugar harvest, however, prompted a searching self-criticism and dramatic rethinking of revolutionary policies and process. Castro himself admitted his personal responsibility for this failure and vowed to make changes to advance the revolution. This led to greater political openness and popular political participation. It also enabled the revolutionary leadership once again to embrace its rebellious youth culture. According to ethnomusicologist Robin Moore, "In the space of only a few years, protest song moved from the margin into the mainstream of socialist music making." Changes in revolutionary state policy, not the surrender of young artists' independence, clearly facilitated this rapid rapprochement.

The Cuban government now increasingly supported this new music, known as *nueva trova* (new ballad), and encouraged its young musicians to represent Cuba at international music festivals organized in Latin America, Spain, and Eastern Europe. It also established performance centers in every province and created the National Movement of the Ballad (MNT), a state organization designed to encourage musical careers and fund the creative arts. Although it refused to support particular songs like Pablo Milanés's "La vida no vale nada" ("Life Is Worthless"), the lyrical content of which it deemed antisocial, the MNT dramatically expanded the resources available to aspiring young musicians, introduced them to new instruments and electronic technologies like the synthesizer, increased their access to studio time, and helped them distribute their recordings.

During the next five years, the government sought to institutionalize the revolution. It created a new executive committee of the Council of Ministers and gave the bureaucracy wider scope of action and more influence. President Osvaldo Dorticós and Carlos Rafael Rodríguez, a veteran Communist who had fought with Castro in the Sierra Maestra, took charge of Cuba's economic development. The government reorganization drew clear lines of separation between the armed forces, the bureaucracy, and the Communist Party. It merged the militia into the army, restructured the military along traditional hierarchical lines, revamped the judicial system, broadened the popular base of the regime, and strengthened the Communist Party. The labor movement played a larger role, and trade unions or the workers' tribunals assumed responsibility for enforcement of labor laws and workers' rights. Workers participated more actively in the formulation of production goals and plans.

The Cuban leadership also drastically overhauled the revolution's policy of economic development. It introduced sophisticated computerized planning techniques, inaugurated a system of material incentives for workers and managers, and implemented a work quota system between 1971 and 1973 that produced a 20 percent increase in pro-

ductivity. The government also differentiated among jobs and paid people according to their productivity. These and other economic reforms led to a dramatic rise in productivity. From 1971 to 1975, the GNP grew at an annual rate of more than 10 percent, compared with an annual growth rate of 3.9 percent for the period from 1966 to 1970.

The first Communist Party congress in December 1975 completed the formal institutionalization of the revolution. The congress adopted Cuba's first socialist constitution, approved by nationwide referendum in February 1976. The constitution, an attempt to make government more responsive to the people, provided for a pyramid of elected bodies. At the bottom, popularly elected municipal assemblies elected delegates to provincial assemblies and to the National Assembly of People's Power. Most of these representatives were Communist Party members. Castro remained entrenched at the top as first secretary of the Communist Party, head of government, and president of the Council of State (elected from the National Assembly).

Political institutionalization accompanied efforts to reorganize and rationalize the economy, whose performance had slowed in the last half of the decade. Still heavily dependent on sugar for its economic well-being, Cuba's economy grew a disappointing 4 percent a year from 1976 to 1980. At the root of the problem was the lack of professional management, quality control, and labor discipline, all of which contributed to poorly manufactured goods, ranging from shoes to televisions.

In 1980, persistent economic problems and political disaffection led to a massive emigration of Cubans, primarily to the United States. More than 125,000 Cubans left, mostly through the port of Mariel, many aboard dangerously overcrowded, leaky boats. Nonetheless, Cuba's outmigration (a rate of less than 2 percent in 1980) compared favorably to that in the rest of the Caribbean, where émigrés constituted about 20 percent of the population. Great political and social upheavals historically have caused similar flights of disaffected people; after the American Revolution, 10 percent of the population left for Canada or England rather than live under the new republican rule.

Between 1981 and 1985, Cuba seriously attacked its chronic economic problems, and the economy experienced a significant quantitative and qualitative improvement. The average annual growth rate for the period was 7.6 percent. Export diversification grew, with reexports of Soviet oil accounting for more than 40 percent of Cuba's hard-currency earnings in 1985, but this fell to 17 percent because of lower prices on the world market in 1988. Despite Cuba's many economic problems, economists Claus Brundenius and Andrew Zimbalist have concluded that Cuba's economic growth between 1960 and 1985 was the second highest in Latin America. Moreover, the distribution of income generated by this growth was the most equitable by far, both within and outside the region.

ACHIEVEMENTS

Despite its mixed economic record, the revolution's achievements in the areas of employment, equitable distribution of income, public health, and education were remarkable. Until 1990, Cuba had the lowest rate of joblessness in Latin America. Workers laid off because of plant closings continued to receive 60 percent of their wages. The revolution dramatically reduced inequalities in the standard of living from the days of Batista. The working classes in particular benefited from government policies that controlled rents (limited to no more than 10 percent of income), rationed food, and regulated prices (except in open farmers' markets). Eighty percent of Cubans owned their own homes. Agricultural workers on state farms and cooperatives received furnished houses with televisions and community recreational centers. Cuban city streets had virtually no beggars or sidewalk vendors, which set them apart from those in other Latin American countries. Education and health care were free and equally accessible to all.

The revolution had always promised equality and social justice, but these were special goals of the Cuban Women's Federation (FMC), organized in 1960 under Vilma Espín's leadership. The FMC played a crucial role early in the development of revolutionary social services. Literacy crusades reduced illiteracy from 24 to 4 percent, and a national childcare system freed women, irrespective of class, to pursue their own careers. An innovative rural education program taught vocational skills and provided peasant women with modern health-care information. Schools for maids and prostitutes discouraged exploitation of women and retrained them as professionals in socially productive activities.

Since 1960, the FMC, Latin America's largest women's organization with a membership of 3.6 million, continued to influence Cuban policy regarding health care, education, women's employment, daycare, sexual discrimination, and family life. For example, it secured passage of the 1975 Family Code, which recognized the equal right of both spouses to education and career, required them to share in household duties and child care, and established divorce as a legal remedy for any spouse whose mate refused to comply. Although a 1988 survey showed that men worked only 4.52 hours per week at home, whereas women worked 22.28 hours, it also revealed the law's potential: Most respondents acknowledged that this inequity was diminishing steadily.

Women gained enormously from the revolution. In 1953, 20 percent of women were illiterate, without hope of either education or rewarding employment, but the revolution had eradicated illiteracy and established equal access to a free education by the early 1960s. After the revolution, higher education, long the redoubt of elite women, who had composed 45 percent of a small university student population in 1956–1957, also opened its doors to women of every class; by 1990, women represented 57 percent of a university population that was ten times larger.

Before the revolution, women composed 13 percent of the workforce, one-third of them employed as domestic servants. By 1990, however, women represented 38.6 percent of Cuba's workers and constituted 58 percent of technical, 85 percent of administrative, and 63 percent of service workers. Yet the percentage of women managers, Communist Party leaders, National Assembly members,

This witty cartoon reminds Americans, who still lack universal health care, that socialist Cuba, against all odds, has transformed itself into a world-class health-care provider.

and People's Power delegates was 27, 16, 33, and 17, respectively. Distressing as these figures were, they resembled the gender inequality typical of industrial countries and represented a vast improvement on the records of Cuba's Latin American and Caribbean neighbors. Nonetheless, Castro, clearly disturbed by this inequality, called for increased women's representation commensurate with "their participation and their important contribution to the building of socialism."

Children were special objects of the government's solicitude. Children ages seven and under and pregnant women received a daily distribution of milk and enjoyed the best medical care in Latin America. With the region's lowest doctor-to-patient ratio, according to a 1990 study in the *Latin American Re-*

search Review, Cuba had "transformed itself into a world-class health-care provider, an extraordinary achievement." Sophisticated medical procedures performed in Cuba included heart transplants, heart-lung transplants, and microsurgery. The education budget amounted to 7 percent of the nation's GNP, the highest in Latin America. The population had an average ninth-grade education, and illiteracy was eliminated.

The revolution also aimed to end the unspoken racism that historically had shaped public policy in Cuba. Castro himself called on Cubans in 1959 "to end racial discrimination at the workplace" and in "cultural centers." The structural transformation of Cuban society since 1959 led most scholars to conclude that "the revolution has achieved racial equality" even as a "racist mentality" endured within Cuban culture. Yet Afro-Cubans, who undeniably benefited from the revolution and held prestigious positions throughout Cuban society, still remained statistically underrepresented in higher education, professional employment, and leadership positions in both the government and mass organizations; they were also overrepresented in vocational schools, blue-collar jobs, and *solares* (substandard tenement houses). More disturbingly, they made up 58 percent of the *jóvenes desvinculados* (alienated youth who neither worked nor studied).

Undoubtedly, most Cubans benefited from the revolution, which explains their extraordinary support for it, even thirty-five years later in the midst of a deep economic crisis. According to an independent 1994 poll commissioned by the *Miami Herald* and conducted by a Costa Rican affiliate of the Gallup Organization, 69 percent of Cubans identified themselves as revolutionaries, Socialists, or Communists, and 58 percent believed the revolution had produced more achievements than failures. For nearly thirty years, the Cuban Revolution's success had derived from a searching self-criticism, careful attention to its mass political base, and an enduring socialist pragmatism. The Cubans renewed *rectificación* (the ongoing effort to correct past mistakes) in the mid-1980s, even before dramatic changes in Eastern Europe created seemingly insuperable economic difficulties.

Meanwhile, the revolution's successes and failures reverberated throughout Latin America and greatly influenced other regional reform movements that sought to learn from the Cuban experience. Fairly or unfairly, the Cuban Revolution became the standard against which others, revolutionary opponents and proponents alike, measured the success of their movements for social change. In the Andean republics, in Chile, Central America, and Venezuela, each sought its own national solutions to the general crisis of populism that characterized the late twentieth century, but all were conscious of the Cuban model.

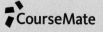

16

Storm over the Andes: Indigenous Rights and the Corporatist Military Alternative

FOCUS QUESTIONS

• Why did military officers, a class commonly regarded as the staunchest defenders of the old order in Latin America, lead revolutions in the Andean republics of Bolivia, Peru, and Ecuador?

• What economic and social reforms did these military leaders propose, and what interests did they represent?

• How did indigenous resistance to political, social, and economic inequality affect these revolutions?

• How did military corporatism aim to promote the rise of an autonomous native capitalism?

• Why did the military reformers fail to make a clean break with the model of dependent development and the problems it generated?

EVEN AS CUBA'S ARMED REVOLUTION offered a model for other Latin American nations in the second half of the twentieth century, a different path to reform occurred in the Andean republics of Peru, Bolivia, and Ecuador, whose economic and social structures were among the most archaic in Latin America. The 1968 Peruvian Revolution, largely carried out by military officers seeking to secure corporatist reforms, provided the clearest alternative to the Cuban revolutionary model. Developments in Peru and Ecuador between 1968 and 1975 exposed the fallacy of the common assumption that the Latin American military constitutes one reactionary mass. Moving with greater speed and vigor than any civilian reformist regime in Latin American history, a Peruvian military junta headed by Gen. Juan Velasco Alvarado decreed nationalization of key industries and land reform that transformed great estates into peasant and worker cooperatives. This created novel new forms of economic organization that claimed to be "neither capitalist nor communist." In 1975, the Peruvian Revolution halted its advance and began a retreat that threatened even its major conquests—the agrarian reform and the great nationalizations—with erosion and even destruction. Yet it ranks among the more serious recent Latin American efforts to achieve a breakthrough in the struggle against backwardness and dependency.

Nevertheless, the Peruvian experience was the culmination of historical events that had long

1879–1883	War of the Pacific engulfs Chile, Peru, and Bolivia
1884	Treaty of Ancón grants resource-rich lands to Chile, weakening Peru and Bolivia
1903	Brazil claims rubber-rich province of Acre from Bolivia
1921–1927	Indigenous Aymara and Challanta rebellions sweep the Andes
1924	Haya de la Torre organizes American Revolutionary Popular Alliance (APRA)
1932–1935	Paraguay seizes more Bolivian land in Chaco War
1948	Gen. Odría overthrows Peru's APRA government
1952	Bolivian Revolution initiates populist reforms such as nationalization of tin mines and land redistribution
1963	Peru elects populist Belaúnde to end decade of dictatorship; Ecuadorian military junta overthrows introduces populist reforms
1964	Gen. Barrientos overthrows Paz Estenssoro in Bolivia and initiates repressive military rule
1968	Gen. Juan Velasco Alvarado leads populist Peruvian "Revolution from Above"; José María Velasco seizes dictatorial power in Ecuador
1972	Gen. Rodríguez Lara overthrows Velasco in Ecuador and initiates populist reforms
1975	Peruvian Revolution ends when Gen. Morales Bermúdez ousts Velasco Alvarado
1980	Shining Path guerrillas escalate rural violence in Peru
1982	Bolivian military cedes power to populist Hernán Siles Zuazo
1983	U.S. and European nations link resumption of Bolivian aid to government austerity program

characterized the entire Andean region. As elsewhere on the continent, Andean reformist movements fused the effort to modernize with the struggle for greater social justice for the masses: economic sovereignty, industrialization, and land reform. However, the presence of large, compact indigenous groups, ranging from some 70 percent of the population of Bolivia to about 40 percent of the populations of Peru and Ecuador, gave a distinctive character to these nationalist movements. Still another common feature of the Andean struggle was the leading role played by nationalist military officers, who, fearing autonomous indigenous rights and militant working-class movements, sought to contain them by advancing a moderate corporatist reform agenda rooted in the idea of a mestizo nation. Military **corporatism** (a state-centered political economic system) gave indigenous, peasant, and working-class communities representation in the affairs of state but simultaneously denied them power by requiring them to subordinate their respective racial and class interests to serve an idealized nation-state that protected all sectors of society equally. The historical origins of military corporatism lay in early twentieth-century struggles over land, indigenous rights, and international capitalist development.

Neocolonialism, the Military, and Indigenous Resistance

The War of the Pacific left a heritage of political and social turbulence as well as economic ruin. Military caudillos and civilian leaders in Peru disputed one another's claims to power and mobilized *montoneros* (bands of guerrillas and outlaws) for their armed struggles. In some areas, the indigenous peasantry, having acquired arms during the war with Chile, rose in revolt against oppressive hacendados and local officials. Banditry was rife in parts of the sierra; on the coast, factions armed by landowners or their agents fought among themselves for control of irrigation canals or over property boundaries.

From the struggle for power, the militarists once again emerged victorious: In 1884, Andrés Cáceres battled his way into Lima, seized the National Palace, and initiated a slow, painful process of economic recovery. His first concern was the huge foreign debt. In 1886, his government negotiated the so-called Grace Contract with British bondholders to create a Peruvian Corporation that assumed responsibility to service Peru's foreign debt and received in exchange Peru's railways for a period of sixty-six years. The agreement confirmed British financial domination of Peru but also initiated a new flow of investments that hastened the country's economic recovery. Particularly important was the resulting rehabilitation of the railways and their extension to important mining centers, especially into La Oroya, whose rich silver, zinc, and lead mines began to contribute to the economic revival.

Economic recovery strengthened the political hand of the planter aristocracy and the commercial bourgeoisie, who were increasingly impatient with the military caudillo's unpredictability. In 1895, their leader was the flamboyant Nicolás Piérola, who sought to bring the military under civilian control and led a successful revolt against Cáceres. Piérola presided over four years of rapid economic recovery. On the coast, he promoted an intensive "modernization" that expanded sugar plantations at the expense of small landholders and indigenous communities. In the Andes, the economic revival spurred a renewed drive by hacendados to acquire indigenous communal lands in regions hitherto free from land grabbing. An 1893 law, which effectively reenacted Bolívar's decree concerning the division and distribution of communal lands, facilitated the process of land acquisition. In this period, the *enganche* (a new contract labor system) arose, which attempted to solve the labor problem of coastal landlords now that Chinese contract labor was no longer easily available. This system forcibly recruited indígenas from the sierra to labor for prolonged periods on coastal haciendas, sometimes under conditions of virtual serfdom.

INDIGENOUS RESISTANCE

The War of the Pacific had a similarly catastrophic impact on Bolivia, which it left landlocked and deprived of revenues from rich deposits of nitrates and copper. Bolivia's national government remained discredited and weak, rendering local landlords still more powerful. Here also, however, indigenous struggles unfolded within the historical context of racial, class, and gender conflicts unleashed by foreign investment, transatlantic market growth, and dependent capitalism. During the late nineteenth century, highland indigenous communities had agreed to pay tribute and provide seasonal labor services to Hispanic hacendados in exchange for their recognition of indigenous communal land rights, but the lure of larger profits produced by a growing market demand for exports led them to expand their haciendas at the expense of the indígenas.

As a result, in the early twentieth century, the *caciques apoderados* (an armed indigenous movement) spread throughout the Andean highlands. These indigenous rebels defended their community lands and cultural traditions in violent uprisings like the 1921 Aymara Rebellion and the Chayanta Rebellion of 1927, which together mobilized thousands of peasants. This rural ferment, further complicated by growing worker unrest in Bolivian mines, factories, and urban centers, where a nascent women's movement also became active, led to greater collaboration among the army, landed oligarchs, and their foreign allies.

The aftermath of the War of the Pacific also saw the birth of a new sensitivity to the social struggle of indigenous peoples in Peru. The rise of this indigenismo among intellectuals was a byproduct of this disastrous war that caused a crisis of conscience. By exposing the incompetence and irresponsibility of a creole elite that had totally failed to prepare materially and morally, the war led many intellectuals to turn to the indigenous peasantry as a possible source of national regeneration. At the University of San Marcos in Lima, a generation of teachers arose to reject the traditional positivist, racist tendency to brand indígenas as inherently

"South of Panama" (New York, The Century Co., 1915), de Edward Alsworth Ross

The Rumi Maqui movement drew upon a long tradition of indigenous resistance to assert traditional communal values in the face of an aggressive expansion of the mining industry, large plantations, and commercial agriculture in Peru and Bolivia.

inferior. The alleged apathy, inertia, and alcoholism of indigenous peoples, these scholars claimed, resulted from the narrow, dwarfed world in which the creole elite forced them to live. Nonetheless, these bourgeois reformers largely ignored the economic conditions of indigenous peoples and focused on a program of education and uplift that would teach them ways to enter the new capitalist society.

The great iconoclast Manuel González Prada (1848–1918) rejected this gradual, reformist approach to the problem. "The Indian question is an economic and social question rather than one of pedagogy," he wrote. Schools and well-intentioned laws could not change a feudal reality based on the economic and political power of the gamonales (great landowners), lords of all they

surveyed. To rescue indigenous people therefore required elimination of the hacienda system, but that change, according to González Prada, would never come through the benevolence of the ruling class: "The Indian must achieve his redemption through his own efforts, not through the humanity of his oppressors." He consequently advised them to spend on rifles and cartridges the money they now wasted on drink and fiestas. His powerful indictment of the oppressors of indigenous peoples, his faith in their creative capacity, and his rebellious spirit, expressed in prose that flowed like molten lava, profoundly influenced the next generation of intellectuals.

For their part, indigenous highland communities, whose passive resistance to the gamonales' encroachment on their lands and autonomy the intellectuals had mistaken for laziness and apathy, now openly rebelled. Sparked by indigenous leaders like Teodomiro Gutiérrez Cuevas, the Rumi Maqui movement, a millenarian insurrection that swept like wildfire through southern Peru and the central sierra between 1915 and 1930, proclaimed the restoration of Tawantinsuyu, the fabled empire of the great Inca kings.

The Leguía Regime: North American Investment and Peruvian Disillusionment

Integration of indigenous peoples was Peru's gravest social problem, but the rapid economic advance that began under Piérola produced the emergence of a working class whose demands also threatened the peace and security of the ruling class. By 1904, an organized labor movement had arisen, and strikes broke out in Lima's textile mills and other factories. In 1918, during World War I, miners, port workers, and textile workers, responding to a catastrophic inflation of food prices, went on strike. Armed clashes took place between the strikers and the troops sent out to disperse and arrest them. News of the success of the Russian Revolution contributed to the workers' militancy. This movement culminated in a three-day general strike in January 1919; the workers demanded the implementation of currently unenforced social legislation, the reduction of food prices, and the imposition of the eight-hour workday. Under pressure from the workers, the government granted some demands, including the eight-hour day for the manufacturing and extractive industries. The labor struggles of that stormy year merged with the struggle of university students for the reform of an archaic system of higher education that made the university the preserve of a privileged few and denied students any voice in determining policies and faculty appointments.

Nevertheless, sections of the oligarchy insisted that this new and unstable political and social atmosphere required a different way of ruling. An astute business leader and politician, Augusto B. Leguía, offered a new **Caesarist** political model that combined unswerving fidelity to the dominant domestic and foreign interests with severe repression of dissidents and a demagogic nationalist corporatist reform program designed to disarm workers. In July 1919, he seized power and established a personal dictatorship that lasted eleven years (1919–1930).

Leguía encouraged by every means at his disposal the influx of foreign—especially North American—capital. This foreign capital was the cornerstone of his economic policies. Oil and copper were major fields of North American investment in Peru in this period. The fruits of Leguía's policy of opening the doors wide to foreign capital soon became evident. In 1927, a vice president of the First National City Bank wrote that "Peru's principal sources of wealth, the mines and oil-wells, are nearly all foreign-owned, and excepting for wages and taxes, no part of the value of their production remains in the country." Perhaps the most scandalous example of Leguía's policy of giving away Peru's natural resources was his cession of the oil-rich La Brea–Pariñas fields to the International Petroleum Company (IPC), a subsidiary of Standard Oil of New Jersey, in return for a minimal tax of about $0.71 a ton. This cession and a 1922 arbitral award confirming the dubious claims of an English oil company, whose rights had passed to the IPC, became an abiding source of Peruvian nationalist resentment.

Peru under Leguía received a plentiful infusion of North American loans, amounting to about $130 million. The bankers were aware of the risks involved, but the prospects of extremely large profits made these transactions attractive. A trail of corruption, involving Leguía's own family, followed these deals; Leguía's son Juan, acting as an agent for Peru, received more than $500,000 in commissions.

Leguía used the proceeds of these loans and the taxes on foreign trade and foreign investment operations for a massive public works program (including a large road-building program carried out with forced indigenous labor) that contributed to the boom of the 1920s. During those years, he largely rebuilt Lima, provided modern drinking water and sanitation facilities, and embellished the city with new parks, avenues, bank buildings, a racetrack, and a military casino. However, these amenities did not improve the living conditions of Andean peoples or dwellers in the wretched *barriadas* (shantytowns) that began to ring Lima.

Convinced that the threat of communism required some concessions to the masses, however, Leguía made some gestures in the direction of reform. The constitution of 1920 had some striking resemblances to the Mexican constitution of 1917. It declared the right of the state to limit property rights in the interest of the nation, vested ownership of natural resources in the state, and committed the state to the construction of hospitals, asylums, and clinics. It empowered the government to set the hours of labor and to ensure adequate compensation and safe and sanitary conditions of work. It also offered corporate recognition of indigenous communities, proclaimed their right to land, and promised primary education to their children. Nonetheless, these and other provisions of the constitution were, in the words of Fredrick Pike, a "model for the Peru that never was."

That same contrast between promises and performance marked Leguía's labor policy. During his campaign for the presidency, he denounced "reactionaries" and made lavish promises to the workers. Indeed, on seizing power in July 1919, he immediately freed the labor leaders imprisoned under Pardo. He also permitted a congress of workers to form a Federation of Workers of Lima and Callao, but when the labor movement displayed excessive independence, he intervened to crush it. Leguía forced workers to accept token reforms and a program of government- and church-sponsored paternalism, crumbs from the well-laden table of the wealthy.

Leguía's performance was especially disillusioning to the university students. Impressed by his promises of education reform, they had proclaimed him "Mentor of the Youth" and supported his presidential campaign in 1919. Once in power, however, he sought to drive a wedge between students and workers, jailing student leaders and outlawing the Popular University of González Prada, organized by the students to provide workers with political education. Frequent jailings and deportations

of dissident journalists and professors brought Leguía into chronic confrontation with students and faculty, who often went on strike, while the government repeatedly closed down the University of San Marcos.

The fledgling women's rights movement also fragmented during the Leguía dictatorship. In 1914, María Jesús Alvarado Rivera had created *Evolución Feminina*, a journal devoted to the cultivation of cross-class, interracial alliances in pursuit of women's liberation and social justice, but patrician women refused to join these mixed-race organizations. According to Carrie Chapman Catt, the U.S. feminist and president of the Pan-American Women's Suffrage Alliance, "the pure Castillian woman would die before she moved equally herself with those of color." As a result, an aristocratic Peruvian National Women's Council supported Leguía, resisted broader social reforms, and largely favored enfranchisement of literate women because it strengthened their elitist cause. Radicals like Alvarado and Magda Portal soon abandoned this feminism dominated by *damas patrióticas civilistas* (polite patriotic ladies) and joined the class struggle against Leguía.

INDIGENISMO AND SOCIALISM

The traditional oligarchical parties' surrender to the dictator and the weakness of the young Peruvian working class meant that the leadership of the opposition to Leguía fell to middle- and lower-middle-class intellectuals who sought to mobilize the peasantry and the workers for the achievement of their revolutionary aims. Socialism, anti-imperialism, and indigenismo provided the ideological content of the movement that issued from the struggles of the turbulent year of 1919, but indigenismo was the most important ingredient.

Influenced by the revered González Prada, these intellectuals believed that the revolution necessary to regenerate Peru must come from the sierra, from the Andean indigenous peoples, who would destroy age-old systems of oppression and unify Peru again, restoring the grandeur that had been the Inca empire. Common to most of the indigenistas was the belief that the Inca empire had been a model of primitive socialist organization, a thesis rejected by modern scholars. They also believed that the indigenous community had been and still was the "indestructible backbone of Peruvian collectivity," even though individual ownership and cultivation of land was nearly universal throughout the nation by the 1920s. The mission of intellectuals, in their view, was to blow life into the coals of indigenous rebellion and link it to the urban revolution of students and workers.

An influential indigenista of this period was Luis E. Valcárcel, author of the widely read *Tempest in the Andes* (1927). In ecstatic prose, Valcárcel hailed indigenous revolts of the sierra as portents of the coming purifying revolution. A more important and systematic thinker, José Carlos Mariátegui (1894–1930) attempted the task of wedding indigenismo to the scientific socialism of Marx and Engels. His major work was the *Seven Interpretive Essays on Peruvian Reality* (1928). Basing his theory on indigenous communal practices and traditions, on the revolutionary experience of other lands, and on his study of history and economics, Mariátegui concluded that socialism offered the only true solution for the indigenous problems.

Like other indigenistas of his time, Mariátegui idealized the Inca empire, which he regarded as the "most advanced primitive communist organization which history records." Nonetheless, he opposed a "romantic and anti-historical tendency of reconstruction or re-creation of Inca socialism," for modern scientific socialism required only its habits of cooperation and corporate life. Moreover, he stressed that the urban proletariat must lead the coming revolution. Before his untimely death, Mariátegui founded the Peruvian Socialist Party in 1928 and sought affiliation with the Communist International.

Indigenismo was a major plank in the program of the *Alianza Popular Revolucionaria Americana* (APRA), a party founded in Mexico in May 1924 by Victor Raúl Haya de la Torre and Magda Portal, student leaders whom Leguía had exiled. Haya de la Torre proclaimed that APRA's mission was to lead the indigenous and proletarian masses of Peru and all "Indo-America" in the coming socialist, anti-imperialist revolution. Despite the high-sounding rhetoric of *Aprista* propaganda, the party's first concern was, and remained, Peru's middle sector: artisans, small landowners, professionals, and small capitalists. These groups' opportunities for development diminished because of the growing concentration of economic power in Peru by foreign firms and a dependent big bourgeoisie.

In a revealing statement in the mid-1920s, Haya de la Torre declared that the Peruvian working class, whether rural or urban, lacked the class-consciousness and maturity needed to qualify it for the leadership of the coming revolution. He assigned that role to the middle class. To this opinion, he joined a belief in the mission of the great man (himself) who "interprets, intuits, and directs the vague and imprecise aspirations of the multitude." Portal's view of Peruvian women was equally condescending: Because of their low "cultural level" and "unquestioning dependence on masculine influence," women required APRA's guidance to vote.

Haya de la Torre early assumed an ambiguous position on imperialism. Refuting Lenin's theory that imperialism was the *last* stage of capitalism, he argued that in weak, underdeveloped countries like Peru, imperialism was the *first* stage. In effect, imperialism provided the capital needed to create industry, a powerful working class, and the middle class that ultimately would lead the nation in a socialist revolution. Switching from this position to the belief that imperialism must be encouraged and defended was an easy step for Haya de la Torre to take. Mariátegui, who was associated with Haya de la Torre in the student and labor struggles of the early 1920s, soon perceived the inconsistencies of his position and assailed APRA for its "bluff and lies" and its personalism. Despite, or precisely because of, its vague, opportunistic ideology, APRA managed to win over an important section of the Peruvian middle class, especially the students, during the three decades after 1920. It also gained great influence over some peasant groups and urban workers, whom it organized into unions that created its main political base.

APRA VERSUS THE MILITARY

The onset of a world economic crisis in 1929, which caused a serious decline of Peruvian exports and dried up the influx of loans, brought the collapse of the Leguía dictatorship. However, neither the small Communist Party nor the stronger APRA movement took political advantage of Leguía's downfall. A *cholo* (indigenous) army officer, Luis Sánchez Cerro, seized power and became the dominant figure in a populist ruling military junta. Sánchez Cerro soon proclaimed the primacy of the indigenous problem, the need for agrarian reform through expropriation of unculti-vated lands, and the aim of regulating foreign invest-ments in the national interest. In effect, Sánchez Cerro had stolen much of APRA's thunder, to the annoyance of Haya de la Torre.

The Apristas nonetheless launched an unsuccess-ful revolt in 1932 that led to mass executions and the assassination of Sánchez Cerro. This created a ven-detta between the army and APRA that transformed them into implacable enemies and enabled the finan-cial and landed oligarchy to consolidate its power. Thereafter, it courted foreign investors like the U.S.-based International Petroleum Company and promoted export production. A stagnant economy ensued, however, because of prices for the country's chief exports (copper, cotton, lead, and wool), a sit-uation only temporarily relieved by growing de-mand and high prices during World War II (1939–1945) and the Korean War (1950–1953).

In the wars' aftermath, however, Peru, despite modest development of its extractive mineral industry, remained a largely agricultural, export-dependent country with a wealthy, powerful landed oligarchy, a weak and fragmented middle class, a marginalized indigenous peasant majority, and a largely unorganized and undeveloped urban working class. Nonetheless, APRA militants con-tinued to agitate for policies designed to restore popular democracy, renew anti-imperialist struggle, and promote social justice. Largely influenced by the *comandos femeninos*, these policies included land reform; civil and political equality irrespective of race, class, or gender; and state regulation of foreign investment. In 1955, Peruvian women finally won the right to vote, but little more. APRA's male leadership, fearful of a growing lower-class power, increasingly abandoned women and their social jus-tice issues to curry favor with landed elites.

Meanwhile, the inequities of Peru's income distribution continued to increase, as did collisions between large landowners and increasingly militant, well-organized indigenous peasants. In some cases, peasants revolted against precapitalist labor systems (like the yanacona, which often required personal service); in others, violence arose because land-owners tried to evict their indigenous tenants and sheep in favor of wage labor and cash rent systems. These evictions increased landlessness and popula-tion pressure in indigenous communities, thereby accelerating the flow of highland emigrants to the coast, where they swelled the population of city slums and shantytowns.

This first generation of *provincianos* (indigenous highland migrants) now found themselves in a foreign environment, surrounded by hostile urban elites who ridiculed their rural lifestyles, scorned their racial ori-gins, and limited their social, economic, and political opportunities. For hundreds of years, Peru's *criollo* elite had preserved its cultural authority and political power by institutionalizing a rigid, race-based, social hierar-chy that defined criollos as "white," civilized, and superior; it likewise identified indigenous peoples, mestizos, and blacks as inferior, barbaric, ignorant, and uncivilized. Not surprisingly, the new migrants sought to assimilate into their strange surroundings by publicly emulating criollo culture even as they pri-vately celebrated their various highland traditions. They settled together in *barriadas* (slums) or *pueblos jóvenes* (squatter communities) and often supported their families by opening small businesses in the infor-mal sector, selling a broad range of commodities on street corners, or working as domestic servants.

The Limits of Populism, 1952–1968

THE 1952 BOLIVIAN REVOLUTION

Against a similar background of indigenous conflicts with creole landlords and class warfare between mineworkers and foreign mine owners, revolution brewed in Bolivia during World War II. The disastrous results of the Chaco War (1932–1935) had doubled the size of Paraguay at the expense of Bolivia, disgraced the Bolivian army, and accelerated revolutionary discontent. (See the map in Chapter 9, p. 219.) Even more problematic, however, was the Bolivian military's desperate effort to force indigenous highland conscripts to fight in the hot, humid lowlands on behalf of a nation they did not recognize. This only exacerbated indigenous unrest. In addition, the social turmoil unleashed by the global economic depression and the growing wartime domination of foreign mining companies, originally inspired by skyrocketing demand for Bolivia's strategic mineral raw materials, combined to alienate middle-class support for successive military dictatorships that had dominated the Bolivian state.

The last straw was the army's 1942 Cataví massacre of unarmed striking miners and their families. Fearing greater social unrest, the mobilization of popular sectors, and its implications for their own power and property, middle-class activists organized the National Revolutionary Movement (MNR) and led a massive protest that brought the reformist government of Gualberto Villaroel to power the following year. After his assassination three years later, the MNR mobilized the countryside and urban centers during a six-year struggle. Women especially played a significant role: The Women Workers' Federation (FOF) and the Barzolas—the MNR's infamous female "secret police" (named for María Barzola, a woman miner who died in the Cataví massacre)—organized street demonstrations, hunger strikes, and other political protests.

By 1952, the MNR, led by Victor Paz Estenssoro, finally overthrew the rule of the great landlords and tin barons with the support of armed miners and peasants. The Bolivian land reform, begun by the spontaneous rising of the peasantry and legitimized by the revolutionary government of President Paz Estenssoro, broke the back of the latifundio system in Bolivia. Like the Mexican land reform, however, the Bolivian reform created some new problems even as it solved old ones. It usually divided the former latifundia into very small farms—true minifundia—and the new peasant proprietors received little aid from the government in the form of credit and technical assistance. Yet, despite its shortcomings, the Bolivian land reform brought indisputable benefits: some expansion of the internal market; some rise in peasant living standards; and, in the words of Richard W. Patch, "the transformation of a dependent and passive population into an independent and active population."

Women, workers, and indigenous communities mobilized politically. Women joined private charitable associations and international organizations like the Inter-American Women's Commission (CIM) to agitate for the right to vote, civil equality, indigenous rights, and greater access to education. Lydia Gueiler Tejada, for example, advocated "the free association of women in legitimate defense of her interests, without distinction of class, race, creed, or even political ideas." Mineworkers, led by Juan Lechín, demanded nationalization of the tin mines and *control obrero*—workers' control in the management of state-owned mines. Indigenous communities called for immediate, wholesale land reform and greater cultural freedom.

In response, the new government nationalized the principal tin mines, most of which three large companies controlled, and recognized its debt to the armed miners by placing the mines under joint labor-government management. It also abolished the literacy and gender restrictions on voting and thus enfranchised women and the indigenous masses. However, the new regime inherited a costly, rundown tin industry, while the initial disruptive effect of the agrarian reform on food production added to its economic problems.

Increasingly fearful of the lower classes' revolutionary demands for equality and social justice, and under strong pressure from the United States, which made vitally needed economic aid to the revolutionary government conditional on the adoption of free-market policies, the MNR leadership gradually abandoned its populist agenda. The government of Paz Estenssoro offered generous compensation to the former owners of expropriated mines, invited new foreign investment on favorable terms, ended labor participation in the management of the government tin company, and reduced welfare benefits to miners.

Likewise, Paz abandoned any particular interest in women's rights or their social agenda and, instead, cynically manipulated the party's historic support for women's enfranchisement to secure their votes. According to Domitila Barrios de Chungara, a militant activist in the mineworkers' Committee of Housewives (CAC), Paz, who excluded women from leadership positions in the government, nonetheless used the Barzolas women to disrupt radical working-class protests: "The Barzolas would jump in front of them, brandishing razors, penknives, and whips, attacking the demonstrators." But the largely middle-class male movement's patriarchal prejudices clearly limited the political ascendancy of women revolutionaries like Gueiler Tejada, a militant feminist and one-time commander of MNR militias, whose political influence dissipated after she accepted a distant diplomatic post in Germany.

Paz also ignored the needs of Bolivia's indigenous peoples, which caused Laureano Machaka, an Aymara peasant leader opposed to the government's policies, to organize a short-lived independent Aymara Republic in 1956. Equally important, Paz agreed to the restoration of a powerful U.S.-trained national army to offset the strength of peasant and worker militias. These retreats broke up the worker–middle class alliance formed during the Revolution, undermined populist reforms, and facilitated the military's seizure of power in 1964.

In the violent ebb and flow of Bolivian politics thereafter, a persistent theme was the conflict among radical workers, women, and students on one side and a coalition of elite business executives and politicians grown wealthy through U.S. aid on the other. The indigenous peasantry, neutralized by a populist agrarian reform that satisfied its land hunger, initially remained passive or even sided with the government in its struggles with labor, but later unrest began to grow because of deteriorating economic conditions and a growing consciousness of their collective indigenous identity. Increasingly, the military intervened in Bolivian politics to resolve these conflicts and impose a social stability through force of arms.

PERU'S BELAÚNDE: INDIGENISTA POPULISM AND BROKEN PROMISES

Following the lead of his populist neighbors in Bolivia, Fernando Belaúnde Terry organized his presidential campaign in Peru with a decided indigenista tinge. Visiting the remotest Andean villages, Belaúnde extolled the Inca grandeur, called on the natives to emulate the energy and hard work of their ancestors, and proclaimed the right of the landless peasantry to land. However, his performance in the field of agrarian reform did not match his promises. The agrarian law that issued from Congress the following year stressed technical improvement rather than expropriation and division of latifundia, with the hope that hacendados would adopt modern methods to improve production. As amended in Congress by a coalition that included Apristas, the law exempted from expropriation the highly productive coastal estates, whose workers APRA had unionized, and reserved archaic hacienda lands in the sierra for redistribution. Moreover, the loopholes or exceptions were so numerous that the law produced modest results.

Meanwhile, Belaúnde's lavish promises had given great impetus to peasant land invasions. By October 1963, invasions had multiplied in the central highlands and spread to the whole southern part of the sierra. The land-invasion movement also changed its character; whereas before the peasants had seized only uncultivated lands, they now occupied cultivated land, arguing that they had paid for it with their unpaid or poorly paid labor of several generations. Militant peasant unions under radical leadership appeared, and a guerrilla movement arose in parts of the sierra. Meanwhile, a wave of strikes broke out in the cities, and workers occupied a number of enterprises in Lima and Callao.

These outbreaks took the Belaúnde administration by surprise. The hacendados, supported by APRA, demanded the use of the armed forces to repress the peasant movement. Indeed, the once "revolutionary" APRA now called for the harshest treatment of rebellious peasants. At the end of 1963, after some vacillation, the Belaúnde government crushed the peasant movement by force, a task the armed forces apparently assumed with reluctance, preferring "civic action" programs of a reformist type. According to one estimate, the repression left eight thousand peasants dead and three thousand five hundred imprisoned, fourteen thousand hectares of land burned with fire and napalm, and nineteen thousand peasants forced to abandon their homes.

Belaúnde had failed to solve the agrarian problem. He also failed to keep his promise to settle the old controversy with the IPC over the La Brea–Pariñas oil fields, which, Peru claimed, IPC had illegally exploited for some forty years. Finally, under strong pressure from U.S. interests, who delayed large planned investments in Peru, Belaúnde's government signed the Pact of Talara, which represented a massive surrender to the IPC. Peru regained the now almost-exhausted oil fields but in return agreed to the cancellation of claims for back taxes and illegal profits amounting to almost $700 million. IPC also received a new concession to exploit a vast area in the Amazon region and retained the refinery of Talara, to which the government agreed to sell all the oil produced from the wells it had regained at a fixed price. A scandal rocked the country when the government, forced to publish the document, claimed to have "lost" the page setting the price that the IPC must pay the state oil company for its crude oil. As public indignation grew, the armed forces, opposition parties, and even the Catholic Church denounced the agreement.

For Peru's military leaders, this was the last straw. For some years, they had engaged in intense soul-searching over the past and future of their country. Now they decided that Belaúnde's government and the social forces that supported it had sold out the national interest and were incapable of solving Peru's problems. In October 1968, the armed forces seized the presidential palace, sent Belaúnde into exile, and established a military governing junta that began a swift transformation of Peru's economic and social structures.

Military Corporatism and Revolution, 1968–1975

THE PERUVIAN MILITARY ABOUT-FACE

Initially, the military seizure of power appeared to be another in the long series of military coups that punctuated the history of Peru and other Latin American countries—coups that changed the occupant of the presidential palace but left the existing order intact. However, under the leadership of Gen. Juan Velasco Alvarado, the self-proclaimed "Revolutionary Government of the Armed Forces" quickly distinguished itself from this tradition. Instead, it decreed laws that called for nationalization of oil, a sweeping agrarian reform, and workers' participation in the ownership and management of industrial concerns.

Observers found these events as startling, in the words of Fidel Castro, "as if a fire had started in the firehouse," for the Latin American military had traditionally functioned as loyal servants of the area's oligarchies. In Peru, however, a social and ideological gulf had developed between the military and civilian elites. Most army officers came from a military family or from the lower-middle class. These officers, fearing the rise of an autonomous, indigenous peasant and working-class radicalism, sought to protect and promote national capitalist development in Peru by shifting power from landed oligarchs, foreign investors, and their government representatives to a socially responsible state controlled by a nationalistic new bourgeoisie.

Within a week, the Velasco junta had nationalized the IPC's oil fields and its refinery at Talara and soon after seized all its other assets. Having settled the IPC question, the junta tackled the country's most burning economic and social questions.

LAND REFORM AND NATIONALIZATION OF RESOURCES

Land reform was the key problem: Peru could not achieve economic independence, modernization, and greater social democracy without liquidating the inefficient, semifeudal latifundio system, the *gamonal* political system that was its corollary, and the coastal enclaves of foreign oligarchical power. Major specific objectives were to expand agricultural production and to generate capital for investment in the industrial sector; thus, the reform compensated landowners for expropriated lands with bonds that they could use as investment capital in industry or

Gen. Juan Velasco Alvarado led the Revolutionary Government of the Armed Forces in 1968 and, invoking the immortal words of the revolutionary Inca Tupac Amaru, proclaimed to Peru's impoverished campesinos and indigenous communities that "the boss will now no longer eat from your poverty!"

mining. On June 24, 1969, President Velasco announced an agrarian reform designed to end the "unjust social and economic structures" of the past. The program deviated from orthodox Latin American reform policies in two respects: first, it did not retain the homestead or family-size farm as its ideal, and second, it did not exempt large estates from expropriation because of their efficiency and productivity. Indeed, it targeted the big coastal sugar plantations for initial expropriation. Largely foreign owned and composed of highly mechanized agroindustrial complexes, these enterprises became cooperatives owned by farm laborers and refinery workers.

Agrarian reform next focused on the haciendas in the sierra. It applied to most highland estates above 35 to 55 hectares and initially aimed to encourage division of estates into small or midsize commercial farms, but this would have reduced the number of potential beneficiaries. Under pressure from militant, unionized peasants, who demanded employment and the formation of cooperatives, the junta moved from parcellation toward cooperative forms of organization. Eventually, fully 76 percent of the expropriated lands became cooperatives, with the remainder distributed in individual plots.

The agrarian reform produced some undeniable immediate and long-range benefits. To begin with, it ended the various forms of serfdom that still survived in the sierra. Second, food production increased, although not substantially or to the level required by Peru's growing population. Third, according to a 1982 field study of the agrarian reform, it "proved a major economic and political benefit to a significant sector of the peasantry," at least in the case of cooperatives with an adequate capital endowment. "In such cooperatives, members' wages and quality of life improved, often dramatically."

Nonetheless, the agrarian reform failed to improve the general material and political condition of the Peruvian peasantry—a failure stemming from incorrect planning and methods on the part of the well-meaning military reformers. First, the reform was neither as swift nor as thorough as the dimensions of the problem required. Delays in implementing the program and the ruses employed by landowners to evade it meant that a considerable amount of land escaped expropriation. As a result, the reform made only a slight impact on the problem of landlessness and rural unemployment and underemployment, especially in the sierra.

Second, the military reformers lacked a coherent strategy for the general modernization of the agricultural sector within an overall plan of balanced, inwardly directed national development. They viewed the agricultural sector as a means of pumping out food and capital to promote development in the urban-industrial area. Reflecting this view, the military government's food-pricing policy aimed to keep food prices low to check inflation and keep the urban working class and middle class content. In the absence of compensating subsidies for small farmers, this policy "served to perpetuate the long-run unfavorable trend of the rural-urban terms of trade." Within the agricultural sector, the allocation of resources and credit skewed in favor of the already well-endowed and efficient coastal estates producing for export, with the bulk of agricultural investment going into large-scale irrigation projects. The military largely neglected the needs of highland small farmers for small-scale irrigation works, fertilizer, and technical assistance. As a result, the coastal sugar, cotton, and coffee cooperatives tended to become "islands of relative privilege in a sea of peasant poverty and unemployment."

The same lack of a coherent strategy for the development of the agricultural sector as a whole appeared in the method of distributing hacienda lands. Only workers who had worked full time on the estates were eligible to become members of the new cooperatives. This left out the temporary laborers and the neighboring peasant villagers who eked out subsistence livings from tiny plots and small herds of sheep. This often led to serious tension and conflict, with the cooperatives defending their privileges and land against invasions by the comuneros (peasant villagers). This pattern of distribution, and the failure to redistribute all the land subject to expropriation, contributed to the continuing flight of campesinos to the coastal cities, where they swelled the ranks of a large unemployed or underemployed population.

Finally, a major flaw of the agrarian reform was that it was a "revolution from above," with little input from below. Despite lip service to participatory ideology, the military technocrats made the final decisions with respect to work conditions, income policy, crop selection, and the like. Because the government's economic policy tended to subordinate peasant interests to the drive for rapid industrial growth, many peasants became disillusioned with the cooperative model. In some cases, particularly after 1975, when a group stressing private enterprise and a free market ousted the nationalist reformist Velasco wing of the military, the disillu-

sionment led to peasant demands to dismantle the cooperatives and parcel out the land.

After land reform, the nationalization of key foreign-owned natural resources was the most important objective of the junta's program. The junta also targeted domestic monopolies that the military regarded as obstacles to development. When the revolution began, foreign firms controlled the commanding heights of the Peruvian economy. Eight years later, state enterprises had taken over most of these firms. The process began with the nationalization of the IPC, whose assets passed into the control of *Petroperu*, the state-owned oil company. Later, the national telephone system, the railroads (the Peruvian Corporation), and Peru's international airline came under state ownership. The military government took over the cement, chemical, and paper industries and nationalized the important fishmeal industry, in which foreigners had invested large amounts of capital. It also seized the sugar industry, in large part controlled by the Grace interests, and the cotton industry, dominated by a U.S. firm, Anderson-Clayton. The 1974 nationalization of the giant U.S.-owned mining complex of Cerro de Pasco gave the state ownership of four thousand concessions and vested control of most copper, lead, and zinc mining and refining in two state companies, *Minoperu* and *Centrominperu*. Nationalization of Marcona Mining in 1975 gave the state control of iron ore and steel. In addition to the takeover of these primarily extractive and manufacturing firms, state companies obtained marketing monopolies of all major commodity exports and most food distribution. Through stock purchases, the government nationalized most of the banking and insurance industries. Thus, the state came to control decisive sectors of the Peruvian economy.

The original intent of the military reformers was not to substitute the state for local private capital but to promote its formation. The military aimed to remove such impediments as the latifundio and foreign monopolistic firms even as it tried to create an industrial infrastructure financed by mineral and agricultural exports. Nevertheless, the radical rhetoric of the nationalistic military frightened the local bourgeoisie, who generally were satisfied with their technological and financial dependence on foreign capital, and they failed to respond to the incentives for industrial investment. As a result, the government had to assume the role of the economy's main investor and by 1972 accounted for more than half the total investment in the economy.

The cost of this investment, added to the large sums expended for compensation for expropriated estates and foreign enterprises, grew high. Tax reform offered one possibility of mobilizing considerable amounts of previously untouched wealth. Such a move, however, would have antagonized the local bourgeoisie, whom the military was wooing, and the middle class, who formed its principal mass base. Because of disputes over expropriation, Peru could not apply for loans to the United States and the multinational agencies it controlled. Accordingly, Peru had to turn to foreign private banks. Encouraged by the high price of copper and other Peruvian exports and by the prospect of rich oil strikes in the Amazon Basin, the banks willingly complied with Peru's requests for loans. They lent $147 million in 1972 and $734 million in 1973, making Peru the largest borrower among developing countries in the latter year.

Although women's rights issues clearly were not a priority for the military regime, a new women's movement, led by Virginia Vargas, founder of the Flora Tristán Peruvian Women's Center, nonetheless emerged. These women were active in grassroots neighborhood organizations, unions, teachers' associations, and social work agencies, which provided experience with collective action and heightened their consciousness of gender-based inequality. Under pressure from this women's movement, the military adopted the eighteenth-century Inca revolutionary leaders, Micaela Bastidas and her husband Tupac Amaru, as the symbols of their 1974 Plan Inca, which demanded civil and political equality for women, laws against discrimination, affirmative action in public employment, and rural education programs.

The military likewise had not intended to unleash a cultural revolution, but its nationalist ideology mobilized popular political participation and reinforced artistic explorations of the country's indigenous and African roots. This led to a dramatic expansion of popular theater and folk music that challenged criollo cultural hegemony and decisively shaped a radically new multiracial Peruvian national identity. In the early 1970s, for example, Yuyachkani, a politically committed theater group that took its name from a Quechua word meaning "thoughts and memories," sought to organize indigenous workers by touring highland mining communities and performing *Fist of Copper*. This play drew on Spanish and European theatrical traditions to extol the virtues of popular resistance to violent police repression of a miners' strike. During postperformance discussions, the young urban actors, who aimed to raise the consciousness of their indigenous audiences, instead learned about the long tradition of Andean indigenous theater, which integrated dance, music, puppets, masks, and colorful costumes. Yuyachkani later incorporated these elements into plays that shared with highland peoples the "good news" about the 1969 land reform that gave them the legal authority to fight for their land against the landowners and their hired thugs. They also became popular in the universities, urban slums, and squatter settlements, where provincianos had migrated in search of jobs.

By early 1975, a new cyclical crisis had begun to ravage the capitalist world. Rising prices for oil and imported equipment and technology, combined with falling prices for Peru's raw material exports, undermined the fragile prosperity that had made President Velasco's reforms possible. These circumstances created unmanageable balance-of-trade and debt service problems. The populist model of development based on export expansion and foreign borrowing had again revealed its inherent contradictions.

The experience of the Peruvian Revolution shows the difficulty of escaping from dependent development without radical structural changes in class and property relationships and income distribution. Like the Mexican Revolution, Peru's experience suggested that the revolution that did not advance risked stagnation and loss of whatever gains it had made. Contemporaneous events in Ecuador reinforced this conclusion.

ECUADOR'S MILITARY REVOLUTION

The military also played a prominent role in Ecuador, the smallest of the Andean republics, which experienced the faint beginnings of a social revolution in 1972. A group of nationalist military headed by Gen. Guillermo Rodríguez Lara ousted the aging, demagogic President José María Velasco Ibarra, who had dominated Ecuadorian politics for the previous four decades. Velasco Ibarra had favored a dependent industrialization, shaped by the Alliance for Progress and based on massive importation of foreign capital and goods. This program rested on the 1964 Agrarian Reform Act, which abolished the *huasipungo* (the country's serflike labor system) and expropriated church lands and inefficient haciendas but also promoted colonization of so-called *tierras baldías* (untitled lands that self-sufficient indigenous communities mostly occupied). The discovery of oil in lowland territories in the late 1960s accelerated incursions into indigenous lands and cultural autonomy, even as petroleum production threatened the environment by contaminating surface and underground water supplies. By the early 1970s, foreign interests were as dominant in Ecuador as in Peru and Bolivia; they controlled some 35 percent of all industrial enterprises, nearly 60 percent of all commercial enterprises, and half of all banking assets in Ecuador.

Promising radical land and social reforms, the new nationalistic military junta offered a program of rapid economic development that stressed industrialization and the modernization of agriculture. It also promised to reverse previous official policy that surrendered the country's rich oil resources in the Amazonian lowlands to foreign companies. The new government counted on revenue from oil to finance the planned reforms and program of economic development.

Five years later, however, the Ecuadorian Revolution stalled. Opposition from the still-powerful hacendado class had almost completely paralyzed agrarian and tax reform. Although modest land distribution benefited peasants, big landowners still controlled 80 percent of the cultivated area. The military government virtually abandoned land redis-tribution in favor of cooperation with hacendados to increase production and state revenues through mechanization, greater concentration of land ownership, and the ouster of peasants from the land. The result was growing peasant agitation for true land reform, accompanied by invasions of estates and clashes between peasants and security forces.

Finally, under pressure from foreign oil companies for lower taxes and wider profit margins—a pressure exerted through a boycott on oil exports—the military regime also retreated from its insistence on tight control over prices, profits, and the volume and rate of oil production. These concessions represented a defeat for nationalist elements in the military junta and sharpened the divisions within it.

In Ecuador, as in other Latin American countries under military control, the late 1970s saw a growing popular movement for social justice and a return to civilian rule. Unlike other countries in the region, however, groups like the Indigenous People's Organization of Pastaza (OPIP), founded in 1979, increasingly played an influential role in these movements, joining with women's rights activists and trade unionists. In addition to a return to democracy, indigenous leaders demanded that the government recognize their communal land titles, cultural identities, and political autonomy.

Ecuador's military leaders had failed to develop the economy or to relieve the dismal poverty and social inequality suffered by the Ecuadorian masses. According to official figures, wage earners' share of national income had declined from 53 percent in 1960 to less than 46 percent in 1973. However, 7 percent of the population received more than 50 percent of the national income. Consequently, the military appeared quite willing to abandon the burden of governing the country. In July 1978, Jaime Roldós, a populist candidate, handily won the ensuing presidential election. During the campaign, the young, energetic Roldós promised to revive agrarian reform and end foreign economic control.

Central to this program was the use of Ecuador's oil earnings to modernize agriculture, promote industrialization, and construct a network of roads to expand the internal market. Roldós's five-year plan called for investment of $800 million in rural development that would bring some 3 million acres of coastal, highland, and Amazonian farmland into new production. He also aimed to accelerate the pace of agrarian reform, targeting almost 2 million acres for distribution to landless peasants by 1984. Roldós's foreign policy stressed greater independence from the United States, reflected in his maintenance of friendly relations with Cuba, expansion of diplomatic and commercial ties with socialist countries, and support for Central American revolutionary movements. However, Roldós's ambitious reform and development program had hardly begun when he died tragically in a plane crash in May 1981.

His successor inherited deteriorating economic conditions because of a developing recession and declining prices for Ecuadorian oil. The economic slump sharpened the social problems created by advances in industrialization and the modernization of agriculture. From 1970 to 1980, the proportion of peasants in the population had fallen from 68 percent to 52 percent. The agrarian reform, stressing mechanization and concentration of landownership rather than distribution of land to the landless, had ended semiservile relations in the countryside but aggravated the problem of landlessness and rural unemployment. This swelled the number of rural people fleeing to the cities in a fruitless search for work. By the early 1980s, the great port city of Guayaquil had a population of 1 million; an estimated two-thirds of its inhabitants were unemployed or underemployed and lacked adequate shelter, food, or medical care. Thus, in an atmosphere of economic and political crisis, social problems and tension accumulated with little prospect for solutions.

Collapse of Military Corporatism, 1975–1990

THE PERUVIAN REVOLUTION UNDER ATTACK, 1975–1983

The economic crisis that stalled Ecuador's top-down military revolution also provoked a sharp struggle within Peru's military establishment. Radical nationalists, who proposed to extend the 1968 revolution's social and economic reforms, confronted moderates who called for measures that would win the confidence of native and foreign capitalists, thereby making possible a revival of private investments. In August 1975, a peaceful coup replaced President Velasco with Francisco Morales Bermúdez, who gradually purged radical nationalists from the government and forced their resignations from the armed forces.

The so-called First Phase of the revolution had ended. To appease foreign and domestic capitalists, the new government introduced a package of severe austerity measures. These included sharp reductions in government investments in state enterprises, steep increases in consumer prices, and a 44 percent devaluation of the currency, only partly offset by 10 to 14 percent wage increases. The government next announced the end of agrarian reform, although it had distributed only about one-third of the land subject to expropriation. In early 1978, after long negotiations, Morales Bermúdez capitulated to the International Monetary Fund (IMF) and accepted its conditions for a new loan, including privatization of state enterprises, heavy cuts in budgets and subsidies, large price increases, and severe restraints on wage increases. These measures provoked widespread strikes and rioting, which the government crushed with a full-scale military operation.

For the thoroughly discredited military junta, the prime concern was how to make a smooth transfer of power to a civilian regime that would continue its policies. A new constitution served this function. It established a bicameral Congress, both elected, like the president, for five years. It contained language ensuring that private property and the free market would remain the foundations of the Peruvian economy. The constitution guaranteed the right to strike and collective bargaining, but these were subject to parliamentary regulation. The biggest novelty was the grant of the right to vote to illiterates.

Predictably, Fernando Belaúnde Terry, a master of populist rhetoric who enjoyed an aura of martyrdom thanks to his ouster by the military in 1968, won the 1980 elections. It soon became clear that he intended to continue and extend the "counterreformation" begun by Morales Bermúdez. Export expansion and debt repayment were the great priorities, which required the familiar arsenal of austerity measures, devaluation, and wage freezes.

The Belaúnde government also dismantled the major reforms of the Velasco Era. A principal objective was to restore a free market in agricultural land by dissolving the cooperative system. A new agricultural promotion and development law gave the government the power to divide cooperative land into small, individual plots and turn them over to cooperative members, who could buy, sell, or mortgage them. This fostered the reconcentration of land in a few hands.

Other legislation empowered the government to sell off state-owned companies and increase private participation in publicly owned firms through stock issues and other programs. The government proposed to ban general and sympathy strikes, drastically reduce public works spending, and phase out subsidies on basic foods and fuel. These proposals caused bitter wrangling in parliament between the government and the opposition parties, but they fomented unprecedented popular protest; for the first time in Peruvian history, all the major labor groups joined in a general strike.

Thus, fifteen years after the military seized power in Peru, the nation again faced a crisis of unprecedented proportions. Its population had doubled between 1960 and 1980, from 10 to 20 million, and its distribution between town and country had changed dramatically. In 1960, 60 percent of the people were rural, but in 1980, 60 percent were urban. Unemployment climbed to new heights; strikes succeeded each other in industry, the railroads, and the banks; and the rural exodus continued to swell the population of the barriadas that ringed Lima.

POPULAR CULTURE AND RESISTANCE

Second-generation provincianos had played a role in many of the urban protests that helped inaugurate the 1968 Peruvian Revolution, and they likewise joined this new popular movement to defend its achievements. Unlike their parents, however, they had become more economically independent of criollo society. They had created their own self-help migrant community associations, usually based on their region of origin (e.g., Punenos from Puno and Ayacuchanos from Ayacucho), joined trade unions, and participated in other grassroots social movements that strengthened their public embrace of indigenous identities. This growing independence of thought and action contributed to the birth of a new cultural form, a popular urban musical style variously called **cumbia andina** or **chicha**, named for the corn beer that was the preferred beverage in highland Andean indigenous communities. No longer interested in assimilating criollo values, these sons and daughters of highland migrants increasingly challenged established social hierarchies based on race, ethnicity, and class power.

Chicha music drew on three radically different sources for its creative inspiration: Colombian cumbia rhythms, whose origins lay in Afro-Colombian cultural traditions; folk melodies indigenous to the Andean highlands; and the electric instruments commonly associated with U.S. and British rock-and-roll. Chicha songs typically explored the everyday lives of poor, hard-working urban provincianos. According to ethnomusicologist Thomas Tutino, one of the earliest chicha bands, Los demonios del Mantaro (Mantaro Devils), sold two hundred thousand copies of "La Chichera," a song that celebrated the life of a street peddler who sold Andean corn beer. Established criollo critics understandably disparaged chicha as crude, amateurish, "mindless" music, and leftist intellectuals either dismissed its lyrical interest in unrequited love as politically disengaged or criticized it for "internalizing criollo values" by promoting upward mobility.

However, young provincianos, often feeling unloved, socially marginalized, out of place, and lacking a clear sense of their own identity, thrilled to its "modern" beat and identified with its lyrical lament about their real-life experiences. In one very popular song, "Ambulante soy" ("I Am a Street

During the 1980s, migrants from highland communities adapted indigenous musical instruments and folk rhythms to reflect a new urban experience of modernity that they found simultaneously exciting and disturbing.

Vendor"), the lead singer of Los Shapis, perhaps the most famous of the chicha bands, bemoaned, "How sad is life, how sad it is to dream" and then proudly announced, "I am a street vendor, I am a proletarian." Similarly, Grupo Alegría's "Pequeño luchador" ("Little Fighter") described the daily survival struggles of "a small child/Who runs through the city/Hawking advertisements that will sell" and then celebrated the heroism of this "Little boy with dirty face/Little fighter/Your hands now know/What it means to work." Even songs like Los Shapis's "Somos estudiantes" ("We Are Students"), which some have criticized for its alleged identification with criollo concerns about "occupational status" and social mobility, clearly stressed the value of professional positions as a means to promote the de-

velopment of their communities, not their own personal self-aggrandizement. "We are teachers/For our children," Los Shapis sang. "Doctors we will be/For the orphans. We are lawyers/Of the poor."

Chicha music soon outsold all its competitors in Peruvian markets, including internationally renowned artists like Julio Iglesias and Michael Jackson. Initially performed on street corners and in vacant lots in the pueblos jóvenes, chicha artists later regularly played to large crowds in *chichadromes* and provided musical entertainment at community religious festivals, weddings, birthday parties, and other social events. Supported by the progressive indigenista policies of Velasco's revolutionary nationalist regime, which had made Quechua an official national language and required radio stations to promote authentic local music, they soon dominated national radio broadcasts, claiming almost 40 percent of airtime by the early 1980s. Chicha music also expanded its popularity from the urban centers of its birth to rural highland communities. As the reformist Velasco government crumbled, chicha artists and their concerts provided young provincianos with useful meeting places to organize popular resistance and promote a return to democracy. Thereafter, they would lend their voice to support reformist state social programs proposed by Aprista and other populist politicians who sought to curry political favor with urban and rural provincianos alike.

APRA IN POWER, 1985–1990

The Aprista candidate who most benefited from Belaúnde's failure was thirty-six-year-old Alán García Pérez, a disciple of the late Haya de la Torre. García campaigned on a populist, reformist program in 1985, promising to defend the agrarian and industrial reforms of the Velasco Era and to reject Belaúnde's free-market policies. In his inaugural address, García proclaimed that henceforth Peru would not deal with the IMF but directly with the creditor banks. He also announced that he would limit interest payments on Peru's foreign debt of about $14 billion to 10 percent of Peru's export earnings—about $400 million. "Peru," García declared, "has one overwhelming creditor, its own people." Other parts of his economic program included measures to halt capital exports, freeze the price of necessities, and raise the minimum wage by 50 percent—all measures opposed by the IMF and the foreign financial community.

García's populist effort to restrict foreign debt payments, prohibit the flight of capital, prevent luxury imports, and raise wages formed part of a coherent program to revive the sluggish Peruvian economy. The long-term goal was to promote the development of an autonomous Peruvian capitalism on the basis of expanded import-substitution industrialization and reduced dependence on imported raw materials. The restriction on debt repayments and the controls on foreign trade aimed to make capital available for internal development; the substantial wage increases sought to expand purchasing power and demand for Peruvian-made goods. Nonetheless, García distinguished his populist policies from the state ownership that had characterized Peru's "military socialism" in the early 1970s. In a speech marking the anniversary of his first year in office, he reassured private business executives that, even as he rejected devaluation and new indebtedness as a regression to "the colonial recipes of the IMF," so too he rejected nationalization. His path, he said, led to "a strong state redirecting the structure of Peruvian industry toward less import-dependent options."

Economic problems remained, however. Business resistance to the price freeze produced shortages of consumer items and forced the government to relax price controls, allowing some prices to rise. Moreover, the gap was growing between the costs of the recovery program and government income from all sources, including export earnings and the savings obtained by limiting debt payments. García had few options. He could try through tax reform to tap the abundant wealth of Peruvian elites, left untouched by the military reformers, but this was an unacceptable solution given the moderate nature of his program. Printing money or a slowdown in economic growth was equally unacceptable and García had ruled out foreign bank loans, but the IMF had in any case declared him ineligible for new credits.

A major obstacle to the sound, balanced economic growth envisaged by García was the continuing cleavage between the sierra and the coast—the contrast between the poverty of the highlands (largely populated by Quechua- and Aymara-speaking indigenous peasants) and the relative prosperity of the coast. Landlessness and unemployment or underemployment continued to be the burning problems of the sierra. The result was that the highlands became the scene of a struggle between the landless peasantry and the giant cooperatives, often controlled by elite groups of managers, engineers, and bureaucrats.

The Maoist *Sendero Luminoso* (Shining Path) entered into this struggle over land, with all its potential for violence. Other left-wing movements repudiated it as terrorist and mistaken in its effort to polarize Peruvian society into militarists and *senderistas*. For the most part led by radicalized students and other middle-class individuals, the Sendero Luminoso organized a terrorist campaign against all who supported the existing bourgeois order; it also encouraged peasants to invade, occupy, and loot cooperatives. The García government responded to this threat by expanding Belaúnde's counterinsurgency campaign, which had placed nineteen of Peru's twenty-three provinces under a state of emergency with the military in overall control and suspended most civil rights. García justified this action, claiming that Sendero Luminoso had killed thousands of officials, police, members of other security forces, and uncooperative peasants. However, church authorities and other independent observers asserted that the security forces had committed many of these repressive acts and that many killings of peasants ascribed to Sendero guerrillas were the work of these forces.

As his term of office ended, a balance sheet of García's record in power pointed to some positive initiatives and accomplishments, including his decision to limit debt interest payments to a certain proportion of export proceeds, thereby making more funds available for development purposes. García's debt strategy marked an advance over that of the military reformers, but it was not enough. Peru needed a program of structural economic and social change. It had to create a self-sufficient industrial base that would lessen dependency on foreign imports and capital, but it also needed a more thoroughgoing agrarian reform that would attack the age-old problem of Andean poverty and backwardness. Finally, it required reforms that would eliminate the need for food imports, expand the domestic market, and reduce the immense inequities in income distribution.

García refused to make these changes, and as a result, by 1987, his project for creating an autonomous Peruvian capitalism ran out of steam. The country had a serious trade deficit, its foreign reserves shrank, and the business class, despite generous incentives from the government, refused to increase its investments. From 1988 to 1989, the per capita gross domestic product declined by

20 percent, the biggest drop in the region. As if the economic crisis were not enough, the war with the Maoist Sendero Luminoso movement grew more intense. Moreover, the indigenous struggle to reclaim ancestral lands led to a wave of **tomas de tierras** (land invasions) that produced a new militancy among peasant leaders and fueled the rural rebellion.

Amid the economic gloom, Peru's illicit coca trade ironically provided the only comfort. In Peru, as in Bolivia, the jobs and dollars generated by the coca boom cushioned the impact of a devastating economic crisis. With opportunities for employment in the legal economy shrinking, thousands of migrants joined the "white gold rush" to the Upper Huallaga Valley, the heart of Peru's coca empire. Coca farmers processed it into a white paste and sold it to Colombian dealers, who pocketed most of the profits. Nonetheless, Peru's share came to about $1.2 billion annually, roughly 30 percent of the value of all Peru's legal exports. Without these illicit dollars, according to one Peruvian economist, the exchange rate would have nearly doubled, making vitally needed imports much more expensive. Like Paz in Bolivia, García liberalized Central Bank rules to permit the purchase of coca dollars, no questions asked.

With APRA and the military disgraced by García's economic fiasco and failure to end the civil war, the 1990 presidential elections became the site of a new contest between neoliberal free-market philosophy and the vague electoral populism of an obscure agronomist, Alberto Fujimori. The son of poor Japanese immigrants, Fujimori insisted that the state's primary obligation was to satisfy people's basic needs before attempting any economic adjustment program. Surprising most political pundits, Fujimori's populist crusade solidified his base and attracted leftist support, thereby ensuring his electoral triumph.

The historical record of Andean military corporatism in promoting authentic national development was ambiguous at best. However, even as the Andean republics had begun experimenting with military corporatism to solve the postwar crisis of populism, another new strategy of national development unfolded in Chile. Eschewing the violence of the Cuban revolution and the hierarchical authority of Andean military corporatism, Chileans opted for a broad-based, popular, participatory, and democratic path to development.

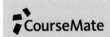

Go to the CourseMate website at **www.cengagebrain.com** for primary sources, additional study tools, and review materials—including audio and video clips—for this chapter.

Chile: The Democratic Socialist Alternative

17

FOCUS QUESTIONS

- What role did copper and nitrates play in the economic, political, and social history of Chile?

- How were women affected by Chile's twentieth-century economic changes, and how did they affect Chilean politics?

- What were the origins of populism in Chile, and what role did the state play in shaping national development?

- What were the foundations upon which populism in Chile rested, and how did this limit its capacity for promoting national development?

- How did the Popular Unity government aim to transcend the limits of populism, what were its major policy objectives, and what were its successes and failures?

- What role did the United States play in the overthrow of the democratically elected Allende regime?

FOR A CENTURY AND A HALF, Chile had set a relatively high standard of political behavior on a continent notorious for its turmoil and dictatorships. Compared with its neighbors, Argentina, Bolivia, and Peru, Chile had been a model of domestic tranquility. Chilean democracy appeared so firmly rooted that it permitted the election and installation of a Marxist head of state, President Salvador Allende Gossens, in 1970. In the regional struggle to overcome the limits of populism and promote a revolutionary national development, Chile seemed to offer a peaceful, democratic model that sharply contrasted with Cuba's armed socialist revolution and the Andean area's "military socialism." Only three years later, however, amid growing economic and political chaos, military rebels violently overthrew Chile's legitimate government and established a terrorist state that ruled through brutal oppression.

How could Chile maintain its parliamentary democracy so long when the rest of Latin America could not? Why, after almost a hundred and fifty years of respect for parliamentary democracy, did it crumble so swiftly? In retrospect, the bounds of Chilean democracy were narrowly drawn; the elite and its foreign collaborators never allowed political freedom or the practice of politics to endanger their basic interests. Instead of seeking to solve the nation's desperate economic and social problems, successive governments merely evaded them by endorsing populist reforms financed by high export prices or foreign loans. When, finally, a coalition government headed by Chile's working-class parties came to power in 1970 and inaugurated structural changes that threatened oligarchical privilege, the elite responded by calling in the army, abolishing parliamentary democracy, and establishing a bloody dictatorship.

1907	Labor strike in the nitrate mines at Iquique leads to creation of Workers' Federation of Chile in 1909
1912	Luis Emilio Recabarren organizes Chilean Socialist Party that joins the Communist International in 1922
1920	Arturo Alessandri wins presidency, calling for populist reforms
1925	New constitution ends Parliamentary Republic, increases presidential power, and limits property rights
1927	Ibáñez del Campo overthrows Alessandri and creates dictatorship
1931	General strike deposes Ibáñez dictatorship and produces the short-lived Socialist Republic of Chile
1934	Chilean Women's Liberation Movement pressures congress to enfranchise literate women
1938–1946	Popular Front coalition wins election and introduces social welfare reforms
1948–1958	Gabriel González Videla bans Communist Party
1958	Jorge Alessandri wins presidency in narrow victory over leftist coalition led by Salvador Allende
1964	Christian Democrat Eduardo Frei Montalva promises "Revolution in Liberty" but fails to deliver
1970	World's first democratically elected Marxist, Salvador Allende, declares a "Chilean Road to Socialism" and nationalizes copper industry; Nixon supports a military coup to prevent Allende's presidency
1971	Allende's Popular Unity coalition wins 50 percent of vote in municipal elections
1971–1973	U.S. funds support an $8 million destabilization campaign to create a "coup climate"
1972	Popular Unity coalition consolidates its democratic control of the state in congressional elections
1973	Gen. Augusto Pinochet leads military coup that inaugurates almost two decades of a brutal dictatorship

Foreign Dependency and the Liberal Parliamentary Republic, 1891–1920

The defeat and suicide of President José Manuel Balmaceda during the civil war of 1891 ushered in an era of unrestrained foreign investment and export-dependent trade, presided over by the so-called Parliamentary Republic, dominated by the Liberal and Conservative political parties, which represented the great landowners of the Central Valley.

A third major party, the Radicals, founded in 1861 by dissident Liberals, enjoyed the support of low-level professionals, bureaucrats, teachers, artisans, and other middle-class groups, as well as that of large landowners on the southern frontier around Concepción, northern mine owners from the Copiapó region, and businessmen from Santiago, the capital. A fourth party, the Democrats, had some base in the lower-middle class and among workers.

The only issue that separated the major parties was the role of the church in education. The chief concerns of the parties appeared to be the preservation of the status quo and the distribution of the spoils of office. Corruption and inefficiency pervaded the political life of the era.

ECONOMIC GROWTH AND THE EXPORT SECTOR

Although politics stagnated in an atmosphere of fraud and apathy, Chilean society underwent a profound transformation. The export sector played a crucial and basically detrimental role in this transformation. Raw material exports generated enormous profits, but relatively few benefits flowed to the nation as a whole. Like the "banana republics" of Central America and the sugar islands of the Caribbean, Chile relied for its revenues on one export commodity, first nitrate and then copper, making it extremely vulnerable to cyclical world market demands for its products. Moreover, the copper industry, which produced the nation's major export in the twentieth century, operated as an enclave, almost totally isolated from the rest of the economy. Finally, and most important, the presence of an export sector that produced sufficient revenue to operate the government and provide employment for a growing middle class enabled the Chilean oligarchy to retain political power and maintain an obsolete system of land tenure and use; these conditions severely hampered the growth of democracy and economic development.

Nonetheless, the nation grew increasingly urbanized and industrialized, and new classes emerged from these processes. An industrial working class rose in the mining regions of the north, first in the nitrate fields and then in the copper mines. Although their wages were higher than elsewhere in the country, the miners suffered from low pay, inadequate housing, the tyranny of company stores, and unsafe working conditions. In the cities, where wages were even lower, workers lived in wretched slums and periodically suffered the ravages of epidemic disease.

After the turn of the century, workers struggled against these dismal conditions. The first major strike broke out in Iquique in the northern mining region in 1901 and lasted for two months. In 1907, the nitrate workers of Iquique again struck against inhuman living and working conditions; the government responded by sending in troops who slaughtered two thousand workers. The wave of strikes continued, with a notable upsurge during World War I. After the war, a cheaper synthetic product displaced Chilean nitrates in world markets and the industry collapsed, leaving thousands of miners unemployed and plunging the entire country into a severe depression. In 1919, faced with growing unrest, the government declared a state of siege (suspending civil liberties) in the mining areas.

Copper soon became Chile's leading export. Initially small-scale, low-technology operations had mined most of Chile's copper, but shortly after 1900, a downturn in copper prices had forced many of these producers to close. At the same time, the introduction of improved methods for the extraction of low-grade ore and the lower transportation costs promised by the opening of the Panama Canal attracted large North American companies, which dominated the industry after World War I. The Guggenheim interests and Anaconda Copper Co. now accounted for more

than 80 percent of the nation's copper production. Foreigners also controlled Chile's other mineral exports: Bethlehem Steel monopolized iron ore and Guggenheim's *Compañía de Salitres de Chile* (COSACH) held 70 percent of the nitrate industry.

Labor in the meantime had begun to organize to achieve better conditions. Luis Emilio Recabarren played a leading part in establishing the Workers' Federation of Chile (*Federación de Obreros de Chile*, FOCH) in 1909. Three years later, he founded the first workers' party, the Socialist, or Socialist Labor, Party. In 1922, it became the Communist Party and joined the Third (Communist) International. By contrast with the Argentine Socialist Party, with its large middle-class base, Chile's first working-class party grew directly out of the labor movement.

In the same period, the middle class became larger and more diverse. The growth of industry and commerce and the expansion of the state created many new white-collar jobs. This growing middle class displayed few of the entrepreneurial traits commonly associated with the North American and European middle classes. The domination of decisive sectors of the economy by large-scale enterprise effectively barred small and midsize entrepreneurs from playing an important role in economic life. Aristocratic control of choice government jobs through clientele and kinship ties also restricted the sphere of middle-class activity. As the twentieth century opened, the middle class began to agitate for a place in the sun.

Meanwhile, the composition of the landed oligarchy was also changing, for it began to incorporate new elements from among industrialists and business executives. More completely than elsewhere in Latin America, the Chilean landed elite fused with the new urban upper and upper-middle classes. They intermarried, and the urban rich acquired land, adopting the values of the traditional elite. This was a serious impediment to reform. Missing in Chile, too, were the large number of immigrants that in some measure had challenged the values and hegemony of the elite in Argentina.

WOMEN AND THE WORKPLACE

The lack of immigrants also meant only a limited supply of native-born Chilean workers could satisfy the growing industrial and agricultural needs, but market demand for cheap labor quickly broke down the gendered walls of work and family. In addition to their unpaid labor in the household, women played an increasingly important role as wage-earning workers in the Chilean economy. By 1913, 21 percent of the labor force was women, almost all of whom were native born and employed in blue-collar occupations; three years later, this figure rose rapidly to 26 percent. Most women worked in *trabajo a domicilio*, sweatshops in which they performed household chores like sewing and weaving for piece-rate wages. In a report on working conditions in the industry, Elena Caffarena showed that these workshops were "neither hy-

gienic nor safe" and that they paid miserably low wages. These poor conditions inevitably damaged women's reproductive capacity; not surprisingly, child mortality rose from an average of 273 infant deaths per 1,000 in 1871 to 325 in 1908. To remedy this, Caffarena and other feminists advocated "strong government regulation" to abolish the sweatshop system and "female exploitation."

Ironically, they drew on traditional gendered ideals of womanhood and the family to lay the foundation for Chile's modern feminist movement. Needleworker and feminist leader Esther Valdés de Díaz, for example, denounced the "wolves" who waited to seduce women, made vulnerable by long hours of work and constant verbal abuse on the shop floor, and she argued the need for a paternalistic state to protect them. Like many working-class feminists, she stressed the class oppression of

© Bettmann/Corbis

The origins of Chile's paternalistic early-twentieth-century populism lay in the private efforts of largely foreign-owned mining companies like Braden Copper, whose El Teniente Mine organized a social welfare office that effectively sought to discipline and control militant working-class resistance.

capitalism rather than the gendered tyranny of patriarchy. "Women who work in factories, pushed by the need to earn their daily bread, not only are not in their place, but, without knowing it, are competing with men and, in so doing, becoming victims of capitalism." Women, she believed, unconsciously and unavoidably contributed to the "devaluation of men's work."

Nonetheless, these feminists insisted that the only remedy for this lamentable state of affairs was an aggressive, activist state that defended women and workers against the predatory interests of capitalists. So, they mobilized to pressure Chile's political leadership to regulate sweatshops, enforce minimum-wage protections for women and children, establish the legal right to equal pay for equal work, and restrict women's workweek to six eight-hour days. They also sought to prohibit work by children under fourteen years of age, abolish night work for women, require companies to provide partially paid pre- and postpartum leaves for pregnant women, compel industries employing more than twenty women to provide on-site child-care facilities, and allow nursing mothers periodic breaks to feed their children.

Alessandri and the Rise of Populism, 1920–1970

By 1920, even sections of the oligarchy were aware that they could no longer ignore the needs of the rest of Chilean society. Foreign interests like the Braden Copper Company actively contributed to this expanded social consciousness. According to Braden, a sturdy nuclear family could stabilize labor turnover; decrease such antisocial behavior as gambling, drinking, and fighting; deter absenteeism and the celebration of "*San Lunes*" (Saint Monday), the unofficial international workers' holiday; and discourage militant trade unionism that frequently led to strikes, industrial sabotage, and worker slow-downs—all of which reduced labor productivity. Braden therefore had developed a comprehensive private social welfare program to encourage family life, but workers typically opposed these paternalistic policies, which transparently aimed to control

their labor; for example, they scorned the company's *Departamento de Bienestar* (Department of Welfare) as the *Departamento de Bienfregar* (Department of Busybodies).

However, state welfare programs enjoyed a social legitimacy that a company's private plan did not. Moreover, public welfare was an effective means of socializing private costs and thus increasing the competitive advantage of large companies over smaller businesses that routinely ignored workers' welfare. Finally, these state-sponsored programs also appealed to middle-class progressives who sought to "moralize" working-class culture and to radicals who sought to cultivate a "proletarian morality" that discouraged workers' fractious individualism and encouraged a politically disciplined, class-based solidarity. The stage was set for a populist reform program that would appeal to diverse political constituencies, and Arturo Allessandri, nicknamed the "Lion of Tarapacá," became its agent.

A former corporation lawyer turned populist politician, Alessandri appealed to the lower and middle classes with promises to reform the constitution and relieve the bleakness of working-class life. He promised a social security system, a labor code, cheap housing, education reform, women's rights, and state control of banks and insurance companies. With considerable support from sections of the oligarchy, which hoped that he could placate the restless masses with a minimum of effective social change, Alessandri became president in 1920.

During the first four years of Alessandri's term, he proved unable to make good his campaign pledges. Congress, representing entrenched oligarchical interests, stood squarely in the way of any meaningful social and political reforms. Accordingly, Alessandri urged the passage of laws that would restore the balance of power between Congress and the executive branch, a balance destroyed after the civil war of 1891. He also sought such social reforms as a shorter workday, labor laws to protect women and children, the right of workers to strike, and health insurance. These modest proposals certainly did not threaten the status quo, but they required money. In view of the catastrophic decline of the nitrate industry, he could raise it only by taxing the oligarchy's land and income, a solution the elite found unthinkable. Because of the parliamentary deadlock, the Chilean government could not cope with the mounting economic and social crisis.

The Chilean military, predominantly of middle-class origins, had observed the unfolding crisis with growing impatience and resentment. Many junior and middle-grade officers favored the enactment of Alessandri's social and political reform program; they also felt that Congress had neglected the needs of the armed forces. A succession of military coups, the last of which was led by reformist officers Carlos Ibáñez del Campo and Marmaduke Grove, ultimately enabled Alessandri to accomplish the political reforms for which he had campaigned. The result was the constitution of 1925, which ended the Parliamentary Republic and restored the balance of power between Congress and the president. It provided for direct presidential elections, six-year terms, no immediate reelection, and presidential control over the cabinet and government finance. The constitution proclaimed the inviolable right of private property but stated that the state could limit this right in the interest of social needs. Other measures included a new and extensive labor code, the grant of the vote to literate males over twenty-one, the establishment of an electoral registry to reduce electoral fraud, a nominal income tax on income over 10,000 pesos a year, and the establishment of a central bank.

Ibáñez and the Great Depression

But Ibáñez and the military remained powerful. Initially, they sought an alliance with the working and middle classes for the achievement of structural reforms, but this ended in the military dictatorship of 1927 to 1931.

To implement his program and secure the position of state employees, which was necessary to maintain political stability, Ibáñez needed substantial amounts of money; his populist program of welfare, public works, and modernization relied above all on huge loans from foreign bankers.

The armed forces were a special beneficiary of government largesse, obtaining generous promotions and salary increases. Most of the protective legislation for which women had lobbied during the previous decade became law. Meanwhile, the Ibáñez dictatorship suppressed all opposition, jailed or deported political foes, and tried to split the Communist-led labor movement by the sponsorship of government-backed unions.

Aided by a temporary revival of copper and nitrate sales and massive foreign loans, the Chilean economy prospered for the first two years of Ibáñez's rule, but the Wall Street crash of 1929 unmasked Chile's dependency on external markets. It cut off the all-important flow of capital and loans, and by the following year, the nitrate and copper markets had both collapsed. Because the government relied heavily on copper taxes for revenue, the Great Depression forced it to curtail daily operations severely and default on its large foreign debt. In 1932, the United States, Chile's main market for copper, adopted a high tariff on copper imports, which caused mine closings and severe unemployment. The Depression also accentuated gender-based wage inequities and unleashed a backlash against women in the workforce. Government supporters called for women's return to the home to stabilize the family and reduce job competition among men, thereby increasing male wages and employment. Although the Socialists and Communists advocated elimination of gendered wage inequalities so all workers could unite against capitalists on the basis of their shared class interest, they nonetheless agreed to identify certain industries, like copper and teaching, as exclusively male or female. In a vain effort to find a solution for the economic crisis, the government tried to limit nitrate sales to push up prices. Ibáñez trimmed social services and his public works program and hiked taxes, but the financial situation grew increasingly desperate.

In July 1931, confronted by a general strike that involved workers, professionals, white-collar employees, women, and students, Ibáñez, faced with growing doubts about the army's loyalty to him, resigned and went into exile in Argentina.

The next seventeen months brought a succession of military coups, one of which, led by Air Force Cdr. Marmaduke Grove, proclaimed a Socialist Republic of Chile. It lasted barely twelve days before a new military revolt overthrew it. Ironically, the program of the socialist republic was not socialist; it proposed, rather, to create jobs through public works financed by the issue of paper money. This coup led to Arturo Alessandri's return to the presidency.

ALESSANDRI AND THE LIMITS OF POPULISM

Alessandri began his second term in the depths of the Great Depression, with one hundred sixty thousand people unemployed in Santiago alone, while a typhoid epidemic ravaged the country. Income from nitrates was one-twentieth the 1927 figure; public employees, including soldiers and police officers, had not received pay for months. In the succeeding five years, 1932 to 1937, the president and his finance minister, Gustavo Ross, presided over an economic recovery that reflected a partial revival and stabilization of the world market. Copper prices recovered in 1935, and by 1937 copper production exceeded pre-depression levels. As the economy revived, government revenues generated from copper taxes enabled the government to avoid taxing large landholdings. Without the spur of equitable taxes, latifundists continued to leave vast tracts of fertile land uncultivated or underutilized. Although it had the potential to feed its own people, Chile had to import foodstuffs—a policy that drained the nation of foreign exchange that would have been better used to purchase capital goods for industrialization or to build roads and harbors.

With its coffers swelled by revenue from the export sector, the Chilean government expanded its role in the economy. A large bureaucracy developed, staffed by an emerging middle class. As the government became the major employer of the middle class and the nation's most important venture capitalist, Chile grew ever more dependent for its economic development on factors beyond its control.

Professor Asuncion Lavrin

In the 1930s, Chile's Women's Liberation Movement mobilized thousands of women and influenced populist policies with a demand that the state guarantee women's right to equality in the home, in the workplace, and in politics.

However, Alessandri had no greater success in solving Chile's structural problems in the 1930s than he had in the 1920s. Foreign capital still controlled the lucrative mining sector of the economy, and the inefficient latifundio continued to dominate Chilean agriculture. He often brutally suppressed workers' strikes for better wages and living conditions.

Middle-class critics of the regime fared little better. Following the example of Ibáñez, Alessandri closed down hostile newspapers, exiled political critics, and dealt highhandedly with Congress. These conditions produced a major new coalition, the Chilean Popular Front, to mobilize workers, peasants, and the urban middle sector to defend democracy and promote social progress.

WOMEN AND THE RISE OF THE POPULAR FRONT

During the 1920s, Chile's progressive tradition had its roots in the Communist Party. The Communists won considerable support among organized labor, particularly the railroad workers' union and the FOCH, which claimed two hundred thousand members. Although they had played a part in framing the constitution of 1925, Communist leaders were imprisoned and exiled during the Ibáñez regime. After the fall of Ibáñez in 1931, however, the party revived under the leadership of Carlos Contreras Labarca and gained considerable popularity among workers and intellectuals.

Chile in the 1930s was fertile ground for the growth of progressive parties and ideologies, many of which coalesced to form the Chilean Popular Front. Composed of Socialists, Communists, and Radicals, the Front's candidate, Radical Pedro Aguirre Cerda, won the presidency in 1938. The Popular Front's electoral platform called for the restoration of constitutional rule and civil liberties and basic social reforms, summed up in the slogan *pan, techo, y abrigo* (bread, clothing, and a roof).

The short, stormy life of the Popular Front yielded some achievements. In 1938, the *Corporación de Fomento de la Producción de Chile* or State Economic Development Agency (CORFO) formed to foster industrialization. Aided by relatively high wartime copper prices, a virtual cessation of imports because of World War II, and government subsidies, low taxes, and protective tariffs on imported consumer goods, native manufacturing made steady progress between 1940 and 1945.

The populist policy of state-supported industrialization also promoted the growth of the Chilean industrial working class; between 1940 and 1952, the number of workers employed in manufacturing rose from 15 percent of the workforce to 19 percent. At least until 1945, the industrialization process accompanied improvement in workers' real purchasing power—up 20 percent between 1940 and 1945—whereas that of white-collar workers increased 25 percent. After 1945, as Radical governments became more conservative and the basis of the Popular Front strategy disintegrated, the working class's relative share of the national income declined.

Women also were active both as workers and mothers, but increasingly they insisted that they would need more than the "aura of dignity and respect, but should also receive the aid of the state when economic conditions demand it." For many women in the 1930s, this meant prenatal health care, subsidies for child care, and state protections against exploitation, but feminists like Clara de la Luz also wanted support for family planning. She defended "scientific procreation"—that is, birth control—and called on women to organize a "strike of the wombs" to liberate themselves from unwanted family responsibilities that increased the supply of new workers for industry and agriculture, lowered workers' wages, and reduced their freedom to resist capitalist exploitation. Others criticized the moral and legal double standard that gave "men impunity and women responsibility" in reproductive matters.

Although Chile's Catholic traditions made abortion illegal, it was widely practiced by midwives and amateurs. In 1936, five hospitals identified 10,514 cases of botched abortions that required medical attention; the following year, the Ministry of Health reported that 24 percent (13,351) of women in public maternity hospitals were there to receive treatment for complications from bungled abortions. Growing numbers of women, especially poor working-class women, viewed abortion, contraception, and family planning as one way to escape what the leftist Women's Liberation Movement (MEMCH) called "compulsory motherhood" and the "slavery of unwanted children."

Women also won basic political and civil rights. Conservatives, influenced by upper-class women's groups like the Club de Señoras, historically had supported enfranchisement of literate women because they believed that, as guardians of home, church, and family life, they were a natural conservative constituency necessary to counter the political advantages accruing to Socialist, Communist, and Radical Parties from the enfranchisement of illiterate men. Meanwhile, MEMCH insisted on the "integral emancipation of women, especially the economic, juridical, biological, and political emancipation." All pressed for civil equality and the right to vote, a campaign that achieved partial success in 1934 with the granting of municipal voting rights to literate women.

Local leftist parties failed to offer women candidates for municipal posts, preferring to emphasize class struggle while ignoring gender difference. This created an electoral void that Conservatives filled by offering women candidates like Elena Doll de Díaz, whose populist campaign defended the moral center of family life. She called for an aggressive program of state intervention to protect it against the injustice of market forces: workers' welfare, equal wages, sanitation, "popular restaurants" to feed the hungry, and electric trolleys to provide workers with cheap transportation. Not surprisingly, by 1941, two-thirds of the women registered to vote identified themselves as Conservatives; thereafter, the Popular Front coalition fractured, and party leaders abandoned any interest in woman suffrage.

World War II decisively reinforced the politics of the Popular Front and reignited the campaign for women's right to vote in national elections. Wartime alliances with the Soviet Union, a growing democratic discourse, and the decline of anti-imperialist rhetoric within the Chilean left contributed to the emergence of a cross-class, gender-based movement in support of women's suffrage. The Chilean Federation of Feminine Institutions (FECHIF), for example, which represented 213 women's organizations, mobilized massive street demonstrations that attracted thousands of women to its militant calls for "social democracy."

Although freed from traditional external constraints during the war, the Popular Front Era produced no structural changes in the Chilean economy or society because the members of the governing coalition had irreconcilable differences over domestic and foreign policy. In the 1946 election, the Socialists, reflecting historic factional disputes within the party, abandoned the Popular Front, but Radical Gabriel González Videla (1946–1952) won with the support of the Communist Party. Soon, responding to the pressures of the cold war, González Videla moved to the right, ousted the Communist members of his cabinet, broke a strike of Communist-led coal miners, and passed the *Ley Maldita* (the Accursed Law), which outlawed the Communist Party and eliminated Communists from Congress. González Videla also established a concentration camp for Communist Party members and other left-wing militants in an abandoned mining camp in the northern desert.

With the repression and disenfranchisement of Communists like Elena Caffarena, who had written the women's suffrage legislation and organized on behalf of women's rights for decades, González Videla finally signed into law a 1949 bill to give literate women the vote in national elections. Thereafter, he tried to consolidate his political support among working-class women by organizing Women's Centers to provide education, training, and career services.

Nevertheless, massive discontent with skyrocketing inflation, the freezing of workers' wages, and González Videla's repressive policies paved the way for a comeback by the ex-dictator Carlos Ibáñez del Campo in 1952. Ibáñez promised repeal of the Ley Maldita, a minimum salary, a family allowance for workers, and a sympathetic hearing for just wage demands, but the decline in Chilean copper revenues following the end of the Korean War made it impossible for Ibáñez to make good on his populist promises. To stabilize the economy, he sought loans from North American banks and the International Monetary Fund; meanwhile, he sought to force the working class to absorb inflation through cuts in real wages. Threatened with labor unrest, Ibáñez embarked on a course of harsh repression. By the end of his term, he had alienated all sectors of the Chilean people.

NEW ALIGNMENTS: CHRISTIAN DEMOCRACY AND POPULISM

Between 1953 and the presidential election year of 1958, the parties of the left restored their unity by forming the *Frente de Acción Popular* (Popular Action Front, FRAP), which included the Socialist Party and the Communists. Simultaneously, a new Christian Democratic Party emerged, led by Eduardo Frei; it appealed to Catholic workers, especially in white-collar sectors, with a vague ideology that claimed to be neither capitalist nor socialist. In its first try for office in 1958, this party demonstrated its electoral force.

Four major candidates contested the presidency in 1958. They were the Conservative Jorge Alessandri, a son of the former president and a leading industrialist; Eduardo Frei, a Christian Democrat; Salvador Allende, of FRAP; and Luis Bossay, a Radical. Surprisingly, Alessandri beat Allende by a threadbare margin of only 33,500 votes. Allende probably would have won if an obscure minor-party candidate had not drawn away some slum and rural poor votes.

Despite booming copper prices, however, Alessandri had no more success than his predecessors in coping with Chile's problems of inflation and economic stagnation. His formula for recovery was to restore the free market, reduce state intervention in the economy, and employ foreign loans and investment as the basis for economic growth.

Although depression and war had slowed the inflow, foreign capital now surged into Chile in the postwar period, not only into the extractive sector but into manufacturing and commerce as well. From 1954 to 1970, foreigners invested $1.67 billion in Chile. U.S. companies continued to dominate copper, nitrate, and iodine production. Foreign companies conducted approximately half the nation's wholesale trade, monopolized the telephone and telegraph industries, and had important stakes in electric utilities and banking. Even the major advertising agencies were foreign subsidiaries or affiliates.

In 1960, the three great mines of the Gran Minería, all owned by the foreign giants Anaconda and Kennecott, accounted for 11 percent of the country's gross national product, 50 percent of its exports, and 20 percent of government revenues. But the millions of dollars in sales, profits, and tax revenues generated by copper mining provided little stimulus for Chilean commerce and industry. Their huge profits, which they remitted to their parent corporations in the United States, added to the outflow of capital from the country.

Chile depended not only on direct investment from abroad but on loans as well. Payment of interest and amortization on the national debt consumed an increasing share of its revenue from the export sector. Because most foreign investment, like the copper enclave, was capital intensive, it provided little employment and few linkages to the rest of the economy. Employment in the mines declined steadily in the post–World War II era, and the surplus of miners made it possible for the companies to pay the largely unskilled labor force relatively low wages. Until the 1950s, Chile imported machinery, equipment, and technical skills entirely from abroad. The benefits to its long-range economic development were minimal. Without a doubt, Chile was not the master of its own economic fate.

Changes in U.S. policy in response to the Cuban Revolution (1959) profoundly affected politics in Chile during the early 1960s. The United States sought to bolster populist reform movements throughout Latin America as an alternative to social revolution. As part of this policy, it covertly financed the Christian Democrats. Combined with the backing of the conservative parties, which Allende's near-election six years earlier had terrified, U.S. support enabled Frei to win the 1964 election with 56 percent of the vote.

Eduardo Frei came to the presidency with populist promises of a "revolution in freedom" that would correct the extreme inequities of Chilean society without a violent class struggle. He especially appealed to women to preserve the sanctity of the Catholic family against Allende's "godless communist revolution" and opened six thousand Women's Centers. The problems he faced were familiar ones: inflation and stagnation, a domestic market too narrow to support an efficient mass industry, an extractive industry dominated by foreign ownership, and inefficient agriculture incapable of supplying the basic needs of the population. To create the market needed for a modern mass industry, Frei proposed agrarian reform, tax reform, and other populist measures to redistribute income to the lower classes.

When Frei took office, landownership was extremely concentrated, the condition of rural laborers was wretched, and the inefficient great landed estates were clearly incapable of providing enough food to feed Chile's growing urban centers. By contrast with the situation in most developing nations, Chile's agricultural sector played only a small role in the economy. The inability of agriculture to provide employment on the one hand and sufficient food on the other resulted in an overurbanized, underemployed, and undernourished population.

The statistics of landholding indicate that these patterns changed little between 1930 and 1970. In 1930, holdings of more than 2,500 acres composed only 2 percent of the total number of farms but constituted 78 percent of the cultivable land. Eighty-two percent of all farms were less than 125 acres but owned only 4 percent of the land. By the 1960s, eleven thousand farms, 4.2 percent of the total, controlled 79 percent of the land. Farms with less than 100 acres—77 percent of all farms—held 10.6 percent of the land. More than seven hundred thousand people, the majority of the rural labor force, had no land at all. The living and working conditions of agricultural laborers were appalling—and getting worse. Agricultural wages had declined consistently since the 1940s, falling 23 percent from 1953 to 1964.

Government credit and tax policies before 1964 ensured that the maldistribution of land and agricultural income would continue. Small landholders, having no access to bank or government loans, had to rely on moneylenders or store owners, who charged outrageous interest. Smallholders and agricultural laborers also bore a disproportionate burden of taxes. Taxes on land, capital, income, and inheritance, on the other hand, were light. The large estates, especially those that remained uncultivated, went virtually untaxed.

Frei's program of agrarian reform had mixed results. He began by attempting to improve conditions in rural areas by increasing wages, establishing peasant unions, and instituting a more equitable system of taxation; he also redistributed some land to the peasants, but inflation eroded wage gains, and land redistribution fell far short of what Frei had promised. As a gradualist, Frei shied away from precipitous or widespread expropriations. Peasants who received land faced a difficult time, for the government did not provide them with credit needed to begin as independent farmers.

Frei's plan for the Chileanization of the copper industry aimed both to appease widespread nationalist sentiment and to obtain new government revenue through increased copper production. The plan required the government to buy 51 percent of the shares in the foreign-owned mines. In return for a promise to increase production and refine more ore in Chile, the foreign companies retained control of management and obtained new concessions with respect to taxation and repatriation of profits, but the plan failed to expand production significantly or to increase government revenues.

Other sectors of the Chilean economy also were concentrated. A few powerful clans controlled a wide variety of industrial and financial enterprises and thus exerted a decisive influence on the national economy as a whole. In 1967, 12 companies out of 2,600 transacted nearly half the total wholesale business in the country. One bank, Banco de Chile, furnished 32 percent of the nation's private bank credit; the five largest banks furnished 57.4 percent.

These facts, however, tell only part of the story, for control of the economy was even more concentrated. Fifteen large economic groups controlled the Chilean economy. The most powerful of the clans, the Edwards family, controlled one commercial bank, seven financial and investment corporations, five insurance companies, thirteen industries, and two publishing houses. It also had close connections to North American companies active in the country. The family's newspaper chain accounted for more than half the circulation of daily newspapers in Chile. Together with another publishing house, it virtually controlled the entire market for periodicals. As early as 1965, concerted opposition from this economic oligarchy convinced Frei to abandon his populist campaign promise to redistribute income, and instead he implemented an economic policy designed to attract foreign and domestic investors. During 1966, the government froze wages and reacted harshly to strikes in the copper mines, at one point sending in troops. Increased worker militancy made Socialist and Communist union leadership more influential.

The need to appease his political constituency and the economic decline after 1966 defeated Frei's efforts at reform. Upper-class Catholic intellectuals had founded and provided the leadership of the Christian Democratic Party. Its membership was overwhelmingly middle class, including urban professionals, white-collar workers (especially from the public sector), skilled workers, and managers, all groups that had emerged during the preceding two decades as the Chilean economy diversified. The party did well in the larger towns, among urban slum dwellers, and among women. In 1964, Frei got considerable support from industrialists and bankers who feared the election of Allende. These were hardly the elements of a revolutionary party. Frei's program of reform depended entirely on a healthy, expanding economy that would enable the government to distribute benefits to the lower class without injuring the middle class or altering the basic economic and social structures.

When Frei came to office in 1964, the economy was expanding rapidly, for the Vietnam War kept copper prices high. Frei's moderate reform goals ensured good relations with the United States and a resulting flow of loans and private investment. Even Chile's chronic inflation slowed. Two good years, however, were followed by four bad ones. After 1967, the economy stagnated while inflation surged again. Income inequalities increased, and living standards declined sharply. Frei's rhetoric brought hope to Chileans, but he fulfilled few of his promises. During his term, the working class grew increasingly restive. Groups like *pobladores* (urban slum dwellers) and rural workers organized for the first time. As the Christian Democrats proved less and less capable of dealing with Chile's economic woes, these newly organized groups and the trade unions became more militant.

Powerful cultural changes, the most significant of which was the birth of *Nueva Canción* (the New Song movement), both reflected and shaped this transformation of Chilean politics. First developed in Peronist Argentina, the New Song movement utilized indigenous musical instruments and typically explored folkloric lyrical themes. In Chile and elsewhere throughout Latin America in the 1960s, however, it quickly became associated with revolution and the democratic struggle against poverty, social injustice, and tyranny. Violeta Parra, the daughter of a schoolteacher and seamstress in Chile's rural south, had pioneered the study of the nation's folkloric art and music in the 1950s. Her ballads, like her paintings and colorful *arpilleras* (tapestries), typically commemorated the struggles of poor folk and condemned the *pitucos* (wealthy people accustomed to privilege and power) who profited from their exploitation.

Parra's work made an indelible impression on a young Víctor Jara, arguably Chile's most famous New Song musician. Born to a poor peasant family, Jara, whose songs celebrated the lives of ordinary Chileans, often combined traditional Catholic rituals with lyrics that reflected his leftist social conscience. Perhaps the most famous of these was his "La plegaria del labrador" ("Farmworkers' Prayer"), modeled on the Lord's Prayer. But Jara, giving voice to Chile's impoverished peasants, did not ask to be saved from some abstract evil; on the contrary, accompanied by his searing *charango* (an indigenous guitar made from an armadillo shell), he raised his powerful voice to demand, "Deliver us from the master who keeps us in misery, thy kingdom of justice and equality come."

In 1969, after Frei's police savagely attacked a group of peasants who illegally had occupied vacant lands in Puerto Montt, Jara wrote a stirring new song that became the battle cry of a generation. "Preguntas por Puerto Montt" ("Questions about Puerto Montt") denounced the barbaric murderers and declared, "All the rains in the south (of Chile) will not be enough to wash your hands clean." Jara believed that artists were cultural rebels. "An artist must be an authentic creator," he once said, "and in essence a revolutionary ... a man as dangerous as a guerrilla because of his great power of communication." Artists became revolutionaries by celebrating a popular culture that all too often a mass media beholden to the wealthy either ignored or scorned. "We should ascend to the people, not feel that we are lowering ourselves to them," Jara once wrote. "Our job is to give them what belongs to them—their cultural roots." Jara and others later collaborated on a popular new musical, "La Cantata de Santa María," which commemorated the 1907 slaughter of three thousand striking nitrate miners, a massacre that sparked the development of Chile's modern trade union movement.

The Christian Democratic Party itself also reflected these cultural changes. In 1969, disillusioned progressives split off to form the Movement for United Popular Action (MAPU), which later joined the Popular Unity Coalition. This break left Frei the leader of the party's traditional faction, and Radomiro Tomic led the progressives who remained. Because Frei was ineligible to run again under the constitution, Tomic became the party's presidential candidate in 1970. He ran on a platform almost indistinguishable from that of Allende, the candidate of the Popular Unity (UP) coalition, whose main elements were the Socialist, Communist, and Radical Parties.

The oligarchy, already alienated by Frei's modest agrarian reform, found Tomic totally unacceptable, refused to join forces with Christian Democrats as it had in 1964, and backed ex-president Jorge Alessandri of the National Party. Allende won the election with 36 percent of the vote, whereas Alessandri got 35 percent and Tomic 28 percent. Preferring to stress class solidarity, Allende had not targeted the women's vote, but his share of it grew by 13 percent from 1958 and doubtlessly provided his razor-thin margin of victory. Because Allende failed to receive a majority, the election went to Congress, which, after much-publicized maneuvering, approved Allende as president.

The Chilean Road to Socialism, 1970–1973

THE OPPOSITION

When Allende took office in 1970, domestic political conditions appeared favorable to his program for the achievement of socialism in Chile within a framework of legality and nonviolence. The assassination in October 1970 of Gen. René Schneider, the commander in chief of the army, who had kept the army neutral during the period after the election just before Allende assumed the presidency, had discredited his opponents. Prospects were

excellent that the Popular Unity would receive the cooperation of the Tomic faction of the Christian Democratic Party in Congress. For the time being, the UP coalition remained united behind a program that called for expropriation of all landholdings greater than 80 hectares and the progressive takeover of large foreign companies and monopolies.

Nonetheless, the forces against the UP were formidable. It did not have a majority in Congress. Both the judiciary and the *Controlaría General* (the government's fiscal arm) opposed Allende's policies. The entire domestic economic establishment, foreign interests, much of the officer corps of the military and national police, and the Catholic Church also aligned against the UP. The anti-UP political coalition, the *Confederación Democrática* (Democratic Confederation), controlled virtually all of the nation's media —two of the three television stations, 95 percent of the radio stations, 90 percent of the newspaper circulation, and all of the weekly magazines.

Even more significantly, however, substantial shifts had occurred in global markets. The European and Japanese economies had fully recovered from their wartime collapse and had emerged as vigorous competitors with the United States, whose economic and technological strength the Vietnam War and a host of other military interventions in developing countries had sapped. By the early 1970s, the leading capitalist countries were on the verge of an international trade war, looking to industrially developing, "semiperipheral" countries like Chile to earn profits otherwise unavailable to them in their own markets.

This meant that foreign interests no longer tolerated nationalistic, statist restrictions on their activities, no matter how popular these might have been with local democratic electoral constituencies. Consequently, when the democratically elected UP coalition of Socialists and Communists sought to implement their campaign promises, U.S. government leaders like Henry Kissinger, President Richard Nixon's National Security Council adviser, imperiously intervened. "I don't see why we have to let a country go Marxist," Kissinger arrogantly insisted, "just because its people are irresponsible."

Salvador Allende, president of Chile, died during the military coup of September 1973.

Nixon immediately ordered the Central Intelligence Agency (CIA) to orchestrate a coup to overthrow Allende before the Congress could validate his election, but even after this failed, he advised U.S. operatives to "make the economy scream." The ensuing economic chaos, according to Nixon, would undermine Allende's legitimacy and force his government to reopen Chile to foreign control.

A lack of internal cohesion also hindered the UP, however. The old problem of how to satisfy the claims of both the working-class—even more militant than during the Popular Front days—and the middle-class sectors—who worried that their interests were being threatened by the structural reforms undertaken by the UP—was never fully resolved.

This competition between middle- and working-class constituents also revealed itself in cultural con-

flict among the nation's youth. During the tumultuous 1960s, the folk music of Parra and Jara, with its social conscience, political protest, and identification with Chile's popular classes, had starkly contrasted with a Chilean rock music that self-consciously emulated British and U.S. (counter)culture. Jara had campaigned for the UP, and he wrote "Venceremos" ("We Shall Overcome"), which quickly became the campaign's theme song.

Conversely, rock musicians like Los Macs identified more with foreign cultures they defined as modern; they especially appealed to alienated upper- and middle-class youth who, like the later supporters of Pinochet's bloody dictatorship, rebelled against the Chilean popular traditions they associated with backwardness. Chilean rockers typically sang their songs, even original compositions, in English and acknowledged the musical influence of Elvis Presley, the Beatles, the Kinks, and the Byrds. So disgusted were these bands with Chilean popular cultural traditions and the nation's stormy politics that some rock musicians, like Juan Mateo O'Brien of Los Vidrios Quebrados (Broken Glass), "thought only about leaving Chile" and declined invitations to return to play for a Chilean audience. Others, like Willy Morales of Los Macs, specifically cited Allende's democratic socialist revolution, "the social and political events between 1970 and 1973," for his disinterest in returning to Chile.

Ironically, countercultural *gringos* who visited Chile to help build a peaceful, democratic socialist alternative to western capitalism often discovered to their amazement that the young Chilean rockers, who dressed like them, wore long hair, smoked marijuana, and listened to Jimi Hendrix, increasingly were politically more sympathetic to Richard Nixon. Middle- and upper-class countercultural Chilean rockers defined the dominant culture against which they rebelled as primitive, uneducated, undeveloped, and working class; in 1970, Salvador Allende had become its political symbol. However, the countercultural gringos and folk enthusiasts like Víctor Jara defined the dominant culture against which they rebelled as modern, capitalistic, socially unjust, and foreign dominated; its political symbols were Richard Nixon and Jorge Alessandri, upon whom the Nixon administration had lavished covert financial support in the 1970 presidential elections.

THE FIRST YEAR, 1971

The UP's immediate goal was to improve the living standard of the working class and get the economy moving. The government accomplished this by increasing purchasing power, which in turn stimulated demand, industrial production, and employment. During the first year of Allende's term, worker income rose a startling 50 percent. The government instituted a massive program of public spending, especially for labor-intensive projects, such as housing, education, sanitation, and health. At the same time, the government ex-

panded its appeal to women. It developed a Ministry of the Family, created community daycare centers, organized low-income milk distribution programs, financed *Almacenes del Pueblo* (People's Grocery Cooperatives), and established price controls, which were monitored by local, housewife-operated price and supply committees. The rate of inflation fell to 22.1 percent in 1971 from 34.9 percent in 1970, and as a result, real income rose 30 percent. The Organization of American States independently confirmed that Allende's program had produced "high growth levels" during its first year.

During this first year, middle-class business executives, industrialists, and peasants fared very well and cooperated with the Allende regime. Larger owners sabotaged their own property in scattered cases, but for the most part, business was not hostile. The government also employed coercion to gain cooperation from industry, threatening companies with intervention if they did not agree to increase production. Coercion and increased demand combined to bring about an expansion of industrial production and employment.

The short-term policies of the UP government increased popular support for the minority regime, a success reflected in the municipal elections of April 1971, in which the Popular Unity won more than 50 percent of the vote. In the long run, however, the depletion of stocks, the outflow of foreign exchange to pay for the import of consumer goods, and the fall of profits in what was still basically a market economy proved damaging to the government's economic program.

Allende's first problems arose when the United States in effect declared economic war on Chile's fragile democratic socialist experiment. The United States covertly embargoed Chilean loans, imports, and exports, especially copper, whose price declined sharply, leading to an imbalance in terms of trade and the depletion of foreign-exchange reserves. In addition, the expropriation of the Gran Minería in July 1971 virtually halted the flow of private investment capital from the United States. The resulting economic difficulties led Allende to stop servicing the national debt, but he eventually managed to reach satisfactory agreements with all of Chile's creditors except the United States.

DEMOCRATIC SOCIALIST DILEMMA: CAUGHT IN THE MIDDLE, 1972–1973

The first year's gains gave way to economic stagnation and a resurgence of inflation. Although Allende's popularity remained high in 1971, he struggled unsuccessfully to reach a delicate balance between the needed structural reform demanded by the working class and the special interests of the middle class. The government's policy of expropriating large enterprises alienated owners of small and midsize businesses, which employed 80 percent of the working population. Workers began occupying and operating factories. State enterprises were badly mismanaged.

The socialist government was also unable to solve the agricultural crisis. Chile's inefficiently managed agricultural production was perhaps the biggest economic roadblock, for it neither raised enough to feed the country's inhabitants nor provided employment for the large pool of rural labor. A hostile Congress forced Allende to operate with reform laws inherited from the Frei administration; nonetheless, by the end of 1972, Allende had effectively liquidated the latifundio system. Expropriation and redistribution proceeded, but with considerable cost to production. The amount of land under cultivation decreased by 20 percent, and the harvest of 1972–1973 was poor.

The Allende administration faced a full-fledged economic and political crisis by the fall of 1972. UP government mistakes and conflicts within the coalition aggravated the inevitable disruptions that accompany revolutionary conditions. Moreover, the Chilean oligarchy and its North American allies were formidable, unrelenting opponents. The United States was deeply involved in Chilean politics. According to the CIA director, William Colby, the agency spent $11 million between 1962 and 1970 to help prevent Allende's election as president. Thereafter, the CIA, with authorization from President Richard Nixon and Henry Kissinger, spent $8 million between 1970 and 1973

to "destabilize" the Chilean economy. Nixon told the U.S. ambassador to Chile that he would "smash that son-of-a-bitch Allende."

The Chilean upper class, although it had lost much of its economic base because of the nationalization of large industries and expropriation of large landholdings, retained control over much of the mass media, the judiciary, a majority in Congress, and the armed forces. The struggle hinged, however, on the middle sectors. Soaring inflation eroded their economic position. All of Allende's efforts to reassure and win over the middle class failed to overcome its traditional hostility toward socialism and its association with the bourgeoisie. This middle class provided the mass base for the coup that overthrew the Popular Unity.

Allende's opponents took advantage of the growing economic crisis to embark on a program of sabotage and direct action that included the mobilization of middle-class women in "empty pots" protest marches and a strike of truck drivers (subsidized by the CIA), which developed into a full-scale lockout by a majority of Chilean capitalists. The strike ended when Allende made major concessions to his opponents, guaranteeing the security of small and midsize industries. He also agreed to the inclusion of generals in his cabinet to ensure law and order and to supervise the congressional election scheduled for March 1973.

Relying on long-established electoral trends, which saw the party in power lose congressional seats, the opposition expected to gain a sweeping victory in the election; it hoped to have the two-thirds majority needed to impeach Allende and legally oust his government. Instead, the UP vote rose from 36 percent (in 1970) to 44 percent, proof that its socialist policies had substantially increased its support among the working class and peasantry. Once again, women now known as *hacedoras de presidentes* (makers of presidents) provided Allende his margin of victory. The UP coalition received 41 percent of the women's vote, a 14 percent increase since the last congressional elections in 1969 and an 11 percent improvement over the 1970 presidential election totals. Allende also benefited from 1971 electoral reforms that enfranchised younger voters and eliminated literacy restrictions, all of which boosted women's participation from 47 percent of the electorate in 1970 to 56 percent in 1973.

Nevertheless, the opposition still commanded a majority in Congress, and it redoubled efforts to create economic and political chaos by disruptive strikes, the organization of terrorist bands, and calls on the armed forces to intervene. The United States greatly influenced the Chilean military, itself internally divided over the Allende government. Many Chilean officers had received counterinsurgency training either in the United States or in the Panama Canal Zone. Throughout the Allende presidency, even after the United States economically embargoed Chile, U.S. military aid continued. The United States even doubled its usual contribution in 1973.

By the spring of 1973, the balance of forces within the military had shifted in favor of Allende's opponents. On June 29, under the direction of Gen. Carlos Prats, loyal troops put down a premature coup. Following it, workers called for occupation of the factories and distribution of arms among them. Instead, Allende renewed his efforts to achieve a compromise with the Christian Democrats, foolishly relying on the armed forces, which raided factories in search of illegal weapons while making no effort to disarm hostile paramilitary groups. Control of many localities effectively passed from the UP administration to the armed forces. On September 11, 1973, a military coup led by Gen. Augusto Pinochet toppled Allende and inaugurated a brutal neoliberal dictatorship.

The coup killed thousands and imprisoned or exiled thousands more. It effectively ended Chile's pioneering effort to transcend the limits of populism and promote national development with revolutionary changes enacted through peaceful, democratic means. In the process, it left a much-disputed legacy for other Latin Americans struggling to throw off the chains of underdevelopment and exploitation. By the mid-1970s, then, the only successful alternative to a bankrupt populism or self-serving personal dictatorship appeared to be Cuba's experience with armed revolution. Consequently, it was no surprise that movements for national liberation in Central America, a region long dominated by foreigners and oligarchical dictatorships, opted for armed struggle and prolonged popular war as the most effective means for achieving their objectives.

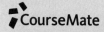

CourseMate

Go to the CourseMate website at **www.cengagebrain.com** for primary sources, additional study tools, and review materials—including audio and video clips—for this chapter.

18

Twilight of the Tyrants: Revolution and Prolonged Popular War in Central America

FOCUS QUESTIONS

- How was Central America's development affected by "liberal" reforms, the rise of a new export dependency, foreign control of key natural resources, and U.S. strategic hegemony?
- What were the policies of Juan José Arévalo and Jacobo Árbenz, how did U.S. intervention affect them, and how did this affect Guatemalan national development?
- What was the program of Nicaragua's Sandinista Revolution, and how did U.S. policy affect it?
- What were the objectives of the Salvadoran Revolution, and how did U.S. intervention affect it?
- What roles did women, workers, and the Catholic Church play in the region's twentieth-century development?

CENTRAL AMERICA, like Chile and the Andean area, was the site of significant movements for social change in the 1970s. Brutal military dictatorships, powerful landed oligarchies, and foreign domination plagued the region throughout much of the twentieth century. In response to these obstacles to national development, a determined revolutionary resistance arose to combine the strategies of armed guerrilla insurgency pioneered in the 1959 Cuban Revolution and popular political mobilization practiced in Chile. This idea of prolonged popular war characterized the struggles for national liberation in Nicaragua, El Salvador, and Guatemala.

The July 1979 victory of the Sandinista Front for National Liberation (FSLN) over one of Latin America's oldest tyrannies—the Somoza family

dynasty of Nicaragua—was an extraordinary event that reverberated throughout Latin America and the United States. Like the Cuban Revolution, this anti-imperialist social revolution challenged U.S. power in a part of the world that for almost a century had been its own secure preserve. In Washington, the Sandinista triumph caused gloom and disarray as to how to deal with the new Nicaragua and prevent the spread of the revolutionary virus to its Central American neighbors. It heartened Latin American revolutionaries, their supporters, and all the democratic forces of the region, ending the discouragement caused by a long series of defeats for radical and progressive causes—from the Brazilian counterrevolution of 1964 to the destruction of Chilean democracy in 1973. Moreover, the Nicaraguan revolution's unique blend of Marxism and

1909	U.S. intervention overthrows Zelaya in Nicaragua
1912–1933	U.S. troops occupy Nicaragua and organize Nicaraguan National Guard
1927–1932	Sandino and Farabundo Martí lead popular resistance to dictatorship in Nicaragua and El Salvador
1931–1934	Dictators Ubico, Hernández Martínez, and Somoza take power in Guatemala, El Salvador, and Nicaragua
1944	Arévalo promises populist reforms like social security and land redistribution
1951	Árbenz wins Guatemala's presidency and deepens reform agenda
1954	U.S.-sponsored coup overthrows Guatemala's Árbenz
1961	Sandinista National Liberation Front (FSLN) organizes in Nicaragua
1967	Anastasio Somoza Debayle succeeds brother Luis in Nicaragua
1972	Earthquake levels Managua corrupt Somoza dictatorship siphons international aid
1977	Farabundo Marti National Liberation Front (FMLN) expands guerrilla war in El Salvador
1979	FSLN overthrows Somoza family dictatorship; Salvadoran death squads kill thirty thousand, including Monsignor Oscar Romero
1982–1989	The United States organizes, finances, trains, and equips Contra rebels to attack Sandinista health clinics, schools, and peasant cooperatives
1984	Duarte wins Salvadoran presidential elections; FSLN's Ortega wins fair elections in Nicaragua; World Court condemns U.S. mine attack on Nicaragua
1991	FMLN transforms from guerrilla army into political party to implement UN peace accord

progressive Catholic thought and its effort to maintain a mix of state and private enterprise excited the imaginations of those committed to social change and national development in Latin America.

In El Salvador, meanwhile, guerrilla activities against a repressive military-civilian junta had developed into a full-scale civil war by the spring of 1980. The guerrillas had created a revolutionary government (the *Frente Democrático Revolucionario*) with its own army, the *Frente Farabundo Martí de Liberación Nacional* (FMLN). Ten years later, despite massive infusions of U.S. military and economic aid (more than $4.5 billion) to the government, rebel forces held much of the country and proved capable of disrupting its economic life and launching powerful offensives at will. By the spring of 1990, popular discontent with the U.S.-supported government, revulsion in the United States at the atrocities committed by the Salvadoran military, and the demonstrated strength of the guerrillas had forced the government to accept rebel proposals for U.N.-sponsored peace talks without preconditions. The resulting peace accords provided for demilitarization and democratic elections in which the FMLN participated. Their opponents won the 1994 elections that were less than completely "free and fair," but the FMLN obtained a strong presence in the national legislature and prepared for a long political struggle for the social transformation of El Salvador.

Guerrilla movements had risen and waned in Guatemala since 1954, when a counterrevolutionary coup, organized and armed by the Central Intelligence Agency (CIA), overthrew a reformist regime and the social changes it had instituted. The armed struggle gained in intensity and popular support in the late 1970s, even as the level of violence on the part of government security forces and death squads reached new heights. After the Guatemalan military government adopted a scorched-earth policy, accompanied by massacres of indigenous villagers thought to have supported the guerrillas, the rebels faded into the mountains and jungles. The roots of revolution—massive poverty, injustice, and repression—remained, however, even after the civilian government of Vinicio Cerezo took office in 1986. By the spring of 1990, the guerrilla war had revived, and rebel units maintained a presence only thirty miles from the capital, Guatemala City. Here, too, peace talks made slow progress against the bitter resistance of the dominant military, but they finally produced the Peace Accords of 1996.

Why was Central America, a region so richly endowed by nature and where U.S. economic, political, and cultural influence had been so strong, such a violent land and why did it present such immense contrasts of wealth and poverty? How did prevailing social and economic conditions shape the strategy of prolonged popular war in the region? The answer to these questions requires a more detailed survey of the twentieth-century history of Guatemala, Nicaragua, and El Salvador, where armed revolutionary movements shaped the contours of modern life.

Guatemala

In Guatemala, the historic sources of political violence and late-twentieth-century revolution lay in the nation's growing external dependence, its domination by foreign monopoly, and the collaboration of a rapacious landed oligarchy that supported a series of military dictatorships between 1898 and 1944. Manuel Estrada Cabrera, a tyrant famous for his cruelty, led the first of these dictatorships. He ruled ruthlessly for two decades before his own previously obedient Congress declared him insane and sought his removal. During his presidency, Estrada Cabrera invested in the national infrastructure, particularly road and port facilities for transporting and shipping coffee.

Although initially funded with Guatemalan resources, the financing and construction contracts for this infrastructure soon passed into the hands of foreign, predominantly U.S., companies. A U.S. firm, International Railways of Central America (IRCA), affiliated with the United Fruit Company (UFCO) through interlocking directors, acquired monopolistic control over land transport in Guatemala and virtual ownership of the major Atlantic port of Puerto Barrios. The UFCO secured a contract in 1901 to carry Guatemalan mail from Puerto Barrios to the United States in its "Great White Fleet" and to carry bananas, obtained from producers at fixed prices, to

the North American market. In time, the company acquired vast banana holdings of its own on favorable terms from the Guatemalan government.

The enormous U.S. economic influence, based on direct investments, loans, and control over Guatemala's chief foreign market, translated into a growing U.S. tutelage over Guatemala. After World War I, the U.S. embassy became in effect a branch of the Guatemalan government, which routinely sought favors from U.S. ambassadors in return for cooperation with U.S. corporations.

By the end of Estrada Cabrera's brutal regime, Guatemala's economy was utterly dependent on the export of bananas, and its land was concentrated in the hands of a few, but unlike Nicaragua and El Salvador, a single foreign company, UFCO, owned much of it. During the next decade, coffee oligarchs battled each other, sought to renegotiate the state's relationship with UFCO, pursued constitutional limitations on the military, and simultaneously worked to preserve their control over indigenous communities, peasants, and workers. The resulting instability provided fertile ground for the emergence of a new military strongman, Jorge Ubico, who seized power in 1930 and dominated Guatemala until a 1944 revolution overthrew him.

During his reign, Ubico consistently supported UFCO and IRCA, but he also cultivated close relations with the nation's coffee oligarchy, whose interests the Great Depression threatened. During the 1930s, coffee prices declined to less than half the 1929 level. By cutting off European markets, World War II deepened dependence on the U.S. market and further depressed coffee prices. The crisis in foreign trade led to rising unemployment, wage cuts, and business failure for many small producers. The Guatemalan planter oligarchy and associated export-import interests, closely linked to U.S. enterprises, made peasants and workers pay for the depression through wage cuts, intensified exploitation, and reduced government services. In the 1930s, the level of official repression rose; in 1933 alone, the government executed some one hundred labor leaders, students, and political dissidents.

Ubico was determined to guarantee the planter class a reliable, cheap source of labor. In 1934, he abolished debt peonage, replacing it with a vagrancy law that required all persons owning less than a stipulated amount of land to carry **libretas** (cards) to show that they had worked at least one hundred and fifty days a year on the haciendas. He jailed those who failed to comply with this obligation to do "useful work." Fearing popular uprisings and peasant land invasions, Ubico also legalized murder for landlords seeking to protect their properties.

The fall of the detested Ubico regime came because of popular democratic opposition movements, fostered by the antifascist climate of opinion created by U.S. and Latin American participation in the war against the Axis powers. Although Guatemala, under U.S. pressure, had declared war on the Axis in December 1941, Ubico's profascist views and the ties of many of his close advisers and ministers to German interests were well known. In June 1944, a general strike and antigovernment demonstrations forced Ubico to resign. A triumvirate of two army officers and a civilian took over and scheduled congressional and presidential elections in December 1944. The overwhelming victory of Juan José Arévalo, a prominent educator and scholar who had spent many years in exile, confirmed the demand of the Guatemalan people for the establishment of a government pledged to democracy and social progress.

REVOLUTION AND COUNTERREVOLUTION, 1944–1983

The Guatemalan Democratic Revolution of 1944 was largely the work of a coalition of urban middle-class groups and discontented junior military, with the small working class as a junior partner and the indigenous peasantry in a marginal role. In fact, historian Greg Grandin shows that *principales* (indigenous communal leaders) consistently opposed the revolutionary nationalist regime because it challenged their traditional authority and proprietary claims. Although the revolutionary leadership favored a capitalist course of development and was friendly to the United States, the Arévalo administration (1945–1951) also launched an ambitious social welfare program that stressed a national literacy campaign and construction of schools, hospitals, and housing.

The 1945 constitution abolished all forms of forced labor, enfranchised literate women, prohibited press censorship, limited presidential power, criminalized racial discrimination, required equal pay for equal work, and established civil equality for men and women. The 1947 labor code guaranteed to workers the right to decent working conditions, social security coverage, and collective bargaining through trade unions of their own choosing; it also provided for compulsory labor-management contracts and mandatory paid maternity leaves. These reforms spurred a rapid organizing drive among urban, banana, and railroad workers, who made a number of limited gains.

Following the example of many Latin American governments in this period, Arévalo began a program of industrial development and diversification, employing a newly created state bank and other agencies for this purpose. As for the existing foreign economic enclaves (chiefly UFCO and IRCA), Arévalo's policy was not to nationalize but rather to regulate their operations in the national interest. The government insisted, for example, that UFCO submit wage disputes to arbitration. New laws stipulated that in the future the state or predominantly national companies should exploit natural resources; in industry, foreign investors could operate on the same terms as nationals.

Although the 1945 constitution permitted expropriation of private property in the national interest, Arévalo's agrarian program was equally moderate. Government programs offered state support to cooperatives and provided agricultural credit and technical assistance. A new law protected tenants from arbitrary ouster by landlords and required them to rent uncultivated lands to landless peasants, but the latifundia remained intact.

Urban, middle-class ladina women played an influential role in the Arévalo government. The Democratic Union of Women (UMD), organized in 1946, included former students at the University of San Carlos who had mobilized against Ubico. They agitated for women's rights, participated as teachers in the literacy crusade, and hosted a 1947 Inter-American Women's Conference that advocated greater democracy, human rights, and national industrial development. The Guatemalan Women's Alliance (AFG), founded in 1947 and closely associated with the clandestine Communist Party, championed working-class interests, agrarian reform, and indigenous rights. Its most famous member arguably was María Vilanova de Arbenz, whose husband became Guatemala's president in 1950.

The pace of reform quickened with the election of Maj. Jacobo Arbenz, who sought to convert Guatemala from a dependent nation with a semicolonial economy into an economically independent country. His major strategy to achieve this objective was **import-substitution industrialization**, which relied heavily on private enterprise. However, the creation of a modern capitalist economy was impossible without an expansion of the internal market—that is, of mass purchasing power—through agrarian reform, and this required a forceful state.

Prompted by indigenous peasant uprisings, the phenomenal growth of the Guatemalan National Peasant Confederation (CNCG), which claimed more than two hundred thousand members, and a 1950 census report showing that 2 percent of Guatemalans controlled 74 percent of the arable land, Arbenz supported a 1952 agrarian reform law. It provided for the expropriation of holdings greater than 223 acres and their distribution to the landless, with compensation made through twenty-five-year bonds. By June 1954, approximately one hundred thousand peasant families had received land, together with credit and technical assistance from new state agencies.

The agrarian reform inevitably affected UFCO, which cultivated no more than 15 percent of its holdings of more than five hundred and fifty thousand acres; the company claimed that it needed these large reserves against the day when its producing lands were worn out or ruined by banana diseases. The land expropriation, coming on top of a series of clashes between the government and UFCO over its labor and wage policies, brought their relations to the breaking point.

Meanwhile, in its struggle with the landed oligarchy, a weak middle class needed allies, and workers used this situation to expand their demands. They organized independent trade unions like the Guatemalan Confederation of Labor (CTG) and the Guatemalan Syndicalist Federation (FSG) and pressed for higher wages and greater worker autonomy. The establishment of the General Confederation of Guatemalan Workers (CGTG), with more than one hundred thousand members, also reflected their success. Coupled with the growing politicization of indigenous peasants organized in the CNCG, these popular working-class organizations pressured Arbenz to pursue a more radical agenda that frightened his supporters in the agroindustrial middle class, inducing them to seek a modus vivendi with the planter aristocracy and its U.S. associates.

The U.S. government already had attacked the moderate Arévalo as being procommunist. Arbenz's deepening of the revolution, threatening the profits and properties of UFCO, evoked a much angrier reaction in the United States and caused UFCO's friends in high places to prepare for direct action against Guatemala. By 1953, President Dwight D. Eisenhower had approved Operation Success, a Central Intelligence Agency (CIA)–State Department plan to remove Arbenz and replace him with Col. Carlos Castillo Armas. Deeply involved in the conspiracy against Guatemala were Secretary of State John Foster Dulles and his brother, CIA director Allen Dulles (both former partners in UFCO's legal counsel), United Nations (U.N.) Ambassador Henry Cabot Lodge, and Assistant Secretary of State for Latin America John Moors Cabot (both UFCO stockholders). Headquartered in Miami, a CIA official served as field commander for the operation and funneled guns and ammunition to Castillo Armas's army. The man in charge of psychological warfare was E. Howard Hunt, later of Watergate fame.

Because the United States had imposed an arms embargo against Guatemala, Arbenz purchased a shipment of Czech arms, whose arrival in May 1954 provided the pretext for implementing Operation Success. In June, Castillo Armas advanced six miles from the Honduras border into Guatemala and waited for his U.S. allies to do the rest. While U.S. pilots in CIA planes dropped propaganda leaflets and incendiary bombs on the capital, Guatemalan army officers refused to arm workers and peasants who wanted to defend the revolution. Instead, they pressured Arbenz to resign, turning over the government to a three-man junta, but the United States insisted on the installation of Castillo Armas, the CIA candidate, as president. On July 3, he arrived in the capital in a U.S. embassy plane and promptly launched a campaign of terror against supporters of the revolution. According to one estimate, his regime executed eight thousand people. Thereafter, Castillo Armas surrounded himself with an entourage of "grafters and cutthroats."

The counterrevolution returned power and property to the landed oligarchy, its foreign allies, and their new middle-class partners. It revoked the 1952 land reform, returning formerly expropriated lands to UFCO and other latifundistas. After 1954, the size of the average peasant landholding decreased, whereas the percentage of land devoted to commercial farming increased, but the Guatemalan economy did not stand still. The new ruling coalition promoted the growth of a small dependent industry and some major shifts in the composition of agricultural exports.

Despite a modest advance of industry, mostly of the *maquiladora* type controlled by foreigners, Guatemala remained a producer of foodstuffs and raw materials. The composition of its exports changed considerably because of declining coffee prices. Coffee was still the leading export in 1980, but cotton, sugar, and cardamom ranked second, third, and fourth in value, respectively. While commercial agriculture gained, Guatemala had to import basic grains (wheat and maize) from the United States. This reflected the continuing concentration of the best lands in the hands of latifundistas, often by usurpation of the plots of mestizo and indigenous smallholders, with army and security forces present to suppress armed resistance. Because the law forbade peasant unions and landowners ignored minimum wage laws, extremely low wages were the rule.

The post-1954 regimes were militaristic and repressive because their social base was so narrow and they depended on flagrant foreign intervention to preserve their power. In the thirty-four years after 1954, only one civilian president was elected—Mario Méndez Montenegro (in 1966)—and he escalated the repression, directing counterinsurgency

operations as much against peasants as guerrillas. Aided by U.S. military advisers, the Guatemalan military slaughtered an estimated fifteen thousand people in the department of Zacapa alone between 1966 and 1968.

Despite the crushing blows inflicted by this and subsequent counterinsurgency campaigns, the guerrilla movements survived and reached a new height of activity in the mid-1970s with the formation of the Guerrilla Army of the Poor (EGP). The resurgence reflected growing cooperation among guerrilla movements, trade unions, and peasant organizations. Another significant development was a cleavage in the church between Archbishop Mario Casariego, who was firmly loyal to the military regime, and some bishops who were sympathetic to liberation theology, as well as working clergy active in the Catholic **comunidades de base** (grassroots communities). Their involvement in the daily struggles of the poor brought charges of subversion and, in 1981 alone, attacks by government and paramilitary forces killed twelve priests and threatened many others, including some bishops, with death.

The guerrilla struggle achieved a high point of organizational unity in 1981 following the decision of the three major guerrilla organizations and the Guatemalan Communist Party to form a unified command to coordinate their military operations. By the end of 1981, they had scored considerable successes. The widespread violence and the growing power of the guerrillas intensified the flight of capital, adding to the economic gloom brought on by low commodity prices and declining industrial activity.

The guerrilla advances produced discord among the military. One group of officers favored a more defensive strategy, controlling what was feasible; others favored an aggressive policy, including "scorched earth" tactics against the areas that purportedly supported the guerrillas. This group gained the upper hand in March 1982 and installed General Efraín Ríos Montt as head of a new three-man junta, whose policy was to eradicate the mainly indigenous population. "Troops and militias move into the villages, shoot, burn, or behead the inhabitants they catch," *Latin America Weekly Report* wrote, "the survivors are machine-gunned from helicopters as they flee. Any survivors are later rounded up and taken to special camps where Church and aid agencies cope as best they can."

These conditions did not deter the Reagan administration from certifying to Congress that the human rights situation in Guatemala had improved, thereby renewing military aid and arms sales to its government. Nonetheless, the United States, carefully avoiding the subversive term *reform*, also continued to pressure the military government to build a broader domestic political constituency by implementing periodic programs of "agrarian transformation." This typically meant the relocation of landless indigenous peasants to inaccessible, uncultivated, relatively infertile, state-owned jungle lands, where they received minimal credit and technical assistance, all of which increased their dependence on markets and eroded traditional autonomy.

RETURN TO DEMOCRACY, GUATEMALAN STYLE, 1983–2003

In August 1983, a military coup toppled Ríos Montt. The desperate state of the economy, the country's international isolation, and growing internal opposition from social movements that overcame traditional racial, ethnic, gender, and class divisions all persuaded the military to withdraw in favor of civilian elites. The domestic opposition particularly frustrated the army. Despite savage repression, hundreds of thousands of indigenous peoples, Catholic activists, homeless people, urban workers, and housewives bravely resisted the government by joining organizations like the Committee of Peasant Unity (CUC), Catholic Action, the National Movement of Shantytown Dwellers (MONAP), the National Committee of Union Solidarity (CNUS), and the Consumers' Defense Committee (CDC). Together these groups organized the Democratic Front Against Repression (FDCR) to demand democracy and social justice, but specific conditions limited the return to democracy. For example, no future civilian government could hope to survive if it interfered with the military's conduct of the ongoing counterinsurgency war or attacked the oppressive land system.

The first step in the transition to this curious democracy was the election of a constituent assembly. Notable for its repressive atmosphere and a "reactionary pluralism" that severely limited political debate, this election resulted in the abstention of 57 percent of eligible voters. It produced a constituent assembly controlled by oligarchic parties who scheduled elections in 1985 and wrote a new constitution that ignored social problems, institutionalized the military repression, and sanctified the rights of private property.

Despite constitutional provisions that criminalized voter abstention, fewer than 50 percent of eligible Guatemalans voted in successive elections that empowered Vinicio Cerezo Arévalo and José Serrano Elías, both of whom promised to honor the military's autonomy, curb inflation, create jobs, respect human rights, and expand democracy. Although the military distrusted these civilian leaders, it understood that their governments, with connections to powerful sister parties in Europe and patrons in Washington, had the best chance of securing urgently needed foreign aid and overseeing the "recomposition" of the state and civil society.

Under Cerezo and Serrano, the military retained effective control of rural Guatemala, scene of a prolonged counterinsurgency war that transformed 38 percent of urban women and 56 percent of rural wives into widows, and caused an immense flow of indigenous refugees, an estimated 10 percent of the population. In Phase One of the process, the army burned down Maya villages, laid waste fields, and killed more than thirty thousand villagers, according to estimates. Phase Two, designed to turn indigenous communities against the guerrillas, created "model villages" (reservations) in which to resettle surviving indígenas and those who had returned home after fleeing and living like hunted animals in the mountains. The military also reorganized indigenous society, forcing hundreds of thousands of Mayans to participate in a civil defense patrol program. Israel, a major supplier of arms to Guatemala, provided it with a wide range of sophisticated hardware and furnished advisers on counterinsurgency.

Meanwhile, the guerrilla struggle, after suffering severe defeats that drove the partisans into remote parts of the mountains and jungles, revived. Guerrilla territory surrounded many model villages; the guerrilla presence was particularly strong in three zones: the Petén, Quiché and Huehuetenango, and Solola. Despite the increase in guerrilla activities, the *Unidad Revolucionaria Nacional Guatemalteca* (URNG), which led and coordinated the guerrilla movement, sent Cerezo an open letter expressing willingness to discuss peace talks. In April 1989, preliminary talks occurred between a reconciliation commission approved by the government and rebel leaders, and the talks continued under Serrano.

Cerezo and Serrano did not deliver on their economic promises. An economic austerity program that reflected the dominant influence of landowning and business elites kept both unemployment and inflation high. Economic aid from the United States and European countries fell below expectations. The economy continued to stagnate, and poverty skyrocketed. Between 1980 and 1987, according to the U.N., the proportion of poor people rose from 79 to 87 percent; the percentage of people in "extreme poverty" grew from 52 to 67 percent. Guatemala's historically high income inequality also worsened substantially. Naturally, this led to dramatic declines in the "physical quality of life," measured by infant mortality, literacy, and life expectancy. Still worse, this crushing poverty was disproportionately concentrated among women and indigenous people.

Nevertheless, popular sectors took advantage of greater political freedoms to create a powerful opposition. Guided by the United Guatemalan Workers (UNSITRAGUA), a new independent labor confederation, students, teachers, workers, shantytown dwellers, human rights activists, peasants, women's groups, and indigenous rights organizations joined together to form a cross-class coalition that called for nationwide general strikes to protest policies that produced greater unemployment and higher prices for bread, milk, and urban transportation. Although they succeeded in winning some important concessions, these popular social movements still lacked the power of the army, international bankers, and Guatemala's propertied elites; but they functioned effectively, consciously or not, as a civilian front for the rural guerrilla insurgency.

Although Cerezo and Serrano pledged to work for peace and end human rights abuses, a wave of assassinations contradicted their promises. The U.S.-based Council on Hemispheric Affairs found that Guatemala, closely followed by El Salvador, was the worst human rights violator in Latin America in 1990. In that year, according to one human rights organization, 773 people were killed, including the murders of dozens of street children, mostly at the hands of the military, the national police, and death squads.

By 1993, a number of factors combined to produce a crisis for the Serrano regime. One was the public anger caused by a series of drastic electricity rate increases. A second shock was the 1992 award of the Nobel Peace Prize to the Maya activist Rigoberta Menchú, which provided the indigenous masses of Guatemala with an internationally recognized leader in their struggle for political and social rights. Against a background of mounting unrest and popular demonstrations, Serrano announced the dissolution of Congress and the Supreme Court and took all power into his own hands. By a certain irony, the United States—which in 1954 had plotted the ouster of the democratic nationalist government of Jacobo Arbenz—now suspended economic assistance to Guatemala to protest the coup, producing consternation in business circles and wavering within the military, which finally withdrew its support from Serrano. The coup promptly collapsed, and Serrano fled to Panama.

There followed prolonged negotiations among the military, political, and business elite, which searched for a presidential candidate who was acceptable to them and the United States but hostile to Serrano. They selected Ramiro de León Carpio, a lawyer and human rights critic who opposed the guerrillas and supported the neoliberal economic policies sponsored by the International Monetary Fund (IMF) and the World Bank.

The military undoubtedly believed that he would improve Guatemala's image without threatening the existing order, a judgment that his first

© Reuters/Corbis

The 1992 awarding of the Nobel Peace Prize to the Maya activist Rigoberta Menchú gave a large boost to the struggle against genocide of indígenas and for indigenous political and social rights in her native Guatemala and throughout Latin America.

presidential acts confirmed. After firing some members of the military high command who allegedly backed the coup, he promptly replaced them with similar individuals. Against the advice of human rights groups, León Carpio decided to keep the Presidential Guard, a group implicated in numerous human rights violations, including the assassination of anthropologist and activist Myrna Mack. He reopened negotiations with the guerrillas, but the talks proceeded slowly and haltingly, largely because León Carpio insisted on separating the negotiations for a cease-fire from discussion of the social and economic issues—land, labor, and political reform—that were the cause of the war.

In general, despite his populist rhetoric, León Carpio showed little interest in the problems of the 90 percent of the population who lived in poverty. Even by low Latin American standards, the dimensions of those problems were staggering: The share of national income received by the poorest 10 percent of the population dropped from 2.4 percent in 1980 to 0.5 percent in 1991. The problems were especially acute for indigenous people (55 to 60 percent of the population). According to official statistics, the indigenous infant mortality rate was 134 per 1,000 live births, twice that of the nonindigenous population. Only 10 percent of the indigenous population was literate; three out of four indigenous children suffered to some degree from malnutrition; and the average life expectancy of forty-five years represented a sixteen-year gap separating the indigenous people from other Guatemalans. The root cause of indigenous poverty was lack of access to land. According to a U.S. Agency for International Development study, 2 percent of the country's farms held two-thirds of the farmland, whereas 70 percent of the farms possessed 17 percent of the land. Government efforts to promote highland production of winter vegetables for export replaced grain production for local consumption, promoted concentration of landownership, and spurred the flight of the indigenous population to the cities.

Many indigenous (and nonindigenous) people found employment in the free-trade zone factories or *maquilas*, the fastest-growing sector of the Guatemalan economy. A 1984 law exempted these factories from import duties and (for ten years) from taxes. Koreans owned the majority of these maquilas, which accounted for 36 percent of Guatemala's exports to the United States. Seventy percent of the workers were women, and they earned about $2.50 a day. "I work from 7:30 in the morning to 10:00 o'clock at night," said one machine operator, "and what I earn doesn't cover what I need to eat." Nonetheless, employers successfully resisted demands for higher wages, shorter hours, and better working conditions.

The repression continued, but it met with growing resistance from thousands of Guatemalan refugees returning from exile in Mexico and from thousands of indigenous people who had lived for a decade in the so-called communities in resistance, refugees in their own country. The award of the Nobel Peace Prize to Rigoberta Menchú gave indigenous people new hope and courage. In November 1993, thousands of indigenous Guatemalans held a protest march in the capital to demand total abolition of the civil defense patrols imposed by the army. This social ferment accompanied a renaissance of Maya culture, which included the formation of centers for the study of Maya culture, an association of Maya writers, and a publishing house devoted to the publication of books in the Maya languages.

Four decades of military dictatorship, death squads, and oligarchic rule had left Guatemala politically divided, economically devastated, and socially unstable. By the 1990s, the terrain of popular struggle had shifted decisively from the battlefield to politics, where social movements increasingly mobilized a constituency that transcended class, racial, and gender divisions. The strategy of revolution and prolonged popular war had won some significant victories; it ended the scourge of dictatorship, harnessed the death squads, and forced the oligarchs to share power, but the ultimate goal of social justice and national development remained elusive. In Nicaragua, however, the strategy actually brought to power a popular movement determined to implement the structural reforms necessary to promote national development, but it faced an equally determined opposition from the U.S. government, whose vast resources ultimately overwhelmed revolutionary Nicaragua.

Nicaragua

LIBERALISM, U.S. INTERVENTION, AND SANDINO, 1894–1934

Like Guatemala, foreign economic dependency and gross inequality in the distribution of land shaped Nicaragua's twentieth-century history; but unlike its northern neighbor, it also suffered from recurrent U.S. military intervention that weakened progressive local elites and decisively undermined national sovereignty. José Santos Zelaya, the late-nineteenth-century liberal dictator, had opened his nation to foreign investment and trade, but he nonetheless remained an ardent nationalist. He successfully asserted Nicaragua's claim to sovereignty over the Atlantic Mosquitia coast in 1894 and long championed a Central American federation. He also angered the United States by turning down its canal treaty proposal and negotiating with other countries for construction of a Nicaraguan canal that would have competed with the United States–controlled route in Panama. Like Mexico's Porfirio Díaz in the same period, Zelaya, alarmed over the extent of U.S. economic influence in his country, sought to dilute U.S. power by granting concessions to nationals of other countries.

These signs of independence convinced the United States, where imperialist attitudes and policies had flowered since 1898, that Zelaya must go. With U.S. encouragement, a revolt broke out in 1909. The U.S. Marines landed at Bluefields on the Atlantic coast and protected the anti-Zelaya forces there against government attack. Under military and diplomatic pressure from the United States, Zelaya resigned, and in 1910 his opponents came to power. Their triumph represented a victory for the traditional landed oligarchy and a defeat for the progressive nationalist faction that sought independent capitalist expansion. They installed Adolfo Díaz, an obscure bookkeeper in a U.S. mining firm in eastern Nicaragua, as president of a puppet regime that hastened to satisfy all the U.S. demands. A U.S. banking firm made loans to the Nicaraguan government, receiving as security a controlling interest in the national bank and state railways and the revenues from the customhouse.

The servility and unpopularity of Díaz and his puppet regime provoked a revolt in 1912, led by the young liberal Benjamín Zeledón. The rebels were on the brink of victory when U.S. Marines again intervened at the request of the Díaz government. Ordered by U.S. officials to end his revolt, Zeledón fought on, warning the U.S. commander that he and his country would bear "a tremendous responsibility and eternal infamy before history … for having employed your arms against the weak who have been struggling to reconquer the sacred rights of their fatherland." Zeledón, fighting to the last, suffered defeat and execution, apparently with U.S. approval. The first U.S. occupation of Nicaragua followed, with the United States ruling the country through a series of puppet presidents from 1912 to 1925. In return for U.S. protection, these quisling regimes made certain important concessions, notably the Bryan-Chamorro treaty of 1916, which gave the United States the exclusive right to construct an interoceanic canal across Nicaragua and imposed limitations on Nicaraguan national sovereignty similar to those included in the 1903 Panama Canal treaty. Because the Panama Canal already existed, the Bryan-Chamorro treaty's real purpose was to prevent any other country from constructing a competing canal, thereby guaranteeing U.S. strategic hegemony in the region.

In August 1925, convinced that the U.S. occupation was no longer necessary, the United States withdrew the Marines, but they returned a few months later, ostensibly to protect U.S. and other foreign property. This time they stayed until 1933. The new U.S. strategy was to arrange a peace settlement among rival elite factions that would give all an opportunity to share in the political spoils, but the real power remained in the hands of the United States. Only Augusto César Sandino refused to accept the U.S.-sponsored peace treaty of 1927. The mestizo son of a liberal landowner and an indigenous servant girl, Sandino had lived in postrevolutionary Mexico, where he encountered radical nationalist and social revolutionary ideas. He had returned to Nicaragua in 1926 to join the struggle against a puppet regime, but José María Moncada, leader of one faction, immediately distrusted Sandino because Sandino spoke of "the necessity for the workers to struggle against the rich and other things that are the principles of communism." Although no Marxist, Sandino was a revolutionary leader who had profound sympathy for all the disinherited and planned to make far-reaching social and economic changes after achieving his primary goal: the departure of U.S. troops.

Unable to secure an independent command under Moncada, Sandino organized his own force, consisting mainly of miners, peasants, workers, and indígenas. "I decided," he wrote, "to fight, understanding that I was the one called to protest the betrayal of the Fatherland." For seven years (1927–1933), Sandino's guerrilla army waged war against the U.S. Marines and the U.S.-sponsored Nicaraguan National Guard. Learning from early defeats and heavy losses when he attempted to meet the enemy in frontal combat, Sandino developed a new kind of warfare based on hit-and-run attacks, ambushes, and temporary occupation of localities. Most important of all, he cultivated close ties with the peasantry, who provided a supply base for the guerrillas and gave them accurate information about enemy movements and other assistance.

In the United States, meanwhile, the war was growing increasingly unpopular, and eventually

General Sandino (*second from left*) and his staff. Third from left is Salvadoran Agustín
Farabundo Martí. (The soldiers at left and right are unidentified.)

Congress cut off all funding for it. The new Hoover administration decided to extricate itself from the Nicaraguan quagmire, but without loss of control. The instrument of that control was a powerful National Guard, which the Marines created, trained, and equipped in 1927. In February 1932, Secretary of State Stimson announced the withdrawal of one thousand Marines from Nicaragua, the rest of whom he recalled after the U.S.-supervised presidential election in November.

Juan B. Sacasa won the elections and sought to promote national reconciliation. First, he accepted the advice of the U.S. Minister to Nicaragua, who had picked Anastasio Somoza García as the new National Guard director. Second, Sacasa proposed a peace conference with Sandino, who had promised to lay down his arms after the Marines left on

January 2, 1934, but Sandino profoundly mistrusted Sacasa's entourage, especially Somoza, who demanded that Sacasa order the total disarmament of the Sandinistas. During the negotiations that followed, Sandino angered Somoza by insisting on the National Guard's dissolution. Unbeknownst to Sacasa, Somoza promptly ordered his arrest and execution. It was Somoza's first step toward the establishment of a tyranny that would oppress the Nicaraguan people for well over four decades.

THE SOMOZA ERA, 1934–1979

Following Sandino's assassination, Somoza gradually consolidated his political power, more and more openly defying President Sacasa. With the aid of a paramilitary force known as the Blue Shirts,

Somoza easily secured election to the presidency in 1936, taking care to combine the post with that of director of the National Guard. With the Guard at his disposal, Somoza had no difficulty extending his term of office indefinitely, ruling directly as president or indirectly through puppet presidents until 1956, when he was assassinated, or *ajusticiado* (brought to justice) as Nicaraguans saw it, by the young poet Rigoberto López Pérez.

Thoroughly cynical and self-seeking, Somoza was obsequiously pro-U.S. because he understood that his power depended on U.S. support. The saying ascribed to President Franklin D. Roosevelt, "Somoza is an S.O.B. but he is our S.O.B." may be apocryphal, but it accurately summarized Somoza's relations with the U.S. government, which rewarded him with loans and assistance in establishing a military academy to turn out officers for the National Guard. Graduates of the school usually spent their senior year at the School of the Americas, the U.S. military training center in Panama. Following Somoza's assassination in 1956, his two sons, Luis and Anastasio Somoza Debayle, took over and ruled Nicaragua either directly or indirectly until 1979. Differences between the Somozas' ruling styles reflected their adaptations to the changing phases of U.S.–Latin American policy. The relative mildness of Luis's rule appeared to reflect the reformist and developmentalist stress of the Alliance for Progress of the 1960s. In fact, all three dictators ruled Nicaragua as a personal estate for their benefit and that of their domestic and foreign allies. By 1970, the Somoza family controlled about 25 percent of the country's agricultural production and a large proportion of its industry; the total wealth of the family approximated $500 million.

U.S. firms also enjoyed profitable investment opportunities in the food-processing industry and mining. Both foreign and domestic employers benefited from the regime's repressive labor policies, but Nicaraguan capitalists grew increasingly unhappy with the Somoza family's penchant for monopoly. The church, originally aligned with the Conservative Party, shifted its support to the first Somoza and generally remained loyal to the family until the 1960s, when it joined the Christian

Democratic Party (PDC) in opposition to Anastasio Jr.'s plans for his perpetual reelection. From first to last, however, the ultimate domestic foundation of the family's power was the National Guard, whose top command always remained in the hands of a Somoza.

While the dynasty and its allies prospered, the Nicaraguan people's economic and social condition steadily worsened because of the unchecked exploitation of rural and urban labor and the developmental programs of the Somoza Era. Responding to growing world demand for new products, especially cotton, the Somozas opened up new lands to the planter class. Once again, as during the coffee boom a century earlier, they drove peasant families from the land and into the cities. Nicaragua under the Somozas had one of the more extreme disparities in income distribution in Latin America; in 1978 the lower 50 percent of the population had an annual per capita income of $256.

Resistance to the Somoza dictatorship had begun in the 1950s, with a series of unsuccessful revolts led by the irrepressible Pedro Joaquín Chamorro, publisher of the highly respected *La Prensa* and son of parents from two of the most powerful oligarchic clans. Because of his elite background, Somoza pardoned him and allowed his return to Managua after each revolt. However, a more serious threat to the dictatorship arose with the formation in 1961 of the FSLN founded by Carlos Fonseca, Silvio Mayorga, and Tomás Borge. Composed largely of students, its initial efforts to organize guerrilla warfare in the mountains met with defeat, but the rebels gradually improved their tactics and organization, attracting a growing number of recruits. Over time, they combined the tactics of rural insurgency and clandestine political organization, which characterized prolonged popular war.

A turning point in Nicaragua's recent history was the devastating 1972 earthquake that killed ten thousand Nicaraguans and reduced the entire center of Managua to rubble, wiping out almost all businesses. The public was immensely indignant over the shameless behavior of the Somozas, who diverted large amounts of foreign international aid into their own pockets and those of the National

Guard. The center of Managua remained "an unreconstructed moonscape," for Somoza and his cronies had bought large parcels of land on the periphery of the city where they built new houses and shops, profiting from the disaster.

In January 1978, the Somozas committed an act of folly that largely contributed to their downfall. *La Prensa* had published a series of articles about a commercial blood-plasma operation through which Somoza sold the blood of his people in the United States. Stung by the criticism and resulting popular outrage, the family or one of its supporters ordered publisher Pedro Joaquín Chamorro's assassination. The murder of the popular journalist provoked an effective general strike that ended only after considerable violence and repression by the National Guard, but its repercussions continued. The crime alienated elites who had tolerated the regime's murder, jailing, and torture of peasants and Sandinistas but condemned the killing of a member of an old privileged family like Chamorro.

The FSLN gained organizational strength from the Chamorro affair, the general strike, and a brutal National Guard attack on an indigenous community commemorating the forty-fourth anniversary of Sandino's assassination. These events contributed to a general broadening of the resistance movement. In August 1978, twenty-five Sandinista guerrillas audaciously invaded the National Palace and seized as hostages most members of the Chamber of Deputies and some two thousand public employees. After frantic negotiations, Somoza agreed to release fifty-nine Sandinista prisoners, pay a huge ransom, and arrange a safe flight to Panama for the guerrillas and released prisoners. This encouraged a prolonged general strike and a spontaneous uprising in the city of Matagalpa by *muchachos* (youngsters), who held out for two weeks and forced the National Guard to retreat to their barracks. On September 8, the FSLN launched coordinated uprisings in five cities. With their headquarters surrounded by civilian and FSLN combatants, the Guard called in Somoza's air force for a ferocious bombing of the cities before government ground forces retook the cities one at a time. Thereafter, a house-to-house search resulted in a

genocidal Operation Cleanup, with a death toll of some five thousand people.

Alarmed by the September uprisings, the United States attempted to mediate a compromise between Somoza and his traditional elite opponents through a committee of the Organization of American States (OAS). Some anti-Somoza factions soon withdrew from the mediation process, charging that the OAS commission wanted "*Somocismo* without Somoza." This and Somoza's obstinate refusal to resign frustrated the U.S. initiative. Meanwhile, the FSLN, overcoming tactical differences among three internal factions, created a unified nine-man directorate to lead the popular movement to victory.

Both sides now mobilized for a final struggle. Somoza prepared for the worst by liquidating his vast assets and shipping his capital abroad. Meanwhile, the FSLN, aided by Western European Social Democratic Parties and governments as politically diverse as those of Costa Rica, Cuba, Panama, and Venezuela, restocked its arms supply with weapons purchased on the international arms market. The regular FSLN army expanded from a few hundred to several thousand. Throughout the country, the network of neighborhood defense committees established after the September revolts worked feverishly to prepare for the coming struggle by stockpiling food and medical supplies. *Comunidades de base* (Catholic grassroots organizations) took an active part in these preparations.

In June 1979, the FSLN announced a general strike and launched a final offensive, infiltrating Managua and occupying *barrios* (slum neighborhoods) on both sides of the central zone. Somoza, retreating into his recently constructed bunker in the fortress of La Loma, ordered a counterattack that included a massive air and artillery bombardment of the city. By July 5, the Sandinistas had encircled the capital, leaving only one way out via the airport six miles east of the city. The Sandinistas could have taken it at will but allowed it to remain in the government's hands, perhaps to give the Somozas and their entourage an opportunity to leave the capital. With victory in sight, the Sandinista directorate named a provisional government—a five-member junta that included three Sandinistas;

Alfonso Robelo, the leader of the business opposition to Somoza; and Violeta Chamorro, the widow of the martyred Pedro Joaquín Chamorro.

Meanwhile, the United States made last-minute efforts to prevent a radical revolutionary regime from coming to power. It called on the OAS to send a "peacekeeping" force to Managua, but it was unanimously rebuffed. Then it sent a special envoy to Nicaragua to try to persuade the FSLN to broaden the base of the new junta, but the Sandinistas pointed out that they already had made a large concession by including wealthy business representatives, Robelo and Violeta Chamorro, in the government. Inclusion of the persons nominated by the United States—a general of the National Guard and a personal friend of Somoza—would have ensured the preservation of "Somocismo without Somoza."

Under intense pressure from Archbishop Miguel Obando y Bravo and people in other influential quarters to accept his inevitable defeat and to spare the capital a new assault, Somoza agreed on July 16, 1979, to go into exile in Florida. The next day, he drove to the airport and left Nicaragua forever. Two days later the FSLN and its government entered Managua.

The Sandinistas in Power, 1979–1990

The cost of the Sandinista victory in lives and material destruction was enormous. Estimates of the dead ranged up to fifty thousand, or a loss of 2 percent of Nicaragua's population. The material damage approached $1.3 billion; the national debt, a large part of which represented sums that Somoza had diverted into his foreign bank accounts, stood at $1.6 billion.

The government of national reconstruction included the five-member junta, its cabinet or ministries of state, and the council of state, a legislative and consultative assembly that represented a broad variety of popular organizations. The composition of these bodies reflected the Sandinista leaders' desire to create a pluralistic system to solve the country's problems. The first cabinet included Marxists like Tomás Borge, minister of the interior, and Jaime

Wheelock Román, minister of agriculture; two bankers; and two Catholic priests, the Maryknoll Father Miguel D'Escoto and the Trappist monk Ernesto Cardenal, which, according to historian Thomas P. Anderson, made "Nicaragua probably the only country in the world with Catholic priests in the cabinet." These formal organs of government were responsible to the nine-member directorate of the FSLN that had created them. The directorate had direct control of the Sandinista armed forces and police. Although it had promised elections, the directorate soon found itself at war because of CIA-organized efforts to overthrow the Sandinista regime, which delayed elections until 1984.

Economic problems dominated the new government's agenda. One immediate goal was to repair the ravages of the war and the 1972 earthquake, a task mainly entrusted to the municipalities and the Sandinist Defense Committees. This occurred with such speed that visitors to Nicaragua in the fall of 1979 marveled at the relatively normal appearance of the country. Food shortages were another serious problem and required the importation of great quantities of foodstuffs, mostly financed with foreign donations. Meanwhile, Sandinistas planted emergency food crops so domestic supplies of food would be available by the middle of 1980. The work of repair combined with food-for-work schemes to provide a temporary solution for the vast unemployment that was a legacy of the war.

What to do about the national debt was a vexing question for the new government, for it knew well that many of the more recent loans had served only to swell the bank accounts of Somoza and his cronies. Nonetheless, it agreed to pay all the loans, even the corrupt ones, for both economic and political reasons. The Sandinistas wanted to retain access to Western loans and technology; they also wished to disprove the charge that the new Nicaragua was a Soviet or Cuban "puppet," solely dependent on the socialist bloc for economic and political support. The socialist countries, particularly the Soviet Union and Cuba, in fact did give considerable aid in the form of food shipments and other supplies. Cuba also sent large numbers of teachers and doctors to assist in the work of reconstruction.

The international lending agencies and Western governments hoped financial aid to Nicaragua would enable the country's private sector to survive and keep the economy pluralistic. The principal difficulty in renegotiation arose with the United States. The Carter administration agreed to make a new loan of $75 million, chiefly for aid to the private sector. When Ronald Reagan came to the presidency, however, he froze the remaining $15 million of the loan, alleging without evidence that Nicaragua had sent arms to rebels in El Salvador. Thereafter, Nicaragua had to rely for aid on the socialist countries, friendly social democratic governments of Western Europe, and developing countries, including Brazil.

Although some Sandinista leaders viewed socialism as a more or less distant goal, the regime pursued a mixed-economy strategy of national development and recognized that private enterprise had a vital role to play in the country's economic reconstruction. However, the state became the most decisive and dynamic element in the economy, providing social services, particularly health, education, and housing. The state sector also grew because of the nationalization of extensive Somocista properties, which became the basis of the People's Property Area, including half the large farms greater than 500 hectares, a quarter of all industry, large construction firms, hotels, real estate, an airline, a fishing fleet, and more. The expropriation of Somocista holdings placed approximately 40 percent of the **gross national product (GNP)** (the total annual value of goods and services) in the state's hands. The Sandinistas also nationalized the banking system and foreign trade.

These expropriations, however, left 60 percent of the GNP in the hands of the Nicaraguan capitalist class, which continued to control 80 percent of agricultural production and 75 percent of manufacturing. Thus, the country remained capitalist, with the state sector no larger than that of France, Mexico, and Peru in the 1970s. The Sandinista government's policy was to avoid radical changes that might cause a rupture with the

"patriotic bourgeoisie," the results of which would be disastrous for the economy. Accordingly, it courted and maintained an alliance with some of the country's largest entrepreneurs. At the same time, the government insisted on safeguards with respect to working conditions, wages, hours, and the like that would at least modestly improve the life of Nicaraguan workers. It also encouraged trade unions to monitor privately owned factories to prevent decapitalization, slowdowns in production, and other sabotage by capitalists hostile to the revolution. The result was a built-in tension between the government and a section of the business class. Partly because of this tension and partly because of objective conditions—lack of foreign exchange to buy inputs, obsolete machinery, and other problems—private businessmen began dropping out of manufacturing or failing to invest.

The growth of the public sector was most marked in agriculture. By the end of 1979, the *Instituto de Reforma Agraria* (INRA) had confiscated without compensation all Somocista lands, which, in the words of political scientist Forrest D. Colburn, were "almost universally held to be little more than stolen property." The government proposed to maintain the integrity of these estates, which accounted for one-fifth of Nicaragua's cultivable land, rather than to divide them into small parcels. Most of these lands were large farms that had operated as capital-intensive enterprises, so parcelization would have resulted in heavy production losses. Consequently, many of these private estates became state farms. Others became production cooperatives, called Sandinist agricultural communes. In late 1980, about 1,327 of these cooperatives were in operation. INRA simultaneously tried to improve the living conditions of state-sector workers through the establishment of clinics, schools, and housing projects. In 1980, more than fifty thousand workers worked full time in the state sector.

Although the government favored state farms and production cooperatives as basic agricultural units, it did not neglect small independent farmers. Agricultural credit for small producers greatly expanded, and the Sandinistas encouraged them to form credit and service cooperatives. In 1979–1980,

1,200 of these co-ops received more than 50 percent of the agricultural credit extended by the government in the same period. Even after the confiscation of Somocista estates, large commercial farms producing such crops as cotton, coffee, cattle, and sugar still held 66.5 percent of Nicaragua's cultivable land. The relationship between this private agricultural sector and the revolutionary government was an uneasy one. Most of the large landowners despised the Somozas, resented their hoggish propensities, and welcomed their overthrow. However, the rules of the game had changed, and the new rules were not always to their liking. Landowners no longer could mistreat their workers; they had to comply with reform legislation defining the rights of tenants and workers.

Despite the government's assurances that it wanted to preserve a private sector, large landowners were understandably nervous about their future. The commercial farmers and cattle ranchers defended their interests through their own associations, which negotiated with the government over prices, acreage quotas, and the like. The commercial farmers had access to credit at low interest rates, and the Sandinistas established a coffee stabilization fund to protect growers against fluctuations in the world market. This economically important sector accounted for 62 percent of cotton production and 55 percent of coffee production in 1979–1980.

The difficulties of Nicaraguan agriculture were not primarily due to inadequate volume of production but rather stemmed above all from falling world prices for its major export crops. Sugar, which sold for $0.24 a pound in 1981, sold for $0.09 in 1983. Natural disasters also hurt production of staple foods in 1982. In May, flooding wiped out twenty thousand acres of just-planted basic grain crops, destroyed $3.6 million in stored grains, and caused $350 million in damage to the national economic infrastructure, according to a U.N. survey. A drought in July and August caused estimated losses of $47 million. Finally, the CIA greatly increased the scale of its counterrevolutionary activity that had begun in 1981, which forced the Sandinista government to divert workers and resources to military purposes. This caused serious

damage to Nicaraguan agriculture and to the economy in general—a major aim of the U.S. destabilization program.

The implacable pressure of the Reagan administration on Nicaragua represented a threat to its economy and to the revolutionary government's existence. Reagan authorized formation of a paramilitary force of ex-National Guardsmen, with an acknowledged budget of $19 million. In a move recalling the 1954 coup against Guatemala, Honduras became a staging area for Nicaraguan operations. Beginning in 1981, Argentine and U.S. advisers trained the Somocistas (familiarly called the **contras** by both sides) and helped them make terrorist raids into Nicaragua, killing hundreds of Nicaraguan soldiers and civilians and destroying bridges, construction equipment, clinics, and agricultural cooperatives.

The "secret war" against Nicaragua escalated when Ambassador John Negroponte arrived in Honduras in 1982 to mastermind the operation. The CIA station in Honduras grew to an admitted fifty employees, plus a large number of secret agents, including many Vietnam veterans who were now mercenaries under contract to the CIA. To secure the Honduran military's cooperation in this secret war, U.S. military aid to Honduras, less than $2 million in 1980, grew to $10 million in 1981, and may have reached as high as $144 million in 1982–1983, with some of it coming from a hidden budget.

In March 1983, the operation moved into high gear when several thousand Somocistas and other mercenaries, supported by Honduran troops, invaded Nicaragua at several points on its northern border with Honduras. Simultaneously, in a gesture of "gunboat diplomacy," several U.S. warships sailed to Nicaragua's Pacific coast, ostensibly to monitor suspected movements of arms from Nicaragua to rebels in El Salvador. By the end of March, despite claims of victory from the invaders' radio, the Nicaraguan armed forces and militia had crushed the counterrevolutionary attacks, although the contras continued to make raids, mostly of the hit-and-run variety.

Under the hardest conditions, Nicaragua's Sandinista leadership continued its difficult struggle to stabilize the economy, expand social reforms, re-place the revolutionary government with a parliamentary democracy, and solve long-standing problems like the demand for autonomy from the Miskito and Sumo peoples of Nicaragua's Atlantic coast. In the same period, the United States intensified its secret war against Nicaragua, provided the contras with supplies and logistical support, mined Nicaraguan harbors, and even issued a manual for use within Nicaragua instructing the contras in terrorist methods—including the liquidation of government officials and progovernment activists. The secret war flouted U.S. laws, treaty obligations, and international law. In June 1986, the World Court, acting on a complaint by Nicaragua, ordered the United States to halt all its military and paramilitary actions against Nicaragua, but the Reagan administration, refusing to accept the court's jurisdiction, disregarded this order.

Despite hundreds of millions of dollars' worth of U.S. financial and military aid to the contras, in early 1986, Nicaraguan President Daniel Ortega celebrated the rebels' "strategic defeat." A major factor in this victory, despite stepped-up U.S. aid, was growing Sandinista military effectiveness and superior morale. But the Reagan administration had not sought a contra military victory. The administration's aid to the contras aimed to sustain a "low-intensity conflict" designed to wear down the Nicaraguan government and disrupt its economy. It sought to create hardships that forced the Sandinistas to divert precious resources from social programs to its army, undermined the regime's popular support, and thereby eventually produced an internal collapse.

The war contributed to a sharp decline in the Nicaraguan economy between 1983 and 1990. The GDP fell by 30 percent in 1985 alone and continued to fall until the secret war ended; inflation reached an annual rate of 10,000 percent in 1988; and severe shortages of goods of every kind prevailed. However, the war was not the sole factor responsible for the economic decline. Other causes included deterioration in the terms of trade for Nicaragua's exports; the U.S. trade embargo of May 1985, which isolated Nicaragua from its traditional export market and from a source of goods and technology difficult to replace; and the unwillingness of some private sector interests to invest in the expansion of Nicaragua's production.

The Nicaraguan government responded to the economic crisis with measures to stimulate production by increasing prices paid for basic grains and other staples, while protecting the real value of salaries and wages by periodic adjustments to compensate for inflation. It expanded trade with the European Economic Community and the socialist bloc to compensate for the loss of the U.S. market. Last, it redesigned the agrarian reform to make more land available to individual peasants to stimulate production of basic grains.

In 1979, the Sandinistas had promised to hold elections by 1985, but the need to refute U.S. charges that their regime was undemocratic and illegitimate led to an acceleration of the timetable. In November 1984, Nicaraguans went to the polls to vote for a president, a vice president, and a ninety-member national assembly that would draft the country's constitution. Opposition poll watchers and a large number of foreign observers, including a task force of the Latin American Studies Association (LASA), the major organization of Latin American scholars in the United States, found no evidence of irregularities in the voting or the vote-counting process. The Sandinista Front received 67 percent of the vote, the rest going to opposition parties. In January 1985, Daniel Ortega Saavedra and Sergio Ramírez Mercado took office as president and vice president, respectively.

The new constitution, adopted after intense democratic discussion and debate at mass meetings throughout the country and in the national assembly, established as its guiding principles political pluralism, a mixed economy, and nonalignment, and it divided power among the executive, legislative, judicial, and electoral branches. It guaranteed individual and social rights, including the rights to a job, education, and health care; free expression of opinion and association; the right to strike; and the right to a fair trial. The constitution also sought a definitive solution for the troubled relations between the central government and the indigenous peoples of the Atlantic coast.

SELF-DETERMINATION FOR ATLANTIC COAST PEOPLES

The Sandinistas inherited a long history of state neglect of coastal peoples, who consequently distrusted government. The Sandinistas acknowledged that they had made serious errors in their effort to integrate indigenous peoples into the revolution because the government failed to take account of their unique culture and traditions. Complicating matters, Reagan and his contra surrogates exploited Sandinista errors and misunderstandings to draw Atlantic coast peoples to the side of counterrevolution.

In 1981, the Nicaraguan government, to prevent their use as a contra military base, forcibly evacuated thousands of Miskitos and Sumos from ancestral lands along the Coco River, destroyed their villages, and resettled the refugees in camps away from the threatened coastal area. Although the camps provided them with improved health care, food subsidies, education, and improved housing and electricity, they remained strongly attached to their village lands and viewed the camps as prisons. As a result, several antigovernment native-based guerrilla groups arose on the Atlantic coast. U.S. efforts to pressure the Miskitos into an alliance with the major contra groups, as a condition of military and financial aid, also produced splits that the Sandinistas exploited to negotiate cease-fire agreements with individual indigenous commanders.

Two major Nicaraguan government initiatives paved the way for a solution of the Atlantic coast problem. First, in 1984, the government created a commission to define an autonomous status for the Atlantic coast peoples under the new constitution. The ensuing dialogue led to a compromise that recognized the right of the Atlantic coast peoples to autonomy and guaranteed the preservation of their languages, religions, cultures, and social organization. They would elect their own representatives to the national Congress and use their resources to satisfy their own needs, as determined by a regional assembly. Second, in 1985, Interior Minister Tomás Borge announced that the Miskitos living in relocation camps could return to the Coco River area.

WOMEN AND THE REVOLUTION

Women also gained appreciably from the revolution, in which they had played a large role militarily, economically, and politically. Making up one-third of all combatants, many women had joined the guerrilla army; others had organized all-women battalions like the Juana Elena Mendoza Infantry Company; and some, like Doris Tijerino and Dora María Téllez, had become respected field commanders. Although their participation in the regular army after 1979 declined to about 20 percent, women were especially active both in local civil defense committees and in the popular militias, where they made up 60 percent of urban contingents.

Most women always had worked both inside and outside the home, but before the revolution, their waged labor (estimated at 48 percent of the labor force) had tended to be relatively invisible and greatly undervalued, concentrated in the informal sector and domestic service. After the revolution, labor legislation guaranteed equal pay for equal work, paid maternity leave, and provided legal protections against the dismissal of pregnant women. Private employers frequently ignored these laws, and the revolutionary government, because of the contra war, often lacked the necessary financial resources to enforce them. Nevertheless, these laws, instead of providing traditional protections to employers, now placed the state on the side of women, their trade unions, and mass organizations like the Nicaraguan Women's Association (AMNLAE).

Moreover, as the state sector of the economy grew and an escalating contra war absorbed more men, women's waged employment expanded: In 1985, women accounted for 50 percent of state employees, 70 percent of coffee harvesters, and 70 percent of textile workers. This naturally raised the issue of the inequitable "double workday," wherein women, in addition to laboring eight hours in the factory or field, worked nine to twelve hours at home, whereas their husbands worked less than an hour at household chores. To remedy this injustice, the Sandinistas encouraged men to assume their fair share of domestic responsibilities and, by 1988, also funded daycare centers—182 at urban workplaces and 69 on state farms. Once again, however, wartime fiscal demands sabotaged this initiative.

Women made up nearly two-thirds of the *brigadistas* (volunteers) who participated in the Sandinista literacy crusade that between 1979 and 1980 reduced illiteracy from 50 to 12 percent. Thereafter, Popular Education Collectives (CEPs) allowed mostly rural people to select local teachers whose instruction would further develop literacy skills; 95 percent of these teachers were women. Free, universal education for adults and children six to twelve years of age was the Sandinista Revolution's commitment; before 1985, it built nearly four thousand new classrooms, and the number of primary school teachers, again mostly women, tripled. Here again, however, the contra war intervened; by the late 1980s, fewer resources were available for education, and illiteracy rates climbed to 23 percent.

Politically, the revolution facilitated women's participation in the leadership of the FSLN Party, the national government, and grassroots organizations. In the 1984 and 1990 parliamentary elections, women accounted for almost 20 percent of the FSLN candidates and almost 22 percent of those Sandinistas elected to the legislature. In 1994, the party decided to allot 30 percent of leadership positions to women, who also made up 34 and 43 percent, respectively, of their department and national legislative candidates in the 1996 elections. By decade's end, almost one-third of FSLN legislators were women.

By 1990, prolonged popular war and revolution had produced some startling achievements in the Sandinista effort to reorganize Nicaraguan society and promote a more egalitarian national development, but there remained powerful opponents, domestic and foreign. Moreover, a decade of U.S. intervention had destroyed Nicaragua's economy, fractured its fragile political alliances, and destabilized the social order. U.S. intervention had a similar impact on the revolutionary movement in El Salvador.

El Salvador

The history of El Salvador, the smallest and most densely populated country in Central America,

presents in exaggerated form all the region's economic and social problems. It suffered from extreme dependence on a single crop, making the economy vulnerable to fluctuations in price and global market demand; a marked concentration of land and wealth in a few hands; and intolerable exploitation of the peasantry, accompanied by ferocious repression of all protest or revolt.

THE POPULIST FLIRTATION

Ironically, however, the early twentieth century bore witness to considerably more political freedoms, at least among the landed aristocracy. Although nineteenth-century liberal reforms had promoted a concentration of land ownership in El Salvador, the coffee oligarchs, largely orchestrated by the Meléndez and Quiñónez families, had developed a political consensus that allowed them to deploy various weapons of social control. Moreover, before World War I, the demand for coffee had not appreciably affected the nation's labor markets, and *finqueros* (oligarchical owners of coffee plantation) still relied on a healthy supply of migrant and resident workers. Consequently, in addition to the National Guard's usual repressive violence, the Salvadoran elite also created mass-based political organizations like the Liga Roja to co-opt and contain urban middle-class peasant and working-class challenges to its power.

Driven by a postwar prosperity, however, coffee markets expanded by 50 percent during the 1920s. The coffee oligarchs responded, both by dedicating more acreage to coffee and by securing new supplies of labor. This deprived more peasants of their traditional milpas, the subsistence plots that were the bedrock of peasant survival and transformed them into full-fledged proletarians: propertyless people whose survival depended exclusively on the sale of their labor.

The economic and social problems generated by the coffee monoculture became more acute with the advent of the Great Depression in 1929. Campesinos who made $0.50 a day before the Depression saw their wages fall to $0.20 a day. The price of coffee was cut in half between July 1929 and the end of the year, ruining many small producers and forcing them to sell their lands. High unemployment and below-subsistence-level wages added to the discontent caused by harsh treatment by overseers and frauds practiced by company stores.

Even before the depression, the National Guard had busily suppressed peasant revolts, but in the 1920s urban workers and some peasants had begun to form unions. In 1925, a small Communist Party operated underground; its leader, Agustín Farabundo Martí, had studied Marxism at the national university. Expelled from El Salvador in 1927 for his radical activities, Martí joined Augusto César Sandino in his fight against the U.S. Marines in Nicaragua. Martí returned to El Salvador in 1930 and again plunged into political activity. Aided by a small group, mostly university students, he carried out propaganda and organizational activities among peasants in the central and western parts of the country.

Against this background of depression and growing radicalism, perhaps the first free presidential election in Salvadoran history occurred. The winner was the wealthy landowner and civil engineer Arturo Araujo, whose admiration for the British Labour Party led him to conclude that an enduring social peace required class harmony and modest populist reforms, like improving education, defending the rights of women and workers, and promoting limited land redistribution. His election caused much disquiet among the coffee planters and the military. The new president immediately ran into storms: Teachers and other public servants clamored for back pay, and peasants demanded land and other reforms, while the coffee oligarchy and the military pressed him to make no concessions.

On December 21, 1931, a military coup ousted Araujo and installed Gen. Maximiliano Hernández Martínez as president. The coup signified the end of direct rule by the oligarchy and the beginning of a long era of military domination. The fall of Araujo and the rise of Hernández Martínez to power closed the door to popular participation in politics. Convinced that the new regime did not intend to allow reforms or free elections, Martí and other radical leaders decided on insurrection. They planned simultaneous uprisings for several towns on January 22, 1932, but the authorities got wind of the plot and arrested Martí and two of his aides. Other rebel leaders then tried to call off the revolt, but communications had broken down, and the largely indigenous revolt began without its ladino leadership.

In town after town, these campesinos rose up, often armed only with machetes. Having taken over much of the western area of the country, they attacked the regional center of Sonsonate. Here, the cacique José Feliciano Ama led a revolt that fused long-standing class, racial, and ethnic grievances. The unequal combat between peasants armed with machetes and the garrison, supported by the Guard and other police units, all armed with modern weapons, ended in total defeat for the insurgents. In a few days, the Guard retook the captured towns. Then the oligarchy took its revenge, relentlessly hunting down the "communists"—that is, any peasant whom landowners refused to protect. As many as thirty thousand peasants died in this *matanza* (massacre), which verged on genocide by wiping out indigenous dress, languages, and cultural traditions. Ferocious repression was the coffee oligarchy's way to teach the peasantry a lesson and ensure social stability. The history of El Salvador since 1932 revealed just how vain that expectation was.

OLIGARCHS AND GENERALS, 1932–1979

The coup that installed Hernández Martínez in the presidency marked a turning point in modern Salvadoran history. Terrified by the peasant uprising of 1932, the oligarchy struck a bargain that allowed the military to hold the reins of government while the oligarchy directed the country's economic life. A network of corruption that permitted the officer class to share in the oligarchy's wealth cemented their alliance. Nevertheless, the persistence of reformist tendencies among junior officers and a growing faction of agroindustrialists involved in the coffee-processing industry periodically produced tensions that threatened the alliance.

Hernández Martínez, known as *El Brujo* (the Witch Doctor) because of his dabbling in the occult, maintained a tight rule over the country through his control of the army and the National Guard until 1944. In addition, power and access to wealth were concentrated in a clique of Hernández Martínez's cronies. This created discontent among junior officers, who allied with agroindustrialists and urban professionals, inspired by wartime rhetoric about democracy, to overthrow Martínez and demand political reform, women's suffrage, economic modernization, and agricultural diversification. This populist "Revolution of 1948," championed by Col. Oscar Osorio, inaugurated a decade of import-substitution industrialization, expanded cotton cultivation, and greater export dependency, all under the watchful eye of the military and its oligarchical allies. Then, in 1961, alienated by the civilian-military junta's increasingly progressive program, its mobilization of popular sectors, and its friendly relations with Cuba, Col. Julio Alberto Rivera joined with the U.S. embassy to organize an "anticommunist" coup d'état that restored the military's monopoly of power.

Rivera established a system patterned on the Mexican idea of a single dominant party that would perpetuate itself in power by holding elections every five years and employing fraud, coercion, and co-optation to maintain control. This allowed a number of opposition parties to exist. The most important were the PDC, headed by José Napoleon Duarte, mayor of San Salvador from 1964 to 1970; the Social Democratic Party, *Movimiento Nacional Revolucionario* (MNR), led by Guillermo Manuel Ungo; and the *Unión Democrática Nacionalista* (UDN), a front for the Communist Party, which had been illegal since 1932.

As the economic difficulties of the country multiplied during the 1960s and 1970s, however, the strains within the system grew, and it became increasingly unworkable. The roots of the problem lay in the monoculture that made the country dependent on a world market over which it had no control and a system of land tenure and use that progressively reduced the land area available to small landowners and staple food production.

Land monopoly and the prevailing system of land use led to population pressure on land, a problem greatly aggravated by the population explosion.

Thanks to the eradication of yellow fever and malaria and to the successes of preventive medicine, the population shot up from 1,443,000 in 1930 to 2,500,000 in 1961 and 3,549,000 in 1969. By 1970, the population density was about four hundred per square mile. The swelling population put great pressure on wage levels: The average daily wage for a field hand in the early 1960s was about $0.62 a day, for an overseer or *mayordomo*, a little over $1.00 a day. Because labor on coffee plantations was seasonal and a peon was lucky to get one hundred and fifty days of work a year, the labor of an entire family for that period might yield a total yearly cash income of $300.

With land reform ruled out as a solution for land hunger and population pressure, Rivera attempted another remedy: industrialization and economic integration through the creation of the Central American Common Market (CACM) in 1961. He expected that unrestricted flow of goods and capital throughout the area would stimulate an expansion of markets and industrialization, relieving population pressure and unemployment. Unfortunately, this industrial expansion took place without a corresponding growth in employment, for the new industries were capital intensive and required relatively few workers. Moreover, foreigners owned much of the new industry, which catered to export markets and largely involved the assembly of imported components.

The problem of population pressure on the land grew much more acute because of the "Soccer War," which took several thousand lives and left at least one hundred thousand Salvadorans homeless. The war followed a series of hotly contested games between Honduras and El Salvador in the qualifying rounds of the 1970 World Cup. Its causes, however, included a long-standing border dispute and Honduran resentment over the marked imbalance of trade between the two countries that resulted from CACM's operations. Honduras, an extremely underdeveloped country whose economy largely depended on bananas, lumber, and cattle, felt that it subsidized the industrial development of El Salvador. The third and decisive cause of the war was the presence in Honduras of some three hundred thousand illegal Salvadoran settlers. Following adoption of an agrarian reform law, Honduras had ordered the expulsion of some eighty thousand settlers. El Salvador retaliated by invading Honduras. The war, which was popular in El Salvador, nonetheless negatively affected the country. El Salvador lost the Honduran market for its manufacturers for more than a decade, and the return of Salvadorans from Honduras swelled the number of landless and homeless peasants.

These developments contributed to the growing economic and social crises of the 1970s. Population growth continued to outstrip the food supply; among the Latin American countries, only Haiti's people had a lower caloric intake than El Salvador's. By the early 1970s, unemployment was 20 percent and underemployment was 40 percent; in 1974, the annual inflation rate reached 60 percent. The proportion of landless peasantry rose from 11.8 percent in 1950 to 41 percent in 1975. The calamitous economic situation gave opposition parties hope for victory in the 1972 presidential election, prompting the PDC, the MNR, and the Communist UDN to form a united front: the *Unión Nacional Opositora* (UNO). Its presidential candidate, José Napoleón Duarte, clearly won the election, but the electoral commission fraudulently announced a victory for the military candidate, Col. Arturo Molina.

The military and the agrarian wing of the coffee oligarchy had become impatient with the agroindustrialists and their modest reform agenda, which, despite their protests to the contrary, never seemed to pacify the nation but instead merely provided political space for popular sector mobilization. As a result, the Molina regime increasingly relied on repression to preserve order. In 1975, hoping to promote the emerging tourist industry, Molina hosted the 1975 "Miss Universe" pageant and spent about $30 million on the show. In a country with so many unfilled social needs, this impressed many Salvadorans as a scandalous extravagance and they protested. Units of the National Guard—without any provocation—fired on them, killing at least thirty-seven people, while many others "disappeared." The massacre was part of a pattern of growing violence. With increasing frequency, guerrilla organizations proliferated, kidnapping members of the oligarchy for ransom. In the countryside, the National Guard, aided by paramilitary organizations like ORDEN (*Organización Democrática Nacionalista*), conducted sweeps against "subversive" peasants, surrounding and destroying villages, killing many villagers, and abducting others who eventually "disappeared."

After another fraudulent election in 1977 ended all hope of reform via the electoral process, the spiral of violence marked the opening of a pre-revolutionary stage of Salvadoran political development. Revolutionary organizations mobilized their forces and attempted to overcome their ideological and tactical differences. They robbed banks, seized radio stations to broadcast propaganda, kidnapped oligarchs for ransom, and assassinated persons identified with official or unofficial repression. Labor and peasant unions grew rapidly along with other mass movements, known collectively as *Fuerzas Populares* (Popular Forces), and umbrella organizations, such as the Front for United Popular Action (FAPU), which organized many groups for joint action against the government. Meanwhile, the National Guard, the National Police, and other security forces, as well as death squads and terrorist organizations like ORDEN and the White Warrior Union, continued their repressive activities.

A major development of this period was the changing posture of the Catholic Church toward the Salvadoran crisis. Before the Second Vatican Council (1962) and the Medellín Bishops' Conference, the church in El Salvador—as elsewhere in Latin America—had supported the regime and the oligarchy. Although most of the hierarchy continued that tradition, Archbishop Luis Chávez y González and his successor Oscar Romero embraced the teachings of Vatican II and Medellín, committing themselves to what Romero called "the preferential option for the poor." One result of this ferment in the church was the formation in a few short years of hundreds of *comunidades de base*, which combined Bible study with attention to the economic and social problems of their localities. The messages the priests brought to their parishioners was that

God is "a God of justice and love who acts on the side of the poor and oppressed" and that the people "have a basic human right to organize in order to begin taking control of their own lives."

Their social activism inevitably marked the priests as targets for security forces and paramilitary death squads like the White Warrior Union, which murdered the Jesuit priest Rutilio Grande in March 1977. A few months later, leaflets circulated around San Salvador, urging Salvadorans to "Be a Patriot! Kill a Priest!" Altogether, between 1977 and 1979, death squads or security forces killed seven priests. Father Grande's death, three weeks after Romero became archbishop, contributed to what the archbishop referred to as his "transformation." Thereafter, Romero used his position to denounce the regime's human rights violations and to plead for social justice. His sermons, transmitted via radio to almost every part of the country, "became the single most-listened-to program in the nation."

The church also helped organize human rights groups like COMADRES (mothers of the imprisoned, assassinated, or "disappeared"). Created in 1977, COMADRES courageously protested against the repression with public demonstrations, hunger strikes, and sit-ins at government buildings. According to a founding member, Alicia, their attire symbolized their objectives: a black dress to mourn the dead, a white scarf to celebrate "peace with justice, not … impunity," a red carnation to recall the bloody dictatorship, and its green leaves to represent "the hope for life." In response, military and paramilitary forces bombed their offices five times, threatened to "decapitate" them, and kidnapped, tortured, and raped more than forty members.

As the crisis deepened month after month, divisions began to appear within the military. A group of reformist junior military watched with profound anxiety the revolutionary course of events in Nicaragua in July and August 1979; they became convinced that a reformist coup offered the only alternative to revolution. After regular consultations with Archbishop Romero, representatives of the PDC, and the U.S. embassy, which indicated it would not oppose such an action, the coup took place on October 15 with virtually no resistance

from any garrison. A military-civilian junta, including two moderates, Román Mayorga Quiroz, rector of the Central American University, and the Social Democrat Guillermo Ungo, and two military representatives, Col. Adolfo Majano and Col. Jaime Abdul Gutiérrez, now governed the nation. The junta's program called for dissolution of the terrorist ORDEN organization, respect for human rights, agrarian reform, freedom for the Popular Forces to operate, and improved relations with revolutionary Nicaragua.

However, the October 15 coup did not end repression by the security forces, which killed more people in the three weeks after the coup than in any similar prior period. Efforts by civilian junta members Mayorga and Ungo to restrain the official violence were totally ineffective. As a result, they resigned in protest, and the military joined the PDC in a secret deal to create a new government. With two Christian Democrats replacing Mayorga and Ungo, the military committed itself to a limited program of agrarian reform, nationalization of banks, a cessation of all repression, and dialogue with the Popular Forces. Barely one week after accepting these conditions, however, security forces fired on a massive demonstration of the Popular Forces, the largest in Salvadoran history, killing about twenty persons. This and similar repressive acts demonstrated the military's bad faith and caused a split in the PDC.

Typical of its strategy of reform and repression, the junta announced a state of siege on the same day that it promulgated an agrarian reform that largely resulted from intense pressure by the United States. Eager to give a reformist face to its protégé, the U.S. chargé d'affaires advised the junta to conduct a "clean counterinsurgency war." The plan was to implement agrarian reform in three stages. Phase I called for nationalization of 376 estates larger than five hundred hectares, belonging to 244 owners and consisting largely of pasture and cotton land. The owners received thirty-year bonds as compensation, and the estates became cooperatives with 29,755 peasant members. Just three years later, however, only twenty-two cooperatives had received final title, although 130 previous owners

Many women, like the Salvadoran guerrilla shown here, took part in recent Central American revolutionary struggles, and some held high positions in the guerrilla commands.

had received their compensation. According to the *Central America Report*, Phase II, which would have affected about two hundred farms of one hundred to five hundred hectares, including most of the coffee fincas, "died before it was born."

Phase III, called "Land to the Tiller," allowed peasants who rented up to forty-two hectares of land to buy it from the owner. Three years later, there were only 58,152 applications, roughly half the number eligible under Phase III provisions. Moreover, the junta issued only 1,050 permanent titles. The Salvadoran Peasants' Union charged that even this limited achievement resulted from the need to provide the U.S. Congress with evidence that El Salvador had made progress in essential economic reform to secure continued economic and military aid.

This curious land reform accompanied a wave of repression directed above all against the peasantry. The junta assigned responsibility for land redistribution to the army and the security forces, which used their authority to favor members of the terrorist ORDEN organization in exchange

for their help in targeting peasants who belonged to the Popular Forces or to the guerrilla movements. Sometimes they collaborated with landowners to evict tenants from lands they had recently acquired under land reform provisions.

In December 1981, the Peasants' Union reported that the "failure of the agrarian reform is an immediate and imminent danger." The union claimed that ex-landlords and their allies, including members of the local security forces, murdered at least ninety of its officials and "a large number of beneficiaries" of the agrarian reform. The report also charged that landowners had evicted twenty-five thousand former *aparceros* (sharecroppers) from their plots before they could obtain provisional titles. The junta's inability to carry out the agrarian reform or to check the terror in the countryside showed that it merely provided, in the words of political scientist William LeoGrande, "a civilian façade" for a military dictatorship.

The most prominent victim of the terror that accompanied the agrarian reform was Monsignor

Oscar Romero, archbishop of San Salvador. For years, his attacks on the military and the security forces for their violations of human rights had been a thorn in the government's side. Increasingly disillusioned with the PDC's role in the junta, he gradually moved toward supporting armed struggle as the only remaining resort. In a sermon on February 2, 1980, he proclaimed, "When all peaceful means have been exhausted, the church considers insurrection moral and justified." On March 23, responding to the repression that accompanied the land reform, he appealed to soldiers not to turn their guns on unarmed civilians. The next day, as he celebrated mass in a chapel in San Salvador, an unknown assassin, probably a military officer, gunned him down. Romero's martyrdom had profound political and military repercussions.

THE SALVADORAN REVOLUTION, 1980–1992

"If I am killed," Archbishop Romero had prophesied shortly before his death, "I shall rise again in the struggle of the Salvadoran people." His death served as a powerful catalyst for the growth of that struggle. In particular, it hastened the breakup of the PDC and the unification of its opposition. In April 1980, a broad coalition of political parties, professional associations, trade unions, and revolutionary groups formed the Democratic Revolutionary Front (FDR), which soon set up a government-in-exile, headed by the Social Democratic leader Guillermo Ungo.

By midsummer of 1980, the five major guerrilla groups also united in a single command under the name *Frente Farabundo Martí de Liberación Nacional* (FMLN), in honor of the leader of the abortive 1932 revolt. In January 1981, the FMLN launched its first general offensive and achieved significant successes, capturing M-16s from U.S.-equipped government soldiers. Within a few months, the rebels captured six hundred fifty firearms, including mortars and heavy machine guns, and about eighty thousand rounds of ammunition. By the spring of 1983, they had considerably expanded the zones of their control. They dominated areas inhabited by some two hundred thousand

people and governed through a system called the *Poder Popular Local* (PPL).

To combat rebel successes, the military leadership changed and pursued a more aggressive strategy that relied on increased military aid from the Reagan administration, but this required it to improve the regime's image, holding elections to legitimize it with a "democratic" face. The elections, it was assumed, would give victory to the PDC and its leader, José Napoleón Duarte, who would preside over a modest reform program to win "hearts and minds" for the government. These reforms, combined with expanded military aid, aimed to accelerate pacification of the country.

In compliance with U.S. wishes, elections for a sixty-member Constituent Assembly occurred in March 1982. However, the FDR and guerrillas, insisting that fair elections were impossible under existing conditions, boycotted them. Less than a year earlier, gunmen had assassinated the FDR's entire leadership. If the government could not guarantee the security of political leaders, it certainly could not protect grassroots campaign workers. As a result, oligarchical parties dominated these "demonstration elections," organized for the benefit of the U.S. government on which the Salvadoran military depended.

In any event, the electoral outcome did not conform to the Reagan administration's expectations. With only 35 percent of the vote, Duarte and the Christian Democrats proved unable to form a majority government. The Nationalist Republic Alliance (ARENA) of Roberto D'Aubuisson, the terrorist who orchestrated Romero's murder, garnered one-fourth of the vote and pressed for a coalition that excluded the Christian Democrats. Thus, the elections appeared to legitimize D'Aubuisson and ARENA even as they imperiled U.S. congressional support for the military. Undaunted, however, Reagan pressured all parties to sign a pact for cooperation in the transition to a new constitutional government. As part of the deal, the U.S.-supported "moderate" banker Álvaro Magaña became provisional president, limiting D'Aubuisson to leadership of the Constituent Assembly.

The Reagan administration's policy in El Salvador had one overriding purpose: to prevent, at all costs, the FMLN-FDR from coming to power. To ensure congressional support for the large infusions of military and economic aid needed to achieve this objective, the Reagan administration again strongly supported Duarte's 1984 presidential candidacy. At the same time, however, Washington demanded a more aggressive war against the rebels, which strengthened the Salvadoran military. With massive use of air power and large-scale sweeps into rebel territory, the armed forces attacked the civilian population to isolate the insurgents, thereby denying them the material and logistical support they needed to survive.

Soon it became evident that Duarte lacked the power, the resources, and perhaps the will to carry out his promises of social and economic reform. He presided over a moribund economy that survived only because of the immense largesse of the United States, which lavished $2.7 billion in military and economic aid on El Salvador. Nonetheless, his political rhetoric had encouraged the labor movement to organize, call strikes, and engage in political activity even as paramilitary forces responded with more repression, including a revival of death-squad killings and disappearances. Duarte simply could not satisfy labor's economic and social demands over the opposition of the oligarchy, the army, and even the Reagan administration. On the other hand, he could not openly support repression without alienating the U.S. Congress and losing his base in the Salvadoran labor movement. Duarte solved his dilemma by denouncing repression in words, while sanctioning it in practice.

In 1986, the Duarte government announced an economic austerity program to help pay the costs of the war against the FMLN-FDR. The program included a 100 percent devaluation of the currency, steep taxes on basic goods and services, large increases in fuel prices, and reductions in already minimal social services, all measures that hit workers the hardest. In response, thousands of angry workers abandoned Christian Democratic trade unions to join a newly organized labor federation, the National Union of Salvadoran Workers (UNTS) and

participated in an avalanche of strikes that ominously linked economic demands to calls for a negotiated end to the civil war. Archbishop Arturo Rivera y Damas, head of the Salvadoran church, strongly supported these demands, and Duarte's labor base virtually collapsed. But the Reaganites still sought a military victory, and a massive influx of new U.S. military aid, including gunships and helicopters, undoubtedly changed the balance of forces in the civil war. U.S. reconnaissance flights from Honduras and the Panama Canal Zone helped pinpoint rebel columns and command posts, using infrared tracking systems. Unable to compete with the army in numbers and firepower, the FMLN developed a new strategy. The large battalion-size units broke up into small units of classic guerrilla warfare, evaded the army's sweeps, and returned after the army had left. The rebels, however, were still capable of launching major surprise attacks.

Believing a military triumph unlikely, the FMLN now aimed to mobilize trade unions, a growing antiwar movement, and other popular forces to create conditions for a "negotiated peace." However, success also required a separation of the two oligarchical factions, the hardline coffee planters, or "agrarians," and the moderate coffee processors, or "agroindustrialists," whose unstable marriage had contributed to the government's historical oscillation between repression and reform. The FMLN sought to encourage negotiations by making the war too expensive for the agroindustrialists, led by Alfredo Cristiani, a wealthy coffee processor and past president of their trade association, ABECAFE. U.S. sources estimated the 1979–1985 loss through economic sabotage at $1.2 billion.

By 1988, the failure of the U.S. counterinsurgency strategy in El Salvador was apparent to all. The economy was in ruins, with industry operating at 40 percent of capacity. Riddled with corruption, the Duarte administration had proved unable to end the war, implement serious reforms, or check the repression. The March congressional and local elections repudiated both Duarte and his U.S. sponsors. Most of El Salvador's eligible voters stayed away from the polls, allowing D'Aubuisson's ARENA to control parliament.

One year later, after a bomb at the National Federation of Salvadoran Workers (FENESTRAS) killed ten persons and wounded many others, the FMLN launched its most powerful offensive since 1981, striking at a number of cities, including San Salvador. Its main objective was to take control of the working-class quarters in the city's densely populated northern outskirts, where it enjoyed considerable political support. The government responded with a ferocious aerial bombing of these working-class barrios, but the FMLN held sections of the city for up to two weeks before withdrawing. The concentrated bombardment of densely populated working-class barrios caused many civilian casualties and provoked an international outcry. A new wave of government repression, directed against church and labor critics, accompanied the bombardment. The military executed six Jesuit priests and professors at San Salvador's Central American University, whom the military regarded as the "brains" of the uprising, as well as their housekeeper and her daughter.

The FMLN's offensive aimed to prove to the Salvadoran government and to the United States that, after nine years of war, the FMLN was stronger than ever. Moved by this demonstration of rebel power, and even more, perhaps, by the threat of a congressional halt to U.S. aid to El Salvador in reaction to the murder of the six Jesuits, the ARENA government agreed to U.N.-mediated peace negotiations without preconditions. This ultimately led to peace accords that ended the decade-long civil war in 1992. The agreement required the dissolution of the National Guard and Treasury Police, and their replacement by a new professionally trained National Civil Police that was open to both former national police and FMLN guerrillas. The accord stipulated a 50 percent reduction in the size of the armed forces and disbandment of the U.S.-trained Immediate Reaction Infantry Battalions, which had committed numerous atrocities. FMLN had to dismantle its military structures under U.N. supervision and integrate their members into the political and institutional life of the country, but the FMLN could form its own party and set up its own radio and television facilities.

The accords also dealt with economic and social issues. The government agreed to implement the existing agrarian code and respect de facto land tenancy in "conflictive zones" under FMLN control during the war until it purchased land from absentee owners. The FMLN conceded the government's right to press on with "structural adjustment" policies, but the government in turn agreed to take measures to alleviate the social cost of those policies. With the support of the U.N. Development Programme, the government agreed to develop a National Reconstruction Plan for the conflictive zones, involving infrastructural development as well as employment, education, housing, and health programs. Finally, the accords provided for the creation of a Truth Commission, composed of three foreigners, who would investigate human rights abuses during the war and recommend prosecutions or other punishment for violators.

In 1993, the U.N.-sponsored Truth Commission released its long-awaited report. The report relied on the testimony of two thousand people who had come forward, under promises of confidentiality, to testify as witnesses about the fate of thousands of victims. The report found that government-supported death squads and the military committed 85 percent of the nine thousand human rights abuses investigated and 95 percent of the killings. Government atrocities included the 1980 assassination of Archbishop Romero and the U.S.-trained Atlacatl Battalion's massacre of nearly one thousand civilians—men, women, and children—in the village of El Mozote and nearby hamlets. The report found that the FMLN had also committed human rights violations, but on a much smaller scale. The report implicitly blamed the United States by noting that the majority of the human rights abuses were directly attributable to graduates of the School of the Americas at Fort Benning, Georgia, where many of El Salvador's death-squad leaders received counterinsurgency training.

The Truth Commission's report and newly declassified documents lifted a veil of deception practiced by the Reagan and Bush administrations to persuade Congress to provide continued military assistance to the Salvadoran armed forces. In 1981, for example, the CIA called ARENA party leader D'Aubuisson "the principal henchman for wealthy landowners and a coordinator of right-wing death squads that have murdered several thousand suspected leftists and leftist sympathizers" and described him as "egocentric, reckless, and perhaps mentally unstable." The CIA also reported that D'Aubuisson trafficked in drugs, smuggled arms, and directed the meeting that planned Romero's assassination. Nonetheless, confronted with the documents, William Walker, Bush's special envoy to San Salvador and Reagan's deputy assistant secretary of state for inter-American affairs, displayed no compunction and responded: "We had to deal with D'Aubuisson."

THE SALVADORAN REVOLUTION: A RECKONING

After twelve years of fighting, seventy-five thousand dead, 2 million displaced, an estimated 1 million war refugees, and billions of dollars in economic losses, what was the legacy of the revolution and its strategy of prolonged popular war? First, it demilitarized Salvadoran society and created space for popular mobilization that the military had suppressed since the 1932 *matanza* (massacre). This transformed domestic power relations and produced a new pluralism that contrasted starkly with the nation's traditional political culture, which limited competition to two factions within the coffee oligarchy: murderous planters and slightly less brutal processors. As a result, an ongoing movement for social justice and national liberation was not only possible, but irrepressible.

Second, it engendered a new male and female consciousness. Women, traditionally consigned to family roles within the household, became active participants in public life, first as defenders of their families in human rights organizations like CO-MADRES and later in other organized popular movements like the Salvadoran Women's Association (AMES). Her COMADRE activism, for example, taught one woman that "the fight for human rights is all about … the rights of workers, the rights of women—before I didn't know this." The war also depleted the male labor force,

expanded women's presence in trade unions, and created new demands for women workers, whose participation in the waged economy increased dramatically to 40 percent by 1992.

Last, women sought to escape the prison of patriarchy by joining the revolution, where they made up 30 percent of FMLN combatants and 20 percent of the military leadership: "We grew up with a mentality … that a woman is no more than a person to look after the house, raise the children," explained María Serrano, a guerrilla mayor. "But with the revolution this stopped; women found that they could do the same things as men." Naturally, this new feminist consciousness also had implications for men; one guerrillero who fought in a predominantly female unit acknowledged the difficult "process of coming to see women as compañeras and not as sex objects." Their shared experiences gave a gendered meaning to the revolution's national liberation struggle, which now included freedom from patriarchal as well as racial, class, and imperialist domination.

These potentially momentous changes, however, while clearly evinced in the peace accords, required a vigilant popular struggle and unflagging international pressure to secure their fullest development. A vigorous participatory democracy was the best guarantor of social justice, without which there could be no enduring peace. Nevertheless, with the infamous Atlacatl Battalion dissolved, a new police force organized, and the FMLN prepared to participate as a political party in its first elections, dark clouds still threatened the fragile peace.

After the collapse of populist experiments in Central America, armed insurrection and prolonged popular war clearly had mixed results as a strategy for national development. In Nicaragua, it defeated a kleptocratic dictatorship and showed great promise for promoting an authentically independent development that would benefit historically marginalized women, indigenous communities, peasants, and workers. Like the revolutionary strategy in Guatemala and El Salvador, however, it ultimately fell victim to a persistent and determined foreign intervention, leaving only a common legacy of popular mobilization and greater political participation. In

Colombia and Venezuela, vastly different circumstances and a correspondingly diverse set of strategies that also included a progressive military component combined to produce radically dissimilar movements for national development.

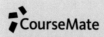 Go to the CourseMate website at **www.cengagebrain.com** for primary sources, additional study tools, and review materials—including audio and video clips—for this chapter.

19

Lands of Bolívar: Military Crisis, State Repression, and Popular Democracy

FOCUS QUESTIONS

- How did the "Oligarchic Republic" affect Colombia's development?
- How did the Great Depression and World War II affect development in Colombia and Venezuela?
- How did *La Violencia* reflect the limits of Colombian populism, and how did it affect national development?
- How did Juan Vicente Gómez's liberal economic policies affect Venezuela?
- How did the populist programs of Rómulo Betancourt and Carlos Andrés Pérez affect national development?
- How did Hugo Chávez's movement for popular democracy affect Venezuela's military, and how did its policies affect national development?

MODERN VENEZUELA AND COLOMBIA often appeared as oases of democratic and economic stability in a turbulent, poverty-ridden continent. A closer look at their recent history, however, suggests they did not escape the fate of their neighbors. Instead, both sought to organize constitutional systems that cooperated with the military to limit popular representation and participation in government, thereby strengthening oligarchical power. However, these transparently corrupt political institutions did not shield them from the socioeconomic problems bequeathed by the general crisis of Latin American dependent capitalism. Its effects were evident in the devastating impact of Venezuela's foreign debt on a country whose oil wealth once made it the envy of the continent. Between 1981 and 1987, the number of Venezuelans living in poverty had risen from 22 to 54 percent of the population.

In February 1989, after Venezuela's populist President Carlos Andrés Pérez announced drastic price increases for basic goods and services to satisfy International Monetary Fund (IMF) requirements for new loans to his government, the country exploded into riots that authorities crushed with the loss of hundreds of lives. However, this crisis of Venezuelan populism sparked a new movement for popular democracy, whose charismatic leader, Hugo Chávez, drew upon his good relations with nationalistic Venezuelan military officers and well-organized grassroots social activists to defend his Bolivarian Revolution from its foreign and domestic enemies.

Neighboring Colombia presented a darker picture. Home of the Cali drug cartel, which accounted for most of the refined cocaine smuggled into the United States, Colombia variously relied on this illicit income and growing U.S. aid to

1899–1903	The War of the Thousand Days strengthens Colombian military
1902	European navies blockade Venezuela to collect debts
1903	Colombia rejects Hay-Herrán Treaty
1908–1935	Venezuelan dictator Juan Vicente Gómez favors foreign investment
1934	Populist Alfonso López initiates *La Revolución en Marcha*
1945–1948	Rómulo Betancourt and reformist military organize populist Venezuelan government
1948	Populist Jorge Eliécer Gaitán is assassinated, sparking Colombia's *La Violencia*; Pérez Jiménez overthrows Rómulo Gallegos in Venezuela
1958	Pact of Punto Fijo and National Front limit democracy in Venezuela and Colombia, respectively
1966	Revolutionary Armed Forces of Colombia forms
1973	Populist government nationalizes Venezuelan oil and steel industries
1989	Venezuela's Carlos Andres Pérez imposes neoliberal program that leads to Caracazo
1998	Hugo Chávez wins Venezuelan presidency and reverses neoliberalism
2002	Uribe wins Colombian presidency military coup temporarily overthrows Venezuela's Chávez
2006	Chávez wins campaign for a "socialist revolution" in Venezuela

repress popular resistance to oligarchical rule. Under an ostensibly democratic regime, death squads linked to the army, security forces, and the drug mafia operated with impunity against radicals, trade unionists, and human rights activists. Meanwhile, a guerrilla war—the longest continuing insurgency in Latin America, reflecting the vast

accumulation of unsolved social problems in this oligarchical democracy—raged in Colombia's jungles and mountains. As elsewhere in Latin America, the twentieth-century origins of these problems resided in the growth of unregulated market forces, external economic dependency, internal social inequality, and an increasingly resolute popular resistance. This pattern began in Colombia with the rise of Rafael Reyes, who governed in the tradition of modern dictators like Rafael Nuñez, Antonio Guzmán Blanco, Manuel Estrada Cabrera, and Porfirio Díaz.

Populism, Military Repression, and Authoritarian Politics in Colombia

THE OLIGARCHICAL REPUBLIC, 1903–1930

For Colombia, the twentieth century began inauspiciously with the War of a Thousand Days, which raged for three years at the cost of thousands of lives and untold damage to the nation's economic infrastructure. The savage civil war slowed economic growth and weakened, at least momentarily, the power of the nation-state, even as it strengthened a military establishment with powerful links to the traditional landowning oligarchy. Quick to seize on this vulnerability, Panamanian separatists, who had struggled in vain for years to establish their independence from Colombia, now seized the twin opportunities afforded by both the civil war and a renewed U.S. interest in the construction of a trans-Isthmian interoceanic canal through Panama. The Colombians had made clear their refusal to approve the Hay-Herran Treaty, which provided for a $40 million payment to a French concessionary company and a mere $10 million for Colombia, in exchange for Colombia's surrender of its sovereignty over the proposed canal zone. Suddenly, the Panamanian nationalists had a new and powerful ally, and with the assistance of President Theodore Roosevelt, they established Panama's official independence in 1903. This dealt a profound psychological shock to Colombians.

At the war's end, Gen. Rafael Reyes (1904–1909) dissolved Congress and established his personal dictatorship, ruling by decree through a puppet national assembly. Despite his dictatorial methods, Reyes's policies of enforcing peace and order, construction of railroads and highways, encouragement of export agriculture, and protection and subsidies for industry initially attracted much elite support.

Reyes's downfall came when he attempted to conclude a treaty with the United States under which Colombia was to receive an indemnity in return for its recognition of Panama's independence. Colombia's governing class, aware of the growing importance of the North American market for its coffee and hopeful of attracting North American capital, accepted the new relations. But the wound of Panama was still fresh, and news of the treaty aroused a public fury of which Reyes's enemies took advantage to force his resignation.

This political crisis led to the convocation of a constituent assembly to reform the 1886 constitution. The assembly agreed to weaken the executive, increase the powers of Congress, and ensure minority representation in elective bodies. Other changes included direct election of the president, establishment of elected departmental assemblies, and abolition of the death penalty. Seemingly progressive, these reforms left intact the privileged position of the church, however, as well as property and literacy qualifications for voting that excluded all women and 90 percent of the adult male population from the suffrage. Although constitutional reforms made one-party rule more difficult, they left control of the electoral process in government hands. The constitutional changes also preserved the *gamonal* system under which landowners, public officials, and priests exerted influence on rural voters.

The characteristic blandness of Colombian politics between 1910 and 1930 contrasted sharply with stormy developments in economic and social life. Reflecting the rapid overall growth of Colombian capitalism, coffee exports increased dramatically. Increasingly, capital that had accumulated in the export industry shifted from commerce to industry, and a partial shift from the old semiservile forms of rural labor to free, capitalist wage labor took place. As elsewhere in the region, a wave of

strikes, land invasions, and clashes between landowners and peasants accompanied these transitions. Successive governments also adopted racist immigration laws designed to "whiten" Colombia by prohibiting "the entrance of those elements whose organic and racial conditions may be inappropriate for the nation." Last, the emergence in cities and plantations of the first true trade union movements, radical political parties, and struggles between workers and employers marked this period.

U.S. capital also began to flow into Colombia, facilitated by the 1914 treaty by which the United States paid Colombia for its loss of Panama. The "dance of the millions" began in 1921–1922, initially fueled by the first installment of a $25 million U.S. indemnity. Between 1922 and 1928, the U.S. government and private investors poured $280 million into Colombia, most of which paid for a vast, chaotic program of public construction. The boom lured workers from agriculture into the cities and created low-wage, unskilled employment opportunities for working-class women, who functioned as a "reserve army" for industry, but it reduced food production and raised living costs, leaving workers worse off than before. Naturally, trade unions, energized by the fiery oratory of labor leaders like María Cano, Colombia's *"flor de trabajo,"* grew more militant, culminating in the 1928 United Fruit Company banana strike whose savage repression claimed thousands of workers' lives.

The extraordinary prosperity ended in 1929 with the New York stock market crash and the Great Depression, which soon spread to Colombia. Growing unemployment, food shortages, and the government's severe fiscal problems completely discredited a regime weakened by political scandals, public outrage over the massacre of banana workers, and its own internal divisions. Moreover, a 1926 Supreme Court ruling that original land titles were the only legal proof of land ownership sparked a series of land invasions by peasants organized in leagues and unions. Alarmed by the rise of peasant unrest, urban strikes, and new radical ideologies, the nation's oligarchs temporarily closed ranks to avoid revolution and supported fellow latifundista Enrique Olaya Herrera in the 1930 election.

The Limits of Populism: The Revolution on the March and Oligarchical Resistance, 1934–1958

Olaya spent his term waiting for the Great Depression to end and for infusions of U.S. loans and investments to resume. His failure to respond to popular expectations for change caused growing tension. In departments where the problem of latifundismo and landlessness was particularly severe, such as Cundinamarca, Tolima, and Cauca, clashes between peasants and landowners or police were frequent. This growing social instability strengthened the appeal of populists like Alfonso López, who won the 1934 elections. He promptly announced a program called *La Revolución en Marcha* (The Revolution on the March). In 1936, he obtained the congressional majority needed to implement his policies.

López and other reformers knew that social justice and national economic interest required land reform. The backwardness of agriculture, especially the food-producing sector, which could not even provide enough food for the growing urban population, blocked the advance of Colombian capitalism. The 1936 agrarian reform law returned to the state all lands not rationally exploited by their owners, but it gave the latifundists ten years to make the transition to efficient land exploitation based on wage labor. The law also prohibited payment of rent in labor or in kind; this had the effect of speeding up the spread of wage labor and the rise of a land market. The law confirmed the property titles of the great landowners, but it also gave peasants "squatters' rights" on unused public and private lands that they had improved. The eviction of squatters thus became more difficult and dropped sharply.

Other legislation adopted during López's administration defined the rights of labor. Congress passed a law that established a minimum wage and paid vacations and holidays, forbade the use of strikebreakers, set up the eight-hour day and the forty-eight-hour week, and created a special tribunal to provide arbitration in labor disputes. With López's support, the number of organized workers quadrupled between 1935 and 1947. Equally important was the formation in 1936 of the Colombian Confederation of Labor (CTC), headed by syndicalists and Communists. One of the most revolutionary innovations of the López reform era was a new progressive tax law, the enforcement of which broke with Colombian tradition and almost doubled the state's revenue-raising capacity.

Despite the moderate character of these reforms, they came under bitter attack from traditional oligarchs, and López began to retreat. In 1936, he announced a "pause" in reform that created a bitter division between moderates and progressives, whose leading advocate was Jorge Eliécer Gaitán, the wildly popular mayor of Bogotá.

Gaitán's political opponents denounced him as a demagogue. He was in fact a magnetic speaker of burning sincerity, capable of presenting his economic and social ideas to audiences of peasants and workers in a clear way, but there was nothing exotic or extravagant about those ideas. Although he used socialist terminology, the essence of Gaitán's program was the need for state intervention in the economy to democratize capitalism, control the great private monopolies, and ensure that peasants owned the land they cultivated. In 1945, he proposed limiting landownership to a maximum of one thousand hectares and suggested a minimum size of four hectares for landholdings to avoid the low productivity of minifundios.

In the 1946 presidential race, however, Mariano Ospina Pérez took advantage of these political divisions to win election with only 42 percent of the vote. After his inauguration, in a conciliatory gesture to his moderate opponents, Ospina Pérez sought to form a National Union government, but he made no effort to consult Gaitán. The snubbing of Gaitán aimed to isolate him politically, deepen the rift between his followers and the moderates, and form a bipartisan coalition to barricade against Gaitán's program of social and economic change. High inflation, static wages, and growing unemployment in the postwar period added to the anger and frustration of workers as they saw their hopes for change crushed by what they perceived as a conspiracy of the "double oligarchy"—the Liberal and Conservative Parties—that controlled government.

Meanwhile, in the face of the National Union government's failure, Laureano Gómez emerged as the gray eminence, the power behind the throne. Scarcely concealing his scorn for the National Union policy, Gómez quickly purged all moderates and organized armed paramilitary groups to attack and persecute his political enemies in preparation for the 1947 elections. Despite these authoritarian methods, however, the outcome was a clear victory for the radicals. Claiming the need to restore law and order, Ospina organized a new security force, the *policía política*, widely known as the "creole Gestapo." Beatings, killings, and outrages of every kind spread throughout the countryside, provoking a growing polarization and armed responses by peasants, sectors of the middle class, and even some large landowners.

As 1948 opened, the violence in some areas assumed the proportions of a civil war. In this tense atmosphere, a stranger approached Gaitán and fired four bullets into him. Mortally wounded, he collapsed on the sidewalk. Generally expected to run and win the election for president in 1950, Gaitán had been regarded by the masses as the sole hope for their liberation. His murder unleashed long-suppressed racial, ethnic, and class antagonisms and signaled a formidable popular insurrection that tore Bogotá apart and spread to the provinces before the army smashed it at the cost of thousands of lives. The spontaneous rising of the masses—accompanied by peasant expropriation of haciendas, establishment of revolutionary committees and workers' control over foreign-owned oil installations, and other radical measures—frightened Colombian elites, who blamed the violence on the "genetically imprinted resentments" of blacks and indigenous people. The coalition government began to come apart in 1949 as the official and unofficial violence in the countryside widened to become a persistent national phenomenon generically called *la Violencia*.

As the 1950 presidential election drew nearer, the threatening, repressive atmosphere visibly deepened. In the countryside, goon squads, backed by the military, compelled peasants to turn in their voting cards. In some areas, landowners took revenge for the land invasions of the 1930s, using

hired thugs to kill or expel peasant occupants. In this stage of the Violencia, however, the conflict was primarily political, based on the peasants' loyalty to party bosses. Finally, in response to a move by a congressional majority to impeach him, Ospina decreed a state of siege, dissolved Congress and all departmental legislatures and municipal councils, granted extraordinary powers for the governors, and established national censorship of the press and radio. With the suppression of all effective opposition, Laureano Gómez assumed the presidency.

Ideologically, the Gómez regime (1950–1953) appeared "feudal" in its effort to restore the intellectual atmosphere of sixteenth-century Spain. In its economic policies, however, the regime showed itself quite favorable to modern corporate capitalism. In the spirit of economic liberalism, it removed all import and export restrictions and encouraged foreign investment in all possible ways. But labor suffered. Wages lagged behind prices, and the state regularly intervened in labor struggles in favor of employers, permitting the use of strikebreakers and blacklists.

In the Colombian countryside, meanwhile, the Violencia gained in intensity, expanded into new regions, and increasingly assumed the nature of a class struggle as peasants resisted the efforts of landowners and their hired thugs to eject them from their parcels. Peasant leaders and Communist Party activists organized strongholds of self-defense among uprooted campesinos. Between 1949 and 1953, Colombia experienced a surge of official state terrorism and the rise of an extensive, well-organized guerrilla resistance.

The dictatorship's failure to achieve a military solution to the guerrilla problem contributed to its gradual weakening and eventual collapse on June 13, 1953, when Gen. Gustavo Rojas Pinilla assumed the presidency with the support of the armed forces. To resolve the social and political crisis, his campaign of "Peace, Justice, Liberty" sought compromise among political elites and peasant radicals. One of his first initiatives was to proclaim an unconditional amnesty to all guerrillas who would return to civilian life.

Several thousand accepted the amnesty, surrendered their weapons, and returned to their old homes, but the leaders of some guerrilla fronts, especially the Communist leadership, distrusted Rojas Pinilla's sincerity. Recalling his role as army commander in a famous massacre in Cali in 1949, they warned their comrades not to "believe the false promises of propaganda thrown from planes of the dictatorship." These guerrilla fronts preferred to maintain an armed truce and await further developments.

Events proved the skeptics right. The honeymoon between Rojas Pinilla and the nation waned as he moved to establish a personal dictatorship with some populist features, not unlike Argentina's Peronist system. One of his reformist measures was giving women the vote in 1954.

Despite some reforms, Rojas Pinilla's policies were essentially reactionary. He revived the Violencia and gave a free hand to notorious *pájaros* (hired assassins), vigilante gangs, and army-police forces to wreak vengeance on veterans of the guerrilla war who had accepted amnesty. As a result, many former guerrillas left their farms and rejoined the surviving guerrilla fronts. The renewal of the civil war combined with other repressive measures and the effects of a deepening depression to unify all elite elements against Rojas Pinilla, whose military colleagues prevailed on him to resign and surrender power to a five-man caretaker military junta.

In July 1957, leaders of the two major political parties, Alberto Lleras Camargo and Laureano Gómez, met to sign an agreement creating a National Front coalition, which in effect provided for a monopoly of shared power for sixteen years. The two parties had parity in both national and local legislatures and the presidency alternated between them. The Colombian experiment in bipartisan rule and "controlled democracy" had begun.

THE NATIONAL FRONT: REFORM AND REPRESSION, 1958–1974

The constitutional pact that created the Colombian National Front in 1958 bore an obvious resemblance to a similar pact signed between Venezuela's oligarchical parties the same year. In both cases, the intent was to preserve elite rule and to marginalize or isolate political movements that might threaten

its property or power. Both were variants of what some scholars have called "controlled democracy" or, more correctly, "restricted democracy."

The Colombian power-sharing pact, which provided for a monopoly of political power for the Conservative and Liberal Parties, excluded the Communists, Christian Democrats, and all future parties. Thus, it denied the electorate an opportunity to reject the policies of the National Front coalition or exercise the sovereign right to change the government. The relative absence of issues between the parties promoted voter apathy and alienation, reflected in low turnout rates; participation in congressional elections fell from a high of 68.9 percent in 1958 to a low of 36.4 percent in 1972.

The rules of the political game established by the National Front, designed to prevent the hegemony of either party, tended to immobilize its governments. Their social policies reflected their fundamentally oligarchical orientation and did nothing to alter the great inequalities in income distribution. Although trade unions gained legal recognition, the government repeatedly intervened in labor conflicts on the employers' side.

To stop the rural violence, Lleras Camargo issued an amnesty for all guerrillas who returned to peaceful life in 1958. The establishment of the National Front coalition marked the official end of the Violencia, a conflict estimated to have taken between two hundred thousand and three hundred thousand lives. In the ensuing decades, the army and police hunted down the remaining outlaw bands, but the continued existence of the latifundio and official repression of some 1 million land-hungry peasants continued to generate violence in the Colombian countryside.

This violence grew so rapidly that, in 1961, evidently fearing that failure to act might produce a Cuban-style revolution, Congress adopted an agrarian reform law that vested apparently limitless power to expropriate and redistribute inefficiently exploited land in a new state agency, *Instituto Colombiano de la Reforma Agraria* (INCORA). In Tolima, the site of the first program, however, only 1,115 out of 90,000 landless agricultural workers had received titles to land by 1969. Naturally,

AP Images

The Colombian army's mobilization of paramilitary violence against unarmed civilians increased the popularity of guerrilla movements like the FARC, whose combatants expanded their power and territorial control.

this failed to satisfy the peasants' hunger for land, and the five-hundred-thousand-member National Association of Peasant Unity (ANUC), originally organized to mobilize rural support for the government, quickly became an outspoken critic.

This innocuous agrarian reform coincided with the launching of a large-scale military effort to destroy the guerrilla zones established under Communist Party leadership in eastern and southern Tolima. Like the agrarian law, this offensive took its inspiration from the anticommunist strategy of the Kennedy administration's Alliance for Progress, a program that combined reform and repression.

The failure of this and later offensives transformed a few guerrilla bases into a network of thirty guerrilla fronts two decades later, all operating in the Colombian backcountry under the military organization of the Communist-led Revolutionary Armed Forces of Colombia (FARC). In addition to the FARC—the largest of the guerrilla groups, created in 1966—the 1960s and 1970s saw the emergence of other revolutionary organizations largely composed of radical students and other urban elements. One such organization, which was led briefly by Father Camilo Torres Restrepo, the radical priest whose 1966 death inspired the 1968 Conference of Latin American Bishops at Medellín to endorse a "preferential option for the poor," advocated agrarian reform, nationalization, social justice, and gender equality. Historian Francesca Miller speculates that the endorsement of women's equality reflected the influence of Torres's feminist mother, Isabel Restrepo Gaviria, who was notorious for her public demonstrations "against her sex's inequalities."

In summary, the National Front's policies successfully promoted the accumulation of foreign and domestic capital but neglected the interests of workers and peasants, whose living standards sharply declined. In 1964, 25 percent of the total labor force lived below the absolute poverty line. By 1973, it had risen to 50.7 percent. Clearly, instead of contributing to the solution of grave socioeconomic problems, the sixteen years of National Front rule merely sharpened them.

DRUG TRAFFICKING AND REPRESSION, 1974–2000

Beginning with the 1974 elections, Colombia returned to the political system of electoral competition, but vestiges of the power-sharing system remained. Despite the renewal of competition, the political system was still a restricted, oligarchical democracy designed to limit the level of conflict between elites and to "keep the masses in their place" with a system of *clientelismo* (electoral mobilization based on machine politics and payoffs).

In addition to their loss of credibility, post–National Front governments faced economic problems of unprecedented proportions. The quadrupling of oil prices in 1974, coming at a time when Colombia had ceased to be self-sufficient in oil production, dealt a heavy shock to the economy. By 1982, Colombia had not only severe inflation but also its worst recession in fifty years.

In this time of economic gloom, some relief came from an unexpected quarter: the drug traffic with the United States. Once negligible and mostly confined to the export of marijuana, this trade mushroomed because Colombia had easy access to both U.S. coasts and abundant sources of cocaine. An efficient distribution system made the new drug available to the ever-swelling U.S. market. A division of labor and profits emerged between the Colombian producers and exporters, centered in Medellín and Cali, and North American domestic wholesalers, bankers, and money launderers. Contrary to a common misconception, Colombia was not a large grower of coca but rather processed the substance, which came from Peru, Bolivia, Ecuador, and Brazil. By the mid-1980s, with cocaine prices dropping, a new product, crack—known as *bazuco* in Colombia and packaged in small quantities that cost only a fraction of cocaine powder—created a large new class of consumers.

Colombia's Medellín and Cali cartels made an estimated $4 to $6 billion annually in cocaine traffic. Of this amount, according to the economist Salomón Kalmanovitz, between $1 and $1.5 billion entered the Colombian black market. This provided a "cushion" for the country's balance of payments and prevented an exchange crisis. The drug mafias enjoyed virtual immunity from the police and army because Colombian **narcocapitalism** stabilized the country's finances and established close ties between the drug lords and traditional oligarchs—landowners, business executives, and government officials.

This situation changed because of three developments. First, President Belisario Betancur (1982–1986) negotiated a series of historic truce agreements with three of the four major guerrilla movements that did not require them to surrender their arms. The accord with the FARC, the largest of the insurgent groups, promised an agrarian reform program; legislation to improve public health, education, and housing; and independent local mayoral and city council elections to broaden popular participation in government. Although the armed forces and other factions effectively blocked implementation of the agreement, the peace process survived momentarily. Second, the United States pressured the Colombian government to wage a more effective war on drug trafficking and offered the incentive of considerable financial aid.

Finally, although the government had collaborated with the drug mafia in training death squads that had freely murdered thousands of trade-union and peasant leaders, radical activists, judges, and others who sought to make Colombia a functioning democracy, it increasingly feared that the drug traffickers threatened the elite's monopoly of power. For example, the drug mafia assassinated prominent members of the elite, including the governor of Antioquia, the country's attorney general, Medellín's police chief, and presidential candidate Luis Carlos Galán. Within hours after Galán's death, the government searched and seized dozens of mansions, hundreds of cars, and more than one hundred airplanes and helicopters that allegedly belonged to the drug traffickers.

Without major social and economic reforms in Latin America, the principal supplier of cocaine, and in the United States, its principal consumer, the drug wars would never end. Without new policies that provided Latin American peasants with a viable alternative to growing coca as a cash crop, its cultivation continued, no matter how many fields the government burned or sprayed with defoliants. As the government destroyed laboratories that processed coca in one part of the region, they moved to another. In both the United States and Latin America, the cocaine epidemic grew dangerously, fueled by mass poverty, despair, and frustration. In the last analysis, military means alone could not solve either the supply side or the demand side of the problem.

In a land famous for the illusions of "**magical realism,**" the Colombian war against the drug cartels provided a perfect cover for the government's thirty-year-old war against the guerrilla insurrection. A network of government agencies, elements of the armed forces and police, landowners, industrialists, and drug lords indissolubly linked the drug and guerrilla problems. The primary target of this alliance was Colombia's radical movement—the guerrillas first, but also trade unions, peasant cooperatives, and opposition parties.

The country's greatest writer, Gabriel García Márquez, says, "The Constitution, the laws ... everything in Colombia is magnificent, everything on paper. It has no connection with reality." The new constitution of July 1991 was typical of that gap between Colombian form and reality. It aimed to open up Colombia's political system, ending the monopoly of power and property long held by a handful of Colombian clans. It provided for the popular election of state governors, limited the president to one term, granted Congress the right to veto cabinet members, established the office of a "people's" defender to investigate human rights abuses, and recognized the authority of traditional courts on indigenous *resguardos*. It also ensured representation for minorities in Congress, barred the extradition of native-born Colombians, and recognized the "collective ownership rights" of Afro-Colombians and indigenous peoples in this multiethnic, multicultural nation.

The new constitution provided a splendid façade for a corrupt, arbitrary social order, but it was still a façade. It did away with the "state of siege" in force in Colombia for most of the previous four decades but conveniently replaced it with the *estado de excepción* (state of exception), utilized to put the country on a war footing and ride roughshod over the rights of workers and others. A voter abstention rate of 70 percent reflected popular cynicism concerning the new Colombian democracy. Colombia's murder rate, among the highest in the world with eighty-six murders per one hundred thousand inhabitants, exposed the thin democratic veneer that masked a lawless state and society. Under cover of the state of emergency, this militarization of the public order also facilitated the imposition of a neoliberal policy featuring the privatization of state enterprises, elimination of subsidies, and other austerity measures promoted by the IMF and the World Bank. These measures, added to the immense costs of the guerrilla war, sharpened all of Colombia's economic and social problems; more than half of Colombia's 33 million people lived below the poverty line, and the official unemployment rate in 1998 was 14.5 percent.

Part of the Colombian "reality" of which García Márquez speaks was that Colombia had been the scene of two wars. One was the drug war. From the official U.S. point of view, this war sought to stem the tide of cocaine flowing into the United States. For the Colombian elite, however, it was a private quarrel with Medellín's "cocaine nouveau riche," who sought too aggressively to join it in the seats of power. By contrast, the Cali cartel, which was more discreet in its dealings with the traditional oligarchy, experienced less interference from the government than did the Medellín cartel. "We do not kill politicians," a member of the Cali cartel explained. "We bribe them." Consequently, by the end of 1994, the Medellín cartel was only a shadow of its former self, with most of its leaders dead or in prison, whereas the rival Cali cartel had taken over most of the heroin and cocaine trade to the United States and Europe.

The other Colombian war was the "dirty war" waged by an alliance of the military, the security services, drug lords, great landowners, and business leaders against Colombia's radical movement, trade unions, peasant leagues, and ethnic minorities. The military made no secret that it was far more interested in fighting guerrillas than in fighting drugs. It repeatedly thwarted efforts to achieve a cease-fire with the guerrilla movements and continued its repressive activity—bombardment, disappearances, torture, and murder. The majority of the victims were not guerrillas but peasants, workers, and radical activists. Despite official government offers to negotiate, successive administrations accelerated the military's counterinsurgency campaign, with a marked increase in aerial bombardments, by U.S.-supplied planes and helicopters, of rural communities. Ostensibly launched to protect the electoral process from "**narcoterrorism**," the operation actually targeted rural areas where guerrilla forces were active.

By 1998, however, the government's military fortunes took a turn for the worse and guerrilla power expanded, reflecting the structural crisis of a corrupt, exclusionary two-party system (or "duopoly"); the poor training and morale of government troops; and a continuing economic crisis that brought recruits and support to the guerrillas. In the government's mad rush to expand private commercial development of export-oriented logging, shrimp aquaculture, plantation agriculture, and cattle raising, it trampled on the traditional rights of indigenous people and Afro-Colombians in the northern Pacific coastal department of Chocó, home to 455,000 Afro-Colombians, 49,000 natives, and 36,000 mestizos. This previously peaceful region had succumbed to violence with the appearance of the army and popular guerrilla groups like the Revolutionary Indigenous Armed Forces (FARIP) and the black *Benkos Biojo*, named for the former African king who escaped Spanish enslavement in the sixteenth century to found the *Palenque de San Basilio*, "the first free village in the Americas."

Guerrilla support also was particularly strong in the long-neglected colonization areas in the southern part of the country, where peasant communities produced coca leaves and poppies as the only alternative to the economic crisis. By compelling "fair" payment by the drug traffickers to the coca growers for their products and by resisting the government's herbicidal spraying of the coca fields, which also destroyed subsistence crops, the guerrillas defended peasants against the government's eradication campaigns and against land-grabbing efforts by the rapacious new **narcobourgeoisie**. In addition to playing a protective role in the regions under their control, according to political scientist Marc Chernick, the guerrillas assumed "many local-level functions of the state, maintaining order, officiating at weddings, births, and divorces, organizing education, mediating conflict and administering justice, and marketing agricultural products." To finance their activities, the guerrillas imposed "taxes" on the drug barons, laboratories, roads, and drug shipments.

The FARC and peasant leaders were well aware of the devastating human, social, and environmental effects of drug cultivation and trade. The FARC proposed a program for the eradication of coca, poppy, and marijuana plantations by the substitution of other crops, with government aid to farmers in land, seeds, and equipment. In 1998, according to *The Nation*, FARC representatives sounded out U.S. officials with a proposal to sever all drug connections in return for a U.S. crop-substitution plan, but neither the Colombian government nor Washington expressed interest.

The dirty war had an unexpected impact on gender balance, family structure, and the labor force. With homicides at seven times the U.S. rate, women headed some 40 percent of families in the 1990s. In addition to their unpaid household labor, these women had to work outside the home, usually for low wages either in unskilled jobs or as self-employed workers in the "informal sector." Within a generation, the proportion of women in the urban workforce rose from approximately 33 percent to 43 percent, but women's wages still lagged 30 percent behind those of men.

The United States, which generously supplied the Colombian military with arms, bore a heavy responsibility for the carnival of death produced by the dirty war. In 1991, the Central Intelligence Agency (CIA) established a new military intelligence network in Colombia, ostensibly to fight drugs. "Instead," says journalist Frank Smyth,

> they incorporated illegal paramilitary groups into their ranks and fostered death squads. These death squads killed trade unionists, peasant leaders, human rights monitors, journalists, and other suspected "subversives." The evidence, including secret Colombian military documents, suggests that the CIA may be more interested in fighting a leftist resistance movement than in combating drugs.

Among the victims of these death squads were leading human rights activists like Jesús María Valle Jaramillo, who publicly had accused certain politicians and military officers of sponsoring death squads. In March 1994, an Amnesty International report further criticized the United States "for remaining silent when aid destined to combat arms trafficking was diverted to counterinsurgency operations and thence to killing of unarmed peasants."

FOREIGN AID AND REPRESSION

With the declining influence of drug trafficking, Colombia's oligarchy increasingly relied on aid from the United States to underwrite its military campaign and avoid serious peace negotiations with guerrilla forces. On January 11, 2000, President Bill Clinton announced a $1.3 billion aid package for Colombia to assist "in vital counter-drug efforts aimed at keeping illegal drugs off our shores" and "to help Colombia promote peace and prosperity and deepen its democracy." The measure, which made Colombia the third-largest beneficiary of military aid from the United States (after Israel and Egypt), formed part of a $7.3 billion Plan Colombia prepared by the two governments; but the hand of Washington showed on every page. Colombia was to contribute $4 billion, although it was unclear where the financially strapped government would find the money; the rest was to come from the United States and countries of the European Union, which showed little enthusiasm

for the plan and eventually withdrew from the project. Announced after formal peace talks between the Colombian government and the FARC had begun, the plan made clear that the United States had chosen war over peace in Colombia.

The ambitious plan had several objectives. Its main goal was the reconquest of the vast area, some 40 percent of the national territory, which the FARC controlled, mostly in southern Colombia. This required a coca-eradication campaign and a crop-substitution program to assist the former coca growers, but the plan ignored altogether the narcotraffickers and their paramilitary allies in the North. As Garry Leech points out in the *Colombia Report*, the plan wielded a huge stick while offering a tiny carrot. Approximately 80 percent of the U.S. aid went to the military and the police, 8 percent to the crop substitution program, 6 percent to human rights programs, 4 percent to displaced farmers, and 1 percent to the continuing peace process.

The plan also had a neoliberal economic component that required Colombia to further restructure its economy, cut government social spending, and privatize state-owned enterprises, including banks, utilities, and the state's coal company. These policies, which complied with commitments to the IMF in return for a $2.7 billion loan in 1999, increased Colombia's combined unemployment and underemployment rate to about 60 percent.

Colombia's former attorney general, Gustavo de Greiff, sharply questioned Plan Colombia's effectiveness in drug eradication. To be successful, he argued, it had to meet four basic tests: (1) reduce the area cultivated to plants from which cocaine, heroin, and marijuana were produced; (2) reduce availability of those drugs in the market; (3) produce higher prices for these drugs; (4) and reduce the number of consumers, habitual and occasional. With data from national and international organizations, Greiff demonstrated that Plan Colombia had failed to obtain any of those results. For Colombia, he cited satellite photographs showing that, after the fumigation of sixty thousand hectares, the area cultivated in coca had grown 60 percent in the previous year. Greiff bristled at the "arrogance" of a U.S. State Department official who, confronted with evidence of increased coca production in Colombia, replied that "we have to do more of what we have been doing, not less."

Plan Colombia was equally ineffective in helping "Colombia promote peace and prosperity and deepen its democracy" because it failed to address the historical causes of the civil war. These causes included the land-grabbing of a selfish elite and massacres of peasants and workers by death squads in its service half a century ago. The successors to those death squads were the contemporary brutal paramilitary outfits, closely linked to the Colombian armed forces, which provided them with intelligence, transport, and weapons. The military officer class, corrupt and incompetent, commanded a rank-and-file consisting mostly of demoralized young workers and peasants who lacked the high school degree necessary to exempt them from the draft. Stung by successive defeats at the hands of the guerrillas, the military chose to "privatize" or "outsource" the war, leaving most of the fighting to the paramilitaries. These gunmen served a variety of masters: drug traffickers, great landowners, especially cattle ranchers, and modern capitalists. They served the interests of the old and new elites by murdering militant peasants, workers, indigenous people, blacks, or anyone they suspected of sympathy with the guerrillas. They threatened, kidnapped, and killed progressive lawyers, human rights activists, and journalists too zealous in the exposure of their crimes. According to Human Rights Watch, the paramilitaries were responsible for 78 percent of the human rights violations in Colombia in 1999.

Early in the twenty-first century, corruption still pervaded the political life of Colombia. Traditionally high abstention rates reflected a pervasive cynicism regarding politics and politicians; only 46 percent of eligible voters turned out for the May 2002 presidential election. Moreover, electoral fraud, including the purchase of votes, was common; in some regions, a vote had one price at 8:00 A.M. and was eight or ten times higher at 3:00 P.M. "Congress," observed *The Economist*, "has come to be seen as a center of shady deals." This corruption, public distrust of

politicians, and resulting high voter abstention rates meant that, in his 2002 "landslide" victory, newly elected president Alvaro Uribe Velez captured only 5.8 million votes—24 percent of the eligible electorate.

If the official justifications for the military aid program for Colombia appeared too glib and unrealistic to be adequate, were other, more pragmatic motives involved? The financial details of the aid package and the new heightened importance of Colombian oil to multinational companies suggested an answer. A major beneficiary was United Technologies Corporation, the Connecticut company that supplied Colombia with some thirty Blackhawk helicopters, each costing $12.8 million. Another was Bell Helicopter Textron, a Texas subsidiary that produced the Huey II helicopter. Indeed, one reason for the delay in getting final approval for the aid package was pork-barrel wrangling between Texas and Connecticut legislators over apportionment of the aid package. Other companies with stakes in it included DynCorp, a defense contractor with a $600 million contract to spray coca crops in Colombia, and Monsanto, producer of the herbicide.

Occidental Petroleum, which operated the Caño-Limón pipeline in northeast Colombia, stood to gain hugely. In 2002, Colombia was the seventh-largest supplier of oil to the United States, and it controlled the largest untapped pool of petroleum in the Western Hemisphere. However, guerrilla attacks between 1982 and 1990 spilled 1.6 billion gallons of Occidental oil along the way. Washington's 1997 decision to reduce its dependence on Middle Eastern oil suggests that its principal interest may not have been drugs but oil. Three years later, the U.S. government confirmed this assessment when it promulgated its Andean Regional Initiative, which increased funding for the counterdrug effort by $731 million and shifted its programmatic emphasis to the war against terrorism. This new program financed a military brigade to protect Occidental's oil pipeline, which of course had nothing to do with drugs.

Still another unspoken justification of Plan Colombia was that it decisively reinforced the militarization of Colombian politics by foreclosing the possibility of peace negotiations with guerrilla armies that claimed to control 40 percent of national territory. Although the expenditure of $4 billion on plant eradication, drug interdiction, and military aid had not reduced cocaine supplies or prices, it had shifted the areas of crop cultivation from Colombia's remote southern provinces, controlled by FARC guerrilla forces, to Pacific and Caribbean coastal provinces increasingly controlled by paramilitary organizations. Although these groups engaged in routine human rights abuses against progressive trade union leaders, peasant activists, and intellectuals, President Alvaro Uribe nonetheless agreed to negotiate their independent demobilization in exchange for their political support for his unprecedented 2006 reelection bid. In the electoral campaign, they explicitly threatened human rights organizations, and on election day, their presence at polling places in small towns and slum neighborhoods intimidated voters. As a result, Uribe won 62 percent of the popular vote, an outcome all the more remarkable because voter abstention rates grew to 54 percent. This meant that Uribe claimed a landslide electoral victory and a popular mandate to rule, even though he had secured the support of fewer than 28 percent of eligible voters. In effect, Plan Colombia funded a realignment of the Colombian political system that allowed the traditional landed oligarchy to sustain its monopoly of power without compromising with the guerrilla insurgency.

Although Plan Colombia was popular in the corridors of power in Bogotá and the United States, the country's southern provinces overwhelmingly opposed it. According to the *New York Times*, six governors of that region, all elected in 2000, "have organized into a formidable bloc that has harshly criticized the central government for everything from the handling of finances to the drug war." Rather than war, these governors demanded "regional public projects and agricultural development programs seen as alternatives to defoliation." The *New York Times* also noted that the group had "the most unlikely governor in Colombia, Mr. Tunubala, a Guambiano Indian who won office in a province

well known for discrimination and social inequality." His political movement, "composed of Indians, union leaders, poor farmers, intellectuals, and others outside the province's circle of power—has already angered some people in the province of Cauca and prompted death threats."

Nonetheless, the 2010 presidential elections largely followed the same pattern. Despite his best efforts to extend his term of office, Uribe's bid for a second reelection foundered on the shoals of an adverse Supreme Court decision and he chose instead to support his political ally, Juan Manuel Santos, who promised that a vote for him was a vote to "reelect" Uribe's policy of "democratic security." Although voter abstention rates rose to a record high of 56 percent, Santos amassed 69 percent of the votes, giving him an electoral "mandate" that amounted to only some 30 percent of the eligible voting population.

Despite some highly publicized claims of victory in the ongoing war against the FARC, Santos seemed increasingly "delusional" as his ineffective security policies coincided with a sharp growth in FARC attacks and the reappearence of rebel checkpoints on major highways. "The Colombian government," writes political scientist Garry Leech, "is intensifying its propaganda campaign in order to offset declining military successes." This apparent contradiction between presidential rhetoric and empirical reality led to a dramatic decline in popular support; in July 2011, 62 percent of urban residents disapproved of the government's security policies, a sharp increase from the 33 percent who disapproved a year earlier.

Santos faced other troublesome problems, including a stubbornly high unemployment rate that averaged more than 11 percent annually, a persistently high poverty rate that approached 46 percent of the population, grotesque income inequality, inadequate economic infrastructure, rising crime rates, intractable drug violence, and increasing inequality in the distribution of land. In 1954, fewer than twenty-four thousand people (3 percent of landowners) owned 55 percent of the arable land; and, by 2011, some sixteen thousand (0.4 percent of landowners) controlled 62 percent of the land.

To remedy these ills, Santos prescribed more of the same: a counterinsurgency war accompanied by greater liberalization of the economy, a key component of which was a free trade agreement with the United States that had stalled in Congress. As a result, a World Bank report, *Doing Business 2011*, ranked Colombia the thirty-ninth "most business friendly environment" in the world. During the previous eight years, however, political violence had claimed the lives of five hundred unionists, some thirty-eight thousand civilians "disappeared" in the previous three years, seven thousand five hundred political prisoners filled Colombian jails, and more than 4.5 million Colombians were internally displaced within the nation's borders. Parmenio Poveda, head of Fensuagro, a farm workers' union, lamented that, "despite all the media hype, this [political violence] is continuing to happen under the Santos government." He insisted that "the only thing that has changed is the tactic: Santos is attempting to present himself as someone open to dialogue and negotiation while the assassinations continue."

With the failure of Colombia's populist Revolution on the March, the nation's oligarchy increasingly relied on military repression to preserve its power and privilege. Although it experimented with various reform initiatives intermittently during the succeeding fifty years, military violence played a primary role in elite efforts to resurrect a political system that protected their property and wealth by limiting popular participation and representation. As a result, prolonged popular war emerged as the primary strategy of resistance, plunging the country into Latin America's longest, bloodiest, and most expensive civil war. With growing dependence on foreign markets, illicit drug revenues, and U.S. military assistance, Colombia had embraced a neoliberal developmental model with a long and largely ignominious history in Latin America. Unlike its neighbors' experience, however, the massive infusions of foreign funds promised to sustain the model for the near future, even though it did not address the underlying sources of poverty and social inequality that underwrote Colombian political instability. Neighboring Venezuela, by contrast, had a somewhat different history that led it to make decidedly different developmental choices in the twenty-first century.

Populism, Authoritarian Politics, and Bolivarian Revolution in Venezuela

Although it shared Colombia's history of dictatorship, militarism, foreign dependence, and oligarchical control, Venezuela's postwar development of its petroleum resources and a fervent nationalism that distinguished its twentieth-century military tradition combined to produce a different set of experiences. Earlier in the century, however, few differences marked Venezuela's liberal social and economic policies.

THE LIBERAL TYRANNY OF JUAN VICENTE GÓMEZ, 1908–1935

Juan Vicente Gómez attempted to placate his foreign patrons and promote a flow of investments into Venezuela by nullifying Cipriano Castro's nationalistic policies, restoring foreign companies' concessionary rights, and allowing foreign nationals to circumvent Venezuelan courts with appeals to their own national courts or to international tribunals. In this and other policies, he shared the ideological interests of his Colombian counterpart, Rafael Reyes.

Gómez especially favored foreign oil companies. The explosive growth of the oil industry eventually transformed Venezuelan economy and society, but the process began slowly. This economic transformation did not reduce Venezuela's dependence or broaden the base of its economy; the monoculture of "black gold" merely replaced the monoculture of coffee and cacao. The oil industry pumped vast wealth into the hands of Gómez, a small native elite linked to the oil industry, and the foreign concessionaires, three of whom—Dutch Shell, Standard Oil, and Gulf—controlled 89 percent of the market. Little of this wealth trickled down to the masses, however, nor did it generate significant industrial progress. Government subsidies failed to stem the decline of agriculture, a sector that traditionally resisted modernization. The

© Corbis

Juan Vicente Gómez, the early twentieth-century liberal dictator, relied on a powerful military to implement unpopular policies that favored foreign investors and local elites.

agricultural crisis contributed to a wave of rural migration to the oil fields of the Maracaibo Basin and other petroleum areas and to the growing cities.

Committed to progress based on private investment and the exploitation of wage labor, Gómez and the generation of liberal intellectuals who served his dictatorship realized that Venezuela's "salvation" could not rely solely on the nineteenth century's failed racist immigration policy of "whitening." This recognition largely reflected Venezuela's growing export dependency and its demand for abundant, cheap labor, which discouraged potential European immigrants even as it attracted Caribbean blacks and Asians. Increasingly, the Gómez regime celebrated race-mixing to erase indigenous and African traditions by submerging them within a dominant European cultural motif, now labeled the "social race," whose unstable compound justified dictatorship.

In the 1920s, nationalist resentment of foreign economic domination and hostility toward Gómez began to pervade the growing middle class. Venezuelan professionals and aspiring entrepreneurs chafed at the difficulties of operating in an economic climate dominated by monopoly, nepotism, and corruption. They also resented foreigners' racist discrimination against their multiracial origins. In 1928, a celebration of the Week of the Student turned into a protest against the dictatorship, as students joined trade unionists and other anti-Gómez political factions.

The student protest also inspired a military revolt, led by young officers of the Caracas garrison and cadets of the *Escuela Militar*. Grievances over the favoritism shown in pay and promotions to officers of unquestioned loyalty to Gómez, and awareness that the army had become a repressive force designed to maintain internal order, fueled discontent. An informer revealed the conspiracy to military authorities, and government troops easily crushed the revolt before it had begun. Some students who had collaborated with the rebellious cadets, including Rómulo Betancourt, future president of Venezuela, escaped and made their way abroad.

Although separated by class and racial status, women also played a powerful role in the emerging anti-Gómez coalition. The Venezuelan Women's Association (AVM) largely represented elite women, who shunned politics and the struggle for equal rights. They limited themselves to social advocacy on behalf of issues central to home and family: charity for the poor, child care, orphanages, prenatal medical care, and sex education. However, even these modest reforms typically envisioned an activist role for the state in the regulation of civil society and, in the words of political scientist Elisabeth Friedman, "proved too challenging to accepted notions of gender relations."

Unlike the AVM, the Feminine Cultural Group (ACF), whose founding members included Cecelia Núñez Sucre and Mercedes Fermín, was a predominantly middle-class social movement that aimed to improve Venezuelan women's social condition, establish civil equality, and secure political rights. In addition to calls for greater access to jobs and education for women, they demanded limits on women's workday, increased wages, and pre- and postmaternity leave. They also called for women's suffrage and reform of the Civil Code, which, according to one contemporaneous observer, gave a "woman no rights whatever against her husband, either personal or financial, even no rights to her own child."

Working-class women like Olga Luzardo, however, typically joined trade unions and actively identified with leftist political parties that, although dominated by men, nonetheless advocated "improvement of the entire exploited sector." Condemning "feminism" as a middle-class idea incapable "of resolving the problems of working women," Luzardo, a Communist and working-class militant, scorned the bourgeois values of a social movement that limited itself to demands for gender equality and the "freedom" to work outside the home. "What would the women comrades of the soap and perfume factories, the polishers, the seamstresses, say [to the idea] that we ought to pull woman from her idleness and push her into work?" Luzardo asked contemptuously. "Wouldn't they laugh at such an unbalanced way of thinking?"

In 1931, Gómez was at the peak of his power, but in the next few years, his health declined and the prospect of his early demise led to intense factional maneuvering in his inner circle. Amid growing signs that Gómez's illness was terminal, his minister of war, Eleazar López Contreras, wove a network of alliances, including the solid support of most army commanders, to ensure his own peaceful rise to power without a civil war or dangerous rebellion of the masses.

Announcing Gómez's death, López proclaimed two weeks of public mourning, but Venezuelans responded to the announcement with rejoicing; in Caracas, angry crowds sacked the palaces of Gómez's most prominent supporters. The jubilation at the news of Gómez's death and popular demands for reform made a mockery of López's eulogy of the dead dictator and foreclosed the possibility of an easy transition that nevertheless perpetuated the old regime. The entrance of the Venezuelan middle classes and workers onto the political scene opened two decades of complicated struggle, culminating in the victory of a new populist model of capitalist development and its associated political form of representative democracy.

In an atmosphere of great social and political effervescence, however, many exiles with various ideologies returned home and joined activists emerging from the underground in organizing trade unions, political parties, and professional organizations. López found himself under siege from the entire political spectrum. He sometimes yielded to pressures for reform and then stubbornly resisted demands for change to the undemocratic Gómez political system. For example, he supported a new constitution in 1936 but insisted on retaining a Gómez clause that defined communism and anarchism as treason, effectively outlawing the major opposition parties, the reformist *Partido Democrático Nacional* (PDN) led by Rómulo Betancourt and the Venezuelan Communist Party of Gustavo Machado.

World War II, having created insatiable demand for Venezuela's oil, enabled López's handpicked successor, Gen. Isaias Medina Angarita, to renegotiate old inequitable contracts and wrest more favorable terms from the oil companies. Moreover, domestic social movements of workers, peasants, women, and industrialists pressured him to support progressive policies like Venezuela's first social security and income-tax legislation. His government also encouraged the formation of trade unions, which gained considerable strength, particularly in the oil industry. Pushed by Mercedes Fermín and the ACF, a largely middle-class women's rights organization that had opposed Gómez, Medina viewed favorably a movement toward a more democratic system with enfranchisement of women and direct popular election of the president.

Medina also tackled the country's urgent agrarian problem. Near the end of his administration, he asked his minister of agriculture, Angel Biaggini, to draft an agrarian reform bill that would distribute the extensive state landholdings to landless peasants. Congress passed the law, but one month later, it died stillborn because of a military-civilian coup led by Marcos Pérez Jiménez and Rómulo Betancourt, two men who dominated Venezuelan politics for the next two decades.

Betancourt was the most influential personality among that famous generation of student leaders who had electrified Caracas in 1928 by leading a public protest against Gómez. Of middle-class background, during his years of exile Betancourt had read widely in the classics of Marxist literature. But the most decisive influence on his thought was a nationalist, reformist ideological current best represented in Latin America by the Peruvian Victor Raúl Haya de la Torre, who argued that in Latin America's specific conditions, characterized by economic backwardness and a small, weak working class, the immediate historical task of social revolutionaries was to complete the unfinished bourgeois revolution.

Betancourt thus appeared as the standard-bearer of the Venezuelan bourgeois revolution, which sought to end dependency on oil by diversifying the economy through industrialization, to expand the internal market by improving living standards, and to initiate land reform to increase agricultural productivity. He hoped to achieve these goals within the framework of parliamentary democracy. Betancourt assigned a decisive role in this process to the state, which was to plan, regulate, and assist economic development. The political instrument that Betancourt and his colleagues created to achieve Venezuela's bourgeois, democratic revolution was *Acción Democrática* (AD), a multiclass party and mass organization that enjoyed rapid growth from 1941 to 1945, gaining a clear superiority over its closest rival, the Communist Party, in numbers and influence among the middle class, workers, peasants, and women.

The women's strategy for securing civil and political equality had four key elements. First, women sought to organize and maintain unity across the seemingly insurmountable dividing lines of class and political party. Reflecting this strategic consensus among middle-class women, Ana Luisa Padra announced in 1941 that "we have different interests, but a common problem: the conquest of our rights for which we ought to [fight] together without rancor or distinctions." Second, rather than seek equality with men, the women's movement in Venezuela sought to mobilize the state's resources to protect children and mothers. Third, women raised the issue of equality without addressing it directly, at least initially by seeking merely to reclaim for married women liberties freely granted to widowed mothers—property rights and custody of their children. Thereafter, they insisted that political rights for women logically flowed directly from the successful attainment of civil equality, rather than vice versa; lacking "voice or vote within the boundaries of her home," a feminist newspaper editorialized, "it would be laughable that [women] would be granted the vote within the boundaries of her country."

This particular strategy also aimed to preserve a gender-based unity, but it fractured later when the women's movement exercised a wartime demand for equal voting rights with men, whose franchise already was limited to literates. This immediately raised issues of class inequality by largely excluding working-class women. Class issues, always lurking in the shadows of the women's movement, took center stage in a 1944 competition to elect the queen of the Amateur Baseball World Series, a cultural event, according to political scientist Friedman, widely viewed as a "primer for universal suffrage." One woman advertised herself as the candidate of the "respectable people," by contrast with her opponent, Yolanda Leal, a poor school teacher, who was "for the common folk." When Leal, "daughter of the people," won overwhelmingly, it created a national furor over the franchise that weakened middle- and upper-class support for universal suffrage.

Even as middle-class women abandoned their working-class counterparts, AD, in its populist struggle to fashion a multiclass electoral movement, came to power in 1945 and established universal suffrage two years later. Ironically, after enfranchisement ended women's political segregation and integrated their participation into male-dominated institutions, women's rights organizations lost much of their traditional autonomy, their memberships fragmented, and their political agenda dissipated.

A STRANGE ALLIANCE: BETANCOURT, MILITARY POPULISM, AND DICTATORSHIP, 1945–1958

After the 1945 military-civilian coup that overthrew the Medina regime, a provisional government headed by Betancourt as president seized power. The motives for this coup, born of an alliance between young military officers and the AD's populist leadership, continue to provoke historical debate. The officers, organized in the *Unión Patriótica Militar* (UPM), complained about promotion, salary, and appointment policies within the military, displayed little interest in government affairs, and appeared content to leave government to the AD. Although Medina's progressive record included support for sweeping constitutional reforms, including universal suffrage, his government, composed almost entirely of white elites, had continued to discriminate against nonwhite immigrants and appeared insensitive to the historical links among race, class, and political order that bound together Venezuela's *café con leche* society (that is, the mixed-race nature of many Latin American societies). Consequently, the Medina government was totally unprepared for the furor over the racist refusal of three posh Caracas hotels to serve the African American singer Robert Todd Duncan. Eager to use race as a powerful organizing tool, the AD seized on public outrage to expand and mobilize its political supporters in a bid to control the state.

However dubious the motives that inspired the 1945 coup, it proved a milestone in Venezuelan history. The AD government between 1945 and 1948—a period Venezuelans call the *Trienio*—represented the first serious effort to transform the country's archaic economic and social structures. Because AD was, in effect, the government, it had a distinct advantage over its political rivals. AD control of the distribution of land and agricultural credits under the agrarian reform enabled it to build a clientele of peasant union leaders that gave it a commanding majority of the peasant vote. AD established a similar relationship of influence and leadership over most of the more than five hundred trade unions organized in this period and affiliated with the Venezuelan Confederation of Workers, which included both trade and peasant unions.

The AD also drafted a new constitution that guaranteed many civil and social rights, including labor's right to organize and strike and the principle that land should belong "to him who works it." The constitution established universal, secret voting for all persons over eighteen, with direct election of the president and both houses of Congress.

Among the economic issues with which the AD government had to deal, oil policy was most important, for it involved fundamental questions of dependency, economic sovereignty, and the revenues needed for economic diversification and modernization. In 1946, the government primarily targeted the oil companies with a supertax of 26 percent on all company profits greater than 28 million bolívars. This tax alone increased government income in 1947 by 230 percent over its income in 1938.

In view of the great importance the AD program attached to agrarian reform, the junta's approach was timid. Evidently fearing the political and economic repercussions of a frontal attack on the latifundio, the government preferred to distribute land to the peasants from the extensive state holdings taken over on the death of Gómez, Venezuela's premier latifundist. Out of a landless peasant population estimated at about three hundred and thirty thousand, only between fifty-five thousand and eighty thousand received land during the Trienio. Because the average peasant received only 2.2 hectares of land to cultivate, "the problem," as Judith Ewell points out, "then changed from *latifundia* to *minifundia.*"

The creation of an independent national economy through industrialization was a major government goal. The Venezuelan Development Corporation (CVF) formed in 1946 to promote this process through loans to private entrepreneurs and direct investment in state corporations. In three years, it lent nearly 50 million bolivars to industrial enterprises, but, by the Trienio's end, the program of "sowing the petroleum" to diversify and modernize the economy had achieved only modest results. Nonetheless, the government made impressive progress in health and education, whose respective budgets for 1948 quadrupled and tripled. The government virtually eliminated the country's principal health scourge, malaria, by spraying DDT (dichlorodiphenyltrichloroethane) on the breeding grounds of mosquitos that carried the disease.

The principal danger to the regime came from military officers like Col. Marcos Pérez Jiménez, who increasingly opposed what they regarded as the radical excesses of their civilian partners. On November 24, the government fell in a virtually bloodless coup, and Minister of Defense Carlos Delgado Chalbaud, seizing power as president of a military junta, arrested and imprisoned many of the leading members of the AD regime. Betancourt escaped, taking refuge in the Colombian Embassy, and, along with other prominent AD leaders, he later went into exile.

In a proclamation issued on November 25, Delgado Chalbaud declared that the junta was provisional and did not intend to destroy Venezuelan democracy or prohibit the activities of political parties, but its actions contradicted these claims. Soon after the coup, it dissolved Congress, annulled the 1947 constitution, voided the petroleum law, and abandoned other progressive programs like agrarian reform and school construction. The junta also imposed a strict censorship, forbidding any criticism of the regime. In 1949, the junta launched an offensive against the unions, arresting leaders of the Venezuelan Labor Confederation, forbidding union meetings, and freezing the funds of most unions.

Initially, opposition to the junta and its repressive policies was limited largely to student protests and the activities of the illegal Communist Party, whose members played a leading role in the organization of the resistance movement. With the ACF and other women's rights organizations under attack, women activists also quickly joined clandestine opposition movements like the Venezuelan Union of Women and the Communist Women's Organization. In 1949, AD leaders who remained in the country also formed an underground organization.

Against the objections of the strongly anticommunist Betancourt and other AD leaders in exile, the AD underground cooperated with the Communists and other groups in the resistance movement's struggle against the dictatorship.

After the assassination of Delgado Chalbaud in 1950, the military regime intensified its repressive activity. By the fall of 1952, the regime, evidently convinced that the repression had intimidated the Venezuelan people into accepting its rule, decided that it could safely hold elections for a Constituent Assembly.

Despite the repressive conditions and the call issued by the exiled AD leadership to abstain from voting—a position it reversed at the last moment—Venezuelans gave a two-thirds majority of the popular vote to the opposition parties. Furious at this outcome, Pérez Jiménez nullified the election and announced he was taking office as provisional president in the name of the armed forces.

For the next five years (1953–1958), Pérez Jiménez was the absolute ruler of Venezuela. In place of the AD's focus on education, health, agrarian reform, and balanced economic development, the Pérez Jiménez regime limited the right to organize and strike, which contributed to a decline in labor's share of the national income. It also emphasized grand works of infrastructure—highways, urban freeways, and port improvements—and urban constructions, some of little or no social utility, like the Officers Club in Caracas or the many-storied shopping center built on the side of one of Caracas's hills. The regime's social and economic policies generated discontent among ever-wider sections of the population, but a brutally efficient repression, imposed by the secret police or *Seguridad Nacional*, made antigovernment activities quite difficult. Nonetheless, a resistance movement uniting persons of all political tendencies survived and continued its struggle against the dictatorship.

Women's roles in Venezuelan society once again changed dramatically in this period. First, as Pérez Jiménez promoted economic growth by offering incentives to private, especially foreign, businesses, demand was greater for low-cost labor, which increased women's participation in the workforce, to be sure, mostly concentrated in menial jobs as domestics, laundresses, and waitresses. As a share of the wage-earning workforce, women's participation increased from 17 to 22 percent. Second, because the dictator dismissed women as political actors, his brutal repression largely targeted men, the effect of which was to create more opportunities for women in popular resistance movements. One of the more active organizations in the antidictatorial struggle was the Venezuelan Teachers' Federation (FVM), 75 percent of whose membership was female.

Although the movement's public leadership remained overwhelmingly male, women shouldered a large measure of the daily organizational responsibilities, ranging from intelligence collection to communications work. The Women's Committee, arguably the most influential of all the women's groups involved in the resistance, was especially successful at building cross-class alliances and uniting women politically even as it mobilized thousands in their opposition to dictatorship. Women also were effective in organizing cultural foundations, like the Gabriela Mistral Center, that efficiently disguised clandestine political objectives. However, when the dictatorship collapsed and a fragile democracy reemerged, the women's movement once again suffered a decline. In the words of Argelia Laya, a prominent activist, guerrilla leader, and founder of Socialist Women, male domination or machismo "was stronger than a military dictatorship!"

Signs of defection from the regime multiplied in 1957. Especially significant was the increasingly critical attitude of the Catholic hierarchy, which issued statements deploring the government's disregard for the interests of the poor. Disaffection also grew among national capitalists, who complained of the government's neglect. With the end of the oil export boom in the late 1950s, the regime's capacity to generate business activity and employment through public works programs ran out of steam. Finally, the armed forces increasingly resented Pérez Jiménez's arbitrary decisions and his reliance on the secret police to watch over the loyalty of officers.

By mid-1957, an underground organization called the *Junta Patriótica* formed to unite the major political parties. This group became the principal motor of the resistance movement and its preparation for a popular revolt. On January 21, 1958, the Junta Patriótica proclaimed an overwhelmingly effective general strike that provoked clashes between the people and the regime's security forces. Barricades appeared in the streets of Caracas. The next day, the insurgents seized key strategic points in the capital. The majority of military units refused to obey Pérez Jiménez and fraternized with the rebels. Fearing the radicalism of the popular opposition, a new military junta demanded that Pérez Jiménez resign, and, shortly thereafter, he fled the country for the Dominican Republic.

The military junta became a provisional government: Its first decrees proclaimed the restoration of all democratic freedoms, amnesty for all political prisoners and exiles, and legalization of all political parties. Almost ten years of rule by a repressive military dictatorship had ended.

LIMITED DEMOCRACY AND POPULIST RESURGENCE, 1958–1969

The military-civilian junta presided over the transition to democratic elections in 1958 and invited the return of political exiles like Betancourt. Chastened by his experience with the military, Betancourt had moderated his political views. He now sought to reassure Venezuela's economic elite about his intentions, chose moderates as his principal political allies, and joined with the nation's other centrist parties to endorse the Pact of Punto Fijo, which provided that, whatever the election results, they would form a coalition government to carry out a program of democratic socioeconomic and political reforms.

The Pact of Punto Fijo was important far beyond its impact on the 1958 elections because it created a unique Venezuelan model of representative democracy. It consciously tailored the Venezuelan political system to isolate Marxist parties, making it virtually impossible for them to wield political power. Second, although the Pact of Punto Fijo provided for a three-party coalition, the system evolved toward hegemonic control of political life by two parties, the social democratic

AD and the social Christian COPEI (*Comité de Organización Política Electoral Independiente*), whose reformist programs were broadly similar.

A third distinctive feature of the Venezuelan populist model of representative democracy was the major role that it assigned to the state as regulator and arbiter of relations between the classes and interest groups. The massive influx of petroleum revenues over the previous three decades had strengthened the state and endowed it with the financial resources necessary to balance and mediate the conflicting demands and interests of labor, the peasantry, capitalists, the middle class, the armed forces, the church, and the political parties.

Finally, the architect of this model, Rómulo Betancourt, sought to use the state to recapture the nation's natural resources from foreign control, reform its socioeconomic structures, and promote a balanced economic development. Betancourt hoped that, in time, this would lead to the rise of an autonomous Venezuelan capitalism capable of providing Venezuelans with a high standard of living and culture. Indeed, over the next three decades, Venezuela significantly improved the nation's health and literacy, but the vast sums expended in "sowing the petroleum" did not achieve Betancourt's main goals; poverty increased and income distribution remained as inequitable as in Mexico and Brazil. Moreover, Venezuela remained deeply dependent, burdened with an unpayable foreign debt.

Although the major parties had approved a common program of economic, social, and political reform broadly similar to the one carried out during the Trienio, the continuing economic crisis and Betancourt's own contentious nature aggravated political disputes. The victory of the Cuban Revolution in January 1959 and Cuba's gradual turn toward socialism created an especially divisive issue. Younger activists hailed the revolution as a model that Venezuela could well emulate, but the virulently anticommunist Betancourt regarded the Cuban socialist regime as a direct challenge to his own populist philosophy. He fully supported U.S. efforts to isolate Castro's regime economically and politically.

In 1961, Betancourt promulgated a new constitution that proclaimed the government's responsibility for its citizens' social well-being, provided for proportional minority representation in Congress, and prohibited the president from succeeding himself. However, it also gave him significant powers to suspend constitutional guarantees of personal and civil liberties. Moreover, although he had campaigned on the need for redistribution of land, which earned him an overwhelming majority of the peasant vote, the results of his agrarian reform were mixed at best and fell far short of solving Venezuela's acute agrarian problem.

By 1969, fewer than half of the three hundred and fifty thousand peasant families without land had received plots. Combined with the estimated two hundred thousand new families formed in those eight years, four hundred thousand families remained without land. Government investments in irrigation, roads, and credit and technical assistance primarily benefited large and midsize commercial farms that produced the lion's share of profitable crops and accounted for most of the 150 percent increase in agricultural production between 1959 and 1968.

Still, Betancourt's administration made large advances in health and public education. His Ministry of Health and Social Assistance controlled nearly 9 percent of the national budget and launched a concerted attack on the problems of endemic disease, infant mortality, and malnutrition that lowered infant mortality from 64 per 1,000 live births in 1955–1959 to 46.5 in 1966. The Betancourt years also saw a significant growth of public education.

Industrialization also was a major objective of the Betancourt regime, which increased its share of oil profits to make more funds available for loans and direct subsidies to support industrial development. A 1958 law therefore raised the tax rate on oil profits to 65 percent. The slogan "Venezuela must industrialize or die" expressed the militant spirit of the AD's new campaign.

The campaign for "economic independence," however, had a peculiar outcome: It fastened more firmly the chains of dependence on Venezuela. Confronted with high tariff walls and unwilling to lose the large consumer market created by oil wealth, a growing number of U.S. and other foreign firms chose to establish branches in Venezuela, frequently in association with local capital. The label "made in Venezuela" increasingly came to mean an article made with raw materials and intermediate materials imported from the United States and finished or assembled in Venezuela.

Between 1958 and 1970, the number of plants producing such items as cans, foodstuffs, clothing, automobiles, auto tires, paint, and cigarettes mushroomed. The alliance of foreign and native capital achieved the goal of import substitution, but because the dominant partner in the alliance was foreign capital, most of the profits flowed back to the home offices of foreign firms. By 1971, Venezuela had accumulated $5.57 billion worth of foreign investment, the largest in any developing country, but the export of profits reached an annual average of $672 million. Venezuela, observed one economist, had become a "fiscal paradise of foreign monopoly capital."

The drive for import-substitution industrialization accompanied the incorporation of labor as a less-than-equal partner in an alliance with the state and industry. In 1958, labor leaders signed a pact with management that committed the unions to seek conciliation of conflicts with employers, and they completed the subordination of labor during the following decade of AD rule.

POPULIST PROBLEMS IN A PETROLEUM REPUBLIC, 1969–1988

In response to growing nationalist sentiment and charges that the foreign oil companies withheld further investment in Venezuela in reprisal for higher taxes and increased government control, Rafael Caldera of the Social Christian Party won the presidency on a campaign to nationalize all existing oil concessions beginning in 1983. The proposed law required private companies to surrender unexploited concessions to the state petroleum company, *Corporación Venezolana del Petróleo* (CVP), in 1974. In addition, the oil companies had to post bonds guaranteeing that they would turn over their plant and machinery in good condition. Caldera also nationalized the foreign-owned natural gas industry and gave the government power to control oil-production levels.

Finally, during his last months in office, Caldera issued a decree that forbade foreign interest in radio and television stations and electric companies.

Despite the establishment of representative democracy in 1958 and Caldera's reforms, a 1973 survey of Venezuela's economic and social conditions gave no cause for satisfaction. No basic change in economic structure had occurred; the government's populist reforms remained heavily dependent on oil income. True, import-substitution industrialization had achieved some economic diversification, but it was a dependent industrialization that relied largely on foreign capital, inputs, and technology. Despite the agrarian reform, agriculture remained the most backward branch of the national economy. In 1971, Venezuela still imported 46 percent of its basic foodstuffs. The agrarian reform also failed to correct fundamental problems like the continuing high concentration of landownership; 1.4 percent of the large estates held 67 percent of all privately owned land in 1973.

Thanks to improved health care and the eradication of such scourges as malaria, the Venezuelan population had grown rapidly, increasing from 7,524,000 in 1958 to 10,722,000 in 1971. However, the quality of life for the majority of Venezuelans had not improved markedly after fifteen years of democratic rule. Although women's share of the labor force had doubled, they still made up a small percentage of wageworkers, mostly employed in low-wage service jobs. Prostitutes typically made more money. In 1974, 30 percent of all Venezuelan children suffered from malnutrition; 12 percent of all adults suffered from mental retardation from the same cause, combined with other difficult living conditions. In the early 1960s, a United Nations study described Venezuela's income distribution as one of the most unequal in the world. A decade later, the situation had not improved.

Carlos Andrés Pérez, a Betancourt protégé, emerged an easy winner in the 1973 election. The flamboyant Pérez, a master of populist rhetoric, had promised a "war on poverty" and against "privilege." Despite his rhetoric, his program did not differ substantially from those of his predecessors, even though his government benefited from the 1973 Arab oil embargo, which raised oil prices from $2.01 a barrel in 1970 to $14.26 in January 1974 and vastly increased state revenues. Pérez promised to "manage abundance with the mentality of scarcity," but the flood of oil riches and the irresistible drive to modernize overwhelmed his administration and frustrated his good intentions.

On August 29, 1975, Pérez signed a law that nationalized the Venezuelan oil industry, effective on January 1, 1976, and created a state oil company, Petroven, to control a sector of the economy whose annual sales volume exceeded $10 billion. In addition to a generous compensation of $1 billion to the foreign companies, the nationalization agreement authorized the state to contract with them for technological assistance, equipment, and marketing agreements for the international transshipment of Venezuelan oil exports. Pérez's populist economic program called for the creation and expansion of heavy industries, especially petrochemicals, steel, and shipbuilding, which supplied the needs of Venezuela's consumer-goods industry. Gradually, this list expanded to include other projects—a fishery industry, a national rail system, the Caracas metro, and modernized port facilities.

During his campaign, Pérez had pledged to direct "priority attention to the needs of Venezuelan agriculture as the essential motor of economic development," but, like his predecessors, he equated it with large commercial farmers. Although Pérez claimed in 1975 to have achieved an "agricultural miracle," the reality was quite different. Domestic food production increased, but imports of the country's basic foodstuffs rose from 46 percent in 1971 to almost 70 percent by the close of his administration. The rapid growth of the urban population contributed to this increased food dependence.

The immense oil revenues that flowed to the state from 1974 to 1979 proved inadequate to cover the costs of the government's ambitious development program, and Pérez, fearful of alienating business leaders, refused to raise taxes. Increasingly, Pérez, like other Latin American populist leaders, had to resort to foreign loans to finance his reforms; between 1974 and 1978, Venezuela's foreign debt grew by almost $10 billion.

Pérez cultivated a populist image that did not correspond to his social policies. Because of the orgy of state spending during his administration, the economy heated up and inflation cut deeply into workers' living standards. For the business, financial, and political elites, however, the boom created vast opportunities for enrichment, resulting in an explosion of conspicuous consumption even as the standard of living for peasants and workers deteriorated. The intimate ties among the state, the ruling party, and the economic elites generated outlandish corruption.

Finally, the Pérez economic program had clearly failed to solve the dilemma of dependency that continued to plague Venezuela. Measured by the yardsticks of foreign indebtedness and the degree of its reliance for revenue on a single resource—oil—Venezuela was more dependent in 1980 than it had been in 1974.

The crisis of Venezuelan populism deepened after 1978 as Pérez's presidential successors struggled with the devastating combined effects of recurrent drops in oil prices and the massive outflow of funds to service the foreign debt. In a New Year's Eve 1989 address to the nation, one of them, Jaime Lusinchi, proclaimed that debt "is strangling our country's social and economic development and that of the majority of the world's people." Faced with a choice between paying foreign bankers and paying for his populist reform agenda, Lusinchi announced a moratorium on the repayment of all debts accumulated with foreign banks before 1983.

NEOLIBERALISM AND THE DILEMMAS OF A PETROLEUM REPUBLIC, 1988–2003

The 1988 election saw the return of Carlos Andrés Pérez to the presidency. Despite a populist campaign that denounced subservience to foreign bankers, once in office, Pérez inaugurated an economic austerity program in response to conditions demanded by the IMF in exchange for a $4.5 billion loan over a three-year period. The program included massive currency devaluation, higher interest rates, and the lifting of controls and subsidies on a wide range of products and services such as gasoline, bread, and electricity. The price increases, announced in advance of their application, caused goods to vanish from the shelves as shopkeepers prepared to profit from the higher prices.

In February 1989, a popular explosion rocked Caracas when the government announced a significant rise in bus fares. For many poor Venezuelans, this measure alone cut their wage increases in half and drove them to open rebellion. Tens of thousands of people took to the streets, rioting and looting shops; from Caracas, the rioting spread to the poor barrios surrounding the city, then to the nearby port of La Guaira, and later to distant cities and towns.

The Pérez government responded with a display of force that many observers found excessive; in contrast to the officially admitted death toll of around three hundred, unofficial estimates placed the number of dead at between four hundred and one thousand. The shock waves of the explosion soon reached Washington, where the U.S. Treasury hastened to make a $453 million "bridging loan" to the Pérez government in advance of its signing an IMF economic adjustment program. In another apparent reaction to events in Venezuela, U.S. Treasury Secretary Nicholas Brady announced a plan partially to reduce Latin American debt. Pérez continued to insist that his "six-month shock" economic program was correct in its essentials and, in time, would create "a new Venezuela."

In the meantime, however, this neoliberal program deepened the recession. Prices for many basic foods and household items, transport, and electricity rose between 50 and 100 percent. Real wages fell between 20 and 50 percent.

Pérez faced a dilemma. The IMF, World Bank, and foreign bankers demanded he continue his austerity program as a condition for obtaining the new loans needed to reactivate the economy, but labor and the middle class insisted that he change course and relieve the suffering caused by his economic adjustment program and a deepening recession. He opted for the international bankers and a neoliberal plan that included the privatization of a large number of state-owned enterprises. Ironically, Pérez himself had nationalized the iron and steel industries, proclaiming that "evolutionary socialism" was his long-term

goal. Pérez even called his IMF-style austerity program *el gran viraje* (the great turnabout). For many suffering Venezuelans, however, it was *la gran perfidia* (the great betrayal).

Pérez's privatization program caused significant loss of jobs in a country already burdened with high unemployment. It also transferred ownership of those enterprises to foreign multinationals. The first privatizations resulted in the sale of 40 percent of the state-owned telephone company to the U.S. telecommunications giant GTE, the national airline to the Spanish Iberia, and several large hotels to various international private interests. The sales prices also grossly undervalued these assets and led to considerable corruption.

The economy partially revived from its deep recession because of a one-time bonanza of $2 billion in government revenues from the sale of state companies and a reduction in import duties that helped spur a boom in the import-led commercial sector. But the recovery was mainly in the realm of stock market speculation; industry and agriculture continued to stagnate. Some economic and social indicators reflected the failure of neoliberal economic policy to improve the life of most Venezuelans. The real minimum wage in 1991 was only 44 percent of its 1987 value, the number of people living below the poverty line jumped from 15 percent at the end of 1988 to 41 percent in 1991, and inflation reached a record high of 80 percent in 1989.

Mounting anger over Pérez's austerity program, the growing gap between rich and poor, and revelations of corruption in official circles sparked a series of strikes and protests demanding Pérez's resignation. The growing discontent reached into the middle and lower echelons of the military, whose members were unhappy with their own deteriorating living conditions and with Pérez's privatization program; in 1992 a coup attempt, led by Lt. Col. Hugo Chávez Frías, involved 10 percent of the nation's armed forces and came perilously close to overthrowing the regime. Its program included putting all those engaged in corruption on trial, a reversal of Pérez's neoliberal policies, an emergency program to combat misery and poverty, dissolution of the government, and election of a constitutional assembly. Although defeated, Chávez became a folk hero overnight among the poor in Caracas's "belt of misery."

The foiled coup combined with the unending wave of strikes and popular protests to pressure the Supreme Court to indict Pérez, charging him with misappropriating $17 million from a secret fund earmarked for national security. Congress then voted to remove him from office. Meanwhile, more than a thousand small and midsize companies closed, causing the loss of fifty-nine thousand jobs. High interest rates, inflation approaching 40 percent, an influx of imports, and weak demand caused by low purchasing power produced an increasingly severe recession. Foreign investment fell by more than 40 percent.

The 1993 elections represented a crushing repudiation of Pérez, his neoliberal policies, and the two-party rule that had prevailed since the fall of Gen. Marcos Pérez Jiménez in 1958. Rafael Caldera, the seventy-seven-year-old populist whose own party had rejected him because of his opposition to neoliberal policies, won the presidential election. His victory and the large gains made by progressive parties testified to the strength of the movement for social and economic change.

Although it provoked alarm among Venezuelan business elites and foreign investors, in reality Caldera's reform program was quite modest. It called for a new labor law—strongly opposed by big business—the provisions of which discouraged layoffs in a time of deep recession. Other goals included a monthly minimum wage increase, repeal of an IMF-inspired value-added tax that sharply increased prices on items of popular consumption, new taxes on luxury items, and a reform of the income tax system that improved tax collection by imposing heavy fines on tax evasion, estimated at 70 percent of all taxpayers.

As his program evolved, however, Caldera's response to the desperate economic crisis deviated more and more from his campaign promise to abandon the discredited neoliberal policies. Soon, reform-minded ministers in his government resigned, and he replaced them with neoliberals who renewed the drive to privatize practically all state companies and bail out eight private banks.

The business sector hailed Caldera's return to economic orthodoxy, but it damaged his image as a crusading populist president among workers and shantytown dwellers. Apparently fearing uprisings like the failed 1992 military coup and the food riots of 1989, Caldera suspended constitutional guarantees, including the rights to liberty, personal security, and free travel, and to protection against unreasonable search. Security forces searched the homes of activists, former military officials, and politicians; they rounded up hundreds of persons in Caracas's slums. Human rights activists and church leaders condemned the suspensions of constitutional guarantees. Caldera, like Pérez before him, perfectly modeled what had become a sadly familiar tendency among populist politicians throughout Latin America: They promised sweeping social and political change to win elections, but they governed like the neoliberals they criticized.

In 1996, for example, Caldera, who in 1993 had denounced his electoral rivals as "IMF-package candidates," nonetheless accepted a package agreement with the IMF that lent his government $3.3 billion. In return, he cut federal spending, eased regulations on foreign investment, and opened the way for privatization of the economy's crown jewels—the oil industry and the aluminum, steel, and electrical companies operated by the public Venezuelan Corporation of Guyana.

The Caldera regime's acceptance of neoliberal orthodoxy and especially its privatization proposals provoked bitter debates. Aware of the immense public opposition to the privatization of oil, the neoliberal politicians chose a more indirect route. In 1997, Congress passed the so-called "oil opening," which invited private capital to participate in the exploration for, and exploitation of, oil reserves, but it limited the state's participation in the development of potentially rich reserves to between 1 percent and 35 percent of the total capital of each joint venture. Despite the circumlocutions of the "opening," as an anonymous eight-page advertisement in *Time* magazine explained, it represented "the back-door route to privatization" of the state-owned oil industry. "Undoubtedly," says Steve Ellner, "the arrangement generates substantial public revenue, but the state's relinquishment of its status as a major investor points in the direction of the early days of the industry when Shell and Standard ruled the oilfields." Meanwhile, continuing public opposition and the refusal of foreign investors to pay Venezuela's price stalled the privatization of the steel and aluminum industries.

These debates took place against a background of chronic economic crisis, reflected in high inflation and unemployment rates, a crisis worsened in 1998 by depressed oil prices and a resulting decline of 35 percent in the central government's revenues. Poverty nearly doubled during the 1990s. A 1996 study by Mark Ungar noted that "62 percent of Venezuelans live below the poverty line, while prices for basic foodstuffs have risen beyond the reach of 75 percent of the population." Caldera's neoliberal remedies of austerity and other "structural adjustments" sharpened the pain and contributed to Venezuela's social devastation.

POPULAR DEMOCRACY, THE MILITARY, AND BOLIVARIAN REVOLUTION

As the 1998 presidential election approached, the price of oil had dropped by a third, the stock market had lost 70 percent of its value, foreign reserves dwindled, and fears of devaluation raised lending rates to around 100 percent a year. This did not favor Venezuela's traditional political parties and their neoliberal programs of privatization and public-spending restraints. "Their political mood," wrote a *New York Times* reporter, "seems to be swinging in precisely the opposite direction, with an overwhelming majority apparently convinced that the oil wealth should guarantee decent salaries, government services, job protection, and retirement benefits."

Despite a final effort to stop his populist juggernaut, retired Lt. Col. Hugo Chávez Frías, promising to combat poverty and misery, scored a decisive victory in the election, which the *New York Times* described as "freighted with a sense of history in the making." His electoral program stressed protection of domestic industry, a two-year moratorium on debt payments, a review of concessions to foreign oil companies, a halt to privatization of state assets, and reform of the constitution.

Chávez swiftly moved to secure from Congress for six months all the powers he needed to enact by decree a package of economic and financial legislation. He ordered army teams to enter the poor barrios of their towns to sell food at low fixed prices, repair schools, and engage in other public works. By 2000, it had become clear that Chávez, fortified by a series of sweeping electoral victories, contemplated nothing less than an economic and social revolution. A new constitution, adopted in 1999 and ratified by an overwhelming majority of voters, swept away the elitist, corruption-ridden political system established by the 1958 Pact of Punto Fijo and cleared the way for the construction of what Chávez called "Bolivarian Democracy." "The fight for justice, the fight for equality and the fight for liberty," Chávez told a Spanish interviewer in April 2002, "some call socialism, others Christianity; we call it Bolivarianism."

His government's ambitious program spelled out in careful detail a series of reforms, down to the number of new hospitals to be constructed and the medical care they would provide. But Chávez did not threaten to destroy Venezuelan capitalism. He sought reforms designed to make it socially responsible and to reduce inequality. An early achievement of the Chávez revolution was the sense of dignity that it gave to the popular masses. Proud of his indigenous, African, and Spanish ancestry, Chávez helped to eradicate the social stigma historically attached to the terms *mulato*, *mestizo*, and *black*. This new sense of dignity, not just the hope for improvement in economic status, helped explain the fierce loyalty of these mixed-race masses toward Chávez.

Because Venezuela still imported half of its food supply, agrarian reform was fundamental. Consequently, Chávez passed a law that limited farm size in some regions to two hundred and fifty acres and permitted the government to expropriate uncultivated land more than five thousand hectares. Traditionally, the vast majority of land was in private hands, and this law targeted vast cattle ranches and the great, frequently uncultivated estates called latifundios. "We have to finish off the latifundios," the president proclaimed in 2001. "The latifundio is the enemy of the country." The agrarian reform proposed to give land to as many peasants as possible, chiefly from the public domain, but it also redistributed private properties that lacked a clear title. From 2001 to 2009, the Chávez government confiscated 6.2 million acres of privately owned latifundio land and redistributed it to individuals or organizations that cultivated staple crops for domestic consumption. This land reform, combined with the construction of housing for poor families and other programs for the development of small and midsize industry, aimed to correct the enormous imbalance between rural and urban populations. Eighty percent of Venezuelans were urban dwellers, and most lived in shantytowns on the hillsides that surrounded Caracas and a few other large cities.

Improved access to education for poor children was another important goal of the Chávez revolution. The education reform eliminated the fees that students formerly had to pay. More than 1.5 million children enrolled in public schools, where they also received breakfast, lunch, and an afternoon snack. A massive vaccination program was launched in poverty-ridden areas, and the infant mortality rate, which had stood at twenty-three per thousand, declined to fifteen a decade later. A special bank provided micro credit to women who wished to start their own enterprises. Another important component of the Chávez program included the "Bolivarian Circles," neighborhood organizations that met to discuss and seek solutions for local problems; they received modest subsidies from the state to carry out local improvements.

The state oil company, Petroleos de Venezuela (PDVSA), was the main source of state revenue on which Chávez's reform program in education, housing, health, and other areas depended. Chávez doubled the royalties paid by foreign oil companies that operated in Venezuela. In cooperation with other members of the Organization of Petroleum Exporting Countries (OPEC, the oil-producing countries' organization) and independent producers, he sought to keep oil prices at satisfactory levels by reducing production quotas when necessary. Finally, he insisted that the state oil company have a controlling interest in new mixed enterprises with foreign oil companies. His nationalistic positions led to conflicts with the state oil company's established bureaucracy, traditionally dominated by the AD machine and more favorable to foreign companies.

Oil played an important role in Chávez's foreign policy to strengthen Venezuela's ties with its Latin American neighbors. In 2000, delegates from Venezuela and ten Central American and Caribbean countries met in Caracas to sign a document that lowered oil prices for signatory countries and eased the terms of payment when the international price of crude became too high. Venezuela also contracted to supply Cuba with up to fifty-three thousand barrels a day; in exchange, Cuba, whose health system was famous for its high quality, agreed to provide medical services in Venezuela's poorest barrios.

The warming relations between Venezuela and Cuba were not lost on the United States. Chávez frequently quoted Simón Bolívar's celebrated remark that "the United States appeared destined by Providence to plague America with misery in the name of liberty." He also defined neoliberalism as "the road to hell for Latin America," urged defeat of "the savage and irrational cart of globalization that destroys and excludes millions," and flatly rejected the U.S. proposal for a "Free Trade Area of the Americas." His political sins included visits in defiance of the United States to countries like Iraq, Libya, and Iran; his embrace of Mercosur, the South American common market; and his refusal to endorse President George W. Bush's "war on terrorism," especially U.S. military operations in Afghanistan.

Thus, it seemed inevitable that if an opportunity arose to topple this Venezuelan "troublemaker," Washington would not hesitate to seize it. In early 2002, the United States temporarily withdrew its ambassador to Venezuela, and high-ranking U.S. policy makers like Elliot Abrams, Otto Reich, and John Negroponte, all of whom had been active in the covert Reagan wars against revolution in Central America, met regularly with Chávez's Venezuelan opponents. These included large business interests, labor leaders, dissident officials of the state oil company's bureaucracy, and a few active military officers. Meanwhile, the press, radio, and television carried out a campaign of demonization against him and his programs. Attorney Eva Golinger painstakingly documented U.S. intervention that channeled hundreds of thousands of dollars to opposition business and labor groups, using as a transmission belt the National Endowment for Democracy, a nonprofit agency created and financed by Congress.

This agitation took place against a background of economic decline, the result of falling international prices for oil, which reduced state revenue and compelled Chávez to make budget cuts in all areas except social programs. Chávez also allowed the overpriced *bolívar* (the national unit of currency) to float, causing a measure of inflation that the large middle class bitterly resented. The economic downturn and inflation also fed the racist hostility of many white members of that class toward Chávez, whom they contemptuously dubbed *el Mono* (the monkey) or *el Negro* (the black).

The long-prepared blow fell on April 11, 2002, when two large demonstrations—one for and one against Chávez—milled about in the streets of Caracas and marched on the presidential palace of Miraflores. In the resulting melee, shooting began, and some fifty people, mostly Chávez supporters, died in four days of revolt and counterrevolt. Meanwhile, a group of military plotters had invaded the palace, tried in vain to make the president sign a letter of resignation, and then spirited him away to an island off the coast of Venezuela. In Caracas, a prominent business leader, Pedro Carmona, assumed the presidency, "with a cabinet of conservative fanatics," in the words of *The Economist*, a British magazine generally known for its neoliberal sympathies. Carmona promptly decreed the immediate closure of the Supreme Court and the National Assembly, while a hunt began for prominent members of the Chávez government. A classic military coup or **"Pinochetazo"** seemed to be in the making.

However, the oligarchy, its military and clerical collaborators, and its allies in Washington had badly miscalculated. The generals and admirals of elite origins who supported the coup did not represent the middle-level commanders and the rank-and-file troops. After the initial reaction of surprise and bewilderment, the presidential guard and loyalist military, spearheaded by the parachute division that

Chávez had formerly commanded, swiftly crushed the revolt and arrested its leaders. Meanwhile, a torrent of Chávez's humble supporters, furious at the conspiracy to topple their leader, poured into Caracas from the surrounding shantytowns and took command of the streets.

Restored to power, Chávez promised a full investigation of the coup and trials for those who orchestrated it, but he also struck a conciliatory note. Stressing that he was president of all the classes of Venezuelan society—upper, middle, and lower— he admitted that he had made mistakes, replaced a number of officials the opposition had sharply criticized, and regretted the harsh language he had used against his critics. Two weeks after the coup, Chávez informed the country in an interview that his peaceful Bolivarian Revolution continued on course, with the aim of transforming an oil-dependent, neoliberal economy and channeling funds into social programs to achieve social equality in a country that the wealthy had plundered for centuries. He made tactful reference to charges that the United States had supported the recent coup, saying it would be "horrible" if the United States was involved. "What I have said is that I ask God that it turns out to be false."

Despite Chávez's conciliatory attitude and gestures to win over some of his enemies, the diehard opposition, centered in the economic elite, remained sullen and unrelenting. It conducted an unsuccessful two-month general strike that crippled the economy in early 2003 but failed to destabilize Chávez's democratically elected government. Thereafter, his opponents seized on a constitutional provision for a recall election and organized a referendum campaign that also failed to bring Chávez down in 2004.

Each of these victories provided Chavez's allies with opportunities to extend and consolidate the Bolivarian Revolution, which triumphed again in 2007 with Chavez's stunning reelection. With 75 percent of Venezuela's 16 million voters turning out, Chávez captured 63 percent. During the campaign, Chavez had championed state regulations to redistribute wealth, property, and power to the nation's poor majority, and in its exuberant aftermath, he cried out to his delirious, flag-waving supporters, "Long live the socialist revolution! Destiny has been written. That new era has begun. We have shown that Venezuela is red! ... No one should fear socialism.... Socialism is human. Socialism is love."

After the election, Chávez used his democratic mandate to reverse the denationalization of the Venezuelan economy. "Everything that was privatized will be nationalized," Chávez promised his supporters, and in June 2007, his government made good on this pledge. It ordered foreign oil companies that earlier had received concessions to operate in the Junín, Ayacucho, and Carabobo oil fields to renegotiate their contracts to make PDVSA, the state-owned oil company, a majority shareholder. It also expropriated private cement companies, steel manufacturers, and one-third of the nation's banking sector, arguing that it had failed to make more resources available to local development initiatives. "Private banking must give priority to financing the industrial sectors of Venezuela at low cost," Chávez announced. "If banks don't agree with this, it's better that they go, that they turn over the banks to me, that we nationalize them and get all the banks to work for the development of the country, and not to speculate and produce huge profits."

Chávez also sought greater solidarity among Latin American nations through expansion of the Bolivarian Alliance for the Peoples of Our America and admission to Mercosur (Southern Common Market), both of which were regional trade associations that promoted the free movement of goods, labor, and capital among member nations. However, Chávez sought the "decontamination of neo-liberalism from Mercosur" and its transformation into an organization that "truly develops the region and its people." As an alternative to the World Bank, for example, he called for the creation of Bancosur (Bank of the South) to fund regional infrastructure development and social programs. Interestingly, according to a classified document released by Wikileaks, U.S. leaders, who opposed Chávez and Mercosur, nonetheless seemed to agree that Chávez's participation in Mercosur had changed the organization "from an imperfect customs union into a more restrictive and anti-American political organization."

After 2007, the Chávez administration faced a series of natural and economic crises. A severe drought drastically reduced hydroelectric energy production and required state intervention to ration electricity supplies. Later, torrential rains produced massive flooding that swept away the houses and lives of many mostly poor Venezuelans, some of whom received temporary shelter in the Miraflores presidential palace. Meanwhile, the global economic collapse in 2009 flattened a Venezuelan economy whose average annual growth of 10.3 percent between 2004 and 2008 had been the highest in all of Latin America. International oil prices fell from $150 to $30 per barrel, and gross domestic product (GDP) declined 3.3 percent. Nonetheless, in 2011, with oil prices once again rising, the government pledged to spend 45 percent of its $47.5 billion budget on public sector investments in health, housing, education, and economic diversification.

Although the Chávez government's policies had transformed Venezuela into the most egalitarian society in the entire region and reduced both poverty and extreme poverty rates from 49 and 22 percent, respectively, in 1999 to 26 and 7 percent in 2010, the 2009 economic crisis exposed its ongoing vulnerability—its extreme dependency on oil exports, the price of which fluctuated wildly. Moreover, unlike its neighbors who found lucrative new export markets for their raw materials in China and India to cushion the blow, Venezuela's economic recovery awaited the resurgence of oil prices that attended new political crises in Libya and the Middle East more broadly in 2011.

As President Chávez prepared for his reelection campaign in 2012, he confronted two challenges, one personal and the other political. After his arrival in Cuba for a routine medical procedure, his doctors discovered a cancerous tumour that they surgically removed, but the ensuing uncertainty about his prognosis and the charismatic nature of his presidential leadership further complicated the county's political future. Venezuela remained largely divided into two nations: a majority struggling

Reflecting the nation's belief in regional cooperation, this mural in downtown Caracas depicts the members of Mercosur as a soccer team led by Venezuela's Hugo Chávez, who enthusiastically exclaims that "Mercosur will mean more jobs, more growth, and improved welfare."

to emerge from poverty and backwardness and a minority determined to hold on to its power and privileges. Increasingly, however, it looked as if popular democracy, buttressed by strong military support, rising international oil prices, and a distracted superpower, might provide the key to unlock the potential for development and a measure of social justice. Venezuela's experience might yet become a model for other Latin American nations struggling to overcome the developmental disabilities imposed by the late-twentieth-century collapse of neoliberalism.

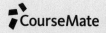

Go to the CourseMate website at **www.cengagebrain.com** for primary sources, additional study tools, and review materials—including audio and video clips—for this chapter.

20

Deconstructing the State: Dictatorship and the Origins of Neoliberal Markets

FOCUS QUESTIONS

- What were the principal characteristics of neoliberalism?
- What was the relationship between neoliberalism and military dictatorship in Argentina, Brazil, and Chile?
- What was the relationship between neoliberalism and Mexico's authoritarian state?
- How did U.S. intervention affect Nicaraguan democratic institutions and the emergence of neoliberalism?
- How did neoliberal policies variously affect foreigners and different Latin American social classes or interest groups, such as large landowners, industrialists, middle-class sectors, women, workers, peasants, Afro-Latinos, and indigenous peoples?

OTHING ABOUT NEOLIBERALISM and the popular movement that resisted it was uniquely Venezuelan. Certainly, by the end of the twentieth century, neoliberalism had become the dominant developmental paradigm in Latin America. Its resurgence was largely a response to the collapse of populism and elite fears of revolutionary alternatives that had been pursued with varying degrees of success in Chile, Cuba, Nicaragua, and Peru. Populist reforms historically had united elites and subalterns under the banner of nationalism because they promised social and political inclusion without fundamentally redistributing property and power. In the absence of such a radical transformation of existing social structures, however, high export prices, low-interest foreign loans, or some combination of both were necessary to finance populist reforms. In the 1970s, high interest rates, high oil prices associated with the Arab oil embargo, and plunging prices for Latin America's agricultural and mineral raw materials produced a perfect storm that destroyed the material foundation of populism.

The strong, nationalistic regulatory state—the centerpiece of populism—quickly became the target for those seeking to explain the reasons for Latin America's limited development. Of course, a powerful voice for policies later associated with neoliberalism always had reigned supreme in the foreign policy of the United States, which routinely supported the idea of an "open door"—that is, "a fair field and no favor," in the immortal words of Secretary of State John Hay. This idea became a founding principle in the postwar reconstruction of the global economy, the institutional pillars of which were the World Bank, the International Monetary Fund (IMF), and the General Agreement of Tariffs and Trade (later the World Trade Organization, or WTO). Increasingly, these institutions used their global economic power and Latin America's

1964–1967	Roberto Campos denounces state-owned industries and supports neoliberal reforms in Brazil
1968–1985	Brazil's dictatorship increases repression and abandons privatization
1968	Tlatelolco Massacre sparks dirty war in Mexico
1969	Assassination of Carlos Marighella, leader of peasant resistance to Brazil's dictatorship
1973	Pinochet overthrows Allende in Chile and initiates neoliberal reforms
1976	Videla leads military coup in Argentina and promotes neoliberal reforms
1978	Popular resistance to dictatorship intensifies in Argentina, Brazil, and Chile
1979	FSLN leads successful revolution against Somoza dictatorship in Nicaragua
1980	Pinochet imposes constitution that institutionalizes military control in Chile
1981–1989	U.S. support for *contras* in Nicaragua and Salvadoran military increase human rights abuses
1982	Britain defeats and discredits Argentine dictatorship in Falkland/Malvinas Islands war
1983–1985	Popular resistance to Argentine and Brazilian dictatorships ends formal military control but limits civilian power
1988	Fraudulent elections in Mexico lead to neoliberal privatization policies; popular movement wins plebiscite against Chilean dictatorship
1993	Mexico and United States sign North American Free Trade Agreement
1994	Zapatista Army leads revolt against Mexico's authoritarian political system and its neoliberal policies

extraordinary accumulated debt to encourage deregulation and denationalization. Local elites, many of whom were educated in the United States, added their voices to the growing international chorus that sang the praises of neoliberalism.

But what were the common characteristics of neoliberalism? Generally, neoliberals believed that development required an "open economy" in which the state's role was limited largely to policing functions—in other words, securing law and order—and promoting individual private enterprise. In the area of economic policy, therefore, neoliberals typically stressed free trade, export production, privatization of publicly owned resources, reduced import tariffs, deregulated capital flows, abolition of state subsidies to consumers, and encouragement of foreign capital investment. In most cases, although these policies successfully produced economic growth, measured in terms of rising gross domestic product (GDP), they uniformly accentuated the region's historical inequality.

Neoliberals also argued that the deconstruction of state power associated with these liberal economic reforms would disperse economic power and create the material foundation for a thriving political democracy that would bring the blessings of individual freedom to all Latin American people. Unfortunately, the historical record of neoliberalism's spread throughout Latin America seemed to contradict its major tenets. Far from promoting democracy, neoliberal ideas first emerged during military dictatorships in Argentina, Brazil, and Chile. In Mexico, its emergence depended on an authoritarian state that employed corruption and electoral fraud systematically to exclude effective popular political participation. In Nicaragua, U.S. intervention effectively subverted the sovereignty of democratic elections. In each case, however, popular mobilization against dictatorship, political corruption, and foreign intervention became the foundation for expansion of democratic rights and representation. Typically, these democratic social movements forced authoritarian leaders—military dictators and civilian elites—to cede their formal authority to elected successors; however, even a decade later, electoral deception and fear of

EL FISGÓN

Inspired by Pedro de Alvarado's sacking of Tenochtitlán, a famous scene described in the sixteenth-century Florentine Codex, El Fisgón's cartoon depicts the destruction of rain forests and indigenous communities as the second conquest of Latin America. In the 1990s, the conquistadors include the International Monetary Fund, modern technology, and transnational corporations (symbolized by the Coca-Cola bottle).

military power often conspired to preserve neoliberal policies.

Military Dictatorship and the Origins of Neoliberalism in Brazil

Although some scholars trace the origins of neoliberalism to Chile during the 1970s, policies closely associated with it—if not the doctrine itself—first emerged in Brazil in the aftermath of the 1964 military coup that toppled the democratically elected populist government of João Goulart. The military leaders of the self-proclaimed "democratic revolution" revealed their long-range intention to use the force of dictatorship to empower private sector property owners, foreign and domestic. On April

9, 1964, the Supreme Revolutionary Command issued the First Institutional Act, permitting the president to rule by decree, declare a state of siege, and deprive any citizen of civil rights for a period of ten years. A docile Congress approved the military's choice for president: Gen. Humberto de Alencar Castelo Branco. Like many of his colleagues, Castelo Branco was a fierce advocate of fanatical anticommunism, favorable treatment of foreign capital, and acceptance of U.S. leadership in foreign affairs.

ENCOURAGEMENT OF FOREIGN CAPITAL AND REPRESSION OF LABOR

The new government most clearly defined its neoliberal ideas and long-range aims in the area of economic policy. Roberto Campos, minister of planning, implemented a program to stimulate foreign capital investment by offering incentives that included the free export of profits, lower taxes on the income of foreign firms, and a special type of exchange for the payment of external financing in case of devaluation. He also favored privatization of state companies like Petrobras, the national oil corporation, and quoted Castelo Branco's belief that "If it is efficient, it doesn't need a state monopoly; if it needs one, it doesn't deserve one." However, the rest of the military leadership blocked its implementation and expanded investment in state-owned enterprises. Undeterred, Campos severely reduced internal credit in compliance with the antiinflationary prescriptions of the IMF, and imposed a wage freeze that depressed the real value of wages and further limited domestic consumption. These policies placed Brazilian-owned companies in an unfavorable position and caused massive bankruptcies.

The new government's economic policies accelerated the foreign takeover of Brazilian industry. By 1968, foreign capital controlled 40 percent of Brazil's capital market, 62 percent of its foreign trade, 82 percent of its maritime transport, 77 percent of its overseas air transport, 100 percent of its motor vehicle production, 100 percent of its tire production, more than 80 percent of its pharmaceutical industry, and 90 percent of its cement industry. The United States led, with about half of the total foreign investment, followed by Britain, France, Germany, and Switzerland.

To ensure foreign and domestic capital of an abundant supply of cheap labor, the government froze wages and banned strikes, which reduced workers' living standards sharply. In 1968, the minister of labor estimated that the real value of wages had fallen between 15 and 30 percent in the preceding four years. The appointment of military intervenors to oversee more than two thousand of the country's leading industrial unions further shackled organized labor.

Furthermore, the government suppressed dissent in all areas of Brazilian life, suspended the political rights of thousands of so-called extremists, fired thousands of federal employees, and either retired or dismissed hundreds of nationalist military officers. The government shut down the Brazilian Institute of Higher Studies, a major center of nationalist economic theory, suppressed the National Student Union, and outlawed the Peasant Leagues.

In 1965, Castelo Branco issued the Second Institutional Act, which dissolved all political parties and instituted indirect elections of the president and vice president. The Third Institutional Act (February 1966) ended the popular election of state governors and mayors of state capitals. Yet Brazil's military rulers chose to maintain a façade of democracy and representative government that Argentine political scientist Guillermo O'Donnell later famously labeled "**bureaucratic authoritarianism**." They established an official party and a legal opposition party, whose ranks they carefully screened to exclude "subversives." Its elected representatives had little or no impact on policy and legislation.

THE ECONOMY AND DENATIONALIZATION

This vicious assault on Brazilian democracy and civil liberties aimed to preserve the military's power and protect its economic policies, which favored foreign investment and export production but attacked the living standards of Brazil's impoverished majority. Although this promoted significant economic growth in Brazil's gross national product, averaging 8 percent annually, there was no parallel development of mass capacity to consume. Moreover, by 1970 the denationalization of key sectors of Brazilian industry was almost complete. One or a few giant multinational firms dominated each major industry. In the automotive industry, for example, three firms—Volkswagen, General Motors, and Ford—typified the concentration of industrial ownership and production. The military champions of free enterprise did not dismantle the state sector, however, as some would have preferred. Instead, they assigned to it the function of providing cheap steel, power, and raw materials to the profitable foreign-owned enterprises.

The regime's economic planners emphasized Brazil's exports to resolve the contradiction between a highly productive, technologically advanced industrial plant and an extremely small domestic market. Primary products continued to dominate the export trade, but exports of manufactured goods increased at a rate of about 12 percent between 1968 and 1972. Although most Brazilians lacked shoes and adequate clothing, Brazil became a major exporter of footwear and textiles. Increasingly, however, the regime stressed the export of durable consumer and capital goods, such as cars, electrical products, and machine tools.

Government planners also hoped that exports would solve the increasingly acute balance-of-payments problem, but even as the volume of exports increased, so too did the deficit. Meanwhile, the foreign debt, which stood at $12.5 billion in 1973, climbed to $17.6 billion in 1974 and approached $30 billion by the end of 1976. Service on this foreign debt, an important component of which was the increased cost of imported oil, amounted to nearly the total value of Brazil's exports in 1977. The problem was compounded by the heavy drain of interest and dividends in amounts considerably greater than the foreign investments that generated them. The deficits in the balance of payments contributed to a steep fall in the exchange value of Brazil's national currency, the *cruzeiro*, and an inflationary spiral that reached a rate of about 46 percent in 1976.

The recession that spread throughout the capitalist world in 1973–1974, combined with much higher oil prices, added to Brazil's economic difficulties. The passage of "antidumping" laws, designed to protect markets in industrial countries like the United States, cut into Brazil's exports of manufactured goods, creating overproduction and unemployment in various industries. By the mid-1970s, the bloom was off Brazil's "economic miracle."

The government's figures documented the devastating effect of the "economic miracle" on the general welfare. By 1974, the minimum wage was only half the minimum income required to buy food for subsistence. Including the costs of rent, clothing, and transportation, a worker needed four times the minimum wage. Official data revealed an intolerable situation with respect to public health. Nearly half the population over the age of twenty suffered from tuberculosis, and about one hundred and fifty thousand people died every year from the disease. According to the president of the National Institute of Nutrition, 12 million preschool children—70 percent of all children in that category—suffered from malnutrition in 1973.

The government's agrarian reform likewise helped great landowners to transform their estates into agribusinesses at the expense of their tenants. It threatened to expropriate latifundia that had not produced for four years, but the stress on "voluntary" adherence gave landowners time to delay and circumvent the law by dividing the land among relatives or forming it into commercial enterprises exempt from the law's provisions. Thus, its principal result was to stimulate the development of capitalist large-scale agriculture, accelerating a process that had been under way since the 1930s. Sociologists warned that the "agrarian reform" was spurring a new wave of rural emigration, throwing a new mass of cheap labor on an overstocked urban labor market.

Cultural Resistance to Dictatorship

As popular disenchantment with dictatorship grew, nationalists inside and outside the armed forces soon called for a return to the state-centered model of economic development, workers called for an end to the wage freeze, and intellectuals and students called for an end to censorship and a return to academic freedom. A portion of the clergy, headed by the courageous archbishop of Recife and Olinda, Helder Câmara, added their voices to the general cry for social, political, and economic reforms. With electoral politics closed to serious democratic debate, opposition to the military dictatorship increasingly infused popular youth culture, where lyrical metaphors and a driving musical beat initially avoided dictatorial censorship and substituted for political manifestos. Born in urban musical theaters that sponsored socially conscious plays like *Roda Viva* (*Commotion*), this new Brazilian popular music (*Música Popular Brasileira* or MPB) soon provided a catalyst for youthful protest against the dictatorship. It quickly reached a mass audience because, to attract a younger generation of consumers, television, radio, and record companies all sponsored competitions among musicians who were eager to play at music festivals originally held in large theaters and later in outdoor stadiums. Six months before each festival and following the carnival tradition, the radio repeatedly played songs and invited the most popular artists to perform at the festival. Among them were musicians like Geraldo Vandré and Chico Buarque, who used love songs and traditional ballads to thinly disguise lyrics that railed against social injustice and oppression. Vandré's "Disparada" ("Stampede"), for example, tells the story of a cowboy from Brazil's arid and poverty-stricken Northeast who, tired of having the fazendeiro treat him worse than the cattle, violently rebels.

However, perhaps the most popular song was "Caminhando" ("Walking"), which became a national anthem of youthful social protest, even after the dictatorship, citing its "subversive lyrics, its offensiveness to the armed forces, and its use as a slogan for student demonstrations," banned its dissemination. It called on workers, peasants, students, and intellectuals to mobilize against dictatorship in defense of song, a metaphor for freedom and democracy: "Walking and singing and following the song/ We're all equal, arms linked or not/In the schools, in the streets, fields, and construction sites/Walking and singing and following the song." More ominously still for Brazil's military leaders, "Caminhando" insisted that "those who know, take action now and don't wait for it to happen."

During this period, a new musical force appeared that made a dramatic impact on Brazilian popular culture and the struggle against dictatorship. Known as *tropicalía*, this new genre criticized the bossa nova and another musical style, *a jovem guarda* (new guard), as hopelessly romantic, fundamentally "bourgeois," and insufficiently willing to confront the brutality of the repressive military dictatorship. It called not only for the ouster of the military regime but also for a revolution of Brazilian culture and national identity.

Ironically, tropicalía music alienated both the military regime and traditional left-wing political opponents because it self-consciously fused Brazilian and foreign instruments and musical styles to create a "universal sound." This contradicted the interests of the dictatorship, which sought to maintain social control by celebrating Brazil's national cultural traditions, but it also undermined the nationalist critique of foreign domination and cultural imperialism. Led by artists like Caetano Veloso and Gilberto Gil, the *tropicalistas* acknowledged the musical influence of the Beatles' album *Sergeant Pepper's Lonely Hearts Club Band* and drew heavily on Oswaldo de Andrade's concept of "cultural cannibalism" to shock their audiences with raucous, electric guitars and lyrics that juxtaposed contradictory images of modernity and repression. At the International Music Festival, Veloso and his band, Os Mutantes (the Mutants), dressed like futuristic automatons, initially were booed off the stage when they performed "To Prohibit Is Prohibited." Veloso, in an angry rage, chastised his audience for seeking "to police Brazilian music" in the same way that the dictatorship sought to police Brazil; by contrast, he and his tropicalía comrades aimed "to abolish the imbecility that rules Brazil." Indeed, Veloso, Gil, and their comrades equally savaged the dictatorship and its agenda of capitalist modernization. According to cultural historian Christopher Dunn, in the title song of his first album in 1968, "Tropicalía," Veloso contrasted the bossa nova, cultural symbol of Brazilian modernity in the late 1950s with *palhoça*, "the ubiquitous mud huts of the Brazilian

Gilberto Gil, Caetano Veloso, Tom Ze, and Os Mutantes shocked Brazilians with their new sound, which combined traditional Brazilian rhythms with the electrified guitar sounds of Jimi Hendrix. Before their arrest and exile in 1968, their psychedelic music scorned middle-class Brazilian consumerism and the military dictatorship that protected it.

backlands." Although this seemed harmless enough, the song concluded with still more disturbing images, ultimately describing a modern metaphorical Brasilia inhabited by a "smiling, ugly dead child" begging for coins.

The tropicalistas' sophisticated allegories confused the military censors and even secured their approval for a time. In fact, the military dictators were unsure how to classify the political meaning of the tropicalía movement, especially because it was also the target of their nationalist opponents. By late 1968, however, the dictatorship, according to Veloso, was convinced that their music "represented anarchy, violence, and a threat to families, relations between generations, respect, and religion." According to Gilberto Gil, the military viewed tropicalía as "a threat, something new, something that can't quite be understood, something that doesn't fit into any of the well-defined compartments of existing cultural practices." The military government consequently incarcerated Gil and Veloso and later exiled them to Europe because they were "sort of illegible, and that won't do; that is dangerous."

Heartened by a growing popular resistance to dictatorship, Congress and the Supreme Court reasserted their independence. The Supreme Court defied military officials by granting a writ of habeas corpus for three student leaders whom they had imprisoned for three months. Congress protected the immunity of a deputy who had bitterly criticized the military for its brutal treatment of political prisoners and student dissenters. These acts of defiance led the military to dissolve Congress, impose greater censorship, suspend the constitution, and grant the president dictatorial powers. This escalated the use of terrorist tactics by a variety of police forces, local and national. Vigilante groups, operating with the covert approval of the government, joined the official security forces. The systematic use of torture by special units of the military police and the "death squads" reached a level without precedent in Brazilian history. The victims included intellectuals, students, workers, and even priests and nuns, as well as common criminals. Increasingly, Brazilians could express their opposition only in the allegorical style by now made famous by Brazilian popular music and the tropicalistas. On December 14, 1968, *Jornal do Brasil* published such a weather report that forecast "black weather, suffocating temperature, unbreathable air, and a country beset by strong winds." It could not have been more accurate.

The intensified campaign of repression convinced some elements of the Brazilian resistance that they had no alternative to an armed struggle against the dictatorship. Some half-dozen guerrilla groups arose, but they never achieved a mass character. The slaying in 1969 by members of a death squad of the most prominent guerrilla leader, Carlos Marighella, dealt a heavy blow to the movement, which soon ceased to pose a serious problem for the regime. Brazil remained a police state.

Ruled by a brutal military dictatorship, the Brazilian people continued to express their dissent and discontent through the few available cultural channels. Strongly influenced by a decade of rigid internal military censorship of Brazilian artists and the regime's free-market exposure to the innovative electric sounds of foreign music (especially jazz), a new generation of Brazilian youth grew up less interested in a song's words but very much aware of the liberating power of its sound. Milton Nascimento, perhaps the best known of these young artists, reflected this awareness in his "Milagre dos peixes" ("Miracle of the Fish"), a popular song sung without lyrics to protest military censorship. To overcome the limitations imposed by television and radio censors, these musicians increasingly relied on massive outdoor music festivals to communicate their ideas to the public; these festivals became important sites for the organization of popular opposition to dictatorship.

Urban theater was another form of popular culture that expressed opposition to the military. Professional theater battled the dictatorship, using metaphor and historical narrative to escape the censors' disapproval. Chico Buarque's "Calabar: O elogio da traição" ("Calabar: In Praise of Treason"), for example, used a famous story of betrayal in the seventeenth-century Portuguese–Dutch colonial wars to celebrate Brazilian independence from Portuguese tyranny, an all-too-obvious metaphor that, after three months, ultimately failed to survive the regime's censorship. Largely because of the military's omnipresent censors, local, decentralized amateur theater dramatically increased. These dramas likewise challenged the power of the military and sought to avoid individual recriminations by collectivizing all production decisions. They used narratives of well-known historical events to communicate themes of popular rebellion and resistance to oppression that resonated with contemporary antidictatorial struggles. *Teatro da rua* (street theater) also flourished during this dark period. It used the techniques of mime and clowning to scorn dictatorship and helped galvanize popular resistance in the nation's favelas, whose residents could not afford the price of a theater ticket. By the mid-1970s, a thriving national subculture of popular protest and rebellion belied the surface calm imposed by the military regime's brutal repression.

Influenced by liberation theology and its "preferential option for the poor," Christian Base Communities also emerged to play a key role in this struggle. Under church protection, women organized community and neighborhood groups that initially limited themselves to "feminine" demands for clean water, better housing, and lower food prices but increasingly became more overtly "political," agitating for the release of political prisoners and a restoration of democracy. According to *Brasil Mulher* (*Brazil Woman*), the media voice of an emerging feminism, women sought the "reconquest of lost equality." By decade's end, its editors, many of whom had been political prisoners, claimed a circulation of ten thousand readers and concluded that this effort had spawned a new revolutionary women's movement increasingly committed to the idea that "capitalism is the origin of numerous forms of the oppression of women."

Afro-Brazilians also created cultural organizations like the Center for Black Culture and Art, which advocated the abolition of racial discrimination and cultivated racial pride associated with a Pan-African consciousness. By 1978, however, these organizations had begun to coalesce in the Unified Black Movement (MNU), which organized *centros de luta* (struggle centers) to protest against racism, "the inevitable consequence of capitalist development." Likewise, a substantial minority of the Catholic Church hierarchy, led by Archbishop Helder Câmara, openly began to oppose capitalism and neocolonialism.

Meanwhile, workers, whose average wages under the military regime's economic program had fallen to two-thirds of their 1964 levels and one-half of their 1957 high, had become more vocal. A "new unionism" emerged to challenge the military government's policies and led directly to the formation of the Workers' Party (PT), which participated in the social struggle demanding an end to dictatorship, respect for human rights, and economic justice. Finally, congressional elections in 1978 reflected Brazilians' immense discontent with the economic and social results of dictatorial rule and the increasing strength of an opposition that united growing sections of the population.

THE DICTATORSHIP IN CRISIS, 1978–1983

Three major developments on the Brazilian scene took place between 1978 and 1983. First, a weak recovery from the recession of 1974–1975 soon gave way to an even more severe recession, culminating in a balance-of-payments crisis that brought Brazil to the verge of national bankruptcy. Second, the living standards of the masses continued to decline because of mounting unemployment, skyrocketing inflation, and the government's austerity measures, causing increased discontent and resistance on the part of the working class and peasantry. At the same time, opposition to the military regime grew among the middle class and sections of the capitalist class. Third, in an effort to defuse the growing opposition, the regime applied the policy of *abertura* (opening toward democracy). This policy of limited political concessions aimed to create a democratic veneer that preserved the military's fundamental power.

The economic crisis resulted from the interplay of domestic and external factors. An important cause was the inability of the domestic market to absorb the growing output of Brazilian industry. For almost two decades, the dictatorship had pursued a policy of promoting the growth of profits and capital by keeping wage increases below the cost of living; this policy sharply limited the purchasing power of the people. The economic downturn of the 1970s and the 1980s, however, also reduced the purchasing power of the middle classes, who provided a major part of the market for cars, television sets, and other durable consumer goods.

The most direct cause of the crisis was an unmanageable balance-of-payments and debt service problem. By 1980, Brazil had a foreign debt of $55 billion, the largest among the developing countries, and service of the debt absorbed 40 percent of the nation's export earnings. Even Brazil's president complained that because of the drain of interest, Brazil had "nothing left over for development." The high interest rates caused by the monetarist tight money policies of the Reagan administration added to Brazil's debt service burden. The export of a considerable part of the profits made by multinational companies in Brazil also increased Brazil's payments deficit. By 1980, these companies controlled 40 percent of the major industrial and mining enterprises of the country and sent home 55 percent of their profits.

By 1982, the balance-of-payments problem had reached a critical point. Brazil had almost exhausted the foreign exchange it needed to meet its financial obligations. The foreign debt stood at about $89 billion, and many of the approximately one thousand four hundred banks that had lent money to Brazil, grown suddenly nervous, were refusing to renew outstanding loans to Brazilian entities. A Brazilian default, however, would have sent shock waves through the world financial system. Once more, the Western Hemisphere's financial community's self-interest dictated a rescue operation. The plan, organized by the IMF with strong support from the U.S. government, provided for rollover loans that allowed Brazil to continue paying the interest on its debt, thus maintaining the profits of the international banks. At the same time, austerity measures imposed by the agreement meant that the mass of impoverished Brazilians, already hard-pressed, suffered further. The new loans gave Brazil breathing space, but the balance-of-payments problem remained as intractable as ever, and the government could not indefinitely repeat the financial juggling act of 1982.

The austerity program imposed by the IMF was a new blow at popular living standards, which had sharply declined since the establishment of the military dictatorship in 1964. In mid-1978, one study concluded that at least 70 percent of the population lived below the officially calculated economic survival level. In 1982, the minimum monthly wage was 23,000 cruzeiros, about $95. According to Brazilian sociologists, however, a family of five needed three times that amount to survive. The superexploitation of Brazilian workers took its heaviest toll on the weakest group of the population—its children. A partial census taken in 1982 indicated that half of all Brazilian children over ten worked.

These abysmal social conditions led to rural conflict that was intensified by an explosion of land concentration and land-grabbing. In part, this process of land concentration reflected the expansion of capitalist, mechanized agriculture primarily into previously uncultivated marginal and frontier land, producing export crops like soybeans or sugar cane for biofuel. This expansion was partially due to the pattern of Amazonian land settlement ignited by the construction of the Trans-Amazonian Highway and other roads. Instead of settling thousands of landless peasant families on the new agricultural frontier, the Amazon Development Agency gave big companies large sums of money to set up vast cattle ranches. As a result, some 95 percent of the new landholdings in the Amazon were of ten thousand hectares or more. Unlike coffee plantations, the large, new soybean and sugar-cane farms and cattle estates employed little labor. Many of the dispossessed or discharged tenants and rural laborers migrated to the cities, aggravating urban social problems and swelling the ranks of the unemployed and underemployed.

Thousands of others drifted to the Amazon frontier, becoming *posseiros* (squatters) who raised subsistence crops of rice, cassava, and maize on their small plots. They enjoyed considerable rights under Brazilian law, but these rights had little value on the violent frontier. Powerful land-grabbers, who arrived with their gunmen and sometimes enjoyed the open or covert support of the local military or other officials, frequently threatened the posseiros with eviction. The posseiros responded by organizing rural unions and defending their land by all the means at their disposal; they found allies in courageous Catholic clergy, whom authorities occasionally arrested, tortured, and even murdered for their humanitarian activities.

Discredited and isolated because of its failed economic policies and corruption, the military regime sought a way out of its impasse by a strategy of détente with the opposition. This policy of abertura included the lifting of most censorship, an amnesty that permitted the return of political exiles and the restoration of their political rights, and an overhaul of the political system that allowed the formation of new parties in addition to the official government and opposition parties.

These concessions were significant, but constitutional amendments, designed to ensure the continuation of military rule, limited their impact. Although the legislative opposition made large gains in the 1982 elections, the military's constitutional reforms had created an all-powerful president who controlled both the federal budget and the operating funds of the states. It still seemed certain that a military officer or a civilian nominee of the military would be the next president of Brazil, but the march of events upset the calculations of the military rulers. The dictatorship had counted on an easy win over opposition candidate Tancredo Neves, but popular mobilization against the military swept Neves to victory. On the eve of his inauguration, however, Neves died, leaving his vice president, José Sarney, to carry out Neves's program of structural reforms, which included land reform and the grant of a larger voice in government to workers and unions. Nevertheless, Sarney took office without Neves's mandate and with little popular support.

THE MILITARY AND EXTERNAL CONSTRAINTS ON DEMOCRACY

The transition to democracy and civilian rule, made under the watchful eyes of the military, was a gradual process. Behind the scenes, the military continued to influence the decision-making process on all major issues. Consequently, the Sarney administration made little progress in solving Brazil's great social and economic problems, the chief of which was land reform. This was not simply a question of redistributive justice; it was a prerequisite for the creation of a modern national capitalism based on a large domestic market. In 1985, for example, Sarney signed into law an agrarian reform bill that provided for the distribution of 88 million acres of land to 1.4 million families through 1989, but a 1986 decree limited the land available for distribution and expropriation to state-owned lands and to private holdings whose production was below the land-use standards set by government agronomists.

So sluggish was the program's implementation that Minister of Agrarian Reform and Development Nelson Ribeiro resigned in protest. The major obstacle to land reform was the fierce resistance of the landowners. Organized under the Rural Democratic Union (UDR) and the Brazilian Society for the Defense of Tradition, Family, and Property, the landowners hired thousands of former military personnel to staff private militias, reportedly paying salaries three times higher than those of the army.

If land reform was the most acute, violence-ridden issue of the New Republic, Brazil's greatest external problem remained the immense foreign debt, which in 1990 stood at about $120 billion. The continuous drain of foreign exchange had a profoundly negative impact on Brazil's efforts to achieve social reform and economic growth. To many Brazilians, it appeared that the nation must choose between paying the interest and supporting social and economic development.

Sarney defined his position on the debt in a 1985 speech to the United Nations General Assembly: "Brazil will not pay its foreign debt with recession nor with unemployment, nor with hunger…. A debt paid for with poverty is an account paid with democracy." These were brave words, in sharp contrast to the docility with which military governments had accepted the debt status quo, but this revolt by a timid president did not last long. Under pressure from foreign bankers and domestic oligarchs, Sarney lifted the debt moratorium and in 1988 began negotiations with the banks for a conventional rescheduling.

On taking office, the Sarney administration found the economy in recession, racked by galloping inflation and high unemployment. To combat this economic crisis, he announced an austerity program, *Plan Cruzado*, which established a freeze on wages, prices, and rents, and replaced Brazil's monetary unit, the cruzeiro, with a new and strong monetary unit, the *cruzado*. He also announced a series of currency devaluations designed to maintain export effectiveness. To reduce government expenditures, he immediately closed or merged fifteen state companies and scheduled thirty-two more to close in the coming months. Most painful of all, he decreed large increases in postal rates, the cost of utilities, fuel, and sugar, and 100 percent increases in taxes on cigarettes and alcoholic beverages.

An explosion of popular wrath followed these announcements. Brazilian wage earners' purchasing power, already slashed 30 percent since 1986, faced another decline of 29 percent. Consequently, the two national labor federations, the *Central Unica dos Trabalhadores* (CUT) and its rival, the *Central Geral dos Trabalhadores* (CGT), joined in a general strike to seek repeal of the austerity program. By mid-1987, Sarney's popularity had declined to the vanishing point. The U.S. banker David Rockefeller astutely noted the source of this decline: "In all my visits to Brazil, I have never before come across such desperate poverty."

In 1988, the national Congress, acting as a constituent assembly and influenced by this massive popular mobilization, gave the country a new democratic constitution that represented a sweeping rejection of all the late military regime had stood for. It provided for popular election of the president, abolished presidential rule by decree (so often used by the military regime), reduced the workweek from forty-eight to forty-four hours, and guaranteed basic civil rights, including freedom of assembly, speech, and press. Other provisions nationalized oil- and mineral-mining rights and protected workers' rights to strike and engage in collective bargaining.

The constitution promised protection of indigenous rights but contained no concrete measures to prevent the destruction of their culture and habitat, the Amazon rain forest. With the financial support of the military regimes and their civilian successors, big ranchers and mining companies, both Brazilian and foreign, cut down or burned vast stretches of forest to graze cattle or strip-mine, threatening the survival of indigenous peoples and *seringueiros* (rubber tappers). Hired gunmen, protected by corrupt and racist government officials, often murdered those who protested the exploitive practices of the ranchers and mine owners.

Sarney's administration received a stunning rebuff from Brazilian voters in the 1988 municipal elections, in which labor and socialist parties captured control of the major Brazilian cities and a majority of state capitals. Led by the militant trade union leader Luís Inácio da Silva (Lula), the PT, with a membership that grew into millions, was among the most dynamic of these new progressive political parties. Popular political protest seemingly had succeeded once again in transforming an elite effort to limit democracy and institutionalize military power into an instrument of mass mobilization. Nonetheless, the popular movement's focus in the 1980s had been largely procedural rather than substantive: It sought to end military dictatorship and open state policy to the influence of democratic participation. Although the devastating social consequences of the military's economic policy drove this political project, it was not yet the target of mass mobilization.

Military Dictatorship and Neoliberalism in Chile, 1973–1990

Like Brazil, Chile experienced a similar pattern of military dictatorship, followed successively by implementation of economic "reforms," popular resistance to dictatorship, and expansion of limited democratic rights. After a violent military coup, led by Gen. Augusto Pinochet, toppled the democratically elected Socialist president, Salvador Allende, Chileans endured a brutal and large-scale repression. The four-man military junta, with Pinochet in control, set about "regenerating" Chilean society. To this end, they abolished all political parties, suppressed civil liberties, dissolved the Congress, banned union activities, prohibited strikes and collective bargaining, and erased the Allende administration's agrarian and economic reforms. The junta jailed, tortured, and put to death thousands of Chileans, including Víctor Jara, who had reportedly defied military authorities by singing "Venceremos" ("We Shall Overcome"). The dreaded secret police, DINA (*Dirección de Inteligencia Nacional*)—with guidance from Col. Walter Rauff, a former Nazi who had supervised the extermination of Jews at Auschwitz—spread its network of terror throughout Chile and carried out assassinations abroad. The military junta also set up at least six concentration camps and arrested one of every one hundred Chileans at least once.

Pinochet, State Terrorism, and Free Markets

Meanwhile, Pinochet worked to legitimize his brutal regime and, under cover of The Feminine Power (EPF), an organization of aristocratic and middle-class women who had opposed Allende, he sought to cultivate a female constituency committed to "traditional family values," self-sacrifice, and loyalty to the motherland. He established a National Ministry of Women, and his wife, Lucía Hiriart, rejuvenated the Mothers' Centers, eventually organizing ten thousand groups that claimed two hundred and thirty thousand members. Nevertheless, the family was an early victim of the regime's political terror, and its economic policies alienated working-class women.

Pinochet, influenced by the "Chicago Boys," a group of economists who had studied with Milton Friedman at the University of Chicago, implemented his neoliberal, free-market doctrines. He slashed public spending drastically, privatized almost all state companies, devalued the peso, and reduced import duties sharply. The social consequences of the "shock treatment" soon became apparent. GDP fell 16.6 percent in 1975. Manufacturing suffered particular injury, with some industries, like textiles, devastated by foreign imports. Wages had fallen by 1975 to 47.9 percent of their 1970 level. Unemployment stood at 20 percent, or 28 percent when including people who worked in government emergency programs.

A recovery partly based on export products—minerals, timber, and fish—but above all on a speculative spree of immense proportions began in 1977 and turned into a boom that lasted until 1980, with annual growth rates averaging 8 percent. The Chilean "economic miracle," however, was superficial and short-lived. Hoping to attract heavy foreign investment to turn Chile into a South Korea or Taiwan, the Chicago Boys deliberately kept interest rates high. Foreign capital poured in, but almost all of it came in the form of loans to Chilean banks, which profited enormously by borrowing abroad at 12 percent and lending at 35 to 40 percent. The borrowing companies, subsidiaries of a few huge conglomerates, did not invest in production, which high interest rates made unprofitable, but used the loans for speculation in real estate or to buy up state companies sold at fire-sale prices under the privatization program.

The bubble burst in 1980. By the end of 1981, the government, contrary to its own free-market principles, had to take over the nation's largest banks to forestall economic calamity. Bankruptcies multiplied, and production declined sharply. Between 1982 and 1986, unemployment rose to more than 30 percent, and real wages fell by as much as 20 percent. An earthquake in 1985 added to the country's economic woes. By the late 1980s, the economy was heavily dependent on foreign loans. With a population of 12.5 million, Chile's foreign debt in 1991 stood at $17 billion, in per capita terms one of the heaviest debt burdens in the world. In its last years, the Pinochet regime swapped debt for ownership of Chilean industries and natural resources, with a resulting growth of foreign control of the nation's economy.

Great landowners who controlled the production, commercialization, and export of agricultural products profited handsomely. Exports of fruit and agricultural products sharply increased in these years, but the modernization and expansion of Chilean agriculture did not benefit the mass of the rural population, who lost most of the land and other gains made during the Allende years, suffered police repression, and endured chronic unemployment. Farm workers, prevented from forming labor unions and denied welfare benefits, worked no more than three or four months at a time and often lived in intolerable conditions.

The situation was even worse in urban areas, whose high levels of unemployment and underemployment forced workers to live with their families in squalid, overcrowded shantytowns. Even the middle class suffered a sharp decline in its standard of living. Between 1978 and 1988, the wealthiest 20 percent of the population increased their share of the national income from 51 to 60 percent. The next 60 percent, which included Chile's large middle class, suffered a substantial drop in income, their share falling from 44 to 35 percent. The poorest 20 percent continued to receive a meager 4 percent.

During the 1980s, as mobilization against the Pinochet dictatorship grew in numbers and audacity, images of Víctor Jara and Salvador Allende, two martyred champions of social justice and popular democracy, proliferated in public protests.

WOMEN AND RESISTANCE TO DICTATORSHIP

During the dictatorship's first decade, the opposition to Pinochet was fragmented. Nonetheless, Pinochet's harsh repression and unsuccessful economic policies soon gave rise to mass opposition. Although the Catholic Church initially supported the *Pinochetazo*, the Vicariate of Solidarity organized community support networks to provide legal aid, health care, and employment in craft workshops to working-class communities devastated by the dictatorship's political terror and economic war against the poor. Within a few months after the coup, the Vicariate served seven hundred thousand people, many of whom were women who became involved in what political anthropologist James Scott calls "infrapolitics," a dissident political culture largely hidden from the powerful but actively engaged in everyday forms of resistance. For example, these women hid people fleeing Pinochet's terror, baked and distributed bread containing secret messages about clandestine opposition activities, circulated information about the "disappeared," and created *arpilleras* (a folk art that used burlap and other common materials to fashion powerful political indictments of the dictatorship). These *arpilleristas* later participated in hunger strikes and *encadenamientos* (chain-ins), chaining themselves to the Supreme Court building, Pinochet's house, and various other government buildings to protest against the dictatorship.

The dictatorship especially damaged women's social position in Chilean society. It restored the *potestad marital*, which authorized a husband's legal control over his wife and her property, eliminated women's protective labor legislation, restricted women's access to unemployment compensation, disqualified women for legislative positions, and reduced women's median income from 68 to 36 percent of men's. These reverses in women's wage rates, coupled with skyrocketing male unemployment, created greater market demand for women's labor and the female workforce grew 4.5 percent by 1985 even as the proportion of female heads of households increased 4 percent.

Women therefore played an active role in the political opposition; for example, to commemorate International Women's Day on March 8, 1978, the Women's Department (DF), a women's trade union group, organized the first public demonstration against Pinochet. Women's antidictatorial struggles also became increasingly antipatriarchal, however. A decade later, at the Days of Protest demonstrations, women's groups like the Feminist Movement (MF) called for "Democracy in the Nation and in the Home." This described a comprehensive democratic agenda to end the dictatorship; reform the constitution; eliminate misogynistic civil, criminal, and labor legislation; create a ministerial office for women's issues; revise education curricula; and establish a government affirmative action goal of 30 percent female employment.

Under growing pressure from this swelling democratic movement, Pinochet made limited concessions to the demands for democratization and amnesty for political prisoners and exiles, even as the repression sometimes intensified. Maneuvering to remain in power, Pinochet called a plebiscite for October 1988, in which Chileans voted by a resounding 54.6 percent to 43 percent to deny Pinochet a new term as president; but the old dictator had fallback positions. By the terms of an undemocratic constitution imposed on the country in 1980, even if defeated, Pinochet was to remain in power for one more year until new elections determined his successor.

Pinochet still presided over a military council with broad powers, appointed one-third of the new Senate, and became a senator for life. In the aftermath of their electoral triumph, thousands of Chileans jubilantly jammed Santiago streets to demand the general's resignation from the army, but the civilian opposition leadership instead cut a deal with Pinochet. In exchange for the military's agreement to respect the plebiscite's mandate for a return to civilian governance, these leaders accepted his imposed constitution, which sustained the reign of Pinochet's economic model and his power to veto any significant political or social change. It also prolonged an abiding impunity for the military killers and torturers protected by the dictatorship's self-serving amnesty law.

Military Dictatorship and Neoliberalism in Argentina, 1976–1990

Like Brazil and Chile, the chaotic collapse of populism in Argentina produced a military coup that overthrew the democratically elected, but wildly unpopular, government of Isabel Perón, wife of the deceased populist caudillo. In the ensuing years, the military, led by Gen. Jorge Rafael Videla, adapted the Brazilian bureaucratic authoritarian model to Argentine conditions, unleashed a reign of terror unprecedented in the nation's history, and imposed an equally harsh neoliberal economic policy that decimated Argentine society. By the summer of 1982, the annual rate of inflation shot up to a catastrophic 500 percent, the highest in the world. Economic growth fluctuated wildly. Worst of all, the free-market policies of finance minister José Alfredo Martínez de Hoz led to record numbers of bankruptcies and bank failures. By eliminating tariffs on imported industrial goods and reducing government involvement in the economy, Martínez de Hoz presided over the destruction of many of Argentina's largest corporations. The real wages of Argentine workers plummeted 40 percent between 1976 and 1979, before

Mass opposition to the economic policies and repressive tactics of President Augusto Pinochet erupted in 1983 and 1984. Here thousands of Chilean youths march through Santiago calling for democracy and jobs for unemployed copper workers.

recovering in 1980 and falling again in the severe crisis of 1982.

ECONOMIC CRISIS AND DIRTY WAR

Between 1975 and 1990, Argentina experienced a prolonged period of economic stagnation, low or erratic growth coupled with high inflation, and declining manufacturing production. This produced sharply rising unemployment that contributed to falling real wages, increasing income inequality, and the dramatic growth of an "informal sector" composed mostly of impoverished urban female street vendors. Misery spread as the share of households earning income below the poverty line steadily expanded from 2.6 percent in 1974 to 7.5 percent in 1980 to a record high of 38.3 percent in 1989.

Naturally, this economic devastation contributed to political discontent and social turmoil. To defend its power, Videla's military junta banned all normal political activity and embarked on a dirty war against its opponents. Under military rule, some thirty thousand Argentines disappeared, many victims of illegal paramilitary death squads. Argentines came to fear the knock on the door at midnight, after which unknown kidnappers would take family and friends, who were never to be heard from again.

Opposition to the military's barbaric cruelty grew steadily, if clandestinely. Popular movements among human rights advocates, labor, youth, community groups, and women replaced direct political action. Human rights organizations, with a longer history of social activism, were most influential. These included veteran groups like the Communist Party–affiliated Argentine League for Human

Rights, established in 1937, and the Permanent Assembly for Human Rights, co-founded in 1977 by Raúl Alfonsín, who later parlayed his prestige into a convincing presidential electoral victory in 1983.

Labor, on the other hand, long the most powerful organized social group in Argentina, suffered dramatic declines because it was a special target of the military's political and economic violence. Determined to eradicate all vestiges of working-class resistance and heroic struggle, military officials attacked the gender identities of union leaders by subjecting them to what Jean Franco calls the "feminization" of torture: systematic assaults on the reproductive organs of men and women. Economically, union membership fell as privatization, government budget cuts, and foreign competition combined to increase unemployment. Under these conditions, important sectors of the labor movement, especially the leadership of the General Labor Confederation (CGT), collaborated with the military government. Some even testified years later that they "did not remember" the massive disappearance of workers and shop stewards during the dictatorship.

Young people also resisted the military's invasion of their schools, disruption of home life, and wholesale assault on youth culture. With traditional vehicles for expressing youth activism closed, their outrage found new channels of discontent, the most influential of which was "national rock." Outdoor concerts during the dictatorship regularly drew as many as sixty thousand youth who routinely defied the authorities with collective chants of "Se va a acabar" ("The dictatorship will soon end") and thrilled to the subversive lyrics of Argentine rock stars like Fito Paez, León Gieco, and Charley García. For example, García's "Los dinosaurios" ("The Dinosaurs") lampoons the military as witless prehistoric beasts destined to extinction, and Paez's "Tiempos difíciles" ("Hard Times") envisions the fires of hell emerging from the nation's cemeteries to avenge the youthful disappeared.

Community organizations offered a similar outlet to adults threatened by the military's economic and political war against citizens. With the moral, logistical, and financial support of local parish priests, squatters—impoverished, homeless, and

unemployed families—organized to reclaim vacant lands in urban centers. The first such group, the Neighbor's Commission, organized some twenty thousand people for a land invasion in San Francisco Solano, a working-class neighborhood in Buenos Aires. Thereafter, these neighborhood groups spread rapidly, protesting higher taxes, skyrocketing food prices, decreased social services, the lack of affordable housing, and inadequate schools and health clinics.

WOMEN, WAR, AND RESISTANCE

Drawing on a rich historic legacy of "social motherhood," Argentine women, according to literary critic Jean Franco, "subverted the boundaries between public and private and challenged the assumption that mothering belonged only to the private sphere." The best known of these women's groups, the Mothers and Grandmothers of the Plaza de Mayo, became the country's moral conscience. They refused to be intimidated by the military's daily death threats and routinely marched in the Plaza de Mayo, the nation's "symbolic center," demanding the return of their "disappeared" children and calling for the end of a dictatorship whose political and economic policies destroyed family life.

Women also campaigned for the abolition of compulsory military service, joint child custody, reproductive rights, sex education, and legal rights for children born to unmarried mothers. An organization known as Housewives of the Country denounced the high cost of living, sponsored shopping boycotts, and coordinated voluntary blackouts to protest the regime's neoliberal economic policies. Collectively, these popular protest movements weakened the military dictatorship and laid the organizational foundation for a return to democratic civilian government in 1983.

Facing growing domestic opposition and international pressure, the military sought to divert the nation from the government's program of economic and political violence by manipulating traditional *Peronista* populist themes of nationalism and anti-imperialism. Suddenly, Argentine soldiers, who earlier had sought to root out domestic opposition to the dictatorship's sale of the national patrimony, now defended Argentina's national dignity against British colonialism by capturing the Malvinas Islands (also known as the Falklands) in the south Atlantic, three hundred miles off the coast.

The invasion was the culmination of a series of colossal miscalculations by the Argentine military. First, it had not expected Britain to fight to retain the islands. The British, however, sensitive to their position as a declining world power, chose to fight as a matter of national honor. The Argentines also misjudged the position of the United States. They believed that their support of the illegal, covert U.S. intervention in Central America would secure its neutrality in the conflict. Instead, after an initial period during which it tried to mediate a peaceful agreement, the United States actively supported the British.

The war was a disaster for Argentina. Thoroughly humiliated and discredited, the military faced an unprecedented political and economic crisis. Inevitably, the generals had to yield power to a civilian government. Argentina ended nine years of nightmarish military rule in the fall of 1983 with the landslide victory of Raul Alfonsín, whose visibility in the human rights movement had earned him popular support.

Alfonsín first attacked inflation, which soared to 1,200 percent in 1985, by instituting the Austral Plan. This plan established wage and price controls, replaced the peso with a new currency, the *austral*, and reduced government spending. Almost overnight, currency stabilized, and inflation fell to 25 percent. Although the immediate crisis ended, the nation's economic problems remained. Argentina's industrial base was technologically backward, its foreign debt exceeded $50 billion by the late 1980s, and it still depended on primary export markets plagued by low prices. Unemployment in 1985 was the highest it had been in twenty years.

Alfonsín faced the difficult problem of the trials of the military accused of atrocities during the so-called dirty war of the 1970s and failures during the war with Great Britain. When the military re-

fused to try officers in its own courts, the president transferred the cases to civilian jurisdiction and appointed a commission to investigate military terrorism. The commission found the armed forces responsible for 8,971 disappearances; it documented torture, kidnapping, and other crimes, and labeled the acts as "the greatest and most savage tragedy in our history." The subsequent trials convicted several generals, who received long prison sentences. But in 1987, against overwhelming public opposition, Alfonsín ended prosecutions of lower-rank military for human rights abuses because they allegedly had simply carried out orders.

Alfonsín also faced an economic crisis of unprecedented proportions in 1989 when Argentina's per capita gross product fell more than 15 percent. To cope with the crisis, he pushed exports and enacted austerity measures—cuts in government services and wage restraints—demanded by the IMF as a condition for new foreign loans to keep the Argentine economy afloat. By spring 1989, the foreign debt stood at about $60 billion. Payment on the debt took some $6 billion a year, but the country's earnings in 1988 were below $3 billion. The deficit required new loans that only increased the country's dependency. The policy of austerity and faithful service of the foreign debt meant that little capital was available for development. The economic program contributed to a deterioration of the infrastructure, with long daily blackouts and energy rationing.

The situation sparked a week of food riots that spread across the country, with desperate thousands of people swarming supermarkets and cleaning out the shelves, although leaving the cash in the registers. The government responded by declaring a nationwide state of emergency and banning all demonstrations and strikes, but this popular uprising effectively marked the political demise of policies openly associated with neoliberalism in Argentina. Without the coercive power of a discredited military dictatorship, these policies seemed incompatible with Argentina's new democracy, but international pressures and electoral deception combined to prolong it for another decade in Argentina.

Neoliberalism and the Authoritarian State in Mexico, 1977–1994

Quite unlike the democratic states overthrown by violent military dictatorships in Argentina, Brazil, and Chile, Mexico boasted a stable one-party authoritarian state that had consolidated its authority through the exercise of populist policies and the creation of powerful state institutions. As a major petroleum exporter, Mexico, like Venezuela, also benefited from the skyrocketing oil prices produced by the 1975 Arab oil embargo. As a result, the emergence of neoliberal ideas in the aftermath of populism's collapse in Mexico was decidedly different than in the southern cone, although it also relied heavily on a clandestine dirty war, political corruption, and electoral fraud. The transition began with José López Portillo, who assumed the presidency on December 1, 1976. He continued the long-established policy of favoring the country's elites, opposing further large-scale land distribution and protecting efficiently run large estates even if their size exceeded legal limits. In the words of one Mexican weekly, "The constitution is to protect peasants wearing collars and ties, and not those wearing rope sandals."

Debt, Crisis, the IMF, and Populist Collapse

Amid growing optimism over Mexico's economic prospects, López Portillo announced the discovery of vast new oil and gas deposits on Mexico's east coast. Figures for the country's estimated and proven oil reserves steadily rose to two hundred billion barrels by 1980, and Mexico ranked among the world's major oil producers. With record high oil prices, government planners counted on the oil and gas bonanza to alleviate Mexico's balance-of-payments problem and to finance the purchase of imported goods needed for further development. The resulting expansion of production, however, was largely concentrated in capital-intensive industries—petrochemical factories, steel mills, and the like—that generated relatively few jobs and required expensive imports of capital equipment. In agriculture, too, the main growth was in capital-intensive, export-

oriented agribusiness operations that created little employment and diverted labor and acreage from staple food production, which actually declined during the 1970s; by 1980, one-third of the maize consumed in Mexico came from the United States.

The high cost of imported equipment and technology required to expand oil production required new loans. Despite increasing revenues from oil and gas exports, Mexico's trade deficit steadily rose from $1.4 billion in 1977 to $3 billion in 1979. Inflation again moved upward; Mexican workers lost 20 percent of their purchasing power between 1977 and 1979. Despite these troubling signs, international bankers appeared eager to lend more, advancing Mexico $10 billion in 1980. Who could question the credit of a country that seemed to float on a sea of oil?

The oil boom and the massive infusions of foreign loans exacerbated the familiar problem of corruption in Mexican political life. One Mexican newsmagazine, *Proceso*, estimated that López Portillo's administration had misused or stolen $3 billion of public funds. Much of this money financed a wave of private construction, but "the dance of the billions" soon ended. In the first months of 1981, responding to weakening demand and a growing world oil glut, oil prices fell sharply. Mexico's projected earnings in 1982 from oil and gas exports, the source of 75 percent of its foreign exchange, fell from $27 billion to less than $14 billion. Many wealthy Mexicans, losing confidence in their currency, hurried to buy dollars and deposit them in U.S. banks. In February 1982, with the government's foreign-exchange reserves dwindling at an alarming rate, López Portillo allowed the peso to fall by 60 percent. Fear of further devaluations provoked another flight of dollars. The growing shortage of dollars, vitally needed fuel for Mexican industry, caused a widening recession and unemployment.

Bankruptcies and closings multiplied as more and more businesses lacked the funds needed to obtain imported parts and raw materials or to pay debts contracted in dollars. With the Banco de México almost drained of reserves, López Portillo, desperate to avoid national economic collapse, announced the nationalization of all private (but not foreign) banks and the establishment of stringent exchange controls. Although the PRI and its client organizations joined with trade unions and progressive parties to support the bank nationalization, which was the most radical measure taken by a Mexican president since Cárdenas seized the oil industry in 1938, the private banking sector howled in protest.

In Washington, usually so allergic to populist measures smacking of collectivism or socialism, the bank nationalization did not arouse the hostility that might have been expected, probably because, given the circumstances, even U.S. officials regarded it as a necessary step. The Reagan administration's primary concern was to save Mexico, the third-largest trading partner of the United States, from a default that could wreck the international banking system and bring down the great U.S. banks to which Mexico owed $25.8 billion, almost a third of its foreign debt. Nonetheless, U.S. officials, in exchange for short-term loans to bridge the debt crisis, seized on Mexico's economic vulnerability to negotiate a rescue operation that required Mexico to open its industry to foreign investments, sell off state-owned enterprises, reduce protective tariffs against foreign trade, and abandon regulation of direct foreign investment. The plan specifically provided for U.S. aid of $2.9 billion for Mexico's current-accounts problem; a seven-month freeze on the repayment of principal due to foreign bankers; and an eventual IMF loan of $3.9 billion, which could initiate a new cycle of commercial bank loans to Mexico. The IMF loan was subject to the usual neoliberal conditions: Mexico must accept certain austerity measures, including reduction of state subsidies, restraints on wage increases, and other economies that were bound to hit Mexico's poor the hardest.

Even before he took office, the PRI's designated successor, Harvard-trained economist Miguel de la Madrid, had indicated his approval of the strong financial medicine prescribed by the IMF. These politically unpalatable steps included price increases of 100 percent and 50 percent on gasoline and natural gas, respectively, and the lifting of price controls and subsidies for consumer items ranging from shoes to television sets. Another measure was a new devaluation of the peso that aimed to stimulate

exports. However, it also made imports more costly, increased the burden of foreign debt service, reduced real wages, and imposed heavy new burdens on already impoverished Mexicans. This solution to the Mexican crisis, in essence, added new debts to old ones, without the slightest prospect that Mexico could ever pay the huge $85 billion foreign debt or even significantly reduce it without a large write-off. Four years after the rescue operation, the debt problem was more intractable than ever, rising to more than $100 billion by the fall of 1986.

Thus, Mexico faced a profound crisis of the populist, import-substitution model of development institutionalized by Cárdenas and continued by his successors. That model relied on state ownership of key industries, protection and subsidies for private industry, and such redistributive policies as the provision of social services, subsidized food prices, and land reform. It also called for the alternate use of co-optation and repression by the one-party state to keep restive labor, peasants, and intellectuals in line. By the early 1980s, however, that model, encumbered by a suffocating foreign debt, had exhausted its possibilities for growth.

Electoral Fraud, Maquiladoras, and NAFTA

Confronted with this crisis, a dominant section of the Mexican elite opted for a new, neoliberal model of development that abandoned the internal market in favor of exports of manufactured goods and integration with the world economy, especially with the United States. De la Madrid's economic program marked the formal transition to the new economic order. Two important steps in that direction were Mexico's signing in 1986 of the General Agreement on Tariffs and Trade, designed to lower tariffs and eliminate quotas and other restrictions on trade, and, under U.S. and Japanese pressure, the liberalization of foreign investment laws. The neoliberal remedy imposed by the IMF and embraced by Mexican propertied elites was politically possible in Mexico only because its one-party authoritarian state, like the military dictatorships in Argentina, Brazil, and Chile, prevented independent popular political participation.

The full implementation of the neoliberal project, however, had to await the outcome of the historic 1988 presidential election, which pitted the PRI candidate, another Harvard-trained economist, Carlos Salinas de Gortari, against Cuauhtémoc Cárdenas, son of former president and national hero Lázaro Cárdenas. Cárdenas's populist program called for an end to political corruption and electoral fraud, suspension of foreign debt payments, renegotiation of the debt with creditor banks and governments, a mixed economy, and state assistance to the ejido farming sector. His candidacy inspired a wave of popular enthusiasm and mobilization unknown since the election of 1934 that had brought his own father to power.

Most political observers believed that Cárdenas actually won the general election, but the PRI counted the votes and declared Salinas the winner with 50.1 percent of the 19 million ballots cast. Despite mass protests, including a march of thousands on Mexico City, Salinas assumed office and immediately slated for privatization almost all of Mexico's remaining 770 state-owned enterprises. He presided over a fire sale of some of Mexico's choicest properties, including mines, sugar mills, a five-star hotel chain, and the national insurance company. He sold two government airlines, state-owned steel companies, 70 percent of the petrochemical industry, and the Teléfonos de México, many well below their market value, and only some operated inefficiently at a loss. The privatization process also produced widespread layoffs, wage cuts, and growing foreign conquest of Mexican industry, aided by repeal of the law that restricted foreign control to 49 percent ownership of Mexican businesses. Salinas sold these state companies to the same small group of people and their foreign partners who already controlled most of Mexico's economy, with no effort to promote "popular capitalism" through stock offerings in the open market. "Crony capitalism," ran one comment, "seems to be the current government's style."

The removal of most tariff barriers destroyed many small and midsize domestic businesses and reinforced the denationalization of Mexican industry sparked by privatization. These developments reflected a general tendency on the part of Mexico's recent rulers to abandon the struggle for economic independence that had been a major goal of the Mexican Revolution, Lázaro Cárdenas, and his nationalistic successors. The foreign conquest of the Mexican consumer goods market since 1986 was very evident: "Everything from Italian pasta and Diet Coke to European cookies and Italian loafers is now available.... In many cases local manufacturers have closed down because imports are cheaper and better made."

The Mexican government's encouragement of the maquiladora program reflected the decision to abandon the struggle for economic independence. It permitted U.S. companies to establish plants for export production of parts and their assembly on the Mexican side of the border. The program allowed duty-free entry of parts and machinery into Mexico and total U.S. ownership of the plants. U.S. customs regulations permitted the finished products to enter the United States with duty paid only on the value of the labor, not on that of the goods themselves. The lure of low wages (averaging between $3.75 and $4.50 per day) caused an explosive growth of maquiladora plants, whose number grew from some 455 with 130,000 workers in 1982 to more than 2,000 with more than 600,000 workers, two-thirds of them women, in 1998. In these plants, workers assembled television sets, radios, and computer hardware for the U.S. market.

Many of these plants lacked unions, and government-controlled unions represented workers in others. These usually offered employers "protection contracts" that kept wages low and did not meet the labor standards mandated by the Mexican Federal Labor Law. The predominantly male supervisors in these U.S. companies routinely subjected a mostly poor, uneducated female labor force to sexual violence, harassment, and discrimination. To avoid the expense of complying with Mexican laws that mandated paid pre- and postpartum maternity leaves, these companies, according to a 1998 U.S. Labor Department report, often screened out pregnant job applicants, forced women employees to take birth control pills, and checked their menstrual flows. In addition, they often required women workers to submit to regular urine tests and arbitrarily fired pregnant women or reassigned them to physically challenging tasks designed to induce voluntary resignations or miscarriages. Moreover, according to University of Chicago sociologist Leslie Salzinger, this "sexualization of factory life," symbolized by annual industrywide "Señorita Maquiladora" beauty contests, discouraged worker solidarity and contributed directly to skyrocketing rates of violent crime against women.

Nonetheless, Mexican officials defended the program by arguing that it relieved high Mexican unemployment. However, because many of the plants were true sweatshops, with health and safety problems widespread among the workers, the program tended to institutionalize poverty on both sides of the border, for it inevitably depressed wages in the U.S. border zone. In the United States, unions feared the loss of thousands of jobs and the prospect of more to come. Environmentalists and health workers criticized the shockingly poor environmental and health record of the maquiladoras, which freely released various toxins into the air and water and routinely neglected to treat hazardous wastes. The American Medical Association declared that the maquiladoras had created "a virtual cesspool" on the border.

The neoliberal assault on state regulation especially affected women. Privatization eliminated relatively high-paying jobs for men and thereby placed additional burdens on women to supplement family income by working outside the home, often as salaried employees but more commonly as self-employed street vendors in the "informal sector." The maquiladoras especially sought out women workers, largely because management viewed them as more docile and likely to accept lower wages. Consequently, between 1970 and 1993, women's waged employment almost doubled from 17.6 to 33 percent of the total workforce. But, according to a recent study, 40 percent of women workers earned less than the minimum wage, and 60 percent received no additional benefits; moreover, 44 percent worked part time (less than thirty-five hours per week), and more than 54 percent were self-employed, working in microenterprises or on the streets.

The North American Free Trade Agreement (NAFTA), approved by the U.S. and Mexican Senates in November 1993, exacerbated all these economic, social, and environmental problems. NAFTA eliminated tariffs between Canada, the United States, and Mexico over fifteen years and permitted the free flow of investment capital across borders. This provided foreign investors with lucrative incentives to relocate their companies to take advantage of Mexico's low wages, which, according to the Economic Research Institute of Vienna, averaged only $2.35 per hour in 1993, compared with $17.02 in the United States, $16.16 in Japan, and $25.94 in Germany. NAFTA, however, also created an unprecedented crisis for the ejido sector of Mexican agriculture, which could not compete with corporate agribusiness in the United States. The agreement allowed duty-free imports of U.S. corn into Mexico and doomed Mexican ejidatarios, who accounted for 45 percent of all maize producers. Moreover, U.S. farmers still benefited from various government subsidies that enabled them to undersell their Mexican competitors.

A 1992 constitutional reform of Article 27 further threatened the very existence of the ejido system. It allowed the division of ejidos into individual lots and their rental, sale, or joint cultivation with domestic or foreign partners. The provision for rental of ejido land legalized a previously existing practice, but the lure of cash induced many impoverished ejidatarios to sell their land. Others lost their land through bank foreclosure. Increasingly, companies with easier access to credit and capital bought the most productive areas of the Mexican countryside.

Where did the hundreds of thousands of farmers who abandoned the land because of NAFTA and the agrarian reform go? Many left for the overcrowded cities, swelling the numbers of unemployed or underemployed Mexicans; others found low-wage jobs in the border maquiladoras or on farms producing fruit or vegetables for the U.S. market. Many headed for the United States to join the pool of undocumented Mexican workers, numbering in the millions and growing between two hundred thousand and three hundred thousand a year, who worked in agriculture, domestic service, small industry, and food service. The existence of this pool of low-paid, vulnerable workers —vulnerable precisely because they were undocumented, subject to deportation—represented a source of superprofits to employers and contributed to the weakness of organized labor.

Despite widespread poverty and repression, the PRI's monolithic control of Mexican politics and its neoliberal economic program faced little effective political opposition. This changed when the PRI held the traditional *destape* (unveiling) of its presidential candidate, Luis Donaldo Colosio, who had managed the fraud-riddled 1988 election. Then a succession of dramatic events shattered Mexico's surface calm, raising serious doubts about the ruling party's secure grip on power and its internal unity. On New Year's Day 1994, a revolt led by a self-styled Zapatista Army of National Liberation broke out in the southern state of Chiapas, one of the poorest regions of Mexico, with a largely Mayan population. The rebels proclaimed NAFTA and its free-trade program "a death certificate" for the native peoples of Mexico and demanded sweeping political and economic reforms, including self-rule for Mexico's indigenous communities, repeal of the reforms to Article 27, and fraud-free elections. They seized the highland city of San Cristóbal de las Casas before melting back into the Lacandon rain forest after a savage counteroffensive by fourteen thousand Mexican army troops, accompanied by village bombing, summary executions, torture of suspects, and other repressive measures.

With some specific features that reflected its tragic history, Chiapas's problems epitomized those of rural Mexico. The Mexican Revolution of 1910 never really reached Chiapas, with the result that no agrarian reform took place there. The great landowners still owned about 40 percent of the land, whereas 63 percent of the campesinos owned plots smaller than 2.5 acres. Emboldened by the crisis and the standoff with the government, land-hungry campesinos, not willing to wait for the government to act, occupied nearly one hundred thousand acres of farmland, resulting in armed clashes with paramilitary groups whom the great landowners had organized.

Severely eroded soils, the Salinas administration's cutbacks in credit and subsidies, and the collapse of world coffee prices aggravated the campesinos' problems. According to economist José Luis Calva, the "time bomb" that exploded in Chiapas resulted from the government's structural adjustment plan and the official free-trade policy, which resulted in a greatly increased importation of cheap corn from the United States. In his view, the reforms to Article 27 of the constitution, threatening what remained of the communal ejido system, "detonated" the crisis.

The Chiapas crisis deeply wounded the PRI and the Salinas regime, exposing sharp disagreements that widened appreciably with the shocking assassination of Colosio. Although Salinas quickly named another U.S.-trained economist, Ernesto Zedillo Ponce de León, as the PRI's new presidential candidate, a large majority of the Mexican public did not expect honest elections. So widespread skepticism greeted the government's announcement that Zedillo's margin of victory topped 50.08 percent, the "magic number" needed to retain control of the Congress and ensure a presidential mandate. Charging "colossal fraud," Cuauhtémoc Cárdenas's opposition party discovered more than six thousand polling places in which more votes were cast than the number of voters on the voting list. An unknown number of persons had disappeared from the voting rolls; the independent observer group Civic Alliance (AC) found that 65 percent of the nation's polling stations featured shaved registries.

In the midst of the regime's crisis of delegitimacy, the Zapatistas of Chiapas convened a National Democratic Convention in the Lacandon forest, to which it invited all sectors of "civil society," including all political parties except PRI, "the common enemy to us all." The convention, modeled on the 1914 revolutionary convention summoned by Zapata and Villa, reflected the Zapatista decision to broaden the scope of their movement—to develop electoral activity as an adjunct to armed struggle, leading to the drafting of a new constitution.

Consequently, Zedillo faced a sea of troubles. In Chiapas, the military standoff continued, but disorder was widespread and growing. Meanwhile, indigenous and mestizo farmers established four autonomous zones in different regions of Chiapas. They blocked roads, refused to pay taxes and electricity bills to federal and state authorities, and ejected local PRI officials. The Zapatista leadership proclaimed these areas "zones of rebellion." A wave of land takeovers continued, producing the unfamiliar spectacle of more than one hundred wealthy landowners staging a hunger strike in Mexico City to call attention to their plight. Zedillo had to choose between coming to terms with the rebels or crushing them with armed force. From the PRI's point of view, both options could have had dangerous consequences.

Mexican public opinion, as expressed in polls and demonstrations, favored a peaceful solution that took into account the just grievances of the Chiapas peasants. But PRI hardliners and foreign investors demanded a military solution of the problem. A January 1995 memorandum, written by Chase Manhattan Bank advisor Riordan Roett and leaked to an investigative newsletter, warned that "the government will need to eliminate the Zapatistas to demonstrate [to the investment community] their effective control of the national territory and of security policy." In addition to calling for the Zapatistas' liquidation, the memo warned the Zedillo administration "to consider carefully whether or not to allow opposition victories if fairly won at the ballot box," because "a failure to retain PRI controls runs the risk of splitting the government party."

Facing these rival pressures, Zedillo initially sought compromise, but on February 9, 1995, he sent thousands of troops, backed by tanks and heavy artillery, into the rebel-held territory, with orders to arrest the Zapatista leadership. The rebels, along with thousands of their supporters, fled into the jungle area near the Guatemalan border. The government's action provoked angry protests, including a march of almost a hundred thousand people in Mexico City that forced Zedillo to halt the military operation. A decade of neoliberal policies that depended on the PRI's monopoly of power effectively had mobilized a popular insurrection that delegitimized Mexico's authoritarian state. This forced a new democratic opening that required Mexico's neoliberal allies to reduce their dependence on the PRI and traditional authoritarian practices. In the process, like their counterparts in Argentina, Brazil, and Peru, they developed novel electoral strategies to prolong their political power.

Foreign Intervention and Subversion of Democracy in Nicaragua

Foreign intervention had always played a large role in neoliberalism's development elsewhere in Latin America, but it was the defining characteristic of Nicaragua's transition in 1990. Here, international economic forces and U.S. foreign policy decisively shaped the social, economic, and political conditions within which Nicaragua's democratic presidential elections occurred. In the process, they subverted the sovereign will of the Nicaraguan people.

LOW-INTENSITY CONFLICT AND DEMOCRATIC DESTABILIZATION

Ironically, by the end of 1986, external opposition to the Sandinista revolution had begun to fragment. The U.S. congressional elections had handed a heavy defeat to President Reagan. His administration suffered another blow with the revelation that it had sold arms to Iran and illegally diverted the proceeds to the Nicaraguan *contras* through secret Swiss bank accounts. The scandal—with new revelations of Central Intelligence Agency involvement in drug smuggling—increased opposition to the additional contra aid that President Reagan requested. By the end of the Reagan presidency, Congress had rejected an administration request for military aid and voted to limit funding to so-called humanitarian aid.

The Iran-contra scandal and its repercussions created a favorable atmosphere for new peace negotiations. Eager to end the contra war that was sapping its popularity, Nicaragua's revolutionary government soon scheduled new elections as part of a regional peace agreement negotiated in 1987 by all five Central American presidents. Significantly, the agreement barred foreign intervention, provided for release of political prisoners, and called for honest democratic elections in all countries.

In the 1990 elections, the FSLN, which had governed the nation since the 1979 overthrow of dictator Anastasio Somoza Debayle, faced a united political opposition, largely financed and organized by the United States. The National Opposition Union (UNO) was an unlikely coalition of fourteen small parties, ranging from former Somocistas to the Communist Party (PC de N). Although the overwhelming majority of foreign observers found that the elections were free and fair, some noted astutely that they took place "within a climate of U.S.-generated military and economic pressure."

On election eve, largely because of the decade-long U.S.-sponsored contra war, the national economy teetered on the verge of collapse. Purchasing power had declined 90 percent since 1980, and per capita GDP had fallen almost 20 percent since 1988. Basic food shortages were epidemic, and inflation raged at more than 5,000 percent. Foreign debt service payments consumed 62 percent of export income, and unemployment had reached a postrevolution high. Confronted with this desperate state of affairs, the Sandinista government reluctantly acceded to a modest program of *compactación* (structural adjustment), which meant still more pain for Nicaragua's impoverished majority. As if the deck were not sufficiently stacked against the FSLN, the Bush administration also illegally intervened directly in the election, plowing millions of dollars into the campaign of the UNO presidential candidate Violeta Chamorro, who triumphed with 55 percent of the vote.

What factors caused the UNO victory? Most observers concurred that the election results did not represent a popular repudiation of the Sandinista program of social reforms. They generally agreed that the key factors in the Sandinista defeat were the contra war and the disastrous state of the economy. In a country of fewer than 4 million people, the war had left sixty thousand dead, twenty-eight thousand wounded, and thousands of others kidnapped. For years, the war had forced the Sandinistas to divert scarce resources from popular social programs to finance military needs; by 1990, the war had consumed more than half the national budget. UNO campaign literature had concentrated on the public's war-weariness and opposition to the military draft, omitting mention that the contra war was the cause of the draft. UNO also neglected to mention that the Reagan administration, in flagrant violation of international and congressional laws, had almost singlehandedly financed the contra war for a decade. UNO campaign rhetoric also blamed the Sandinista government alone for the economic crisis.

Washington's strategy of bringing Nicaragua to its knees by a combination of economic blockade and low-intensity warfare had finally achieved its goal, but the initial aftermath of the election produced new surprises. In a stinging defeat for U.S. foreign policy, Chamorro announced that Gen. Humberto Ortega, chief of the Sandinista army and brother of the outgoing president, would remain. Moreover, Chamorro loyalists next joined FSLN deputies in electing a slate of National Assembly officers that included two Sandinista deputies. Chamorro's appointment of three Sandinistas to cabinet positions, including the strategic position of agrarian reform, sealed her temporary alliance with the FSLN. "In a strange twist of events," commented *Latinamerica Press*, the "coalition that Chamorro led to victory in 1990 has switched places with the Sandinistas and now considers itself the opposition." Chamorro's moderation also irritated Bush administration officials, who warned that Nicaragua could lose $300 million in U.S. aid if she made appointments that did not meet with Washington's approval.

The Chamorro government quickly reviewed its policies and began to implement a harsh neoliberal economic austerity program, including periodic devaluations that weakened the earning power of workers, termination of subsidized prices for staple products, and massive layoffs of government workers. Chamorro also sought to dismantle the agrarian reform and other social conquests of the 1979 Sandinista revolution. Although designed to achieve "stabilization," this policy produced political and social conflicts that threatened civil war. Promising to "rule from below," the Sandinistas vowed to continue their resistance inside and outside the halls of government.

The first major confrontation between Chamorro's neoliberal government and Sandinista unions ended in victory for the latter. A ten-day general strike produced a settlement with terms favorable to workers. These included wage increases, major political concessions like union consultation on economic policies, protection of government workers against large-scale layoffs, and a moratorium on the reversal of Sandinista agrarian reforms. The agreement proved to be only a truce in a continuing struggle between the Chamorro government, which sought to dismantle most of the Sandinista reforms, and unions determined to preserve their social and economic gains. Nevertheless, the agreement gave the government breathing space to seek relief from its desperate economic crisis through foreign loans and U.S. aid. Chamorro officials admitted that they needed "the Sandinistas to keep the country from exploding."

Sandinista supporters of this temporary alliance pointed to other victories as well as some defeats. If the Sandinistas could not prevent the return of many large properties to their former owners, with Chamorro's support, they succeeded in defeating UNO's plan to undo the Sandinista agrarian reform. If they could not prevent the privatization of almost all the state enterprises, they succeeded in including a provision for the workers' right to own 25 percent of the privatized firms and in some cases acquire total ownership of such firms.

Meanwhile the Chamorro government had expected Washington and the international financial community to reward its free-market policies of austerity and privatization with the aid and loans it needed to rebuild a shattered economy. However, U.S. aid was slow in coming and limited in amount, largely due to the opposition of Republican Senator Jesse Helms, who contended that the Sandinistas were still in power. Combined foreign aid and loans were clearly insufficient. During its first two years, the Chamorro government received about $715 million in donations and about $997 million in new loans, but in the same period, it paid more than $1.2 billion to service its foreign debt of more than $11 billion and another $456 million for oil imports.

By the end of the 1990s, neoliberalism had failed to offer a permanent solution to the developmental crisis that afflicted Latin America. Moreover, its dependence on U.S. government intervention and local authoritarian regimes threatened to poison popular enthusiasm for its policies. Increasingly, neoliberal proponents joined with popular opponents of dictatorship to demand the restoration or expansion of democratic electoral institutions. Nonetheless, neoliberals, noting the unpopularity of the neoliberal prescription, often sought to insulate economic policy from popular political debate. They also advocated institutional limits on democratic participation and routinely engaged in an electoral populism that postelection neoliberal policies often contradicted.

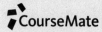

Go to the CourseMate website at www.cengagebrain.com for primary sources, additional study tools, and review materials—including audio and video clips—for this chapter.

Transcending Neoliberalism: Electoral Engaños and Popular Resistance to the Dictatorship of Markets

21

FOCUS QUESTIONS

- What were the electoral campaign promises of Collor and Cardoso in Brazil, and how did they contrast with the government policies that each implemented?

- How did Carlos Menem's presidential campaign and subsequent government policies in Argentina compare or contrast with those of his contemporaries in Brazil?

- How were the presidential campaigns and government policies pursued by Alberto Fujimori similar to or different from Menem's and Cardoso's?

- How did the long, brutal military dictatorship of August Pinochet limit the democratic process in Chile after 1990?

- How did electoral fraud in Mexico sustain neoliberal policies?

- What role did electoral deception play in shaping the neoliberal experience in Bolivia and Ecuador?

- How did Cuba handle the economic crisis of the 1990s, and how did this affect the Cuban people?

- What was the Pink Tide and how did it reflect the reactions of popular social movements to these electoral *engaños* and the neoliberal policies that they made possible?

- What roles did Chinese trade and investment play in shaping the global environment for the progressive nationalist policies of the Pink Tide?

B Y THE LAST DECADE of the twentieth century, popular political mobilization against dictatorship and other forms of authoritarianism had effectively eroded the power of these institutions in Latin America, establishing the foundation for the fuller development of formal democratic political systems. Very early in this process, however, politicians who benefited from and supported neoliberalism understood that success under the new political rules required them to disguise their practical policy prescriptions in the ambiguous language of electoral populism. Throughout the region, neoliberal candidates packaged their wine in populist bottles, but these electoral deceptions, so successful in the short term, had long-term negative consequences that

1989–2000	Era of "Washington Consensus" promotes privatization, exports budget cuts, and deregulation of business in Latin America
1989	Menem wins populist election in Argentina, but governs as a neoliberal
1990	Collapse of Soviet Union and socialist bloc alternative to capitalist development; Cuba announces "Special Period" of limited market reforms; Brazil and Peru elect populist presidents who govern as neoliberals
1995	Southern Common Market (Mercosur) forms to expand regional trade within the Southern Cone
1998	Hugo Chávez of Venezuela wins presidency campaigning against neoliberalism
2000–2011	Chinese economic growth diversifies Latin American dependency but threatens independent national development
2002	Lula da Silva wins Brazilian presidency, campaigning against neoliberalism; Argentine economy collapses
2003	Argentina elects Néstor Kirchner, a populist critic of neoliberalism
2006	Lula wins reelection and reduces Brazilian poverty; Socialist Michelle Bachelet becomes first woman president of Chile; Socialist Evo Morales wins presidency in Bolivia; Ecuador elects Rafael Correa to end neoliberalism
2007	Cristina Fernández de Kirchner becomes Argentina's first freely elected woman president
2008	Fidel Castro retires from public life, succeeded by brother Raúl
2010	Dilma Roussef becomes first woman president of Brazil
2011	Peru joins the Pink Tide with the election of Ollanta Humala

Gouverneur Morris, a sharp North American critic of popular democracy, predicted two centuries earlier. Equating democracy with "mob rule," the aristocratic Morris had argued that, in a democracy, "wealthy people" could only preserve their power through deception, but he feared that with each election they might "deceive the people and again forfeit a share of their confidence. And if these are instances of what with one side is policy, with the other perfidy, farewell aristocracy." In effect, Morris acknowledged that "aristocracy" required "perfidy" to preserve its power and property in a democracy, but he anticipated that "the people" would quickly lose "confidence" in their perfidious leaders and use the power of numbers to constrain the power of property.

Similarly, neoliberalism's initial electoral successes depended greatly on false promises, producing contradictory policies that deepened external dependency and widened the enormous chasm of social inequality. Predictably, new popular social movements soon arose to challenge these neoliberal policies and to insist that the nation-state had a central role to play in regulating market forces to guarantee growth and development. Among the models of national development that influenced them was the Cuban experience. While neoliberal policies ravaged other Latin American societies during the 1990s, Cuba suffered its own peculiar crisis, losing virtually overnight all of its major trading partners. Nonetheless, Cuba's revolutionary state system, modified to allow a greater role for private markets and foreign investment, retained its regulatory responsibilities. By the decade's end, Cuban leaders proudly trumpeted their achievements; whereas hunger, homelessness, illiteracy, inequality, and lack of medical care were pervasive throughout the region, they remained relatively rare in Cuba.

Even as they dissented from many Cuban policies, leaders recently elected in what many observers called Latin America's "Pink Tide" acknowledged their respect for Cuba's social and economic achievements. Like Cuba, these democratically elected governments in Argentina, Bolivia, Brazil, Chile, Ecuador, Nicaragua, Paraguay, Uruguay, and Venezuela all opposed neoliberalism and advocated national development through regional integration and state regulation of market forces.

Ironically, a major transformation in global markets accompanied and reinforced this progressive nationalist developmental strategy. The emergence of China as a world economic power early in the twenty-first century provided the region with alternatives to the traditional markets of Europe and the United States, without their colonial baggage and geostrategic interests. According to a confidential U.S. embassy cable published by Wikileaks, Chinese President Hu Jintao toured the region a second time in November of 2008 to emphasize "a common focus on economic development and shared values as developing world partners [which] underlie rapidly growing trade and investment ties" that already had increased by 49 percent over the previous year. China was very much interested in Latin America's agricultural and mineral raw material exports, as well as new markets for its manufactured goods.

During the past decade, Chinese demand buoyed the region's global export prices, softened the economic blow of the 2009 recession, and, combined with low-cost imports, created surplus funds that progressive nationalist governments reinvested in domestic infrastructure projects. Latin America also sought to attract Chinese direct and portfolio investments that would allow them to utilize local resources to finish products, finance infrastructure development, create more employment, and improve domestic purchasing power. In 2009, China joined the Inter-American Development Bank and donated $350 million. A year later, China's EximBank offered $200 million in credits to finance Latin American imports of high-tech Chinese goods.

Moreover, Chinese assistance often came without the political and ideological conditions customarily attached to U.S. and European aid. Unlike the "Washington Consensus," sociologist Adrian Hearn argues, the "Beijing Consensus" presupposes "endorsement of national sovereignty and state-coordinated development." Thus, although Hu's goal in Cuba was to "introduce China's economic situation, including its transition from a socialist to market economy," a Chinese representative told

U.S. embassy officials that China "would refrain from offering suggestions that could be viewed as interfering in Cuba's affairs." In a luncheon with Mexican business executives and government leaders, Vice President Xi Jinping more candidly contrasted Chinese relations with Latin America to their European and U.S. counterparts. "There are some well fed foreigners who have nothing better to do than point fingers at our affairs," Xi argued, but "China does not, first, export revolution; second, export poverty and hunger; third, cause troubles for you." This message appealed to Latin Americans with memories of a century of U.S.-sponsored coups and destabilization programs.

Nonetheless, potential dangers also accompanied the advantages offered by the Chinese market. In particular, progressive nationalist governments in Latin America, according to Chinese authorities, "preferred longer term investment in roads, railroads, and ports," in sharp contrast to the Chinese penchant for extractive resources "that would yield quick profits." Moreover, Chinese light manufactured exports also competed with similar products produced in Argentina, Brazil, and Mexico, all of whom, according to Wu Hongying, Director of the Chinese Institute of Contemporary International Relations, "brought anti-dumping and other unfair trade suits against China in the WTO [World Trade Organization]." Mexico and Peru offered perhaps the best examples of the potential disadvantages of the China market. Because Mexico was not a major mineral raw materials exporter, it routinely incurred extraordinarily large trade deficits; on the other hand, Peru maintained a consistent trade surplus with China, but it largely depended on substantial mineral raw materials exports like copper, which reinforced the nation's historical dependency and produced economic growth without significant development.

Nevertheless, since 2000, the growing China market provided development opportunities that strengthened the Pink Tide, whose leaders often had spent their youth protesting military dictatorship only to face the dictatorship of markets in their adulthood. Two decades earlier, however, despite the absence of a propitious international environment, local Latin American popular movements challenged military dictatorships, which began a transition to civilian rule, electoral populism, and the institutionalization of neoliberal policies.

Electoral Deception in Brazil

Brazil's experience with electoral populism and neoliberal governance developed early in the transition from dictatorship to formal democracy. The startling results of 1988 municipal elections and, a few months later, a general strike that mobilized 20 million workers, sounded an alarm bell to Brazil's elites and their political managers, who were preparing for the first popular presidential election in nearly thirty years. The new democratic environment required proponents of neoliberalism to present a populist, charismatic presidential candidate who could convince the Brazilian people to swallow the ill-tasting free-market prescription of austerity and privatization.

Neoliberal Wine in Populist Electoral Bottles, 1990–2002

Fernando Collor de Mello, a dapper sportsman and athlete from a wealthy family, was one such candidate. Sharply critical of official state corruption and inefficiency, his campaign focused on promises to reduce the bloated bureaucracy, attract foreign capital, and institute a free-market economy. Although he combined populist initiatives with policies that reflected his hardline free-market principles, the basic thrust of Collor's program conformed to the most traditional International Monetary Fund (IMF) recipes for economic solvency. Reduction of government spending and services, a halt to wage indexation (adjustment of wages to changing price levels), an end to collective bargaining except on the firm level, and wholesale privatization of state enterprises became the order of the day. A freeze of savings and banking deposits, designed to check inflation, helped produce the desired effect but had major recessive results; by 1990, industrial production had plummeted 25 percent, and layoffs nationwide were well over three hundred thou-

sand. Caught between the scissors of declining sales and interest rates of 6 percent a month, many companies filed for bankruptcy; almost a million workers were unemployed.

Meanwhile, Brazil's land problem remained without solution. Amazonia continued to be the scene of violent clashes between great landowners who frequently acquired their land illegally and small farmers whose tiny plots would not support their families. Peasants who resisted usurpation and exploitation faced threats, harassment, and murder. *Agências de pistolagem* (rent-a-killer agencies) operated in many areas; they offered a sliding scale ranging from $600 for a peasant to $4,000 for an elected official. In southern Pará, they killed 172 rural activists. A judge in Rio Maria (Pará state) expressed surprise about the excitement caused by such killings: "They were only peasants," he said. The Collor government did little to protect peasant leaders or punish their assassins. Responding to the devastating effects of the Collor program on wages, employment, and living standards, many unions went on strike and in some cases wrung concessions from employers and government. In the face of declining popularity, reflected in growing congressional and judicial resistance to his decrees, Collor's administration suddenly collapsed amid accusations of personal corruption on a large scale. Congressional investigations established that Collor and his associates had accumulated at least $32 million in public funds and payoffs, but that was only a fraction of the total involved. After months of investigations, revelations, and legal maneuvering, Collor, who had campaigned on an anticorruption platform, resigned just before Congress would have voted to subject him to an impeachment trial.

Electoral Engaños and Popular Protest

Following Collor's resignation, his vice president, Itamar Franco, who originally had opposed Collor's neoliberal market reforms, including the privatization of state companies, announced that he would continue Collor's privatization program and honor Brazil's debt commitments. Claiming that the income of Brazil's poorest citizens had fallen 30 percent as a result of Collor's "false modernization program," Franco assigned priority to a campaign against hunger and poverty. Governing elites seemingly understood clearly that the unadulterated neoliberal reforms so enthusiastically championed by the IMF, foreign investors, and Brazil's bourgeoisie were widely unpopular with the lower classes and therefore impossible to realize within the context of democracy, however carefully circumscribed.

This shaped a new debate between two groups within Franco's coalition cabinet. One advocated social reform and argued that growth to relieve hunger and poverty should be a priority in a country where millions of destitute people constituted a ticking "social time bomb." The other advocated neoliberal economic reform and prioritized the need to achieve fiscal stability through reduced government spending, the sale of state companies, and improved tax collection. The conflict between the cabinet's "social sector" and its "economic sector" sometimes sent confusing signals about the government's goal, but the neoliberal tendency generally prevailed. To head his economic reform team, Franco appointed the prominent sociologist Fernando Henrique Cardoso, whose program centered on deficit reduction, budget cuts, tax reform, promotion of foreign investment, and privatization of state companies in sensitive areas such as oil, mining, and telecommunications.

But Cardoso's program encountered strong resistance from progressives who opposed the austerity and privatization plans and from state governments dismayed by demands that they pay their large debts to the federal government. It quickly became the focus of political debate in the 1994 elections, the most sweeping in Brazilian history, with the president, two-thirds of the Senate, the Chamber of Deputies, the governors of all twenty-seven states, and deputies in the state assemblies all coming up for election. For the first time in Brazil's history, voters had the opportunity to choose between a neoliberal profit-driven model of economic growth, based on exports and foreign investment, and a more statist, autonomous model of development, oriented toward the solution of the country's great social problems. Workers' Party

(PT) leader Lula da Silva, an automobile worker and trade unionist who had opposed the military dictatorship, championed the latter and campaigned throughout the country, repeating his pledge to implement agrarian reform, fight unemployment, increase agricultural production, and improve health and education.

But Lula's chief rival was Cardoso, a distinguished academic who ran as a representative of the "viable left" (in contrast to Lula's "utopian left"). This reflected the increasingly leftward leanings of the Brazilian electorate. Cardoso's trump card was a new economic stabilization plan, the *Plano Real* (Real Plan). Under this tight-money plan, the monthly inflation rate fell from 50 percent in June to 6.1 percent in July 1994. Cardoso counted on the support of workers, whose salaries rose every two months but quickly lost their value because of uncontrollable price increases. His plan, combined with populist promises of sweeping social reform and oligarchical fear of a socialist victory, produced Cardoso's decisive win.

Cardoso faced staggering problems when he took office in 1995. True, the Brazilian economy grew strongly, with exports for the first five months of the year reaching $15.5 billion, an all-time record. However, these exports consisted mainly of raw materials like soy products, coffee beans, iron ore, and some manufactured goods like footwear and auto parts that were extremely vulnerable to fluctuations in market demand. Moreover, the growth of these exports, produced mostly by highly mechanized agribusinesses and plants, had little or no multiplier effect. Thus, high unemployment continued and the "informal sector," estimated between 30 and 60 percent of the economically active population, grew rapidly. Cardoso's program of a balanced budget and the Real Plan tamed the monster of inflation, but other economic and social problems still loomed large.

Revealing once again Brazil's extraordinary vulnerability to global economic changes, the Asian financial crisis in the fall of 1997 panicked the Brazilian stock market and unleashed a speculative assault on its currency, the *real*. To defend the *real* against devaluation and still attract the foreign capital that financed the nation's fiscal deficit, Cardoso doubled interest rates to 40 percent and announced an austerity package of spending cuts and tax increases designed to save $17.7 billion, or 2.5 percent of gross domestic product (GDP). Although Cardoso, facing reelection in the fall of 1998, sought to immunize social spending from these draconian budget cuts, they plunged Brazil into a severe recession. Industrial production fell and unemployment rates continued to climb; in São Paulo, the country's industrial heartland, even official estimates of unemployment rose to 17 percent in 1997.

Another major social problem was the grossly inequitable distribution of land. Less than 3 percent of the population owned almost 60 percent of Brazil's arable land, 62 percent of which lay uncultivated and unoccupied. Meanwhile, 5 million rural families were landless and lacked the means to earn an income with which to purchase their survival. Although Cardoso acknowledged that "we need agrarian reform," his government was slow to enforce a 1993 law permitting the government to expropriate (with adequate compensation) lands that were 75 percent idle. Consequently, under the auspices of the Catholic Church, some forty-two thousand landless families joined together to form the Landless People's Movement (MST), which organized a campaign of direct action to invade uncultivated lands. The MST soon established "squatter" communities that gave more than one hundred and forty thousand families access to land and pressured the Cardoso government to promise land to an additional two hundred and eighty thousand families.

But these popular victories came with a heavy price. Police officers and hired thugs often engaged with impunity in the wholesale slaughter of squatters, once in full view of television cameras. Despite international protests, however, no one was ever arrested, much less tried and convicted. For his part, although he deplored the violence, President Cardoso also chastised the MST as a "threat to democracy," thereby revealing the extraordinary shadow that historical memories of military dictatorship still cast over Brazil's "free institutions." Lest Cardoso's

subtle allusion was lost, the local president of a landowners' organization was characteristically more blunt: If the government failed to curb the MST's activities, he boldly announced, "we could have a repeat of the coup d'état."

Widespread poverty was yet another problem that neoliberal policies failed to relieve. According to government figures, the number of people living in poverty increased steadily from 50.9 million in 1979 to 64.7 million in 1989 and jumped 10 percent in 1990 to 69.8 million, almost half the entire population. Moreover, 32 million people, 21 percent of all Brazilians, lived in extreme poverty. Although poverty fell from 42 percent in 1993 to 34 percent in 1995, largely due to the Real Plan's elimination of inflation, it remained disturbingly high at 34 percent, despite steady economic growth over the next seven years.

Sixty percent of this indigent population lived in the Northeast, racked by recurrent droughts that wiped out crops and jobs and produced a water shortage that threatened the area with a large-scale spread of cholera. Anthropologist Nancy Scheper-Hughes noted that throughout the 1980s, diseases like typhoid, tuberculosis, leprosy, and bubonic plague, once thought to be under control, resurfaced in Brazil, especially in the Northeast. Calling them diseases of "disorderly development," she traced their roots to the "social relations that produce rural to urban migration, unemployment, *favelas* [shantytowns], illiteracy, and malnutrition." She described an area that was still "in a transitional stage of state formation that contained many traditional and semifeudal structures, including its legacy of local political bosses (coroneis) spawned by an agrarian latifundista class of powerful plantation estate masters and their many dependents." Moreover, she quoted the words of a woman factory worker who was disillusioned with civilian and military governments: "We need a government that will take care of the people, but I have begun to think that this doesn't exist; that it is another *engano* [deceit]."

The Northeast and the Amazon provided the extreme illustrations of the "disorderly development" that characterized contemporary Brazil, but the crisis pervaded every part of the country and especially affected urban women, who shouldered increasing burdens in the waged workplace. They worked for low wages, even as their unpaid familial responsibilities in the home grew proportionally with the decline of public services in health care, education, and child care. This crisis actually sharpened under the civilian, democratically elected regimes in power since 1985, regimes that embraced neoliberal economic policies and the model of dependent capitalist development even more ardently than the discredited military rulers. Official figures told the story of an increasing income gap between the rich and poor. According to Brazil's 1991 census, the poorest 10 percent of the population had less than 1 percent of the nation's wealth. The richest 10 percent, on the other hand, held 49 percent of the nation's wealth.

POPULAR RESISTANCE AND STATE-SPONSORED DEVELOPMENT, 2002–2012

But this "disorderly development" could have created still more problems without the determined opposition of a social protest movement that included trade unions like the Central Federation of Workers, environmental clubs, and mass organizations like the MST—all of whom defended popular interests against the worst excesses of neoliberalism. Senator Benedita da Silva, the nation's first elected *favelada* (slum dweller) and most prominent Afro-Brazilian woman activist, proudly claimed that "Brazil is perhaps the country in Latin America that has most resisted the neoliberal model, and our unions are on the forefront of this resistance."

Although politically divided, this social movement nonetheless influenced the contours of Brazilian political debate. Even Cardoso, defending his progressive, nationalist credentials, sought to identify his policies with these popular interests, insisting that his privatization of government services never sought to eliminate the state's role in Brazil's national development but merely to transform its function from a "producer state" to a "regulatory state." State social programs, he conceded, "are necessary because we cannot expect the market to solve the problem of poverty." This blend of market-centered policies and state-supported social services made Cardoso an elu-

sive target for his political enemies, enabling him to win reelection in fall 1998 with slightly more than 50 percent of the votes.

For almost a decade, Cardoso worked to integrate the nation's economy into the global marketplace, adopting neoliberal reforms endorsed by the IMF and relying on a steady expansion of exports, foreign investment, privatization, and overseas loans to finance modest social programs. This produced economic growth that averaged 2 percent since 1997, but it increased Brazil's external dependence. Debt service as a share of export income rose steadily from 26 percent in 1993 to an improbable 122 percent in 1999. More distressingly, however, income inequality remained the highest in Latin America, and poverty likewise stayed stubbornly high. Despite this record, Cardoso's populist rhetoric and a divided political opposition ensured his repeated electoral successes.

Cardoso was unable to pass his good fortune to his successor, however. By 2002, the collapse of neighboring Argentina's economy, growing uncertainties in U.S. money markets, and a generalized global market contraction reduced foreign investment and external demand for Brazilian exports. With a stalled economy and few state resources left to sell, Brazil could not pay its oppressive $245 billion public debt, stimulate renewed growth, and still satisfy popular demands for greater equality. In the 2002 presidential elections, the Brazilian people spoke loudly and overwhelmingly elected veteran presidential candidate and leader of the progressive PT, Lula da Silva, who promised to "break with the current economic model" and "suspend or reevaluate the privatization program." Presenting himself as a more mature, sophisticated candidate, Lula nonetheless criticized existing agreements and promised to "negotiate new ones with an eye to protecting national interests and without accepting impositions."

During the course of his presidential term, Lula pledged to "create the conditions so that all the people in our country can eat decently three times a day, every day, without needing donations from anyone." Poverty and income inequality, which had worsened during the nation's neoliberal experience, were a special target of presidential action. Lula insisted that "Brazil can no longer continue to live with such inequality. We need to overcome hunger, misery, and social exclusion." To that end, his government established the Bolsa Familia and Fome Zero, state-funded social programs designed to reduce poverty and eliminate hunger. By 2010, on the condition that their children regularly attend school and receive appropriate professional medical care, some 12.9 million families (52 million Brazilians) earned state subsidies under Bolsa Familia that, for Brazil's poorest families, doubled their annual incomes and reduced poverty from 22 percent to 7 percent.

Development for the great majority of Brazilians was the goal, but steady economic growth, averaging 5 percent per year, and reduction of foreign dependency were the primary means to achieve it. During his first term, despite heavy criticism from traditional political allies, Lula's government pursued budgetary austerity, price stability, and an aggressive export strategy designed to accumulate significant foreign exchange reserves, which climbed to $180 billion by 2008. The state then used these funds to pay off its foreign debt to the IMF, liberating the country from financial constraints imposed during the Neoliberal Era. Shortly after he won reelection in 2006 with 60 percent of the popular vote, Lula proudly announced the expansion of both social welfare programs and infrastructure investments in transportation, energy, housing, and sanitation that created some 4 million new jobs. His Accelerated Growth Plan, supervised by chief of staff Dilma Rousseff, a former urban guerrilla in the 1970s, invested half a trillion dollars in various projects designed to develop the impoverished rural interior and urban shantytowns.

Lula's progressive nationalist government also understood that socioeconomic inequality was an enduring obstacle to the nation's development, so it sought to confront Brazil's unspoken history of racial discrimination. Although 46 percent of the nation's 187 million people were black, they did not enjoy proportionate representation in government, education, and business. Under pressure from social movement organizations like the Coalition of Black Brazilian Women to remedy this sad state of affairs, Lula supported affirmative action policies in higher education and government employment. He also signed the Maria da Penha Law, which provided women protection from domestic violence, and created two Special Secretariats, one on Policy for Women and the other on the Promotion of Policies for Racial Equality.

Despite the legacy of a severe 2009 global economic recession that significantly reduced government tax revenues, newly elected president Dilma Rousseff, the daughter of a first generation Bulgarian immigrant family and Brazil's first woman chief executive, continued the policies that had earned Lula an 80 percent popular approval rating. To address the fiscal crisis, she raised taxes on foreign investors and announced drastic cuts totaling more than $30 billion in government spending, but she protected state investments in national infrastructure and social programs like Bolsa Familia, whose budget grew by almost 20 percent to $1.26 billion. She also inaugurated a new $5.7 billion program, *Rede Cegonha* (Stork Network), to finance maternal and infant health care. She increased the minimum wage, which had grown by 60 percent during Lula's tenure. State-financed initiatives to develop basic infrastructure and prepare for the 2014 World Cup championship and the 2016 Olympic Games contributed to a drastic decline in the unemployment rate to a record low of 6.4 percent.

Moreover, early in 2011, Rousseff signed a $7 billion agreement with China to finance local production of 6 million tons of soybeans, tripling Brazil's output over last year. This reflected Brazil's "strategic partnership" with China, the product of Lula's negotiation of a Joint Plan of Action for 2010–2014, but Rosseff also encouraged the export of high-value finished manufactured products to China. In a clear statement of the government's view of foreign investment in general and Brazil's special relationship with China, Brazil's attorney general insisted that "nothing is preventing investment from happening, but it will be regulated."

After years of blindly submitting to the will of unregulated markets, Brazil's future remained unclear, but one conclusion was inescapable: The

The Greek playwright, Euripides, wrote "What anger worse or slower to abate than lovers' love when it turns to hate." This cartoon captures these contradictions in the new economic romance between Brazil and China, which drove Brazil's rapid recovery from the global recession in 2009 but now threatens the nation's long-term autonomous industrial development.

popular political mobilization that brought Lula to power and elected Brazil's first female president had charted a different course of development in southern South America's largest nation.

Electoral Populism in Argentina

Building on Brazil's example, Argentina's military dictators had implemented a neoliberal agenda that greatly benefited foreign investors and wealthy, politically well-connected, local elites, but it had alienated a broad cross-section of Argentine society by its failure to produce sustained popular well-being. The economic crisis during the 1980s and a disastrous war against Britain over the Malvinas Islands led military officials to accept a democratically elected civilian government that nonetheless remained subordinate to, and fearful of, them.

MENEM'S REVERSAL OF FORTUNE, 1990–2000

Against a background of economic collapse, the Peronist candidate, Carlos Saúl Menem, campaigned against neoliberal liquidation of the national patrimony. His followers, including the powerful Peronist-controlled unions, naturally expected him to repudiate the policies that had led to an unprecedented economic and social crisis. What followed was a stunning surprise. Convinced that an even more powerful dose of those policies offered the only solution for the crisis, Menem, who professed his admiration for Ronald Reagan, Margaret Thatcher, and Augusto Pinochet, abandoned his party's traditional economic and political positions in favor of a neoliberal program.

First, Menem's cabinet included many big business executives from firms like Bunge and Born, a powerful multinational corporation, with links to the agricultural oligarchy that Peronists traditionally had distrusted. He also announced a program to privatize state-owned companies, dismiss thousands of state employees, and cut billions in government social spending over the next year. The program deepened and expanded the failed policies of the brutal military governments between 1976 and 1983.

The process of privatization occurred with frenzied haste and clearly favored large economic groups. Typical of the process was the fire-sale aspect of the privatization of two profitable state firms: Entel (the telephone company) and Aerolíneas Argentinas (the national airline). The *Wall Street Journal* commented that these two privatizations "more resemble corporate raids than stockholders' sales. Both Aerolíneas Argentinas and Entel are being sold for a fraction of their net worth." In July 1993, bidding began for the jewel of the state properties, the state oil company, Yacimientos Petrolíferos Fiscales, a profitable company with assets calculated at $7.4 billion and projected revenues of $5 billion. Among Latin America's oil producers, Argentina alone sold off its oil state monopoly, usually regarded as a "strategic" asset.

Menem's "shock therapy" on his way to the goal of a free-market economy provoked resistance. The Peronist trade union movement, once his ardent supporter, split into pro- and anti-Menem wings, followed by a series of strikes to which Menem responded by firing strike leaders and seeking to curtail the right to strike by law or decree. The once-powerful labor movement's ineffective resistance to Menem's policies reflected the decline in size of the blue-collar labor force and the increase in the number of unemployed and underemployed, which weakened labor militancy. Labor's traditional loyalty to the Peronist Party and the greedy opportunism of Peronist labor bosses, who lived off state money and collaborated with the party, whatever its policies, also paralyzed its opposition to Menem.

To combat inflation, Menem's finance minister, Domingo Cavallo, unveiled the "ultimate anti-inflation shock," a plan that made the Argentine currency convertible in relation to the dollar and forbade the Central Bank from printing any money that was not backed by gold or foreign currency. To ensure wage and price stabilization Cavallo pledged government budget cuts of $6 billion, largely at the expense of public sector jobs, in health, education, welfare, and pensions. From the government's point of view, the Cavallo Plan was a great success. Prices plummeted, the stock market exploded, and the Buenos Aires financial district hailed the start of the "Argentine miracle." The United States and the IMF rewarded Menem's fiscal orthodoxy by approving a Brady Plan that refinanced $21 billion of Argentina's foreign debt over thirty-five years.

This latest round of neoliberal orthodoxy deepened national income inequality, especially damaging women workers. During the next few years, unemployment soared from 13.1 percent in 1993 to 17.4 percent in 1995; the share of households that fell below the poverty line similarly increased from 13 percent in 1993 to 20 percent in 1996. During Menem's administration, women compensated for the decline in family income caused by higher male unemployment and falling real wages by entering the job market at much lower wage levels than men. In 1992, 45.9 percent of women worked for wages, but only three years later, the rate climbed to 52 percent. Even as more women entered the job market, however, unemployment among women grew, from 6.3 percent in 1992 to more than 20 percent in 1995.

These neoliberal policies had a significant impact on family relations. The number of families with a primary male breadwinner declined steadily from 73 percent in 1980 to 65 percent in 1994, with these trends intensifying between 1992 and 1994, when the number of families with primary female breadwinners increased by 62 percent. The resulting double burden on women both within the household and in the public sector undermined the traditional family; divorce rates rose markedly, and since 1980, the number of single-mother households increased by 93 percent and the number of nontraditional families tripled between 1992 and 1994. Moreover, under the relentless pressure of global market forces, the working conditions of wage-earning women deteriorated. Sociologist Rosa Geldstein concludes that, under the neoliberal regime, women suffered greater gender discrimination in the workplace and were required to work faster, with shorter and less frequent breaks, longer and less flexible hours, for lower wages.

Another legacy of Menem's neoliberalism was the appearance of a class of "new poor," including many members of Argentina's once substantial middle class. Nearly 30 percent of Argentina's population over age sixty fell into this category. An agricultural crisis—itself the result of low international prices, declining local markets, and the high cost of credit—contributed to this state of affairs. Moreover, the removal of tariff protections, which caused a flood of cheap textiles and other imports, forced many small businesses to close. Last, budget cuts for education and other social welfare programs were savage. This prompted Argentine social scientist Atilio Borón to disparage a democracy that "has no obligation to the poor and weak and has no concern for their fate, a democracy that manipulates injustice to protect the powerful and its favorites while it imposes the law of the jungle on the shantytowns." More to the point, he wondered, "Can a democracy of this kind consolidate itself through successive endorsements at the polls?"

DEMOCRACY OR DICTATORSHIP OF THE MARKET, 2000–2012

With the utter collapse of the economy in 1999, however, growing popular discontent removed all doubt about this possibility. If poverty and social inequality grew ominously even during Argentina's "miraculous" growth in the early 1990s, they skyrocketed thereafter when Menem's economic house of cards, battered by low export prices, high debt, and the flight of foreign investment, came crashing down. Between 1999 and 2002, the economy shrank 3 percent per year, unemployment increased from 15 to 25 percent, and Argentina's capital account fell from a surplus of $16.8 billion to a deficit of $4.1 billion. Poverty, which rose during Argentina's prosperous years from 7 percent in 1987 to 19 percent in 1996, swelled to

half the population in 2002. Increasingly, families scoured garbage piles, competing with flies and maggots in their search for scraps of food to eat. One such man, cooking a small pot of fetid potatoes retrieved from a local dumpster, reflected simultaneously the anger and resiliency of a proud people victimized by foreign bankers and Argentina's elite: "Tell Mr. Bush we still want to pay back the debt, but give us more time," he laughed derisively.

Indeed, as the new millennium opened, Argentina found itself mired in a virtually unpayable foreign debt that, since 1990, had grown steadily to $155 billion. To service this debt between 1990 and 1996, Argentina had paid foreign bankers $3 of every $10 that it earned in export sales, but thereafter this rose precipitously to an average of $6. Nonetheless, to be eligible for low-interest loans that might have prevented national bankruptcy, the IMF insisted that the national government ignore the urgent cry of its own citizens and implement a domestic austerity program that balanced its budget on the backs of the Argentine people. Not surprisingly, "capitalism in Argentina," according to an investment banker at Salomon Smith Barney, "has become a dirty word; profit has become a dirty word." Another banker put the issue much more starkly: "We're somewhat less popular than serial killers."

Soon this simmering contempt for the inequities produced by unregulated markets boiled over in open revolt, as unemployed *piqueteros* (picketers) blockaded roads and middle-class youth burned cars, smashed windows, and looted stores. This popular wrath also ignited a political tempest that led to the resignations of President Fernando de la Rua, only recently elected in 1999 on a populist platform, and Alejandro Rodríguez Saa, his interim successor. To combat the economic mess bequeathed by Menem and generate the revenues necessary to appease the foreign bankers, de la Rua had deserted his own constituents and slashed pension benefits, cut state workers' wages 13 percent, reduced public expenditures 20 percent, and raised taxes. This apparent surrender to wealthy foreign interests again reinforced a growing popular disdain for politicians and the political process. In the 2001 elections, 40 percent of voters registered their protest by casting blank or defaced ballots. At weekly demonstrations throughout the nation, protesters ritualistically abused politicians, sometimes physically, chanting, "*Que se vayan todos!*" ("Throw the bums out!").

By early 2002, Eduardo Duhalde, a Peronist and frequent critic of Argentina's decade-long neoliberal experiment, assumed the presidency with a popular mandate to defy the foreign bankers and rescue the nation from this devastating crisis. He immediately defaulted on the external debt; abandoned the dollar as Argentina's monetary standard; and devalued the peso to make Argentine exports more affordable, raise the cost of imports, and create more jobs. He regulated the largely foreign-owned utilities industries to lower electricity, gas, and telephone rates; imposed new energy taxes that mostly affected foreign companies; and developed contingency plans for price controls. He also continued to limit the amounts that bank depositors could withdraw, regulated currency convertibility, expanded an emergency relief program that paid $42 per month to more than a million families, and allowed Argentines to use devalued pesos to repay credit card debt at par. Although foreign bankers expressed skepticism about these reforms, workers, farmers, and small-business owners clearly approved. In 2003, they elected as president Néstor Kirchner, Duhalde's populist political ally, who pledged not to be "a prisoner of the big corporations."

Following through on that electoral promise, Kirchner's government devalued the Argentine peso, expanded Argentine exports, and forced private utility companies to renegotiate their contracts. He also confronted the IMF, whose demands for austerity budgets had discredited his elected predecessors, and renegotiated the nation's foreign debt, reducing its value by 30 percent. In 2005, he used the nation's accumulated savings to liquidate IMF debt and thereafter announced temporary price controls that would become permanent if inflation persisted. "We are once again giving the state the neurons that have been taken away from it," he triumphantly announced to Congress. With successive years of 9 percent economic growth and

a dramatic reduction of poverty from 57 percent to 40 percent, it was hard to argue with his success. Moreover, Argentines rewarded his policies with a landslide victory in the 2005 congressional elections, in which Kirchner's allies won 54 percent of the contested seats. Polls showed that the president consistently enjoyed popular approval ratings around 75 percent.

This personal popularity greatly assisted his wife, Cristina Fernández de Kirchner, who won the presidency in 2007, becoming the second woman head of state in Latin America. Long a prominent lawyer and senator, Fernández, who had fought against the military dictatorship thirty years earlier, had campaigned on a nationalist platform that called for state regulation of private markets. She proposed expansion of Mercosur to include Hugo Chávez's Venezuela, greater regional collaboration with Brazil and Bolivia in the production and distribution of energy resources, and substantial investment in basic infrastructure like schools, transportation, and health care to reduce poverty and eliminate illiteracy. Additionally, she moved aggressively to limit increases in public utilities charges, prohibited foreign oil companies from exporting Argentine oil to reduce Argentine energy prices, and similarly imposed high taxes on agricultural exports like soybeans to encourage production of subsistence crops for the domestic market. She solidified her support among Argentine workers by supporting 20 percent wage increases for the CGT, which became a model for other labor unions.

During Fernández's presidency, Argentina also reformed its political system, limited the influence of private campaign contributions, increased the role of popular participation in candidate selection, reduced the number of minor party candidates, and made it possible for a candidate to win with less than a majority of the votes. The Fernández government negotiated a substantial discount of the nation's external debt and incorporated $30 billion worth of private pension funds into the social security system. It legalized same-sex marriages and established a state program to reduce poverty by paying poor families to keep their children in school. To shape the nation's growing economic relationship with China,

Reflecting Argentina's expanded economic relations with China, President Fernández toasts with Hu Jintao after signing trade agreements in Beijing.

she sought to increase the export of higher value Argentine products, reduce Chinese imports that competed with Argentine industry, and regulate Chinese investment. With an economy growing at 7.5 percent, unemployment at historic lows, and reliable polls showing her with 47 percent of the vote while her nearest challenger earned less than 20 percent, Fernández de Kirchner seemed poised to win reelection handily in 2012.

Although her policies experienced resistance from foreign investors, private oil companies, and landed oligarchs dependent on agricultural raw material export production, they appeared to be overwhelmingly popular with Argentines. According to reliable public opinion polls, she remained personally popular with 66 percent of the public. More important, however, the poll showed that 58 percent endorsed her vision of state intervention to control markets and protect average Argentine citizens.

Luís D'Elía, a prominent piquetero leader, earlier had identified the stark choices that Fernández de Kirchner and the Argentine nation confronted: "democracy or dictatorship of the market." Increasingly, it looked as if the Argentine people were determined to use the power of democracy to tame the market. After a decade of neoliberal addiction to unregulated foreign markets and privatization, however, it remained unclear whether this prescription of state regulation and regional integration would be sufficient to induce a sustained independent development.

Electoral Smoke and Mirrors in Peru

Like Menem in Argentina and Brazil's Collor and Cardoso, Alberto Fujimori had offered himself as a populist candidate for the presidency of Peru in 1990. As a political novice and ethnic outsider, this son of Japanese immigrants was particularly adept at securing the votes of subaltern indigenous and mixed-raced peoples too long scorned by the traditional creole elites that had dominated Peruvian politics.

FUJIMORI'S FRAUD, 1990–2000

Following his election, however, Fujimori caused consternation among his supporters by enacting severe austerity measures akin to those they had soundly rejected at the polls. "Fujishock," as the program was immediately dubbed, included the removal of customer subsidies. The result was soaring price increases, with the price of such staple foods as milk and bread nearly tripling. The program provoked widespread rioting and looting in Peru's shantytowns. Contrary to his pledge against privatization of major public enterprises, Fujimori, hoping to attract foreign capital, offered to sell 232 state-owned companies, including the controlling shares of the state copper mines. Despite their many problems, these firms provided one-half of Peru's foreign exchange earnings.

Fujimori confronted a comatose economy kept alive only with large injections of coca dollars, a fanatical guerrilla movement rampaging in the countryside and gaining ground in the cities, and a Congress that became increasingly restive over his use of the special decree powers it had granted him. Fujimori used those powers to promote his extreme neoliberal program and to give the military absolute control over the counterinsurgency. When Congress finally reacted to his abuse of the decree powers by overturning or amending some of the most offensive decrees in a special session, Fujimori aggressively attacked Congress and the judiciary for their alleged inefficiency and corruption. Then, on April 5, 1992, he carried out his famous *autogolpe* ("self-coup"), closing Congress and the judiciary, suspending the 1979 constitution, and proclaiming a "Government of Emergency and National Reconstruction."

Public support for this coup, revealed in polls that showed approval rates between 70 and 90 percent, reflected widespread fear of the Shining Path guerrilla insurgency, which played into Fujimori's hands by its merciless killing of popular community leaders who organized communal soup kitchens and glass-of-milk programs. As a result, the public applauded government victories in its fight against the Shining Path and the smaller Tupac Amaru Revolutionary Movement (MRTA), capped in 1992 by the capture of Shining Path leader Abimael Guzmán.

This terrorism provided a convenient pretext for the security forces' equally indiscriminate repression of those who opposed Fujimori's program: popular organizations, progressive parties, and journalists, a number of whom he arrested on charges of promoting terrorism. Fujimori apparently had come to the same conclusion as Carlos Menem in Argentina: "free markets" worked more efficiently in the context of an authoritarian political system.

To remove the taint of dictatorship and gain international respectability for his regime, in 1992, Fujimori drafted a new constitution that fully conformed to his authoritarian temper and neoliberal economic views. It permitted his reelection in 1995 and concentrated all power in the president by allowing him to dissolve Congress at will, veto laws, and promulgate laws by decree. The document provided for a laissez-faire economy, with the private sector assigned the dominant role, and for privatization of state enterprises. State activity in education would decline, with less support for free education. The constitution established a strongly centralized nation-state, eliminating regional governments, subordinating the provinces to the executive branch, and denying provinces the right to keep a portion of the profits generated by the exploitation of natural resources in their territory. Finally, the document adopted the death penalty for terrorism.

In 1995, Fujimori sought to lower inflation, expand consumption, and guarantee his reelection by opening Peru to a flood of cheap foreign imports. Although this produced short-term benefits, it also doubled the trade deficit, increased the nation's balance-of-payments deficit by 80 percent, and, over time, drove small and midsize industrial manufacturers and agricultural producers into bankruptcy. He also borrowed heavily from foreign bankers to pay for dramatically higher expenditures on poverty relief in poor communities devastated by his neoliberal structural adjustments. External debt grew by 72 percent from 1993 to 1995, and interest payments on that accumulated debt skyrocketed to 31 percent of export revenues.

In addition, the crafty president, dressed in indigenous garb, traveled daily to the *pueblos jovenes* (squatter cities), composed of indigent highland migrants forced off their lands or fleeing the grinding poverty of the countryside, and directly dispensed presidential patronage, agreeing to build schools, roads, or public infrastructure. Government spending on poverty relief increased nearly 60 percent in 1994 and another 90 percent in 1995. Social spending more than doubled from 3 percent of the GDP in 1993 to 7.8 percent in 1995; whereas Fujimori had spent only $12 on the social welfare of each Peruvian in 1990, he paid out $176 in 1995. Despite the long-term risks for national development, the strategy worked, and Fujimori captured 60 percent of the vote in the 1995 elections. Moreover, according to political scientist Kenneth Roberts, "Fujimori's support in 1995 was highest in Peru's poorest departments, especially in the southern and central Andean highlands, where opposition to the constitution had been strongest in 1993."

Although backing for Fujimori's economic policies was solid among foreign investors, the IMF, and domestic elites, it remained highly volatile among the impoverished masses. If every year were a presidential election year, the poor majority might be convinced to vote for Fujimori, and poverty rates might have declined from their historic highs in 1993, when 53.6 percent of Peruvians lived in poverty and 21 percent lived in "extreme" poverty. His 1995 reelection effort alone reduced poverty by almost 10 percent, but thereafter poverty grew at an alarming rate.

Despite the dramatic increase in 1995 GDP and Fujimori's effective anti-inflation program, the nation's economy did not expand sufficiently during his tenure to justify the sacrifices that his neoliberal policies imposed on Peru. Growth rates averaged 4.7 percent per year since 1991, but unemployment, averaging almost 9 percent a year, remained

EL FISGÓN

FUJIMORI: A MAN WHO SUITS ALL OCCASIONS.

El Fisgón/NACLA

Peru's President Fujimori quickly learned how to manage democratic capitalism's potentially fatal contradiction: to serve the powerful minority of international bankers and local elites who supported neoliberalism, successful politicians had to deceive their lower-class constituents with populist rhetoric and election-year patronage.

stubbornly high, and the poorly paid "informal sector," composed of part-time and self-employed street vendors, experienced the most sustained growth. As a result, despite a decade of growth, in 2002 54 percent of Peruvians remained in poverty. External debt, trade deficits, and net outflows of wealth all increased steadily since Fujimori took over in 1991. In 2000, the external debt was a whopping $28 billion, almost twice as large as when he took office. The trade deficit averaged almost $1 billion per year during his administration, almost three times higher than the annual average $500 million surplus accumulated in the two economically depressed years before Fujimori took office.

However, this economic picture of growing poverty and increased external dependency tells only part of the story. Fujimori's government continued to rely on authoritarian methods to preserve his power and implement his neoliberal agenda. But this weakened his standing among both political elites and popular sectors. After a constitutional tribunal ruled unconstitutional his bid to run for reelection in 2000, he promptly fired the justices. Next, reports surfaced that he had authorized his security forces to tap the telephones of 167 political opponents, including the former secretary-general of the United Nations, Javier Perez de Cuellar. Fujimori's military then virtually declared war on the opposition press, engaging in beating, kidnapping, and torture. When a television reporter criticized the $600,000 salary of the president's intelligence chief, Fujimori revoked the station owner's citizenship and transferred ownership to minority shareholders.

Determined to remain in power, no matter the cost, Fujimori pressed his National Intelligence Service (SIN), the equivalent of the U.S. Central Intelligence Agency, to intervene boldly in the electoral process to guarantee it. Emboldened by popular opposition to these high-handed, overtly authoritarian tactics, Alejandro Toledo, born to poor indigenous parents, denounced the impending fraud and withdrew from the elections. International observers quickly followed suit, and even the U.S. State Department, which had supported Fujimori's neoliberal economic policies, described the 2000 election as "invalid." Popular grassroots movements quickly organized a general strike, and a wave of social protests, some of which became violent, swept the countryside. Suddenly, the issue that galvanized all Peruvians, regardless of their other disagreements, was Fujimori. Toledo, an economist educated in the United States, seized on this popular mobilization to energize his own presidential ambitions; he now denounced Fujimori's authoritarianism, his "antipopular economic measures," corruption, and failure to reduce poverty among the 55 percent of the nation that earned less than $2 per day. The resulting tumult forced the Congress to dismiss Fujimori, who sought exile in Japan.

POPULAR MOBILIZATION AND RESISTANCE, 2000–2012

Ironically, this messy transition dramatically increased Toledo's popularity but without requiring him to spell out his vision of a post-Fujimori Peru. Although he supported free trade, his populist campaign called for a review of Fujimori's privatization program, specifically promised not to sell off the state's public utilities, and pledged to reduce unemployment and poverty. As a result, when he assumed the presidency in 2001, public expectations were understandably high. The popular sectors that had supported his candidacy had one agenda, but the Peruvian business elite and foreign bankers urged another. Toledo quickly made clear which program would shape his presidential administration. After meeting with officials of the IMF, he agreed to raise $700 million in 2002 and almost $1 billion in 2003 by selling off state assets, but this required him to break his campaign pledge to the people who had elected him. Thereafter, he announced the privatization of two profitable state-owned electric companies—Egasa, which earned $14 million on sales of $50 million in 2001, and Egesur—which were to be sold to a Belgian company, Tractebel, for $167 million, one-half their declared value.

This naturally ignited a storm of violent popular protests that led to the declaration of a state of emergency and produced two deaths, hundreds of arrests, and $100 million in damages. Pressed by this "democracy in the streets," Toledo, whose popularity already had plunged from a historic high of 60 percent to 16 percent, at least temporarily abandoned his privatization plans and apologized publicly for having violated his campaign promises. Toledo also had failed to make good on a promise to create 2 million jobs, restore workers' rights that had been usurped by Fujimori, and reduce unemployment and poverty, both of which rose as a result of his neoliberal policies.

The 2006 presidential election occurred in the midst of a growing popular clamor to "pay the poor, not the foreign debt." The top two candidates, Alán García and Ollanta Humala, a political newcomer and charismatic former military officer, both attacked Toledo's neoliberal policies and called for national development based on regional integration and state regulation of private enterprise. Ultimately, García cultivated neoliberal support and triumphed over Humala, who had identified himself with the radical nationalist policies of Bolivia's Evo Morales and Venezuela's Hugo Chávez. With 53 percent of the vote to Humala's 45 percent, Peru appeared poised to abandon its decade-long experiment with unfettered free enterprise in search of a more socially productive mix of state regulations and market forces.

Nevertheless, a year into his new administration, García appeared to follow the well-trod path of his mendacious predecessors. He appointed Toledo's neoliberal finance minister, Luís Carranza, to his cabinet and endorsed a free-trade agreement negotiated with the United States. He also supported an education law that the Peruvian United Education Workers Union (SUTEP) condemned as an underhanded attempt to privatize education. García, lacking a legislative majority, apparently compromised his populist electoral promises in exchange for a neoliberal agenda.

Meanwhile, Humala announced that his party would use its plurality in the Congress to "make sure García complies with his electoral promises." Even as Humala led the political opposition to García's government, popular movements joined the struggle. The Peruvian Peasant Confederation (CCP) denounced the free-trade pact and organized a strike that paralyzed much of the countryside. Teachers' strikes closed down 70 percent of the nation's schools, and copper miners, unable to negotiate a satisfactory contract, joined the national protest movement organized by the General Confederation of Peruvian Workers (CGTP). Indigenous communities also protested García's efforts to open the Amazon rainforests to foreign oil exploration.

Despite a steadily growing economy averaging 6.8 percent, largely the product of expanded copper exports to China, García's popularity fell precipitously from 63 to 42 percent in his first year and continued its slide to 27 percent in 2010. Presidential elections in the following year pitted Ollanta Humala against Keiko Fujimori, the daughter of the criminally convicted and imprisoned former president. Extolling the virtues of her father's corrupt dictatorial rule, Keiko promised to sustain García's neoliberal policies and a *mano dura* (iron fist) to deal with growing popular protests against them. Humala, by contrast, stressed the bankruptcy of

neoliberalism and, citing Lula's model in Brazil, called for greater state regulation of market activities and redistribution of national wealth. Humala won a narrow victory with 51.5 percent of the vote, but he lacked a reliable majority in the Congress, so the future remained unclear. By 2012, it seemed as if the Pink Tide had washed ashore in Peru, but it may have brought more of the same old flotsam and jetsam instead of the real change that the nation's impoverished majority demanded.

"Limited" Democracy in Chile

Like the Brazilian and Argentine experiences with dictatorship, Chile's military government proved unable to sustain a stable social order that guaranteed private property rights beneficial to both Chilean elites and foreign investors alike. In opposition to the growing demand for restoration of popular democracy, these military leaders and their oligarchical supporters sought to reconstruct state institutions to permit popular electoral participation without surrendering social, economic, or political control.

NEOLIBERALISM IN A LIMITED DEMOCRACY, 1990–2000

Despite many differences, prodemocratic forces coalesced around Patricio Aylwin, who won the 1989 elections. The first democratically elected government since 1970 faced enormous problems. First, the power of Augusto Pinochet and his military dictatorship remained solidly entrenched in the state apparatus, especially the judiciary and security forces.

His 1980 constitution, which made it a crime even to think Marxist thoughts, also severely limited the new government's democratic options. Nonetheless, popular movements pressed for the release of all political prisoners, dissolution of the security forces, abolition of torture and other human rights abuses, and punishment of officials who had committed such abuses. Here a major obstacle was the amnesty decreed by Pinochet for acts committed during the so-called internal war between 1973 and 1978, but that amnesty did not cover the many brutal murders committed after that date.

The discovery early in 1990 of secret cemeteries, generally located near armed forces bases, that contained the remains of numerous victims who frequently had been tortured before being murdered, brought home to all Chileans the full horror of the regime under which they had suffered for seventeen years. One year later, a Commission of Truth and Reconciliation documented the horrific record of human rights violations committed under the Pinochet dictatorship. It identified 2,279 known deaths and disappearances, assigned direct responsibility for these crimes to the armed forces, and charged the courts with negligence for failing to respond properly to such violations of human rights.

However, the process of settling accounts with the military murderers and torturers proceeded with excruciating slowness, in part because of the grim resistance offered by Pinochet and the army and in part because of the government's anxiety to achieve compromise and "reconciliation" with the military. This led the president to support a "gentle accommodation" with them and to abandon efforts to make Pinochet step down as commander in chief, which angered organizations of relatives of the "disappeared" and many other Chileans who claimed that Aylwin's policies tended to institutionalize impunity.

Another major problem facing the new democratic government was the need to define its attitude toward the economic and social policies of the old regime, which benefited foreign transnationals and their domestic allies at the expense of long-range national interests and the welfare of Chilean workers. Here again, Pinochet's constitution, which prohibited new government investments that competed with the private sector, constrained public policy. Aylwin had to promise to make no major changes in the old regime's free-market policies but also committed himself to improve the living and working conditions of the Chilean masses. In fact, under Aylwin, the government considerably increased spending for health care, education, and social services. This resulted in a significant reduction in poverty. Overall poverty fell from 40 percent of the population in 1990 to 28 percent in late 1994, and absolute poverty

(defined as insufficient income to buy a basic food basket) fell from 14 percent to 9 percent.

However, the decline in Chile's poverty rate did not reverse historic patterns of income inequality. After almost a decade of democratic reforms, the wealthiest 10 percent of the Chilean population still received almost 50 percent of national income, while the poorest 40 percent, who had received only 10.5 percent in 1989, watched their share fall steadily during the 1990s.

This growing inequality was largely the product of the government's neoliberal economic model, which privileged employers' rights at the expense of labor. "Over the past twenty years," writes Orlando Caputo, a prominent Chilean economist, "$60 billion has been transferred from salaries to profits." Like its predecessor, the Aylwin government prohibited farm workers' strikes during harvest season, which effectively undermined their collective bargaining power. It also disguised unemployment rates by "privatizing" unemployment— that is, by forcing the unemployed into the "informal sector" of low-income, self-employed peddlers who composed 50 percent of the workforce. Real wage and salary income, which was still 18 percent lower than it was during the Allende period, declined 10 percent since 1986. By the late 1990s, a third of the nation earned less than $30 a week.

Aylwin continued to stress such export products as seafood, lumber, fruit, and agricultural products, with production and commercialization dominated by agribusiness companies, many of them foreign-owned. Typical was the case of wood exports. There was a veritable explosion of Chilean lumbering, which increased by 57 percent and grew 6.4 percent per year in the 1990s. In south-central Chile, the new tree farms replaced such traditional crops as wheat, corn, and rice. Environmentalists charged that the new forests were damaging the soil, drying up water sources, and causing a rapid decrease of many species of plants and animals. Chile's export-based economic strategy also had serious health costs. A study carried out in the large fruit-growing region around the city of Rancagua, south of the capital of Santiago, revealed an alarming increase in children born with physical deformities to parents whose work exposed them to dangerous pesticides.

The explosive growth of raw-material exports accompanied the collapse of large-scale industry in such areas as textiles and construction, which resulted in a decline in the number of unionized workers, who composed only 12 percent of the total labor force in 1996, compared with 41 percent in 1972. Meanwhile, the number of Chileans who worked alone or owned firms with fewer than four employees (the so-called *microempresas*) greatly increased, employing more than 45 percent of the labor force in 1992. Typically, they serviced the large conglomerates called AFPs (*Asociaciones de Fondos Provisionales*) or Mutual Funds, controlled by the ten richest families in Chile. "Workers in *microempresas*," writes Cathy Schneider, "are paid salaries barely above subsistence, without fringe benefits or job security. Irregular hours, unstable employment, and low caloric intake have increased levels of physical and mental exhaustion."

The AFPs also managed Chile's privatized pension system, to which all workers (but no employers) had to contribute. This system empowered employers to withhold employees' contributions from their paychecks, but no mechanisms could ensure that the employers promptly deposited those sums into AFPs, leading to frequent complaints about delays of months or even years in so doing. Moreover, because so many Chileans held marginal jobs in the "informal sector," almost half the enrollees did not keep their contributions up to date and consequently accumulated less than a $1,000 balance, clearly insufficient to support retirement. Finally, because the return on pensions depended on the value of the stocks in which fund managers invested, a prolonged decline in the Chilean stock market promised to have a catastrophic effect on workers' retirement incomes and the system's health.

POPULAR STRUGGLE FOR DEMOCRACY AND SOCIAL JUSTICE, 2000–2012

In December 1993, Chilean voters elected Eduardo Frei of the ruling center-left coalition, son of the reformist president of the same name. Frei's populist program pledged to eradicate extreme poverty by the year 2000, reform the labor laws and the public health system, and regain civilian control of the military, but he also declared his support for free markets. This meant that Chile's prosperity and democratic institutions, already severely compromised by civil society's Faustian bargain with the military, would depend on increasing exports, attracting new foreign investment, and expanding domestic consumer credit, all of which could easily collapse as the world market fluctuated. The 1997 Asian economic crisis, which briefly panicked the Chilean stock market, alerted many Chileans to the fragility of their government's developmental model.

As a result, significant indicators of growing popular resistance appeared. First, labor unions became more defiant. The Teachers' Guild (*Colegio de Profesores*), led by Jorge Pávez, a long-time Communist Party militant, organized a successful strike in 1996 and continued to coalesce with youth groups, environmentalists, women, and indigenous organizations like those of the Mapuches and Aymaras, all of whom had been damaged by the expansion of unregulated market forces.

Second, disenchanted with the political options available to them, none of which seemed to challenge the neoliberal orthodoxy, Chileans increasingly abandoned the political process altogether. In the December 1997 congressional election, 41 percent of eligible voters failed to register, abstained from voting, or defaced the ballot. Young people especially lost interest in politics and increasingly associated all political parties with corruption; during the last decade, the percentage of eighteen- and nineteen-year-olds registered to vote declined from 5 percent of the electorate to less than 1 percent. Even more startling, the share of voters between twenty and twenty-four plummeted from 15.6 to 4.8 percent.

Third, greater public support emerged for bringing to justice those accused of brutal crimes during the fifteen-year Pinochet dictatorship. A particularly courageous judge, Juan Guzmán Tapia, successively indicted Pinochet on murder and kidnapping charges. He also authorized a criminal investigation into the murders of two U.S. citizens,

Charles Horman and Frank Teruggi, who had supported Allende's Socialist government thirty years ago, and declared former U.S. Consul General Fred Purdy *inculpado* (a suspect) in the crime. Intimating that he formally would seek their extradition to Chile if he could not secure their voluntary cooperation, Guzmán also respectfully asked the United States to make available to his investigation some sixteen other former U.S. government officials, including then U.S. Ambassador Nathaniel Davis and National Security Adviser Henry Kissinger. A recently declassified U.S. State Department document seemed to confirm the wisdom of Guzmán's inquiry into the activities of these U.S. government officials: "There is some circumstantial evidence," it reported, "to suggest U.S. intelligence may have played an unfortunate part in Horman's death."

Finally, Chileans elected Ricardo Lagos, presidential candidate of the ruling *Concertación* coalition and a lifelong member of the Socialist Party. Although Lagos's political platform was not remotely similar to that of Salvador Allende, the Socialist president who had died defending democracy against a vicious military coup, the martyred president was clearly on the minds of the massive crowd that wildly celebrated Lagos's election with electrifying cries of *"¡Se siente! ¡Se siente! ¡Allende está presente!"* ("I feel it! I feel it! Allende is here among us!"). However, Lagos found himself in an awkward political position. He had campaigned on social themes, promising to sustain Chile's economic expansion, reduce unemployment, eliminate extreme poverty, promote equality for women and indigenous peoples, and guarantee workers' rights. But, thanks to undemocratic constitutional provisions imposed by the Pinochet dictatorship, his political opponents still controlled the Senate and blocked most of his legislative agenda, including a national heath-care initiative, a dramatic increase in the minimum wage, and greater spending on education.

Meanwhile, as global markets began to contract, unemployment continued to grow from 5.3 percent in 1997 to almost 10 percent in 2002; before the Asian economic crisis flattened Chile, its GDP had peaked at 6.6 percent, but it averaged a meager 2.9 percent during the first two years of the Lagos presidency. Equally disheartening was the steady growth of Chile's external debt and the steady rise in the share of export revenues diverted to repay it.

Nonetheless, Lagos could point to some modest successes. He reformed the nation's labor laws to defend workers' rights, make workplace discrimination illegal, and strengthen trade unions. This legislation extended state protection to some four hundred thousand women, annually hired as temporary workers by **enganchadores** (labor contractors who recruited workers by coercion or deceit) to harvest fruit in Chile's booming export industry. His government cut the military budget by severing its historic connection to copper exports and reallocated the resulting savings to social programs. During the Pinochet dictatorship, the military had received $225 million or 10 percent of all export revenues earned by the state-owned copper company, Corporación Nacional del Cobre (CODELCO), whichever was higher. Even though world copper prices generally rose during the 1990s, successive Christian Democratic presidents, still fearful of the military's power, had continued this practice, paying as much as $341 million to the military account in 1995.

Finally, he worked to reduce Chilean poverty, which had rocketed to 40 percent by the end of the Pinochet dictatorship, the "glory days" of the "free market." Steady economic growth and increasing state social programs since 1990 had produced a gradual decline in poverty rates to 20 percent in 1996, but Lagos sought to reduce these numbers still further and to eliminate extreme poverty by the end of his presidential term in 2006. Declaring that "the poor cannot wait, and these poor families will no longer have to wait," Lagos pledged to pay a monthly "protection bonus" of $16 to indigent families earning a dollar per day or less.

Lagos's successful management of Chile's "free market" created considerable public support for the Concertación's 2006 presidential candidate, the self-described Socialist Michelle Bachelet, the first Latin American woman to win the presidency independently of her husband. Like Argentina's

Kirchner and Brazil's Lula, Bachelet had spent time in prison for her political opposition to the dictatorship during her youth, but her fragile political coalition restrained her presidential policies. Sustaining a 5 percent average rate of economic expansion, she nonetheless pledged "to make sure that everybody in this country will have the benefits of this growth" and immediately appointed a cabinet with gender parity.

Moreover, she stressed the need to provide free health care to the elderly, reform the social security system, and free electoral procedures from the remaining constraints originally imposed by Pinochet's dictatorship. Bachelet's 2007 budget reflected these priorities, reducing the military's share and allocating 68 percent of funds to social expenditures— an 11 percent increase over the previous year. The bulk of these investments was in health care, social security, housing, and education. Because of these state-sponsored social services, Bachelet insisted that in 2007 the poorest 10 percent saw their household incomes triple, and "the gap between the wealthiest and the poorest 20 percent of Chileans declined by one half." Despite a severe economic recession in late 2008, Bachelet's popular approval ratings two years later rose to 85 percent, largely because her government had moved rapidly to promote growth with a $4 billion stimulus package that included dramatic increases in transfer payments to low-income families. Nevertheless, her popularity did not transfer to her Concertación political coalition, which lost the 2010 presidential elections to a conservative populist, billionaire business executive, Sebastián Piñera.

During the first year of his presidency, Piñera benefitted greatly from the dramatic rescue of thirty-three Chilean miners trapped beneath the earth's surface for more than two months. Thereafter, however, his neoliberal policies steadily eroded his popularity, which fell steadily to 30 percent. First, students and teachers declared a national strike that mobilized tens of thousands to protest in the streets in support of free, universally accessible, public education, most of which the old Pinochet dictatorship had privatized in 1981. Dressed as zombies and dancing to the beat of Michael Jackson's inter-

national hit, students debuted the "Thriller for Education," a correeographed "flash mob" that lampooned a private educational system that allegedly crushed their souls and transformed them into an army of the undead.

Next, in a protest against Piñera's privatization policies, mineworkers shut down CODELCO, the world's largest copper producer and the source of $5.8 billion in government revenues, 40 percent of the total in 2010. They complained that Piñera's appointee, CODELCO chief executive Diego Hernández, a former head of the Chilean operations of a foreign-owned private mining company, BHP Billiton, planned to attract private investment to CODELCO by eliminating 2,600 jobs and reducing workers' health benefits. Representing some 45,000 workers, union leader Raimundo Espinoza denounced the plan as "covert privatization." Piñera sought to resolve the crisis, at least temporarily, by reorganizing his cabinet. In his address to the public, however, he unintentionally paid tribute to the decades of popular mobilization and resistance that had brought down a dictator and restrained the dictatorship of unfettered markets. "Our institutions, our leadership," he asserted, "are being tested by citizens who are more empowered, who are demanding greater participation and, above all, greater equality." This was the legacy of Salvador Allende and the popular movement that defended his memory.

Clearly, history would judge Chile by its performance over time. This judgment ultimately depended on two factors: popular struggle to overcome the considerable institutional constraints imposed by almost two decades of dictatorship and a growing global economy upon which thirty years of neoliberal policies had rendered the nation utterly dependent. By 2012, progress on the former seemed certain even as the latter appeared increasingly doubtful; thus, its troubled past continued to cloud the fate of Chile's peculiar democracy.

Electoral Corruption in Mexico

The Partido Revolucionario Institucional (PRI), which had come to power on the crest of a rising tide of populism early in the twentieth century, had embraced the neoliberal prescription for development in the 1980s, but its bitter medicine had alienated popular support. As elsewhere in Latin America, this forced PRI leaders to rely increasingly on scarcely concealed electoral fraud to secure their power. The "colossal fraud" that brought Ernesto Zedillo to the presidency in 1994 exposed the growing weakness of Mexico's long-standing authoritarian one-party state, and persistent popular political pressure finally destroyed it.

NEOLIBERAL CRISIS AND POPULAR RESISTANCE, 1994–2012

The immediate threat to the Zedillo regime was the prospect of an economic collapse. NAFTA, which was supposed to bring prosperity to Mexico, instead had deepened the recessive tendencies of the Mexican economy. The removal of trade barriers had ruined many small farmers, who found themselves unable to compete with the influx of cheaper U.S. grain, milk, and other agricultural products. Moreover, competition from more technologically advanced U.S. and Canadian producers threatened to destroy Mexican national industries like shoe and textile manufacturing because Zedillo deliberately overvalued the peso to promote confidence in the Mexican economy, ensure the passage of NAFTA, and attract foreign investment. This reduced prices and contributed to the flood of imports. Ironically, over time it caused a growing trade deficit, a decline in the value of the peso against the dollar, and the flight of domestic and foreign capital out of the country. With $20 billion in short-term loans coming due in a few months, Mexico faced a replay of the 1982 debacle of inflation and looming default.

Once again, foreign governments, led by the United States and international lending agencies, came to Mexico's rescue with a bailout package of loans and loan guarantees amounting to some $50 billion to pay or renegotiate the huge loans coming due and to stem the peso's collapse. However, the price of the February 1995 bailout was high. In return for $20 billion from the United

States in loan guarantees, Mexico had to deposit $7 billion a year in oil-export revenues at the New York Federal Reserve as collateral. Another $27.5 billion came from the IMF and the Bank for International Settlements, with the usual conditions: Mexico must cut social spending, restrain wage increases, and expand the privatization program to include PEMEX, the nation's prized petrochemical industry. Many Mexicans viewed the deal not as a bailout but as a sellout. "The gringos have us by the throat again," commented one Mexico City taxi driver.

By the decade's end, recurrent economic troubles, combined with the regime's growing vacillation, had produced a crisis of state legitimacy, fractured elite consensus, and fueled widespread popular discontent. In 1996, the government signed the San Andrés Accords, halting troop movements in Chiapas and recognizing indigenous rights to create "autonomous municipalities." A grassroots coalition of human rights groups in the neighboring oil-rich state of Tabasco promptly mobilized ten thousand Chontal natives, declared local petroleum reserves "an autonomous region," and blocked access to sixty wells; meanwhile, the powerful oil workers' union successfully lobbied the PRI leadership to condemn Zedillo's plans to privatize PEMEX. The Chiapas revolt continued to seethe, even as its rebellious message spread.

Still another guerrilla group, the Popular Revolutionary Army (EPR), emerged in Guerrero and coordinated an armed campaign in six southern states that included seizure of radio stations, raids on police stations, and assaults on army posts. Although government leaders scoffed at the EPR's popularity and dismissed its threat to regime stability, Father Máximo Gómez, a local parish priest, concluded that "90 percent of the people here support the guerrillas in their hearts."

Popular opposition to the PRI and its neoliberal program, although clearly centered in the impoverished south, also continued to grow in central Mexico. *El Barzón*, a debtors' group initially composed of middle-class farmers and ejidatarios damaged by free trade and high interest rates, filed some three hundred and fifty thousand lawsuits to block mortgage foreclosures; organized mass protests to obstruct the nation's commercial highways; and staged sit-ins in government buildings, banks, courtrooms, and factories to demand debt relief. Under the leadership of leftist Juan José Quirino, the *barzonistas* expanded and became more politically partisan. With an estimated membership of half a million to a million, the Barzón demanded that the banks return to ejidos over a million acres of land illegally foreclosed during the debt crisis and announced an alliance with the Zapatistas to establish a democratic front to resist neoliberalism.

A Fox in the Henhouse

Nevertheless, the most convincing evidence of massive popular resistance to the PRI and its neoliberal agenda were successive electoral repudiations in 1997 and 2000. This first secured a majority for opposition parties in the Chamber of Deputies that denied the PRI its traditional veto-proof Senate, thereby undermining the presidency's nearly unlimited de facto power, and gave mayoral candidate Cuauhtémoc Cárdenas control of metropolitan Mexico City, home to a quarter of the nation's people. The second shattered the PRI's historic monopoly of presidential power, which dated to its founding in 1929, and elected Vicente Fox Quesada, the candidate of the National Action Party (PAN), to the presidency. Fox, a wealthy former Coca-Cola business executive, had campaigned on populist themes, and he was a founding member of "Latin American Alternatives." This group had denounced neoliberalism for its failure "to generate growth and development, and particularly to meet the challenge of achieving a more equitable distribution of income and wealth." He promised to support indigenous rights and negotiate a peaceful resolution of the Chiapas crisis; dismantle the structure of political authoritarianism; promote economic growth; protect the state-owned oil company, PEMEX, from privatization; reduce poverty and inequality throughout Mexico; and double state funding of education.

Once in office, however, Fox abandoned his populist promises and surrounded himself with neoliberal advisors from the Mexican and transnational corporate business community: the World Bank, Union Carbide, DuPont-Mexico, Procter and Gamble, and Avantel, a subsidiary of WorldCom. His Minister of the Interior, Santiago Creel, was heir to an agricultural, mining, and timber fortune whose origins lay in the nineteenth-century world of Porfirio Díaz. Given their social backgrounds, these men understandably supported policies that favored investors, not social justice. During its first year in office, the Fox administration sought to cut subsidies to small farmers, privatize Mexico's energy and telecommunications industry, eliminate legal protections for workers, and facilitate debt collection. He also secured passage of a regressive 15 percent, value-added tax on food and medicine, which, opponents insisted, would fall disproportionately on 40 million poor people, 17 million of whom were desperately poor. Largely because he lacked a congressional majority, however, Fox failed to win legislative support for these proposals. His own party helped defeat a presidential initiative that would have protected indigenous rights, while other legislative coalitions blocked the president's remaining agenda. Fox even failed to win congressional authorization to leave the country to meet with Microsoft CEO Bill Gates. By December 2001, polls showed that his popularity had declined to 50 percent from a historic high of 75; moreover, according to another poll published by the Mexico City newspaper *El Universal*, only 37 percent said they would vote for Fox again.

Meanwhile, the economy, which grew at an annual average rate of 5.5 percent between 1997 and 2000, nonetheless produced greater income inequality in Mexico than ever: The poorest 10 percent of the population earned 1.3 percent of national income in 1998, whereas the wealthiest 10 percent received 41.7 percent. This growing inequality was largely a function of unregulated markets that empowered investors rather than workers, but fewer than 2 percent of Mexican households relied on investment income, whereas 72 percent depended on waged labor. Poverty rates also rose dramatically. After two decades of neoliberal policies and steady economic growth, punctuated by major declines in 1982 and 1994, the share of poor Mexicans, according to the World Bank's conservative estimates, had grown from 34 percent in 1977 to 68.5 percent in 2000. Using different standards and methods, Julio Bolvitnik, an economics professor at the Colegio de México and an early advisor to the Fox government, reported in March 2001 that some 70 million Mexicans were poor, 27 million of whom earned less than was necessary to purchase their basic nutritional requirements. According to Bolvitnik, data for 2002 and 2004 showed a further increase in poverty aggravated by the Fox government's 2 percent reduction of its financial support for Procampo, the state's rural antipoverty program.

By 2007, Mexico remained utterly dependent on foreign export and investment-capital markets. Since 1990, its external debt, which had risen steadily from $104 billion to $166 billion in 1999, declined to $117 billion in 2006, well above the 1990 figure. Nonetheless, it still relied on the United States for 80 percent of its export sales, and it paid foreign bankers $1 of every $3 that it earned. Mexico's economy withered between 2000 and 2005, as the U.S. market contracted: Export prices fell, export income dropped, economic output declined, and urban unemployment grew from 3.4 to 5.3 percent in 2004 before declining slightly to 4.6 percent during an economic boomlet in 2006. The economy's resurgence surely helped Felipe Calderón win the 2006 presidential election over his progressive opponent, Andrés Manuel López Obrador, a persistent vocal critic of the nation's neoliberalism. But allegations of electoral fraud continued to haunt the nation, as López Obrador released evidence of erroneous ballot tallies and other irregularities in a close election decided by fewer than two votes in each electoral district. Under considerable popular pressure, Mexico's Electoral Commission nonetheless denied López Obrador's request for a total recount and instead agreed to reexamine vote totals from only 9 percent of the nation's polling places. However, even this modest recount reduced Calderón's margin of victory from 0.58 to 0.56 percent of the total vote. According to Mark Weisbrot of the nonpartisan

Center for Economic and Policy Research (CEPR), this constituted "a significant percentage of votes in an election this close" and "certainly casts doubt on the electoral authorities' decision to reject a full recount."

In the election's aftermath, Calderón faced widespread popular opposition. Millions occupied the Zócalo, the main public square in Mexico City, to protest the election outcome and to demand a recount "vote by vote." Later, they proclaimed López Obrador the "legitimate president" and called for the creation of a shadow "government in rebellion." From Chiapas, the EZLN continued its "Other Campaign," a grassroots movement to build a unified national popular resistance to a capitalist economic system that routinely relied on marginalized and exploited workers. In the southern state of Oaxaca, meanwhile, a teachers' strike and protest against a corrupt governor blossomed into an open rebellion that mobilized some four hundred thousand militants. In the face of such determined opposition, Calderón found his government constrained to court his rivals. He announced a 2007 budget that seemed to increase public expenditures on social services. He also allocated $300 million to a National First Job program that paid employers to hire first-time workers and announced a Tortilla Price Stabilization Pact that secured agreements with the nation's major tortilla producers to limit price increases, although the caps permitted a 30 percent increase.

Notwithstanding these concessions to popular pressures, Calderón continued the decades-old policy of privatization, tax cuts, and free trade, which resulted in greater inequality, rising unemployment and poverty, declining investments in infrastructure, and the growth of oligopolies in industries ranging from telecommunications to mining, transportation, energy, and finance. The 2008 economic crisis deepened Mexico's external dependency and facilitated the dramatic expansion of a violent, illegal drug trade fueled by insatiable demand in the United States and the free flow of guns from its northern neighbor. Moreover, stiff competition from low-cost Chinese exports drove increasing numbers of Mexican workers into the informal sector, where some 13.5 million Mexicans, more than half the economically active population, earned low wages with no pensions or medical insurance. Another four hundred thousand annually immigrated to the United States in search of work and sent $20 billion a year back home to support their families. Ten million Mexicans had fallen below the poverty line since 2006. As Mexicans prepared for the 2012 presidential elections, Calderón's popularity declined steadily to 44 percent, popular protests grew exponentially, and the political fortunes of the PRI, perhaps chastened by its historic association with neoliberal policies, seemed again on the rise as it denounced the government's failure to reduce poverty.

Whatever the outcome of these ongoing struggles, at the heart of Mexico's continuing economic, political, and social crisis was the debt problem and the system of dependent capitalism that produced it. North American scholar Peter Evans had presciently written in 1979:

> Like Brazil, Mexico has found that dependent development requires a mass of imported outputs even larger than the exports it generates, and that even when the multinationals cooperate in the promotion of local accumulation they still ship more capital back to the center than they bring in.... Dependent development does not correct the imbalances in semi-peripheral relations with the center; it replaces old imbalances with new ones.

Electoral Snake Oil in Bolivia

Like their counterparts in Argentina, Brazil, and Chile, the Bolivian military had largely governed Bolivia between 1964 and 1982. Although it periodically permitted elections in which highland indigenous peoples, who constituted a majority of the population, did not participate, the military routinely intervened to prevent the triumph of Progressives like Walter Guevara Arze in 1979. Instead, it presided over the systematic looting of the nation's economy and left a legacy of social

unrest that plagued the nation for decades. Bolivia's continuing crisis endured largely because of the collapse in the price of tin (the country's major traditional export), the meteoric rise of cocaine as its chief dollar earner, and heavy international pressure on Bolivia to adopt neoliberal policies of austerity and privatization. Discredited by two decades of failure, the Bolivian military withdrew to its barracks, but its unmistakable presence constrained elected governments thereafter and produced a sharp contrast between populist electoral promises and neoliberal government policies.

COVERT SUBVERSION OF DEMOCRACY, 1985–2000

This pattern of covert subversion of democracy began in the 1985 presidential election, in which two-thirds of the electorate, disillusioned with military-controlled politics, stayed away from the polls. Neither former dictator Gen. Hugo Banzer Suárez nor Víctor Paz Estenssoro, the seventy-eight-year-old populist leader of the 1952 revolution, commanded more than 50 percent of the vote. Although Congress, with the support of Progressive deputies, eventually elected Paz president, pressure from Banzer and the IMF forced him to implement a severe austerity program as a condition for badly needed new IMF loans. In quick succession, he slashed government subsidies for basic services and food, froze wages, devalued the currency more than 1,000 percent, removed all restrictions on foreign imports and investments, and resumed payments on Bolivia's foreign debt.

In alliance with Banzer, Paz announced a neoliberal plan designed to end hyperinflation and stabilize the economy. Drafted by Harvard economist Jeffrey Sachs, it called for closing down as many as eleven unprofitable state-owned mines, laying off thousands of workers, selling other state enterprises to the private sector, making deep cuts in public services, and increasing taxes. Paz's decision to close down Bolivia's largest tin mine brought the conflict between the government and the labor movement to a head. The miners' union called a general strike, and thousands began a march on the capital of La Paz. The government imposed a state of siege, arresting hundreds of labor and community leaders and sending troops, tanks, and planes to patrol the mining regions.

The mining crisis added to the tension caused by a 1986 decision to invite U.S. troops to join with the Bolivian military in Operation Blast Furnace, a campaign to eradicate the country's cocaine laboratories. Ironically, the cocaine trade was the most dynamic sector of Bolivia's economy—despite these well-publicized antinarcotic raids, this chief source of dollars compensated for the sharp decline in the country's export earnings. Sale of coca paste generated $600 million annually, 50 percent more than the nation's legal export earnings of $400 million.

The conflict between the miners and the government took a dramatic turn when some one thousand miners, protesting the state of siege, other repressive measures, and government plans to close mines, occupied mineshafts and launched a hunger strike. The miners' plight and the stubborn refusal of the government to negotiate a solution to the conflict caused growing public sympathy and demonstrations of support for the miners. In a momentous show of solidarity, the Bolivian National Federation of Peasant Women led national sympathy strikes and blockades to protest the government's neoliberal policies.

Aware of the unpopularity of its position, the Paz government accepted the offer of church mediation in its dispute with the miners. Eleven days of talks produced an agreement that called for the release of one hundred labor, peasant, and community leaders; a moratorium on mine closings; compensation for miners who lost jobs; and termination of the blockade on the flow of supplies to the mining regions.

The miners, the backbone of the *Central Obrera Boliviana* (Bolivian Workers' Central, COB), historically Latin America's strongest labor movement, had defeated government efforts to destroy their union. However, the government showed no indication of a change to its overall economic policy, a neoliberal, free-market policy that sought to eliminate or sell off state-owned industries, remove tariff barriers to foreign imports, and lift all restrictions on foreign investment. The fruits of that policy were apparent in the decline of traditional industries, a 40 percent drop in purchasing power in 1985–1986, and an unemployment rate of 30 percent.

Paz and Sachs celebrated their program's successful conquest of inflation. However, the resulting high unemployment contradicted their free-market theory that assumed the tens of thousands of displaced miners would find work in the private sector. But the only expanding private sector economic activity in Bolivia was coca and cocaine production. Thousands of miners, finding no alternative employment, invested the indemnification money they received from the government in land and began to grow coca. Bolivian coca-leaf production increased 60 percent—from fifty thousand metric tons before the Sachs plan to eighty thousand afterward—making Bolivia the second-largest producer of coca. It was also the second-largest producer of cocaine. An estimated five hundred thousand Bolivians were now dependent on the coca economy, which made cocaine "like a cushion that is preventing a social explosion."

The neoliberal policies that made Bolivia dependent on coca cultivation also increased its reliance on U.S. military and financial aid, which ironically depended on its agreement to mobilize the Bolivian army, as an instrument of the U.S. war on drugs, to eradicate coca plantings. Joint U.S.-Bolivian sorties soon regularly occurred in the Chaparé region, where peasants cultivated most of Bolivia's coca. However, no evidence indicated that the sorties, the destruction of access roads, and other military measures won the Bolivian war on drugs. Increasing or declining supplies of coca from the Chaparé region seemed above all to reflect the movement of peasants into and out of coca cultivation according to fluctuations in coca leaf prices.

Meanwhile, indigenous peasant communities, whose livelihoods increasingly depended on coca leaf cultivation, fiercely resisted all Bolivian and U.S. military efforts to eradicate it. Under their relentless pressure, the Bolivian government in 1992 sought to decriminalize the coca leaf, as opposed to cocaine. This "coca diplomacy" stressed the coca leaf's alleged medical benefits. Bolivian and other

Andean indigenous peoples had used coca for centuries to alleviate hunger and counter the debilitating effects of living at high altitudes. However, U.S. drug policy sternly opposed any proposal to end the illegal status of the coca leaf.

During the 1990s, successive presidential elections provided a forum for populist campaign promises that invariably disguised neoliberal policies. Gonzalo Sánchez de Lozada, a millionaire business executive, won a comfortable victory in 1993 with 36 percent of the vote in a field of four candidates. At his inauguration, attended by Fidel Castro, to whom the new president granted his first formal audience, and by Rigoberta Menchú, the Guatemalan Nobel Peace Prize winner, Sánchez proclaimed his commitment to the country's poor and promised to redistribute income.

Nevertheless, the core of his economic program was the privatization of state enterprises and state restructuring demanded by the IMF and the World Bank as the condition for continued economic aid to Bolivia. One month after the inauguration, he fired ten thousand state workers, sparking a wave of strikes and demonstrations, led by the COB, which paralyzed the country for weeks.

The crisis over state restructuring, combined with a renewed crisis in the tin-mining industry, itself the result of falling world market prices, led to the closing of hundreds of small mining cooperatives employing thirty-five thousand workers and to accumulating losses by the much-diminished state-owned Corporación Minera de Bolivia (Comibol). Because tin accounted for almost 49 percent of Bolivia's total exports, the fall in its price had a disastrous impact on the country's trade balance.

By the end of Sánchez's term, Bolivian society remained desperately poor; despite moderately high annual economic growth rates, population increases produced an annual per capita income of only $800—next to Haiti, the lowest in the western hemisphere. Nonetheless, even this figure understated the social crisis because real wealth in Bolivia was so unequally distributed; 78 percent of urban households lived below the poverty line and, of these, 40 percent were "indigent," meaning that their income did not cover their most basic needs.

Moreover, poverty there as elsewhere had a distinctively feminine cast: 10 percent of women were single heads of households, 67 percent of whom were raising one or more children. Two-thirds of rural women were illiterate and therefore limited to extremely low-wage jobs. Thirty-three percent of all children were chronically malnourished. Even Sánchez conceded that "while the economy is going well, what is going poorly are the social problems of the country."

POPULAR RESISTANCE AND RESURRECTION OF THE STATE, 2000–2012

The decade ended with neoliberalism firmly entrenched in the policies of the new president and former dictator Hugo Banzer, who soon resigned for health reasons in favor of his vice president, Jorge Quiroga, an industrial engineer, graduate of Texas A&M University, and a self-described "corporate yuppie." Quiroga produced a stable, even impressive, economic growth rate averaging 4 percent annually, which as elsewhere in the region was largely financed by high interest rates to attract foreign capital. By 1999, this capital had expanded external debt from $385 to $494 million. It also left more than 5 million people—60 percent of the nation's population—impoverished, with the second-highest infant mortality rate (fifty-seven of one thousand) in the western hemisphere and the third-lowest life expectancy (sixty-four years). Underemployment was widespread, and unemployment rates hovered around 12 percent. Bolivian women, workers, trade unions, indigenous rights activists, and debtors' organizations increasingly joined together to protest neoliberalism's negative social consequences; they often won modest victories—for example, reversing the privatization of parts of the state-owned Comibol in 2002.

More than a decade of neoliberal policies had brought Bolivia no closer to prosperity or balanced development. Even *The Economist*, the English tribune of free trade, had to acknowledge that Bolivia's experience had sorely tested faith in market forces: "Market economics, whatever its promise for the future, has not brought prosperity to the poor." Bolivians increasingly agreed. In the 2002 elections, none of the presidential candidates sang the praises of privatization and unfettered markets. Former president and millionaire mine owner Gonzalo Sánchez de Lozada, popularly known as Goni, won a narrow plurality (22 percent) of the vote, promising to improve the free market by using state revenues to create jobs. All the other candidates severely criticized neoliberalism and called for its rejection or reform. The candidate of the Movement Toward Socialism (MAS), Evo Morales, a defiant leader of indigenous coca growers, shocked all observers by finishing second in the balloting with 20.94 percent. He advocated indigenous rights, suspension of foreign debt service, renationalization of industries privatized over the previous two decades, and state regulation of the economy to reduce poverty and promote greater social equality. Because no candidate received 50 percent of the vote, the new Congress selected Goni, but a powerful popular opposition, led by Evo Morales and galvanized by a resurgent indigenous rights movement, soon drove him from office.

The key event that prompted Goni's impromptu exit was the 2004 Gas War, a conflict over Bolivia's abundant gas reserves and their exploitation. Labor and indigenous rights activists, led by Felipe Quispe, joined forces to demand the renationalization of gas and the use of the resulting state revenues to promote national economic development beneficial to Bolivia's impoverished masses, especially Aymara and Quechua indigenous communities. Strikes, roadblocks, and other forms of direct action ultimately induced Goni's resignation, and his successor, Carlos Mesa, organized a national referendum to end the crisis. The overwhelming majority (between 87 and 92 percent) supported repeal of Goni's privatization law, reclamation of national ownership of hydrocarbons, and reestablishment of the state-owned oil company *Yacimientos Petrolíferos Fiscales Bolivianos* (YPFB). Defying this national mandate but seeking to mollify its supporters, the government passed a law in 2005 that merely increased the state's share of royalties, which failed to satisfy the social movement. New protests over Mesa's refusal to sign the act into law led to his resignation.

In the aftermath of the Gas War and referendum, the 2006 presidential elections offered Bolivians an opportunity to exercise their collective democratic voice, and they elected Evo Morales with 54 percent of the votes, a clear electoral mandate in Bolivian politics. Shortly after his stunning triumph, Morales, distinguishing himself from his predecessors, declared his unwavering support for popular democracy. "We are not a government of mere promises," he thundered. "We follow through on what we propose and what the people demand." On May 1, 2006—the International Workers' holiday—he signed a decree that nationalized the gas and oil industries and directed foreign companies to renegotiate their existing contracts within six months in conformity with the law.

As if to reemphasize his point, Morales ordered the army and YPFB engineers to occupy and secure the companies. The reassertion of state control over the industry aimed to subordinate hydrocarbon production to the needs of national industrialization and to expand state revenues by some $780 million, six times greater than in 2002. Some of these funds paid for social programs designed, with assistance from Cuban doctors and educators, to meet United Nations Millennium Development Goals that included free medical services, eradication of malnutrition, and elimination of illiteracy. For example, early in 2008, the Morales government used 30 percent of the new revenue generated by the nationalization of oil to fund a "dignity pension" that paid $315 monthly to some seven hundred thousand poor people, disproportionately of indigenous descent. The clear goal, according to a government spokesman, was to "reduce incidences of poverty in the country from 59.9 percent to 42.4 percent by 2015."

Two years after Morelos' inauguration, the Economic Commission on Latin America reported modest success in reducing extreme poverty from 35 to 31 percent and moderate poverty from 64 to 54 percent. Although Bolivians recognized these initial successes by reelecting Morelos in 2009, with 64 percent of the vote and two-thirds majorities in both houses of congress, social movements remained vigilant. In late 2010, for example, they mobilized against proposed cuts in state subsidies for gas and diesel fuel, forcing Morales to rescind them.

Naturally, many obstacles confronted both Morales and the social movements that brought him to power. Domestically, they faced a determined opposition from the regional autonomy movement in the eastern department of Santa Cruz, home to the nation's richest deposits of gas and oil. Fearing the redistributionist policies of Morales's national government, these groups, led mostly by wealthy, Euro-identified mestizo businesspeople, insisted on considerable autonomy in economic and political affairs. Substantial opposition also came from foreign investors and international lending agencies like the IMF and the World Bank, traditional proponents of neoliberalism. Bolivian political analyst, Carlos Toranzo, had concluded in 2002 that Morales and his social movement allies represented "ideas that are in style all over the world—antiglobalization, antineoliberalism, anti-imperialism." A decade later, those words seemed prophetic, but the history of Bolivia suggested that a more confident assessment must await the passage of time.

Electoral Populism in Ecuador

Like its neighbors, Ecuador's recent history amply demonstrated the tortured conflict between popular democratic processes and neoliberal programs, whose initial public appeal relied heavily on the unfulfilled promises and chaos bequeathed by populism's gradual collapse. Here, as in Bolivia, the political mobilization of indigenous peoples played a key role.

POPULIST RHETORIC AND NEOLIBERAL PRACTICE, 1984–2000

In the mid-1980s, Ecuador, like Bolivia, became the scene of a determined effort to implement the free-market, neoliberal policies for which the United States under the Reagan administration provided a model. In 1984, León Febres Cordero won the presidency and signed an agreement with the IMF to defer payment on Ecuador's foreign debt, which stood at about $7 billion and consumed

more than 30 percent of Ecuador's export earnings to pay interest. The price exacted was that usually demanded of developing countries by the IMF: Ecuador must take steps to encourage foreign investment, restrict domestic consumption, lower tariffs on foreign imports, and modify the monetary exchange system in favor of exporters. In this and in other ways, Febres justified the tribute paid to him by President Reagan when he visited Washington in January 1986: Febres, declared Reagan, was "an articulate champion of free enterprise."

A balance sheet of the impact of Febres Cordero's economic and social policies on Ecuadorian living standards made dismal reading. A study by Ecuador's Catholic University disclosed that foreign corporations took $3 out of the country for every $1 they invested. Between 1981 and 1984, workers' share of national income fell from 32 to 20 percent, and employers' profits rose from 60 to 70 percent. Ninety percent of schoolchildren suffered from parasitic diseases, and the infant mortality rate, according to various estimates, stood at between one hundred and fifty and two hundred and fifty per thousand.

Understandably, the 1988 general elections provided Ecuadorians an opportunity to voice their displeasure with neoliberalism. The country's trade unions mobilized behind a program calling for the nationalization of the oil industry, the rescinding of price hikes, and a 100 percent increase in the country's $80-per-month minimum wage. They helped elect Rodrigo Borja Cevallos, whose campaign stressed social needs over debt interest payments to foreign banks, but he faced what he called "the worst economic crisis" in Ecuador's history. In the last four years, food prices had jumped 240 percent, and half the labor force was unemployed or underemployed. The crisis sharply limited Borja's options in economic and social policy. A moderate leftist in the social democratic mold, Borja assured businesspeople that his government would carry out no nationalizations but would seek to regulate the economy and support the private sector.

Nonetheless, his efforts to achieve debt payment relief met with resistance from the foreign banks that forced him to accept IMF demands for a currency devaluation, fuel price increases, and other austerity measures as a condition for starting debt rescheduling talks. As a result, the Borja regime faced growing opposition from both traditional elites and progressives who formerly had supported it. Denouncing Borja's economic policies as unjust and dictated by the IMF, these groups joined to censure the ministers responsible for the austerity measures.

Indigenous peoples, who made up more than 40 percent of the country's population, matched the growing militancy of Ecuadorian labor, reflected in a 1991 general strike. In 1990, organizations like the Ecuadorian Confederation of Indigenous Nationalities (CONAIE) spearheaded the Inti Raymi uprising, which mobilized hundreds of thousands of supporters from eight provinces in the sierra and several in the Amazon. The indigenous demands included land redistribution and a constitutional declaration that Ecuador was a multiethnic country that respected indigenous rights. Although the government agreed to speak with indigenous leaders, the great planters and ranchers pressured the government to abandon its promises. The new militancy of indigenous peoples, traditionally reputed to be peaceful and docile, caused alarm among the country's landed elite.

By 1992, Ecuadorians had come to distrust Borja's promises and opted instead for the populist pledges of Sixto Durán-Ballén, who campaigned on a program of state reconstruction and modernization. However, his governing plan specifically called for the dismissal of up to one hundred and twenty thousand employees out of a total state sector of four hundred thousand over the following four years and the privatization of one hundred and sixty state companies. Durán-Ballén also announced a structural adjustment package that included a 35 percent devaluation of the national currency, fuel price increases of more than 125 percent, rises in electricity rates of up to 90 percent, and a 190 percent increase in cooking-gas prices.

Received with enthusiasm by international financial institutions, this plan caused an immediate drastic decline in Durán-Ballén's popularity at home. The major trade union, the United Workers' Front (FUT), and CONAIE both opposed him. Two

months into his four-year term, a poll showed that half of those who had voted for him would not have done so again, and 75 percent disapproved of his policies. In mid-1993, the unions claimed that living standards had fallen by 50 percent since Durán-Ballén had taken office. The minimum wage was about $30 a month, but unofficial estimates put the cost of a shopping basket of basic goods at about $250.

In 1993, this opposition mounted a successful "guerrilla campaign" of strikes and demonstrations to limit the government's neoliberal "modernization" program. Peremptory dismissals of state employees were abandoned, and privatization of state companies in strategic areas, such as oil, telecommunications, and electric power, required the passage of special laws by Congress.

A nationwide teachers' strike, the longest such strike in Ecuador's history, grew into a major battle in the war between the president and labor. It began when Durán-Ballén pushed through Congress changes in the code that governed teachers' salary scales and school administration. The strike became a battle of wills; it ended after Congress passed a new package of changes that restored the status quo and ensured the National Educators' Union's participation in school policymaking. The union declared that the strike was a turning point in the grassroots struggle against "the IMF-dictated policies that [the government] is implementing."

Another front in Ecuador's social wars opened when indigenous Huaoranis, who live deep in the Ecuadorian Amazon, traveled to Quito in 1993 to protest the intrusion of oil companies into their territory. The protest aimed to halt the construction of a highway by the Dallas-based company Maxus that would run through the heart of the Huaorani reserves. The Huaorani complained that the road would bring in thousands of settlers and land speculators, leading to deforestation, loss of animal and plant species, and destruction of the indigenous economy and way of life.

Although Durán-Ballén met with the Huaorani, he made no promises. However, even the state oil company (Petroecuador) admitted that, since Ecuador began large-scale oil production in 1972, pipeline failures had dumped four hundred and fifty thousand barrels of oil into the Amazon forest. According to a 1993 "Letter from the Amazon" in *The New Yorker*, "A spill filled the Napo [River] with a slick that stretched from bank to bank for forty miles." The Huaorani, wrote reporter Joe Kane, "were trapped in the path of an American juggernaut, their fate bound up with a culture whose thirst for oil was second to none." Kane noted sardonically, "It is likely that the Huaorani will be wiped out for the sake of enough oil to meet United States energy needs for thirteen days."

The Huaorani promised to use force if necessary to prevent construction of the highway. In 1993, other Ecuadorian indigenous groups filed a billion-dollar class action suit in New York against the Texaco oil conglomerate over massive environmental devastation of the Oriente rain forest. According to the suit, Texaco knowingly had dumped millions of gallons of crude oil into open pits and lakes in the region at the rate of three thousand gallons a day for twenty years. A Harvard University study confirmed that most residents of the area suffered severe health problems because of the dumping.

PLURICULTURAL RESISTANCE AND STATE RECONSTRUCTION, 2000–2012

By the 1996 presidential elections, Durán-Ballén's popularity had declined from more than 70 percent to less than 10 percent because of his neoliberal economic policies. Simultaneously, indigenous peoples joined with Afro-Ecuadorians, women, students, trade unions, and peasant organizations to form the Movement of National Pluricultural Unity Pachakutik, a political coalition that won many state offices. It also successfully lobbied for the creation of CONPLADEIN, an independent state agency, to represent the autonomous cultural and economic interests of black and indigenous Ecuadorians. Pachakutik, though a successful and growing political party, still functioned as a powerful social movement that mobilized "pluricultural" opposition to the newly elected President Abdala Bucaram, a wealthy business executive who also violated his 1996 populist presidential campaign promises by privatizing state assets and cutting state

spending on social services. By February 1997, outrage over this violation of campaign promises, fueled also by charges of widespread corruption, led directly to Bucaram's ouster, an ensuing political crisis, and economic chaos, exacerbated by devastating El Niño–inspired floods that wiped out whole villages and destroyed basic infrastructure.

In 1998, after campaigning on a populist platform, new president Jamil Mahuad, a Harvard graduate, faced an economic crisis aggravated by a steep decline in global oil prices and sought relief by implementing a neoliberal austerity program in exchange for an $800 million IMF loan. His government promptly declared a state of emergency, abolished income taxes, bailed out the nation's private banks, doubled gasoline prices, and reduced spending on social services for the 60 percent of the nation's population classified as poor. Strikes and massive, angry protest marches proliferated. Unemployment grew to more than 50 percent, and Mahuad's popularity fell to 16 percent, prompting even his congressional allies to abandon him.

In January 2000, the FUT and CONAIE, representing indigenous peoples, together organized massive protests against Mahuad's neoliberal privatization plans. They especially opposed his dramatic price increases for bus transportation and cooking gas, all of which targeted the nation's poor majority and curried favor with wealthy Ecuadorian business leaders and foreign bankers. Angered by military budget cuts, elements of Ecuador's army later joined the opposition and effectively forced Mahuad to resign. Fearing the radicalism of this popular rising, especially its indigenous complexion, military officers in this racially and class-stratified nation organized a countercoup to restore Mahuad's vice president, Gustavo Noboa, to power.

Although he initially made concessions, Noboa soon confronted an economic crisis in which inflation surpassed 90 percent, unemployment exceeded 10 percent, and external debt almost equaled the total value of the nation's GDP. To tame inflation and generate revenues to repay foreign bankers, Noboa adopted the U.S. dollar as the nation's currency, slashed social spending, and sought to privatize an array of state resources, prompting domestic business elites to celebrate and popular forces to renew their resistance. Now joined by university students, CONAIE and the popular coalition launched yet another massive demonstration to "combat the neoliberal economic model." But this time, with thousands of indigenous peoples camped out in Quito, they also pressed the Noboa government to end its cooperation with U.S. and Colombian forces seeking to use Ecuadorian military bases to support Plan Colombia, a U.S. proposal for a military solution to neighboring Colombia's decades-long conflict.

Negotiations to end the protest ultimately reinforced the social movement's power and its grassroots democratic structure; the protestors won various concessions, including increased spending on national indigenous health, education, and development projects and a pledge to end "the regionalization of Plan Colombia and the involvement of Ecuador in foreign conflicts." Emboldened, the protesters mobilized in support of the 2002 presidential candidacy of Lucio Gutiérrez, a retired colonel who had joined the 2000 rebellion of workers and indigenous people. Gutiérrez promised to reduce poverty, create jobs, and stimulate national production. He pledged to root out business corruption, reform tariffs, and allocate 15 percent of the budget to public works projects. This progressive coalition mobilized against him, however, when he failed to carry out his populist electoral promises and instead declared his support for the neoliberal Free Trade Area of the Americas. In 2005, amid considerable social turmoil and political chicanery, this social movement induced the Ecuadorian Congress to restore order by voting to impeach Gutiérrez.

Thereafter, this powerful popular coalition shifted its political support to Rafael Correa, who won the 2006 presidential election with 57 percent of the vote. Pledging to end the "long dark night of neoliberalism," Correa steadfastly opposed free trade, called for the renegotiation of foreign oil contracts to increase Ecuador's revenues, and advocated expansion of state antipoverty programs, including subsidies for housing, food, public utilities, health, and education. Defending the country's

sovereignty against foreign bankers, he defied the IMF, expelled a World Bank official, threatened to default on Ecuador's $10 billion external debt, and insisted on its renegotiation to exclude those funds lent to "illegitimate" military governments in the past. Seeking to change the nation's political structure, he secured the support of 82 percent of voters in a referendum to convene a popular assembly to reform the nation's constitution. Finally, Correa advocated the removal of some four hundred U.S. military troops from an Ecuadorian airbase on the border with Colombia and established cordial relations with regional allies in the hemispheric opposition to neoliberalism, Venezuela's Hugo Chávez and Brazil's Lula da Silva.

Although Correa's policies had alienated traditional elites and foreign investors, he also found himself frequently at odds with the militant social movements that had propelled his electoral victories. Nonetheless, he won reelection in 2009 with 52 percent of the vote and remained exceedingly popular thereafter, with approval ratings of 67 percent in 2010, shortly before a police protest against looming budget cuts morphed into an attempted coup. In the coup's aftermath, however, Correa reiterated his determination to implement his electoral promises: "We are going forward," he told the Mexican newspaper, *La Jornada*. "Even more: we will radicalize the revolution."

Notwithstanding these important victories for the popular opposition to neoliberalism, the contest over Ecuador's future had not ended. The immediate obstacle to sustained national development was the nation's burdensome foreign debt, annual repayment of which cost more than the government spent on education, health, and social services combined. Although Correa successfully defaulted on $3 billion worth of external debt that his Public Debt Audit Commission determined was "illegitimate" and restructured its outstanding liabilities to reduce its 2010 debt by 26 percent, its accumulated obligations remained perilously high at $13.4 billion. Political pressure from organized social movements and the Correa government's commitment to implement its state-centered strategy for poverty reduction and national development combined to

After his 2007 presidential victory, Rafael Correa used his popular democratic support to elect a solid 60 percent majority in the constituent assembly that was "fully empowered to draw up a new constitution and reform the institutional framework of the state" to end oligarchic control.

produce modest successes that augured well for the future. Nonetheless, this long-term project required the political determination reflected in the words of a Pachakutik representative: "The struggle will continue in other forms."

Market Forces and State Regulation in the Cuban Model, 1990–2012

Although the leaders whom the Pink Tide swept into office sought diverse practical solutions to their respective nation's problems, they all seemed to agree that a stable national development required a mix of state and market activities. Many, like

Hugo Chávez, Evo Morales, and Rafael Correa, specifically acknowledged that they had drawn inspiration from the Cuban experience. Although denying that his Bolivarian Revolution was "copying anything," Chávez, for example, nonetheless admitted his admiration for the Cuban system because "in Cuba, there is no child that is not in school, no sick person who is not tended to." Although critical of Cuba's limits on political freedoms, Correa also indicated his appreciation for the way Cuba had endured its worst crisis since the 1959 Revolution without sacrificing the education or health of its citizens. The Cuban system also underwent significant reform, however, requiring the cultivation of private sector market activities to complement the decisive role played by the state in promoting sustainable national development.

RECTIFICACIÓN AND THE "SPECIAL PERIOD"

During the early 1990s, the socialist collapse in Europe threatened Cuba's progress in streamlining its economy and creating greater equality. As they transitioned toward a market economy, Cuba's Eastern European trading partners began to trade on international prices, conducted in hard currency. However, Cuba needed its limited stock of hard currency to pay interest on its foreign debt and purchase certain vital products from Western Europe. Anticipating increased difficulties with some of its former socialist trading partners, Cuba diversified its trade links, doubling its trade with China and increasing its trade with Latin America by 20 percent.

Nonetheless, the Soviet collapse dealt a devastating blow to the Cuban economy, resulting in a national income decline of approximately 45 percent between 1989 and 1992. Before 1990, Cuba had received 13 million tons of oil annually from the Soviet Union, but this fell sharply to 1.8 million tons in 1992 (from Russia). In addition to routine blackouts and factory shutdowns, the resulting energy crunch led to a revival of horse-drawn carriages, the use of oxen-drawn tractors, and wholesale replacement of cars with bicycles—good for the environment and health, but economically inefficient and uncomfortable. The shortfall in oil dealt a heavy blow to another of Cuba's major hard-currency earners: the nickel industry. Cuba had the world's third-largest nickel reserves, but the Soviet collapse caused production to fall 36 percent, from 46,600 metric tons in 1989 to 29,900 in 1994. To make matters worse, world-market prices for nickel, which had peaked at more than $6 per pound in 1989, plummeted more than 50 percent during the next five years to $2.87. Foreign-exchange earnings therefore declined disastrously.

The economic crisis also temporarily reversed the trend of steadily improving social conditions and produced a temporary decline in living standards. During the early years of this Special Period, most Cubans lived on a drab diet of white rice and red beans, supplemented by some vegetables and fruit, an occasional chicken, and other goods available in the open market. The food-rationing system, however, prevented the emergence of the massive hunger and malnutrition so common in the rest of Latin America.

This crisis grew worse because the United States intensified its efforts to strangle socialist Cuba through passage of the 1992 Torricelli Act, which extended the U.S. trade embargo against Cuba to U.S. subsidiaries in third-world countries and barred any ship docked in Cuba from entering a U.S. port for one hundred and eighty days. The Helms-Burton Act of 1996 tightened the noose by allowing U.S. citizens to sue foreign corporations whose trade or investment profits derived from properties expropriated more than forty years earlier. These laws drew angry protests from Canada and the European Community, which felt that the United States had no right to apply its laws extraterritorially. Each year since 1992, the United Nations General Assembly had voted by overwhelming majorities (157 to 2 in 1998) to condemn the embargo, and in July 1993, a summit of the leaders of Latin America, Spain, and Portugal unanimously called for an end to the embargo against Cuba. Pope John Paul II, during a much-celebrated visit to Cuba in 1998, added his voice to those protesting the embargo, as did Nobel laureate and former U.S. president Jimmy Carter in 2002.

In the midst of crisis, the socialist government showed its revolutionary pragmatism. In 1992, the National Assembly adopted sweeping changes in the constitution and electoral law, including enhanced constitutional protections for all religious faiths and provisions for a direct, secret election by voters of National Assembly deputies. It also authorized 100 percent foreign-owned companies and joint-venture enterprises with foreign capital. The first direct, competitive elections for deputies of the National Assembly resulted in a lowering of their average age to forty-three—a reflection of the generational change of guard taking place in Cuba. In another sign of the new political atmosphere, candidates for office no longer needed approval by the Communist Party, and other reforms aimed to make the

National Assembly "a more independent and effective body for legislation, governmental monitoring and oversight, and economic planning."

According to Cuban Vice President Carlos Lage, the revolutionary government during this Special Period also sought economic reform "without altering its socialist essence." In fact, unlike the rest of Latin America, where domestic elites and the IMF pressed governments to slash social spending, Cuba actually increased its investment in social services from an average 17 percent of GDP during the 1980s to 24 percent in 1993, the depth of the national crisis.

The government monitored foreign investment, closely regulated its relations with Cuban labor, and scrutinized its impact on the environment. Ironically, Cuba's socialist infrastructure of national planning, free universal health care, and education may have been the most attractive feature to foreign investors, who grudgingly endured inevitable state interventions in exchange for the benefit of a healthy, disciplined, productive, highly educated workforce. They also benefited from relative labor peace and freedom from the extraordinary expense of unemployment or medical insurance payments. In effect, they gained access to scarce resources and First World workers at Third World costs. "It's one of the advantages of a centralized economy," a Cuban economist explained. "We can actually make a company's investment more secure than it would be in an unregulated economy."

As a result, foreign firms eagerly engaged in joint ventures in fields ranging from a new overseas telephone system to tourism. In June 1994, a Mexican company signed a $1.5 billion deal to rehabilitate Cuba's telephone system. New hotels built by joint ventures with Spanish companies rapidly sprang up on Cuban beachfronts, with the number of foreign tourists topping five hundred thousand in 1993 and rising to 1 million annually thereafter. In 2000, tourism earned $1.9 billion in reserves, Cuba's largest source of hard currency. More than three hundred joint ventures with some fifty-seven countries in forty different sectors of the economy attracted investments in excess of $5 billion; domestic investment also increased, rising to

9 percent in 1997. Cuba still depended greatly on sugar, but the economy also had diversified. Income from manufacturing netted $415 million, tobacco and cigars brought in $100 million, a relatively new biotechnology industry earned $100 million, and nickel production grossed $90.8 million. Moreover, the government invested heavily in modernizing the sugar industry, building new mills and harvesting most cane by machine.

After five years of declines, Cuba's GDP rose steadily after 1993, averaging 3.3 percent per year between 1994 and 2000. Trade also rose consistently: The annual average increase in the value of exports and imports since 1993 was almost 20 percent. As a percentage of GDP, budget deficits had grown astronomically to 40 percent in 1993 but thereafter declined to 4 percent in 1996, producing dramatic improvement in consumer confidence and strengthening the Cuban peso by 40 percent. More important, these macroeconomic indexes of national recovery reflected the experiences of everyday life in Cuba. Ascribing this apparent renaissance to Cuba's "entrepreneurial socialism," a visitor concluded that "in Havana some of the new wealth is clearly starting to be felt in the population generally. On almost every block, it seems, is a freshly painted house. The discos are jammed every night with both Cubans and foreigners."

Cuba hoped to overcome its energy crisis through the development of large offshore oil and gas reserves, which the U.S. Geological Survey estimated at 4.6 billion barrels and 9.8 trillion cubic feet, respectively. In June 1994, two Canadian firms announced that they had found commercial quantities of oil at offshore wells in Matanzas Province. Utterly dependent on frequently expensive oil imports since its independence, Cuba contracted with Chinese, Indian, and Brazilian state oil companies to collaborate with its own Cubapetróleo (Cupet) to produce almost 4 million metric tons of oil in 2006, an increase of 400 percent during the decade. Moreover, with assistance from Venezuela's state oil company, Cuba refurbished its Cienfuegos oil refinery facilities, which enabled it to process some sixty-five thousand barrels per day, almost half of the nation's total energy needs. This reduced the nation's import bill, lowered its energy costs, improved industrial efficiency, and contributed to greater economic independence.

In addition to promoting such traditional exports as sugar and nickel and expanding tourism, the Cuban government made the development of biotechnology and medical exports an essential part of its economic survival strategy. In the 1980s, Havana's center for genetic engineering produced interferon, an important drug in the treatment of cancer. Thereafter, Cuba invested more than $1 billion in biotech research, organized thirty-eight biotech centers, and developed four hundred patents on products ranging from fetal monitors to vaccines against hepatitis B and meningitis B. Ironically, in 2002, Cuba contracted with Glaxo SmithKline, a multinational pharmaceutical company, to market this meningitis B vaccine around the world, including the United States, where annually three thousand cases of meningitis claimed three hundred lives, mostly in impoverished, high-risk areas. But the U.S. government, which usually opposed restraints on private trade and investment, nonetheless prohibited the use of this life-saving vaccine unless Glaxo agreed to pay Cuba its royalties in kind—for example, through the export of medicines—rather than in cash.

In response to the economic crisis of the early 1990s, the Cuban government had instituted additional reforms. Most important, a new law reorganized agriculture and replaced large state farms with autonomous cooperatives in land "ceded for an indefinite period by the state." These Basic Units of Cooperative Production (UBPC) operated on a profit-sharing basis and administered their own resources. The state provided them credits to purchase farm equipment, seeds, and other inputs in exchange for a commitment to sell a fixed amount of their harvest to the government; they could sell any surplus crops at prevailing prices in the open market. By 1998, more than 1,500 UBPCs controlled 3 million hectares of land and employed almost 122,000 workers, 114,000 of whom were co-op members. This decentralization of agriculture, appealing to the workers' self-interest, led to greater efficiency and contributed to a 17.3 percent growth of agricultural production in 1996.

Cuba also launched a vast technological experiment in agriculture that aimed to end dependence on costly foreign agricultural inputs by converting from conventional modern agriculture to large-scale organic farming. The "alternative model," as the Cubans call it, sought "to promote ecologically sustainable production by replacing the dependence on heavy farm machinery and chemical inputs with animal traction, crop and pasture rotations, soil conservation, organic soil inputs, and what the Cubans call biofertilizers and biopesticides—microbial pesticides and fertilizers that are nontoxic to humans." Two agricultural scientists who have studied the program, Peter Rosset and Shea Cunningham, stress its "potentially enormous implications for other countries suffering from the declining sustainability of conventional agricultural production."

A second general reform authorized self-employment in a long list of trades and occupations. In reality, these new rules simply legalized long-existing activities, but they also generated tax revenues and provided regulatory controls, inspections, and licenses. This "informal sector" expanded rapidly, averaging between ten thousand and fifteen thousand self-employed Cubans in 1993 and mushrooming to one hundred and eighty thousand by decade's end. Cuba's informal sector, however, contrasted sharply with the poverty and economic insecurity of its counterparts in the rest of Latin America. Because socialism guaranteed them inexpensive housing, basic subsistence, free health care, and education, self-employed Cubans typically spent their income on discretionary consumer goods. In a 1997 article in the *Atlantic Monthly*, Joy Gordon reported the example of a woman with a *paladar* (private home restaurant) that served $4 dinners, who could afford a Sony stereo system, a VCR, and new color television. "Yet," Gordon concludes, "this is possible in Cuba only because and insofar as it has remained socialist."

Finally, in an obvious move to encourage the inflow of dollars through family remittances from the United States, the government announced that it would no longer penalize the holding of foreign currencies and would authorize Cubans to spend

U.S. dollars in a network of government stores. These measures eased the government's cash crisis and put a dent in the flourishing black market, but they created a privileged class of people with access to U.S. currency and increased inequality. According to one Cuban economist, "The 4:1 income gap between best-paid and worst-paid has widened in ten years to 25:1." But this still left Cuba the most egalitarian society in the western hemisphere.

A Mix of State Ownership, Regulation, and Markets

These reforms and Cuba's growing insertion into the world economy gradually increased Cuban officials' confidence that the crisis had ended. Some professional economists agreed that, in defiance of neoliberal orthodoxy, this "Cuban miracle" had "confounded its critics," but many problems remained unsolved. Largely because of the U.S. economic blockade, which increased the cost of Cuban imports and limited income from exports, Cuba suffered from massive trade deficits that also increased its reliance on short-term foreign loans at high interest rates. By 2001, its foreign debt was $13 billion.

During the late 1990s, the nation had relied on dollar remittances and a rapidly growing $1.5 billion a year tourism industry to cushion the impact of its trade deficit. An important consequence of the September 11 terrorist attacks on the World Trade Center, however, was a dramatic decline in worldwide tourist travel, which threatened to reduce national revenues. Finally, the rising cost of oil and the fall of sugar prices damaged Cuban prospects for a full economic recovery. Although Cuban socialism guaranteed every citizen free access to health care, education, and a basic subsistence diet, Cubans interested in resurrecting pre-1990 living standards had to access private markets; but this required dollars that they could secure only in the tourist industry or through family remittances from abroad. Naturally, this tended to undermine the revolution's long-standing commitment to social and economic equality.

As a result, a new debate about racism, civil rights, and equal opportunity emerged among Cuban intellectuals and in popular culture. Historian Alejandro de la Fuente suggested that a recent proliferation of Cuban scholarly studies of race in its historical and contemporary context reflected concerns about rising inequality in Cuba. To be sure, dollarization immediately privileged families with relatives living in self-imposed exile in the United States, and these overwhelmingly tended to be light-skinned Cubans of Spanish ancestry. However, more disconcerting was the virtual invisibility of Afro-Cubans in the tourism industry, the only other source of dollars. In 2000, Fidel Castro himself admitted that Cuba was not "a perfect model of equality and justice" and acknowledged that, although "we established the fullest equality before the law and complete intolerance for … sexual discrimination in the case of women, or racial discrimination," these racial, gender, and class prejudices persisted.

These prejudices, growing social inequality, and their collective impact on Afro-Cuban identity also became lyrical themes in the rapid emergence of a new hip-hop culture in Cuba. Initially influenced by rap music broadcast by Miami commercial radio stations, young, mostly black males fused hip-hop styles with traditional Afro-Cuban rhythms to deplore injustices associated with the Special Period: racism, class inequality, prostitution, and selfishness. According to an official of a Cuban state organization that promoted rap artists, "Cuban rap is criticizing the deficiencies that exist in society, but in a constructive way, educating youth and opening spaces to create a better society." Indeed, Cuban rappers increasingly recognized the nation's enduring cultural identification with "whiteness" as the historical source of its lingering racism. Thus, a Cuban hip-hop producer, responding to a reporter's question about whether there were any "white" rappers, mischievously replied, "Well, let's say there are lighter-skinned rappers," he replied, "because no one in Cuba is white."

Despite all these problems, the collapse of its major trading partners two decades earlier, and fifty years of implacable opposition from the United States, including a trade blockade that openly violated international law, Cuba made a remarkable recovery. It ranked fifty-one in the 2007–2008 United Nation's Human Development Index of one hundred eighty countries. Cuba's doctor-to-patient ratio ranked first in the world, with 591 physicians per 100,000 people. Among one hundred eight developing countries, Cuba had the sixth-lowest poverty index. Its infant mortality rate, at six per one thousand live births, was the lowest in Latin America and lower than that of the United States (seven per one thousand). Its adult literacy rate was the highest in Latin America (99.8 percent). It had the largest number of scientists and engineers per capita of any Latin American nation (1,611 per 1 million people), twice that of second-place Argentina. With understandable pride, Cuban president Fidel Castro surveyed the devastation wreaked by the early 1990s economic armageddon and remarked, "In spite of this, we did not close down a single health care centre, a single school or daycare center, a single university, or a single sports facility.... What little was available we distributed as equitably as possible." No other nation in the region could make a similar claim.

Further Cuban development would of course be greatly facilitated and hastened by a change in U.S. policy that would result in economic advantages for both countries. Unfortunately, the United States continued to harbor cold war prejudices and illusions about Cuba that it abandoned long ago about a much more powerful Communist state, the People's Republic of China. U.S. government officials openly promoted the overthrow of Cuba's socialist state and planned for a post-Castro reorganization of Cuban society, but reports of the Cuban Revolution's early demise were greatly exaggerated—even after Fidel Castro retired in 2008 and the National Assembly elected his brother Raúl, also a leader of the 1959 Revolution, to the presidency. Short of a massive U.S. invasion, prospects that Cuba's socialist regime would collapse remained very low. In Cuba, unlike in Eastern Europe, socialism did not arrive in the wake of a victorious Red Army. It emerged from an indigenous popular revolution that linked the ideals of socialism and independence, and it still enjoys considerable popular support. Despite many economic problems, the Cuban Revolution

had a record of social achievement without parallel in Latin American history and presented a vivid contrast to the economic and social crises that gripped most of the capitalist societies of Latin America.

Early in the twenty-first century, however, Cuba's economy exploded, averaging an annual growth rate of 6.5 percent between 2001 and 2008, according to the Economic Commission on Latin America. Chief among the major sources of new economic activity was a dramatic expansion in the export of services. For example, Cuba paid for valuable oil imports from Venezuela by providing Cuban doctors to dispense medical services to poor Venezuelans under joint programs like Barrio Adentro and Operation Miracle. Like the rest of the region, Cuba also benefited from relatively high export prices, but this, combined with increased exports and growth in the service sector, reduced the nation's debt service as a share of export income. By 2007, its foreign debt was $15 billion, but its debt service ratio declined from 17 percent in 2002 to 11 percent.

This economic renewal placed additional pressure on the U.S. government to lift its economic blockade. Influential newspapers called for rolling back the embargo. The *New York Times* complained that U.S. policy toward Cuba remained frozen in the past and appeared to be dictated by the most radical factions of the anti-Castro Cuban exile community. Fearing the impact of global economic competition on U.S. trade and investment, "an exponential increase" of U.S. companies became interested in Cuban markets, according to testimony of the United States–Cuba Trade and Economic Council, a business group that supported a gradual dismantling of the embargo. Eager to claim a share of Cuba's health-care market, worth $500 million to $1 billion, and its bulk-food commodity imports, valued at $800 million, influential corporate executives like Dwayne Andreas of Archer Daniels Midland Company, Ted Turner of Time Warner, and Donald Fites of Caterpillar also opposed the embargo. Because removal of the embargo would produce between $3 and $7 billion of trade, at least $2 billion in exports, and some forty thousand new jobs, doing so would bring substantial economic benefits to both the United States and Cuba.

Even as U.S. citizens debated proposals to end the blockade, however, Cuban authorities sought to deal with three major problems: a succession of hurricanes in 2008 that wreaked $10 billion worth of damage, the 2009 global economic crisis, and the resulting decline of raw material prices that especially affected foreign exchange earnings from nickel exports. These economic shocks, Cuba's own experience in dealing with economic crisis in the 1990s, and the success of its Latin American allies encouraged the government to introduce broad reforms designed to promote further expansion of private markets. Seeking to boost labor productivity and eliminate redundant workers in an economy in which the state historically had guaranteed full employment and free, universal access to education and health services, Raúl Castro announced a plan to reduce state expenditures and transform five hundred thousand state jobs into private sector, self-employed small businesses. This "privatization" of state resources, however, aimed to preserve the essence of Cuban socialism and the state's investment in its social infrastructure.

Despite the ravages of the global recession, for example, public spending on health care and education grew steadily, peaking at 10.6 and 13.6 percent of GDP respectively, the highest in the region.

With political allies in power throughout the region, Fidel Castro retiring from public office after a serious surgery, and his brother Raúl in the presidency, the outlines of an institutionalized post-Fidel political transition seemed unmistakable. After fifty years, during which the Cuban Revolution and Fidel Castro had become virtually synonymous, the island nation's future remained uncertain, but one conclusion seemed unequivocal. Cuba's revolutionary commitment to social justice had inspired political leaders and popular movements throughout the region to embrace a dynamic mix of state ownership and market regulation designed to promote sustainable national and regional development.

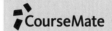 Go to the CourseMate website at **www.cengagebrain.com** for primary sources, additional study tools, and review materials—including audio and video clips—for this chapter.

22

The Two Americas: United States–Latin American Relations

FOCUS QUESTIONS

- What were the permanent long-term U.S. objectives in Latin America, and how did successive U.S. governments variously seek to achieve them before 1898?
- How did U.S. policy change between 1898 and 1933?
- What were the origins of the Good Neighbor Policy, and how was it applied?
- How did U.S. policy change in the aftermath of World War II, and what roles respectively did the cold war and U.S. economic interests play?
- How did U.S. policy change after 1981?
- How did U.S. policy affect the development of Latin America?

Two Consistent Themes appear in the examination of U.S. relations with Latin America over two centuries. First, the United States sought to protect and expand its economic and strategic interests in the region. Ever since the administration of James Monroe, the United States attempted to establish and maintain Latin America as an economic appendage. U.S. policy makers displayed resourcefulness and flexibility in pursuit of this goal, adapting their methods to meet the varying domestic political pressures, the changing requirements of U.S. business, and the shifting conditions in Latin America. Thus, U.S. policy never relied exclusively or even primarily on unilateral military conquest and subjugation of Latin America. Instead, it sought to establish its hegemony—that is, to "manage" hemispheric events by securing Latin America's consent to a multilateral system of inter-American relations whose "general rules," though expressed in universal,

humanitarian terms, nonetheless incorporated U.S. political, economic, and strategic interests.

Second, U.S. leaders consistently justified U.S. policy by portraying the region as hopelessly backward, desperately in need of beneficent U.S. tutelage to save its people from the ravages of barbarism and promote the development of virtuous, democratic republics modeled on an idealized U.S. experience. In this process, according to Mark T. Berger, the work of historians and social scientists in Latin American studies was complicit. This "discourse" of a U.S. "civilizing mission" drew on white supremacist ideas in the nineteenth century and the discursive language of modernization theory in the twentieth. It thereby facilitated "the creation and maintenance of the national and international organizations, institutions, interstate relations and politico-economic structures that sustain and extend U.S. hegemony in Latin America and around the world."

1819	Adams-Onis Treaty annexes Florida to the United States
1823	Monroe Doctrine declares U.S. solidarity with Latin American independence struggles
1846–1848	U.S. invasion of disputed land triggers war with Mexico
1893–1895	Economic crisis of surplus production reinforces U.S. imperialism
1898	Spanish-American-Cuban-Filipino War results in U.S. colonial expansion
1903	Platt Amendment and Hay-Bunau Varilla Treaty shape new U.S. empire
1904–1930	Theodore Roosevelt corollary to Monroe Doctrine promotes "gunboat diplomacy"
1933	Good Neighbor Policy abandons military intervention but expands non-military interference
1952–1954	U.S. policy undermines elected governments in Argentina, Bolivia, British Guiana, Cuba, Guatemala, and Venezuela
1955	Military dictatorships rule thirteen nations with U.S. support
1961	Kennedy creates Alliance for Progress to discourage rebellion and encourage private investment; U.S.-sponsored the Bay of Pigs invasion fails
1964–1977	U.S. support stabilizes military dictatorships in Argentina, Brazil, Chile, Dominican Republic, and Uruguay
1981–1993	U.S. military intervenes in Grenada, Haiti, El Salvador, Nicaragua, and Panama
1991	Soviet Union and Socialist bloc collapse, ending the cold war
1993–2001	U.S. economic intervention in Latin America increases
2001	Al-Qaeda assault on World Trade Center and Pentagon shifts U.S. attention to Asia
2002–2011	"Pink Tide" governments reject "Washington Consensus" and rely increasingly on China market

U.S. Policy Objectives

U.S. policy toward Latin America changed over time to accommodate its burgeoning economic activities in the region. During the early years of the nineteenth century, U.S. commerce with its southern neighbors demanded little more than policing the Caribbean for marauding pirates. As the United States grew into a commercial, industrial, and, eventually, financial power, its foreign policy broadened in scope. The hunt for new markets brought it into competition with European nations, especially Great Britain. As a result, it became one of the major aims of U.S. policy to check the further penetration of European commerce and capital into Latin America.

By the turn of the century, Latin America had become not only a substantial market for U.S. products but also an important source of raw materials and a major area for capital investment. Having recently built a powerful navy, the United States assumed the responsibility of protecting its commerce and investment by forcibly maintaining order in the region. Uninvited, it assumed the role of the Western Hemisphere's police force. In this capacity, the United States focused its attention on the weak and chaotic nations of the Caribbean and Central America, where U.S. economic activity was concentrated.

At mid-century, South America replaced the Caribbean as the focus of U.S. economic expansion. Geography, logistics, and the anti-imperialist temper of the times required the United States to abandon the old policies of military intervention in favor of more subtle and sophisticated ways of achieving its ends; these new methods included the lure of grants and loans, the threat of economic sanctions, and subversion. When these methods failed, however, as they did in Guatemala in 1954, in Cuba in 1959, and in the Dominican Republic in 1965, the United States did not hesitate to resort to the open or covert use of force.

Ideology always figured in U.S. policy toward Latin America. Thus, Theodore Roosevelt vowed to "civilize," Woodrow Wilson to "democratize," and John F. Kennedy to "reform" Latin America.

© Cengage Learning

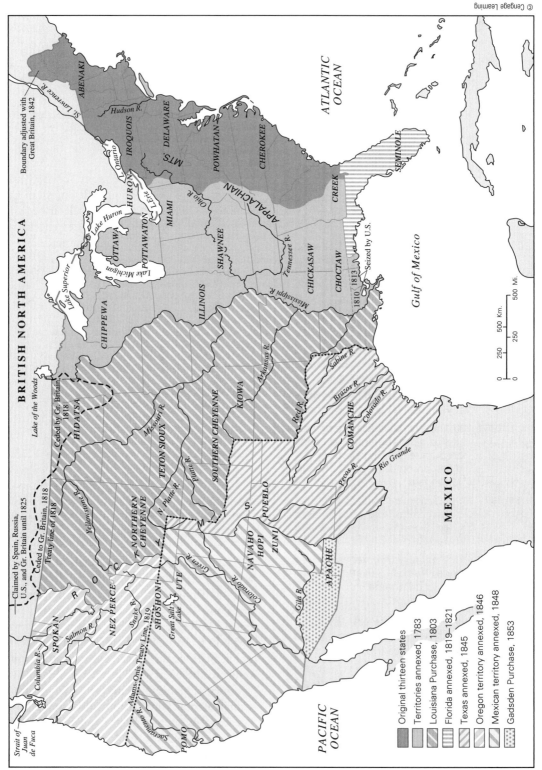

BRITISH NORTH AMERICA

Boundary adjusted with
Great Britain, 1842

ATLANTIC
OCEAN

St. Lawrence R.

ABENAKI

Hudson R.

IROQUOIS

DELAWARE

MTS.

POWHATAN

CHEROKEE

APPALACHIAN

CREEK

SEMINOLE

Seized by U.S.

1810 1813

Gulf of Mexico

Lake Ontario

L. Erie

Lake Huron

HURON

OTTAWA

POTTAWATON

MIAMI

Ohio R.

SHAWNEE

Lake Michigan

Lake Superior

CHIPPEWA

ILLINOIS

Tennessee R.

CHICKASAW

CHOCTAW

Mississippi R.

500 Mi.

500 Km.

250

250

0

0

Lake of the Woods

Ceded by Gr. Britain,
1818

HIDATSA

Missouri R.

TETON SIOUX

Platte R.

SOUTHERN CHEYENNE

KIOWA

Arkansas R.

Red R.

Sabine R.

Brazos R.

Colorado R.

COMANCHE

Pecos R.

Rio Grande

MEXICO

Claimed by Spain, Russia,
U.S., and Gr. Britain until 1825

Ceded to Gr. Britain, 1818
Treaty line of 1818

Yellowstone R.

NORTHERN
CHEYENNE

R

C

O

S.

PUEBLO

M

NAVAHO

HOPI

ZUNI

APACHE

Gila R.

SPOKAN

Columbia R.

NEZ PERCE

Salmon R.

Snake R.

SHOSHONI

Adams-Onis Treaty Line, 1819

UTE

Green R.

Great Salt Lake

Colorado R.

Sacramento R.

POMO

PACIFIC
OCEAN

*Strait of
Juan
de Fuca*

Original thirteen states

Territories annexed, 1783

Louisiana Purchase, 1803

Florida annexed, 1819–1821

Texas annexed, 1845

Oregon territory annexed, 1846

Mexican territory annexed, 1848

Gadsden Purchase, 1853

U.S. Territorial Expansion

Nevertheless, ideology always served the material needs of United States–Latin American policy, and the presidents who made these pious professions were ready to use force in defense of the U.S. empire in Latin America. They were also ready to support the most oppressive regimes in the area as long as they cooperated with the United States. Highlighting this link between high ideals and capitalist class interests, Wilson, for example, argued in 1912 that "if America is not to have free enterprise, then she can have freedom of no sort whatever."

The two Americas, both born in wars of national liberation, followed very different historical paths. In two centuries, the United States rose to become the industrial and financial giant of the capitalist world; despite its many economic and social problems, it provided the majority of its people with a satisfactory material standard of living. Latin America fell far behind the other America in terms of its capacity to meet the economic needs of its citizens.

Many Latin Americans are convinced that these divergent trends are related, that Latin American underdevelopment is the other side of North American development, and that Latin American poverty and misery have accumulated as the economic and political power of foreign (chiefly North American) multinational corporations have grown.

Prelude to Empire, 1810–1897

MANIFEST DESTINY, 1810–1865

During the early decades of the nineteenth century, westward expansion and nascent commerce brought the United States into its first contact with its southern neighbors. However, U.S. military and economic weakness, lack of information, and British predominance in the area limited U.S. activities in Latin America. U.S. trade with Latin America began in earnest in 1797, when Spain opened the ports of its New World colonies to foreign trade. By 1811, the Spanish colonies accounted for 16 percent of all U.S. trade. A dozen years later, despite the disruptions of the War of 1812, the figure had increased to 20 percent.

With only a small navy and few funds at its disposal, the U.S. government could offer little aid

to the Spanish American nations during their wars of independence (1810–1826). During the first stage of these wars, the War of 1812 consumed the attention and resources of the United States. From 1817 to 1819, it undertook delicate negotiations with Spain for the purchase of Florida and chose not to jeopardize these dealings by helping the Spanish American insurgents. Their victory offered powerful strategic and commercial advantages to the United States. First, with the French retreat from Haiti and the Louisiana territories in 1803 and the British pursuit of a U.S. alliance in the 1820s, Latin American independence eliminated Spain, the hemisphere's last potential military threat to U.S. security. This enabled the United States to spend less on defense and invest more in the development of its civilian economy.

Second, it meant, in Thomas Jefferson's words, that the United States could absorb "piece by piece" the old Spanish American empire, "a huge, helpless and profitable whale." Similarly, John Quincy Adams, anticipating U.S. economic relations with a "free" Latin America, expected that the United States would grow wealthy from the region's dependence on it. "As navigators and manufacturers," he wrote,

> we are already so far advanced in a career upon which they have yet to enter that we may, for many years after the conclusion of the [independence] war, maintain with them a commercial intercourse, highly beneficial to both parties, as carriers to and for them of numerous articles of manufacture and foreign produce.

When the Latin American independence movements clearly had succeeded, the United States acted to prevent other European nations from reestablishing colonies or undue influence in the region, developments that could shut off U.S. access to potentially lucrative markets. In his message to Congress on December 2, 1823, President James Monroe declared that, as a matter of principle,

> the American continents, by the free and independent condition they have assumed

and maintain, are henceforth not to be considered subjects for future colonization by any European powers…. We should consider any attempt on their [the European powers'] part to extend their system to any portion of this hemisphere as dangerous to our peace and safety.

Monroe went on to say that the United States would not interfere with existing colonies and would not meddle in European affairs.

The Monroe Doctrine was ineffective for much of the nineteenth century because the United States had neither the resources nor the inclination to back it up. The doctrine, furthermore, failed to prevent repeated European interventions in Latin America. Following the accepted practice of the time, French and British gunboats regularly bombarded or blockaded Latin American ports to force payment of debts or reparations. The United States, too, adopted this practice, landing troops in the Falkland Islands, Argentina, and Peru during the 1830s; in Argentina, Mexico, Nicaragua, Panama, Paraguay, and Uruguay during the 1850s; and in Columbia, Mexico, Panama, and Uruguay during the 1860s.

Nineteenth-century westward territorial expansion involved the United States in countless wars against Native Americans and two wars against Mexico. After the purchase of Louisiana (1803) and Florida (1821), the country began to covet Mexico's northern provinces, where U.S. citizens conducted a flourishing commerce. In 1825, President John Quincy Adams authorized the U.S. minister to Mexico to negotiate the purchase of Texas. The Mexican government rejected the proposal. During the early 1830s, U.S. settlers poured into Texas and quickly found themselves at odds with Mexican authorities over the issues of local autonomy and the illegal introduction of slavery into the area. In 1836, the settlers rebelled, defeated Mexico in a short war, and won their independence. Texas remained an independent nation for ten years, for the bitter debate over the extension of slavery prevented its annexation to the United States until 1845.

In 1845, President James Polk sent an emissary, James Slidell, to Mexico to arrange the acquisition of California. Outraged at the annexation of Texas, the Mexicans refused to cede any of their territory. Consequently, Polk trumped up a border incident along the Rio Grande, provoking a military clash that led to the war against Mexico (1846–1848). The victorious United States took the territories of Arizona, New Mexico, and California. Barely some seventy years old, the United States, building on its conquest of Native American lands, had successfully waged another war of territorial acquisition.

COMMERCE AND THE CANAL

From 1815 to 1860, U.S. foreign commerce increased dramatically; exports grew by nearly 400 percent and imports by 300 percent. The nature of U.S. trade changed, for instead of reexporting foreign-made goods, U.S. merchants exported agricultural commodities and manufactured goods produced in the United States. Because of the increased economic activity in the Caribbean, especially Cuba and Central America, the United States began to pay close attention to the region. Cuba became one of the most important U.S. overseas markets, ranking third behind Great Britain and France in total U.S. trade. Throughout the 1850s, sentiment was strong, particularly among southern slave owners, to annex the island. President Millard Fillmore tried unsuccessfully to purchase Cuba from Spain in 1852.

Central America became important because of the prospect of a canal through the Central American isthmus. After discussions began in 1825, the United States signed an 1846 agreement with New Granada (Colombia) that guaranteed U.S. access to any canal built in its province of Panama. This concern over a canal and commercial interests in Central America brought the United States into direct confrontation with Great Britain, which had colonies in the region. Each nation sought to keep the other from dominating the area or controlling any canal that would be built. As a result, in 1850 they agreed to the Clayton-Bulwer Treaty, which provided that neither country would try to dominate Central America or acquire exclusive rights to a canal. Thus, they eliminated a potential cause of hostilities.

The gold rush to California in 1849 increased the importance of transportation across the isthmus. U.S. entrepreneurs invested heavily in steamships and railroad construction in the region to satisfy the demand for cheap and fast transport across the isthmus to California. Despite the treaty with Britain and these heavy investments in transportation, U.S. interest in a canal continued.

THE AWAKENING GIANT, 1865–1887

In the two decades after the U.S. Civil War (1861–1865), U.S. policy makers focused their concerns on territorial expansion and increased trade in Latin America, finding little success in either. The major diplomatic triumph of the era came in 1866 when Secretary of State William H. Seward, belatedly invoking the Monroe Doctrine, demanded that France remove its troops from Mexico, where they propped up the rule of the Emperor Maximilian, the Austrian archduke. Emperor Napoleon III of France complied the following year, more because of growing tensions with Prussia in Europe than because of fear of the United States.

A succession of U.S. presidents and secretaries of state attempted to acquire new territories, but Congress inevitably thwarted them. They also sought to expand U.S. trade to Latin America through the negotiation of reciprocal trade treaties and establishment of inter-American diplomatic conferences. The United States signed bilateral reciprocal trade agreements with six Latin American nations during the 1880s, but no real benefits accrued. The first Inter-American Conference met in Washington, D.C., in 1889. It resulted in little more than the airing of long-simmering grievances and mistrust.

ADVENTURES IN LATIN AMERICA, 1888–1896

U.S. adventurism in Latin America in the last years of the nineteenth century stemmed from severe domestic economic and social problems, pervasive racism, and the country's growing stake in commerce and investment in the region. The United States experienced a deep depression from 1893 to 1898, the third such downturn in twenty-five years (the others had occurred in 1873–1878 and 1882–

1885). It became evident that the domestic market could not profitably absorb the rapidly growing output of U.S. agriculture and industry. U.S. leaders unanimously agreed that the answer to the problem was to expand foreign markets. The depression of 1893 created deep-seated social unrest as well, resulting in a series of bitter and bloody strikes. Business executives and politicians alike feared that continued depression would lead to class warfare.

At the same time, U.S. capitalists increased their investment in Latin America. Paradoxically, despite the depression, U.S. banks had surplus funds to invest. Because investments in the United States were unattractive, the bankers turned to potentially more lucrative foreign enterprises. These investors poured millions of dollars into Cuban sugar and Mexican mining and railroads. By 1900, the U.S. stake in Mexico alone had reached $500 million.

U.S. interest, however, was not limited to areas like Mexico and Cuba, where it already had large investments. The United States was willing to go to great lengths, even at the risk of war, both to protect potential markets and to reinforce its political dominance in the region. This was particularly true of the Caribbean, which leaders tended to view as an "American lake." Thus, in 1888, the United States intervened in a civil war in Haiti to secure a favorable commercial agreement and a naval base at Môle St. Nicolas. The U.S. fleet actually broke a blockade to bring about the victory of the faction it favored. Once entrenched in power, however, this group reneged on its promises to the Harrison administration (1887–1893). Then Secretary of State James G. Blaine also tried unsuccessfully to obtain Samaná Bay from Santo Domingo.

Naturally, the same doctrines of white supremacy that sought to justify a domestic racial apartheid, the lynching of thousands of African Americans, disfranchisement of 8 million southern blacks, the "tribalization" of sovereign Native American nations, and the exclusion of Chinese immigrants also shaped U.S. relations with Latin America. U.S. policy makers increasingly came to share the view of Atlanta's Henry Grady, an influential "New South" publisher, who argued that white supremacy reflected "the right of character, intelligence, and property to rule." This, according to diplomatic historian Walter LaFeber, "anticipated some of the arguments Americans later used to justify their new foreign policies."

As the depression of 1893 deepened, U.S. leaders looked southward with growing anxiety. President Grover Cleveland declared in his annual message to Congress in 1893 that unrest and European meddling had threatened U.S. interests in Brazil, Costa Rica, Guatemala, Honduras, and Nicaragua in 1892; the U.S. fleet found it difficult to keep up with its "responsibilities." Local disorders and European, particularly British, competition threatened markets desperately needed by U.S. corporations.

In 1894, the United States became involved in another revolution when it intervened in Brazil to protect a potentially important market and to check British influence there. The United States had signed a reciprocal trade agreement with the newly proclaimed republic of Brazil in 1891, but the rebels who rose up in 1893 opposed the pact. The main strategy of the rebel forces was to blockade the harbor of Rio de Janeiro, the nation's principal city; they hoped to strangle the government by denying it the all-important customs revenue. The United States helped undermine this strategy by refusing to recognize the blockade. U.S. vessels unloaded their cargoes without interference.

Late in 1894, however, with clandestine aid from the British, the rebellion regained momentum. At this time, important mercantile and oil (Rockefeller) interests, fearing the loss of their Brazilian market, brought pressure on the State Department to intervene. The United States responded by sending most of the Atlantic fleet to the harbor of Rio de Janeiro. By maneuvering to prevent rebel bombardment of the capital, the U.S. warships played a crucial part in the defeat of the revolt.

Shortly thereafter, the United States intervened in Nicaragua to protect its rights to an isthmian canal and the substantial holdings of U.S. investors. In 1893, a nationalist government, headed by Gen. José S. Zelaya, took power in Nicaragua; it threatened to cancel a concession granted by a previous administration to the Maritime Canal Company to build a canal through Nicaraguan territory. Later, Zelaya also threatened the prosperous U.S.-run banana plantations in the indigenous Miskito reservation (an area claimed by Nicaragua but controlled by the British) by invading the reservation in 1894. In response, British troops landed and quickly subdued the Nicaraguan force. U.S. interests, with a $2 million stake in the Miskito region, were unwilling to accept either British or Nicaraguan rule. To protect its property, the United States stationed two warships off the coast and in July dispatched marines to restore order. U.S. troops landed three more times, in 1896, 1898, and 1899, to protect U.S. lives and property.

THE TURNING POINT: VENEZUELA, 1895–1896

The Venezuelan crisis of 1895–1896 ended in full British recognition of U.S. hegemony in the Western Hemisphere. The United States intervened in a boundary dispute between Venezuela and Great Britain that had festered for more than half a century. The controversy concerned the region at the mouth of the Orinoco River, the major commercial artery for northern South America, which both Venezuela and the British colony of Guiana (present-day Guyana) claimed. In the 1880s, Britain extended its claims, causing Venezuela to break off diplomatic relations.

During 1893 and 1894, the Venezuelan government, confronted with mounting economic difficulties and political unrest, appealed to the United States to help settle the controversy. President Cleveland's entrance into the dispute reflected his deep concern about the apparent resurgence of European intervention in Latin America. Between 1891 and 1895, the British had actively intervened in Brazil, Chile, and Nicaragua. The French had become involved in a dispute with Brazil over the boundary of their colony of Guiana and had threatened intervention in Santo Domingo to obtain satisfaction for the killing of a French citizen. The simultaneous scramble for territories in Africa magnified the threat; what the European rivals did on one continent, they could do on another. Specifically,

President Cleveland feared that British control of the mouth of the Orinoco would exclude U.S. commerce from northern South American markets.

In 1895, in an obvious effort to intensify U.S. support, the Venezuelan government granted a lucrative concession to a U.S. syndicate for the exploitation of rich mineral resources located in the disputed zone. In July 1895, Secretary of State Richard Olney spelled out the U.S. attitude toward European meddling in Latin America. Citing the Monroe Doctrine, he declared that the United States would intervene whenever the actions of a European power in the Western Hemisphere posed a "serious and direct menace to its own integrity and welfare." In effect, Olney claimed hegemony for the United States in Latin America.

The British initially responded to Olney's claims with disdain; the English foreign secretary denied the validity of the Monroe Doctrine in international law and brushed aside the U.S. assertion of supremacy in the Western Hemisphere. President Cleveland, however, firmly supported Olney's position and made it clear that the United States was willing to go to war to uphold it. Meanwhile, international developments worked to soften the British stand; the threat of a war with Germany and British problems in South Africa took precedence. Accordingly, in late 1896, the British agreed to submit the dispute to arbitration. The government of Venezuela neither participated in nor was informed of this agreement.

The Venezuelan affair marked the end of British military predominance in Latin America. Its attention now focused on the growing German power and the competition for territory in Africa, Britain could no longer commit substantial resources to the region. With the growing threat of a general war in Europe, British leaders also could not afford to alienate the United States, a powerful potential ally. Thus, the British formally recognized U.S. hegemony in Latin America with the signing of the Hay-Pauncefote Treaty of 1901, which allowed the United States unilaterally to build, control, and fortify an isthmian canal. In 1906, Britain withdrew its fleet from the Caribbean. Great Brit-

ain retained its predominant economic position in southern South America but was fated to lose that also to the United States after World War I.

An Imperial Power, 1898–1945

By 1898, the United States had emerged as an industrial, financial, and naval power. It surpassed Great Britain as the world's leading manufacturing state. Giant U.S. banks and corporations invested heavily overseas. Increasingly, the nation looked abroad for markets, raw materials, and profits. Recurring economic difficulties and mounting social unrest spurred U.S. leaders to seek solutions in overseas economic expansion and foreign adventures.

THE WAR WITH SPAIN

The war with Spain in 1898 established the United States as a full-fledged imperial power. The primary goal of its Cuban policy during the 1890s was to protect the very large (more than $50 million) U.S. investment in the island by stopping the chronic political disorder there. When Spain proved unable to end the turmoil, and it appeared that ungovernable native rebels might take over, the United States intervened. In declaring war against Spain, the U.S. Congress pledged to free Cuba from Spanish tyranny and, in the Teller Resolution, disavowed any intention to annex the island. Nevertheless, to the dismay of Cuban rebels, the McKinley administration had opposed the Teller Amendment and defeated the Turpie-Foraker bill, which would have recognized the Cuban government-in-exile. The U.S. government proceeded to conduct the war and negotiate the peace without consulting the Cubans.

The United States occupied and ruled the island from 1898 to 1902, departing only after the Cubans agreed to include in their constitution the notorious Platt Amendment, which made the country a virtual U.S. colony. U.S. forces occupied the island three more times—1906–1909, 1912, and 1917–1922. As noted in Chapter 1515, instead of bringing the Cubans liberty and economic progress, U.S. intervention promoted and perpetuated racism, corruption, violence, and economic stagnation.

AN "AMERICAN LAKE": THE "BIG STICK" AND "DOLLAR DIPLOMACY" IN THE CARIBBEAN

From 1898 to 1932, the United States intervened militarily in nine Caribbean nations a total of thirty-four times. Its occupation forces ran the governments of Cuba, the Dominican Republic, Haiti, Nicaragua, and Panama for long periods; Costa Rica, Guatemala, Honduras, and Mexico experienced shorter invasions. Military intervention was not the only method employed by the United States to control the region; other effective means included threats, nonrecognition, and economic sanctions.

The U.S. economic stake in the Caribbean was substantial. Moreover, the nature of this investment, which was concentrated primarily in agricultural commodities, mineral extraction, oil production, and government securities, made it particularly vulnerable to political disorders. From 1887 to 1914, U.S. investment in Cuba and the West Indies rose almost sevenfold, from $50 million to $336 million. Investment in Central America more than quadrupled, from $21 million to $93 million. By 1914, U.S. investment in Mexico had risen to more than $1 billion. In 1914, 43 percent of this investment was in mining, 18.7 percent in agriculture, 10 percent in oil, and 13 percent in railroads, which U.S. corporations built to transport export products to market. The owners of these enterprises often had considerable influence on U.S. policy.

The United States justified its actions in the Caribbean by the so-called Roosevelt Corollary (1904) to the Monroe Doctrine, so named because President Theodore Roosevelt maintained that the United States, as a "civilized" nation, had the right to end "chronic wrongdoing" and thus could intervene in the Caribbean to maintain order. The Roosevelt Corollary was a logical outgrowth of the increasingly aggressive policies successively advanced by Seward, Grant, Cleveland, and Olney.

THE PANAMA CANAL

U.S. interest in a canal across Central America to join the Atlantic and Pacific oceans had intensified as the nation filled out its continental boundaries

and expanded its commercial activities throughout the Western Hemisphere. But the first to attempt to build a canal was Ferdinand de Lesseps, the Frenchman who had constructed the Suez Canal. He began a project to dig a sea-level canal across Panama in 1878. After eleven years of effort, de Lesseps, thwarted by tropical disease and engineering problems, gave up the project. Throughout this period, the United States pressured France to abandon the undertaking; it asserted its "rightful and long-established claim to priority on the American continent." The growth of a large U.S. Navy, which had two coasts to defend, added to the urgency of constructing an isthmian passageway.

In the 1880s and 1890s, support grew for building a canal through Nicaragua. In 1901, a presidential commission endorsed the Nicaraguan route, despite the more favorable engineering and logistical characteristics of the Panamanian alternative, because the French company that controlled the canal concession in Panama wanted the fantastic sum of $109 million for its rights. At this point, two extraordinary entrepreneurs, William N. Cromwell, an influential New York attorney, and Philippe Bunau-Varilla, chief engineer of the de Lesseps project and an organizer of the New Panama Canal Company (the French company that had rights to the canal), acted to change the course of U.S. policy. Cromwell, as lawyer for the canal company, bribed the Republican Party to end its support of the Nicaraguan route. He and Bunau-Varilla then convinced the company to lower the price for its concession to a more reasonable $40 million.

The two men faced the problem of convincing the United States to purchase their company's concession before it expired in 1904. In 1902, Bunau-Varilla and Cromwell managed to push through Congress the Spooner Amendment, which authorized President Roosevelt to buy the New Panama Canal Company's rights for the asking price of $40 million if he could negotiate a treaty with Colombia. In 1903, Secretary of State John Hay pressured the Colombian ambassador to the United States to sign a pact that gave the United States a ninety-nine-year lease on a strip of land across the isthmus in return for $10 million and an annual payment of $250,000. The Colombian Senate, demanding more money, rejected the proposal.

In the meantime, Bunau-Varilla undertook to exploit the long tradition of Panamanian nationalism and rebelliousness for his own end. From the time that Colombia won its independence from Spain in 1821, it had never been able to establish its rule in Panama. During the nineteenth century, the Panamanians revolted fifty times against their Colombian masters. On two occasions, when the Panamanian rebels seemed near success (1855–1856 and 1885), the United States intervened militarily to protect its interests and end the revolts. After a terrible civil war (1899–1902) had severely weakened Colombia, Panamanian nationalists again prepared to rise in revolt. Working closely with the U.S. State Department and the Panamanians, Bunau-Varilla triggered a successful uprising in early November 1903. With the help of the U.S. Navy and bribes paid to the Colombian officers who were supposed to crush the revolt, Panama won its independence.

The Panamanians, to their own undoing, entrusted to Bunau-Varilla the subsequent negotiations with the United States over the canal concession. Feverishly working to complete the arrangements before the New Panama Canal Company's rights expired, he produced a treaty that gave the United States control over a ten-mile-wide canal zone "as if it were a sovereign of the territory." The United States was to have "in perpetuity the use, occupation, and control" of the zone. In return, the United States was to pay Panama $10 million and assume a virtual protectorate over the new nation. The Panamanian government indignantly protested the terms of the agreement but eventually accepted the pact, fearing that the United States might either seize the canal with no compensation or build one in Nicaragua instead.

U.S. Marines were stationed in Panama from late 1903 until 1914 to protect U.S. interests while the canal was built, largely by black workers recruited from the West Indies. During this period, the United States disbanded the Panamanian army and assumed the responsibility of defending Panama

against any external threat. The United States established its own postal system, customhouses, and commissaries in the Canal Zone, privileges that seriously undermined the Panamanian economy and badly injured Panamanian pride. The canal was completed in 1914.

THE DOMINICAN REPUBLIC, HAITI, AND NICARAGUA

The United States occupied and administered the governments of the Dominican Republic (1916–1924), Haiti (1915–1934), and Nicaragua (1912–1925 and 1926–1933) to the detriment of these nations' long-range political and economic development.

President Ulysses S. Grant had sought to annex the Dominican Republic (then known as Santo Domingo) in 1869; only rejection of the agreement by the U.S. Senate, influenced by fears of mingling with "people of the Latin race mixed with the Indian and African blood," prevented him from acquiring the nation, which shares the island of Hispaniola with Haiti. In the decades that followed, a series of venal and brutal dictators, often supported by loans from U.S. banks, produced a debilitating cycle of repression and rebellion. In 1893, the Santo Domingo Improvement Company, a U.S. firm, purchased the country's heavy foreign debt in return for the right to collect its customs revenue. In both 1903 and 1904, the United States dispatched marines to protect the interests of the influential New York financiers who were principals in the company. In 1905, the U.S. government assumed the administration of Dominican customs.

However, unrest persisted. In 1916, President Woodrow Wilson sent in Marines after the Dominican government refused to accept broader U.S. control over the nation's internal affairs, and the U.S. Navy maintained a military dictatorship until 1924. The Marines brutally repressed guerrilla activities that threatened U.S.-owned sugar plantations. In addition, several U.S. officers subsequently were court-martialed for the commission of atrocities.

The U.S. occupation forces attempted administrative and fiscal reforms and built some roads, but these projects were abandoned when the soldiers

U.S. Interventions in the Caribbean and Central America, 1898–1945

departed. One institution that remained intact after the occupation ended was the *Guardia Nacional*, the national police force. Rafael Trujillo, with U.S. support, rose through the ranks of the Guardia to become dictator of the Dominican Republic in 1928. His rapacious rule, extending over three decades (he was assassinated in 1961), was the bitter legacy of U.S. intervention.

Events in Haiti followed a similar course. For a century after winning independence from France in 1804, Haiti experienced ruinous political turmoil. Seizing the opportunity presented by the brutal murder of the Haitian president in 1915, Woodrow Wilson sent in the Marines, ostensibly to prevent Germany from taking advantage of the chaos to

establish a base on the island, which would endanger U.S. commerce and the access routes to the Panama Canal. A treaty signed the next year placed the United States in full control of the country. Although Haitians held public office, they served only at the pleasure of U.S. authorities. Here, too, U.S. troops ignored civil liberties and committed atrocities while engaged in the suppression of rural guerrillas. U.S. control lasted until 1934.

The United States also intervened in Nicaragua to protect the interests of U.S. companies operating there. The U.S. investment totaled only $2.5 million, but the largest company, the United States–Nicaraguan Concession, had considerable influence in the Taft administration (1909–1913); Secretary of

State Philander C. Knox had been the company's legal counsel. In 1909, Gen. José Zelaya, an old nemesis of the United States, canceled a concession to one U.S. company and threatened the Nicaraguan Concession. The same year, the United States backed a revolution that overthrew Zelaya. In 1912, at the request of the Nicaraguan government, President William Howard Taft sent in the Marines to crush a new rebellion; the Marines remained for thirteen years. In 1916, the United States secured its monopolistic control over transisthmian canal rights by signing the Bryan-Chamorro Treaty with Nicaragua. President Calvin Coolidge withdrew U.S. troops for a short period in 1925 but dispatched them again to subdue yet another revolution the following year; the soldiers stayed until 1933.

Puerto Rico

The United States became a colonial power with the conquest and acquisition of the island of Puerto Rico in 1898 during the Spanish-American-Cuban War. From December 1898 until May 1900, U.S. military governors ruled the island. In 1900, the U.S. Congress passed the Foraker Act, which established a new civilian government for the island with a governor and an executive council appointed by the U.S. president. In 1917, an elected Senate replaced the executive council, but the president maintained the power to veto legislation passed by the Puerto Rican Congress. The same year, the U.S. Congress granted Puerto Ricans U.S. citizenship to make them eligible for the military draft for World War I.

U.S. occupation cost Puerto Ricans dearly politically. At the time of the Spanish-American War, the island had won a large degree of autonomy from Spain. The new colonial regime stripped that from them and ruled Puerto Rico with tactless, condescending mainlanders who had no experience in dealing with different cultures. When Puerto Ricans protested against unresponsive government, U.S. authorities reacted harshly. In 1909, for example, members of the Puerto Rican House of Delegates refused to pass the year's appropriation bill because of their objections to the indifference shown in the court system to struggling coffee

growers. President Taft angrily demanded rescission of the House of Delegates' right of appropriations, and the U.S. Congress enacted this legislation in the so-called Olmstead Amendment. Puerto Rico did not have a native-born governor until 1947 or an elected governor until 1948.

Puerto Rico also underwent drastic economic changes because of the U.S. occupation. In 1898, its leading crop, coffee, was exported to Europe. U.S. policies transformed the island into a mono-crop sugar economy with landownership concentrated in a few hands, mostly absentee foreign corporations. Puerto Ricans became dependent on the U.S. sugar quota. The decline of sugar prices during the 1920s and their collapse during the Great Depression of the 1930s brought chronic economic problems. By 1929, near starvation prevailed in many parts of the island. New Deal agencies, such as the Puerto Rican Emergency Relief Administration and the Puerto Rican Reconstruction Administration, poured some $230 million into the island from 1933 to 1941.

During the 1930s and for decades thereafter, the influence of two Puerto Ricans, Pedro Albizu Campos and Luis Muñoz Marín, dominated Puerto Rican politics. Harvard-educated Albizu became the foremost advocate of independence. He formed the Nationalist Party and took an ardently anti-U.S. stand. He spent many years in prison for supporting violent confrontation with the island's colonial master. Muñoz Marín, whose father had led the Unionists in the early years of U.S. rule, was also educated in the United States. He did not live in Puerto Rico permanently until 1931. During the dark depression days of the 1930s, Muñoz Marín became the star protégé of the New Deal.

The terrible plight of Puerto Rico during the Great Depression led U.S. policy makers to reevaluate its status in the late 1930s. It was, as historian Arturo Morales Carrión has said, "a crisis of the whole colonial system." North Americanization had brought the "rise of absentee landownership, the collapse of coffee culture, the migration to growing slums, and shocking poverty in rural areas." U.S. rule had been a "mixture of paternalism and neglect, self-righteousness and condescension." The U.S. administrators of the island reacted harshly to such criticism and to nationalist protests. In March 1937, during a parade of the Nationalist Party in San Juan, police killed seventeen protesters in an unprovoked attack. In the crisis that followed in the aftermath of the massacre, old political coalitions realigned, and Muñoz Marín emerged as the leading political figure. Based on his grassroots organization in the countryside, Muñoz Marín's Popular Democratic Party (PPD) rose meteorically, sweeping elections from 1944 until 1968. With Washington's help, he led Puerto Rico into a new era of industrialization and economic expansion.

Characteristic of Puerto Rican development was its dependence on the U.S. economy. North American corporations effectively monopolized the key sectors of banking, transport, tourism, and high-tech industrialization. This discouraged native capital formation. For North American corporations, however, the combination of low wages and tax breaks proved a bonanza, with profits in the range of $10 billion a year.

The combination of economic, political, and legal dependency adversely affected Puerto Rican political culture, breeding a colonial psychology that made dependency appear a natural condition and independence an impossible dream. Accurately summarizing the island's colonial legal status since 1898, Attorney General Richard Thornburg declared that "the Congress of the United States holds full powers over Puerto Rico, a relationship that Puerto Ricans are incapable of altering." He went on to say that this relationship remained inalterable until changed by an amendment to the U.S. Constitution.

THE MEXICAN REVOLUTION

In Chapter 12, we discussed some aspects of U.S. policy toward the Mexican Revolution (1910–1920). That policy aimed above all to safeguard the vast U.S. investment below the border and secure the favorable political and economic climate required by U.S. interests in Mexico. The specific policies and tactics employed by the administrations of Presidents Taft and Wilson varied with the shifting conditions in Mexico, political pressures in the United States, and the changing international background. The United States twice resorted to military intervention in Mexico. In 1914, U.S. Marines occupied the gulf ports of Veracruz and Tampico in an effort to bring down Gen. Victoriano Huerta, considered too friendly to British and German investors. The second intervention, Gen. John J. Pershing's incursion into northern Mexico in 1916 in pursuit of Pancho Villa, aimed to pressure the regime of Venustiano Carranza to disavow allegedly radical constitutional constraints on foreign investment.

The United States more decisively influenced the military course of the revolution by regulating the flow of arms and munitions across the United States–Mexican border. Through selective application of its neutrality laws, the U.S. government prevented "undesirable" factions from instigating disruptive activities on the U.S. side of the border. Woodrow Wilson introduced a new tactic in U.S. relations with Mexico by announcing that he would withhold recognition of governments that did not measure up to his standard of "morality." Wilson used this ploy against Huerta, Carranza, and Obregón.

Ultimately, U.S. efforts to control the course of the revolution failed because of stubborn resistance on the part of nationalist Mexican leaders like Carranza, divisions among U.S. investors in Mexico— some favoring and others opposing military intervention—and finally, growing involvement of the United States in World War I. Its entry into the war in 1917 sharply limited policy alternatives because the country lacked the military resources to fight in both Mexico and Europe. The threat of a Mexican alliance with Germany—a threat strongly posed by the famous Zimmerman telegram—forced the United States to adopt a more moderate policy toward its neighbor.

QUIET IMPERIALISM: THE GOOD NEIGHBOR IN WORDS AND ACTION, 1921–1945

U.S. investment in Latin America grew rapidly in the period between 1914 and 1929. The world war enabled U.S. entrepreneurs to buy up much of the large British and German investment in the region.

Total U.S. investment in Cuba and the West Indies, for example, rose from $336 million in 1914 to $1.2 billion in 1929—nearly a fourfold increase. U.S. capital in Central America more than tripled, while investment in South America increased eightfold. In 1929, total U.S. investment in Latin America had reached the staggering sum of $5.4 billion, or 35 percent of all U.S. foreign investment.

Much of the new investment went into oil: U.S. companies channeled $235 million to Venezuela, $134 million to Colombia, $120 million to Mexico, and $50 million to Peru for oil exploration and production. Another $163 million went to manufacturing enterprises in South America. U.S. companies also invested heavily in Chilean copper and nitrate, Argentine beef, and Cuban sugar.

This period marked the full-fledged involvement of large U.S. corporations, later called multinationals, in Latin America. Such giants as Standard Oil of New Jersey, the American Smelting and Refining Company, International Telephone and Telegraph, American Foreign Power, and Armour established or added to their vast stake in the region.

The basic goal of U.S. policy in Latin America did not change during the postwar period; it remained the protection of U.S. economic interests. Nonetheless, public opinion and realism dictated modifications. U.S. citizens were weary of overseas adventures and crusades. The United States remained dominant in the Caribbean, exerting decisive influence in the affairs of Mexico and Cuba and continuing to occupy the Dominican Republic, Haiti, and Nicaragua during the 1920s, but opposition was growing to the old-style imperialism.

U.S. leaders also realized that growing popular hostility to U.S. policy in Latin America, primarily a response to U.S. actions in the Caribbean, posed a serious long-term danger to U.S. economic interests. An early sign of this policy shift came in 1921, when the Colombian government threatened to cancel U.S. companies' concessions to explore and drill for oil. The United States responded by paying Colombia $25 million to compensate for the loss of Panama. This had a dual meaning: It protected U.S. economic interests, and it symbolized a less aggressive policy toward Latin America. The shift in U.S.

tactics became even clearer when the United States removed its troops from Cuba in 1922, from the Dominican Republic in 1924, and from Nicaragua in 1925. Despite these actions, the United States encountered bitter criticism of its role in the hemisphere at the Pan-American conferences in Santiago in 1923 and Havana in 1928.

The most important indication that the United States had largely abandoned military intervention as a major tactic was its restraint in dealing with Mexico, the biggest trouble spot in the hemisphere during the 1920s. The Mexican constitution of 1917 was a most radical document by contemporary standards. The constitution's provisions on landownership and ownership of subsoil rights seriously endangered U.S. investments. U.S. oil companies, in particular, objected to the new laws, which sought to reclaim statutory control of Mexico's rich natural resources even as they confirmed foreign usufruct rights.

Throughout the 1920s, the United States and Mexico haggled over application of the constitution, but the basic disagreement inflamed relations until World War II. The United States did not intervene militarily to protect its large investments in Mexico because three circumstances discouraged such action. First, public opinion opposed further foreign adventures. Second, a military invasion would have been prohibitively costly in terms of both manpower and finances. Finally, U.S. entrepreneurs with interests in Mexico disagreed sharply over the proper course of action. The oil companies, which were most threatened by the constitution, favored intervention. The banks and mining companies, whose interests would have been in greater danger in the event of war between the United States and Mexico, opposed intervention. The controversy abated during the late 1920s, after the U.S. government conceded that Mexico's nationalist regulations did not threaten the oil companies' right to profit from oil production.

President Herbert Hoover and Secretary of State Henry L. Stimson continued to shift toward moderation and stepped up U.S. efforts to win goodwill in Latin America. Hoover abandoned Wilson's policy of denying recognition to "unworthy" governments. The Clark memorandum, a milestone in Hoover's efforts, declared that the Roosevelt Corollary had no support in the Monroe Doctrine; consequently, the United States would no longer interfere militarily in the internal affairs of Latin American nations under the provisions of the doctrine. However, the president carefully refrained from rejecting intervention outright. In 1933, he withdrew U.S. troops from Nicaragua and planned to remove them from Haiti, but the Haitians objected to the withdrawal terms.

Building on these experiences, Franklin D. Roosevelt assumed the presidency in 1933 and, officially proclaiming the United States to be a "good neighbor" to the rest of the world, he rejected "interference in the internal affairs of other nations." The following year, the United States abrogated the Platt Amendment, thus abandoning its protectorate over Cuba; the same year, it withdrew its occupation troops from Haiti.

Events in Cuba soon tested the nonintervention policy. In 1933, political unrest there threatened the substantial U.S. investment on the island. Roosevelt dispatched Sumner Welles to Havana to try to arrange an accommodation between dictator Gerardo Machado and his opponents. After several months of unsuccessful negotiations, Machado fled, and power fell into the hands of a disorganized and disunited junta. Eventually, Dr. Ramón Grau San Martín emerged as leader of the government. He quickly fell into disfavor with the United States when he suspended loan repayments to a large New York bank and seized two U.S.-owned sugar mills. As a result, the United States refused to recognize the Grau government. With U.S. warships lingering in Havana harbor, Welles collaborated with Fulgencio Batista to force Grau to relinquish his leadership. Supported by the United States, Batista emerged as the strongman of Cuba. Despite government protestations to the contrary, the United States had not entirely abandoned the "big stick."

Mexico again tested U.S. nonintervention in 1938. The long dispute between the Mexican government and the oil companies culminated in the expropriation of foreign oil holdings when the oil companies defied an order of the Mexican Supreme Court in a labor dispute. While the oil companies clamored for reprisal, Roosevelt tried to settle matters peacefully. In the face of isolationist sentiment in the United States, intervention was unthinkable. Moreover, with war in Europe on the horizon, the United States did not want to endanger an important source of oil, and it eventually reached a settlement during the 1940s.

Roosevelt's Good Neighbor Policy toward Latin America also involved efforts to achieve reciprocal trade agreements as a means of increasing U.S. trade and influence in the area. Secretary of State Cordell Hull ardently supported such agreements, believing they would help the United States emerge from the Great Depression. From 1934 to 1941, Hull succeeded in signing reciprocal trade treaties with fifteen Latin American nations. Had those treaties succeeded in significantly increasing U.S. trade, which they did not, they would have adversely affected Latin America's nascent industrialization, which was critically dependent on protective tariffs for its survival. In this area, U.S. policy was in direct conflict with the goal of Latin American economic development.

In the 1930s, the United States grew increasingly concerned over the spread of German economic and political influence in Latin America. In response to this influence, the United States pushed for closer cooperation among the nations of the Western Hemisphere by promoting a series of meetings to consider common problems. The participants in successive inter-American conferences agreed to consult in the event of war, approved a joint declaration of neutrality, proclaimed the existence of a safety zone around the hemisphere, and warned belligerents not to wage war within it. They decided to administer French and Dutch colonies in the Western Hemisphere in the event they were in danger of Nazi takeover. They also proclaimed that they would construe an attack on any of the conferring nations as an attack on all. In early 1942, shortly after the Japanese attack on Pearl Harbor, the conferees agreed to cooperate against the Axis; most Latin American nations severed diplomatic relations with the Axis powers.

Every Latin American country but Argentina contributed to the Allied war effort.

The war strengthened the economic links between the United States and Latin America. The United States served as the sole market for the region's exports and the only supplier of its requirements of arms, munitions, industrial equipment, and manufactured goods. A growing proportion of U.S. capital went into manufacturing enterprises instead of raw material extraction. By the end of the war, Argentina accounted for 16 percent of U.S. investment in Latin America, Chile 16 percent, Brazil 13 percent, and Peru 4 percent. For the first time, South America accounted for more than half the total U.S. investment in Latin America.

Defending the Empire and Capitalism, 1945–1981

In the postwar era, four factors determined United States–Latin American relations: (1) the need for the United States to protect U.S. interests in the region, (2) its broader efforts to construct global markets open to trade and investment, (3) the desire of Latin American nations to industrialize and diversify their economies, and (4) the rivalry between the United States and the Soviet Union.

INVESTMENT AND TRADE

Several important trends characterized U.S. investment in and trade with Latin America after World War II. First, the amount of investment increased enormously. Furthermore, the type of investment changed from mostly extractive industries, such as mining and oil, to manufacturing, and it became concentrated in the hands of a few large corporations and banks. Last, although the amount of U.S. trade with Latin America grew substantially, the relative importance of this trade to the economies of the United States and individual Latin American nations decreased.

These trends did not mean that the United States had changed its policies. Its leaders continued to protect U.S. economic interests in the region, as trade and investment represented huge sums, despite declining importance. Accordingly, the editors

of *Fortune* magazine, an influential voice of corporate America, urged postwar U.S. leaders "to organize the economic resources of the world so as to make possible a return to the system of free enterprise in every country." Policy makers like then–Assistant Secretary of State Dean Acheson, a corporate lawyer, shared this worldview; fearing a replay of the Great Depression, he conceded in 1944 that the major postwar challenge was "a problem of markets. The important thing is markets. We have got to see that what the country produces is used and sold under financial arrangements which make its production possible.... You must look to foreign markets." Thus, every overt or covert U.S. intervention in Latin America during this period—in Chile, Cuba, the Dominican Republic, and Guatemala, for example—took place in countries where local governments enacted policies that endangered the security of large U.S. investments. Moreover, each of these countries challenged the U.S. vision of a global open-door system.

POST–WORLD WAR II ADJUSTMENTS

Despite the high degree of wartime cooperation, sharp differences between the United States and Latin America surfaced in the immediate postwar years. These disagreements emerged initially at the Chapultepec Conference in February 1945. Latin American leaders felt the United States should reward them for their contributions and sacrifices during the war, but Washington regarded European recovery as its first priority. There were also major disagreements over trade, industrialization, the overall direction of Latin American economic development, and the role of the United States in this development. The United States insisted on an open door to Latin American markets and investment opportunities, but it was unwilling to make any concessions that might injure its own producers. Latin Americans, however, feared that such free access to Latin American markets would destroy much of the industrial progress the region had made in the preceding two decades.

U.S. and Latin American interests clearly conflicted. The major Latin American obstacle to U.S.

objectives was the region's nationalism. Contrary to the open-door philosophy, according to the State Department's Office of Intelligence Research, in Latin America "the idea that the government has direct responsibility for the welfare of the people has resulted in a phenomenal growth of social and economic legislation designed to protect labor, distribute land more widely … and increase opportunities for education." Whereas U.S. leaders regarded private capital investment and free trade as the best routes to development, Latin American nations favored a massive government role in industrialization and restrictions on foreign trade and investment as the only means of modernizing and regaining control over their economies.

After the war, Latin America vainly sought help from the United States to finance industrialization and access to U.S.-manufactured goods, especially capital equipment needed to further industrialization. These efforts encountered further obstacles in the next few years as high prices for manufactured products dissipated the dollar reserves Latin American nations had accumulated during the war; declining prices for raw materials eroded Latin America's terms of trade even further.

Moreover, evidence mounted that the United States had reverted to its traditional disregard for Latin American sensitivities and to intervention in the region's internal affairs. In 1946, the United States interfered in the internal political affairs of three South American nations. It meddled disastrously in the Argentine presidential campaign of that year, ensuring the election of Juan Perón; it forced the González Videla government in Chile to oust the Communist members of its coalition cabinet; and it helped undermine a revolutionary regime in Bolivia that it had accused of fascist tendencies.

THE COLD WAR

Alarm in the United States over the vast expansion of communist influence in Eastern and Central Europe because of World War II, the communist victory in the Chinese civil war, and the gains of Communist parties in Western Europe had the effect of pushing Latin America to the back burner.

In this initial stage of the cold war, which lasted into the 1950s, the United States focused its attention on checking the further spread of communism in Western Europe and Asia by aiding the revival of the shattered capitalist economy. Nevertheless, according to a secret 1951 U.S. Intelligence Estimate entitled "Latin America's Support of U.S. Objectives," the cold war with the Soviet Union remained an indispensable source of U.S. leverage to secure support from the region's increasingly nationalistic regimes: "Latin American cooperation with the US," the report concluded, "is unlikely, in the absence of more generalized East-West hostilities, to increase substantially in the near future."

During this first stage of the cold war, U.S. leaders tended to view the world as two camps, one committed to the United States and its free enterprise system and the other loyal to communism. Because it regarded the world in such black-and-white terms, the United States viewed with implacable hostility governments and movements that disagreed with its policy or attempted to institute structural social and economic reforms. On two occasions, in Guatemala and Iran, cold war fears of communism provided the pretext for covert U.S. operations, undertaken by the Central Intelligence Agency (CIA), to topple such governments.

A second stage of the cold war began in the mid-1950s, when a "Third World" (that is, the developing world) emerged, made up of the many newly independent states of Africa and Asia, which proclaimed themselves unaligned in the struggle between the blocs led by the Soviet Union and the United States. The two superpowers, faced with the unacceptable consequences of nuclear war, fought out the cold war in the developing world. In this second stage, the United States became intensely concerned with Latin America, especially after the 1959 Cuban Revolution led to the establishment of the first socialist state in the Americas. U.S. preoccupation with the threat of more Cubas in the hemisphere produced the Alliance for Progress as an alternative to the Cuban model.

Equally important, however, was the use of military aid to shape the internal policies of recalcitrant Latin American nations. The Military Defense

Assistance Act of 1951 appropriated an initial $38.5 million to finance the build-up of Latin American armies for "country missions"—that is, internal security rather than global or regional defense. This expanded under successive U.S. presidential administrations such that immediate postwar U.S. military aid amounted to more than half a billion dollars for the circum-Caribbean area alone and included paying for the training of thousands of Latin American military officers. By 1954, this policy had borne substantial fruit: Pro-U.S. military dictatorships ruled thirteen of twenty countries.

The third stage of the cold war followed the disastrous U.S. experience in Vietnam and lasted until Ronald Reagan took office as president in 1981. Losing the Vietnam War and its tragic cost brought home to the U.S. government and its people the limitations of U.S. power and the dangers involved in trying to prevent social revolutions. Nonetheless, the United States remained determined to maintain its hegemony in the Western Hemisphere, and, to achieve its goals, the United States adapted traditional methods to suit new conditions.

A fourth stage of the cold war brought to the late 1980s the renewal of provocative anticommunist rhetoric, the simplistic 1950s division of the world into "them" and "us," the resurrection of military force as a policy tool, and a revival of illegal, covert activities. The collapse of the Stalinist-type Communist regimes in eastern and central Europe and the resulting demise of the cold war created a problem for the military-industrial complex that had flourished in the cold war's protective shadow and for U.S.-Latin American policy by depriving it of its traditional enemy, "international communism." In the 1990s, the drug trafficker replaced that traditional enemy as a convenient pretext for intervention in Latin America. After the September 11, 2001, terrorist attacks on the Pentagon and World Trade Center, a new pretext arose and the so-called war on terrorism replaced the war on drugs.

THE LATIN AMERICAN POLICIES OF TRUMAN AND EISENHOWER

The Truman administration (1945–1953) focused its attention on fighting communism in Europe and the Far East, but, as we have seen, it meddled with mixed success in the political affairs of Argentina, Bolivia, and Chile in 1946. Under Truman, the movement for hemispheric cooperation continued, at least outwardly. The Rio Treaty of 1947 brought Central and South America into a military alliance with the United States. The ninth International Conference of American States, held in Bogotá the following year, resulted in the formation of the Organization of American States (OAS). The OAS was to provide collective security, with an attack against one member viewed as an attack on all. The OAS also was to be a mediator in disputes among its members. Truman and his chief advisers were primarily concerned with maintaining the status quo in the region.

The Eisenhower presidency (1953–1961) marked a revival of strong corporate influence in U.S. foreign policy. Eisenhower took office in the middle of the Korean War and at the height of the McCarthy "Red Scare." His administration, particularly the fanatical anticommunist secretary of state, John Foster Dulles, divided the world into two categories: nations that supported the United States and those that did not. It described any foreign government that restricted the activities of U.S. corporations under its jurisdiction as communist and a threat to the security of the United States. During his two terms, Eisenhower faced four challenges of this kind in Latin America: Bolivia, British Guiana, Cuba, and Guatemala. In each case, his administration reacted according to the scale of the U.S. economic interests involved and the prevailing domestic and international conditions.

In Bolivia in 1952, a successful revolution headed by Victor Paz Estenssoro and the National Revolutionary Movement (MNR) ushered in sweeping economic and political reforms. In its first year, the new government nationalized the nation's tin mines, wiped out the latifundio system, replaced the old army with workers' and peasants' militias, and greatly increased the number of eligible voters. The outgoing Truman administration, anxious over the regime's radicalism, withheld recognition and aid from Bolivia. The middle-class leadership of the MNR eventually managed to convince the

Eisenhower administration that it was not Communist; as a result, Bolivia received millions of dollars in grants and loans and substantial technical assistance over the next decade. U.S. aid had a significant moderating influence on the MNR reform program. Indeed, U.S. assistance decisively altered the whole course of Bolivian development; the United States reestablished, equipped, and trained the Bolivian army, which overthrew Paz Estenssoro in 1964, ushering in a period of conservative rule that continued almost uninterrupted until 1981.

The United States employed different tactics to achieve the same general results, to adjust to the differing conditions of another Latin American country. In 1953, Marxist Cheddi Jagan campaigned on a program of structural reform and won election to head the government of the British colony of Guiana, an important source of bauxite and other metals. Several large U.S. companies, including Reynolds Metals and Kennecott Copper, had substantial holdings in the colony. Alarmed at the prospect of nationalization of these holdings by a Marxist regime, the United States urged the British to nullify the election; the British government duly sent troops to Guiana and deposed the new government.

The Eisenhower administration employed yet other tactics in Guatemala in 1954: conspiring to overthrow a democratically elected government whose reforms threatened the interests of a large and influential U.S. corporation. In 1944, a revolution toppled the oppressive regime of Jorge Ubico, who had ruled Guatemala since 1931. The victorious middle-class revolutionaries favored a capitalist course of development and were friendly to the United States. However, the reform programs of Presidents Juan José Arévalo (1945–1951) and Jacobo Arbenz (1951–1954) provoked the hostility of the United Fruit Company (UFCO) and Dulles. UFCO had operated in Guatemala since the 1890s, when it acquired a virtual monopoly on banana production and distribution. It was Guatemala's largest employer, with ten thousand workers, and its largest landowner. The company also controlled the nation's main transportation artery, the International Railways of Central America (IRCA), and major port facilities on the Gulf of Mexico.

The Guatemalan government clashed with UFCO over labor and land reform. Arévalo enacted a new labor code in 1947. Charging that Arévalo discriminated against it, the company protested sharply. The ensuing labor agitation severely hampered banana production for several years. In 1952, the Guatemalan Congress enacted a land reform program, expropriating large tracts of uncultivated land for distribution among landless peasants. Again, UFCO charged the government with discrimination.

Unfortunately for Guatemala, UFCO enjoyed great influence with the U.S. government. It was a client of Dulles's law firm, and the company's headquarters were in Boston, which also made it a constituent of three of the most powerful men in the U.S. Congress: Senator Henry Cabot Lodge, Speaker of the House Joseph Martin, and Democratic Party leader John McCormack. Moreover, the family of the assistant secretary of state in charge of Guatemalan relations, John Moors Cabot, was a major stockholder in UFCO.

Seizing on allegations of Communist participation in the Arbenz government to justify its actions, the United States trained and outfitted a rebel group under the command of Carlos Castillo Armas, who invaded Guatemala through UFCO property and overthrew Arbenz in June 1954. Castillo's repressive regime, which lasted until his assassination in 1957, erased all of the postwar reforms and restored UFCO's privileges.

THE CUBAN REVOLUTION AND UNITED STATES– LATIN AMERICAN RELATIONS

Eisenhower's successful interventions in Bolivia, British Guiana, and Guatemala produced bitter criticism of the United States in Latin America and contributed to the hostile and violent reception accorded Vice President Richard Nixon on his tour of the region in 1958. No major change in policy, however, occurred until the victory of Fidel Castro in Cuba in 1959.

The United States, a steadfast supporter of Batista's cruel dictatorship, consistently had opposed Castro's revolutionary movement and later embarked on a two-pronged program designed to

The United Fruit Company allowed an exile mercenary force, trained, equipped, and financed by the CIA, to use this Puerto Barrios Hiring Hall as a staging area for an invasion that pressured the Guatemalan Army to overthrow Jacobo Arbenz, the democratically elected populist who had favored land and labor reform.

destroy his government. To avert new Cubas, U.S. policymakers simultaneously sought to placate the rest of Latin America with various concessions. Meanwhile, they imposed economic sanctions on Cuba and began clandestinely to train an invasion force of Cuban exiles. To ensure Latin American backing, the United States committed limited funds to a new Social Trust Fund for the region and agreed to support plans for common markets in the area, such as the Latin American Free Trade Association (LAFTA) and the Central American Common Market, proposals that it had long opposed.

Under the new administration of John F. Kennedy, these economic reforms developed into a comprehensive plan for the region: the Alliance for Progress. The United States pledged to spend $10 billion in the region over ten years to build badly needed transportation facilities and to buy technology and industrial equipment. In return, Latin American governments were to institute programs of social and political reform. The United States proposed to foster democracy and economic justice in Latin America through a program of incentives. To guard against radical movements like the Castro-led guerrilla insurgency in Cuba, the U.S. government also undertook to strengthen the region's military forces with arms and training.

The Alliance for Progress, however, brought neither economic development nor democracy to Latin America. In the first place, the program was not philanthropic; it aimed rather to foster capitalist, private-sector economic growth and to expand U.S. trade and investments. Much aid to the region was in the form of loans that eventually required repayment. Moreover, aid recipients had to use the money to buy U.S. products transported on U.S. ships; by eliminating competition, such restrictions reduced the developmental impact of aid. Although the U.S. government and private sources pumped $10 billion into Latin America during the 1960s, more than that amount of capital flowed out from the area. Debt service payments ate up an increasing share of the budgets of Latin American nations, leaving little for social welfare expenditures and investments in economic development. Often, these nations had to obtain new loans just to pay off their old debts. Unfortunately, too, corruption and inefficiency dissipated a significant percentage of aid funds.

U.S. support for the Latin American military was the most effective program of the Alliance. Indoctrinated in the U.S. worldview, officers from the region also received the most modern training in counterinsurgency tactics against both rural and urban guerrillas. Sophisticated torture techniques formed part of the curriculum. One indication of the thoroughness of the training was the success of U.S.-trained and equipped Bolivian rangers in hunting down Che Guevara and his comrades. The United States also urged Latin American military leaders to take a more positive role in their nations' development by participating in civic action programs in which military personnel built roads and other public facilities.

However, despite the Kennedy administration's avowed goal of helping Latin America "strike off the remaining bonds of poverty and ignorance," its major concern clearly was to maintain friendly capitalist regimes in the region. Kennedy continued to interfere in the internal affairs of countries in the area, even after the debacle of the failed Bay of Pigs invasion in Cuba. In 1961, he attempted to destroy the regime of Cheddi Jagan in British Guiana for a second time by refusing to grant much-needed aid and pressing the British to overturn the democratically elected premier. The CIA also helped subvert the Jagan government. Kennedy was involved in attempts to rid the Dominican Republic of Rafael

Trujillo, and the CIA allegedly was responsible for the dictator's assassination in 1961. In his zeal to get rid of Fidel Castro, Kennedy even planned to enlist the aid of the Mafia to assassinate the Cuban leader.

Like its predecessors, the Kennedy administration supported dictatorial regimes in Latin America when U.S. policymakers considered them the only alternative to disorder and possible revolution. In March 1962, the United States made no protest when the Argentine military overthrew the democratically elected President Arturo Frondizi. Four months later, the U.S.-trained and -equipped Peruvian army seized power to prevent a democratically elected president from taking office. For a time, the United States withheld recognition and cut off aid, but it soon reached an understanding with the military regime. Like its predecessors, the Kennedy administration preferred order, even at the expense of democracy.

President Lyndon Johnson carried on Kennedy's Latin American program, although he increasingly shifted the emphasis of U.S. policy from reform to the maintenance of order. Johnson was determined that he, unlike Kennedy, would not "lose" any nation in any part of the world to communism. In the Dominican Republic in 1965, Johnson faced a rebellion against a reactionary military regime that less than two years before had overthrown the nation's first democratically elected president. Johnson claimed that the United States had the right to intervene unilaterally in Latin America to prevent what he feared would be a Castro-like Communist takeover. He dispatched the Marines to suppress the rebellion. Johnson undoubtedly worried about another Cuba in the Dominican Republic, but considerable evidence exists to indicate that his administration's main concern was to ensure Dominican sugar production for several important U.S. firms. Not coincidentally, several of Johnson's key foreign policy advisers, including Ellsworth Bunker and W. Averell Harriman, had close links to the sugar industry.

Under Johnson, the United States also played a major role in the military overthrow of the leftward-leaning regime of João Goulart in Brazil in 1964. Disapproving of Goulart's proposed "radical" reforms—which included a mild land reform and the grant of the vote to illiterates—the United States cut aid to Brazil to a minimum in 1963 and began to channel funds instead to pro-U.S. state governors. In April 1964, the Brazilian military toppled Goulart and instituted fifteen years of brutal, repressive dictatorship. The Johnson administration immediately recognized the new government. In the next five years, the United States poured more than $1.5 billion in economic and military aid into Brazil, one-quarter of all U.S. aid to Latin America.

The lavish aid funneled to the Brazilian military helped persuade the Argentine military that they should overthrow the faltering regime of President Arturo Illia in June 1966. The United States gave the military government $135 million in aid during the three years following the coup.

In political as well as socioeconomic terms, the results of the Alliance for Progress under Kennedy and Johnson were dismaying. When Kennedy took office, Alfredo Stroessner in Paraguay was the only dictator in power in South America. By 1968, military dictators ruled in Argentina, Brazil, and Peru, as well as in Paraguay. In Bolivia and Ecuador, civilian-elected governments served as figureheads for the military. In Central America, the record was worse. Rightist military coups overthrew democratically elected governments in El Salvador, Guatemala, and Honduras. The Somozas tightened their dictatorial grip on Nicaragua. In 1968, a military coup ousted the elected president of Panama. More important, by every measure, the Alliance failed to stimulate economic development or rectify the immense economic and social inequalities of Latin America.

THE VIETNAM ERA

From the late 1960s until 1981, the repercussions of the disastrous U.S. experience in Vietnam and related developments produced readjustments in U.S. foreign policy toward its southern neighbors. Nonetheless, the main goal of this policy—to expand North American economic interests and maintain capitalism as the dominant economic system in the region—remained constant.

In the aftermath of Vietnam, U.S. policy makers did not regard overt military intervention as a realistic option. They relied on such indirect methods as economic sanctions and subversion. The United States used these methods in Chile from 1970 to 1973 to undermine and ultimately to topple a democratically elected socialist government.

The story began in 1958, when the Socialist Salvador Allende narrowly missed victory in the Chilean presidential election. For the next fifteen years, the U.S. government poured millions of dollars into Chile, first to prevent Allende from winning subsequent elections, and then, after his election in 1970, to subvert his administration. The United States helped Eduardo Frei, a moderate reformer, win the presidency and thereafter sent an average of $130 million a year in aid to Chile. Despite this enormous effort and the injection of more millions of dollars in the 1970 campaign, Allende won the presidential election.

The United States then tried to orchestrate a military coup d'état, but when it failed, Nixon imposed economic sanctions on the Allende government, cutting aid by 90 percent and denying credit. Meanwhile, the CIA cooperated with opposition groups to destabilize the Chilean economy. Amid growing economic difficulties and political turmoil, the Chilean military overthrew Allende in a bloody coup in September 1973. The United States promptly recognized the military junta and resumed aid and credit.

The U.S. economic stake in Chile, as we saw in Chapter 17, was large and concentrated primarily in copper mining. The first act of the Allende government, supported by the unanimous vote of the Chilean Congress, had been to expropriate the holdings of the U.S. copper companies without compensation. Later, it expropriated the International Telephone and Telegraph Company, whose president enjoyed considerable influence in the Nixon administration. The United States intervened both to protect these investments and to teach a salutary lesson to other Latin American nations that might wish to construct a socialist society in the future.

Nixon also collaborated with brutal military regimes in Argentina and Brazil to organize an international terrorist network, later known as Operation Condor, designed to destroy leftist, antidictatorial political movements throughout South America. An early example of this cooperation developed in response to popular support for the *Frente Amplio* (Broad Front), a coalition of Socialists, Communists, and Christian Democrats, in the 1971 Uruguayan presidential elections. Determined to reduce "the threat of a political takeover by the Frente," Nixon systematically cultivated Argentine and Brazilian military leaders and, in the words of a U.S. Embassy strategy paper, encouraged them to "collaborate effectively with the Uruguayan security forces" to harass Frente candidates and otherwise intervene in the election to secure their defeat. According to a declassified document published by the National Security Archive, Nixon himself told British Prime Minister Edward Heath that he knew "Brazil helped rig the Uruguayan elections."

Nixon and his National Security Adviser Henry Kissinger especially identified with these dictators. After a series of personal meetings with Brazil's Garrastazu Médici, Nixon described him as a "strong" ruler who, he wished, "were running the whole continent." Kissinger made clear his growing reliance on Brazil's military dictatorship as a proxy for U.S. interests in the region. "In areas of mutual concern such as the situations in Uruguay and Bolivia," Kissinger confided to Médici, referring to Brazilian involvement in a 1971 Bolivian coup, "close cooperation and parallel approaches can be very helpful for our common objectives." However, Kissinger also clearly understood that massive intervention in the internal affairs of sovereign nations, such as he and Médici contemplated, would not endear them to Latin American people. "As Brazil plays a stronger leadership role," Kissinger lectured, "it may find itself in a position similar to that of the U.S.—respected and admired, but not liked."

CARTER'S LATIN AMERICAN POLICY: NATIONALISM, THE CANAL, AND HUMAN RIGHTS

Assuming office in 1977, President Jimmy Carter proclaimed a "new approach" for U.S. foreign policy based on "a high regard for the individuality and sovereignty of each Latin American and Caribbean nation ... our respect for human rights, ... [and] our desire to press forward on the great issues which affect the relations between the developed and developing nations." He immediately put these principles into practice in two major initiatives: the reopening of negotiations with Panama over the canal and the beginning of talks with Cuba about normalization of relations.

Periodically since the signing of the original canal treaty, Panamanians violently protested the U.S. presence in the middle of their country; serious anti-U.S. riots erupted in 1931, 1947, 1959, and 1964. These riots occurred in times of economic hardship in Panama and remained a source of tension that Carter and Gen. Omar Torrijos sought to remove. After four years of sometimes-bitter negotiations, the United States and Panama agreed to a new treaty that gradually returned control of the Canal Zone to Panama by the year 2000. Although Panamanians were unhappy with a provision that gave the United States the right to intervene to maintain the operation of the canal, they generally supported it.

Negotiations with Cuba led eventually to the opening of United States and Cuban Interest Sections in Havana and Washington in September 1977. These initiatives were short-lived, however, for the two nations came into conflict early in 1978 over Cuba's extensive military involvement in Africa, particularly in Angola and Ethiopia. The Carter administration strenuously objected to the presence of thirty-five thousand Cuban troops in Africa and broke off further talks as a result. Relations worsened during 1980 because of the exodus of one hundred and twenty-five thousand Cuban refugees to the United States.

Carter's pursuit of human rights proved to be the most controversial aspect of his foreign policy. He centered his attention on Argentina, Brazil, and Chile, the harshest practitioners of repression in the region. The United States instituted sanctions against all of these nations, ending or reducing economic and military aid and impeding their ability to obtain credit from international lending agencies. In the last two years of his term, because of stepped-up pressure from U.S. business and concern about growing communist influence in Central America, Carter backed off his human rights activism.

Nicaragua proved to be Carter's most difficult and pressing problem in Latin America. The growing insurrection of the Sandinista National Liberation Front (FSLN), a broad coalition movement against the U.S.-backed dictator Anastasio Somoza, brought Nicaragua to crisis in 1978. Carter, worried about leftist elements in the Sandinista coalition, sought a more moderate alternative, proposing at one point that the Sandinistas include members of the hated National Guard in the postrevolution Nicaraguan government. Following the Sandinista victory in 1979, the United States offered economic aid to rebuild the nation devastated by civil war. After considerable debate, the U.S. Congress approved $75 million, most of which was designed to support private sector businesses that opposed the Sandinista government.

The Return to "Gunboat Diplomacy," 1981–2003

Ronald Reagan became president in 1981, aiming to turn back "communism" in Latin America and reassert U.S. military power. In the process, he openly courted repressive regimes in Argentina and Chile and committed substantial amounts of U.S. money and military advisers to the antiguerrilla war in Central America. During the next two decades, the U.S. decision to intervene militarily or to refrain from intervention revealed traditional U.S. open-door objectives, perhaps most concisely articulated by John Hay in 1898: "a fair field and no favor."

GRENADA

On October 25, 1983, the United States invaded the tiny island nation of Grenada in the southern Caribbean to oust its allegedly communist, pro-Cuban government. The Reagan administration proclaimed the invasion its greatest triumph in Latin American policy.

In March 1979, the New Jewel Movement, led by Maurice Bishop, had overthrown the British and U.S.-backed dictatorship of Eric Gairy, who had dominated Grenadan politics since the early 1950s. Bishop's program included a massive literacy campaign, the institution of free medical care, free secondary education, and extensive rehabilitation of housing. He regulated foreign investment and stressed agricultural independence, reducing Grenadan food imports. Bishop began to expand tourism, mainly by building a modern airport. The Reagan administration threatened repeatedly to intervene against the popular Bishop regime but finally invaded Grenada after a radical faction of Bishop's own party had assassinated him.

The invasion of Grenada showed clearly that the United States was as willing as ever to use force to protect its perceived interests in the Caribbean. The action also conveyed the message—as did U.S. policies in Central America—that the United States opposed far-reaching economic and social reform in its "back yard." Moreover, it viewed Grenada, like so many other "crises" in the region, not as a nation struggling to overcome impoverishment but rather as part of a worldwide communist threat or at the very least as "another Cuba."

HAITI

The United States played a decisive role in the history of Haiti, the poorest country in Latin America. A long U.S. military occupation from 1915 to 1934 preserved the Haitian elite's monopoly of property and reinforced its dependence on coffee exports. The United States also trained a national army "specifically to fight Haitians." This army imposed the rule of the sinister François "Papa Doc" Duvalier on Haiti in 1957. Duvalier in turn used the army to centralize power in his own hands to an unprecedented degree. He did not tolerate the existence of any independent institution; distrusting his own army, he organized two parallel paramilitary organizations: a much-feared militia and the dreaded secret police, the Tontons Macoutes. The United States may not have approved of his methods, but it supported him, and when he died in 1971, U.S. Ambassador Clinton Knox personally supervised the transition to the rule of the dictator's son, eighteen-year-old Jean-Claude Duvalier.

The predatory, repressive rule of the Duvaliers aggravated all of Haiti's economic and social problems. The ruin of Haitian agriculture because of long misuse of the land and the exactions of the regime caused many thousands of impoverished peasants to flock into the urban centers, especially the shantytowns of Port-au-Prince and its environs, where between 1.2 and 1.8 million people endured unspeakable conditions. Workers' families usually ate only one meal a day, consisting of cornmeal with onions or boiled plantains with beans.

Acting on U.S. advice, Jean-Claude Duvalier tried to promote economic growth by using this vast underclass to establish export-assembly industries, subcontracted to U.S. firms. However, this program did not diminish the immense inequalities of Haitian society or the growing anger of the masses. In 1986, an explosion of urban rioting forced Jean-Claude to depart from Haiti; the Reagan administration provided a jet that whisked him away to a luxurious exile. The U.S. Agency for International Development (USAID), meanwhile, continued to promote Haiti as a low-wage haven for U.S. firms, expending $100 million in the effort. A delegation of U.S. trade-union leaders, visiting a "model" apparel factory in Haiti's export-assembly sector in 1991, found that the highest-paid workers received the equivalent of $1.47 a day. After paying for transportation and a meager breakfast and lunch, they had $0.71 to take home.

Jean-Claude Duvalier's departure created a political vacuum that U.S. policymakers rushed to fill. They supported Marc Bazin, linked to export-assembly industries and agribusinesses, and opposed Jean-Bertrand Aristide, a populist priest influenced by liberation theology. Aristide represented grass-roots workers, peasants, and student organizations. He supported a massive literacy campaign, land reform, defense of national industries, and an end to Duvalierist violence and corruption. His program included price controls on basic foodstuffs and raising the minimum hourly wage to $0.50. Despite U.S. support and a $36 million campaign, Bazin lost to Aristide, who received 67 percent of the vote, but he held power for only eight months; in September 1991, a military coup headed by Lt.

Gen. Raoul Cédras forced him into exile. The coup unleashed a reign of terror in Haiti, claiming thousands of lives and causing a flood of refugees.

Reflecting the contradictions of U.S. foreign policy, ambiguity marked the Bush administration's response to the coup. The United States rhetorically claimed to support constitutionally elected civilian regimes like Aristide's, but Aristide's anti-imperialism and opposition to neoliberalism contradicted basic U.S. foreign policy objectives. President Bush denounced the coup and said he wanted Aristide's return to power, but this pro-Aristide rhetoric contradicted a policy that limited sanctions against the coup leaders to a "porous" embargo easily breached by exporters and importers. Bush also permitted a State Department–driven media campaign to attack Aristide openly, and the CIA leaked information that cast doubt on Aristide's mental stability. The U.S. government also pressured him to moderate his positions and strike a deal with the coup leaders.

President Clinton continued Bush's Haitian policy, virtually unchanged, when he took office in January 1993. He forced Aristide to negotiate with the coup leaders and sought to impose conditions that would leave Aristide powerless to carry out his program, once returned to power. This was the essence of the 1993 Governors Island Accord, which called for the military rulers to resign, with the promise of amnesty, and for Aristide to return to power under the control of United Nations (UN) monitors and "peacekeeping" forces, an arrangement vehemently opposed by Haitian popular organizations.

Joyful demonstrations by his adoring followers greeted Aristide's return to Haiti in October 1994, but he clearly was no longer his own man; on issue after issue, his U.S. military and political advisers forced him to back down. For example, Aristide wanted to fire the entire army high command and supervise the formation of a new army and police within his government, but the U.S. military vetoed his plan. The new "professionalized" army and police was "retrained," and "candidates" for "professionalization" came largely from the old armed forces, many of the officers and specialists of which the notorious School of the Americas had trained at Fort Benning, Georgia.

The role for former president Jimmy Carter, shown here with the Haitian president Jean-Bertrand Aristide, in negotiating the accord with the military junta that restored Aristide to office in October 1994, displeased many Haitians who believed the accord was too favorable to the military and seriously abrogated Aristide's power.

Under U.S. pressure, Aristide also scrapped his nationalist program to revive Haiti's state industries and accepted a plan of neoliberal structural readjustment for the economy, which required the sale of those industries to private capitalists, both Haitian and U.S. According to Allan Nairn, this plan included commitments from Haiti

> to eliminate the jobs of half of its civil servants, massively privatize public services, "drastically" slash tariffs and import restrictions, eschew price and foreign exchange controls, grant "emergency" aid to the export sector, enforce an "open foreign investment policy," ... "limit the scope of state activity" and regulation, ...

and diminish the power of Aristide's executive branch in favor of the more conservative Parliament."

In return, Haiti received $700 million in financial aid, but $80 million of this immediately went to pay the debt accrued to foreign bankers in the three years since the coup.

Ordinary Haitians were surprised at what had happened to their idol. The Aristide they elected came to power as the representative of a massive grassroots movement, calling itself the *lavalas* (flood), that proposed to attack the country's fundamental social problems and end the traditional monopoly of power by a repressive military allied with a corrupt merchant bourgeoisie and U.S. economic interests. The new Aristide appeared to have cut a deal with the World Bank and the International Monetary Fund (IMF) that sacrificed the popular welfare in exchange for $700 million in aid. Chevannes Jean-Baptiste, leader of Haiti's largest peasant organization, had warned against premature celebration of Aristide's return in the wake of the U.S. invasion: "Don't celebrate and think that the U.S. army is here to liberate us. Only Haitians can free Haiti!"

CENTRAL AMERICA

Ronald Reagan's campaigns against the revolutionary Sandinista regime in Nicaragua and the Farabundo Martí National Liberation Front (FMLN) in El Salvador took on all the characteristics of a holy crusade against communist forces in Central America. Reagan opposed the nationalistic efforts of both groups to use state power to regulate private property and foreign trade to benefit the nation's poor peasants and urban workers. He sought to overthrow the Sandinistas, employing tactics that included economic sanctions, a campaign of public misinformation, support of rightist counterrevolutionary armies (the contras), and covert terrorist operations aided by the CIA.

One of Reagan's first official acts in 1981 was to cut off the last $15 million in aid appropriated by Congress at President Carter's request. More severe economic sanctions followed. By the end of 1985, the United States had effectively foreclosed any possibility of the Sandinistas obtaining loans from any of the major international lending agencies, such as the World Bank or the Inter-American Development Bank. The U.S. government closed Nicaragua's consulates and even forbade the Nicaraguan airline from landing in the United States. The misinformation campaign included unproven allegations against the Sandinistas of running arms to El Salvador, smuggling illegal drugs, and training terrorists.

By far the most damaging U.S. policy against the Sandinistas was support of the armed opposition to the Nicaraguan government. Predominantly led by ex-Somocista National Guardsmen, the contras were the 1979 creation of the CIA, which recruited ex-guardsman Enrique Bermúdez as their leader. In Reagan's first year in office, he secretly funneled $40 million to support these counterrevolutionaries. The CIA forged the Nicaraguan Democratic Force in late 1981, temporarily unifying the contra factions.

Frustrated with Reagan's policy, the U.S. Congress passed the so-called Boland Amendment, which forbade the use of funds to overthrow the Sandinistas; this legislation was in effect from December 1982 until December 1983, but the Reagan administration, in violation of the law, continued to provide covert support. In early 1984, the CIA mined Nicaraguan harbors and staged several helicopter attacks inside Nicaragua. Later that year, a CIA manual became public that advised the contras to employ terrorist tactics, including assassinations. The ensuing furor led the Congress to cut off aid to the contras. Nonetheless, by 1987 the United States had invested $200 million in support of the contras and had little to show for it. With hopeless divisions between civilian and military leaders, the corrupt and quarrelsome counterrevolutionaries had made no military headway in overthrowing the Nicaraguan government.

Evidently fearing that the Sandinistas would win a free and fair election in Nicaragua, the Reagan and Bush administrations obstructed the peace process initiated by the Guatemala City Accords of August 1987 and continued to provide millions in "humanitarian" aid to the contras until February 25, 1990,

the date of the elections. The United States also gave millions of dollars in aid to the anti-Sandinista coalition, *Unión Nacional Opositora* (UNO). Exhausted by almost ten years of U.S.-supported contra war and the U.S. economic blockade, Nicaraguans by a large majority voted in the UNO candidate for president, Violeta Chamorro.

In the process of taking over the counterinsurgency war in El Salvador, the United States also took over the nation's economy and politics. The United States consistently interfered in Salvadoran politics, successfully keeping the far right, led by Roberto D'Aubuisson, from taking power in 1984 and shoring up the tottering centrist government of President José Napoleón Duarte.

The United States poured some $4.5 billion from 1979 to 1990 into a futile military effort to defeat the FMLN guerrillas. This included massive military assistance in the form of equipment and training. Between fifty and a hundred U.S. advisers planned the counterinsurgency campaign, sometimes accompanying Salvadoran government troops in antiguerrilla forays. For a time, during 1984 and 1985, the Salvadoran army kept the guerrillas at bay because of its advantages in equipment. By early 1987, however, the FMLN was again striking at government forces and installations in almost every part of the country at will. Under domestic and U.S. pressure, both Duarte and his successors initiated peace talks with the guerrillas, which led to peace accords in 1992 that provided for reform of the armed forces and security services, dismantling of FMLN military structures, and elections in which leftist parties, for the first time in El Salvador's history, took part.

THE INVASION OF PANAMA

Upon his election as president in 1988, George Bush vigorously continued Reagan's Latin American policy of maintaining and reinforcing U.S. dominance over the region. Meanwhile, the Soviet Union withdrew its troops from Afghanistan and made no effort to prevent the collapse of Stalinist-type regimes in Eastern and central Europe. Washington interpreted this new noninterventionist

Soviet policy to mean that the possibility of a Soviet response no longer hampered its freedom of action. Most Latin American countries, mired in the greatest depression in the continent's history and heavily indebted to U.S. banks, were unlikely to make more than token protests against U.S. interventionist actions. If the end of the cold war deprived U.S. imperialism of its stock in trade, the bogeyman of "international communism," a new villain, the Latin American *narcotraficante*, the drug trafficker, provided a convenient pretext for an armed intervention that advanced traditional U.S. strategic and economic interests.

Bush justified the December 1989 invasion of Panama by the need to protect U.S. citizens (a U.S. Marine had died in a shooting incident), defend democracy, seize dictator Manuel Antonio Noriega on drug charges, and protect the canal. These arguments convinced few foreign governments, but the great majority denounced or deplored the invasion as a violation of the UN charter, the OAS, and the Panama Canal Treaty. However, the U.S. press accepted them without question and "did little more than parrot the Bush administration's transparent legal justifications for the invasion." The press ignored the fact that, until he began to display an inconvenient nationalist independence and stopped being "our man in Panama," Noriega was a prized ally of the United States, receiving, by conservative estimates, more than $1.2 million in payoffs from the CIA just during the last ten years of his thirty-year connection with the agency. As regards his drug connections, as recently as February 1987, Noriega had received a letter from the U.S. Drug Enforcement Administration (DEA), expressing its gratitude for his traditional position of support for the DEA and the cooperation of his army. The notion that Bush, the former CIA director, did not know of Noriega's drug links strains credulity.

The press also overlooked long-standing Republican objections to the Carter-Torrijos canal treaties, which called for the canal to become Panamanian territory in the year 2000 and the dismantling of U.S. military bases. A document, "Santa Fe II: A Strategy for Latin America in the Nineties," circulated during the 1988 campaign and reflected the views of conservative Republicans. In effect, it provided a blueprint for the invasion, stressing the need for the replacement of Noriega by a "democratic regime" with which the United States could hold talks concerning "the United States' retention of limited facilities in Panama ... for proper force projection throughout the Western Hemisphere." These and other recommendations in the Santa Fe document closely conformed to the Bush administration's Panama policies.

The administration proclaimed Operation Just Cause a huge success. Intense bombardment soon broke Panamanian resistance. Twenty-four American soldiers died; Panamanian death tolls ranged from Washington's estimate of 516 to the figure given by an independent commission of inquiry, between three thousand and four thousand, the great majority being civilians. The areas hardest hit by the invasion were the poorest neighborhoods of Panama City, inhabited primarily by black and mixed-race people. Thousands became homeless and resettled in refugee camps that often lacked medical care, sanitary facilities, and food. The invasion cost an estimated $2 billion in damages and reduced the country's economic life, already moribund because of U.S. economic sanctions, to paralysis.

In the midst of the invasion, a new president and two vice presidents took their inaugural oath fittingly enough at a military base of the U.S. Southern Command. The new president, Guillermo Endara, represented the traditional oligarchy of wealthy white families (90 percent of Panama's 2.2 million population was black, mulatto, or mestizo) who had lost their political, but not their economic, power because of the reformist, nationalist 1968 revolution led by Omar Torrijos. This handful of families, linked by intermarriage and corporate boards, controlled some one hundred and fifty of Panama's principal businesses. Once again, U.S. policy had rescued propertied elites and preserved open markets for trade and investment.

LATIN AMERICA AND THE GULF WAR

Latin America felt the impact of the crisis that began with the Iraqi invasion of Kuwait in August 1990 and erupted into the short but destructive Gulf War in February 1991. For most countries of the region, heavily dependent on oil imports, the economic effects of the dramatic rise in oil prices were profoundly negative. Brazil, the largest oil importer, was particularly hard hit, for it had a barter arrangement with Iraq whereby it paid for oil with manufactured goods, and UN sanctions against Iraq forced Brazil to use its limited hard currency to buy oil from other sources at world market prices. The region's oil exporters—Colombia, Ecuador, Mexico, Trinidad and Tobago, and Venezuela—profited by increasing their oil exports to compensate for the loss of Iraqi and Kuwaiti supplies and to take advantage of the sharp rise in crude oil prices. Nevertheless, even they stood to lose in the end: The unexpectedly quick conclusion of the war left them with large oil surpluses, forcing prices down to much lower levels.

Although most Latin Americans condemned Iraq's invasion of Kuwait, polls showed that they opposed the war option by equal or even greater majorities. In Argentina, whose government was the only one to give military aid to the coalition led by the United States, 91 percent of those questioned opposed Argentina's participation in the war and demanded the return of the two warships sent to join the multinational force. In general, editorial opinion was strongly critical of President Bush's haste to abandon reliance on sanctions against Iraq in favor of war, his rejection of various peace proposals, and the massive destruction of life and material resources caused by the war. Skepticism was widespread, too, regarding Bush's professions of concern for self-determination by critics who recalled the U.S. invasions of Panama and Grenada and the covert war against Nicaragua. Many regarded Bush's call for a "new world order" as a thin disguise for the vision of a unipolar world dominated by the United States, the only superpower.

TOWARD A NEW WORLD ORDER?

With the collapse of the Soviet Union, U.S. policy in Latin America focused on promoting free trade. The Clinton and Bush administrations' stands on a series

of issues—economic policy toward Latin America, Cuba, human rights, and the drug problem—reflected this essential continuity in foreign policy.

With the IMF and World Bank as "enforcers," U.S. policy used debt as a powerful coercive weapon to impose on Latin America a neoliberal economic system based on free trade and privatization. That system required Latin American countries to nullify past advances toward economic independence, to sell at bargain prices valuable national enterprises, and to enact austerity programs that helped increase the number of people living in poverty by 39 percent in the course of the 1980s. By the late 1990s, even the World Bank's conservative estimates of Latin American poverty had risen from 31.5 percent of the people in 1989 to 38 percent; worse still, this growing poverty accompanied modest economic growth.

The imposition of this system prepared the way for the logical next step: the incorporation of the area into a U.S.-dominated Western Hemisphere common market that would aid the United States in its growing competition with Japan and Europe. NAFTA with Mexico, negotiated by Bush and pushed through Congress by Clinton over the virtually unanimous opposition of the labor movement that had ensured his election, illustrated the continuity of U.S. policies in this area. U.S. leaders proposed similar free-trade agreements with other Latin American countries, beginning with Chile, but the ultimate objective was a Free Trade Area for the Americas.

Given the absence of strong trade-union movements in many Latin American countries, including some, like Mexico, where democracy was little more than a façade, NAFTA-type agreements in effect placed U.S. and Latin American workers in competition to see who would produce goods for the U.S. and Canadian consumer markets for the lowest possible wages. According to Public Citizen's Trade Watch, although the Clinton administration had promised two hundred thousand new jobs per year in the United States, after five years, it failed to document any new jobs produced by NAFTA even as it certified that nearly 215,000 U.S. workers were casualties of the agreement.

Although maquiladoras lured to Mexico by NAFTA grew by 37 percent and employment skyrocketed, Mexican workers' wages fell by 29 percent since 1994. Because of NAFTA, poverty rates in Mexico in 1999 rose to 60 percent from an annual average of 34 percent between 1984 and 1994.

In conjunction with provisions of the Uruguay Round of the GATT, these free-trade agreements also posed a major threat to environmental standards. The agreements with Canada and Mexico, for example, set up unelected trinational boards, made up of trade experts, as secret and final arbiters in all decisions relating to commerce and trade. These NAFTA disputation boards could identify any federal, state, or local law or regulation, no matter how democratically arrived at, as an impediment to trade and unilaterally void it. The "side agreements" added to Clinton's version of the NAFTA package made the process of challenging a labor rights or environmental violation so difficult and time-consuming that a Mexican government official could "assure concerned industrialists that they should never worry about repercussions from NAFTA's labor and environmental enforcement boards." In fact, since 1993, the boards routinely dismissed complaints filed against corporations like General Electric and Sony, but even when the board certified a complaint against Han Young, a Korean subcontractor for Hyundai, it lacked mechanisms to enforce the decision.

The dangers of environmental pollution posed by NAFTA and GATT were much greater to Latin America than to the United States or Canada. The developing nations already had become what Eduardo Galeano calls "a kingdom of impunity" for environmental polluters. In the absence of strong grassroots opposition, NAFTA and GATT enhanced the trend to make the South "the garbage dump of the North."

Cuba provided another test of Clinton's willingness to rethink old and discredited Reagan-Bush policies. The U.N. Assembly three times voted overwhelmingly to condemn the U.S. embargo against Cuba; two summits of Latin American heads of state unanimously voted the same way; and a growing number of Cuban Americans opposed a policy that inflicted hardships on their relatives on the island and obstructed further liberalization of the Cuban regime. The United States had long maintained normal relations with one great communist power, China, and in early 1994, in apparent response to pressure from U.S. business circles, President Clinton lifted economic sanctions against communist Vietnam, with which the United States once had fought a long and bloody war. As regards Cuba, however, Clinton appeared frozen in the most hardline cold war attitude.

On the subject of human rights, the Clinton administration displayed the opportunism of its predecessors. Clinton claimed to favor civilian regimes and oppose dictatorships and military coups. In practice, however, he applied that position selectively, pragmatically taking account of the relationship of the country in question to the United States and its acceptance or rejection of U.S.-sponsored economic policies. Thus, the Clinton administration remained silent when the Mexican army and paramilitary organizations ran amuck in Chiapas, carrying out summary executions, torture of prisoners, and aerial attacks on civilian populations. Indeed, U.S. military sales and assistance to Mexico suddenly skyrocketed to $78 million in 1994 and annually averaged well over $100 million thereafter. The Clinton administration took the same benign attitude toward Peru's President Fujimori's *autogolpe* (self-coup) after he proved his firm loyalty to the neoliberal economic doctrine and program. In general, in the words of the *Washington Report on the Hemisphere*, "The Administration seems prepared to wink at moderate human rights violations provided they occur in a 'good cause,' like fighting leftist guerrillas."

Despite rhetoric to the contrary, Clinton continued to militarize the war on drugs that he inherited from Bush. Throughout Latin America, the U.S. Southern Command participated in dozens of operations that involved thousands of soldiers or police and billions of U.S. taxpayers' dollars. In fact, Clinton's drug-war budget grew to $16 billion, then the highest in U.S. history. Yet the war failed to reduce the availability or use of drugs in the United States.

After the Soviet Union's disintegration removed strategic restraints on the unilateral exercise of U.S. power, U.S. policy makers struggled to define the appropriate mix of economic, political, diplomatic, and military instruments necessary to govern a "new world order" based on neoliberal principles of privatization, state deregulation, and free trade. In this task, they shared a certain sympathy with their British counterparts like Richard Cooper, foreign policy adviser to Britain's Prime Minister Tony Blair. He boldly declared in 2001 that "when dealing with the more old-fashioned kinds of states outside the postmodern continent of Europe, we need to revert to the rougher methods of an earlier era—force, pre-emptive attack, deception." Perhaps more bluntly than others, Cooper alleged, "The opportunity, perhaps even the need, for colonization is as great as it ever was in the nineteenth century" and called for the mobilization of "a new kind of imperialism."

In the United States, these same ideas emerged less candidly in discussions of "nation-building"—that is, external intervention in the sovereign affairs of developing nations to create institutions to facilitate the process of globalization and manage the growing popular opposition that its expansion inevitably seemed to produce. To this end, in 1994, under the direction of former U.S. Secretary of State Cyrus Vance, the Carnegie Corporation created the Commission on Preventing Deadly Conflict, the purpose of which, according to its 1997 report, was to promote nation-building through multilateral initiatives, including the use of external force. To identify those disputes in which such intervention was justified, the Commission stressed the need to develop "legal standards" against which it might measure regime legitimacy—that is, the degree to which "the responsibilities of governments to themselves and to their peoples" were carried out. This approach provided the intellectual foundation for many Clinton Era interventions in Latin America.

Also in 1997, however, a neoconservative organization, the Project for the New American Century (PNAC), founded by William Kristol and Robert Kagan, a Reagan Era deputy in the State Department's Bureau of Inter-American Affairs, took up a similar task, although it emphasized unilateral interference. Supported by many who would become high-ranking policymakers in George W. Bush's administration (including Vice President Cheney), the PNAC openly called for a reassertion of the aggressive imperialist intervention that had characterized early twentieth-century U.S. foreign affairs. According to its senior fellow, Thomas Donnelly, "American imperialism can bring with it new hopes of liberty, security, and prosperity; its attractions can soften the fear of overweening U.S. military power."

Although candidate Bush in 2000 had denounced "liberal" exercises in nation-building, such as those contemplated by the Carnegie Commission, as president in 2001, he nonetheless continued to support Clinton's global initiatives. Especially after the September 11 terrorist attacks on the Pentagon and World Trade Center, however, the Bush foreign policy team more vigorously embraced the PNAC's idea, if not the specific language, of unilateral imperialist intervention to protect and promote U.S. interests. "Sovereignty entails obligations," according to Richard Haass, director of policy planning in the Bush State Department. "If a government fails to meet these obligations, then it forfeits some of the normal advantages of sovereignty, including the right to be left alone inside your own territory. Other governments, including the U.S., gain the right to intervene."

What were the special "obligations" that the Bush administration expected sovereign nations to satisfy to avoid U.S. intervention? First, the president expected them to oppose terrorists who targeted the United States, but he also insisted that they promote free-market principles and practices. According to one administration spokesperson, U.S. policy stressed "the importance of ruling justly, the importance of investing in one's own people, and the importance of operating in an economic policy framework that creates openings for enterprise and entrepreneurship." This meant "sound economic policies," including "more open markets, sustainable budget policies, and strong support for individual entrepreneurship."

Wherever a government or popular forces threatened these values or resisted market reforms, the Bush administration overtly interfered politically and sometimes threatened serious economic and military intervention.

In Venezuela, for example, in the months before and during an ill-fated April 2002 military coup against the democratically elected populist president Hugo Chávez, high-ranking U.S. government officials met repeatedly with military and civilian coup leaders, including Pedro Carmona, formerly head of the Venezuelan Chamber of Commerce (*Fedecámaras*), whom the coup leaders appointed to replace Chávez. One Venezuelan who attended some of these meetings told *Newsday* that U.S. officials only mildly objected to the idea of a coup, leading him to the inescapable conclusion that "all the United States really cared about was that it was done neatly, with a resignation letter or something to show for it." As the coup unfolded, a State Department official seemingly confirmed this. He allegedly told a Venezuelan diplomat that, although the United States, as a signatory to "the Inter-American Democratic Charter, which condemns any violation of constitutional rule," officially opposed a military coup, it was nonetheless "necessary that the transition currently under way in Venezuela, which [the United States] understands and sympathizes with, conserve constitutional structures." For this reason, the United States unsuccessfully had counseled Carmona against his planned dismissal of the National Assembly.

Although the OAS and every single Latin American government immediately denounced the coup and called for the restoration of democracy, the Bush administration further embarrassed itself by greeting news of the coup with some measure of enthusiasm. Instead of condemning the coup, officials initially blamed it on the alleged "dictatorial" policies of Chávez, the elected president. Chávez apparently had angered U.S. policy makers by his populist rhetoric, his principled opposition to the U.S. war in Afghanistan, his friendly relations with Cuba and other regimes that the United States opposed, and his resistance to neoliberal policies promoted by the United States, the World Bank, and the IMF.

Similarly, the United States openly intervened in Bolivia. First, under the rubric of fighting a hemispheric war on drugs, it funded a mercenary army known as the Expeditionary Task Force, which Bolivians accused of murdering an unarmed peasant union leader and engaging in torture and theft. "These are soldiers with no clearly defined loyalties, and a foreign power is funding them to run around our country with guns," a Bolivian official complained. "The existence of this force is a violation of the Bolivian constitution."

In the summer of 2002, the United States also openly interfered in Bolivian democratic presidential elections. On election eve, the U.S. ambassador announced that the United States would cut off all economic aid to the impoverished nation if it elected Evo Morales, an Aymara indigenous leader who had fiercely resisted a U.S.-sponsored coca eradication program. Morales incurred Bush's wrath with his populist proposals and candid insistence that "capitalism is humanity's worst enemy." Notwithstanding U.S. hostility and covert financial support for his opponents, Morales surprised all political analysts with a second-place finish in the race, with 20 percent of the vote.

The United States also openly intervened in Nicaragua's 2001 presidential elections. After early polls showed that Daniel Ortega, candidate of the FSLN, led his nearest rival by almost 10 percentage points, the United States organized a spirited campaign to secure his defeat. The U.S. ambassador pressured a conservative candidate to drop out of the race to avoid splitting the anti-Ortega vote, vociferously denounced Ortega, loudly supported Enrique Bolaños, and used the distribution of emergency food aid to promote his candidacy. Even Jeb Bush, the president's brother, enlisted in the campaign, alleging that Ortega associated with those "who shelter and condone international terrorism." In the aftermath of September 11 and President Bush's declaration of a war on terrorism, this sent a powerful message to Nicaraguans, who a decade earlier already had endured horrendous privations caused by U.S. economic and military intervention.

Meanwhile, in Colombia and Ecuador, the Bush administration expanded the Clinton government's militarization of U.S. policy. Under the guise of interdicting drug smuggling, Plan Colombia, developed during the Clinton years, had authorized billions of dollars to support the Colombian military's counterrevolutionary war against the Revolutionary Armed Forces of Colombia (FARC), a guerrilla insurgency that claimed a popular base in the rural communities that it controlled. Even U.S. Ambassador Myle Frechette privately acknowledged in a confidential 1996 memorandum that the FARC's reputation as drug traffickers "was put together by the Colombian military, who considered it a way to obtain U.S. assistance in the counterinsurgency." According to one U.S. Special Forces trainer in Colombia, although his mission was "ostensibly to aid the counternarcotics effort," everyone understood "perfectly well" that they were "giving military forces training in infantry counterinsurgency doctrine." He candidly confessed "that narcotics was a flimsy cover story for beefing up the capacity of armed forces, who had lost the confidence of the population through years of abuse."

Nevertheless, U.S. military forces continued to cooperate with Colombian forces accused of human rights violations, despite congressional restrictions on such assistance. In May 2000, according to confidential memoranda released to the National Security Archive, U.S. Ambassador Curtis Kamman alerted the State Department that the U.S. Army's Bravo Company was "bedding down" with, and receiving logistical support from, a Colombian infantry brigade accused of human rights abuses. Although it acknowledged that the United States could not legally assist this brigade, the State Department nonetheless reassured Kamman that its participation was critical "for the success of Plan Colombia."

Shortly after September 11, however, the Bush administration abandoned even these cursory efforts and shamelessly used the new war on terrorism to circumvent congressional controls originally designed to guarantee that U.S. military aid would not support human rights violations. Calling the FARC "the most dangerous international terrorist group based in the Western Hemisphere" and

alleging that it "engaged in a campaign of terror against Colombians and U.S. citizens," President Bush authorized an additional $1.3 billion to support the Colombian military in 2001–2002. He requested another $98 million to fund the training of a special Colombian military unit to defend Occidental Petroleum's Cano Limón oil pipeline. The Bush government also dramatically increased military assistance to neighboring Peru, Bolivia, and Ecuador, whose military base at Manta became an especially key strategic asset for the U.S. military. This "Andean Regional Initiative" widened the arena of conflict and promised additional military aid through the Foreign Military Sales program, whose funding for Latin America almost doubled, to $8.7 million in 2001. This encouraged these impoverished nations to waste precious resources on more military equipment, and it clearly strengthened a sector of Latin American society that historically had been a enemy of democracy and human rights.

However, the Bush administration did not rely exclusively on military initiatives and covert interventions to secure U.S. foreign policy objectives. In a secret memorandum dated June 18, 2007, Ambassador Craig Kelly outlined the various tactics that Washington would use to "counter [Hugo] Chavez and reassert U.S. leadership in the region." In addition to enhanced "military relationships" and "better intelligence," Kelly recommended specific public diplomacy initiatives to appeal to "nonelites," especially because of their growing role in shaping the democratic resurgence of the region's progressive nationalist governments. He specifically encouraged "programs that speak directly to their economic and social needs, particularly in the areas of health and education" and insisted that "we be seen not just with government officials and elites, but also with those who have been marginalized or are on the fringes of society." This mobilization of "soft power" aimed to sustain traditional U.S. objectives in the region to promote free trade and "develop the kind of investment climate that will attract the volume of domestic and foreign investment needed to build new foundational infrastructure at competitive costs."

Despite personal criticism of the "tireless promotion of American-style capitalism and multinational corporations" and soaring public rhetoric that promised a "new era" of mutual respect in U.S. relations with Latin America, newly elected President Barack Obama seemed mostly intent on expanding the role of this "soft power" in U.S. efforts to secure its unorthodox empire of trade and investment. Obama's first test came early in his presidency when the Honduran military overthrew its democratically elected president in July 2009. Manuel Zelaya had opposed neoliberalism, supported higher wages for Honduran workers, and secured the country's admission to the Bolivarian Alliance for the Americas (ALBA), Hugo Chávez's alternative regional trade and development organization. Although the entire region joined in unrestrained denunciation of the coup and expelled Honduras from the OAS until it reinstated Zelaya, the Obama State Department offered tepid criticism that merely encouraged "all political and social actors in Honduras" to respect democracy and eschew violence.

Obama refused to invoke massive economic penalties required by U.S. congressional law in the event of a military coup d'état, despite a confidential memorandum from U.S. Ambassador Hugo Llorens that "there is no doubt that the military, Supreme Court, and National Congress conspired on June 28 in what constituted an illegal and unconstitutional coup against the Executive Branch." Moreover, Secretary of State Hillary Clinton publicly chastised the exiled president for his "reckless" attempt to return to Honduras, which she criticized as "a provocative action that could lead to violence." Finally, unlike the rest of the region's democratic governments, the Obama administration failed to denounce the repression of Honduran political resistance to the coup and agreed to recognize the results of presidential elections held by the coup regime in 2010.

U.S. policy toward Venezuela, Bolivia, and Colombia likewise remained consistent under both the Bush and Obama governments. In Venezuela, the United States continued to fund anti-Chávez political movements, spending $40 million between 2008

and 2011. Obama's 2012 budget targeted $5 million in Economic Support Funds for anti-Chávez activists and millions more for nongovernmental organizations (NGOs) like the National Endowment for Democracy, the International Republican Institute, and the National Democratic Institute, all of which were conduits to fund Chávez's political opponents in the past. Bolivians likewise worried about the role of these U.S.-funded NGOs and insisted on a full, transparent accounting of how these agencies spent the $80 million annually allocated to organizations in Bolivia. The Obama State Department steadfastly refused to release this information. Moreover, it continued to use the World Trade Organization to block Bolivia's enforcement of constitutional provisions to prohibit the privatization of health care, water supply, and other human rights.

Finally, Obama's foreign policy toward Colombia continued the tradition of militarization sustained by Democratic and Republican presidents alike. In July 2009, it negotiated a Defense Cooperation Agreement with Colombia that significantly increased U.S. military presence in South America, much to the chagrin of Chile's president Michelle Bachelet, Brazil's Lula da Silva, and Venezuela's Hugo Chávez. According to a November 2010 secret embassy cable published in 2011 by Wikileaks, Chávez immediately urged "the Venezuelan public [to] 'prepare for war' to defend the country against anticipated Colombian-U.S. cross-border aggression." The crisis defused because of Venezuela's forceful response, the determined opposition of the Union of South American Nations, and a 2010 court decision that the agreement violated the Colombian constitution.

Despite steadfast U.S. opposition, popular movements throughout the region gradually coalesced after 2002 in their fierce rejection of the neoliberal policies that successive U.S. governments had promoted relentlessly for two decades. From *piqueteros* in Argentina to indigenous rights activists in Bolivia, Latin America appeared to be in revolt. Although some sought to portray this as the routine chaos characteristic of the continent, others saw it as a natural, almost inevitable, consequence of unregulated markets that created wealth for a few and misery for the many. To be sure, it was unclear just

AFP/Getty Images

In 2007, Argentina's Cristina Fernández joined Chile's Michelle Bachelet as Latin America's second democratically elected woman president, giving new meaning to the "Pink Tide" that swept the region in defiance of U.S. efforts to promote privatization and hemispheric free trade. From left to right, they are Bachelet, Paraguay's Nicanor Duarte, Uruguay's Tabaré Vázquez, Fernández, Brazil's Lula, Venezuela's Hugo Chávez, and Bolivia's Evo Morales.

how well organized, politically disciplined, and effective these popular movements would remain. However, it appeared that U.S. preoccupation with Afghanistan, Iraq, and the Middle East increasingly had preempted its capacity to intervene effectively in Latin America. The decline of U.S. influence in the region after 2003 doubtlessly encouraged popular support for the Pink Tide that threatened to sweep away the vestiges of neoliberalism. Although it remained uncertain how successful they might be

over time, one thing was indisputable: They challenged a U.S. foreign policy that historically had prized property rights and unregulated markets over human rights and democratic freedoms.

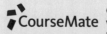

Go to the CourseMate website at **www.cengagebrain.com** for primary sources, additional study tools, and review materials—including audio and video clips—for this chapter.

INDEX